James C. Sheridan,

J. Mitchell 1908-1996

# Up in the Old Hotel

# Up
# in the
# Old
# Hotel

AND OTHER STORIES

# Joseph Mitchell

PANTHEON BOOKS · NEW YORK

All rights reserved under International and Pan-American Copyright Conventions. Published in the United States by Pantheon Books, a division of Random House, Inc., New York, and simultaneously in Canada by Random House of Canada Limited, Toronto.
The stories in this book were originally published in a somewhat different form in *The New Yorker*.

Grateful acknowledgment is made to Saul Steinberg for permission to reprint several illustrations.
Copyright © 1951, 1979, 1964, 1992 by *The New Yorker* Magazine, Inc.
Reprinted by permission of Saul Steinberg.

Library of Congress Cataloging-in-Publication Data
Mitchell, Joseph, 1908–
Up in the old hotel / Joseph Mitchell.
p.    cm.
ISBN 0-679-41263-8
1. New York (N.Y.)—Fiction.   2. New York (N.Y.)—Social life customs.   I. Title.
PS3525.I9714U6       1992
813'.54—dc20                                    91-50835

Book Design by Chris Welch
Manufactured in the United States of America
First Edition

FOR SHEILA MCGRATH

# Contents

# Author's Note

THIS BOOK CONSISTS OF FOUR BOOKS that I wrote years and years ago and that have been out of print for a long time, and of latter-day additions to one of them. The four books are *McSorley's Wonderful Saloon,* 1943; *Old Mr. Flood,* 1948; *The Bottom of the Harbor,* 1960; and *Joe Gould's Secret,* 1965. I have added several stories to *McSorley's Wonderful Saloon.* They are "The Gypsy Women," "A Spism and a Spasm," "The Deaf-Mutes Club," "Santa Claus Smith," "The Mohawks in High Steel," "The Kind Old Blonde," and "I Couldn't Dope It Out." Edmund Wilson used "The Mohawks in High Steel" as the introduction to his book, *Apologies to the Iroquois.* The other stories have never been reprinted. I wrote two Profiles of Joe Gould. I wrote the first one, "Professor Sea Gull," in 1942, and used it in *McSorley's Wonderful Saloon.* Twenty-two years later, in 1964, I wrote the second one, "Joe Gould's Secret." I took "Professor Sea Gull" out of the McSorley book and used it as the first part of the book, "Joe Gould's Secret", but for this book I have put it back in its original place in the McSorley book and *Joe Gould's Secret* now stands by itself. The four short stories, if I can call them that, in the section of the McSorley book numbered II are fictional. The three stories about Black Ankle County in the section of the McSorley book numbered III are fictional. All of the other stories in the McSorley book are factual. The three stories in the Flood book are fictional. All of the stories in *The Bottom of the Harbor* are factual. *Joe Gould's Secret* is factual. All of the stories in all of the books were originally printed in *The New Yorker.*

In going over these stories—rereading some of them for the first time since they appeared in *The New Yorker*—I was surprised and pleased to see how often a kind of humor that I can only call graveyard humor turned up in them. In some of them it is what the story is all about. In some of them it lurks around in the background or in between the lines. It turns up often in the conversations between me and the people I interviewed, or in the parts of the conversations that I chose to quote. I was pleased to discover this because graveyard humor is an exemplification of the way I look at the world. It typifies my cast of mind.

I am sure that most of the influences responsible for one's cast of mind are too remote and mysterious to be known, but I happen to know a few of the influences responsible for mine. One influence dates back to my childhood and youth. I grew up in a farming town in the southeastern part of Robeson County in North Carolina. The name of the town is Fairmont, which happens to be a remarkably inexact name. The town's original name was Ashpole and this was changed to Union City and this was changed to Fairmont. There are no *monts* in or around it or anywhere near it. It is in the middle of a region of flat, rich, black farmland interspersed with swamps and the branches of swamps and with woods in which short-leaf pines predominate. My ancestors on both sides were farmers in this region since back before the Revolutionary War, growing cotton, tobacco, corn, and timber. When I was young, my father and mother and my brothers and sisters and I would leave Fairmont on Sunday afternoons and go for a ride in the country. Some Sundays we would head south and ride around on back roads down in the Marietta, Black Ankle, and Bear Swamp sections, where my father's people came from. The backgrounds of most of the people down there are English and Welsh and most of them are Methodists and Baptists. And some Sundays we would head west and drive around on back roads in the Iona and McDonald sections, where my mother's people came from. The backgrounds of most of the people out there are Scottish (the county adjoining Robeson County on the west is named Scotland County), and most of them are Presbyterians. Scattered all over these sections are family cemeteries in many of which people kin to my family by blood or marriage are buried. Most of the cemeteries are out in the middle of fields—usually in a grove of cedars and magnolias and usually surrounded by an old wreck of a cast-iron fence. Now and then my father would stop the car and we would get out and visit one of those cemeteries, and my father or my mother would tell us gravestone by gravestone who the people were who were buried there and exactly how they were related to us. I always enjoyed those visits.

And once or twice every summer my family and the families of my mother's two sisters—Aunt Annie Parker Lytch and Aunt Mary Parker Davis—would meet in a picnic grove in back of an old church out in the country—old Iona Church, a Scottish Presbyterian church that my mother's ancestors had helped build—and cut some watermelons. The melons had been pulled early that morning in our own gardens—long, heavy, green-striped Georgia Rattlesnakes and big, round, heavy Cuban Queens so green they were almost black. We would place them on the picnic tables and cut them into rashers. After we had finished eating the watermelons, we would stand around and talk for a while. And then, when it was getting late in the afternoon, some us would walk out to the cemetery of the church in a kind of procession. My Aunt Annie would always lead the procession. All of us loved and admired Aunt Annie. She was tall and thin and erect, and she was sure of herself. She had been through a lot in her life and I remember how sad her eyes were, but her disposition was cheerful. She wore old-fashioned clothes and she often talked about "the old times," and we thought of her as our link to the past. She had what her sisters called a dry sense of humor, and she sometimes delighted us by using (or, as my mother called it, "coming out with") words and expressions that were considered "earthy" in those days. She had a lovely garden covering an acre or so in which old-fashioned varieties of vegetables and flowers and herbs and grape vines and peach trees and fig bushes and chinquapin bushes and pomegranate bushes grew side by side. She had a row of old-fashioned roses along one fence, and people came from afar to admire them and get cuttings. She was a fancier of dominicker chickens and had a large flock of them, and she had a flock of tree-roosting guineas.

As I said, Aunt Annie would lead us into the cemetery, and here and there she would pause at a grave and tell us about the man or woman down below. At some of the graves my mother and my Aunt Mary would chime in, but Aunt Annie did most of the talking. "This man buried here," she would say, "was a cousin of ours, and he was so *mean* I don't know how his family stood him. And this man here," she would continue, moving along a few steps, "was so *good* I don't know how his family stood him." And then she would become more specific. Some of the things she told us were horrifying and some were horrifyingly funny.

I am an obsessed reader of Finnegans Wake—I must've read it at least half a dozen times—and every time I read the Anna Livia Plurabelle section I hear the voices of my mother and my aunts as they walk among the graves in old Iona cemetery and it is getting dark.

Another influence on my cast of mind has been a Mexican artist named Posada. I first heard of him in 1933, during the worst days of the Depression, when I was a reporter on *The World-Telegram*. I had gone up to the Barbizon-Plaza Hotel to interview Frida Kahlo, who was the wife of Diego Rivera and a great painter herself, a sort of demonic surrealist. That was when Rivera was doing those Rockefeller Center murals. Thumb-tacked all along the walls of the hotel suite were some very odd engravings printed on the cheapest kind of newsprint. "José Guadalupe Posada," Kahlo said, almost reverentially. "Mexican. 1852–1913." She told me that she had put the pictures up herself so she could glance at them now and then and keep her sanity while living in New York City. Some were broadsides. "They show sensational happenings that took place in Mexico City—in streets and in markets and in churches and in bedrooms," Kahlo said, "and they were sold on the streets by peddlers for pennies." One broadside showed a streetcar that had struck a hearse and had knocked the coffin onto the tracks. A distinguished-looking man lay in the ruins of the coffin, flat on his back, his hands folded. One showed a priest who had hung himself in a cathedral. One showed a man on his deathbed at the moment his soul was separating from his body. But the majority of the engravings were of animated skeletons mimicking living human beings engaged in many kinds of human activities, mimicking them and mocking them: a skeleton man on bended knee singing a love song to a skeleton woman, a skeleton man stepping into a confession box, skeletons at a wedding, skeletons at a funeral, skeletons making speeches, skeleton gentlemen in top hats, skeleton ladies in fashionable bonnets. I was astonished by these pictures, and what I found most astonishing about them was that all of them were humorous, even the most morbid of them, even the busted coffin on the streetcar tracks. That is, they had a strong undercurrent of humor. It was the kind of humor that the old Dutch masters caught in those prints that show a miser locked in his room counting his money and Death is standing just outside the door. It was Old Testament humor, particularly the humor in Proverbs and Ecclesiastes. Gogolian humor. Brueghelian humor. I am thinking of that painting by Brueghel showing the halt leading the blind, which, as I see it, is graveyard humor. Anyway, ever since that afternoon in Frida Kahlo's hotel suite, I have been looking for books showing Posada engravings. I never pass a bookstore or a junk store in a Spanish neighborhood of the city without going in and seeing if I can find a Posada book. My respect for him grows all the time.

Joseph Mitchell
(1992)

# McSorley's
# Wonderful
# Saloon

# The Old House at Home

$M$cSORLEY'S OCCUPIES the ground floor of a red-brick tenement at 15 Seventh Street, just off Cooper Square, where the Bowery ends. It was opened in 1854 and is the oldest saloon in New York City. In eighty-eight years it has had four owners—an Irish immigrant, his son, a retired policeman, and his daughter—and all of them have been opposed to change. It is equipped with electricity, but the bar is stubbornly illuminated with a pair of gas lamps, which flicker fitfully and throw shadows on the low, cobwebby ceiling each time someone opens the street door. There is no cash register. Coins are dropped in soup bowls—one for nickels, one for dimes, one for quarters, and one for halves—and bills are kept in a rose-wood cashbox. It is a drowsy place; the bartenders never make a needless move, the customers nurse their mugs of ale, and the three clocks on the walls have not been in agreement for many years. The clientele is motley. It includes mechanics from the many garages in the neighborhood, salesmen from the restaurant-supply houses on Cooper Square, truck-drivers from Wanamaker's, internes from Bellevue, students from Cooper Union, and clerks from the row of second-hand bookshops just north of Astor Place. The backbone of the clientele, however, is a rapidly thinning group of crusty old men, predominantly Irish, who have been drinking there since they were youths and now have a proprietary feeling about the place. Some of them have tiny pensions, and are alone in the world; they sleep in Bowery hotels and spend practically all their waking hours in McSorley's. A few of these veterans clearly remember John

McSorley, the founder, who died in 1910 at the age of eighty-seven. They refer to him as Old John, and they like to sit in rickety armchairs around the big belly stove which heats the place, gnaw on the stems of their pipes, and talk about him.

Old John was quirky. He was normally affable but was subject to spells of unaccountable surliness during which he would refuse to answer when spoken to. He went bald in early manhood and began wearing scraggly, patriarchal sideburns before he was forty. Many photographs of him are in existence, and it is obvious that he had a lot of unassumed dignity. He patterned his saloon after a public house he had known in his hometown in Ireland—Omagh, in County Tyrone—and originally called it the Old House at Home; around 1908 the signboard blew down, and when he ordered a new one he changed the name to McSorley's Old Ale House. That is still the official name; customers never have called it anything but McSorley's. Old John believed it impossible for men to drink with tranquillity in the presence of women; there is a fine back room in the saloon, but for many years a sign was nailed on the street door, saying, "NOTICE. NO BACK ROOM IN HERE FOR LADIES." In McSorley's entire history, in fact, the only woman customer ever willingly admitted was an addled old peddler called Mother Fresh-Roasted, who claimed her husband died from the bite of a lizard in Cuba during the Spanish-American War and who went from saloon to saloon on the lower East Side for a couple of generations hawking peanuts, which she carried in her apron. On warm days, Old John would sell her an ale, and her esteem for him was such that she embroidered him a little American flag and gave it to him one Fourth of July; he had it framed and placed it on the wall above his brass-bound ale pump, and it is still there. When other women came in, Old John would hurry forward, make a bow, and say, "Madam, I'm sorry, but we don't serve ladies." If a woman insisted, Old John would take her by the elbow, head her toward the door, and say, "Madam, please don't provoke me. Make haste and get yourself off the premises, or I'll be obliged to forget you're a lady." This technique, pretty much word for word, is still in use.

In his time, Old John catered to the Irish and German workingmen—carpenters, tanners, bricklayers, slaughter-house butchers, teamsters, and brewers—who populated the Seventh Street neighborhood, selling ale in pewter mugs at five cents a mug and putting out a free lunch inflexibly consisting of soda crackers, raw onions, and cheese; present-day customers are wont to complain that some of the cheese Old John laid out on opening night in 1854 is still there. Adjacent to the free lunch he kept a quart crock of tobacco and a rack of clay and corncob pipes—the purchase of an ale entitled a man to a smoke on the house; the rack still holds a few of the communal pipes. Old John was thrifty and was able to buy the tenement—it is five stories high and holds eight families—about ten years after he opened the saloon in it. He distrusted banks and always kept his money in a cast-iron safe; it still stands in the back room, but its doors are loose on their hinges and there is nothing in it but an accumulation of expired saloon licenses and several McSorley heirlooms, including Old John's straight razor. He lived with his family in a flat directly over the saloon and got up every morning at five and took a long walk before breakfast, no matter what the weather. He unlocked the saloon at seven, swept it out himself, and spread sawdust on the floor. Until he became too feeble to manage a racing sulky, he always kept a horse and a nanny goat in a stable around the corner on St. Mark's Place. He kept both animals in the same stall, believing, like many horse-lovers, that horses should have company at night. During the lull in the afternoon a stablehand would lead the horse around to a hitching block in front of the saloon, and Old John, wearing his bar apron, would stand on the curb and groom the animal. A customer who wanted service would tap on the window and Old John would drop his currycomb, step inside, draw an ale, and return at once to the horse. On Sundays he entered sulky races on uptown highways.

From the time he was twenty until he was fifty-five, Old John drank steadily, but throughout the last thirty-two years of his life he did not take a drop, saying, "I've had my share." Except for a few experimental months in 1905 or 1906, no spirits ever have been sold in McSorley's; Old John maintained that the man never lived who needed a stronger drink than a mug of ale warmed on the hob of a stove. He was a big eater. Customarily, just before locking up for the night, he would grill himself a three-pound T-bone, placing it on a coal shovel and holding it over a bed of oak coals in the back-room fireplace. He liked to fit a whole onion into the hollowed-out heel of a loaf of French bread and eat it as if it were an apple. He had an extraordinary appetite for onions, the stronger the better, and said that "Good ale, raw onions, and no ladies" was the motto of his saloon. About once a month during the winter he presided over an on-the-house beefsteak party in the back room, and late in life he was president of an organization of gluttons called the Honorable John McSorley Pickle, Beefsteak, Baseball Nine, and Chowder Club, which held hot-rock clambakes in a picnic grove on North Brother Island in the East River. On the walls are a number of photographs taken at outings of the club, and in most of them the members are squatting around kegs of ale; except for the president, they all have drunken, slack-mouthed grins and their eyes look dazed. Old John had a bull-frog bass and enjoyed harmonizing with a choir of drunks. His favorite songs were "Muldoon, the Solid Man," "Swim Out, You're Over Your Head," "Maggie Murphy's Home," and "Since the Soup House Moved Away." These songs were by Harrigan and Hart, who were then called "the Gilbert and Sullivan of the U.S.A." He had great respect for them and was pleased exceedingly when, in 1882, they made his saloon the scene of one of their slum comedies; it was called "McSorley's Inflation."

Although by no means a handshaker, Old John knew many prominent men. One of his closest friends was Peter Cooper, president of the North American Telegraph Company and founder of Cooper Union, which is a half-block west of the saloon. Mr. Cooper, in his declining years, spent so many afternoons in the back room philosophizing with the workingmen that he was given a chair of his own; it was equipped with an inflated rubber cushion. (The chair is still there; each April 4th for a number of years after Mr. Cooper's death, on April 4, 1883, it was draped with black cloth.) Also, like other steadfast customers, Mr. Cooper had a pewter mug on which his name had been engraved with an icepick. He gave the saloon a life-sized portrait of himself, which hangs over the mantel in the back room. It is an appropriate decoration, because, since the beginning of prohibition, McSorley's has been the official saloon of Cooper Union students. Sometimes a sentimental student will stand beneath the portrait and drink a toast to Mr. Cooper.

Old John had a remarkable passion for memorabilia. For years he saved the wishbones of Thanksgiving and Christmas turkeys and strung them on a rod connecting the pair of gas lamps over the bar; the dusty bones are invariably the first thing a new customer gets inquisitive about. Not long ago, a Johnny-come-lately annoyed one of the bartenders by remarking, "Maybe the old boy believed in voodoo." Old John decorated the partition between barroom and back room with banquet menus, autographs, starfish shells, theatre programs, political posters, and worn-down shoes taken off the hoofs of various race and brewery horses. Above the entrance to the back room he hung a shillelagh and a sign: "BE GOOD OR BEGONE." On one wall of the barroom he placed portraits of horses, steamboats, Tammany bosses, jockeys, actors, singers, and statesmen. Around 1902 he put up a heavy oak frame containing excellent portraits of Lincoln, Garfield, and McKinley, and to the frame he attached a brass title tag reading, "THEY ASSASSINATED THESE GOOD MEN THE SKULKING DOGS." On the same wall he hung framed front pages of old newspapers; one, from the London *Times* for June 22, 1815, has in its lower right-hand corner a single paragraph on the beginning of the battle of Waterloo, and another, from the New York *Herald* of April 15, 1865, has a one-column story on the shooting of Lincoln. He blanketed another wall with lithographs and steel engravings. One depicts Garfield's deathbed. Another is entitled "The Great Fight." It was between Tom Hyer and Yankee Sullivan, both bareknuckled, at Still Pond Heights, Maryland, in 1849. It was won by Hyer in sixteen rounds, and the prize was $10,000. The judges wore top hats. The title tag on another engraving reads, "Rescue of Colonel Thomas J. Kelly and Captain Timothy Deacy by Members of the Irish Revolutionary Brotherhood from the English Government at Manchester, England, September 18, 1867." A copy of the Emancipation Proclamation is on this wall; so, inevitably, is a facsimile of Lincoln's saloon license. An engraving of Washington and his generals hangs next to an engraving of a session of the Great Parliament of Ireland. Eventually Old John covered practically every square inch of wall space between wainscot and ceiling with pictures and souvenirs. They are still in good condition, although spiders have strung webs across many of them. New customers get up on chairs and spend hours studying them.

Although Old John did not consider himself retired until just a few years before he died, he gave up day-in-and-day-out duty back of the bar around 1890 and made his son, William, head bartender. Bill McSorley was the kind of person who minds his own business vigorously. He inherited every bit of his father's surliness and not much of his affability. The father was by no means a lush, but the son carried temperance to an extreme; he drank nothing but tap water and tea, and bragged about it. He did dip a little snuff. He was so solemn that before he was thirty several customers had settled into the habit of calling him Old Bill. He worshipped his father, but no one was aware of the profundity of his worship until Old John died. After the funeral, Bill locked the saloon, went upstairs to the family flat, pulled the shutters to, and did not come out for almost a week. Finally, on a Sunday morning, gaunt and silent, he came downstairs with a hammer and a screwdriver and spent the day painstakingly securing his father's pictures and souvenirs to the walls; they had been hung hit or miss on wires, and customers had a habit of taking them down. Subsequently he commissioned a Cooper Union art teacher to make a small painting of Old John from a photograph. Bill placed it on the wall back of the bar and thereafter kept a hooded electric light burning above it, a pious custom that is still observed.

Throughout his life Bill's principal concern was to keep McSorley's exactly as it had been in his father's time. When anything had to be changed or repaired, it appeared to pain him physically. For twenty years the bar had a deepening sag. A carpenter warned him repeatedly that it was about to collapse; finally, in 1933, he told the carpenter to go ahead and prop it up. While the work was in progress he sat at a table in the back room with his head in his hands and got so upset he could not eat for several days. In the same year the smoke- and cobweb-encrusted paint on the ceiling began to flake off and float to the floor. After customers complained that they were afraid the flakes they found in their ale might strangle them to death, he grudgingly had the ceiling repainted. In 1925 he had to switch to earthenware mugs; most of the pewter ones had been stolen by souvenir hunters. In the same year a coin-box telephone, which he would never answer himself, was installed in the back room. These were about the only major changes he ever allowed. Occasionally one of the pictures his father had hung would fall off the wall and the glass would break, and he would fill in the gap. His contributions include a set of portraits of the wives of Presidents through the first Mrs. Woodrow Wilson, a poster of Barney Oldfield in a red racing car, and a poem called "The Man Behind the Bar." He knew this poem by heart and particularly liked the last verse:

*When St. Peter sees him coming he will leave the gates ajar,*
*For he knows he's had his hell on earth, has the man behind the bar.*

As a businessman, Bill was anachronous; he hated banks, cash registers, bookkeeping, and salesmen. If the saloon became crowded, he would close up early, saying, "I'm getting too confounded much trade in here." Agents for the brewery from which he bought his ale often tried to get him to open a checking account; he stubbornly continued to pay his ale bills with currency, largely silver. He would count out the money four or five times and hand it to the driver in a paper bag. Bill was an able bartender. He understood ale; he knew how to draw it and how to keep it, and his bar pipes were always clean. In warm weather he made a practice of chilling the mugs in a tub of ice; even though a customer nursed an ale a long time, the chilled earthenware mug kept it cool. Except during prohibition, the rich, wax-colored ale sold in McSorley's always has come from the Fidelio Brewery on First Avenue; the brewery was founded two years before the saloon. In 1934, Bill sold this brewery the right to call its ale McSorley's Cream Stock and gave it permission to use Old John's picture on the label; around the picture is the

legend "As brewed for McSorley's Old Ale House." During prohibition McSorley's ale was produced mysteriously in rows of barrels
and washtubs in the cellar by a retired brewer named Barney Kelly,
who would come down three times a week from his home in the
Bronx. On these days the smell of malt and wet hops would be
strong in the place. Kelly's product was raw and extraordinarily
emphatic, and Bill made a practice of weakening it with near beer.
In fact, throughout prohibition Bill referred to his ale as near beer,
a euphemism which greatly amused the customers. One night a
policeman who knew Bill stuck his head in the door and said, "I
seen a old man up at the corner wrestling with a truck horse. I
asked him what he'd been drinking and he said, 'Near beer in
McSorley's.'" The prohibition ale cost fifteen cents, or two mugs
for a quarter. Ale now costs a dime a mug.

Bill was big and thick-shouldered, but he did not look strong;
he had a shambling walk and a haggard face and always appeared
to be convalescing from something. He wore rusty-black suits and
black bow ties; his shirts, however, were surprisingly fancy—they
were silk, with candy stripes. He was nearsighted, the saloon was
always dimly lit, and his most rigid conviction was that drink should
not be sold to minors; consequently he would sometimes peer across
the bar at a small-sized adult and say, "Won't sell you nothing, bud.
Get along home, where you belong." Once he stared for a long
time at a corner of the saloon and suddenly shouted, "Take your
foot off that table!" Evidently he had been staring at a shadow; no
one was sitting in the corner. Bill was tyrannical. Reading a newspaper, he would completely disregard a line of customers waiting
to be served. If a man became impatient and demanded a drink,
Bill would look up angrily and shout obscene remarks at him in a
high, nasal voice. Such treatment did not annoy customers but made
them snicker; they thought he was funny. In fact, despite Bill's bad
disposition, many customers were fond of him. They had known
him since they were young men together and had grown accustomed
to his quirks. They even took a wry sort of pride in him, and when
they said he was the gloomiest, or the stingiest, man in the Western
Hemisphere there was boastfulness in their voices; the more ec-

centric he became, the more they respected him. Sometimes, for the benefit of a newcomer, one of these customers would show Bill off, shouting, "Hey, Bill, lend me fifty dollars!" or "Hey, Bill, there ain't no pockets in a shroud!" Such remarks usually provoked an outburst of gamy epithets. Then the customer would turn proudly to the newcomer and say, "See?" When prohibition came, Bill simply disregarded it. He ran wide open. He did not have a peephole door, nor did he pay protection, but McSorley's was never raided; the fact that it was patronized by a number of Tammany politicians and minor police officials probably gave it immunity.

Bill never had a fixed closing hour but locked up as soon as he began to feel sleepy, which was usually around ten o'clock. Just before closing he would summon everybody to the bar and buy a round. This had been his father's custom and he faithfully carried it on, even though it seemed to hurt him to do so. If the customers were slow about finishing the final drink, he would cough fretfully once or twice, then drum on the bar with both fists and say, "Now, see here, gents! I'm under no obligoddamnation to stand here all night while you hold on to them drinks." Whenever Bill completely lost his temper he would jump up and down and moan piteously. One night in the winter of 1924 a feminist from Greenwich Village put on trousers, a man's topcoat, and a cap, stuck a cigar in her mouth, and entered McSorley's. She bought an ale, drank it, removed her cap, and shook her long hair down on her shoulders. Then she called Bill a male chauvinist, yelled something about the equality of the sexes, and ran out. When Bill realized he had sold a drink to a woman, he let out a cross between a moan and a bellow and began to jump up and down. "She was a woman!" he yelled. "She was a goddamn woman!"

Bill was deaf, or pretended to be; even so, ordinary noises seemed to bother him unduly. The method he devised to keep the saloon tranquil was characteristic of him. He bought a fire-alarm gong similar to those used in schools and factories and screwed it to the seven-foot-tall icebox behind the bar. If someone started a song, or if the old men sitting around the stove began to yell at each other, he would shuffle over to the gong and give the rope a series of savage jerks. The gong is there yet and is customarily sounded at a quarter to midnight as a warning that closing time is imminent; the customers grab their ears when it goes off. Bill was consistent in his aversion to noise; he didn't even like the sound of his own voice. He was able to go for days without speaking, answering all questions with a snort or a grunt. A man who drank in McSorley's steadily for sixteen years once said that in that time Bill spoke exactly four intelligible words to him. They were "Curiosity killed the cat." The man had politely asked Bill to tell him the history of a pair of rusty convict shackles on the wall. He learned later that a customer who had fought in the Civil War had brought them back from a Confederate prison in Andersonville, Georgia, and had given them to Old John as a souvenir.

Bill would sometimes take an inexplicable liking to a customer. Around 1911 a number of painters began hanging out in McSorley's. Among them were John Sloan, George Luks, Glenn O. Coleman, and Stuart Davis. They were all good painters, they didn't put on airs, and the workingmen in the saloon accepted them as equals. One night, Hippolyte Havel, the anarchist, came in with the painters. Havel was a long-haired, myopic, gentle-mannered Czech whose speeches often got him in trouble with the police. Even Bill was curious about him. "What's that crazy-looking fellow do for a living?" he asked one of the painters. Playing safe, the painter said Havel was a politician, more or less. Havel liked the place and became a steady customer. Most nights after making a fiery speech in Union Square, he would hurry down to McSorley's. To the amazement of the old-timers, a strong friendship grew up between him and Bill, who was a Tammany Democrat and an utter reactionary; no one was ever able to figure out the basis of the friendship. Bill called the anarchist Hippo and would let him have credit up to two dollars; other customers were not allowed to charge so much as a nickel cigar. Bill had an extremely vague idea about Havel's politics. Charles Francis Murphy, the Tammany boss, occasionally dropped in, and once Bill told Havel he was going to speak a good word to the boss for him. "Maybe he'll put you in line for something," Bill said. The anarchist, who thought no man was as foul as a Tammany boss, smiled and thanked him. A police captain once took it upon himself to warn Bill against Havel. "You better keep your eyes on that long-haired nut," he said. "Why?" asked Bill. The question annoyed the police captain. "Hell fire, man," he said, "Havel's an anarchist! He's in favor of blowing up every bank in the country." "So am I," said Bill. Bill's friendship for Havel was extraordinary in every way. As a rule, he reserved his kindness for cats. He owned as many as eighteen at once and they had the run of the saloon. He fed them on bull livers put through a sausage grinder and they became enormous. When it came time to feed them, he would leave the bar, no matter how brisk business was, and bang on the bottom of a tin pan; the fat cats would come loping up, like leopards, from all corners of the saloon.

Bill had been married but was childless, and he used to say, "When I go, this place goes with me." In March, 1936, however, he changed his mind—why, no one knows—and, to the surprise of the veteran customers, sold both saloon and tenement to Daniel O'Connell, an old policeman, who, since 1900, had spent most of his leisure at a table in the back room. O'Connell retired from the Department two days before he purchased the saloon. He was the kind of man of whom people say, "If he can't speak a good word about you, he won't speak a bad one." He was almost as proud of the saloon's traditions as Bill and willingly promised he would make no changes; that was one of the conditions of the sale. Almost from the day Bill sold out, his health began to fail. He took a room in the house of a relative in Queens. Sometimes, in the afternoon, if the weather was good, he would shuffle into the bar, a sallow, disenchanted old man, and sit in the Peter Cooper chair with his knotty hands limp in his lap. For hours he would sit and stare at the painting of Old John. The customers were sure he was getting ready to die, but when he came in they would say, "You looking chipper today, Billy boy," or something like that. He seemed grateful for such remarks. He rarely spoke, but once he turned to a man he had known for forty years and said, "Times have changed, McNally." "You said it, Bill," McNally replied. Then, as if afraid he had been sentimental, Bill coughed, spat, and said, irrelevantly, "The bread you get these days, it ain't fit to feed a dog." On the night of September 21, 1938, barely thirty-one months after he quit drawing ale, he died in his sleep. As close as his friends could figure it, his age was seventy-six.

The retired policeman made a gentle saloonkeeper. Unlike Bill, he would never throw a quarrelsome drunk into the street but would try to sober him up with coffee or soup. "If a man gets crazy on stuff I sold him, I can't kick him out," he said one day. "That would be evading my responsibility." He was proprietor for less than four years. He died in December, 1939, and left the property to a daughter, Mrs. Dorothy O'Connell Kirwan. A young woman with respect for tradition, Mrs. Kirwan has chosen to remain in the background. At first customers feared that she would renovate the place, but they now realize that this fear was groundless. "I know exactly how my father felt about McSorley's," Mrs. Kirwan said, "and so long as I am owner, no changes will be made. I won't even change the rule against women customers." She herself visits the saloon only on Sunday nights after hours. Even so, early in her ownership, she made a mistake in judgment that brought about a crisis in McSorley's. She had a hard time getting over this mistake, but she now looks back on it as a blessing in disguise and regards the crisis as a kind of inevitable demarcation between McSorley's past under Old John and Old Bill and her father and McSorley's present under her. She enjoys telling about this.

"For some months after my father's death," she says, "I let things drift in McSorley's. I left everything in the hands of my father's two old bartenders, the day bartender and the night bartender, but the responsibility was too much for them and things gradually got out of hand, and I saw I had to find a manager—someone to look after the books and pay the bills and just generally take charge. And the more I thought about it the more I thought that the exact right person for the job was an uncle of mine named Joe Hnida. Well, I grew up in an Irish family that has lived in one of the old Irish neighborhoods on the west side of Greenwich Village for generations, in among the bohemians and the erratical personalities, and I thought I knew quite a lot about human behavior, but I soon found out that

I didn't. Joe Hnida is a Czech, and he's an uncle of mine by marriage—he's my father's sister's husband. He worked for a limousine service that specializes in weddings and funerals; he was the supervisor of the drivers. Joe's a kind, decent, hardworking, trustworthy man, and I spoke to him and asked him if he would care to take over the management of McSorley's. He thought it over and decided he would. Well, Joe started out in McSorley's on a Monday morning and by the end of the week I was getting telephone calls from some of the real old-timers among the customers, all of them old friends of my father's, complaining about him. What I hadn't taken into account is that Joe is a man of few words, a very few— he just doesn't have any small talk. In addition, he's unusually self-sufficient. And also in addition, and I think he himself would agree, if he has any sense of humor at all it's a Czech sense of humor— it certainly isn't an Irish sense of humor. Anyway, it seemed that some of the old men who sit in those chairs along the wall in McSorley's all day long and do a lot of talking and arguing back and forth among themselves would try to start conversations with Joe and Joe just wouldn't participate. As one of them told me, 'He'll go so far as to say "Good morning" or "How do you do?" and he'll answer you yes or no, but that's about the full extent and sum total of what he has to say. He won't even comment on the weather.' 'If he's behind the bar,' another one told me, 'he'll draw an ale for a customer and take his money and give him his change, and that's the end of it. He just will not speak a single unnecessary word.' A few of the old men developed a liking for Joe, but they were ones who never had much to say themselves. And before long, little by little, most of the old men convinced themselves that Joe considered them to be just a bunch of old bores and windbags and they also convinced themselves that he looked down on them, and to get back at him they began to mock him behind his back and call him 'that stuck-up Czechoslovakian hearse-driver.' When the old men telephoned me I tried to explain Joe to them and stand up for him and smooth things over. 'After all,' I said, 'Bill McSorley didn't exactly knock himself out talking. According to my father, there were days you couldn't get a word out of him.' But that didn't do any good. Bill McSorley was different—he owned the place and he had earned the right to do as he pleased, and he might not necessarily care if you lived or died but he didn't give you the impression that he looked down on you. This new man comes in here out of nowhere and he won't even be polite. It went on and on like that. Weeks went by and months went by and things didn't get any better. And then one day the oldest of the bartenders, a man I completely trust, telephoned me and said that just about the worst that could happen had happened. 'It's completely ridiculous, Dot,' he said, 'but the old men have discovered that Joe doesn't like ale. He's done his best to hide this, but it somehow slipped out, and they began right away picking on him about it, whereupon he got his back up and told them that he not only doesn't like the taste of ale, he doesn't like the smell of it. In fact, he said that the smell of it sometimes gives him a headache. Well, as I said, it sounds ridiculous, but the old men are acting as if they have found out something about Joe that is shocking beyond belief. And I know them—they're not going to let this die down. And furthermore, to add to everything else, a number of them have suddenly become very sensitive and touchy— the situation in general has brought back to the surface differences between them that they thought they had buried and forgotten long ago, and they have stopped speaking to each other, only sometimes they can't exactly remember why they stopped speaking, and they go around avoiding each other and at the same time looking puzzled. It's a mess.' I saw I had to do something. It was up to me. Now, it so happens that my husband, Harry Kirwan, grew up in an old, old town in Ireland named Ballyragget, down in Kilkenny. Bally-ragget is a market town that is noted for its old public houses. Harry's mother died when he was a child and he lived with his grandmother. And quite early in his schooldays he started working for an old public house called Staunton's. On his way to school, he would stop off and sweep the place out, and after school he would stop off for the rest of the afternoon and wash glasses and fill the coal box and run errands and generally make himself useful. Harry has a studious nature; he's always read a lot. He wanted very much to be a professor in Ireland, but he couldn't afford the education. So when he was around nineteen he came to the United States and got a job in a manufacturing chemist company in the Bronx, and by the time we got married—which as a matter of fact was less than a year before the death of my father—he had worked himself up to where he was head bookkeeper. And so, anyway, when Harry came home that night, I said to him, 'Sit down, Harry. I've got something very serious I have to discuss with you.' I filled him in on the situation in McSorley's, and then I said to him, 'Harry, I know how much you love your job, and I hate to ask this, but do you think you could possibly find it in your heart to give it up and take over the management of McSorley's?' 'Well, Dot,' he said, and I remember every word he said that night, 'first of all, I don't love my job, I pretend to, but I hate it. And second of all, Dot, why in the name of God did it take so long for this thought to occur to you? You've heard me talk a lot about Staunton's back in Ballyragget, and most of the customers in there were hard-to-get-along-with old men, and I got along with them. I not only got along with them, I enjoyed getting along with them. I enjoyed observing them and I enjoyed listening to them. They were like actors in a play, only the play was real. There were Falstaffs among them—that is, they were just windy old drunks from the back alleys of Ballyragget, but they were Falstaffs to me. And there were Ancient Pistols among them. And there was an old man with a broken-hearted-looking face who used to come in and sit in a chair in the corner with a Guinness at his elbow and stare straight ahead for hours at a time and occasionally mumble a few words to himself, and every time he came in I would say to myself, "King Lear." There were good old souls among those men, and there were leeches among them, leeches and lepers and Judases, and I imagine the cast of characters down in McSorley's is about the same. In other words, Dot,' he said, 'in answer to your question, yes, I'm willing to take a chance and go down to McSorley's and see if I can handle it.' The changeover didn't take long. Early next morning I went to Joe Hnida's apartment and had a heart-to-heart talk with him and begged him to forgive me for getting him into all of this, which he did, and he went back to the limousine service. And the very same day Harry gave notice up in the Bronx.

And two Mondays later, he started in at McSorley's. I remember that day so well. I was worried half sick that I might've made another big mistake, so in the middle of the afternoon I telephoned McSorley's and asked to speak to Harry. 'Everything's O.K., Dot,' he said. 'I'm amazed at how much I'm enjoying this. I feel like I'm back home again—back home in Ballyragget, back home in Staunton's.' And when he got home that night and opened the door, the first thing he said was, 'I think I have finally found my right and proper place in the world.' "

Like Old John and Old Bill and like his father-in-law and his wife, Harry Kirwan is strongly opposed to change, and since he took over he has made only one change and that was a fiscal one and long overdue. He gave raises to the old bartenders, Eddie Mullins and Joe Martoccio, and he gave a raise to Mike Boiko, the cook, who is an old Ukrainian, and he gave a raise to Tommy Kelly, who broke down and cried when Harry told him about it. Tommy Kelly is perhaps the most important member of the staff of McSorley's, but his duties are so indefinite that the old men call him Kelly the Floorwalker. When business is brisk, he acts as the potboy—he carries mugs of ale from the bar to the tables, hooking his fingers through the handles of the mugs and carrying two in each hand. He is sometimes the fill-in bartender. He makes an occasional trip to the butcher or the grocery store for Mike. He answers the coin-box telephone. In the winter he keeps the fire going in the stove. When he shows up, around 8:30 A.M., he is just a sad-eyed little man with a hangover, but by noon lukewarm ale has given him a certain stateliness; by six he is in such a good humor that he stands near the door and shakes hands with incoming customers just as if he were the proprietor. Some strangers think he is the proprietor and speak to him as Mr. McSorley. Kelly says that he had a long succession of odd jobs before he wound up in McSorley's. "And when I say odd," he says, "I mean odd." Once, for a brief period, he took a job as night clerk and night watchman in a large funeral parlor in Brooklyn, quitting because a corpse spoke to him. "I sat up front in the office all night," he says, "and I used to keep a pocket-sized bottle of gin in my coat hanging up in the locker in the back room, and I would go back there every little while and take a sip—not a real swallow, just a sip, just enough to keep me going through the night—and to get back there I had to pass through the parlor, the room where the coffins and the corpses were kept, and on this particular night I had to go past an open coffin that had a corpse in it, a man all laid out and fixed up and ready for the funeral in the morning, and I must've already gone past him a half a dozen times, passing and repassing, and this time, as I was going past him, he spoke to me, and quite distinctly too. 'Take off your hat,' he said, 'and put out that cigar and pour out that gin and turn off that damn radio.'"

To a devoted McSorley customer, most other New York City saloons are tense and disquieting. It is possible to relax in McSorley's. For one thing, it is dark and gloomy, and repose comes easy in a gloomy place. Also, the barely audible heartbeatlike ticking of the old clocks is soothing. Also, there is a thick, musty smell that acts as a balm to jerky nerves; it is really a rich compound of the smells of pine sawdust, tap drippings, pipe tobacco, coal smoke, and onions. A Bellevue intern once remarked that for some mental states the smell in McSorley's would be a lot more beneficial than psychoanalysis or sedative pills or prayer.

At midday McSorley's is crowded. The afternoon is quiet. At six it fills up with men who work in the neighborhood. Most nights there are a few curiosity-seekers in the place. If they behave themselves and don't ask too many questions, they are tolerated. The majority of them have learned about the saloon through John Sloan's paintings. Between 1912 and 1930, Sloan did five paintings, filled with detail, of the saloon—"McSorley's Bar," which shows Bill presiding majestically over the tap and which hangs in the Detroit Institute of Arts; "McSorley's Back Room," a painting of an old workingman sitting at the window at dusk with his hands in his lap, his pewter mug on the table; "McSorley's at Home," which shows a group of argumentative old-timers around the stove; "McSorley's Cats," in which Bill is preparing to feed his drove of cats; and "McSorley's, Saturday Night," which was painted during prohibition and shows Bill passing out mugs to a crowd of rollicking customers. Every time one of these appears in an exhibition or in a newspaper or magazine, there is a rush of strangers to the saloon. "McSorley's Bar" was reproduced in Thomas Craven's "A Treasury of Art Masterpieces," which came out in 1939, and it caused hundreds to go and look the place over. There is no doubt that McSorley's has been painted more often than any other saloon in the country. Louis Bouché did a painting, "McSorley's," which is owned by the University of Nebraska. A painting, "Morning in McSorley's Bar," by a ship's purser named Ben Rosen won first prize in an exhibition of art by merchant seamen in February, 1943. Reginald Marsh has done several sketches of it. In 1939 there was a retrospective exhibition of Sloan's work in Wanamaker's art department, and a number of McSorley patrons attended it in a body. One asked a clerk for the price of "McSorley's Cats." "Three thousand dollars," he was told. He believed the clerk was kidding him and is still indignant. Kelly likes the Sloan paintings but prefers a golden, corpulent nude which Old John hung in the back room many years ago, right beside Peter Cooper's portrait. To a stranger, attracted to the saloon by a Sloan painting, Kelly will say, "Hey, Mac, if you want to see some real art, go look at the naked lady in the back room." The nude is stretched out on a couch and is playing with a parrot; the painting is a copy, probably done by a Cooper Union student, of Gustave Courbet's "La Femme au Perroquet." Kelly always translates this for strangers. "It's French," he says learnedly. "It means 'Duh Goil and duh Polly.'"

McSorley's bar is short, accommodating approximately ten elbows, and is shored up with iron pipes. It is to the right as you enter. To the left is a row of armchairs with their stiff backs against the wainscoting. The chairs are rickety; when a fat man is sitting in one, it squeaks like new shoes every time he takes a breath. The customers believe in sitting down; if there are vacant chairs, no one ever stands at the bar. Down the middle of the room is a row of battered tables. Their tops are always sticky with spilled ale. In the centre of the room stands the belly stove, which has an isinglass door and is exactly like the stoves in Elevated stations. All winter Kelly keeps it red hot. "Warmer you get, drunker you get," he says. Some customers prefer mulled ale. They keep their mugs on the hob until the ale gets as hot as coffee. A sluggish cat named Minnie sleeps in a scuttle beside the stove. The floor boards are warped, and here and there a hole has been patched with a flattened-out soup can. The back room looks out on a blind tenement court. In this room are three big, round dining-room tables. The kitchen is in one corner of the room; Mike keeps a folding boudoir screen around the gas range, and pots, pans, and paper bags of groceries are stored on the mantelpiece. While he peels potatoes, he sits with early customers at a table out front, holding a dishpan in his lap and talking as he peels. The fare in McSorley's is plain, cheap and well cooked. Mike's specialties are goulash, frankfurters, and sauerkraut, and hamburgers blanketed with fried onions. He scribbles his menu in chalk on a slate which hangs in the bar-room and consistently misspells four dishes out of five. There is no waiter. During the lunch hour, if Mike is too busy to wait on the customers, they grab plates and help themselves out of the pots on the range.

The saloon opens at eight. Mike gives the floor a lick and a promise and throws on clean sawdust. He replenishes the free-lunch platters with cheese and onions and fills a bowl with cold, hard-boiled eggs, five cents each. Kelly shows up. The ale truck makes its delivery. Then, in the middle of the morning, the old men begin shuffling in. Kelly calls them "the steadies." The majority are retired laborers and small businessmen. They prefer McSorley's to their homes. A few live in the neighborhood, but many come from a distance. One, a retired operator of a chain of Bowery flophouses, comes in from Sheepshead Bay practically every day. On the day of his retirement, this man said, "If my savings hold out, I'll never draw another sober breath." He says he drinks in order to forget the misery he saw in his flophouses; he undoubtedly saw a lot of it, because he often drinks twenty-five mugs a day, and McSorley's ale is by no means weak. Kelly brings the old men their drinks. To save him a trip, they usually order two mugs at a time. Most of them are quiet and dignified; a few are eccentrics. Some years ago one had to leap out of the path of a speeding automobile on Third Avenue; he is still furious. He mutters to himself constantly. Once, asked what he was muttering about, he said, "Going to buy a shotgun and stand on Third Avenue and shoot at automobiles." "Are you going to aim at the tires?" he was asked. "Why, hell no!" he said. "At the drivers. Figure I could kill four or five before they arrested me. Might kill more if I could reload fast enough."

Only a few of the old men have enough interest in the present to read newspapers. These patrons sit up front, to get the light that comes through the grimy street windows. When they grow tired of reading, they stare for hours into the street. There is always something worth looking at on Seventh Street. It is one of those East Side streets completely under the domination of kids. While playing stickball, they keep great packing-box fires going in the gutter; sometimes they roast mickies in the gutter fires. In McSorley's the free-lunch platters are kept at the end of the bar nearer the street door, and several times every afternoon kids sidle in, snatch handfuls of cheese and slices of onion, and dash out, slamming the door. This never fails to amuse the old men.

The stove overheats the place and some of the old men are able to sleep in their chairs for long periods. Occasionally one will snore, and Kelly will rouse him, saying, "You making enough racket to wake the dead." Once Kelly got interested in a sleeper and clocked him. Two hours and forty minutes after the man dozed off, Kelly became uneasy—"Maybe he died," he said—and shook him awake. "How long did I sleep?" the man asked. "Since the parade," Kelly said. The man rubbed his eyes and asked, "Which parade?" "The Paddy's Day parade, two weeks ago," Kelly said scornfully. "Jeez!" the man said. Then he yawned and went back to sleep. Kelly makes jokes about the constancy of the old men. "Hey, Eddie," he said one morning, "old man Ryan must be dead!" "Why?" Mullins asked. "Well," Kelly said, "he ain't been in all week." In summer they sit in the back room, which is as cool as a cellar. In winter they grab the chairs nearest the stove and sit in them, as motionless as barnacles, until around six, when they yawn, stretch, and start for home, insulated with ale against the dreadful loneliness of the old. "God be wit' yez," Kelly says as they go out the door.

(1940)

# Mazie

$A$ BOSSY, YELLOW-HAIRED BLONDE named Mazie P. Gordon is a celebrity on the Bowery. In the nickel-a-drink saloons and in the all-night restaurants which specialize in pig snouts and cabbage at a dime a platter, she is known by her first name. She makes a round of these establishments practically every night, and drunken bums sometimes come up behind her, slap her on the back, and call her sweetheart. This never annoys her. She has a wry but genuine fondness for bums and is undoubtedly acquainted with more of them than any other person in the city. Each day she gives them between five and fifteen dollars in small change, which is a lot of money on the Bowery. "In my time I been as free with my dimes as old John D. himself," she says. Mazie has presided for twenty-one years over the ticket cage of the Venice Theatre, at 209 Park Row, a few doors west of Chatham Square, where the Bowery begins.

The Venice is a small, seedy moving-picture theatre, which opens at 8 A.M. and closes at midnight. It is a dime house. For this sum a customer sees two features, a newsreel, a cartoon, a short, and a serial episode. The Venice is not a "scratch house." In fact, it is highly esteemed by its customers, because its seats get a scrubbing at least once a week. Mazie brags that it is as sanitary as the Paramount. "Nobody ever got loused up in the Venice," she says. On the Bowery, cheap movies rank just below cheap alcohol as an escape, and most bums are movie fans. In the clientele of the Venice they are numerous. The Venice is also frequented by people from the tenement neighborhoods in the vicinity of Chatham Square, such as Chinatown, the Little Italy on lower Mulberry Street, and the Spanish section on Cherry Street. Two-thirds of its customers are males. Children and most women sit in a reserved section under the eyes of a matron. Once, in an elegant mood, Mazie boasted that she never admits intoxicated persons. "When do you consider a person intoxicated?" she was asked. Mazie snickered. "When he has to get down on all fours and crawl," she said. In any case, there are drunks in practically every Venice audience. When the liquor in them dies down they become fretful and mumble to themselves, and during romantic pictures they make loud, crazy, derogatory remarks to the actors on the screen, but by and large they are not as troublesome as a class of bums Mazie calls "the stiffs." These are the most listless of bums. They are blank-eyed and slow-moving, and they have no strong desire for anything but sleep. Some are able to doze while leaning against a wall, even in freezing weather. Many stiffs habitually go into the Venice early in the day and slumber in their seats until they are driven out at midnight. "Some days I don't know which this is, a movie-pitcher theatre or a flophouse," Mazie once remarked. "Other day I told the manager pitchers with shooting in them are bad for business. They wake up the customers."

Most Bowery movie houses employ bouncers. At the Venice, Mazie is the bouncer. She tells intimates that she feels fighting is unladylike but that she considers it her duty to throw at least one customer out of the theatre every day. "If I didn't put my foot down, the customers would take the place," she says. "I don't get any fun out of fighting. I always lose my temper. When I start swinging, I taste blood, and I can't stop. Sometimes I get beside myself. Also, a lot of the bums are so weak they don't fight back, and that makes me feel like a heel." Mazie is small, but she is wiry and fearless, and she has a frightening voice. Her ticket cage is in the shadow of the tracks of the City Hall spur of the Third Avenue elevated line, and two decades of talking above the screeching of the trains have left her with a rasping bass, with which she can dominate men twice her size. Now and then, in the Venice, a stiff throws his head back and begins to snore so blatantly that he can be heard all over the place, especially during tense moments in the picture. When this happens, or when one of the drunks gets into a bellowing mood, the women and children in the reserved section stamp on the floor and chant, "Mazie! Mazie! We want Mazie!" The instant this chant goes up, the matron hastens out to the lobby and raps on the side window of Mazie's cage. Mazie locks the cash drawer, grabs a bludgeon she keeps around, made of a couple of copies of *True Romances* rolled up tightly and held together by rubber bands, and strides into the theatre. As she goes down the aisle, peering this way and that, women and children jump to their feet, point fingers in the direction of the offender, and cry, "There he is, Mazie! There he is!" Mazie gives the man a resounding whack on the head with her bludgeon and keeps on whacking him until he seems willing to behave. Between blows, she threatens him with worse punishment. Her threats are fierce and not altogether coherent. "Outa here on a stretcher!" she yells. "Knock your eyeballs out! Big baboon! Every tooth in your head! Bone in your body!" The women and children enjoy this, particularly if Mazie gets the wrong man, as she sometimes does. In action, Mazie is an alarming sight. Her face becomes flushed, her hair flies every which way, and her slip begins to show. If a man defends himself or is otherwise contrary, she harries him out of his seat and drives him from the theatre. As he scampers up the aisle, with Mazie right behind him, whacking away, the women and children applaud.

Mazie's animosity toward a stiff or a drunk usually lasts until she has driven him out to the sidewalk. Then, almost invariably, she becomes contrite and apologetic. "Look, buddy, I'm sorry," she said one afternoon recently to a drunk she had chased out because he had been screaming "Sissy! Sissy!" at George Raft during the showing of a prison picture called "Each Dawn I Die." "If you didn't see the whole show," she continued, "you can go back in." "Hell, Mazie," said the drunk, "I seen it three times." "Here, then," she said, handing him a dime. "Go get yourself a drink." Although the drunk's ears were still red from Mazie's blows, he grinned. "You got a heart of gold, Mazie," he said. "You my sweetheart." "O.K., buddy," Mazie said, stepping back into the cage. "You quit acting like a god-damn jackass and I'll be your sweetheart."

The Venice is a family enterprise. It is owned by Mazie and two sisters—Rosie, the widow of a horse-race gambler, and Jeanie, an acrobatic dancer. Mazie's sisters let her run things to suit herself. She is profoundly uninterested in moving pictures and is seldom able to sit through one. "They make me sick," she says. Consequently, she employs a manager and leaves the selection and ordering of films entirely up to him. For a theatre of its class, the Venice is prosperous, and Mazie could afford to hire a ticket girl and take things easy, but she enjoys the job and will not relinquish it, as her sisters often urge her to do. From her cage she has a good view of Chatham Square, which is the favorite promenade of Bowery drunks and eccentrics. "The things I see, by God, you wouldn't believe it," she says proudly. When she catches sight of a person she knows among the passers-by, she sticks her face up to the round hole in the front window of her cage and shouts a greeting. Sometimes she discusses exceedingly personal matters with people out on the sidewalk. "Hey there, Squatty," she yelled one afternoon to a dreamy-eyed little man, "I thought you was in Bellevue." "I was, Mazie," the man said. "They turned me loose yesterday." "Where'd they put you this time—the drunk ward or the nut ward?" "I was in with the drunks this time." "How'd they treat you?" "They didn't do me no harm, I guess." "You get drunk last night, Squatty?" "Sure did." "Guess you had to celebrate." "Sure did." "Well, take care yourself, Squatty." "Thanks, Mazie. You do the same."

Sitting majestically in her cage like a raffish queen, Mazie is one of the few pleasant sights of the Bowery. She is a short, bosomy woman in her middle forties. Some people believe she has a blurry resemblance to Mae West. Her hair is the color of sulphur. Her face is dead white, and she wears a smudge of rouge the size of a silver dollar on each cheek. Her eyes are sleepy and droopy-lidded. On duty, she often wears a green celluloid eyeshade. She almost always has a cigarette hanging from a corner of her mouth, and this makes her look haughty. Like a movie croupier, she can smoke a cigarette down to the end and not take it from her mouth once, even while talking. She has a deep cigarette cough; she smokes three and a half packs a day and says tobacco is murdering her. On her right hand she wears four diamond rings. She likes vigorous colors, and her dresses are spectacular; they come from shops on Division Street. The glass-topped Bowery and Chinatown rubberneck wagons often park in front of the Venice, and now and then a band of sightseers stand on the sidewalk and stare at Mazie. She despises sightseers and says they give the Bowery a black eye. Sometimes she thumbs her nose at them. Actually, however, she does not mind being stared at. "People walk past here just to give me the eye," she once said. "I got a public of my own, just like a god-damn movie-pitcher star."

Mazie is a talkative woman, and on most subjects she is remarkably frank, but she rarely says anything about her private life, and some people on the Bowery consider her a mystery woman. A man who had been stopping by to chat with her several times a week for years suddenly realized recently that he did not know whether she was Miss or Mrs. Gordon. "You ever been married, Mazie?" he asked. "That's for me to know, you to find out," she said sharply. A moment later she added, "I'll ask you this. Do I look and act like a girl that never had a date?" People around Chatham Square believe, among other things, that she was a belly dancer in the Hurtig & Seamon burlesque houses when she was a young woman, which isn't true. They claim, with not much relevance, that she gives her spare money to bums because she was once disappointed in a love affair. Furthermore, they believe she was born in Chinatown. Actually, she is a native of Boston, a fact which gives her a lot of satisfaction. Every winter she takes a week off and spends it in Boston, just walking around. She believes the people of Boston are superior to the people elsewhere. One night a blind-drunk bum stumbled into an "L" pillar in front of the Venice, skinning his nose, and she rushed out and dragged him into her lobby. Then she went into a nearby saloon and yelled, "Gimme some hot water and a clean rag!" "You want to take a bath, Mazie?" asked the bartender. This remark enraged her. "Don't you talk like that to me, you yellow-bellied jerk," she said. "I come from Boston, and I'm a lady."

Mazie says her real name is Mazie Phillips, but she will not tell anything about her parents. Her intimates say that around 1903, when she was a schoolgirl in Boston, her older sister, Rosie, came to New York and married Louis Gordon, an East Side gambler and promoter. They established a home on Grand Street, and a few years later Mazie and her younger sister, Jeanie, came to live with them. The family of Belle Baker, the vaudeville singer, lived nearby on Chrystie Street. Irving Becker, Belle's brother, now the manager of a road company of "Tobacco Road," once had a job loading rifles in a shooting gallery Gordon operated at Grand Street and the Bowery. "We and the Gordons were great friends," Becker said recently. "Louie Gordon was as fine a gambler as the East Side ever produced. He was a big, stately gentleman and he gave to the poor, and the bankroll he carried a billy goat couldn't swallow it. He hung around race tracks, but he would gamble on anything. He made a lot of money on horses and invested it in Coney Island. He and his brother, Leo, helped back the original Luna Park, which opened in 1903. He was one of those silent gamblers. He never said nothing about himself. He gave everybody a fair shake, and he didn't have a thing to hide, but he just never said nothing about himself. All the Gordons were that way."

In 1914, Gordon opened a moving-picture theatre in a building he owned on Park Row, naming it the Venice, after an Italian restaurant in Coney Island whose spaghetti he liked. After operating it four years, he found that it kept him away from the tracks and he gave it to Rosie, who had been working in the ticket cage. The next year he sold his Bowery shooting gallery, in which, for several months, Mazie had been running a candy-and-root-beer concession. Rosie did not like selling tickets, so Mazie took her job. Around this time, Mazie began calling herself Mazie Gordon. She will not explain why she took her brother-in-law's name. "That's my business," she says. The Gordons left Grand Street in the early twenties, moving to a house on Surf Avenue in Coney. Mazie continued to live with them. Louis was away much of the time, following the horses. Mazie says that once, after a good season in Saratoga, he gave her a Stutz which, with accessories, cost $5,000. She used to ride down to Coney in the Stutz every night after work; one of the ushers at the Venice was her chauffeur. In October, 1932, Louis fell

dead of a heart attack at the Empire City race track. Mazie and her
sisters left Coney Island a few years later and returned to the East
Side, eventually taking an apartment together in Knickerbocker
Village, four blocks from the Venice. They live quietly. Rosie, a
taciturn, sad-eyed woman, looks after property left by her husband.
Besides her interest in the Venice, this property includes a number
of lots along the boardwalk in Coney and an ancient red-brick
tenement at 9 James Street, a block from the Venice. This tenement
has sixteen cold-water flats, all occupied by unmarried Chinese men.
Jeanie, a handsome young woman, boasts that she has gone to the
West Coast and back ten times while working in vaudeville as an
acrobatic dancer. Now and then she spells Mazie in the cage at the
Venice.

Mazie's hours would kill most women. She works seven days a
week, seldom taking a day off, and is usually on duty from 9:30
A.M. until 11 P.M. Her cage is not much more spacious than a
telephone booth, but she long ago learned how to make herself
comfortable in it. She sits on two thick pillows in a swivel chair
and wears bedroom slippers. In summer she keeps an electric fan,
aimed upward, on the floor, replacing it in winter with an electric
heater. When the weather is especially cold she brings her dog,
Fluffy, an old, wheezy Pomeranian bitch, to the theatre. She lets
Fluffy sleep in her lap, and this keeps both of them warm. Mazie
makes change as automatically as she breathes, and she finds time
for many domestic chores while on duty. She mends clothes, puts
red polish on her fingernails, reads a little, and occasionally spends
half an hour or so cleaning her diamonds with a scrap of chamois
skin. On rainy days she sends out for her meals, eating them right
in the cage. She uses the marble change counter for a table. Once,
hunched over a plate of roast-beef hash, she looked up and said to
a visitor, "I do light housekeeping in here." When she gets thirsty
she sends an usher across the street to the King Kong Bar & Grill
for a cardboard container of beer. She used to keep a bottle of
Canadian whiskey, which she calls "smoke," hidden in her cash
drawer, but since an appendix operation in 1939 she has limited
herself to celery tonic and beer.

There are two cluttered shelves on one wall of her cage. On the bottom shelf are a glass jar of "jawbreakers," a kind of hard candy which she passes out to children, a clamshell that serves as an ashtray, a hind leg of a rabbit, a stack of paper towels, and a box of soap. When a bum with an exceptionally grimy face steps up to buy a ticket, Mazie places a couple of paper towels and a cake of soap before him and says, "Look, buddy, I'll make a bargain with you. If you'll take this and go in the gents' room and wash your face, I'll let you in free." Few bums are offended by this offer; most of them accept willingly. Occasionally she gives one fifteen cents and sends him to a barber college on Chatham Square for a shave and a haircut. If she is in a good humor, Mazie will admit a bum free without much argument. However, she says she can tell a bum by the look in his eyes, and ordinary citizens who have heard of her generosity and try to get passed in outrage her. "If you haven't got any money," she tells such people, "go steal a watch."

On Mazie's top shelf is a pile of paper-backed books, which includes "Old Gipsy Nan's Fortune Teller and Dream Book," "Prince Ali Five Star Dream Book," and "Madame Fu Futtam's Spiritual Magical Dream Book." Mazie is deeply interested in dreams, although at times she seems a little ashamed of it. "A dream just means you et something that didn't agree with you," she sometimes says, rather defiantly. Nevertheless, she makes a practice of remembering them and spends hours hunting through her books for satisfactory interpretations. Also on her top shelf are a rosary, some back numbers of a religious periodical called the *Messenger of the Sacred Heart,* and a worn copy of "Spiritual Reflections for Sisters," by the Reverend Charles J. Mullaly, S. J., which she borrowed from an Italian nun, one of the Daughters of Mary Help of Christians, who conduct a school in Chinatown. Lately Mazie has been reading a page of this book every day. She says that she understands hardly any of it but that reading it makes her feel good. Mazie is not a Catholic; she is Jewish, but she has been entranced by Roman Catholicism for many years. One of her oldest friends in the neighborhood is Monsignor William E. Cashin, rector of St. Andrew's, the little church back of the Municipal Building. She frequently shows up for the Night Workers' Mass, which is said every Sunday at 2:30 A.M. in St. Andrew's by Monsignor Cashin. She sits in a middle pew with her head bowed. Surrounded by policemen, firemen, scrubwomen, telephone girls, nurses, printers, and similar night workers who regularly attend the mass, she feels at home. On the way out she always slips a dollar bill into the poor box. Now and then she calls on the Monsignor and has a long talk with him, and whenever he takes a walk on the Bowery he pauses at her cage and passes the time of day.

Mazie also knows two mothers superior quite well. The rosary she keeps in her cage is a present from the Sisters of Our Lady of Christian Doctrine, who run Madonna House, a settlement on Cherry Street. Sister Margaret, the superior there, has known Mazie for years and has made an attempt to understand her. "On the Bowery it's probably an asset to have a reputation for toughness," Sister Margaret once told a friend, "and I'm afraid Mazie tries to give people the worst possible impression of herself, just for self-protection. She isn't really tough. At heart, she's good and kind. We can always count on her for help. A few weeks ago there was a fire in an Italian tenement near here. One of the families in it had a new baby. It was late at night and we didn't know exactly how to help them. Two of the sisters went to Mazie, and she came right down and found the family a new flat and gave the mother some money." Mazie's favorite saint is St. John Bosco. There is a statue of him in a niche in the steeple of the weatherbeaten Church of the Transfiguration in Chinatown. At night the saint can be clearly seen by the light of the galaxy of neon signs on the chop-suey joints which surround the church. When she passes through Mott Street, Mazie looks up at the saint and crosses herself. "I asked a sister once if it was O.K. for me to give myself a cross, and she told me it was," Mazie says.

Mazie became interested in Catholicism in the winter of 1920. A drug addict on Mulberry Street, a prostitute with two small daughters, came to her cage one night and asked for help. The woman said her children were starving. "I knew this babe was a junky," Mazie says, "and I followed her home just to see was she lying about her kids. She had two kids all right, and they were starving in this crummy little room. I tried to get everybody to do something—the cops, the Welfare, the so-called missions on the Bowery that the Methodists run or whatever to hell they are. But all these people said the girl was a junky. That excused them from lifting a hand. So I seen two nuns on the street, and they went up there with me. Between us, we got the woman straightened out. I liked the nuns. They seemed real human. Ever since then I been interested in the Cat'lic Church."

Mazie does not spend much time at home, so she encourages people to visit her while she is working. Her visitors stand around in the lobby at the rear door of her cage. She frequently gets so interested in a caller that she swings completely around in her swivel chair and presents her back to customers, who have to shout and rap on the window before she will turn and sell them tickets. In the morning, practically all of her visitors are bums with hangovers who come to her, scratching themselves and twitching, and ask for money with which to get their first drinks of the day. She passes out dimes regularly to about twenty-five of these men. Because of this, she is disliked by many of the hard-shell evangelists who hold hymn-singings in the gutters of the Bowery every evening. One of them, a grim, elderly woman, came to the cage not long ago and shook a finger at Mazie. "We sacrifice our nights to come down here and encourage these unfortunates to turn over a new leaf," she said. "Then you give them money and they begin using intoxicants all over again." When Mazie is faced with such a situation, she makes irrelevant or vulgar remarks until the complainant leaves. On this occasion she leaned forward and said, "Par'n me, Madam, but it sounds like your guts are growling. What you need is a beer."

Few of the men to whom Mazie gives money for eye-openers are companionable. They take her dimes with quivering fingers, mutter a word of thanks, and hurry off. Two of them, however, invariably linger a while. They have become close friends of Mazie's. One is a courtly old Irishman named Pop, and the other is an addled, sardonic little man who says he is a poet and whom Mazie calls Eddie Guest. She says she likes Pop because he is so cheerful and

Eddie Guest because he is so sad. "I come from a devout family of teetotallers," Pop once said. "They was thirteen in the family, and they called me the weakling because I got drunk on Saturday nights. Well, they're all under the sod. Woodrow Wilson was President when the last one died, and I'm still here drinking good liquor and winking at the pretty girls." "That's right, Pop," Mazie said. Pop works bus stops. He approaches people waiting on corners for a bus and asks for a nickel with which to get uptown or downtown, as the case may be. When he gets a nickel, he touches his hat and hurries off to the next bus stop. At night he sings ballads in Irish gin mills on Third Avenue. Mazie thinks he has a beautiful baritone, and every morning, in return for her dime, he favors her with two or three ballads. Her favorites—she hums them—are "Whiskey, You're the Divil," "The Garden Where the Praties Grow," "Tiddly-Aye-Aye for the One-Eyed Reilly," and "The Widow McGinnis's Pig." Sometimes Pop dances a jig on the tiled floor of the lobby. "Pop's a better show than I got inside," Mazie says on these occasions.

Eddie Guest is a gloomy, defeated, ex–Greenwich Village poet who has been around the Bowery off and on for eight or nine years. He mutters poetry to himself constantly and is taken to Bellevue for observation about once a year. He carries all his possessions in a greasy beach bag and sleeps in flophouses, never staying in one two nights in succession, because, he says, he doesn't want his enemies to know where he is. During the day he wanders in and out of various downtown branches of the Public Library. At the Venice one night he saw "The River," the moving picture in which the names of the tributaries of the Mississippi were made into a poem. When he came out, he stopped at Mazie's cage, spread his arms, and recited the names of many of the walk-up hotels on the Bowery. "The Alabama Hotel, the Comet, and the Uncle Sam House," he said, in a declamatory voice, "the Dandy, the Defender, the Niagara, the Owl, the Victoria House and the Grand Windsor Hotel, the Houston, the Mascot, the Palace, the Progress, the Palma House and the White House Hotel, the Newport, the Crystal, the Lion and the Marathon. All flophouses. All on the Bowery. Each and all my home, sweet home." For some reason, Mazie thought this was extraordinarily funny. Now, each morning, in order to get a dime, Eddie Guest is obliged to recite this chant for her. It always causes her to slap her right thigh, throw her head back, and guffaw. Both Eddie Guest and Mazie can be grimly and rather pointlessly amused by the signs over flophouse entrances and by the bills of fare lettered in white on the windows of pig-snout restaurants. When Mazie passes the Victoria House and sees its sign, "ROOMS WITH ELECTRIC LIGHTS, 30C," or when she looks at the window of the Greek's on Chatham Square, "SNOUTS WITH FRENCH FRY POTS & COFFEE, T, OR BUTTERMILK, 10C," she always snickers. Mazie has considerable respect for Eddie Guest but thinks he is kidding when he calls himself a poet. Once he read to her part of a completely unintelligible poem about civilization in the United States, on which he says he has been working for twenty years and which he calls "No Rags, No Bones, No Bottles Today." "If that's a poem," Mazie said when he had finished, "I'm the Queen of Sweden."

Mazie's afternoon visitors are far more respectable than the morning ones. The people who stopped by to talk with her between noon and 6 P.M. one Saturday included Monsignor Cashin, Fannie Hurst, two detectives from the Oak Street station, a flashily dressed young Chinese gambler whom Mazie calls Fu Manchu and who is a power in Tze Far, the Chinatown version of the numbers lottery; two nuns from Madonna House, who wanted to thank her for buying a phonograph for the girls' club at their settlement; a talkative girl from Atlanta, Georgia, called Bingo, once a hostess in a Broadway taxi-dance hall and now the common-law wife of the chef of a chop-suey restaurant on Mott Street; the bartender of a Chatham Square saloon, who asked her to interpret a dream for him; and the clerk of a flophouse, who came to tell her that a bum named Tex had hanged himself in the washroom the night before. When she was told about Tex, Mazie nodded sagely and said, as she always does when she hears about the death of someone she has known, "Well, we all got to go sooner or later. You can't live forever. When your number's up, rich or poor, you got to go." Most of the visitors on that afternoon happened to be old friends of Mazie's. Miss Hurst, for example, she has known for eleven years. She calls her Fannie and likes to tell about their first meeting.

"One night," she says, "a swell-looking dame came to my cage and said she often took walks on the Bowery and would like to meet me. She said her name was Fannie Hurst. 'Pleased to meet you, Fannie,' I said. 'My name is Mary Pickford.' It turned out she really was Fannie Hurst. At first I thought she was going to put me in a book, and I didn't go for her. Since she promised not to write no books about me, we been pals." Miss Hurst visits Mazie frequently. Each time she comes, Mazie looks at her dress, fingers the material, asks how much it cost, tells her she got gypped, and advises her to try one of the shops on Division Street. Miss Hurst does not mind this. "I admire Mazie," she said. "She is the most compassionate person I've ever known. No matter how filthy or drunk or evil-smelling a bum may be, she treats him as an equal." Until recently, Miss Hurst occasionally took friends down to meet Mazie. "I'm afraid they looked on her as just another Bowery curiosity," she says. "So I don't take people down any more. I used to invite Mazie to parties at my house. She always accepted but never came. I think she's still a little suspicious of me, although I've never written a line about her and never intend to. I simply look upon her as a friend."

From callers like Fu Manchu and Bingo, Mazie hears considerable gossip about the sleazy underworld of Chinatown. She says she never repeats such gossip, not even to her sisters. Detectives know that she has many Chinese friends and sometimes stop at her cage and ask apparently innocent questions about them; she shrugs her shoulders and says, "No spik English." In general, however, she cooperates with the police. Drunken tourists often come down to Bowery joints to see life, and when she notices them stumbling around Chatham Square she telephones the Oak Street station. "Such dopes are always getting rolled by bums," she says. "I got no sympathy for out-of-towners, but bums are the clumsiest thieves in the world. They always get caught, and it's best to get temptation out of their way." Although her language frequently shocks the Oak Street cops, they admire Mazie. Detective Kain, for instance, says that she has "the roughest tongue and the softest heart in the Third Precinct." "She knows this neighborhood like a farmer knows his farm," he says. "I believe she's got the second sight. If anything out of the way is happening anywhere along the Bowery, she senses it."

Detective Kain has for some time been trying to solve a mystery in which Mazie is involved. Mazie has a telephone in her booth, of course, and in June, 1929, a man whose voice she did not recognize began calling her daily at 5 P.M., asking for a date or making cryptic remarks, such as "They got the road closed, Mazie. They won't let nobody through." After three months he stopped calling. Then, around Christmas of the following year, he began again. He has been calling intermittently ever since. "I won't hear from him for maybe six months," Mazie says. "Then, one day around five, the phone will ring and this voice will say, 'All the clocks have stopped running' or 'Mazie, they cut down the big oak tree' or some other dopey remark. He never says more than a few words, and when I say something he hangs right up. One afternoon he gave me the shakes. He called up and said, 'Mazie, I got a nephew studying to be an undertaker and he needs somebody to practice on.' Then he hung up. A minute later he called again and said, 'You'll do! You'll do!' Somehow, I get to feeling he's across the street in a booth. The worst thing is I suspect every stranger that buys a ticket. I strike up conversations with strangers just to see if I can find one who talks like him. I think he's trying to drive me crazy." Among her friends, Mazie refers to her caller as The Man. If she has visitors around five o'clock and the telephone rings, she says, "Pick up the receiver and see what The Man has to say this time." Fannie Hurst once listened. "It was macabre," she said. Detective Kain has listened often, has warned the man, and has tried vainly to trace the calls. Mazie's number has been changed repeatedly, but that does no good.

Mazie closes her cage shortly after 11 P.M., when the final show is under way, and goes to an all-night diner near Brooklyn Bridge, where she glances through the *Daily News* while having a couple of cups of coffee and a honey bun. The only things in the *News* that she regularly reads from beginning to end are the comics, the "Voice of the People," and "The Inquiring Fotographer." She says she doesn't read political or war stories because she can't understand them and because they make her blue. "The world is all bitched up," she once said. "Always was, always will be." "Do you really believe that?" she was asked. "No," she said, after a moment of deliberation, "I guess I don't." She spends half an hour in the diner. Then, practically every night, before going home to bed, she makes a Samaritan tour of the Bowery and its environs. She carries an umbrella and a large handbag, which contains a flashlight, a number of cakes of soap of the size found in hotel bathrooms, and a supply of nickels, dimes, and quarters.

If it is a cold night, she goes first to an alley near the steps leading to the footwalk of Manhattan Bridge. Bums like to keep fires going in discarded oil drums in this alley. She distributes some change. Then she inspects Columbus Park, a block west of Chatham Square, where every winter a few bums pass out on benches and die of exposure. The police say Mazie has rescued scores of men in this park. Then, passing through Chinatown, she returns to the Bowery and heads uptown, pausing whenever she recognizes a bum and giving him enough money for a meal, a drink, or a flop. Frequently, in addition to small change, she gives a bum a cake of soap. "*Please use it, buddy,*" she says pleadingly. Here and there she gets out her flashlight and peers into a doorway. She pays particular attention to the drunken or exhausted bums who sleep in doorways, on loading platforms, and on sidewalks. She always tries to arouse them and stake them to flops. In warm weather, if they don't seem disposed to stir, she leaves them where they are. "A sidewalk is about as nice as a flophouse cot in the summertime," she says. "You may get up stiff, but you won't get up crummy." In the winter, however, she badgers them until they awaken. She punches them in the ribs with her umbrella and, if necessary, gets down on her knees and slaps their faces. "When a bum is sleeping off his load, you could saw off his leg and he wouldn't notice nothing," she says. Sometimes a bum who has been awakened by Mazie tries to take a poke at her. When this happens, she assumes a spraddle-legged stance, like a fencer, and jabs the air viciously with her umbrella. "Stand back," she cries, "or I'll put your eyes out." If a man is too weak, sodden, or spiritless to get up, Mazie grabs his elbows and heaves him to his feet. Holding him erect, she guides him to the nearest flophouse and pulls and pushes him up the stairs to the lobby. She pays the clerk for the man's lodging (thirty cents is the customary price) and insists on his having at least two blankets. Then, with the help of the clerk or the bouncer, she takes off the man's shoes, unbuttons his collar, loosens his belt, and puts him to bed with his clothes on. This is usually a tumultuous process, and sometimes many of the lodgers are awakened. They stick their heads out of the doors of their cubicles. "It's Mazie!" they shout. "Hello, Mazie!" Now and then an emotional bum will walk out in his underwear and insist on shaking Mazie's hand. "God bless you, Mazie, old girl!" he will cry. Mazie does not approve of such antics. "Go back to bed, you old goat," she says. If she is acquainted with the clerk and trusts him, she leaves some change with him and asks that it be given to the bum when he wakes up. Flophouses are for-men-only establishments, and Mazie is the only female who has ever crossed the threshold of many of them.

At least a couple of times a week, Mazie finds injured men lying in the street. On these occasions she telephones Police Headquarters and asks for an ambulance from Gouverneur or Beekman Street, the hospitals which take care of most Bowery cases. She knows many of the drivers from these hospitals by name and orders them around. Police say she summons more ambulances than any other private citizen in town, and she is proud of this. "I don't over-do it," she says. "Unless a man is all stove-up and bloody, I don't put in a call, but if I had my way, the wagons would be rolling all night long. There's hardly a bum on the Bowery who don't belong in a hospital."

On her walk, Mazie usually tries to steer clear of other well-known nocturnal Bowery characters. Among these are the Widow Woman and the Crybaby. The Crybaby is an old mission bum who sits on the curb for hours with his feet in the gutter, sobbing brokenly. Once Mazie nudged him on the shoulder and asked, "What's the matter with you?" "I committed the unforgivable sin," he said. Mazie asked him what the sin consisted of, and he began a theological description of it which she didn't understand and which she interrupted after a few minutes, remarking, "Hell, Crybaby, you didn't commit no sin. You just prob'ly got the stomach ulsters." The Widow Woman is a bent, whining crone who wears a mourning veil, a Queen Mary hat, and a rusty black coat, and comes hobbling down the Bowery around midnight giving bums little slips of paper on which are scribbled such statements as "God is love" and "The fires of Hell will burn forever." Mazie is afraid of her. "She walks like a woman and she dresses like a woman, but when she talks I get the feeling that she's a man."

Most nights, before going home to bed, which is usually around two o'clock, Mazie makes brief stops in several saloons and all-night restaurants. She does not mind the reek of stale beer, greasy cabbage, and disinfectant in them. "After you been around the Bowery a few years, your nose gets all wore out," she says. She goes into these places not to eat or drink but to gossip with bartenders and countermen and to listen to the conversation of drunken bums. She has found that bums do not talk much about sex, sports, politics, or business, the normal saloon topics. She says most of them are far too undernourished to have any interest in sex. They talk, instead, about what big shots they were before they hit the Bowery. Although their stories fascinate her, Mazie is generally cynical. "To hear them tell it," she says, "all the bums on the Bowery were knocking off millions down in Wall Street when they were young, else they were senators, else they were the general manager of something real big, but, poor fellows, the most of them they wasn't ever nothing but drunks."

(1940)

# Hit on the Head with a Cow

W HEN I HAVE TIME TO KILL, I sometimes go to the basement of a brownstone tenement on Fifty-ninth Street, three-quarters of a block west of Columbus Circle, and sit on a rat-gnawed Egyptian mummy and cut up touches with Charles Eugene Cassell, an old Yankee for whose bitter and disorderly mind I have great respect. Mr. Cassell has Negro, French, Portuguese, and English blood. He calls himself Captain Charley because he had charge of an ammunition barge for a brief period during the First World War and saw no reason why he shouldn't have a title. About fifteen years ago, after he got too contrary to hold down a steady job, he took out some of his savings and opened a museum—Captain Charley's Private Museum for Intelligent People—in a Harlem apartment house; some time later, after a series of robberies, he moved to the basement on Fifty-ninth Street. The Captain is a relentless and indiscriminate collector, and stored in his place are thousands of curious odds and ends he gathered during the fifty-five years he worked as a sailor or cook on navy and merchant ships, and during other years when he was a servant in clubs and hotels in Manhattan. The most valuable exhibit is a group of stuffed animals. They are moth-cut and mangy, but several times a year the Captain is able to rent them to moving picture theatres for lobby displays during the showing of jungle films. The Captain charges fifteen cents admission to his museum, but half the time he forgets to collect it. The majority of his visitors are passers-by attracted by big cardboard signs which he puts up at the head of the steps leading down to

the basement—signs such as "IF YOU CONSIDER YOURSELF INTELLI-
GENT, STEP INSIDE," "CAPTAIN CHARLEY WILL SELL A FEW ODDS AND
ENDS FROM TEN CENTS TO FIFTEEN HUNDRED DOLLARS," and "IF YOU
ARE SO DAMN SMART, WHY AIN'T YOU RICH?" A few of the visitors
are women hunting for bargains in antiques.

I like to sit in the gloomy, moldy basement and listen to the
Captain. After I have listened to him for fifteen minutes or so, I
get to thinking about something that happened to me when I was
ten years old. My father and a hired man named Alonzo were
butchering a cow in the hall of the barn in back of our house in
the small town in North Carolina that I come from, and I was
helping. We were hoisting the cow up in the air with a block and
tackle so we could skin her, and Alonzo and I had hold of the rope.
We had the cow off the ground when something went wrong with
the gear, and when I came to I was out in the barnyard running
around in circles and screeching, and my head was bloody. When
I was caught and subdued by Alonzo and stretched out on the
green grass under a pecan tree, I looked up at my father and said,
"What happened, Daddy?" My father had a faraway look in his
eyes and he said, "Son, you were hit on the head with a cow."
For at least a week after I received the blow on the head everything people said to me seemed illogical or disconnected; every
conversation I heard seemed to end unerringly and pleasantly in
confusion. That is the way I feel after I have listened to Captain
Charley for a little while. I feel as if I had been hit on the head
with a cow.

The last time I went to see him I took a notebook along, and
while he rummaged through the museum—he was searching for a
bone which he said he hacked off an Arab around 9 P.M. one full-
moon night in 1907 after the Arab had been murdered for signing
a treaty—I wrote down everything he said. He didn't pay much
attention to me while he talked; most of the time he was talking
to himself. And while he rambled along he kept plucking objects
out of the clutter on the floor of the basement. He said he wanted
to find the Arab's bone and send it to Police Commissioner Grover
A. Whalen by parcel post. "I dreamt about old Grover last night,

and I made up my mind to send him a present," he said. "In this dream old Grover was a engineer on a fast freight on the New York Central, and I was the fireman, and we was arguing over who had the right to blow the whistle. Toot! Toot! Old Grover won." (Captain Charley is a great admirer of Mr. Whalen, and I once asked him why. Mr. Whalen is noted for his sartorial daring, and it turned out that that is the reason. "I like the way old Grover dresses," Captain Charley said. "He dresses like he means it.") Before long the Captain had piled up a dusty mound of objects which included a stuffed barn owl, an old gilt picture frame, a tin lunch bucket, a stack of theatre programs and restaurant menus of the 1890's, a woman's hat with a green ostrich feather on it, a dirty beaded bag, a bashed-in pith helmet, a cigar box full of seashells, political campaign buttons, and Chinese coins; a big roll of yellowed newspapers around which a necktie had been knotted, a cutlass, a parasol which he said was once the property of a famous New Orleans madam named Mrs. Lilly-belle Sue-belle Russell, and the lengthy skin of a boa constrictor that killed a girl and a goat in South America at a moment when the girl was milking the goat.

"Where were you born, Captain Charley?" I asked.

"I'm born in Boston," he said. "I'm born in the Hub. I'm a bluenosed Yankee, fed on codfish and cranberries. My type of people are all dead. They broke the mold. I consider myself different from other men, on a higher plane, always been a boss, never wore overalls. Take the biggest man in the country and no matter what big deeds he did, I did twice as much. I don't smoke and I don't hang out in none of them low-down Columbus Avenue saloons. I drink in high-class places. Nothing but champagne wine and brandy, that's all I drink. High-class people invite me to their houses for dinner, just for the honor of it, send me home full of brandy. I'm very particular about my something to eat. When I got cash on hand I set a fine table, don't eat nothing but lobsters and fresh peaches and T-bone steaks. There's people that could live high on what I throw away. Use to take advantage of women, but somewhere along the line I lost my animal spirits. I can look a gangster in the eye and make him change his mind, but I can't do a thing with a woman no more. At one time I had nine big switch-tail women on my personal payroll and they all stole from me, picked me clean. Buzzards! One of these days I'm going to pack my grip and go up to Boston and die. Won't even bother to get me a cemetery lot; I'll just find me a convenient gutter and lie down in it and die. Sad, sad! Made up my mind to die in Boston because I was born there. Ashes to ashes, dust to dust. Older I get the more disgusted I get. I'm yet to find a honest man, a honest woman. I don't even believe in good deeds; once I tried to help a man out of a well and I tumbled in and broke both legs. I believe in assassination, it makes elbow room. I believe in gassing off all the old people, except me. I'm too smart to gas. I'm a taxidermist. I can mount a mosquito. I can mount a strawberry. I can mount any old fish you ever see."

At this moment a cowbell hanging from the knob on the street door began to tinkle and a middle-aged woman came in. When her eyes got used to the gloom, she peered at us and said, "May I look at the antiques?" The Captain said, "Help yourself, friend." He shambled over and collected fifteen cents admission, and then returned to his search for the Arab's bone. The woman stood stock still for a few moments and stared at the Captain. He is small, grimy, and surly. His eyes are always bleary. He wears a white, waxed mustache. He had on his customary outfit—ragged duck pants, a turtleneck sweater, a pea jacket, a captain's cap, and tennis sneakers painted with silver radiator paint. He was decorating some seashells one day with the silver paint and decided that it would look good on his sneakers.

"Look at this lunch bucket," he said. "Use to belong to Al Smith when he was in Fulton Fish Market. Never used such a common thing myself. Always had money, never broke; had the chicken pox, had the sleeping sickness, had the dropsy, had the yellow johnnies, had the walking, talking pneumonia. Didn't miss a thing in the medical line. My old man was a big man with shoulders like a mule, born on a farm in Nova Scotia, lived most of his life in Boston. He was born in a barn. When he went in a place he always left the door wide open. People would yell at him, 'Shut the door! Were

43

you born in a barn?' and he'd say, 'That's right. How'd you guess it?' He was biggity as sin. What you call a beachcomber. He did odd jobs on the fish docks, and he fed us on fish until the bones stuck out of our ears. Comb my hair in the morning, I'd comb out a handful of bones. It got so my stomach rose and fell with the tide. Fish, fish! I was almost grown before I found out people ate anything else. Use to take me with him to the saloons when I was just a little teeniney baby. He'd set me on the bar beside his glass of whiskey. When he wasn't watching, I'd sneak me a drink of his whiskey, then I'd crawl down on the sawdust and pick a fight with the saloon cats. My old man would tuck me under his right arm like I was a bag of groceries and tote me home and throw me on the bed and I'd sleep it off. I'd grunt and snore like a full-grown man. People said I was the prettiest boy baby ever born in Boston. I was always smart. Worked all my life, never had time for baseball, never spun a top. First job I ever had, I guided a blindman beggar around the streets of Boston, a fellow named Blind Clancy, a gin drinker. I was seven years old, going on eight. He had a grip like steel. He'd hold on to my shoulder, and he had such a grip it made my shoulder ache. He was a smart blindman; he wouldn't ever let me hold the cup. We'd stumble along and he'd sing out, 'All good people please to drop a penny in the blindman's cup.' I got sick and tired of hearing that, and one day I walked off and left him right in the middle of a parade on Tremont Street. I took to knocking around the docks. At sixteen I was an A.B. on the deep sea, drawing down a man's pay. Take those old sea captains; why, I made monkeys out of them because I knew so much astronomy. Use to be an atheist, but I'm getting so old I'm afraid to be an atheist. Take hell and damnation. Didn't use to believe in it, but now I just don't know. It sounds so logical. I'm a Just in Case Christian. Ever so often I hunt me up a church and get right with the Holy Ghost, just in case. Still and all, I can't endure preachers. Deep down in my heart, I don't believe in pie in the sky; I believe in T-bone steak in the here and now. Look at this. Theodore Roosevelt's pith helmet. I was working in a big club full of rich old men that sat around all day in thick leather chairs dozing and grunting and scratching theirselves. And one of these rich old men said to me, 'See here, Charley, you want this helmet? It use to belong to President Roosevelt.' I sure was glad to get it. Old Theodore wore it when he was a rootin' and a tootin' around in them deep jungles. That's what I'd like, big game hunting. Bang! Bang!"

The Captain turned abruptly and scrutinized the woman visitor to make sure that she wasn't stealing anything. He believes every person who enters the museum plans to rob it. The woman pretended to be examining a stuffed crocodile, but from the perplexed look on her face I knew that she had been listening to everything the Captain said.

"The world owes me a lot," continued the Captain, "but I'll never collect. Owes me a lot of sleep. I don't get out of bed until high noon; sometimes I don't even get out of bed then. There's times I get so disgusted I just stay in bed three, four days hand running. Somebody knocks on the door, I holler out, 'Go 'way, go 'way! There's an old man in here with a severe case of the blue-green leprosy. Run for your life, whoever you are.' I just lie in bed and study over a long list of people I wish was dead. Sometimes I sit up and put a mirror in my lap and wax my mustache, wax it so sharp it's dangerous. Sometimes I sing to myself. You know that old number called 'Mother'?" The Captain threw his head back and began to sing in a quavering voice. " 'M is for the many things she gave me, O means only that she's growing old, T is for the tears she shed to save me, H is for her heart of purest gold. . . .' " His voice broke, and he snorted angrily and spat on the floor. "Oh, the hell with it. Use to run with the rowdiest women in this country until I took and married a Buffalo girl. I was up in Buffalo on political business and I seen her and I took and married her. She gave me two beautiful daughters and when they was grown I set them up in a candy store on Amsterdam Avenue, share and share alike, but they was too stuck up to wait on the customers, so I married them off to post office clerks. I didn't see no certain future in doctors or lawyers, so I married them off to post office clerks in the Bronx. Working for the government is sure and

45

certain. If I had to do it all over again, I'd get me a good hold on the public teat and I wouldn't let loose until death do us part. Always been a leader of men, always had high-class people for my friends. Use to know O. Henry right well. Use to ask me questions about countries I had travelled in, and when I gave him an answer he'd give me a dollar. When the first bicycles came out he bought me a bicycle, bought me a suit of clothes. He was that kind of a man. Use to work for a man that ran a hotel. At 10 P.M. he'd go upstairs and leave me to run the damned hotel. I ran it, all right. Never had so much to drink before or since. I use to wash my socks in good liquor. I'm just a case of cabin boy to captain. Where in the hell is that old Arab bone? I hope the cat didn't drag it out of here. My cat's name is Steamboat Bill. I was the first man to collect stamps. If you doubt my statement, disprove it. Try to disprove me, I'll make a monkey out of you. When you think of all the things I've done, people ought to respect me more'n they do. A man don't pay me my due respect, I knock his slats in."

The woman visitor left. The cowbell on the doorknob tinkled as she shut the door.

"I bet she stole something," said the Captain, smacking a fist against a knee in a petulant, childish gesture. "They all steal something. I got a fine cat, best cat I ever had. Jumps up and pulls the electric-light cord. Jumps in bed and scratches my back. Use to have a monkey for a house pet. I got rid of him; monkeys stink. When I talk I get excited. Had so many knocks on the head in saloon fights I don't always remember. It's a nuisance when you can't remember, I be damned if it ain't. It makes you mad. Look at this here snakeskin. South American boa constrictor. You could make a woman fifty-five pairs of pretty shoes out of that snakeskin. Longest damned snakeskin in the United States. Show me any millionaire that's got a snakeskin as long as that. I'm disgusted to the full with this world. What I'd like is an expedition, a scientific expedition. I like brains. I'd kill a man for being stupid or give him credit for robbing me because that would demonstrate he had sense. Brains is what counts. I got a pension from the Brooklyn Navy Yard and I got a pension from the Spanish-American War, and I don't trust nobody. Don't trust the preacher, don't trust the newspaper, don't trust the radio set, don't trust the billboards, don't trust the pretty label on the liquor bottle where it says eight years old; it's all big black lies. When I hear the whistle, I don't even believe the train's coming. I got a radical nature, and I can't help it. When I went to sea, I was always making trouble. I was a scrapper. When I hit a port, the population scattered inland. In some towns, a half hour after I hit port there wouldn't be nobody there but me. The people would take themselves a blanket to lie on and enough groceries to last them, and they'd hide out in the hills until I went back to sea. Once I was a cook on a scientific expedition to the Arctic. I found a mastodon bone and I wanted it. It was just exactly what I wanted. I was always on the lookout for bones and historical odds and ends; even when I was a young man with my head full of women worry I was planning ahead for my museum. But it was a rule you had to turn in everything you found. So a sailor said to me, 'Break it, cook, and they'll let you keep it.' So I hefted this valuable bone high over my head and I slammed it on the deck and it cracked all to hell and gone. Then they let me keep it. That's a piece of it over there in the far corner. Worth fifteen hundred dollars if it's worth a cent."

That is a fair example of the way the Captain answers a question. If you remember, all I asked him was "Where were you born, Captain Charley?" After my last visit I checked up on several of the Captain's remarks, not that it makes any difference to me if they are true or false. First I checked up on his boast that he drinks nothing but champagne wine and brandy. The bartender in a saloon on Columbus Avenue around the corner from the museum said, "Sometimes that old boy comes in here to make a phone call and I invite him to have a beer, and he sure don't refuse." The bartender said he once visited the museum. "Jeez," he said, "what a place! If they really want to find Judge Crater, that's the place to look." Later I telephoned Alfred E. Smith and asked him if he was aware that his old tin lunch bucket was in a museum. "It couldn't be my lunch bucket," said Mr. Smith, "because I never owned a lunch bucket. When I was working in the fish market I always went home to eat."

The Captain becomes evasive and hostile when any one tries to pin him down. Once I asked him the name of the ship of which he was captain.

"It was in 1917," he said. "War time."

"What was the name of the ship?"

"Like I said, it was war time. They called it the World War; to me, it was just a fuss, a commotion."

"What was the name of the ship?"

"Number Four."

"What kind of a ship was Number Four?"

"God damn it, sir, don't interrupt me. Haven't you got any respect for old age?"

"What kind of a ship was Number Four?"

"It was a barge. It was a munitions barge. It was towed between Wilmington and the Navy Yard in Brooklyn, and I was captain. Everybody took orders from Captain Charley. Half of Brooklyn would of blowed up one night if I hadn't cut the barge loose from the tug. The tide was throwing her around, and I took charge and cut her loose. If she'd a bumped into Brooklyn it would of been goodbye Brooklyn. Might of been a good thing. Thinned out some of them slums. I been mixed up in everything. I even been kidnapped. When my museum was situated up in Harlem a fellow and a girl I never seen before came and stood over my bed, and the fellow said, 'Are you the man that took advantage of this here girl?' And I said, 'I don't know. I might be. I'm a mean old man.' And the girl said, 'Let's slit his throat for him.' Then they kidnapped me and took me to the bank and made me draw out my account, two hundred and some odd dollars. Said they'd slit my throat if I told. I found out who the fellow was; he was a brush-boy in a barber shop four or five blocks up the street from my museum. I seen him on the street a couple of times, but I was afraid to notify the Police Department. I never said a mumbling word. I didn't care to risk it. I need my throat to swallow with. There's something about a knife that makes me shrink right up. Like that old saying my mamma use to have, 'When the big bulldog gets in trouble, puppy-dog britches fit him fine.' "

I was surprised to find out about the Captain's streak of timidity. He is small and frail-looking, but he is bellicose. He likes to push his captain's cap on the back of his head, put his fists up like a prizefighter, and give a frightful account of the way he maimed a disrespectful shipmate by throwing pepper in his eyes and striking him in the face with "the business end of a broken beer bottle." He is proud of his captain's cap. He says, "This cap takes me anywhere, right past the ticket window." The Captain seeks to give visitors the impression that he once was a great lover; tacked up in the museum is the old saloon wall-motto which states, "The happiest moments of my life were spent in the arms of another man's wife." This motto usually ends with a dash and "My mother," but the Captain chopped off the last two words. He becomes rather wistful when he tells about his conquests in Paris, among the Eskimos, and on various South Sea islands. He shakes his head, cackles, and says, "I still got the passion, but I ain't got the power. My race is run." He tells visitors that he is "seventy-seven years old, more or less." "I'm not long for this world," he likes to say. "I give myself three more years they'll have me in a box." However, there is still plenty of grit and gristle in him. The basement is so crowded he has to wrestle with exhibits to get from the museum proper back to the tiny room in which he sleeps and eats, and he shoves a massive, old-fashioned bureau or a heavy sea chest out of his way with ease a young pug might envy. He is conscious of his strength and is always threatening to let loose and knock somebody's head off. Like the museum, the room in the rear is stuffed to the ceiling with junk. He has his meals sitting on the bed. The last time I visited him there was a platter on the bed bearing the head and bones of a fish off which his cat was feeding.

Captain Charley has a good reason for his robbery phobia because the museum is frequently entered by petty burglars, a state of things for which he himself is responsible; in talking to visitors he always attributes a fabulous value to even the most worthless trinket. Naturally, some of his visitors believe him when he boasts, holding up a valueless gimcrack, "This is worth fifteen hundred and seventy-five dollars." Occasionally a visitor comes back at night, when the Captain is away, and walks right into the museum and steals a few things. I am certain these thieves are furious after they try to pawn their loot. When the Captain goes away from the museum he usually leaves it unlocked and sticks up a sign just inside the door which warns, "BEWARE OF THE ALIVE SNAKES LOOSE IN HERE." In the daytime the sign is effective, but at night, of course, it does no good. Paradoxically the Captain is proud of the frequency with which he is robbed. He laughs his high, goatlike laugh and says, "*Every*body robs Captain Charley!"

Captain Charley's most remarkable possessions are two objects which look like ironing boards wrapped with strips of brown cloth. The museum is too crowded for chairs, and I sometimes use one of these objects for a seat.

"You know what you sitting on?" the Captain asked me one day.

"No, sir," I said. "What?"

"A Egyptian mummy."

"Is that right?"

"Yes, God damn it, that's right."

"Where did you get it?"

"Got it in Egypt. My boat was tied up in Alexandria and I took a turn around Egypt. They was pulling old mummies out of the tombs by the thousands, so I took three. I took three of the middle-sized ones. I think they're he-mummies. I don't think they mummied no women. I was cook on this boat and I stood 'em up in the kitchen, in the galley. I had 'em stood up in corners. When the crew found out I had the galley full of Egyptian mummies, they became disagreeable to me. They was going to throw my mummies overboard, but that night I took and hid 'em in the lifeboats, under canvas. We was months and months getting back to the United States and it use to give me the snickers every time I thought about them three mummies hiding up in the lifeboats like stowaways. When I went to sneak my mummies ashore a queer thing happened. One of 'em was missing."

"What do you think happened to it?"

"Oh, hell, I don't know. Something real peculiar. When a man takes to meddling with Egyptian mummies fresh out of the tomb, damn near anything's apt to happen."

(1938)

# Professor Sea Gull

*J*OE GOULD IS A BLITHE and emaciated little man who has been a notable in the cafeterias, diners, barrooms, and dumps of Greenwich Village for a quarter of a century. He sometimes brags rather wryly that he is the last of the bohemians. "All the others fell by the wayside," he says. "Some are in the grave, some are in the loony bin, and some are in the advertising business." Gould's life is by no means carefree; he is constantly tormented by what he calls "the three H's"—homelessness, hunger, and hangovers. He sleeps on benches in subway stations, on the floor in the studios of friends, and in quarter-a-night flophouses on the Bowery. Once in a while he trudges up to Harlem and goes to one of the establishments known as "Extension Heavens" that are operated by followers of Father Divine, the Negro evangelist, and gets a night's lodging for fifteen cents. He is five feet four and he hardly ever weighs more than a hundred pounds. Not long ago he told a friend that he hadn't eaten a square meal since June, 1936, when he bummed up to Cambridge and attended a banquet during a reunion of the Harvard class of 1911, of which he is a member. "I'm the foremost authority in the United States," he says, "on the subject of doing without." He tells people that he lives on "air, self-esteem, cigarette butts, cowboy coffee, fried-egg sandwiches, and ketchup." Cowboy coffee, he says, is strong coffee drunk black without sugar. "I've long since lost my taste for good coffee," he says. "I much prefer the kind that sooner or later, if you keep on drinking it, your hands will begin to shake and the whites of your eyes will turn yellow."

While having a sandwich, Gould customarily empties a bottle or two of ketchup on his plate and eats it with a spoon. The countermen in the Jefferson Diner, on Village Square, which is one of his hangouts, gather up the ketchup bottles and hide them the moment he puts his head in the door. "I don't particularly like the confounded stuff," he says, "but I make it a practice to eat all I can get. It's the only grub I know of that's free of charge."

Gould is a Yankee. His branch of the Goulds has been in New England since 1635, and he is related to many of the other early New England families, such as the Lawrences, the Clarkes, and the Storers. "There's nothing accidental about me," he once said. "I'll tell you what it took to make me what I am today. It took old Yankee blood, an overwhelming aversion to possessions, four years of Harvard, and twenty-five years of beating the living hell out of my insides with bad hooch and bad food." He says that he is out of joint with the rest of the human race because he doesn't want to own anything. "If Mr. Chrysler tried to make me a present of the Chrysler Building," he says, "I'd damn near break my neck fleeing from him. I wouldn't own it; it'd own me. Back home in Massachusetts I'd be called an old Yankee crank. Here I'm called a bohemian. It's six of one, half a dozen of the other." Gould has a twangy voice and a Harvard accent. Bartenders and countermen in the Village refer to him as the Professor, the Sea Gull, Professor Sea Gull, the Mongoose, Professor Mongoose, or the Bellevue Boy. He dresses in the castoff clothes of his friends. His overcoat, suit, shirt, and even his shoes are all invariably a size or two too large, but he wears them with a kind of forlorn rakishness. "Just look at me," he says. "The only thing that fits is the necktie." On bitter winter days he puts a layer of newspapers between his shirt and undershirt. "I'm snobbish," he says. "I only use the *Times*." He is fond of unusual headgear—a toboggan, a beret, or a yachting cap. One summer evening he appeared at a party in a seersucker suit, a polo shirt, a scarlet cummerbund, sandals, and a yachting cap, all hand-me-downs. He uses a long black cigarette holder, and a good deal of the time he smokes butts picked up off the sidewalks.

Bohemianism has aged Gould considerably beyond his years. He has got in the habit lately of asking people he has just met to guess his age. Their guesses range between sixty-five and seventy-five; he is fifty-three. He is never hurt by this; he looks upon it as proof of his superiority. "I do more living in one year," he says, "than ordinary humans do in ten." Gould is toothless, and his lower jaw swivels from side to side when he talks. He is bald on top, but the hair at the back of his head is long and frizzly, and he has a bushy, cinnamon-colored beard. He wears a pair of spectacles that are loose and lopsided and that slip down to the end of his nose a moment after he puts them on. He doesn't always wear them on the street and without them he has the wild, unfocussed stare of an old scholar who has strained his eyes on small print. Even in the Village many people turn and look at him. He is stooped and he moves rapidly, grumbling to himself, with his head thrust forward and held to one side. Under his left arm he usually carries a bulging, greasy, brown pasteboard portfolio, and he swings his right arm aggressively. As he hurries along, he seems to be warding off an imaginary enemy. Don Freeman, the artist, a friend of his, once made a sketch of him walking. Freeman called the sketch "Joe Gould versus the Elements." Gould is as restless and footloose as an alley cat, and he takes long hikes about the city, now and then disappearing from the Village for weeks at a time and mystifying his friends; they have never been able to figure out where he goes. When he returns, always looking pleased with himself, he makes a few cryptic remarks, giggles, and then shuts up. "I went on a bird walk along the waterfront with an old countess," he said after his most recent absence. "The countess and I spent three weeks studying sea gulls."

Gould is almost never seen without his portfolio. He keeps it on his lap while he eats and in flophouses he sleeps with it under his head. It usually contains a mass of manuscripts and notes and letters and clippings and copies of obscure little magazines, a bottle of ink, a dictionary, a paper bag of cigarette butts, a paper bag of bread crumbs, and a paper bag of hard, round, dime-store candy of the type called sour balls. "I fight fatigue with sour balls," he says. The crumbs are for pigeons; like many other eccentrics, Gould is a pigeon feeder. He is devoted to a flock which makes its headquarters atop

and around the statue of Garibaldi in Washington Square. These
pigeons know him. When he comes up and takes a seat on the
plinth of the statue, they flutter down and perch on his head and
shoulders, waiting for him to bring out his bag of crumbs. He has
given names to some of them. "Come here, Boss Tweed," he says.
"A lady in Stewart's Cafeteria didn't finish her whole-wheat toast
this morning and when she went out, bingo, I snatched it off her
plate especially for you. Hello, Big Bosom. Hello, Popgut. Hello,
Lady Astor. Hello, St. John the Baptist. Hello, Polly Adler. Hello,
Fiorello, you old goat, how're you today?"

Although Gould strives to give the impression that he is a phil-
osophical loafer, he has done an immense amount of work during
his career as a bohemian. Every day, even when he has a bad hangover
or even when he is weak and listless from hunger, he spends at
least a couple of hours working on a formless, rather mysterious
book that he calls "An Oral History of Our Time." He began this
book twenty-six years ago, and it is nowhere near finished. His
preoccupation with it seems to be principally responsible for the
way he lives; a steady job of any kind, he says, would interfere with
his thinking. Depending on the weather, he writes in parks, in
doorways, in flophouse lobbies, in cafeterias, on benches on elevated-
railroad platforms, in subway trains, and in public libraries. When
he is in the proper mood, he writes until he is exhausted, and he
gets into this mood at peculiar times. He says that one night he sat
for six or seven hours in a booth in a Third Avenue bar and grill,
listening to a beery old Hungarian woman, once a madam and once
a dealer in narcotics and now a soup cook in a city hospital, tell
the story of her life. Three days later, around four o'clock in the
morning, on a cot in the Hotel Defender, at 300 Bowery, he was
awakened by the foghorns of tugs on the East River and was unable
to go back to sleep because he felt that he was in the exact mood
to put the old soup cook's biography in his history. He has an
abnormal memory; if he is sufficiently impressed by a conversation,
he can keep it in his head, even if it is lengthy and senseless, for
many days, much of it word for word. He had a bad cold, but he
got up, dressed under a red exit light, and, tiptoeing so as not to

disturb the men sleeping on cots all around him, went downstairs to the lobby.

He wrote in the lobby from 4:15 A.M. until noon. Then he left the Defender, drank some coffee in a Bowery diner, and walked up to the Public Library. He plugged away at a table in the genealogy room, which is one of his rainy-day hangouts and which he says he prefers to the main reading room because it is gloomier, until it closed at 6 P.M. Then he moved into the main reading room and stayed there, seldom taking his eyes off his work, until the Library locked up for the night at 10 P.M. He ate a couple of egg sandwiches and a quantity of ketchup in a Times Square cafeteria. Then, not having two bits for a flophouse and being too engrossed to go to the Village and seek shelter, he hurried into the West Side subway and rode the balance of the night, scribbling ceaselessly while the train he was aboard made three round trips between the New Lots Avenue station in Brooklyn and the Van Cortlandt Park station in the Bronx, which is one of the longest runs in the subway system. He kept his portfolio on his lap and used it as a desk. He has the endurance of the possessed. Whenever he got too sleepy to concentrate, he shook his head vigorously and then brought out his bag of sour balls and popped one in his mouth. People stared at him, and once he was interrupted by a drunk who asked him what in the name of God he was writing. Gould knows how to get rid of inquisitive drunks. He pointed at his left ear and said, "What? What's that? Deaf as a post. Can't hear a word." The drunk lost all interest in him. "Day was breaking when I left the subway," Gould says. "I was coughing and sneezing, my eyes were sore, my knees were shaky, I was as hungry as a bitch wolf, and I had exactly eight cents to my name. I didn't care. My history was longer by eleven thousand brand-new words, and at that moment I bet there wasn't a chairman of the board in all New York as happy as I."

GOULD IS HAUNTED by the fear that he will die before he has the first draft of the Oral History finished. It is already eleven times as long as the Bible. He estimates that the manuscript contains

9,000,000 words, all in longhand. It may well be the lengthiest unpublished work in existence. Gould does his writing in nickel composition books, the kind that children use in school, and the Oral History and the notes he has made for it fill two hundred and seventy of them, all of which are tattered and grimy and stained with coffee, grease, and beer. Using a fountain pen, he covers both sides of each page, leaving no margins anywhere, and his penmanship is poor; hundreds of thousands of words are legible only to him. He has never been able to interest a publisher in the Oral History. At one time or another he has lugged armfuls of it into fourteen publishing offices. "Half of them said it was obscene and outrageous and to get it out of there as quick as I could," he says, "and the others said they couldn't read my handwriting." Experiences of this nature do not dismay Gould; he keeps telling himself that it is posterity he is writing for, anyway. In his breast pocket, sealed in a dingy envelope, he always carries a will bequeathing two-thirds of the manuscript to the Harvard Library and the other third to the Smithsonian Institution. "A couple of generations after I'm dead and gone," he likes to say, "the Ph.D.'s will start lousing through my work. Just imagine their surprise. 'Why, I be damned,' they'll say, 'this fellow was the most brilliant historian of the century.' They'll give me my due. I don't claim that all of the Oral History is first class, but some of it will live as long as the English language." Gould used to keep his composition books scattered all over the Village, in the apartments and studios of friends. He kept them stuck away in closets and under beds and behind the books in bookcases. In the winter of 1942, after hearing that the Metropolitan Museum had moved its most precious paintings to a bombproof storage place somewhere out of town for the duration of the war, he became panicky. He went around and got all his books together and made them into a bale, he wrapped the bale in two layers of oilcloth, and then he entrusted it to a woman he knows who owns a duck-and-chicken farm near Huntington, Long Island. The farmhouse has a stone cellar.

Gould puts into the Oral History only things he has seen or heard. At least half of it is made up of conversations taken down verbatim or summarized; hence the title. "What people say is history," Gould says. "What we used to think was history—kings and queens, treaties, inventions, big battles, beheadings, Caesar, Napoleon, Pontius Pilate, Columbus, William Jennings Bryan—is only formal history and largely false. I'll put down the informal history of the shirt-sleeved multitude—what they had to say about their jobs, love affairs, vittles, sprees, scrapes, and sorrows—or I'll perish in the attempt." The Oral History is a great hodgepodge and kitchen midden of hearsay, a repository of jabber, an omnium-gatherum of bushwa, gab, palaver, hogwash, flapdoodle, and malarkey, the fruit, according to Gould's estimate, of more than twenty thousand conversations. In it are the hopelessly incoherent biographies of hundreds of bums, accounts of the wanderings of seamen encountered in South Street barrooms, grisly descriptions of hospital and clinic experiences ("Did you ever have a painful operation or disease?" is one of the first questions that Gould, fountain pen and composition book in hand, asks a person he has just met), summaries of innumerable Union Square and Columbus Circle harangues, testimonies given by converts at Salvation Army street meetings, and the addled opinions of scores of park-bench oracles and gin-mill savants. For a time Gould haunted the all-night greasy spoons in the vicinity of Bellevue Hospital, eavesdropping on tired internes, nurses, orderlies, ambulance drivers, embalming-school students, and morgue workers, and faithfully recording their talk. He scurries up and down Fifth Avenue during parades, feverishly taking notes. Gould writes with great candor, and the percentage of obscenity in the Oral History is high. He has a chapter called "Examples of the So-called Dirty Story of Our Time," to which he makes almost daily additions. In another chapter are many rhymes and observations which he found scribbled on the walls of subway washrooms. He believes that these scribblings are as truly historical as the strategy of General Robert E. Lee. Hundreds of thousands of words are devoted to the drunken behavior and the sexual adventures of various professional Greenwich Villagers in the twenties. There are hundreds of reports of ginny Village parties, including gossip about the guests and faithful reports of their arguments on such subjects as reincarnation, birth control, free love, psychoanalysis, Christian Science, Swedenborgianism, vegetarianism, alcoholism, and different political and art isms. "I have fully covered what might be termed the intellectual underworld of my time," Gould says. There are detailed descriptions of night life in scores of Village drinking and eating places, some of which, such as the Little Quakeress, the Original Julius, the Troubadour Tavern, the Samovar, Hubert's Cafeteria, Sam Swartz's T.N.T., and Eli Greifer's Last Outpost of Bohemia Tea Shoppe, do not exist any longer.

Gould is a night wanderer, and he has put down descriptions of dreadful things he has seen on dark New York streets—descriptions, for example, of the herds of big gray rats that come out in the hours before dawn in some neighborhoods of the lower East Side and Harlem and unconcernedly walk the sidewalks. "I sometimes believe that these rats are not rats at all," he says, "but the damned and aching souls of tenement landlords." A great deal of the Oral History is in diary form. Gould is afflicted with total recall, and now and then he picks out a period of time in the recent past— it might be a day, a week, or a month—and painstakingly writes down everything of any consequence that he did during this period. Sometimes he writes a chapter in which he monotonously and hideously curses some person or institution. Here and there are rambling essays on such subjects as the flophouse flea, spaghetti, the zipper as a sign of the decay of civilization, false teeth, insanity, the jury system, remorse, cafeteria cooking, and the emasculating effect of the typewriter on literature. "William Shakespeare didn't sit around pecking on a dirty, damned, ninety-five-dollar doohickey," he wrote, "and Joe Gould doesn't, either."

The Oral History is almost as discursive as "Tristram Shandy." In one chapter, "The Good Men Are Dying Like Flies," Gould begins a biography of a diner proprietor and horse-race gambler named Side-Bet Benny Altschuler, who stuck a rusty icepick in his hand and died of lockjaw; and skips after a few paragraphs to a story a seaman told him about seeing a group of lepers drinking and dancing and singing on a beach in Port-of-Spain, Trinidad; and goes from that to an anecdote about a demonstration held in front of a moving-picture theatre in Boston in 1915 to protest against the showing of "The Birth of a Nation," at which he kicked a policeman; and goes from that to a description of a trip he once made through the Central Islip insane asylum, in the course of which a woman pointed at him and screamed, "There he is! Thief! Thief! There's the man that picked my geraniums and stole my mamma's mule and buggy"; and goes from that to an account an old stumble-bum gave of glimpsing and feeling the blue-black flames of hell one night while sitting in a doorway on Great Jones Street and of seeing two mermaids playing in the East River just north of Fulton Fish Market later the same night; and goes from that to an explanation made by a priest of Old St. Patrick's Cathedral, which is on Mott Street, in the city's oldest Little Italy, of why so many Italian women always wear black ("They are in perpetual mourning for our Lord"); and then returns at last to Side-Bet Benny, the lockjawed diner proprietor.

Only a few of the hundreds of people who know Gould have read any of the Oral History, and most of them take it for granted that it is gibberish. Those who make the attempt usually bog down after a couple of chapters and give up. Gould says he can count on one hand or on one foot those who have read enough of it to be qualified to form an opinion. One is Horace Gregory, the poet and critic. "I look upon Gould as a sort of Samuel Pepys of the Bowery," Gregory says. "I once waded through twenty-odd composition books, and most of what I saw had the quality of a competent high-school theme, but some of it was written with the clear and wonderful veracity of a child, and here and there were flashes of hard-bitten Yankee wit. If someone took the trouble to go through it and separate the good from the rubbish, as editors did with Thomas Wolfe's millions of words, it might be discovered that Gould actually has written a masterpiece." Another is E. E. Cummings, the poet, who is a close friend of Gould's. Cummings once wrote a poem about Gould, No. 261 in his "Collected Poems," which contains the following description of the history:

> . . . a myth is as good as a smile but little joe gould's quote oral
> history unquote might (publishers note) be entitled a wraith's

*progress or mainly awash while chiefly submerged or an amoral
morality sort-of-aliveing by innumerable kind-of-deaths*

Throughout the nineteen-twenties Gould haunted the office of
the *Dial,* now dead, the most highbrow magazine of the time. Finally,
in its April, 1929, issue, the *Dial* printed one of his shorter essays,
"Civilization." In it he rambled along, jeering at the buying and
selling of stocks as "a fuddy-duddy old maid's game" and referring
to skyscrapers and steamships as "bric-a-brac" and giving his opinion
that "the auto is unnecessary." "If all the perverted ingenuity which
was put into making buzz-wagons had only gone into improving
the breed of horses," he wrote, "humanity would be better off."
This essay had a curious effect on American literature. A copy of
the *Dial* in which it appeared turned up a few months later in a
second-hand bookstore in Fresno, California, and was bought for a
dime by William Saroyan, who then was twenty and floundering
around, desperate to become a writer. He read Gould's essay and
was deeply impressed and influenced by it. "It freed me from
bothering about form," he says. Twelve years later, in the winter
of 1941, in Don Freeman's studio on Columbus Circle, Saroyan saw
some drawings Freeman had made of Gould for *Don Freeman's Newsstand,* a quarterly publication of pictures of odd New York scenes
and personalities put out by the Associated American Artists. Saroyan
became excited. He told Freeman about his indebtedness to Gould.
"Who the hell is he, anyway?" Saroyan asked. "I've been trying to
find out for years. Reading those few pages in the *Dial* was like
going in the wrong direction and running into the right guy and
then never seeing him again." Freeman told him about the Oral
History. Saroyan sat down and wrote a commentary to accompany
the drawings of Gould in *Newsstand.* "To this day," he wrote, in
part, "I have not read anything else by Joe Gould. And yet to me
he remains one of the few genuine and original American writers.
He was easy and uncluttered, and almost all other American writing
was uneasy and cluttered. It was not at home anywhere; it was
trying too hard; it was miserable; it was a little sickly; it was literary;
and it couldn't say anything simply. All other American writing was
trying to get into one form or another, and no writer except Joe

Gould seemed to have imagination enough to understand that if the worst came to the worst you didn't need to have any form at all. You didn't need to put what you had to say into a poem, an essay, a story, or a novel. All you had to do was say it." Not long after this issue of *Newsstand* came out, someone stopped Gould on Eighth Street and showed him Saroyan's endorsement of his work. Gould shrugged his shoulders. He had been on a spree and had lost his false teeth, and at the moment he was uninterested in literary matters. After thinking it over, however, he decided to call on Saroyan and ask him for help in getting some teeth. He found out somehow that Saroyan was living at the Hampshire House, on Central Park South. The doorman there followed Gould into the lobby and asked him what he wanted. Gould told him that he had come to see William Saroyan. "Do you know Mr. Saroyan?" the doorman asked. "Why, no," Gould said, "but that's all right. He's a disciple of mine." "What do you mean, disciple?" asked the doorman. "I mean," said Gould, "that he's a literary disciple of mine. I want to ask him to buy me some teeth." "Teeth?" asked the doorman. "What do you mean, teeth?" "I mean some store teeth," Gould said. "Some false teeth." "Come this way," said the doorman, gripping Gould's arm and ushering him to the street. Later Freeman arranged a meeting, and the pair spent several evenings together in bars. "Saroyan kept saying he wanted to hear all about the Oral History," Gould says, "but I never got a chance to tell him. He did all the talking. I couldn't get a word in edgewise."

As LONG As HE can remember, Gould has been perplexed by his own personality. There are a number of autobiographical essays in the Oral History, and he says that all of them are attempts to explain himself to himself. In one, "Why I Am Unable To Adjust Myself To Civilization, Such As It Is, or Do, Don't, Do, Don't, A Hell Of A Note," he came to the conclusion that his shyness was responsible for everything. "I am introvert and extrovert all rolled in one," he wrote, "a warring mixture of the recluse and the Sixth Avenue auctioneer. One foot says do, the other says don't. One foot says shut your mouth, the other says bellow like a bull. I am painfully shy, but try not to let people know it. They would take advantage of me." Gould keeps his shyness well hidden. It is evident only when he is cold sober. In that state he is silent, suspicious, and constrained, but a couple of beers or a single jigger of gin will untie his tongue and put a leer on his face. He is extraordinarily responsive to alcohol. "On a hot night," he says, "I can walk up and down in front of a gin mill for ten minutes, breathing real deep, and get a jag on."

Even though Gould requires only a few drinks, getting them is sometimes quite a task. Most evenings he prowls around the saloons and dives on the west side of the Village, on the lookout for curiosity-seeking tourists from whom he can cadge beers, sandwiches, and small sums of money. If he is unable to find anyone approachable in the tumultuous saloons around Sheridan Square, he goes over to Sixth Avenue and works north, hitting the Jericho Tavern, the Village Square Bar & Grill, the Belmar, Goody's, and the Rochambeau. He has a routine. He doesn't enter a place unless it is crowded. After he is in, he bustles over to the telephone booth and pretends to look up a number. While doing this, he scrutinizes the customers. If he sees a prospect, he goes over and says, "Let me introduce myself. The name is Joseph Ferdinand Gould, a graduate of Harvard, *magna cum difficultate,* class of 1911, and chairman of the board of Weal and Woe, Incorporated. In exchange for a drink, I'll recite a poem, deliver a lecture, argue a point, or take off my shoes and imitate a sea gull. I prefer gin, but beer will do." Gould is by no means a bum. He feels that the entertainment he provides is well worth whatever he is able to cadge. He doesn't fawn, and he is never grateful. If he is turned down politely, he shrugs his shoulders and leaves the place. However, if the prospect passes a remark like "Get out of here, you bum," Gould turns on him, no matter how big he is, and gives him a shrill, nasal, scurrilous tongue-lashing. He doesn't care what he says. When he loses his temper, he becomes fearless. He will drop his portfolio, put up his fists, and offer to fight men who could kill him with one halfhearted blow. If he doesn't find an audience on the trip up Sixth, he turns west on

Eleventh and heads for the Village Vanguard, in a cellar on Seventh Avenue South. The Vanguard was once a sleazy rendezvous for arty people, but currently it is a thriving night club. Gould and the proprietor, a man named Max Gordon, have known each other for many years and are on fairly good terms much of the time. Gould always hits the Vanguard last. He is sure of it, and he keeps it in reserve. Since it became prosperous, the place annoys him. He goes down the stairs and says, "Hello, Max, you dirty capitalist. I want a bite to eat and a beer. If I don't get it, I'll walk right out on the dance floor and throw a fit." "Go argue with the cook," Gordon tells him. Gould goes into the kitchen, eats whatever the cook gives him, drinks a couple of beers, fills a bag with bread crumbs, and departs.

Despite his shyness, Gould has a great fondness for parties. There are many people in the Village who give big parties fairly often. Among them are a rich and idiosyncratic old doctor, a rich old spinster, a famous stage designer, a famous theatrical couple, and numbers of painters and sculptors and writers and editors and publishers. As often as not, when Gould finds out that any of these people are giving a party, he goes, and as often as not he is allowed to stay. Usually he keeps to himself for a while, uneasily smoking one cigarette after another and stiff as a board with tenseness. Sooner or later, however, impelled by a drink or two and by the desperation of the ill at ease, he begins to throw his weight around. He picks out the prettiest woman in the room, goes over, bows, and kisses her hand. He tells discreditable stories about himself. He becomes exuberant; suddenly, for no reason at all, he cackles with pleasure and jumps up and clicks his heels together. Presently he shouts, "All in favor of a one-man floor show, please say 'Aye'!" If he gets the slightest encouragement, he strips to the waist and does a hand-clapping, foot-stamping dance which he says he learned on a Chippewa reservation in North Dakota and which he calls the Joseph Ferdinand Gould Stomp. While dancing, he chants an old Salvation Army song, "There Are Flies on Me, There Are Flies on You, but There Are No Flies on Jesus." Then he imitates a sea gull. He pulls off his shoes and socks and takes awkward, headlong skips about the room, flapping his arms and letting out a piercing caw with every skip. As a child he had several pet gulls, and he still spends many Sundays on the end of a fishing pier at Sheepshead Bay observing gulls; he claims he has such a thorough understanding of their cawing that he can translate poetry into it. "I have translated a number of Henry Wadsworth Longfellow's poems into sea gull," he says.

Inevitably, at every party Gould goes to, he gets up on a chair or a table and delivers some lectures. These lectures are extracts from chapters of the Oral History. They are brief, but he gives them lengthy titles, such as "Drunk as a Skunk, or How I Measured the Heads of Fifteen Hundred Indians in Zero Weather" and "The Dread Tomato Habit, or Watch Out! Watch Out! Down with Dr. Gallup!" He is skeptical about statistics. In the latter lecture, using statistics he claims he found in financial sections in newspapers, he proves that "the eating of tomatoes by railroad engineers was responsible for fifty-three per cent of the train wrecks in the United States during the last seven years." When Gould arrives at a party, people who have never seen him before usually take one look at him and edge away. Before the evening is over, however, a few of them almost always develop a kind of puzzled respect for him; they get him in a corner, ask him questions, and try to determine what is wrong with him. Gould enjoys this. "When you came over and kissed my hand," a young woman told him one night, "I said to myself, 'What a nice old gentleman.' A minute later I looked around and you were bouncing up and down with your shirt off, imitating a wild Indian. I was shocked. Why do you have to be such an exhibitionist?" "Madam," Gould said, "it is the duty of the bohemian to make a spectacle of himself. If my informality leads you to believe that I'm a rum-dumb, or that I belong in Bellevue, hold fast to that belief, hold fast, hold fast, and show your ignorance."

GOULD IS A NATIVE of Norwood, Massachusetts, a suburb of Boston. He comes from a family of physicians. His grandfather, Joseph Ferdinand Gould, for whom he was named, taught in the

Harvard Medical School and had a practice in Boston. His father, Clarke Storer Gould, was a general practitioner in Norwood. He served as a captain in the Army Medical Corps and died of blood poisoning in a camp in Ohio during the First World War. The family was well-to-do until Gould was about grown, when his father invested unwisely in the stock of an Alaska land company. Gould says he went to Harvard only because it was a family custom. "I did not want to go," he wrote in one of his autobiographical essays. "It had been my plan to stay home and sit in a rocking chair on the back porch and brood." He says that he was an undistinguished student. Some of his classmates were Conrad Aiken, the poet; Howard Lindsay, the playwright and actor; Gluyas Williams, the cartoonist; and Richard F. Whitney, former president of the New York Stock Exchange. His best friends were three foreign students—a Chinese, a Siamese, and an Albanian.

Gould's mother had always taken it for granted that he would become a physician, but after getting his A.B. he told her he was through with formal education. She asked him what he intended to do. "I intend to stroll and ponder," he said. He passed most of the next three years strolling and pondering on the ranch of an uncle in Canada. In 1913, in an Albanian restaurant in Boston named the Scanderbeg, whose coffee he liked, he became acquainted with Theofan S. Noli, an archimandrite of the Albanian Orthodox Church, who interested him in Balkan politics. In February, 1914, Gould startled his family by announcing that he planned to devote the rest of his life to collecting funds to free Albania. He founded an organization in Boston called the Friends of Albanian Independence, enrolled a score or so of dues-paying members, and began telegraphing and calling on bewildered newspaper editors in Boston and New York City, trying to persuade them to print long treatises on Albanian affairs written by Noli. After about eight months of this, Gould was sitting in the Scanderbeg one night, drinking coffee and listening to a group of Albanian factory workers argue in their native tongue about Balkan politics, when he suddenly came to the conclusion that he was about to have a nervous breakdown. "I began to twitch uncontrollably and see double," he says. From that night on his interest in Albania slackened.

After another period of strolling and pondering, Gould took up eugenics. He has forgotten exactly how this came about. In any case, he spent the summer of 1915 as a student in eugenical field work at the Eugenics Record Office at Cold Spring Harbor, Long Island. This organization, endowed by the Carnegie Institution, was engaged at that time in making studies of families of hereditary defectives, paupers, and town nuisances in several highly inbred communities. Such people were too prosaic for Gould; he decided to specialize in Indians. That winter he went out to North Dakota and measured the heads of a thousand Chippewas on the Turtle Mountain Reservation and of five hundred Mandans on the Fort Berthold Reservation. Nowadays, when Gould is asked why he took these measurements, he changes the subject, saying, "The whole matter is a deep scientific secret." He was happy in North Dakota. "It was the most rewarding period of my life," he says. "I'm a good horseman, if I do say so myself, and I like to dance and whoop, and the Indians seemed to enjoy having me around. I was afraid they'd think I was batty when I asked for permission to measure their noggins, but they didn't mind. It seemed to amuse them. Indians are the only true aristocrats I've ever known. They ought to run the country, and we ought to be put on the reservations." After seven months of reservation life, Gould ran out of money. He returned to Massachusetts and tried vainly to get funds for another head-measuring expedition. "At this juncture in my life," he says, "I decided to engage in literary work." He came to New York City and got a job as assistant Police Headquarters reporter for the *Evening Mail.* One morning in the summer of 1917, after he had been a reporter for about a year, he was basking in the sun on the back steps of Headquarters, trying to overcome a hangover, when the idea for the Oral History blossomed in his mind. He promptly quit his job and began writing. "Since that fateful morning," he once said, in a moment of exaltation, "the Oral History has been my rope and my scaffold, my bed and my board, my wife and my floozy, my wound and the salt on it, my whiskey and my aspirin, and my rock and my salvation. It is the only thing that matters a damn to me. All else is dross."

GOULD SAYS THAT HE RARELY has more than a dollar at any one time, and that he doesn't particularly care. "As a rule," he says, "I despise money." However, there is a widely held belief in the Village that he is rich and that he receives an income from inherited property in New England. "Only an old millionaire could afford to go around as shabby as you," a bartender told him recently. "You're one of those fellows that die in doorways and when the cops search them their pockets are just busting with bankbooks. If you wanted to, I bet you could step over to the West Side Savings Bank right this minute and draw out twenty thousand dollars." After the death of his mother in 1939, Gould did come into some money. Close friends of his say that it was less than a thousand dollars and that he spent it in less than a month, wildly buying drinks all over the Village for people he had never seen before. "He seemed miserable with money in his pockets," Gordon, the proprietor of the Vanguard, says. "When it was all gone, it seemed to take a load off his mind." While Gould was spending his inheritance, he did one thing that satisfied him deeply. He bought a big, shiny radio and took it out on Sixth Avenue and kicked it to pieces. He has never cared for the radio. "Five minutes of the idiot's babble that comes out of those machines," he says, "would turn the stomach of a goat."

During the twenties and the early thirties Gould occasionally interrupted his work on the Oral History to pose for classes at the Art Students' League and to do book-reviewing for newspapers and magazines. He says there were periods when he lived comfortably on the money he earned this way. Burton Rascoe, literary editor of the old *Tribune,* gave him a lot of work. In an entry in "A Bookman's Daybook," which is a diary of happenings in the New York literary world in the twenties, Rascoe told of an experience with Gould. "I once gave him a small book about the American Indians to review," Rascoe wrote, "and he brought me back enough manuscript to fill three complete editions of the Sunday *Tribune.* I especially honor him because, unlike most reviewers, he has never dogged me with inquiries as to why I never run it. He had his say, which was considerable, about the book, the author, and the subject, and there for him the matter ended." Gould says that he quit book-reviewing because he felt that it was beneath his dignity to compete with machines. "The Sunday *Times* and the Sunday *Herald Tribune* have machines that review books," he says. "You put a book in one of those machines and jerk down a couple of levers and a review drops out." In recent years Gould has got along on less than five dolllars in actual money a week. He has a number of friends—Malcolm Cowley, the writer and editor; Aaron Siskind, the documentary photographer; Cummings, the poet; and Gordon, the night-club proprietor, are a few—who give him small sums of money regularly. No matter what they think of the Oral History, all these people have great respect for Gould's pertinacity.

GOULD HAS A POOR OPINION of most of the writers and poets and painters and sculptors in the Village, and doesn't mind saying so. Because of his outspokenness he has never been allowed to join any of the art, writing, cultural, or ism organizations. He has been trying for ten years to join the Raven Poetry Circle, which puts on the poetry exhibition in Washington Square each summer and is the most powerful organization of its kind in the Village, but he has been blackballed every time. The head of the Ravens is a retired New York Telephone Company employee named Francis Lambert McCrudden. For many years Mr. McCrudden was a collector of coins from coin telephones for the telephone company. He is a self-educated man and very idealistic. His favorite theme is the dignity of labor, and his major work is an autobiographical poem called "The Nickel Snatcher." "We let Mr. Gould attend our readings, and I wish we could let him join, but we simply can't," Mr. McCrudden once said. "He isn't serious about poetry. We serve wine at our readings, and that is the only reason he attends. He sometimes insists on reading foolish poems of his own, and it gets on your nerves. At our Religious Poetry Night he demanded per-

mission to recite a poem he had written entitled 'My Religion.' I
told him to go ahead, and this is what he recited:

> '*In winter I'm a Buddhist,*
> *And in summer I'm a nudist.'*

And at our Nature Poetry Night he begged to recite a poem of his
entitled 'The Sea Gull.' I gave him permission, and he jumped out
of his chair and began to wave his arms and leap about and scream,
'Scree-eek! Scree-eek! Scree-eek!' It was upsetting. We are serious
poets and we don't approve of that sort of behavior." In the summer
of 1942 Gould picketed the Raven exhibition, which was held on
the fence of a tennis court on Washington Square South. In one
hand he carried his portfolio and in the other he held a placard on
which he had printed: "JOSEPH FERDINAND GOULD, HOT-SHOT POET
FROM POETVILLE, A REFUGEE FROM THE RAVENS. POETS OF THE
WORLD, IGNITE! YOU HAVE NOTHING TO LOSE BUT YOUR BRAINS!"
Now and then, as he strutted back and forth, he would take a leap
and then a skip and say to passers-by, "Would you like to hear
what Joe Gould thinks of the world and all that's in it? Scree-eek!
Scree-eek! Scree-eek!"

(1942)

# A Spism and a Spasm

*A* GARRULOUS OLD SOUTHERNER, the Reverend Mr. James Jefferson Davis Hall, is the greatest and the most frightening street preacher in the city. He is an Episcopal priest in good standing, but he hasn't had a church since 1904. "The gutter is my pulpit," he says, "and the roaring traffic is my pipe organ. Halleluiah!" He has preached in the streets and squares of Manhattan for twenty years. Before coming here, he had been, successively, a rector in several cotton-gin towns in Alabama, a convict-camp chaplain, and the superintendent of a nickel-a-meal, dime-a-flop mission for down-and-outs in Philadelphia. Hall used to preach in Wall Street at noon, in Madison Square or Union Square in the afternoon, and in Columbus Circle at night, but for the last seven years he has concentrated on the theatrical district, an area which he once described as "the belly and the black heart of that Great Whore of Babylon and mother of abominations, the city of New York." He has a little band of disciples, the majority of whom are elderly spinsters or widows, and they sometimes refer to him as the Bishop of Times Square.

Every fair evening, after a dinner which customarily consists of an onion, a bulb of garlic, and a head of cabbage, all raw, he leaves his flat in a tenement on Forty-fifth Street, just east of Ninth Avenue, and walks around for three or four hours, shouting at people and threatening them with the delirium tremens, the electric chair, potter's field, and the blue and bubbly flames of hell. As a rule, he goes forth alone, carrying a couple of oilcloth banners, a batch of newspaper clippings about women suicides neatly pasted on pieces of cardboard, and a pocketful of tracts of his own composition. He has written and published scores of tracts; among them are "Seven Communists the Night Before DEATH," "A Conversation Between a Whiskey Flask and a Cigarette," and "The Cry of the Meat-eaters is 'MORE HOSPITALS!' " Hall is especially outraged by drunken women, and he edges up to every one he sees and hands her a suicide clipping. "It's a souvenir of the Great White Way, sister," he told one woman not long ago, "a souvenir and a warning. Nay, nay! Don't throw it down. Put it in your purse and read it the first thing in the morning. Are you an actress? I bet you're an actress! You're riding on the hell-bound train, sister, right up with the engineer. Next stop, the padded cell! Next stop, the Bellevue morgue!" He despises the theatre and has an idea that most of the drunken women he encounters are actresses; the very word "actress," when he says it, sounds sinister.

Hall has a frantic voice. When lifted, particularly in a dimmed-out street, it is extraordinarily disquieting. "I can speak on any old subject, just about, and make my audience uneasy," he once said. "A street preacher's job is to frighten people—shake them up, put the everlasting fear of God into them, and I reckon my voice is my best asset." He developed a quality of hysteria in it years ago in Alabama by going deep into a cypress swamp for an hour or so a day and screaming warnings of one kind or another at an imaginary crowd. "Look out! Look out!" he would scream. "Here comes a mad dog running loose! Fire! Fire! The barn's on fire!" "After a while," he says, "I got so good I scared myself."

His appearance is also an asset. He is tall and bony, with sunken cheeks, haunted eyes, a pale face, and a grim, cackling laugh. He is a bachelor. He likes to be asked his age. "I'm seventy-nine," he says. "No aches or pains, no pills or powders, no doctors or drugstores." His hair is white and unkempt, and he has a mustache and a goatee, both badly trimmed; he brags that he hasn't put foot in a barber shop in twenty-some-odd years. He owns a set of barber's tools which he ordered from Sears Roebuck, and once a month he and a colleague, an old colporteur from Staten Island, get together and cut each other's hair. He disapproves of barber shops because he thinks they charge too much and because of what he calls "the shame and the disgrace of the manicure woman." "I won't be seen in a place," he says, "that has a pretty woman a-sitting in there for the pure and simple purpose of holding hands with any man that'll pay the price. No good can come of that."

Hall is fully as opinionated on a number of other subjects. For example, he is opposed to the use of coffins (he calls them "boxes" or "bone boxes"), and sometimes he puzzles a street audience by denouncing "the funeral-parlor trust." He thinks that people should be buried in winding sheets, as in Biblical times. Fifteen years ago he got the directors of the Elmwood Cemetery, in Birmingham, Alabama, in which he owns a plot, to sign a document permitting him, when the time comes, to be put away in this manner. "I'm not a reactionary," he says. "I wouldn't be against the coffin custom if they were made out of old packing cases and sold for two or three dollars. That would be all right. If coffins just *have* to be used, they should be stacked on top of each other, a whole family in one grave. Think of the saving in space! Otherwise, in a few more generations the U.S.A. will be one vast and widespread cemetery." Hall is also opposed to soda fountains. "First the sody fountain," he says. "Then comes the saloon. Ice water, milk shakes, ginger ale, beer, hot toddies, straight whiskey, the D.T.'s—those are the steps the drinker takes." He is a confident prohibitionist. He is convinced that, one way or another, liquor will be illegal within five years. He corresponds with other street preachers all over the country, and recently, to one of them, he wrote, "My dear brother in Christ: I am so sure of Prohibition I have quit fretting about it. I have a good, bedrock reason that if the Whiskey Trust knew about it they would be quite agitated. This is it. For years upon years every time I brought up the subject of Prohibition on the streets of New York the people would snicker and snort. Well, they do not snicker any more. Nay, nay. Quite the contrary. They look serious, and some nod their heads. Even the liquor-head sots, they know it's coming. They feel it in their bones. Over a year ago Dr. Gallup said that thirty-six per cent of the people were ripe and ready to vote for it. Facts and figures. And the per cent is rising, rising, rising, like water in a tub. Five more years, I estimate, and we'll put King Whiskey in the tomb, R.I.P. And the first grand rascal that D-double-dares to open up a speak-easy—why, the good Christians will descend on him and pull him apart."

Other institutions Hall disapproves of are laundries and cleaning and pressing establishments. "This is a democratic country," he says, "and no able-bodied man should have the right to call on some other man to scrub his duds. If people in general, even the highly educated, even Nicholas Murray Butler, had to bend over a washtub once a week, it would give them some sense of proportion; it would keep them from getting biggity." Hall does his own washing and ironing, and now and then he takes a flatiron and puts some crooked creases in his trousers. He is shabbily dressed. He buys his suits in a Ninth Avenue rummage store. He paid $7.15 for his last one, and a hat he has worn for almost three years cost thirty-five cents. "It's still as good as new," he says. He wears a clerical collar, a clerical shirt, and a gold cross. The cross was given to him by a group of converted highwaymen, safe-crackers, and cop-killers in Flattop, an Alabama convict camp, where he was once a chaplain. He keeps a celluloid badge with only a red question mark on it pinned to his left lapel. When asked what it signifies, he narrows his eyelids and says, "Friend, every step you take, Death walks right in behind you. No matter how fat and sassy you may be, you're living every second on the lip of the grave. The question is, 'Are you ready for the shroud and the box, are you ready for the Judgment Day?'"

HALL USUALLY BEGINS AN EVENING'S WORK by delivering brief harangues—he calls them "halleluiah hypodermics"—in the doorways of a dozen or so Eighth Avenue saloons. He never goes inside a saloon and he never tries to take up a collection; he just stands in the doorway and shouts. Bartenders are used to him. They address him as "Dad," "Reverend," or "Shadrach." One evening recently he stopped first at the Dublin Restaurant, a saloon just above Forty-second Street. He stuck his head in, cleared his throat, and cried out, "Distilled damnation and liquid death, that's what you're a-swilling and a-guzzling!" Many of the people along the bar abruptly turned around. While they stared, he unrolled one of his oilcloth banners. Lettered on it in red was this message: "PUT DOWN THAT GLASS AND GO. THE SALOON IS THE GATE TO HELL. DREADFUL ARE THE MORNINGS OF A DRUNKARD. PREPARE TO MEET THY GOD." (Hall is a good amateur sign-painter, and he makes his own banners.) Holding up the banner, Hall shouted, "Brothers! Sisters! That's not the brass rail you're resting your feet upon. Nay, nay! That's the third rail! Whiskey and beer! Wrack and ruin! Death and destruction! The cup that stings, the frolic, the midnight brawl, the strait jacket! Hark to the destiny of the whiskey drinker: forsaken by his friends, his furniture seized, his wife broken-hearted, his babies starving, his liver a sieve, his mind a tangle, his nerves a snarl, not a shoe to his foot. Don't you people ever sleep? Go home! Go to bed! Are you ready for the Judgment Day? You may be taken suddenly. On your way home, rooting and tooting, drunk and disorderly, *you may be taken!* You, sister, a-sitting there in that booth with a cigarette in one hand and a glass of distilled damnation in the other, a sorry sight, are *you* ready?" Hall was interrupted by one of the bartenders, who walked up to the front end of the bar and said, "O.K., Dad, break it up. That's enough racket for one night." "Why, howdy-do, young man, howdy-do," Hall said. "Haven't seen you in quite some time. Have you been on the day shift? Be sure your sins will find you out. I'll go, but I'll be back." "Yes, indeed," said the bartender sadly, "I'm sure you will."

Holding his banner aloft, Hall proceeded up the avenue. In an hour and a half, after making stops at O'Donnell's, Kieran & Dineen's, Larry's, the Eagle Bar, Gilhuly's, Pete Moran's, the Ranch Bar, Morahan's, McGreevy's, Mickey Walker's, and the Ringside, he reached Fiftieth Street, which is about as far uptown as he ever goes. En route he passed out a couple of dozen tracts. He came across one reeling woman and tried to make her take a suicide clipping, but she flung it down and said, "Get out of here, you old wolf. Go to hell, you old wolf." "You'll have to excuse me, sister," Hall told her. "I'm not going your way."

On Fiftieth Street, Hall headed east. Reaching the northeast corner of Broadway and Fiftieth, where most nights horse-race gamblers congregate along the curb to argue over the racing charts in the early edition of the *Mirror,* he got out his second banner and unrolled it. It said, "GAMBLERS ARE THIEVES AND WILL STEAL. SATAN AND THE GAMBLER WALK HAND IN HAND. SMOKING WILL KILL YOU. WHERE WILL YOU SPEND ETERNITY?" Displaying both banners, he stood for about ten minutes in front of the Paddock Bar & Grill, a hangout of racing people, staring upward with a soulful expression on his face, not saying a word. Then, as is his custom, he started south on Broadway, a banner upheld in each hand, walking slowly and preaching, most of the time at the top of his voice.

To stay in one spot on Broadway and preach requires a Police Department permit; by keeping in motion, Hall gets along without one. He walks close to the building line, so that his banners can be read by the lights in the show windows. Even in the busiest blocks, he is seldom caught in a crowd; flustered by his voice, people give him plenty of room. He rarely plans a street sermon but depends upon whatever comes into his head. Occasionally he sings a snatch of a hymn or quotes a verse of Scripture, usually a chilly one from Job, the Revelation, or the Lamentations. Like Father Divine, he makes up words. Also like Divine, he frequently pairs words of similar meanings—"hoot and howl," "shudder and shake," "masses and multitudes," "swill and swig." He deeply accents the first syllable in many words; "disturbed and perturbed," for example, becomes "*dee*sturbed and *pee*turbed."

He is profoundly discursive. This particular evening, in the course of one block, the block between Fiftieth and Forty-ninth, he made the following remarks: "A lost city, hungry for destruction, aching for destruction, the entire population in a fuss and a fret, a twit and a twitter, a squit and a squat, a hip and a hop, a snig and a snaggle, a spism and a spasm, a sweat and a swivet. Can't wait for night to fall, can't wait for day to break. Even the church bells sound jangly in New York City; they ring them too fast. And the women! Into *every*thing! Free livers! They've gone hog-proud and hog-wild. Wearing britches, wearing uniforms, straining their joints for generations to come with high-heel shoes. They're turning into Indians. Their mouths smeared and smiddled and smoodled with paint, *and* their cheeks, *and* their fingernails. And what color do they pick? Old Scratch's favorite. The mark of the beast, that's what it is. And they've taken to painting their toenails! Why don't they get a bucket of paint and turn it over on themselves, top to bottom, like a whooping red Indian, and be done with it? Save time and trouble. Oh, my! Tell you what I saw last Sunday! I visited St. Bartholomew's, and there was an old sister in the pew in front of me with her hair dyed *blue,* and I mean *blue!* Call the doctor!

"My name is Daddy Hall, and I love you one and all. An old-time preacher, believes *every*thing in the Bible, including the crosses on the t's, the dots on the i's. I'm just a stranger here; heaven's my home. Don't claim to be a highly educated man, but I can still read Latin; used to read Greek. If put to the test, I can recite Shakespeare. No degrees but D.D.—Divine Dynamiter; S.S.—Shining Saint; M.A.—Mightily Altered. If your troubles are more than you can bear, give me a ring—Circle 6-6483, the sanctified telephone number. I'll preach you a sermon on the telephone. I pray for you, and I warn you, but all you care for is gluttony, whiskey, movie shows, Reno divorces, cocaine dope, silk underwear, birth control, and stocks and bonds. That, and the almighty dollar; you can't get enough. Like a fine old lady said to me, 'The people this day and time, if the government was to let them back a ten-ton truck up to the front door of the U.S. Mint and haul off a bogging-down load from the million-dollar-bill department, that wouldn't by no means satisfy them.' That it wouldn't! Nay, nay! They'd be back next morning bright and early a-scratching on the door like a dog, a-begging and a-pleading for just one more load. The root of all evil. And what kind of music do you hear now days? 'Praise the Lord and Pass the Ammunition,' that's what you hear. They play it in the saloons, and they dance to it! Blasphemous music, that's what it is, blasphemous and brimstony! It's taking the Lord's name in vain. That big, stout, fool-faced man over yonder at the curb is a-laughing at me. He thinks I'm funny. Let him laugh! As the crackling of thorns under a pot, so is the laughter of fools. He probably thinks he's highly educated. The big professors these days, the highly educated, they don't believe in sin. Oh, no! It's just your glands. Glands, indeed! Glib, glab, gloody-doody! Just wait until those glandy professors hit the fiery pit, the bottomless, shoreless pond of roaring fire; they'll wish they'd kept off the subject of sin.

"The people have strayed, and God is put out and provoked, and He has plunged us into war as a test and a trial, a punishment. It's time for the locusts and the plague of boils. Famine! Food rationing! Why, it's all foretold. 'The tongue of the sucking child cleaveth to the roof of his mouth for thirst. The young children ask for bread, and no man breaketh it unto them. They that did feed delicately are desolate in the street.' People eat too much, anyway. We need a famine or two. Personally, I'm a dead-set vegetarian. There's nothing so fine in the eating line as a good green vegetable—root, stalk, and leaf. The pictures stuck up in front of these theatres along here are a scarlet shame and a purple disgrace. Grown women with their stomachs showing. Why, their very navels are showing. It's a vexation to the men. It puts thoughts of a certain nature in their minds. Sodom and Gomorrah, that's what it is. 'Rock of ages, cleft for me; let me hide myself in Thee.' My name is Daddy Hall, and I love you one and all. If suicide is on your mind, give me a ring. I'll tell you what to do. Write it down—Circle 6-6483. Look at that poor brother. He's certainly under the influence; he's trying to walk on both sides of the street at once. I reckon he was bit by the brewer's dog. He looks like he had quite a tilt and a tussle with the brewer's big hungry dog. At this hour of the night, all over town, the people are pouring it in—rivers of highballs, rivers of cocktails, whole train-loads of distilled damnation; they're just about washing their faces in it, the boozy, bedaddled old buzzards.

"A pickpocket I converted here the other day told me they have a school out in Chicago, a pocket-picking school, and the beginning rule they teach is 'No stimulants!' Have to keep their heads clear. Why, friends, you set a bucket of beer in front of a pig and he'll grunt and walk away. Highballs! Cocktails! Winston Churchill! I read in *Life* where it said he drinks a quart of champagne a day and nobody knows how much Scotch whiskey in between. Thinks nothing of it! Just like a Christian man drinks buttermilk. A pig won't touch it, nor a pickpocket, but Mr. Churchill, he'll get right down and wallow in it. A fine example for the soldier boys! Oh, yes! Oh, yes! The city of New York is just about ready for a great religious upswelling. It's a bud, getting bigger by the minute. Pretty soon now it's going to bust wide open and blossom. People are slapping the dust off their Bibles, and regretting their misdeeds, and getting ready for the wrath to come. Back before Pearl Harbor there wasn't much use passing out tracts on the street. People would throw them down and trample on them. Now they fold them up and put them in their pockets. That they do. It's coming! It's on the way! My name is Daddy Hall, and I love you one and all. . . ."

Hall kept this up, even while crossing streets, all the way down to Broadway and Forty-second. There, hoarse but happy, he rolled up his banners and called it a night. "I warned them," he said to a policeman. "I put the fear of God into them. Now I'm going home, and I'm going to eat me a big Bermuda onion and drink me a glass of pure, God-given water. And I'm going to bed. And during the night, if there's a doomsday rumbling in the earth and a flicker of fire in the sky, I'll be ready."

HALL HAS A SOUND REASON for believing in the imminence of a religious upswelling in the city. Off and on, ever since he came here, he has been in the habit, in the course of his street sermons, of announcing his telephone number and inviting people in trouble to call him. "I'll comfort you," he says. "I'll preach you an old-time sermon on the telephone." For seventeen years there was no response. Finally, one morning in December, 1939, a stranger called. He was worried about his daughter. She was sixteen; she had gone out with a sailor without permission, she had drunk some beer, and so on. He asked Hall to pray for her soul. Hall did, then and there. Later in the day the man's wife called and put the wayward daughter on the telephone. Hall gave her such a rampant description of hell that she began to sob and dropped the receiver. The wife picked it up and said, as well as Hall can remember, "Why, Reverend, you made her cry! Why, she's crying like her little heart will break. Thank you! Oh, thank you so much! I'm *so* grateful." "Don't mention it, sister," Hall told her. "If you have friends or neighbors with trouble on their mind, tell them to phone me. Pass the word around." The woman said she certainly would. Next day Hall got four calls from strangers, all wanting a telephone sermon. The third day, according to his records, he got seven. The fourth day he got sixteen. "All of a sudden, among the humble and the heavy-hearted," Hall says, "the fame of Daddy Hall began to spread like wildfire. One told another. Something like a chain letter. Wheels within wheels." One of his converts, a scrubwoman, got so interested that she commenced leaving anonymous notes—"There is a message for you at Circle 6-6483"—on desks in the office building in which she worked at night. She got other scrubwomen to do the same. When the recipient of one of these notes called, Hall would begin, "Yes, siree-bob, friend, I do have a message for you. Are you prepared to die? Are you ready for the shroud and the box, are you ready for the Judgment Day?" Then, if the caller did not snort and hang up, Hall would preach a brief, violent sermon.

Day by day, the number of calls increased. In a couple of years, Hall was getting around seventy-five a day. He was overjoyed. From 6 A.M. until 7 P.M., he sat beside his telephone, going out to preach in the streets only at night. "Things went along real smooth," he says, "until the Monday after Pearl Harbor. That day I preached until my jaw got stiff. There wasn't a moment's letup. The instant I put the receiver down and caught my breath, the phone rang again. I preached I think it was eighty-three sermons in a row, some over five minutes long, and then my head began to swim. I took the receiver off the hook and went in and flopped down on the bed, all wore out." Presently an investigator from the telephone company knocked on the door, aroused him, and told him that scores of people had complained that they got only a busy signal when they dialled his number. Hall sighed, went to his telephone, and started in again. In the morning he summoned to his apartment six of his disciples, all elderly women who make a practice of handing out his tracts and all lay preachers; they agreed to come to his rescue and take turns on the telephone.

Nowadays, Hall seldom preaches on the telephone more than a couple of dozen times a day; he saves his energy for his saloon harangues and his nightly journey down Broadway. His disciples, who model their sermons on his, handle most of the calls. In return, he gives them carfare, an occasional grassy meal, and his blessing. The most zealous is an Englishwoman named Frances Woodcock. She comes in from Queens each day and preaches from around 8:30 until 11:55 in the morning. Then she hastens around the corner to the Gospel Tabernacle, a Fundamentalist, nondenominational mission on Eighth Avenue, in whose work Hall is a believer, and plays the organ at the noon meeting. Frequently she returns in the afternoon. The sole male helper is Joseph Serafin, an elocutionary Rumanian, who is renting agent for an Eighth Avenue loft building owned by the Tabernacle. He drops in whenever he has an hour or two to spare. Calls are answered constantly from 6 A.M. until midnight, when the receiver is removed. Hall says that more than a hundred and fifty thousand sermons have been preached over his telephone since December, 1939. He estimates that around one-fourth of the callers are curiosity seekers, practical jokers, or the victims of practical jokers. Many of these victims are under the impression that horse-race bets are taken at Circle 6-6483. One practical joker spoke double-talk. After listening to him for a few moments, Hall exclaimed, "Speak out, man, speak out! What *are* you, anyhow, a Mohammedan?" Finally he summoned Serafin, who was in the adjoining room, eating a head of cabbage. "Come here, Serafin," Hall said. "I think I've got a poor Mohammedan brother on the wire. He seems to be in sore distress." Serafin, who is more worldly, listened for a moment or two and then explained double-talk to Hall. "I fixed that brother," Hall says, cackling. "I interrupted him and shouted at him in Latin until he got mad and told me to go to you know where."

Hall quizzes his callers, and has come to the conclusion that the majority are repentant backsliders. "They *had* the old-time religion," he says, "but somewhere along the line they lost it. The war makes them ache to find it again. 'Turn over a new leaf,' I tell them. 'Repent. Pray. Read your Bible. Find an old-time church and go to it. Don't go to one of those Fifth Avenue churches that all they have is weddings.' The most of them are hungry to confess. Oh, my! Some confess to sins I never even heard of before. I hear things I wouldn't discuss with *any*body, not even another preacher. Some call from saloons; while I'm exhorting I can hear the racket from one of those monstrous nickel phonographs a-coming over the wire. Some are lonely, some have sons fighting across the water, some have consciences that hurt and hurt, some are unwed girls that got in a family way after heeding a rascal's promise, some are booze-fighters, some are studying suicide. Oh, I get *more* people now days that are studying suicide."

Some of Hall's more desperate callers insist on conferring with him face to face, and most mornings there are a few sitting in his living room, waiting to be admitted to his study. Hall lives in a cold-water tenement at 360 West Forty-fifth Street, paying $30 a month for five small rooms. He has been there for twelve years. He has one of those rear flats whose entrance is through the kitchen and whose windows overlook a blind court with a single, sooty ailanthus tree in it. His telephone has nine feet of cord; in winter it is kept on a stand near the coal range in the kitchen and in summer it is moved to a desk adjacent to a window in the living room. The telephone costs him only $3.54 a month; since he is a clergyman, he gets a reduction of twenty-five per cent below the basic rate. Hall's study is cluttered. In it are an enamelled iron bed, a radio, a bureau, a couple of straight-back chairs, three tables, and a pigeonhole cabinet which holds bales of tracts. Leaning against the wall in one corner are three collapsible cots. Hall is acquainted with scores of itinerant colporteurs and evangelists, and when they are in New York they sleep in his flat. Sometimes he has so many guests that there are not enough cots to go around and he has to spread pallets on the floor. There is a typewriter on one table, and a great rat's-nest of correspondence and manuscripts. Hall is editor of a tiny monthly magazine, the *Church Militant,* which sells for a quarter a year and has thirteen hundred subscribers. The policy of this paper is extraordinary—it favors prohibition, savings banks, osteopathy, and women preachers; it opposes church suppers, vaccination, bingo, and aspirin tablets.

Under the iron bed is a pile of newspapers, mostly tabloids. Hall rarely buys a newspaper; these were picked up by his disciples off subway seats. He says that when the pile gets large enough to bother with he goes through it and clips out stories proving that the wages of sin is death, such as stories about women suicides and electrocutions at Sing Sing; he has two bureau drawers full of clippings. One wall is covered with snapshots of Hall converts. On another wall are two oilcloth signs. One says, "LOST: A HUMAN SOUL OF UNTOLD VALUE. ANYONE BRINGING SAME TO CHRIST WILL BE RICHLY REWARDED." The other says, "CIGARETTE SMOKERS WILL PLEASE CRAWL INTO THE STOVE AND OPEN THE BACK DRAFT." Hall is an enemy of tobacco. "My daddy was murdered by the tobacco trust," he says. "He was a cigar smoker and he dropped dead long before his time." Hall occasionally marries couples in his study, most of whom came to know him by way of the telephone. The study is cleaned for weddings, but not often otherwise. A disciple once pointed at one of the windowsills, on which grit and dust was half an inch thick, and said, "That's a mess if ever I saw one. Why don't you dust it off?" "I don't dust off windowsills," Hall said indignantly. "I dust off human souls."

HALL'S OUTLOOK ON LIFE IS A PRODUCT of the grayness of the Reconstruction period in the South. He was born in 1864, during the winter of the fourth year of the Civil War, in Greenville, Alabama, a small county seat. His family has been in the South since pre-Revolutionary days. His father's forebears came from Scotland, his mother's from Holland. The family, once affluent, was impoverished by the war, in which Hall's father, Dr. James Woodward Hall, served as a Confederate Army physician. "I had a real stony childhood," Hall says. "I was one of eleven children, and there was never enough to go around, duds or vittles. I didn't wear shoes until I was eighteen, except Sundays and cold spells. I went through the fifth grade, living on grits and greens, and then I had to stay home and plow cotton. I plowed with an ox. There weren't any mules in that country when I was a young un; the Yankees had

shot them all to entertain themselves. We had a hard, hard time."
Hall was tutored at night by his mother, who had what he calls "a
rock-bottom Latin and Shakespeare education." When he was
twenty, he quit the cotton fields and became a schoolteacher.

In Anniston, Alabama, in 1888, he had his first memorable encounter with sin. "I was teaching in a boys' school and rooming
and boarding at a hotel, the finest in town," he says. "Some show
people by the name of Graw's Dixieland Grand Opera Company
came to Anniston and put up at my hotel. I had never been to the
theatre and I took a foolish notion to go. I don't know what possessed
me to do so. I'm not what you'd call narrow, but oh, my! I was
shocked! And that night, back in the hotel, those strutty show
women were up and about until fully 2 A.M., a-giggling and a-
carrying on. I suspect they drank. I looked out my door and saw
one a-tiptoeing down the hall in her nightshift. Her hair was down.
It was long, yellow hair, more gold than yellow. I believe until this
day that she was on her way to some man's room. I still pray for
her; I *do* hope she reformed. Next morning I got on my knees and
asked God to forgive me for going to the theatre, and I asked Him
to make me a preacher, so I could go forth and fight such
wickedness." Hall says that he has never been in a theatre again.
He takes great pride in this. Recently, on the Forty-second Street
crosstown trolley, he heard one woman say to another, "I haven't
been to the theatre in months." Hall leaned across the aisle and
said, "Sister, *I* haven't been to the theatre since 1888."

In 1892, when Hall was twenty-eight, he took his school-teaching
savings and entered the Protestant Episcopal Seminary in Alexandria,
Virginia. Four years later he became an Episcopal priest. He started
out with churches in two Alabama small towns, Troy and Union
Springs, which are forty miles apart. "I preached one Sunday here,"
he says, "and the next Sunday yonder." He received $50 a month.
In 1904 he was appointed Episcopal chaplain for Pratt City and
Flattop, two convict camps on the outskirts of Birmingham, at a
salary of $1,000 a year, which is the most he has ever made. Flattop
was a Siberia; only the worst criminals were sent there, to work in
a coal mine. Hall prepared men for the scaffold, and he has since

used his experiences to illustrate many a grisly sermon. He says he converted hundreds. "The best time to convert a convict," he says, "is directly after there's been a hanging. One Good Friday I walked to the scaffold with three train-robbing brothers, and each time the trap was sprung there came forth a certain sound. Ka-chug, *crack!* Ka-chug, *crack!* Ka-chug, *crack!* I went straight from the hanging yard to the cell occupied by Tom Fay, a new convict. Tom was a real boa constrictor; he was the crown prince of the Miller Duncan gang of highwaymen, and he was feared by the whole of Alabama. I described this certain sound to Tom, and I chatted with him on the subject of hell. Lo and behold! Not only did I convert him, but a few months later he became a preacher himself."

Hall's work with convicts got to be well known among evangelists all over the country, and in 1908 he was invited to Philadelphia to take charge of Galilee Mission, on Vine Street. Galilee is a meeting hall and dormitory, supported by Episcopalians, for down-and-outs. It is patterned after the rescue missions on the Bowery. The job paid only $900 a year, but Hall took it. "The main thing I learned at Galilee," he says, "is that the scourges of mankind are adultery, drink, drugs, and doubt. Every night of the year we held a three-hour meeting and the derelicts you might call them stood up, one by one, and testified. They came from every walk of life, even the ministry, but there was a sameness about their confessions—adultery, drink, drugs, or doubt, night after night. Among the derelicts I ran into were sixty-one of the reverend clergy, all sots. I'll say this for the preacher sot. When he hits the bottle, he doesn't do any jackleg, halfway job. He puts his mind to it. He *works* at it. An awful, awful thing to see!" After twelve years as superintendent of Galilee, Hall resigned and became a street preacher. He wandered for four years, seldom staying in one city longer than a couple of weeks. "One night in Los Angeles in 1923," he says, "I decided that I was about ready to unpack my grip and stay a while somewhere, and I asked myself a question. 'Brother Hall,' I said to myself, 'which city is the most wicked city, pluperfect and parboiled, you've ever been in?' Without a bit of hesitation the answer came forth, 'New York, N.Y.' Consequently, I got on a train and came here and took root. If you're determined to fight the devil, you might as well get right up in the front-line trenches."


HALL DIFFERS FROM OTHER STREET PREACHERS in that he never takes up a collection. If he is offered money on the street, he accepts it, but this happens infrequently. "When it comes to religion," he says, "the common run of New York people aren't stingy; they just don't believe in giving anything away." His preaching has been subsidized, ever since he came here, by a succession of old, wealthy, Fundamentalist ladies, most of them of Southern birth. One, for example, the widow of a real-estate man, gave him $75 a month for more than five years, asking only that he preach at noon in front of J. P. Morgan & Company as often as possible. Another, also a widow, who lived at the Plaza, used to hand him an envelope containing from one to five $10 bills every time he went to call on her. In 1930 she gave him $500 and sent him to London to attend the Lambeth Conference. "Once I dropped in on this lady and found her taking a glass of wine," Hall says. "She turned it off by saying it was doctor's orders. Except for wine, she was a good old soul." Since 1933, when Hall reached the retirement age, he has been receiving $50 a month from the Pension Fund of the Episcopal Church.

Among themselves, street preachers are a squabbly lot. Hall is atypical in that he has never fought with his colleagues on matters of doctrine or dogma. "I have preached side by side in Columbus Circle with unknown tonguers, and Jehovah's Witnesses, and Salvation Army soldiers, and Pillar of Fire women, and Father Divine angels, and Happy Am I shouters, and with brothers that had one-man theologies that they thought up for themselves," Hall says, "but I never had any back talk with any of them. Take the matter of baptism. Way I figure, you can sprinkle a man, or you can totally immerse him face forward, sideways, head first, or feet first, and it's all the same, so long as the water is pure and he doesn't drown." The one street speaker with whom Hall has fought a feud is Charles Lee Smith, president of the American Association for the Advancement of Atheism. Smith is also a Southerner. Hall refers to him as the Atheist Pope and has shouted him down in Wall Street, in Union Square, and in the Circle. "It's not so much that he's an atheist," Hall says. "I could overlook that. It's that middle name of his. He was named for Robert E. Lee. Said so himself. How a man named after that great lion-hearted Christian hero General Robert E. Lee could turn into a common, street-corner atheist is more than I can understand." Smith, on the contrary, is fond of Hall. "Next to W. C. Fields," Smith says, "I don't know any man I'd rather listen to than old James Jefferson Davis Hall. I'd pay good money any day to hear him preach his sermon on the D.T.'s. I must've heard him preach that sermon a dozen times, and I've never heard him preach it the same way twice. He digresses quite a lot, and I do enjoy his digressions. They can be really wild." This sermon, "Cases of the D.T.'s I Have Known," is Hall's masterpiece. One of the cases he takes up in the course of it is that of Bobcat Jones, an old song-and-dance man.

"Mr. Jones was a derelict, an old vaudeville actor," Hall says, "and I converted him at the Galilee Mission in 1917, but he backslid. He went on a bat that lasted for weeks, and one day he showed up, a-muttering and a-raving. He was holding his head with both hands; said he was afraid the spiders would crawl in his ears. 'Repent, Mr. Jones!' I said to him. 'Repent!' He began to duck and dodge; said that Old Scratch was throwing a spear at him. I took him up the stairs to the dormitory on the second floor, and no sooner did I get him in bed than he cried out, 'There's an old goat a-coming through the transom. It's the devil. His horns are on fire. Get back there, goat! Don't let that goat butt me!' 'Why, Mr. Jones,' I said, 'I don't see any goat. Repent, repent, and ye shall be saved.' He leaped out of bed and tied three neckties together and he cried out, 'I'm a-going to lasso Old Scratch. I'm a-going to lasso him and tie him down and kick him.' I got him back in bed, but I had a struggle doing so. There was an electric fan in the room, and next he took a notion that the fan was the devil. He picked up an alarm clock and chunked it. It hit the fan and began to ring. And Mr. Jones was a-howling all the time. Oh, my, what a racket! Then he ran over and tried to take hold of the fan, and it scraped his hand, and he leaped backwards about fifteen feet and howled out, 'Old Scratch bit me! Let me out of here!' He shot out of the door, and next thing I knew he fell head over heels down the stairs, hitting every step on the way down. As my good old grandmother a long time ago way back in Alabama would've put it, 'Ass over teakettle,' and it was perfectly all right for my grandmother to use that kind of language, nobody looked down on her for doing so, good old sanctified cow-milking butter-churning biddy-hatching bee-keeping huckleberry-picking hickory-nut-cracking pole-fishing catfish-catching rabbit-trapping snuff-dipping cotton-picking hardworking old countrywoman that she was. She was a living saint, but she was very plainspoken and she was known far and wide for some of her sayings. 'Ass over teakettle,' she used to say about almost anything that happened accidentally. 'Butt, behind, bottom and all!' she used to say. 'Gut, gallus, goozle and all!' So I stood there at the head of the stairs and looked down at Mr. Jones all sprawled out on the floor at the bottom of the stairs, and I was just so afraid that he had hurt himself severely—a broken hip at the very least. He might never walk again! Permanently crippled! Or ruptured on both sides! Ruined! Done for! But nay, nay, in a minute or two the D.T.'s took control of Mr. Jones again, and he got to his feet and began to do a skippy little dance and he sung a song called, 'Cut a Watermelon on My Grave and Let the Juice Soak Through.'" At this point in the sermon Hall slowly shakes his head, and a deeply mournful look comes on his face. "Whiskey! Whiskey! Whiskey!" he exclaims. "I don't even believe in ginger ale!"

(1943)

# Lady Olga

$J$ANE BARNELL OCCASIONALLY CONSIDERS HERSELF an outcast and feels that there is something vaguely shameful about the way she makes a living. When she is in this mood, she takes no pride in the fact that she has had a longer career as a sideshow performer than any other American woman and wishes she had never left the drudgery of her grandmother's cotton farm in North Carolina. Miss Barnell is a bearded lady. Her thick, curly beard measures thirteen and a half inches, which is the longest it has ever been. When she was young and more entranced by life under canvas, she wore it differently every year; in those days there was a variety of styles in beards—she remembers the Icicle, the Indian Fighter, the Whisk Broom, and the Billy Goat—and at the beginning of a season she would ask the circus barber to trim hers in the style most popular at the moment. Since it became gray, she has worn it in the untrimmed, House of David fashion.

The business of exhibiting her beard has taken her into every state in the Union. In fact, she has undoubtedly travelled as widely in the United States as any other person, but she has always been too bored to take much notice of her surroundings and probably would not do well with a grammar-school geography quiz. "I been all over everywhere, up, down, and sideways," she says. "I've hit thousands of towns, but I don't remember much about any of them. Half the time I didn't even know what state I was in. Didn't know or care." Miss Barnell is sixty-nine years old and was first put on exhibition shortly after her fourth birthday; she claims she has been bearded since infancy. As Princess Olga, Madame Olga, or Lady Olga, she has worked in the sideshows of at least twenty-five circuses and carnivals for wages ranging between twenty and a hundred dollars a week. She has forgotten the names of some of these outfits; one circus she remembers only as "that ten-car mess on the West Coast where I and my third husband had to knock the sideshow manager on the noggin with a tent stake to get my pay." She started out with a tramp circus, or "mud show," whose rickety, louse-infested wagons were pulled by oxen, and worked her way up to Ringling Brothers and Barnum & Bailey.

She spent six years in the Ringling circus. She was with it last in 1938, when its season was cut short by a strike in Scranton, an occurrence which made her hysterical. Ringling's sideshow, the Congress of Strange People, is as highly esteemed by freaks as the Palace used to be by vaudeville actors, but she would not sign a contract for the 1939 season. It pained her to make this decision; for six consecutive seasons she had occupied the same berth in Old Ninety-six, the Ringling sleeping car for sideshow people, and had grown attached to it. "Once I heard about a man in the penitentiary who broke down and cried when he finished his term and had to leave his cell for the last time," she says. "It had got to be a home to him. That's how I felt about my berth." She turned down the 1939 contract because she had become obsessed with a notion that out on the road she would somehow be forced to join the circus union. Unions frighten her. Although she has never voted, she is a violently opinionated Republican. Also, she is a veteran reader of Hearst newspapers and believes everything she reads in them. She thinks the average union organizer carries a gun and will shoot to kill. When she sees pickets, she immediately crosses to the other side of the street. "Just as sure as I go back to Ringling's, that union will get me," she told a circus official who tried for hours to reason with her, and added, "To tell you the truth, I think that old union is a corporation, like everything else these days." She also has a fear of corporations; to her, they are as sinister as unions. Since she left, Ringling's has been without a bearded lady. Fred Smythe, manager of the Congress, offers her a contract every spring, but she always tells him that she will never again work for the Big Show. This never surprises Smythe. "Short of blasting," he says, "there's no way of getting a fool notion out of the head of a freak. I'd sure like to get her back. She's the only real, old-fashioned bearded lady left in the country. Most bearded ladies are men. Even when they're women, they look like men. Lady Olga is a woman, and she looks like a woman." Smythe says that bearded ladies are not particularly sensational but they are traditional in sideshows, like clowns in the circus itself. "People don't laugh at clowns any more but they want to see them around," he says. "Likewise, if there isn't a bearded lady in a sideshow, people feel there's something lacking."

Miss Barnell has not been on the road since leaving the Big Show but has stuck pretty close to New York City, which, as much as any other place, she considers home. In the winter she works intermittently in the basement sideshow of Hubert's Museum on West Forty-second Street. She has shown her beard in practically every dime museum in the country and likes Hubert's best of all; she has come to look upon it as her winter headquarters. Professor Le Roy Heckler, who operates the Flea Circus concession in Hubert's, is an old friend of hers. They once lived in the same farming community in Mecklenburg County, North Carolina, and she worked in circuses long ago with his father, the late Professor William Heckler, who was a sideshow strong man before he developed a method of educating fleas and established the family business. She has great respect for Le Roy; she calls him "the young Professor" and says she has known him since he was "diaper size." In the summer she divides her time between Hubert's and Professor Sam Wagner's World Circus Side Show, also a dime museum, in Coney Island. She likes Coney because she feels that salt air is good for her asthma; also, she has a high regard for the buttered roasting-ear corn that is sold in stands down there.

On the dime museum circuit she does not work steadily; she works two or three weeks in a row and then lays off for a week. "I don't want to go nuts," she says. In museums, her hours are from 11 A.M. to 11 P.M. There is an average of two shows an hour and during a show she is on the platform from five to ten minutes.

Between appearances, she is free. At Hubert's she kills most of this time dozing in a rocking chair in her dressing room. Sometimes she visits with other performers, usually with Albert-Alberta, the half-man-half-woman. Twice a week she goes into Professor Heckler's booth and watches him feed his fleas. This spectacle always amazes her, although she has seen it scores of times. The Professor rolls up one sleeve, picks the fleas out of their mother-of-pearl boxes with tweezers, and drops them, one by one, on a forearm, where they browse for fifteen minutes. While the fleas are feeding, the Professor reads a newspaper and she smokes a cigarette. They seldom say anything to each other. Taciturn herself, Miss Barnell does not care for talkative people. At least once an afternoon she wraps a scarf around her beard and goes out for coffee or a mug of root beer. She usually goes to the lunchroom in the American Bus Depot, a few doors west of Hubert's. She finds the atmosphere of a bus terminal soothing to her nerves. When showing in Coney Island, she takes brisk turns on the boardwalk between appearances.

In the past, while filling engagements in and around the city, Miss Barnell always lived in small Broadway hotels. A year or so ago she gave up hotel life. One Saturday night, after working late in Hubert's, she walked into a hotel off Times Square in which she had been living since the Ringling strike and a drunk in the lobby saw her and said, "By God, it's the bearded lady!" He followed her to the elevator, shouting, "Beaver! Beaver!" Next day she moved out and took a furnished apartment in a theatrical rooming house on Eighth Avenue, not far from the Garden. The house was rec-ommended by a colleague, a man who eats electric-light bulbs. Among the other tenants are a magician, an old burlesque comedian, a tattooed woman, and a retired circus cook. Surrounded by such people, she feels at ease; when she meets them on the stairs they simply take her for granted and do not look startled. "If an old baboon was to walk down the hall tooting on a cornet, nobody in my house would give him a second look," she says.

Miss Barnell would like to spend the rest of her life in the city, but she knows that sooner or later she will become a stale attraction in the dime museums and will have to run an "At Liberty" notice in *Billboard* and get a job with a circus or carnival again. She wants to put this off as long as possible because she has grown to like apartment life; it has given her a chance, she says, really to get acquainted with Thomas O'Boyle, her fourth husband, and with Edelweiss, her cat. O'Boyle is a veteran Joey, or clown, but recently he has been employed as a talker—the sideshow term for barker— on the box at the gate at Hubert's. He is nineteen years younger than Miss Barnell and, unlike her, is enthralled by sideshow life. He wears dark-blue shirts, lemon-yellow neckties, and Broadway suits. He believes Miss Barnell is one of the great women of all time and treats her accordingly. When she comes into a room he leaps to his feet, and when she takes out a cigarette he hurriedly strikes a match for her. They were married after working together during the season of 1931 in the Johnny J. Jones Exposition, a carnival. Both are short-wave-radio fans, and O'Boyle says that this mutual interest is what brought them together. "Since our marriage, I and Mr. O'Boyle have travelled with the same outfits," Miss Barnell said recently, "but I never felt like I really knew him until we settled in an apartment. In a sleeping car you just don't feel married. To get to know a husband, you have to cook and wash for him." Next to O'Boyle, Edelweiss is her chief concern. Edelweiss is a sullen, overfed, snow-white Persian, for which she paid twenty-five dollars when it was a kitten and which now weighs sixteen pounds. She has nicknamed it Edie, and when she speaks to it she uses baby talk. She owns a comfortable old canvas chair—it came out of a circus dressing tent—and she likes to loll in this chair, hold the cat in her lap, and sing to it. Interminably, one after the other, she sings "Eadie Was a Lady" and "Root, Hog, or Die," an old circus song. Cats and dogs are not permitted in the sleeping cars of most circuses, so when she is on the road she usually has to board Edie in a pet store. "Sometimes out in the sticks," she says, "I get so lonesome for Edie I feel like I just can't bear it." She thinks Hubert's is much nicer than other museums because the manager there understands how she feels about the cat and lets her bring it with her to work. While she is on the platform, Edie sits beside her, purring. After cats, Miss Barnell likes horses best. She is one of those women who cannot pass a horse standing at a curb without trying to stroke its head; she keeps a handful of wrapped cube sugar in her bag for horses. Once a month, no matter how lean the season, she sends a contribution to the A.S.P.C.A. "To an animal, if you're bearded, it don't make no difference," she says.

Miss Barnell has not only a beard but side whiskers and a droopy mustache. In a white, loose-fitting house dress, she looks like an Old Testament prophet. Her appearance is more worldly when she dresses for a party; on such occasion she uses lipstick and rouge. Monty Woolley saw her once when she was dressed for the evening and said she looked like Elsa Maxwell in a property beard. Someone repeated Woolley's remark to her and she snorted with indignation. "Mr. Woolley must not have good eyesight," she said. She is not as plump as Miss Maxwell. She is five feet five and weighs a hundred and eighty-three pounds. She does not look her age; she has few wrinkles and she walks with a firm step. Her face is round and gloomy. Her bobbed gray hair is brushed pompadour style, and on the platform she wears a Spanish comb and two side combs. Once a year she gets a permanent wave. Before going on the street, she always covers her face with a veil and wraps a Paisley scarf around her neck, hiding her beard. To keep it curly, she sleeps with her beard in a pigtail plait; on days off she does not unplait it. She wears a thick gold wedding ring. Her voice is low and feminine.

Years of listening to barkers has had an effect on her speech; she makes long words longer. To her, a monstrosity is a "monsterosity." She uses some circus slang. The men who haunt the pinball machines on the first floor of Hubert's and never spend a dime to visit the sideshow in the basement are "lot lice" to her; in circuses, this term is applied to townspeople who do not buy tickets but stand around the lot, gaping at everything and getting in the way. She uses the word "old" to express contempt. She once said, "If that old Mayor they have here can't think up anything better than that old sales tax, he ought to lay down and quit." She consistently says "taken" for "took." This is a sample of her conversation: "When I was a young'un I taken the name Princess Olga. After I first got married I changed to Madame, but when every confounded swami-woman and mitt-reader in the nation taken to calling herself Madame So-and-So, I decided Lady was more ree-fined." She has a dim but unmistakable Southern accent, and many of her habits of speech are North Carolinian. She heavily accents the first syllable in words like "hotel" and "police." She uses "one" as a contraction for "one or the other." She says, "I'm going to the movie pitchers this afternoon, or down to Coney Island, one." When she gets ready to do her kitchen shopping, she doesn't say, "I'm going up the street"; she says, "I'm going up street," or, "I'm going down street." Another heritage from her years in rural North Carolina is a liking for snuff. She and O'Boyle own an automobile, and occasionally they get it out of storage and take a long trip. While riding along with the windows lowered, they both dip snuff. "Out in the country, snuff is better than cigarettes," she says. "Of course, I'd never think of using it indoors." She smokes a pack and a half of cigarettes a day. The use of tobacco is her only bad habit. As a rule, sideshow performers are fond of the bottle, but she is a teetotaler and a believer in prohibition.

On a sideshow platform or stage, Miss Barnell is rather austere. To discourage people from getting familiar, she never smiles. She dresses conservatively, usually wearing a plain black evening gown. "I like nice clothes, but there's no use wasting money," she says. "People don't notice anything but my old beard." She despises pity and avoids looking into the eyes of the people in her audiences; like most freaks, she has cultivated a blank, unseeing stare. When people look as if they feel sorry for her, especially women, it makes her want to throw something. She does not sell photographs of herself as many sideshow performers do and does not welcome questions from spectators. She will answer specific questions about her beard as graciously as possible, but when someone becomes inquisitive about her private life—"You ever been married?" is the most frequent query—she gives the questioner an icy look or says quietly, "None of your business." Audiences seem to think that this is admirable. Now and then, after she has told off a persistent or insulting questioner, people will applaud. Miss Barnell's temper has been a blessing; it has kept her from succumbing to utter apathy, which is the occupational disease of freaks. "I don't take no back talk from nobody," she says. She guards her dignity jealously. Once she slapped an apology out of a carnival owner who had suggested that she dye her beard so he could bill her as "Olga, the Lady Bluebeard." Wisecracking professors, or talkers, annoy her; she prefers to be introduced by one who is deadly serious and able to use long medical words. Except for midgets, the majority of freaks in American sideshows are natives, but talkers hate to admit this. Consequently, at one time or another, Miss Barnell has been introduced as having been born in Budapest, Paris, Moscow, Shanghai, and Potsdam. In one carnival she was "the daughter of a Hungarian general," and in another "the half sister of a French duke." She does not have a high opinion of foreigners and is sorely vexed by such introductions. She was grateful to the late Clyde Ingalls, who was once married to Lillian Leitzel and preceded Smythe as manager of Ringling's Congress, because he never seemed to resent the fact that she was born in North Carolina. Ingalls would bow to her, turn to the audience, click his heels, and say, "It gives me the greatest pleasure at this time to introduce a little woman who comes to us from an aristocratic plantation in the Old South and who is recognized by our finest doctors, physicians, and medical men as the foremost, unquestioned, and authentic fee-male bearded lady in medical history. Ladies and gentlemen, Lay-dee Oolgah!"

Among freaks it is axiomatic that Coney Island audiences are the most inhuman, but Miss Barnell has found that a Surf Avenue dime museum on a Saturday night is peaceful compared with a moving-picture studio at any time. She talks bitterly about her experiences in Hollywood, where she has been used in a number of horror and circus pictures. Her most important role was in "Freaks," a Metro-Goldwyn-Mayer study of sideshow life filmed in 1932. It was probably the most frightening picture ever made. In it, among other things, a beautiful trapeze girl of a European circus permits a dwarf to fall in love with her in order to obtain some money he has inherited. At their wedding feast, with a fantastic group of sideshow people around the table, she gets drunk and lets slip the fact that she despises the dwarf. A few nights later, during a terrible storm when the troupe is on the road, the freaks climb into her private wagon and mutilate her, turning *her* into a freak. Miss Barnell thinks this picture was an insult to all freaks everywhere and is sorry she acted in it. When it was finished, she swore she would never again work in Hollywood.

Her self-esteem suffers least of all when she is working in circuses, where sideshow class distinctions are rigidly observed. She herself divides freaks into three classes: born freaks, made freaks, and two-timers. Born freaks are the aristocrats of the sideshow world. She, of course, is a member of this class. So are Siamese twins, pinheads, fat girls, dwarfs, midgets, giants, living skeletons, and men with skulls on which rocks can be broken. Made freaks include tattooed people, sword-swallowers, snake charmers, and glass-eaters. Normal people who obtain sideshow engagements because of past glory or notoriety are two-timers to her. Examples are reformed criminals, old movie stars, and retired athletes like Jack Johnson, the old prizefighter, and Grover Cleveland Alexander, the old ballplayer, both of whom starred for a while on the dime museum circuit. Because Johnson wears a beret and because she has heard that he sips beer through a straw, she particularly dislikes him. "To the general public, old Jack Johnson may be a freak," she says, "but to a freak, he ain't a freak." Paradoxically, she bears no animosity toward fake bearded ladies. They amuse her. She was greatly amused when Frances Murphy, the Gorilla Lady in the "Strange As It Seems" sideshow at the New York World's Fair in 1940, got into an altercation with a truck-driver and was exposed as a male. "If any man is fool enough to be a bearded lady," she says, "it's all right with me."

Some of Miss Barnell's genuine but less gifted colleagues are inclined to think that she is haughty, but she feels that a woman with a beard more than a foot long has a right to be haughty. She undoubtedly does have the most flamboyant female beard in American sideshow history. The beard of Joséphine Boisdechêne, a native of Switzerland and one of P. T. Barnum's most lucrative freaks, was only eight inches long, and she had no mustache. She did, however, have a bearded son—Albert, billed as "Esau, the Hairy Boy"—who helped make up for this shortcoming. Grace Gilbert, who came from Kalkaska, Michigan, and spent most of her professional life in Barnum & Bailey's Circus, had a lush beard, but it was only six inches long. Miss Gilbert used peroxide and was billed as "Princess Gracie, the Girl with the Golden Whiskers." Records of non-professional female beards are scarce. Margaret of Parma, Regent of the Netherlands from 1559 to 1567, had a "coarse, bushy beard." She was proud of it, believing it gave her a regal appearance, and she required court physicians to mix tonics for it. Charles XII of Sweden had a bearded female grenadier in his army, a reputedly beautiful amazon, who was captured by the Russians in the battle of Poltava in 1709 and subsequently taken to St. Petersburg and presented to the Czar, at whose court she was popular for several years. There was a Spanish nun called St. Paula the Bearded, who grew a miraculous beard, according to sacred history. She was being pursued one night by a man with evil intent when hair suddenly sprouted from her chin. She turned and confronted the man and he fled. No reliable statistics on the length of these beards have come down to us.

Most freaks are miserable in the company of non-freaks, but unless she is sunk in one of the morose spells she suffers from occasionally, Miss Barnell welcomes the opportunity to go out among ordinary people. One morning in the winter of 1940 Cole Porter went to her dressing room at Hubert's and asked her to go with him to a cocktail party Monty Woolley was giving at the Ritz-Carlton. Porter told her that Woolley was a student of beards, that he was known as The Beard by his friends, and that he had always wanted to meet a bearded lady. "I'll have to ask my old man," Miss Barnell said. O'Boyle told her to go ahead and enjoy herself. Porter offered to pay for the time she would lose at the museum. "Well, I tell you," she said, "I and you and Mr. Woolley are all in show business, and if this party is for members of the profession, I won't charge a cent." Porter said non-professionals would be present, so she set a fee of eight dollars. Late that afternoon he picked her up at her house. She had changed into a rhinestone-spangled gown. In the Ritz-Carlton elevator she took off the scarf she was wearing around her beard, astonishing the other passengers. There were more than a hundred stage and society people at the party, and Porter introduced her to most of them. Woolley, who got quite interested in her, asked her to have a drink. She hesitated and then accepted a glass of sherry, remarking that it was her first drink in nine years. "I like to see people enjoying theirselves," she said after finishing the sherry. "There's too confounded much misery in this world." She was at the party an hour and a half and said she wished she could stay longer but she had to go home and cook a duck dinner for her husband. Next day, at Hubert's, she told a colleague she had never had a nicer time. "Some of the better class of the Four Hundred were there," she said, "and when I was introduced around I recognized their names. I guess I was a curiosity to them. Some of them sure were a curiosity to me. I been around peculiar people most of my life, but I never saw no women like them before." She was able to recognize the names of the society people because she is a devoted reader of the Cholly Knickerbocker column in the *Journal & American*. She is, in fact, a student of society scandals. "The Four Hundred sure is one cutting-up set of people," she says.

Several endocrinologists have tried vainly to argue Miss Barnell into letting them examine her. She is afraid of physicians. When sick, she depends on patent medicines. "When they get their hands on a monsterosity the medical profession don't know when to stop," she says. "There's nobody so indecent and snoopy as an old doctor." Her hirsuteness is undoubtedly the result of distorted glandular activity. The abnormal functioning of one of the endocrine, or ductless, glands is most often responsible for excessive facial hair in females. Hypertrichosis and hirsutism are the medical terms for the condition. Miss Barnell once read a book called "The Human Body" and is familiar with the glandular explanation, but does not take much stock in it. She says that her parentage was Jewish, Irish, and American Indian, and she believes vaguely that this mixture of bloods is in some way to blame, although she had three beardless sisters.

Miss Barnell has to be persuaded to talk about her early life. "What's the use?" she tells people. "You won't believe me." She says that her father, George Barnell, an itinerant buggy- and wagonmaker, was a Russian Jew who had Anglicized his name. Around 1868, while wandering through the South, he visited a settlement of Catawba Indians on the Catawba River in York County, South Carolina, and fell in love with and was married to a girl who had a Catawba mother and an Irish father. They settled in Wilmington, the principal port of North Carolina, where Barnell established himself in the business of repairing drays on the docks. Miss Barnell was their second child; she was born in 1871 and named Jane, after her Indian grandmother. At birth her chin and cheeks were covered with down. Before she was two years old she had a beard. Her father was kind to her, but her mother, who was superstitious, believed she was bewitched and took her to a succession of Negro granny-women and conjure doctors. Around her fourth birthday, her father inherited some money from a relative and went up to Baltimore to see about starting a business there. While he was away a dismal little six-wagon circus came to Wilmington. It was called the Great Orient Family Circus and Menagerie, and was operated by a family of small, dark foreigners; Miss Barnell calls them "the Mohammedans." The family was composed of a mother, who was a snake charmer; two daughters, who danced; and three sons, who were jugglers and wire-walkers. The wagons were pulled by oxen, and the show stock consisted of three old lions, a few sluggish snakes, some monkeys, a cage of parrots, an educated goat, and a dancing bear. There were many tramp circuses of this type in the country at that time. On the last day of the Great Orient's stay, Mrs. Barnell sold or gave Jane to the Mohammedan mother. "I never been able to find out if Mamma got any money for me or just gave me away to get rid of me," Miss Barnell says bitterly. "She hated me, I know that. Daddy told me years later that he gave her a good beating when he got home from Baltimore and found out what had happened. He had been in Baltimore two months, and by the time he got home I and the Mohammedans were long gone. He and the sheriff of New Hanover County searched all over the better part of three states for us, but they didn't find hide or hair."

She does not remember much about her life with the Great Orient. "My entire childhood was a bad dream," she says. The

Mohammedans exhibited her in a small tent separate from the circus, and people had to pay extra to see her. On the road she slept with the Mohammedan mother in the same wagon in which the snakes were kept. Her pallet on the floor was filthy. She was homesick and cried a lot. The Mohammedans were not intentionally cruel to her. "They did the best they could, I guess," she says. "They were half starved themselves. I didn't understand their talk and their rations made me sick. They put curry in everything. After a while the old Mohammedan mother taken to feeding me on eggs and fruits." The circus wandered through the South for some months, eventually reaching a big city, which she thinks was New Orleans. There the Mohammedans sold their stock and wagons to another small circus and got passage on a boat to Europe, taking her along. In Europe, they joined a German circus. In Berlin, in the summer of 1876, after Jane had been exhibited by the German circus for four or five months, she got sick. She thinks she had typhoid fever. She was placed in a charity hospital. "I was nothing but skin and bones," she says. "The day they put me in the hospital was the last I ever saw of the Mohammedans. They thought I was due to die." She does not remember how long she was in the hospital. After she recovered she was transferred to an institution which she thinks was an orphanage. One morning her father appeared and took her away. "I disremember how Daddy located me," she says, "but I think he said the old Mohammedan mother went to the chief of police in Berlin and told who I was. I guess he somehow got in touch with the chief of police in Wilmington. That must have been the way it happened."

Barnell brought Jane back to North Carolina but did not take her home; she did not want to see her mother. Instead, he put her in the care of her Indian grandmother, who, with other Catawbas, had moved up from the settlement in South Carolina to a farming community in Mecklenburg County, near Charlotte. Jane worked on her grandmother's farm, chopping cotton, milking cows, and tending pigs. She never went to school but was taught to read and write by a Presbyterian woman who did missionary work among the Catawbas. Jane remembers stories this woman told her about

Florence Nightingale; they made her long to become a nurse. In her teens she taught herself to shave with an old razor that had belonged to her grandfather. When she was around seventeen she went to Wilmington to visit her father, and a doctor he knew got her a place as a student nurse in the old City Hospital. She worked in the hospital for perhaps a year, and she still thinks of this as the happiest period of her life. Eventually, however, something unpleasant happened which caused her to leave; what it was, she will not tell. "I just figured I could never have a normal life," she says, "so I went back to Grandma's and settled down to be a farmhand the rest of my days." Three or four years later she became acquainted with the senior Professor Heckler, who owned a farm near her grandmother's; he worked in circuses in the summer and lived on the farm in the winter. Heckler convinced her she would be happier in a sideshow than on a farm and helped her get a job with the John Robinson Circus. As well as she can remember, she got this job in the spring of 1892, when she was twenty-one. "Since that time," she says, "my beard has been my meal ticket." Until the death of her grandmother, around 1899, Miss Barnell went back to North Carolina every winter. She had three sisters and two brothers in Wilmington, and she visited them occasionally. "They all thought I was a disgrace and seeing them never gave me much enjoyment," she says. "Every family of a freak I ever heard of was the same. I've known families that lived off a freak's earnings but wouldn't be seen with him. My parents passed on long ago, and I reckon my brothers and sisters are all dead by now. I haven't seen any of them for twenty-two years. I had one sister I liked. I used to send her a present every Christmas, and sometimes she'd drop me a card. She was a nurse. She went to China twenty-some-odd years ago to work in a hospital for blind Chinese children, and that's the last I ever heard of her. I guess she's dead."

Miss Barnell was with the Robinson Circus for fourteen years. While with it, she was married to a German musician in the circus band. By him she had two children, both of whom died in infancy. Soon after the death of her second child, her husband died. "After that," she says, "I never got any more pleasure out of circus life. I had to make a living, so I kept on. It's been root, hog, or die. When I got sick of one outfit, I moved on to another. Circuses are all the same—dull as ditch water." She left Robinson's to go with the Forepaugh–Sells Brothers' Circus and Menagerie, leaving it to marry a balloon ascensionist. He was killed about a year after they were married; how, she will not say. "He was just killed," she says, shrugging her shoulders. Her third marriage also ended unhappily. "That one treated me shamefully," she says. "If he was in a bottle, I wouldn't pull out the stopper to give him air. I taken out a divorce from him the year before I and Mr. O'Boyle got married."

Miss Barnell is disposed to blame circuses for much of the unhappiness in her life. Consequently she does not share her present husband's enthusiasm for them. O'Boyle was an orphan who ran away to work with a circus, and has never become disenchanted. Every week he reads *Billboard* from cover to cover, and he keeps a great stack of back copies of the magazine in their apartment; she rarely reads it. Like most old circus men, he is garrulous about the past. He often tries to get his wife to talk about her circus experiences, but she gives him little satisfaction. O'Boyle is proud of her career. Once he begged her to give him a list of the circuses and carnivals she has worked for; he wanted to send the list to the letters-to-the-editor department of *Billboard*. She mentioned Ringling, Barnum & Bailey, Forepaugh-Sells, Hagenbeck-Wallace, the World of Mirth Carnival, the Royal American Shows, the Rubin & Cherry Exposition, and the Beckmann & Gerety Shows, and then yawned and said, "Mr. O'Boyle, please go turn on the radio." He has never been able to get the full list.

In the last year or so Miss Barnell has become a passionate housekeeper and begrudges every moment spent away from her apartment. About once a week she rearranges the furniture in her two small rooms. On a window sill she keeps two geranium plants in little red pots. On sunny afternoons during her days off she places a pillow on the sill, rests her elbows on it, and stares for hours into Eighth Avenue. People who see her in the window undoubtedly think she is a gray-bearded old man. She spends a lot of time in the kitchen, trying out recipes clipped from newspapers. O'Boyle has gained eleven pounds since they moved into the apartment. Before starting work in the kitchen, she turns on four electric fans in various corners of the apartment and opens all the windows; she does not trust gas and believes that stirring up the air is good for her asthma. While the fans are on, she keeps Edie, the cat, who is susceptible to colds, shut up in a closet. She has developed a phobia about New York City tap water; she is sure there is a strange, lethal acid in it, and boils drinking water for fifteen minutes. She even boils the water in which she gives Edie a bath. In her opinion, the consumption of unboiled water is responsible for most of the sickness in the city. On her bureau she keeps two radios, one of them a short-wave set. On her days off she turns on the short-wave radio right after she gets up and leaves it on until she goes to bed. While in the kitchen, she listens to police calls. The whirring of the fans and the clamor of the radio do not bother her in the least. The walls are thin, however, and once the burlesque comedian who lives in the next apartment rapped on the door and said, "Pardon me, Madam, but it sounds like you're murdering a mule in there, or bringing in an oil well."

Miss Barnell's attitude toward her work is by no means consistent. In an expansive mood, she will brag that she has the longest female beard in history and will give the impression that she feels superior to less spectacular women. Every so often, however, hurt by a snicker or a brutal remark made by someone in an audience, she undergoes a period of depression which may last a few hours or a week. "When I get the blues, I feel like an outcast from society," she once said. "I used to think when I got old my feelings wouldn't get hurt, but I was wrong. I got a tougher hide than I once had, but it ain't tough enough." On the road she has to keep on working, no matter how miserable she gets, but in a museum she simply knocks off and goes home. Until she feels better, she does not go out of her apartment, but passes the time listening to the police calls, playing with Edie, reading the *Journal & American,* and studying an old International Correspondence Schools course in stenography which she bought in a secondhand-bookstore in Chicago years ago. Practicing short-hand takes her mind off herself. She is aware that such a thing is hardly possible, but she daydreams about becoming a stenographer the way some women daydream about Hollywood. She says that long ago she learned there is no place in the world outside of a sideshow for a bearded lady. When she was younger she often thought of joining the Catholic Church and going into a nunnery; she had heard of sideshow women who became nuns, although she had never actually known one. A lack of religious conviction deterred her. Religion has been of little solace to her. "I used to belong to the Presbyterians, but I never did feel at home in church," she says. "Everybody eyed me, including the preacher. I rather get my sermons over the radio."

Most of Miss Barnell's colleagues are touchy about the word "freak," preferring to be called artistes or performers. Years ago, because of this, Ringling had to change the name of its sideshow from the Congress of Freaks to the Congress of Strange People. Miss Barnell would like to be considered hardboiled and claims she does not care what she is called. "No matter how nice a name was put on me," she says, "I would still have a beard." Also, she has a certain professional pride. Sometimes, sitting around with other performers in a dressing room, she will say, with a slight air of defiance, that a freak is just as good as any actor, from the Barrymores on down. "If the truth was known, we're all freaks together," she says.

(1940)

# Evening with a Gifted Child

$P$HILIPPA DUKE SCHUYLER IS PROBABLY the best example in New York City of what psychologists call a gifted child. She is nine years old. Her mental age, according to the Clinic for Gifted Children at New York University, which tests her periodically, is sixteen. She has an I.Q. of 185. Phillipa reads Plutarch on train trips, eats steaks raw, writes poems in honor of her dolls, plays poker, and is the composer of more than sixty pieces for the piano. Most of these compositions are descriptive, with such titles as "Spanish Harlem," "Men at Work," "The Cockroach Ballet," and "At the Circus." She began composing before she was four, and has been playing the piano in public, often for money, since she was six. She has an agreement with the National Broadcasting Company by which she plays new compositions for the first time in public on a Sunday-morning broadcast called "Coast to Coast on a Bus," and she frequently plays on other radio and television programs. A Schuyler album, "Five Little Pieces," has been published. She has gone on tour several times, playing compositions by Bach, Rimsky-Korsakoff, Debussy, Schumann, and herself in Grand Rapids, Cincinnati, Indianapolis, Columbus, Youngstown, Atlantic City, Trenton, and other cities. On one tour she averaged $175 an engagement, plus all expenses. Philippa is often called a genius by admiring strangers, and her parents find this displeasing. To them, her development is explained not by genius but by diet. They believe that humans should live on uncooked meats, fruits, vegetables, and nuts, and are convinced that the food Philippa has eaten most of her life is largely responsible for her precocity. She particularly likes raw green peas, raw corn on the cob, raw yams, and raw sirloin steaks.

Philippa's father, George S. Schuyler, whom she calls by his first name, is a Negro essayist and novelist, the son of a dining-car chef on the New York Central. He writes an influential column on national and world affairs for the Pittsburgh *Courier,* a weekly Negro newspaper, and is business manager of the *Crisis,* which is the official organ of the National Association for the Advancement of Colored People. He wrote often for the *American Mercury* when H. L. Mencken edited it. Mr. Schuyler's skin is jet black. He comes from one of the oldest Negro families in New York; long before the Revolutionary War, ancestors of his in Albany began using Schuyler as a surname. Since then, Negro Schuylers have occasionally also used the Christian names of distinguished white Schuylers. Philippa is named for Philip John Schuyler, the Revolutionary general. Philippa's mother, Mrs. Josephine Schuyler, is white. She is, in fact, a golden-haired blonde. She is a member of a pioneer west Texas ranching and banking family, and speaks with a Southern accent. When she was in her teens, she ran away from home and went to California; since then she has considered herself "a rebel." Before she and Mr. Schuyler were married in 1928, she had been, successively, a Mack Sennett bathing beauty, a ballet dancer in a San Francisco opera company, a painter, a poet, and a writer for the Negro press. She met Mr. Schuyler in New York when she visited the office of a magazine of which he was an editor and to which she had contributed poems and articles. This magazine was the *Messenger,* the official organ of the Brotherhood of Sleeping Car Porters. Mrs. Schuyler acquired her dietary convictions in California years ago; her husband is a more recent convert and is not quite as dead set. Mrs. Schuyler feels that both alcohol and tobacco are utterly unnecessary; her husband, however, drinks beer and smokes cigars. Mrs. Schuyler still writes occasionally for Negro newspapers under various names, but devotes most of her time to painting and Philippa. On tour, she serves as Philippa's manager. Philippa calls her Jody. The Schuylers live in a large apartment house on Convent Avenue. This house, which is tenanted by both white and Negro families, is on a hill overlooking the western fringe of Harlem, and is several blocks from the Convent of the Sacred Heart, where Philippa is in Grade 6A.

The Schuylers recently invited me to come and hear Philippa play. I went up one evening around eight o'clock. Mrs. Schuyler met me at the door and said that Philippa was in her own room transcribing a composition called "Caprice No. 2," which she had finished just before dinner. We went into the living room, where Mr. Schuyler, in shirtsleeves, was hunched over a desk. At his elbow was a stack of clippings about Philippa from newspapers in the cities in which she had played. He was pasting these in a large scrapbook. "We have nine scrapbooks full of stuff about Philippa, one for each year," he said. "She's never seen them. In fact, so far as we know, she's never seen a clipping about herself. We're afraid it might make her self-conscious. When she gets to be a young woman, we'll bring out all her scrapbooks and say, 'Here are some things you might find interesting.' "

There were paintings, chiefly nudes, on two walls of the living room. I noticed Mrs. Schuyler's signature in the corner of one. Bookcases lined another wall, and arranged on their top shelves were a number of pieces of African sculpture. Mrs. Schuyler pointed to one, a female fetish. "George brought that back from Africa in 1931," she said. "He was down there getting material for a book. Most of these things, however, belong to Philippa. They were sent to her by people in Liberia, Nigeria, and the Ivory Coast who heard her play on the radio. They listen in on short-wave. They write to her, and she answers their letters. They know that part of her background is African, and are proud of her. Their presents to Philippa are brought here by Africans who work on ships plying between New York and various West African ports. She has a slew of medals and prizes she won in tournaments held by the New York Philharmonic, the National Guild of Piano Teachers, and similar organizations, and she keeps them in a fancy inlaid chest that was sent to her by a craftsman in Africa. Philippa is extremely proud of her Negro blood."

Mr. Schuyler looked up from the scrapbook. "She has radio fans all over the world, not only in Africa," he said. "On her last birthday she received six sable skins and a black pearl from Alaska, a scarf from Portugal, and a doll from the Virgin Islands. However, most of her presents did come from Africa."

While we were looking at an ebony elephant, Philippa came into the room. Mr. Schuyler unobtrusively closed the scrapbook and put it in a drawer of the desk. Then he introduced me to Philippa. She shook hands, not awkwardly, as most children do, but with assurance. She is slender, erect, and exquisitely boned. Her face is oval, and she has serious black eyes, black curls, and perfect teeth. Her skin is light brown. She is a beautiful child.

"Did you get through with the piece?" her mother asked her.

"Oh, yes," Philippa said. "Half an hour ago. Look, Jody, do you remember that silly little riddle book I bought at the newsstand in the station at Cincinnati and never got a chance to look at?"

"Yes, I remember."

"Well, I've just been looking through it, and some of the riddles are funny. May I ask one, please?"

Mrs. Schuyler nodded, and Philippa asked, "What has four wheels and flies?"

We were silent a minute, and then Philippa said impatiently, "Give up, please, so I can tell you."

"We give up," Mrs. Schuyler said.

"A garbage wagon," Philippa said.

Mr. Schuyler groaned, and Philippa looked at him and burst out laughing.

"Was it that bad, George?" she asked. "Wait until you hear some of the others."

"Not now, Philippa," Mrs. Schuyler said, rather hastily. "Instead, maybe you'd like to play for us in your room."

"I'd like to very much," Philippa said.

Mr. Schuyler said that he would stay in the living room and listen. Mrs. Schuyler and I followed Philippa down the hall. A large red balloon was tethered by a string to the doorknob of Philippa's room. "I like balloons," she said, spanking it into the air with the heel of her hand. "They remind me of the circus."

The Schuylers have a four-room apartment. I noticed that Philippa's room was the largest. In it there was a grand piano, a bed, an adult-size dressing table, two small chairs, and a cabinet. Mrs. Schuyler opened the doors of the cabinet. "Philippa keeps her music and dolls in here," she said. "She made this doll house. She knitted the little rug herself and sewed dresses for the dolls. She sews very well. She made me an apron the other day." On top of Philippa's piano there was a Modern Library giant edition of Plutarch, a peach kernel, a mystery novel called "The Corpse with the Floating Foot," a copy of the New York *Post* opened to the comic-strip page, a teacup half full of raw green peas, a train made of adhesive-tape spools and cardboard, a Stravinsky sonata, a pack of playing cards, a photograph of Lily Pons clipped from a magazine, and an uninflated balloon. I was standing beside the piano, examining this rather surrealistic group of objects, when Mrs. Schuyler suddenly snapped her fingers and said, "I forgot the peaches!" She started out of the room, then paused at the door and said, "It's a kind of ice cream I make. We're going to have some later on, and I forgot to put the peaches in the icebox. I'll leave you two alone for a few minutes. Philippa, don't start playing until I get back." I took one of the chairs and Philippa sat on the piano bench. Left alone with her, I felt ill at ease. I didn't know how to go about making small talk with a gifted child.

"Do you mind if I smoke in here?" I asked her.

"Of course not," Philippa said. "I'll go get you an ashtray."

When she returned, I asked her if she had been reading the Plutarch on the piano.

"Yes," she said. "I've read most of it. I got it to read on trains."

"Don't you find it rather dry?"

"Not at all. I like biography. I particularly like the sections called the comparisons. Best of all I liked Theseus and Romulus, and Solon and Poplicola. Plutarch is anything but dry. I'm very interested in the Romans. I want to get 'The Decline and Fall' next. It's in the Modern Library, too."

"What are some other books you like?"

Philippa laughed. "Lately I've been reading a Sherlock Holmes omnibus and some mystery books by Ellery Queen."

"What book do you like best of all?"

"Oh, that's almost impossible to answer. You can't just pick out one book and say you like it better than all others. I bet you can't."

"I certainly can," I said. I was not bothered any longer by the difference in our ages, and had completely got over feeling ill at ease.

"What book?"

"Mark Twain's 'Life on the Mississippi,' " I said.

"Oh, I like Mark Twain," Philippa said, clapping her hands excitedly. "I like him very much. What other writers do you like?"

"The ones I like best," I said, "are Mark Twain, Dostoevski, and James Joyce."

Philippa deliberated for a few moments.

"I guess you're right," she said. "I *can* say that there's one book I like best of all. That's the 'Arabian Nights.' George has an eight-volume set. It's an unexpurgated edition. I read it first when I was three, and at least four times since. I based my longest composition on it. I called it 'Arabian Nights Suite.' Oh, the stories in that book are absolutely wonderful!" She laughed. "Goodness!" she said. "I didn't mean to get so"—she paused and appeared to be searching for a word—"impassioned."

Mrs. Schuyler returned, and sat down.

"Look," Philippa said to me, "do you like funnies?"

"You mean comic strips?" I asked.

"Yes," she said. "Funnies."

"Of course I do," I said. "The best comic strip is 'Moon Mullins' in the *News*."

"Oh, no, it isn't," she said. "The best funny is 'Dixie Dugan' in the *Post*, and the next best is the full-page 'Katzenjammer Kids' in the Sunday *Journal*. The *Post* has the best funnies. I like 'Dixie Dugan,' 'Superman,' 'Tarzan,' 'Abbie an' Slats,' and 'The Mountain Boys,' and they're all in the *Post*. You know, I'm almost ready to write a composition about the funnies. I'm going to call it 'The Katzenjammer Kids.' I read a lot of mystery stories, and I've already written a composition called 'Mystery Story.' "

"Philippa tries to describe places and experiences in her music,"

Mrs. Schuyler said. "We used to live in Spanish Harlem, and she put some of the things she saw and heard in that neighborhood into a composition. She wrote 'Men at Work' while the WPA was digging a sewer in front of our apartment house. She likes the playground at Sacred Heart very much, and she described it in a piece called 'In a Convent Garden.' Once she had a canary, and it died. For its funeral she wrote a sad little piece called 'Death of the Nightingale.' Philippa, you're getting fidgety. Are you ready to play for us?"

"Yes, Jody," Philippa said, getting to her feet. She turned to me, curtsied, and said, "Think about cockroaches while I'm playing this piece. It's 'The Cockroach Ballet.' This is the story: Some cockroaches are feasting on a kitchen floor. A human comes in and kills some of them. He thinks he has killed them all. But after he leaves, one little cockroach peeps out, then another, and another. They dance a sad little dance for their dead comrades. But they aren't very sad because they know that cockroaches will go on forever and ever. Unfortunately."

Mrs. Schuyler laughed. "Philippa took that piece to Mother Stevens at Sacred Heart the afternoon she wrote it," she said. "Mother Stevens is head of the music department. She asked Philippa why she didn't write about angels instead of cockroaches. 'But dear Mother,' Philippa said, 'I've never seen an angel, but I've seen many cockroaches.'"

Philippa sat down at the piano, and began playing. I thought it was a nice piece.

Next she played a composition called "Impressions of the World's Fair, 1939." In it the sound of the tractor-train horn—that wornout phrase from "The Sidewalks of New York"—was recurrent. Then she played "Men at Work." When she finished it she asked me to enumerate the noises I had recognized. I told her I thought I had recognized an air drill, the sound of trowels knocking the tar off paving blocks, and the sound of a chisel being hammered into rock. "You're very good," Philippa said, and I felt pleased. "Here's one called 'The Jolly Pig,'" she said. In the middle of it she turned to me and asked, "Hear him laughing?" I didn't, but I said I did. After that came the "Caprice" she had finished that day. Then she played some pieces by other composers. They included Rimsky-Korsakoff's "Flight of the Bumble Bee" and Johann Sebastian Bach's "Two Part Invention No. 1." After she had played for at least an hour without any sign of weariness, she said, "I'll play just one more, one I composed a long time ago, when I was four years old. It's 'The Goldfish.' A little goldfish thinks the sky is water. He tries to jump into it, only to fall upon the floor and die."

"I'll go get the ice cream," Mrs. Schuyler said as Philippa began "The Goldfish." Just as Philippa finished playing, Mrs. Schuyler returned, bringing a tray with four saucers. She called Mr. Schuyler and he came in and sat down on the bed.

"I liked your new piece, Philippa," he said. Philippa smiled proudly.

"Thanks, George," she said. "I'm going to do a little more work on it tomorrow."

"It isn't really ice cream, and you might not like it," Mrs. Schuyler said to me as she distributed the saucers. "It's just fresh peaches and cream sweetened with honey and chilled. In this house we use almost no sugar. In her entire life, Philippa has never eaten a piece of candy. Her taste hasn't been perverted by sweets. Instead, she has a passion for lemons. She eats them the way most people eat oranges, pulp and all. Don't you, Philippa?"

"Yes, Jody," Philippa said. She was eating with gusto.

"We seldom have cooked food of any kind," Mrs. Schuyler continued. "Once in a while I broil a steak very lightly, but usually we eat meat raw. We also eat raw fish that has been soaked in lemon juice. When we're travelling, Philippa and I amaze waiters. You have to argue with most waiters before they'll bring you raw meat. Then they stare at you while you eat. I guess it *is* rather unusual to see a little girl eating a raw steak. Philippa drinks a lot of milk, and she gets quite a large daily ration of cod-liver oil. About the only cooked thing she really likes is a hardboiled egg. She mashes the yolk and squeezes a lemon over it. When she goes to the movies she sometimes takes along an ear of corn. That's better than peanuts. She always fills her pockets with green peas before she goes to school. The other children at Sacred Heart used to stare at her, but now they think nothing of it."

"Jody makes me big birthday cakes," Philippa said. "They're made of ground-up cashew nuts. Once I had one that weighed twenty pounds. It was shaped like a white piano. This year it was shaped like the map of South America. The different countries were colored with berry and vegetable juices. It was a swell cake."

"We eat all kinds of nuts, just so they're raw," Mrs. Schuyler said. "Each year my father sends me all the pecans off one big tree on his ranch in Texas. Some people think we're peculiar, but the best proof that our diet theory is sensible is Philippa's health. She's extremely healthy, mentally and physically. Her teeth, for example, are absolutely perfect. She's never had even a tiny cavity."

Mr. Schuyler looked at his watch. "It's nine-thirty, Philippa," he said.

"May I ask another riddle before I go to bed?"

"Just one," her father said.

"All right. What's smaller than a flea's mouth?"

"Oh, I know that one," Mrs. Schuyler said.

"So do I," said Mr. Schuyler.

"All right, all right," Philippa said. "Wait until tomorrow. I'll ask you some you couldn't guess in fifteen years."

We said good night to Philippa. Mrs. Schuyler went into the kitchen and Mr. Schuyler and I went into the living room. I asked him how many hours a day Philippa studies. He said that during school months she gets up at seven-thirty, has a bath and breakfast, and starts practicing on the piano at eight. She practices for two hours. Then for half an hour she plays anything she likes. At ten-thirty her music supervisor arrives. The supervisor, a young piano teacher named Pauline Apanowitz, is with her an hour and a half. Shortly before one, Philippa walks to Sacred Heart, eating green peas on the way. She spends two afternoon hours a day at the convent, attending history, geography, and English classes. She misses arithmetic, spelling, and reading, which are morning classes. However, her examination grades for these subjects are always good. "There wouldn't be much point in Philippa going to a spelling class," Mr. Schuyler said. "When she was twenty-nine months old she could spell five hundred and fifty words. She has an enormous vocabulary. She likes jawbreakers. At four, she discovered the scientific word for silicosis, which is pneumonoultramicroscopicsilicovolcanoniosis, and she spelled it morning and night. It fascinated her. We certainly got tired of that word." Once a week, Mr. Schuyler said, she goes to Antonia Brico's studio for lessons in score-reading and conducting; William Harms, an assistant of Josef Hofmann, also gives her a weekly piano lesson. Most afternoons she spends an hour in the convent playground; rope-skipping is her favorite exercise. "Philippa isn't a Catholic, and we have no religious affiliations," Mr. Schuyler told me. "My parents were Catholics, however, and Philippa will become one if she so desires. Most of the other children at the convent are Irish Catholics. She gets along with them wonderfully."

Mrs. Schuyler came into the room, bringing several small books. "When Philippa was very little I kept a careful account of the stories and poems she wrote, the words she invented, the questions she asked, and such things," she said. "I wrote them down in the form of letters to her, letters for her to read when she becomes a young woman. The people at the gifted-child clinic saw the books and had the notations transcribed for their files. Perhaps you'd like to look through some of the books."

I opened one. At the top of the page was written "Three years, seven months." Beneath this was the following notation:

You are very interested to know why some people are good and some bad. "What do they do with bad people?" you ask. "If they are very bad, they put them in jail," I say. "What is a jail?" you inquire. "A jail is a building full of little rooms with barred doors." "What do they do to bad people in jail?" "They don't have nice things to eat or wear," I explain. Several days later you heard about how poor most people are in Georgia, and you asked, "The poor people in Georgia who have nothing nice to eat or wear, are they bad?" "No," I said. "They are not bad. They are unlucky. Later, I will explain more fully." That afternoon you laughed and asked, archly, "Jody, when the weather is bad, do they put it in jail?" The same day you asked if flowers get white hair when they are old. And you asked if people who sleep on cots say at night, "I am going to cot." And you asked if mothers ever say to their children, "You must go crooked to bed." Walking along the street you said, "Jody, trees stand on one leg." Yesterday you began to giggle. "There's no Mr. Lady or Mrs. Man," you said, and enjoyed the humor of the idea very much. Today you made up a poem.

> *"Pipes are steel,*
> *But bones are real."*

Tonight you sat on the floor and made up a long story. You said, "Varnetida, a little girl, and her mother, Armarnia, went to see Slowbow, a brother who lived with his father, Solom, in a big house in Channa. They met the grandmother, Branlea, and another little girl, Jolumbow, who had a kitten named Lilgay, and a dog named Cherro. They all sat down in a chilbensian room and ate dishes of wallaga and thaga . . ." and so on, as long as I would listen. If you were at a loss for a word you simply invented one with a perfectly solemn face.

I picked up another book. In it I found a poem Philippa wrote when she was five. She wrote it on Easter morning while sitting in the bathtub:

> *The sun is lifting his lid.*
> *The sun is leaving his crib.*
> *The sun is a waking baby*
> *Who will bring the Spring maybe*
> *Thump, thump, thump! out of the earth.*

I thought that this was a wonderful poem. It was followed by this notation:

Tonight a red light flashed to green while we were walking across Fifth Avenue. The automobiles were whizzing by us. Suddenly you looked up and said, "Jody, will you please name for me all the diseases in the world?"

"Philippa must be hard to deal with at times," I said.

"She is indeed," Mrs. Schuyler said. "Women often tell me, 'You mustn't push her!' Their sympathy is misplaced. If there's any pushing done, she's the one that does it."

A few minutes later, I said good night to the Schuylers. At the door I asked Mrs. Schuyler to tell me the answer to the riddle Philippa had propounded just before she went to bed; it had been on my mind ever since. "That riddle about what's smaller than a flea's mouth?" she said. "That's an old, old nursery riddle. I guess it's the only one I know. The answer is, 'What goes in it.' I'm very sorry she got hold of that riddle book. Tomorrow at breakfast she'll have the drop on us. She'll ask us two dozen, and we probably won't know a single answer."

(1940)

# A Sporting Man

COMMODORE DUTCH IS A BRASSY LITTLE MAN who has made a living for the last forty years by giving an annual ball for the benefit of himself. "I haven't got a whole lot of sense," he likes to say, "but I got too much sense to work." On big showcards which he puts up in drinking places in the theatrical district, he advertises his ball, which is usually held in the spring, as "The Annual Party, Affair, Soirée & Gala Naval Ball of the Original Commodore Dutch Association." Dutch founded this organization in 1901, because he needed the name of a sponsor to print on tickets. At first he called it simply the Commodore Dutch Association, adding "original" during the depression. "It sounds more high-toned that way," he says. "It sounds like I got imitators." No meetings of the organization have ever been held, and its headquarters are wherever Dutch happens to be. He keeps all its records in his pockets. It has one active member and three hundred honorary members. Dutch is the active member. Among the honorary members are eighteen Tammany politicians, thirteen saloonkeepers, six fight managers, six night-club proprietors, four publishers of racing dope sheets, two executives of the New York Giants, the owner of a chain of barbershops, a bail bondsman, a subway contractor, the manager of a Turkish bath, and approximately one hundred and twenty-five professional gamblers. All these men occasionally give Dutch small sums of money; that is the only requirement for membership in the Original Commodore Dutch Association. Dutch refers to these sums as dues, a euphemism which makes some of his members snicker. Joe Madden, an ex-prizefighter, who keeps a West Fifty-sixth Street saloon in which sporting and society people hang out and who has been an honorary officer of the association for twenty-seven years, not long ago defined the attitude of many of the members when he introduced a friend to Dutch and remarked, "Commodore Dutch is a bum, but he's not an ordinary bum. He doesn't make touches; he collects dues. He's the fanciest bum in town." Dutch was not offended by this remark. He beamed at Madden and said, "Thanks, pal."

Dutch lets each member decide how much dues he should pay. "You're the doctor," he says. "Give me what you think is right. I'll take anything from two bits to a million dollars." Practically every time a member pays dues, Dutch hands him a Gala Naval Ball ticket. Dutch keeps a supply in his pockets and passes out hundreds every year; they take the place of receipts. On the back of them, Dutch always writes, with a flourish, "O.K. Pd. Member in Good Standing. C. Dutch (signed)." Only a few members attend the ball, and some do not believe that he actually gives it. Less than twenty-five showed up for the last one, which was held in the back room of an obscure Third Avenue saloon. Dutch's feelings were not hurt. "When my constituents show their respect for me by coming to my swaree, I am gratified," he once said, "only I don't mind admitting that the main thing I am innarested in is dues."

The Original Commodore Dutch Association has a profusion of officers and committeemen, all appointed by Dutch. Their names are printed each year on the showcards with which the ball is advertised. Some of these men dislike seeing their names in print, so their nicknames are used. On the most recent card, interspersed among such names as Herbert H. Lehman, Robert F. Wagner, and Alfred E. Smith, are nicknames like Big Yaffie, Little Yaffie, Gin Buck, Senator Gut, Eddie the Plague, Johnny Basketball, and Swiss Cheese. With the exception of Swiss Cheese, who is the retired operator of a private detective agency, all these nicknamed men are connected with horse racing. Swiss Cheese is called that for two reasons; he has a sallow, pock-marked face, and he is a passionate yodeler. He likes to get pie-eyed, then go to Salvation Army street meetings and make a nuisance of himself by yodeling hymns. At the Gala Naval Ball he is a star performer.

There are thirty-two officers of the association, and Dutch is constantly adding to the list. He holds the highest office, Founder and Standard Bearer. Just beneath him in importance is Head President. Sam H. Harris, the theatrical producer, was Head President from 1916 until his death in 1941. The office is vacant at present. "Out of respect for Mr. Sam, I'm going to wait a year or so before I appoint a successor to him," Dutch says. "He was the most ideal officer I ever had. I put the bite on him real often, and he never bellyached. A sawbuck was the least he ever slipped me. Sometimes he made it a double sawbuck." Joe Madden is Assistant Head President and Nick the Greek, the California gambler, is Second Assistant Head President. Other high offices are Admiral, Rear Admiral, Front Admiral, Captain, Auditor, Field Marshal, Judge Advocate, Floor Manager, Gangway Overseer, High Commissioner, Master of Ceremonies, and Master of Fox Hounds. The majority of the offices are held by gamblers. "I got a lot of respect for gamblers," Dutch says. "They throw money around, and I like to see people throw money around. I figure they might throw some my way."

There are four standing committees, all made up of men who have been especially generous to Dutch. The honorary members committee is the most impressive. Except for Sam Rosoff, the subway contractor; William V. Dwyer, the Tropical Park racetrack man; and Horace Stoneham, president of the Giants, it is composed of public offficials and Tammany district leaders. Former Governor Lehman, who automatically gets out his wallet whenever he catches sight of Dutch, is chairman. Dutch appoints officers and committeemen without consulting them. He was once asked if the Governor had authorized the use of his name on some showcards. "He never told me I couldn't," Dutch said. People in show business predominate on the arrangements committee. The reception committee is a hodgepodge of race-track and night-life characters; Abe Attell, the old pug, who now runs a Broadway saloon called Abe's Steak & Chop House & Bar & Grill, is chairman. The floor committee is made up entirely of prizefighters and James J. Braddock is chairman.

Dutch calls the prizefighters "my adjutants." "Years ago," he says, "anybody that came to my ball with a load on and misbehaved himself, I snapped my fingers and my adjutants rushed up from all directions and piled on top of him. Nowdays, to be an adjutant, it's just honorary."

Dutch enjoys explaining the duties of his officers and committeemen. It makes him giggle. "Except to pay dues, they don't have no duties," he says. "Anybody that slips me a buck off and on, I consider him a member in good standing of the Original Commodore Dutch Association. That entitles him to come to my ball, but it don't get him no privileges. It just makes him an ipso-facto member. If he wants to rise higher, he's got to stake me. If he stakes me, I elect him to a committee. If he stakes me good, I make him a chairman. If he stakes me real good, I elect him to be an officer and confer him with a title. An officer has privileges. He can make a speech at the ball, or sing a song, which nobody can shut him up. Also, he can take part in the grand march, providing enough people show up to have a grand march; such a thing hasn't happened in years. Any officer that gets behind in his dues, I weed him out. Take Joe Madden. I made him a high officer because he slips me a sawbuck every time I hit him for dues. Well, if he was to make a practice of slipping me a deuce instead, God forbid, I would naturally figure on getting me a brand-new Assistant Head President."

Dutch is sixty-two, but he often says that he feels much older. "I feel like I am a hundred and sixty-two," he says. He is small and wizened and hungry-looking. His cheeks are sunken, and he has big ears, a jutting nose, and distrustful pale-blue eyes. He has only one tooth, an upper incisor, and when he smiles his face takes on a distinctly hobgoblin aspect. He has such an extraordinary face that he himself is sometimes taken aback by it. One night in Attell's, after he had stared at the bar mirror for a while, he suddenly clapped his hands over his eyes and groaned. "I scare meself," he said, when he had regained his composure. "I never see such an ugly fella. My ears are a coupla sizes too big for my head, and they ain't even with each other, and I'm the hatchetest damned faced human being God ever made. I wonder why He took the trouble." However, despite Dutch's unusual countenance, he usually looks quite dapper. He keeps himself as neat as possible. He often shaves twice a day, and he gets a manicure whenever he can afford it. Several times a week he ducks into a dry-cleaner's and sits in a booth while his suit is being sponged and pressed. He brags that he was a dandy in his youth. "When I was twenty-five, I had a wardrobe consisting of twenty-five suits," he says, "and most of them hadn't ever been turned." Now, for winter wear, he owns two black suits and a double-breasted imitation camel's-hair overcoat with a belt in the back. In summer he customarily wears a black jacket, a baby-blue rayon polo shirt, seersucker pants, and a stiff straw hat. He keeps a big artificial rose in his lapel; when one gets grimy, he drops into Woolworth's and buys another.

Dutch makes a show of being blithe. Actually, he worries a lot, particularly about his health, which is good. He broods about pneumonia, and wears rubbers almost every day in winter, even though they make his feet ache. He has a germ phobia; in most of the restaurants he goes to, before he will eat anything he shakes out his napkin and painstakingly polishes his knife, fork, and spoon. On the street, he walks close to buildings, keeping as far away from automobiles as possible; he claims that one good whiff of exhaust will give him a headache. "In all the world," he says, "there's nothing I hate as much as a god-damn automobile." His eyesight is poor, but he is too vain to get spectacles. Every night he spends several hours studying the *Daily Mirror*'s horse-racing charts, which are printed in small type, and he uses a magnifying glass he bought in Woolworth's. He holds the newspaper and the glass close to his face, and while he reads his lips work. This always amuses onlookers. "My God, Dutch," Attell once told him, "you look like you're trying to chew the *Daily Mirror*." When not in use, his magnifying glass dangles by its handle from a black ribbon which he wears around his neck. He is disturbed about his hair, which is growing thin. He carries a military brush in a coat pocket and gets it out when he has time on his hands, no matter where he happens to be, and gives his hair exactly one hundred strokes, counting each stroke out loud. Sometimes, standing at a bar or sitting in a restaurant, he will suddenly start brushing and counting, startling the people around him.

Although Dutch spends at least half of his waking hours in saloons, he is a teetotaler. "In my youth," he says, "I was the scourge of the gin mills, and bartenders shuddered when they seen me coming, but I reformed." He has forgotten the year he went on the wagon, but remembers, for some reason, that William Howard Taft was President at the time. When a comparative stranger offers to buy him a drink, he looks uneasy and says, "I got a bum heart. One drink and I would most likely drop dead." He gives a different explanation to his intimates. "If I was to get a skinful," he says, "I would start right in and insult everybody I know. I would make enemies, and enemies don't pay dues. Also, I look at it from a health standpoint. What happened to all the tanks I palled with years ago? We mourn our loss. Gone but not forgotten. When I think of all the dead-and-gone crap-shooters that if they had took it easy on the schnapps they would be here today, I'm glad I swore off." Dutch prefers caffeine to alcohol. He drinks from fifteen to twenty cups of black coffee a day. He frequently gets so fidgety that he begins to stutter, or has a sudden attack of the trembles, or upsets a glass of water by just reaching for it. Although he takes coffee black, he always demands cream on the side. After finishing the coffee, he drinks the cream in one gulp, although he does not like it. "I pay for it, don't I?" he says. He carries a bag of Bull Durham smoking tobacco in his breast pocket and rolls his own cigarettes. He is as expert as any cowboy. "Made butts are too dear," he says. "Also, I think they put chemicals in them. I be damned if I think they're sanitary."

Dutch has lived in furnished rooms practically all his life. At present he has a room in a house on Thirteenth Street, just west of Third. He uses it only as a place to sleep. He customarily gets to bed around 5 A.M. and sleeps until noon. He goes to the races every day a local track is open; he always turns up at the railway station early, and most days he is able to find a member who will buy him tickets for the train and the track. After the races, on the way in, he goes down the aisle of the train looking for any members who might be aboard, soliciting dues from those who have been lucky and listening sympathetically to those who haven't. Dutch himself is an extremely timid horseplayer. He makes only one small, sure-thing bet a day, but he always has a doleful answer when someone asks, "How'd *you* do, Dutch?" "Picked wrong every race," he usually answers. "Even lost my coffee money. Don't know how I'm going to eat tonight, and already my belly thinks my throat's cut. Could you slip me some dues?" Three or four nights a week, he makes a round of saloons, restaurants, cigar stores, bowling alleys, barbershops, and hotel lobbies around Broadway in which sporting people foregather. Other nights, he goes to gambling places. He has been a hanger-on in gambling circles since adolescence and keeps on good terms with every operator of any consequence in town. Gambling-house lookouts and doorkeepers pass him in without question, although he rarely risks a dollar; he just stands around and gazes wistfully at the cash on the tables. When one of his members wins a fistful, Dutch's eyes light up; he knows he can be certain of at least a couple of bucks of it. Now and then he spends an evening away from Broadway. He considers himself a staunch Tammany Democrat, and a number of downtown Tammany district leaders are members of his association. He occasionally drops into their clubhouses, and he shows up for many of their beefsteak parties and moonlight sails; he finds out about such affairs by reading a political-gossip column in the Sunday *Enquirer.* He does not eat anything at beefsteak parties; he shakes hands with the dignitaries and watches for a chance to collect some dues. He always goes to the weighing-in ceremonies before important prizefights, and most fight nights he hangs around the outer lobby of Madison Square Garden. A couple of times a month he puts in an appearance at Jimmy Kelly's night club in Greenwich Village; he and Kelly have been friends since they were in their teens. He makes a practice of attending the funerals of prominent politicians. On these occasions he usually manages to pick up a few dollars. "Some of my big-shot members like Al Smith and Governor Lehman, the best time to put the bite on them is to bunk into them at a funeral," he says.

Dutch's demeanor fluctuates between servility and arrogance. In the company of some of his members, he is meek. "I hate to bother you, pal, but I'm flat," he will say, "and I wonder could you see your way clear to pay some dues. I wouldn't ask it, only I know I can count on you." Toward others he behaves with the wary impudence of an English sparrow among city pigeons. "Either you get yourself in good standing," he will say, "or I'll excommunicate you the hell and gone right out of my association. I don't allow no deadheads, and you know it." The majority of his members probably could not explain exactly why they give him money. Some have known him since they were young men together and are genuinely fond of him. Joe Madden, the Assistant Head President, is one of these. "I'm acquainted with Dutch almost thirty years," he once said, "and if he was to croak, I'd miss him. Whatever money he gets out of me, I figure it well spent. He hands me a lot of laughs. I like to listen to him. He keeps his ears open, and he always knows who beat the dice tables last night, and what millionaire from Hollywood lost five thousand bucks and got sick to his stomach, and who's in hock to who, and what places got thrown in the street by the cops and why. He knows everything. Say a crap game has to float from one little fleabag hotel to another; if you want the new address, Dutch can tell you. A lot of so-called underworld fellows from out of town, as soon as they hit Broadway they look Dutch up, just to hear what's new. Fellows like Boo Boo Hoff, the big Philadelphia gangster that croaked a few months ago. Use to, every time Boo Boo came to town, he and Dutch would get together and cut up touches. In his time, he gave Dutch plenty of dues."

No matter how much his members may like Dutch, practically all of them look upon him as a clown. He does not mind this; he feels that it gives him an advantage over them. "I act like a screwball," he says, "but I know what I'm doing." On his nightly rounds he encourages people to ridicule him, and in places like Lindy's, Madden's, Attell's, the 18 Club, the Paddock Bar & Grill, and the Dublin Café, he is treated as an official butt. He cannot be insulted. In situations that would be painful to the average man, he always behaves with a sort of deadpan, Chaplin-like jauntiness. A stock joke is often played on him. Someone invites him to sit down and have a free meal. He promptly accepts, and then his benefactor refuses to let him order anything but a steak. Dutch's one tooth is useless and he is forced to subsist almost entirely on soups. When a free steak is placed before him, people crowd around and watch his struggle with it. "Don't give up, Dutch, old boy!" they yell. "Keep fighting!" Dutch puts on a show; trying his best to chew the steak, he grunts, groans, looks cross-eyed, and tosses his head about like a turkey gobbler. "I can't really chew it," he says, "but I certainly can gum it."

At least once a night, wherever he may happen to be, Dutch is asked to sing. "Give us a song, Dutch," someone will say, "and I'll slip you some dues." Dutch is convinced that he has a fine baritone, and between not singing and singing and being laughed at, he greatly prefers the latter. He usually sings "My Pearl Was a Bowery Girl," "The Bowery, the Bowery! I'll Never Go There Any More," or "Down in a Coal Mine," all of which were popular in his youth. Sometimes, however, if he has an especially appreciative audience, he will put his right foot forward, clasp his hands behind his back, gaze soulfully into the distance, and sing "The Last Rose of Summer." Almost invariably, while he is singing, someone creeps up from behind and gives him a hotfoot. He has undoubtedly been a hotfoot victim oftener than any other human being. He never appears to mind. "A fella that pays his dues, I don't hold it against him if he gives me a hotfoot," Dutch says. "Maybe he figures he ought to get *something* for his money."

References to Dutch frequently appear in sports and Broadway columns, especially in Damon Runyon's and Dan Parker's. Such references are seldom complimentary, but Dutch always considers them so. Recently, commenting on the attitude of civilians toward soldiers in some parts of the country, Runyon wrote, "It is said that in certain of these spots the appearance of a guy in uniform in the vicinity of a local festivity would produce about the same coolness that might be created if Commodore Dutch showed up at Mrs. Vanderbilt's party." Dutch carried a clipping of this column around until it wore out. "Did you see the swell write-up my pal Runyon gave me?" he would ask, pulling it out. When Dutch is introduced to someone, he usually makes fun of his own face. He shakes hands and says, "Pleased to meet you, pal." Then, opening his mouth as wide as possible and exhibiting his solitary tooth, he giggles and says, "Look, pal! I'm an Elk." He seems most pleased with himself when people are making jokes at his expense and laughing at him. It makes no perceptible difference to him whether their laughter is scornful or good-natured. "When a fella is laughing at me, I'm sizing him up," he once told an intimate. "I'm giving him the old psychology. To put the bite on a man, what I call collecting dues, you got to study him. You got to figure out the right moment to nail him. With some of my members, I wait until they are drunk and happy before I bring up the question of dues. With others, I wait until they pick right in a horse race or beat the tiger in a crap game. With others, I wait until they are sitting with some doll that they want to impress with their great generosity. But with each and every one of them, before I ask for dues, I wait until I got them snickering at me." Dutch has devoted considerable thought to his peculiar position in society. He is profoundly cynical and has come to the conclusion that people enjoy his company because he makes them feel superior. "The fellas on Broadway are so low themselves," he says, "it makes them feel good to have somebody around that they can look down on, and I guess I fill the bill."

Dutch says that he was born on Tompkins Square, a lower East Side neighborhood which was then known as Little Germany. He says that he has been called Dutch for as long as he can remember, but that he doesn't know whether his parents came from Germany or Holland. "I never took no interest in where they came from," he says. He makes a mystery of his childhood and will not tell his real name. He explains that his surname is a long one and hard to pronounce. "I'm the only person in the world that knows it," he says, "and I wouldn't tell it to nobody. I don't hardly remember it myself. I haven't used it since I quit school. When I was fifteen, I just wouldn't go to school no more and had to leave home, so I got a job helping on a Bowery dray wagon. The driver said to me, 'What's your name?' I told him the kids all called me Dutch, and that's what he called me. Since then I never once used my born name, not even to vote. When I die, I don't even want it on my tombstone. Some of my pals around Broadway don't realize Dutch is a nickname, and they figure I ought to have a nickname, so they call me The Tooth."

Dutch's first boss was a drayman who owned his own cart and picked up most of his jobs around the Bowery. In the morning he and Dutch hauled for a second-hand furniture store on Chatham Square and the rest of the day they were on call, working out of a stable on Great Jones Street. At that time, in 1894, the Bowery was just beginning to go to seed; it was declining as a theatrical street, but its saloons, dance halls, dime museums, gambling rooms, and brothels were still thriving. In that year, in fact, according to a police census, there were eighty-nine drinking establishments on the street, and it is only a mile long. On some of the side streets there were brothels in nearly every house; Dutch refers to them as "free-and-easies."

Dutch is excessively proud of this period of his life. "In that day and time," he says, "a good way to get yourself educated was to work on a dray. I hadn't been on a dray a year before I could point out the head madams, the head pickpockets, the head crapshooters, and all like that. Quite a few of the free-and-easies were outfitted by the furniture store we hauled for, and we were in and out of them all the time. Also, the girls were always on the move, and we handled their trunks. And we did trunk work for the classy Bowery hotels, places like the Occidental, the Worden House, and Honest John Howard's Kenmore Hotel. The Occidental was the classiest. We called it the Ox, and I got a thrill out of it even if I only went in to horse some luggage around. It's still standing, at the southwest corner of Broome and the Bowery, but it's just a ghost of bygone days. You can stay there now for three bucks a week. It gives me the awfullest feeling just to walk past it. In my time it had a beautiful barbershop and a beautiful barroom, and the ceiling of this barroom was one enormous painting of some dames giving theirselves a bath. The old Ox was a hangout for politicians, actors, gambling men, fighters, and the like of that, the sporting element. Some of the fighters that put up there to my personal knowledge were Terrible Terry McGovern that Sam Harris managed for years, the original Jack Dempsey that they called the Nonpareil, Charlie Mitchell that throwed himself away fighting in gin mills when he should of been saving his strength for the ring, Jake Kilrain, Joe Bernstein, Tom Sharkey, and Oscar Gardner that they called the Omaha Kid, only he came from Wheeling, West Virginia; names don't mean a damn thing. I knew them all, to speak to.

"Every single night, after I knocked off work, I would wash up and walk the Bowery. I wasn't a teetotaler then by no means, and I would hit four or five gin mills and listen to the personalities, what they call celebrities nowadays, only a personality was somebody, but a celebrity, who the hell is he? Like I would listen to old Silver Dollar Solomon. He was high up in a combination of white slavers, the Max Hochstim Association, that bossed over the free-and-easies, and he ran a saloon that had one thousand silver dollars stuck in the concrete floor. And drunks would bring cold chisels in and they would kneel down when they thought nobody was looking and try to pry themselves up some silver dollars, but they would just get throwed out. And I would listen to Steve Brodie that took a leap off Brooklyn Bridge, only he didn't, and a brewery set him up in a saloon because he got so much attention for himself they figured he would draw trade, and he would wear your ears out discussing Steve Brodie; that's all he knew. I never thought he was so much. All the write-ups about the Bowery I ever read, they made Brodie a hero. People that really knew him, like me, we considered him ninety-nine per cent jaw. But a personality I liked was George Washington Connors that they called Chuck. He had three girl friends and claimed all of them was his wife—one named The Truck, one named The Rummager, and one named Chinatown Nellie, only she was Irish. Chuck was a guide for slummers, and he had Nellie and an old Chinee fella lying in bunks in a fake opium den on Mott Street, and Nellie sometimes couldn't keep a straight face when Chuck brought some slummers in. She would bust out laughing, and the slummers would think it was the opium taking effect. Chuck was the squarest of all the personalities. Some nights there were more slummers around than one man could handle, and Chuck would let me guide a party. Him and I were pals. The first cigar I ever smoked, he give it to me. The first drink of champagne I ever had, it was out of a bottle he bought."

Dutch says that he quit the dray wagon in 1898, when he was nineteen, and began living by his wits. For a while he had a job steering sailors to a saloon at 295 Bowery called John McGurk's Suicide Hall, where in one year five back-room girls killed themselves by swallowing carbolic acid. He says he got the title of Commodore while working for McGurk's. "I wore a sailor cap and a pea jacket," he says, "and I knocked around South Street and gave out cards to the sailors describing the attractions at McGurk's. Sometimes I would collect a mob and take them up. One night I came in with about two dozen sailors and a fella says to McGurk, 'Who the hell,' he says, 'is that little squirt that brings all the sailor trade into here?' 'Why, that's my Commodore,' old McGurk says to him. 'That's Commodore Dutch, the Commodore of the Bowery Navy.' And that's how I got my title. I was proud of it. Back in those days all the personalities had a nickname or a title. If you was known by your real name you didn't have no standing."

Dutch's period of greatest affluence began in the spring of 1899, when Timothy D. Sullivan, the Tammany boss of the Bowery district, gave him a job. Big Tim was the most powerful and the most open-handed politician in the city. He was a member of a syndicate which controlled all the gambling houses in Manhattan, he owned saloons, race horses, and prizefighters, and he had a partnership in a chain of vaudeville and burlesque theatres. His clubrooms were at 207 Bowery, but he also kept a suite on the second floor of the Occidental, where he and other politicians played poker and he received reports from the managers of his various enterprises. One evening he summoned Dutch to the Occidental. "I had run errands for Big Tim and he knew I was O.K., and he asked me did I want a job of a confidential nature," Dutch says. "He was the silent partner in eight saloons and he was anxious to know what went on in them. He trusted his managers, still and all he didn't, and he wanted somebody neutral to circulate around in an unbeknownst way and watch conditions and listen to the talk that went on. That was right up my alley. I would wander in and out of Big Tim's various gin mills every night and enjoy myself to the full, and every afternoon I would go to the Ox and report to him what I seen and heard. Some days he wouldn't have time to hardly listen, other days he'd keep me talking two, three hours. He paid me irregular. One Saturday night it would be a hundred bucks and the next Saturday it would be a ten spot, all according to the humor he was in. Anyway, he seen to it I had plenty of coconuts."

Big Tim had a number of retainers and hangers-on whose duties were similarly vague and confidential. He rewarded some by permitting them to run balls, or "rackets," for which all the saloonkeepers and divekeepers in the Bowery district were obliged to buy so many tickets. Among them were Larry Mulligan, Big Tim's half-brother, who operated a profitable St. Patrick's Eve ball in Terrace Garden Hall, and Harry Oxford, a fixer, who ran one on Washington's Birthday Eve in Webster Hall. Chuck Connors, whose fanciful conversation amused Big Tim, was allowed to run an annual ball in Tammany Hall; it was sponsored by the Chuck Connors Association, of which Chuck was the sole member. Biff Ellison, a gunman who shepherded gangs of repeaters to the polls every Election Day, imitated Connors and formed a Biff Ellison Association, which ran three rackets a year.

On New Year's Eve of 1900, Dutch and a girl friend went on a champagne spree; he woke up owing two saloons a total of $285. He asked Big Tim for a loan. "He wouldn't give me no loan," Dutch says. "He told me that wasn't no way to do business. He says to me, 'Dutch, you have certainly behaved like a fool, but I tell you what I'll do. I'll give you a franchise to run a racket. Hire yourself a date in a hall and get some tickets printed, and I'll pass the word around.' So I told him it might look nicer to the public if I had an association behind me, like Chuck and Biff. It would look more businesslike. So he says, 'Go right ahead. If those hoodlums can be a one-man association, so the hell can you.' I had two thousand tickets printed, a buck a head, ladies free. Everybody on the Bowery knew I was professionally associated with Big Tim in some way or other—why ask too many questions?—so naturally I didn't have no trouble unloading my tickets."

Dutch's racket, the first Gala Naval Ball of the Commodore Dutch Association, was held on the night of April 30, 1901, in Everett Hall, on East Fourth Street, just off the Bowery. Big Tim, of course, was the guest of honor. With him, in a box, sat Photo Dave Altman, his bodyguard; Sarsaparilla Reilly, his valet; and Flatnose Dinny Sullivan, one of his brothers, who later became boss of Coney Island. The music was furnished by Professor Pretzel Wolf's East Side Society Orchestra. Dutch led the grand march with a red-haired Irish girl whose name he has forgotten. He wore an admiral's outfit he had purchased from a theatrical costumer; it consisted of a cocked hat, a pair of swords, and a uniform with gold-starred epaulets and a red, white, and blue belly sash. In the grand march was Connors, who had The Truck on one arm and Chinatown Nellie on the other. The Rummager was escorted by Eat-'Em-Up Jack McManus, a fighter who sometimes worked as night bouncer at McGurk's. Dutch says there were at least fifteen couples in the march, all personalities, but he has forgotten the names of the others.

"After we sashayed two times around the ballroom, bowing to the right and then to the left," he says, "I blowed on a police whistle and the fun began. I had got a cut rate on two dozen kegs of beer from a brewery that was indebted to Big Tim for a favor, and I had them resting in washtubs full of ice. The instant I let loose with my whistle, whoosh, most of the mob descended on the beer, and the way they helped theirselves it was a disgrace to the human race. I was nuts about waltzing—never got enough—and I waltzed around an hour or more, not paying much attention to anything but the music. Then I stopped to get my breath and I took a look around, and I never see so many drunks. The place was swarming with drunks. Each fella was singing at the top of his voice, or slugging somebody smaller than him, or trying to steal some other fella's girl. One fella was flat on his back and he had his mouth right under a spigot on a beer keg, and the spigot was wide open and the beer was pouring into him; it was coming out of his ears. And the girls were wrestling with the fellas and squealing. I took one look and I felt like fleeing out of there. 'Ladies and gentlemen,' I said, 'Jesus Christ!' I thought to myself, 'No good can come of this. People will die before morning, people by the dozens.' But to tell the truth, it was a most successful swaree. Nobody was killed and everybody got all the beer they could hold, and I cleared damned near fifteen hundred bucks. When I told Big Tim how much I drew, he took me off his steady payroll. He says to me, 'Let the racket be your meal ticket. Go ahead and run yourself one every year. All the joints in the district know I'm in back of you, and if any one of them refuses to take their quota of tickets, you just let me know."

For twelve years, with Big Tim's support, Dutch netted an average of $2,000 a year out of the Gala Naval Ball. He abandoned Everett Hall, which had become too small, and switched to the old Tammany Hall, on Fourteenth Street. Shortly after the 1912 ball, however, everything went to pieces. In the summer of that year Big Tim began to suffer from delusions of persecution and had to be placed in a sanitarium. In February, 1913, he was removed to a house in the Williamsbridge section of the Bronx and friends hired a staff of guards to watch him. Occasionally he would tire his guards out and escape, usually turning up hours later at the Occidental on the Bowery, where, according to Dutch, he would "just sit in the lobby and stare until they come and took him away." "I seen him one day," Dutch says, "and I went over to him and I said, 'Jesus Christ, Big Tim, old pal, ain't there something I could do for you?' He just sat and stared at me. It broke my heart." Big Tim's last escape took place on the evening of August 30, 1913. Next morning, around dawn, the body of a man who had been struck by a train was found beside the New York, New Haven & Hartford tracks just north of the Westchester freight yards. It was carried to the Bronx morgue, where it lay unidentified fourteen days. Just before it was to be removed to potter's field a policeman took a look at it and said, "It's Big Tim Sullivan, God rest his soul." Big Tim's funeral, held in old St. Patrick's Cathedral on Mott Street, was one of the largest in the city's history. "I marched in the procession," Dutch says, "and I cried every step of the way."

The decay of the Bowery as a night-life street set in after Big

Tim's funeral. The gamblers drifted up to Broadway and Dutch followed them. He found the going hard. Without political support, he was unable to sell tickets, and his 1914 ball was a flop. "With Big Tim in his grave, I was Mr. Nobody," he says. "Until then, I hadn't paid no attention to the Commodore Dutch Association; it was just a name. I seen I had to do something, so I figured to build up the association. I made honorary officers out of all the Bowery personalities that had moved uptown and for members I took in all the Broadway crowd I could get. And when you have members, naturally you collect dues. I began collecting dues in 1914 and I'm still at it. My ball don't amount to a damn any more, but without I run a ball, what would be the excuse for an association?"

After old Tammany Hall was torn down in 1928, Dutch began the practice of using the back rooms of lower Third Avenue saloons for his balls. For his most recent ball, which was a typical one, he used the Stuyvesant Grill, a neighborhood saloon on Third Avenue near Fifteenth Street. The Stuyvesant's back room has a tiny bandstand and a small dance floor, on either side of which are seven booths, the kind with trellises to which artificial grapevines are fixed. Dutch got it rent free, of course. On his showcards, he had advertised that "festivities will begin with a bang at 9 sharp." However, most guests had sense enough to go late. Dutch himself did not show up until eleven. By that time approximately fifty men and women were sitting at tables in the booths. About half were members of the association. The others were curiosity-seekers from uptown, or regular customers of the saloon who had left the bar to see what was happening in the back room and had stayed. No tickets were collected; Dutch doesn't bother any more. Drinks were brought in from the bar by a waitress; no free beer has been served at a Gala Naval Ball since 1912. Mr. and Mrs. Swiss Cheese sat at one table. Swiss Cheese, in a gay mood, was yodeling "Mexicali Rose" and his wife was urging him to shut up. At another table sat Assistant Head President Madden and eight friends, among whom were Ed and Pegeen Fitzgerald, the radio commentators, and Father A. R. Hyland, chaplain of Clinton Prison, at Dannemora. At still another table sat Fiddler Cronin, F. X. Fitzsimmons, Peanuts Pelletier, and the Iron Horse, all elderly and irritable pugs who have known Dutch since his Bowery days. Pelletier, the youngest, fought last in 1906. They always show up for Dutch's balls. Until they are drunk, they insult each other. After they are drunk, they call each other the greatest fighter that ever lived. "What you doing now, Peanuts?" Cronin asked at the last ball. Pelletier said that he had just got a job as a night watchman for a big steam laundry in the Bronx. "I bet you're one hell of a fine night watchman," Cronin said. "If some robbers was to come around, I bet you would pitch in and help them open the safe." "Listen here, Fiddler," Pelletier said, "you remember the night you fought Boxhead Tommy Hansen at the Pelican A.C.? As I remember it, you didn't last out the first round. If ever I saw a no-good, two-bit fighter, it was you." "Oh, go to hell," said Cronin.

With Dutch, when he came in, was a band he had hired, an outfit called the New York Ramblers, consisting of an elderly piano player, a banjo picker, and a girl violinist. The Ramblers, looking bored, went over to the bandstand, took their places, and promptly started playing "The Star-Spangled Banner." Everybody stood up. Dutch had a pasteboard suitbox under his arm, and after people began to sit down again he ducked into the men's room. When he reappeared, he was wearing his admiral's uniform. He lost his cocked hat and his pair of swords shortly after his first ball, but for forty years he has been lugging the moldy old uniform from one furnished room to the next; it is his most precious possession. Across the chest he had pinned four badges—"Private Detective," "Special Officer," "Sheriff," and "Sharpshooter," The guests clapped as Dutch walked jauntily across the dance floor to the bandstand. It had rained a little during the afternoon and he wore rubbers. He stepped up on the stand, held his clasped hands over his head for several moments like a prizefighter, and then took a bow. "Well, folks," he said, "we're all here for a good time, so let's all have a good time. The world-renowned New York Ramblers will play for you and I want everybody to step out and dance. That's all the speech I'm going to make. I thank you one and all."

Swiss Cheese stood up unsteadily and shouted, "Just a minute,

Dutch. Would it be all right if I entertained the crowd?" "Certainly, Cheese," said Dutch, "go ahead and yodel all you want to." "Yodel, hell," said Swiss Cheese, "I'm going to do a dance." He walked to the middle of the floor, squatted on his heels, and began a Cossack dance. After two kicks, he sat on the floor. He got to his feet, guffawing, and yelled, "Hey, Dutch, you know what I am? I'm a gentleman and a scholar." Dutch looked at him disapprovingly. "You're a very foolish man," he said. "You're going to get your blood pressure all shook up and tomorrow you'll feel awful. I wish you'd come up here and yodel." A few moments later, with Swiss Cheese yodeling happily, the Ramblers started on "My Wild Irish Rose." Several couples stepped out on the floor and began waltzing.

Dutch went over to Madden's table. "I got a party of slummers here that would like to meet you," Madden told him. Dutch was introduced. "Mr. Commodore Dutch," said one of Madden's friends, a young woman who didn't know any better, "I understand you were quite a well-known figure on the Bowery during the gay nineties." "Madam," said Dutch, giving his one-toothed grin, "I am the last of the Bowery Boys." He unbuttoned the stiff, gold-braided collar of his uniform, sat down, and put his elbows on the table. Then, interminably, while the New York Ramblers played waltzes, while Swiss Cheese yodeled, while the old pugs drank beer and insulted each other, and while one curiosity-seeker after another became disgusted with the proceedings and stalked out, Dutch talked about the Bowery in the days of Big Tim Sullivan. He talked steadily until 1 A.M. At that time the music stopped and the piano player came over and said that the New York Ramblers did not propose to play another note until they had been paid. Dutch looked gloomily at his Assistant Head President. "Joe, old pal," he said, "could you slip me a couple of sawbucks? I wouldn't ask it, only I know I can count on you."

(1941)

# The Cave Dwellers

*T*HE WINTER OF 1933 WAS A PAINFUL ONE. It seems like a hundred and thirty-three years ago, but I remember it distinctly. That winter, the fifth winter of the depression and the winter of repeal, I was a reporter on a newspaper whose editors believed that nothing brightened up a front page so much as a story about human suffering. "The man on the street is so gloomy nowadays," one of the editors used to say, "that a story about somebody else's bad luck cheers him up." In the three weeks preceding Christmas there was, of course, an abundance of such stories, and for one reason or another I was picked to handle most of them. One morning I spent a harried half-hour in the anteroom of a magistrate's court talking with a stony-faced woman who had stabbed her husband to death because he took a dollar and eighty cents she had saved for Christmas presents for their children and spent it in one of the new repeal gin mills. "I sure fixed his wagon," she said. Then she began to moan. That afternoon I was sent up to the big "Hoover Village" on the Hudson at Seventy-fourth Street to ask about the plans the people there were making for Christmas. The gaunt squatters stood and looked at me with a look I probably never will get over; if they had turned on me and pitched me into the river I wouldn't have blamed them. Next day I was sent out to stand on a busy corner with a Salvation Army woman whose job was to ring a bell and attract attention to a kettle in the hope that passers-by would drop money into it for the Army's Christmas Fund. "Just stand there three or four hours," I was told, "and see what happens; there ought to be a story in it." The bellringer was elderly and hollow-eyed and she had a head cold, which I caught.

Day in and day out, I was sent to breadlines, to relief bureaus, to evictions; each morning I called on cringing, abject humans who sat and stared as I goaded them with questions. My editors sincerely believed that such interviews would provoke people to contribute to the various Christmas funds, and they undoubtedly did, but that did not help me conquer the feeling that I had no right to knock on tenement doors and catechize men and women who were interesting only because they were miserable in some unusual way. Also, the attitude of the people I talked with was disheartening. They were without indignation. They were utterly spiritless. I am sure that few of them wanted their stories printed, but they answered my questions, questions I absolutely had to ask, because they were afraid something might happen to their relief if they didn't; all of them thought I was connected in some way with the relief administration. I began to feel that I was preying on the unfortunate. My faith in human dignity was almost gone when something happened that did a lot to restore it.

Early one bitter cold morning, only a few days before Christmas, a man telephoned the newspaper and said that the evening before, while walking his dog in Central Park, he had come upon a man and woman who said they had lived for almost a year in a cave in the park. This was one of the caves uncovered when the old lower reservoir was emptied and abandoned, an area since filled in for playgrounds. He said he had discovered the man and woman squatting in the cave beside a little fire, and had been afraid they would freeze to death during the night, so he had persuaded them to leave the Park and had put them up in a furnished room.

"I wish your newspaper would run a story about them," said the man on the telephone. "It might help them get jobs."

I went up to see the man and woman. They were living in one of a cluster of brownstone rooming houses on West Sixtieth Street, off Columbus Avenue, two blocks from the park. They were on the fourth floor. An inch and a half of snow had fallen during the night and there was a ridge of it on the window sill of their furnished room. The man said his name was James Hollinan and that he was an unemployed carpenter. He was small, wiry, and white-haired. He wore corduroy trousers and a greasy leather windbreaker. The woman was his wife. Her name was Elizabeth and she was an unemployed hotel maid. When I arrived, Mr. Hollinan was preparing to go out. He had his hat on and was getting into a tattered overcoat. I told him who I was.

"I'd like to ask a few questions," I said.

"Talk to my wife," he said. "She does all the talking."

He turned to his wife. "I'll go get some breakfast," he said.

"Get egg sandwiches and some coffee," she said, taking a few coins out of her purse and placing them, one by one, in his hand, "and we'll have seven cents left."

"O.K.," he said, and left.

I asked Mrs. Hollinan to tell me about their life in the cave. While she answered my questions she made the bed, and she appeared to get a lot of pleasure out of the task. I could understand it; it was the first bed she had made in a long time.

"Well, I tell you," she said, smacking a pillow against the iron bedstead, "we got dispossessed from a flat up in Washington Heights the middle of last December, a year ago. When we went to the relief bureau they tried to separate us. They wanted to send my husband one place and me another. So I said, 'We'll starve together.' That night we ended up in Central Park. We found the cave and hid in it. Late at night we built a fire. We been doing that almost every night for a year."

She smoothed out the counterpane until there wasn't a wrinkle in it and then rather reluctantly sat down on the bed. There was only one chair in the room.

"Of course," she continued, "some nights it got too cold and rainy. Then we'd go to a church uptown that's left open at night. We'd sleep in a pew, sitting up. Most mornings we'd part and look for work. He hardly ever found anything to do. It was worse for him. He's older than me. Couple of times a week I'd pick up a cleaning job and that would mean a few dollars, and we'd eat on that. We'd carry water to the cave and make stews."

"How did you sleep in the cave?" I asked.

"We'd take turns snoozing on a bed we made of a pile of cardboard boxes," she said. "We kept a fire going. A little fire, so the cops wouldn't run us off. The Park cops knew we were there, but so long as we didn't build up a big fire and attract attention they'd let us alone. Last summer the cave was better than a house. But lately, when it rained, we'd get rheumatism, and it was awful."

Mrs. Hollinan's dress was nearly worn out, but it was clean and neat. I wondered how she had kept so clean, living in a cave. I think she guessed what was on my mind, because she said, "We'd go to a public bath about twice a week, and I used to put my dresses and his shirts in an old lard stand in the cave and boil them." We talked for about fifteen minutes and then her husband returned. He had a cardboard container of coffee and two sandwiches in a paper bag. I knew they didn't want me around while they ate breakfast, so I said goodbye.

"I hope we get some relief this time," said Mrs. Hollinan as I went out the door, and I realized she thought I was a relief investigator. I didn't have the nerve to tell her she was mistaken.

I wasn't especially interested in Mr. and Mrs. Hollinan; compared with some of the people I had seen that winter, they were living off the fat of the land. In the story I wrote about them I mentioned the incident in which Mrs. Hollinan told her husband that when breakfast was paid for they would have seven cents left, and I gave the address of the rooming house in case someone wanted to offer Mr. Hollinan a job. I wrote the story hurriedly and it was printed on the front page of the first edition, which reached the newsstands around noon, and, unlike many stories in the first edition of an afternoon newspaper, it wasn't dropped from subsequent editions but was kept in, and on the front page, throughout the day.

Next day was my day off, but late that afternoon I dropped by the office to get my mail. My box was stuffed with letters and telegrams from people who had read the story about Mr. and Mrs. Hollinan, and attached to many of the letters were bills or checks to be turned over to them. In all, there was eighty-five dollars, and there were two telegrams, offering jobs.

I had promised my wife that I would meet her and help her with some Christmas shopping, and I telephoned her that I couldn't do so, that I had to go give eighty-five dollars to a man and woman who had spent a year in a cave. She wanted to go with me. I met her at Columbus Circle and we walked over to the rooming house. The streets were crowded with Christmas shoppers and store windows were full of holly and tinsel and red Christmas bells. The cheerful shoppers depressed me. "How can men and women be so happy," I thought, "when all over the city people are starving?"

The landlady of the rooming house met us at the door. She appeared to be in an angry mood. I told her I was the reporter who had come to see Mr. and Mrs. Hollinan the day before. She said people had been calling on them since early morning, bringing them money and food.

"They read that story you had in the paper last night," the landlady said. "They keep coming, but I haven't let anybody upstairs this afternoon. That was a lot of baloney you had in the paper. Why, those cave people are upstairs celebrating."

"I don't blame them," said my wife.

"Well, I do," said the landlady.

She wouldn't let my wife go upstairs with me.

"You'll have to wait down here, young lady," she said severely.

I went on upstairs, carrying the fistful of letters. I knocked on their door and someone shouted, "Come on in!" I opened the door. The room was in magnificent disorder. On the table were two big steamer baskets, cellophane-wrapped, with red ribbons tied to their handles. The steamer baskets looked odd in the shabby room. Also on the table were bottles of beer and gin and ginger ale and some half-eaten sandwiches. The floor was strewn with wrapping paper and boxes and cigar butts. Mrs. Hollinan was sitting on the bed with a tumbler in her hand. A cigar was sticking out of a corner of Mr. Hollinan's mouth and he was pouring himself a drink of gin. They were quite drunk, without a doubt. Mr. Hollinan looked at me, but he didn't seem to recognize me.

"Sit down and make yourself at home," he said, waving me to the bed. "Have a drink? Have a cigar?"

"It's that sneak from the newspaper," said Mrs. Hollinan. "Give him hell, Jim."

Mr. Hollinan stood up. He wasn't very steady on his feet.

"What did you mean," he said, "putting that writeup in the paper?"

"What was wrong with it?" I asked.

"You said in that writeup we only had seven cents left, you liar."

"Well, that's what your wife told me."

"I did not," said Mrs. Hollinan, indignantly. She got up and waved her tumbler, spilling gin and ginger ale all over the bed. "I told you we had *seventy* cents left," she said.

"That's right," said Mr. Hollinan. "What do you mean, putting lies about us in the paper?"

Mr. Hollinan took a square bottle of gin off the table. He got a good grip on it and started toward me, waving the bottle in the air.

"Wait a minute," I said, edging toward the door. "I brought you some money."

"I don't want your money," he said. "I got money."

"Well," I said, holding out the telegrams, "I think I have a job for you."

"I don't want your help," he said. "You put a lie about us in the paper."

"That's right, Jim," said Mrs. Hollinan, giggling. "Give him hell."

I closed the door and hurried to the stairs. Mr. Hollinan stumbled out of the room and stood at the head of the stairs, clutching for the railing with one hand. Just as I reached the landing on the second floor he threw the bottle of gin. It hit the wall above my head and broke into pieces. I was sprayed with gin and bits of wet glass. I ran on down the stairs, getting out of Mr. Hollinan's range. All the way down the stairs I could hear Mrs. Hollinan up in the room, yelling, "Give him hell, Jim!"

"Mother of God," said the landlady when I got downstairs, "what happened? What was that crash?"

"You smell like a distillery," said my wife.

I was laughing. "Mr. Hollinan threw a bottle of gin at me," I said.

"That's nothing to laugh about," said the landlady sharply. "Why don't you call an officer?"

"Let's get out of here," I said to my wife.

We went to a liquor store over on Columbus Circle. I bought a bottle of Holland gin and had it wrapped in Christmas-gift paper, and I gave the liquor-store man Mr. Hollinan's address and told him to deliver the order. My wife thought I was crazy, but I didn't mind. It was the first time I had laughed in weeks.

Early the following morning I went back to the rooming house. I had decided it was my duty to make another attempt to give the money to Mr. and Mrs. Hollinan.

"Those cave people are gone," the landlady told me. "A gentleman came here last night in a limousine, with a chauffeur. He took them away. I had a talk with him before he went upstairs, and I told him how they'd been cutting up, but he didn't care. He gave me a five-dollar bill. 'Here,' he said, 'take this for your trouble. If any mail comes for these good people, send it along to me, and I'll see they get it.' He put them in the back seat with him. He told me he was going to give Mr. Hollinan a job on his farm."

The landlady was quite angry. "They were still drunk," she said, "but that man in the limousine didn't seem to care. He was drunk, too. Drunker than they were, if you ask me. He kept slapping them on the back, first one and then the other. And when they got in the limousine they were laughing and falling all over theirselves, and that Mrs. Hollinan, that lowdown woman, she rolled down the window and thumbed her nose at me."

She had the benefactor's name and address written down and I made a note of them. It was a New Jersey address. I went back to the office and wrote letters to all the people who had sent money to Mr. and Mrs. Hollinan, returning it. I told them Mr. Hollinan had found a job and had declined their contributions.

Until perhaps a week before Christmas of the following year, I forgot about Mr. and Mrs. Hollinan. Then I recalled the experience and began to wonder about them. I wondered if the man in the limousine did give Mr. Hollinan a job and if he was getting along all right. I kept thinking about them all that week and on Christmas Eve I decided to try and get in touch with them and wish them a merry Christmas and a happy New Year. I searched through a stack of old notebooks in the bottom drawer of my desk and finally found their benefactor's name and address. I asked Information to get me his telephone number in New Jersey and I put in a call for him. He answered the telephone himself. I told him I was the reporter who wrote the story about the man and woman he had befriended last Christmas, the cave dwellers. I started to ask him if he would let Mr. Hollinan come to the telephone, but he interrupted me.

"Have you seen them lately?" he asked, irrelevantly. His voice was blurry.

"Why, no," I said. "Aren't they out there with you any longer?"

"I certainly would like to see them," he answered. "To tell you the God's truth, I was just thinking about them. I was sitting here by the fire having a few drinks and I was thinking how much I'd like to see them. I used to have a few drinks at night with old man Hollinan. He was good company, and so was the old lady. He was a funny old crock." He paused.

"What happened?" I asked.

"Well," he said, "I have a little farm out here and he took care of it for me when I was in the city. He was the caretaker, sort of. They stayed until about the end of March, and then one day the old boy and his wife just wandered off and I never saw them again."

"I wonder why they left."

"I don't know for sure," he said, "but you know what I think? I think living in that cave ruined them. It ruined them for living in a house. I think they left me because they just got tired of living in a house."

"Well," I said, "merry Christmas."

"Same to you," he said, and hung up.

(1938)

# King of the Gypsies

*T*HERE ARE AT LEAST one dozen gypsy kings in the city. All are elderly, quarrelsome, and self-appointed. One of them, Johnny Nikanov, a Russian, sometimes called King Cockeye Johnny by the detectives of the Pickpocket Squad, is a friend of mine. I became acquainted with him in the fall of 1936. I was covering the Criminal Courts Building for a newspaper and spent a part of every working day in the back office of Samuel Rothberg's bail-bond establishment, diagonally across Centre Street from the Courts, where lawyers, cops, probation clerks, and the loafers of the neighborhood assembled to play pinochle. Among Rothberg's clients were practically all of the gypsy pickpockets, wallet-switch swindlers, and fortune-tellers, and King Cockeye Johnny came in now and then to get a bail bond written for one of his subjects. After transacting his business, he would always swagger into the back office and take a hand in the game. When the pinochle players saw him coming they would pretend to be alarmed. They would slap their hands over the money on the table and shout warnings at each other, such as "Stick your dough in your shoes, boys! Here comes Cockeye Johnny!" or "Make way for the king, the king of the pickpockets!" Johnny was never offended by their remarks; it seemed to give him a great deal of satisfaction to be looked upon as a thief. Whenever the gypsy reputation for thievery came up in conversation, as it frequently did, he would expand. "To a gypsy feller," he said on several occasions, with pride in his voice, "there ain't but two kinds of merchandise. Lost and unlost. Anything that ain't nailed down is lost." He professed to believe, however, that gypsies are far more honorable than *gajos,* or non-gypsies. He leaned across the table toward Rothberg one afternoon and said, "Mr. Rothberg, you never heard of a gypsy feller stealing an oil well, did you?" "I can't say I did," said Rothberg. "Well," said Johnny triumphantly, "I heard of an American feller that did. Some years back a crowd of us was coming up from Florida in a couple of Ford trucks. The womenfolks had been telling fortunes at county fairs and business had been real bad. We was awful broke. So every night we'd hit some city and siphon gas out of cars that was parked on back streets. We'd steal enough gas to run us through the next day. Nothing was safe from us. I remember draining the tank on a hearse. There was a full moon one night in Washington, D.C., and a cop caught me in the act and throwed me in jail. And I got to talking to the man in the next cell and he said to me, 'There's been a lot of excitement in town over the Teapot Dome.' And I asked him what in hell was that, and he told me it was a big oil well that was stole by one of the President's right-hand men. I bet I laughed for ten minutes. You take a poor, starving gypsy feller, he'll steal a tankful of gas— there's no denying it. But you take a high-class American feller, he'll steal a whole damned oil well."

Johnny was by no means spick-and-span and was constantly scratching; this made those who sat near him at the table apprehensive. "Look here, Cockeye," a policeman said one afternoon, "you got the itch?" "No, sir, not at present," said Johnny. "I haven't had the itch in more than a month." He bummed cigarettes shamelessly, and his tongue was rarely still. Furthermore, he was the winner in almost every pinochle game he entered. However, despite all this, he was a popular figure in the back office, and he appeared to be rather proud of his popularity; at least, unlike Rothberg's other gypsy clients, he did not obviously despise *gajos.* Once he invited a few of the Criminal Courts loafers, including myself, to his home on Sheriff Street for a *patchiv,* or gypsy spree. We ate a barbecued pig, drank a punch composed of red wine, seltzer, and sliced Elberta peaches, watched the women dance, and had an exceedingly pleasant time. Since then I have often visited Johnny.

Whenever I am in the Sheriff Street neighborhood I call on him.

Johnny says that he has been a king of the gypsies off and on since he was a young man, but he has no idea how old he is. "Between forty-five and seventy-five, somewhere in there," he says with characteristic vagueness. "My hair's been white for years and years, and I got seventeen grandchildren, and I bet I'm an old, old man." Johnny is short, potbellied, and jaunty. His face is round and swarthy and sprinkled with smallpox scars. He has high cheekbones and a flattened nose. Because of a cast in his left eye, there is always an alert, skeptical expression on his face; he looks as if he does not believe a word he hears. He wears a wide-brimmed black hat and carries a copper-headed cane. Whenever he has to attend a wedding or a funeral he puts on boots, riding breeches, and a scarlet silk pajama top which buttons high around the neck and resembles a Russian blouse, but otherwise he dresses like any other American. He never owns more than one suit at a time. His current one is beetle green. Most nights he sleeps in it. As a rule Johnny is unobtrusively drunk by noon. He is a gin-drinker. He says that he never drinks less than five quarts a week. He mixes gin with Pepsi-Cola, half and half, and calls the mixture old popskull. Johnny is a highly skilled coppersmith, but he brags that he hasn't touched a tool since 1930. "I despise to work," he says. "It makes me bilious. If I had to take a steady job or be exterminated, I would beg to be exterminated."

A gypsy gets to be a king by calling himself one. There is not a king in the city who has the respect of more than fifty families, but all the kings make big, conflicting boasts about the extent of their jurisdiction. Until King Steve Kaslov was sent to a federal penitentiary in the summer of 1942 for swearing to draft boards that certain of his unmarried youths were married, he was perhaps the most powerful. Steve, whose headquarters were on Attorney Street, always claimed to be the *o boro,* or supreme ruler, of all the Russian gypsies in the United States. Actually, he was the spokesman for approximately fifty families on the lower East Side. King Frankie Mitchell, of Williamsburg, Brooklyn, who calls himself a Russian on some days and a Serbian on others, has been disputing Steve's claim to supremacy for many years. "*I* am the head of all the Russians in the United States," Frankie says. "I am also the head of all the Serbians in the same territory." Frankie is the head of about twenty families. King Tene Bimbo, of Spanish Harlem, a Serbian who has a record of a hundred and fourteen arrests, is hated by his people; detectives say that except for members of his own family there is hardly a gypsy who will go near him. He maintains, however, that he is the king of all the Russian, Serbian, and Rumanian gypsies in the United States, Canada, and Mexico.

Johnny is similarly boastful. When he is full of old popskull and talking to a *gajo,* he claims that he is the head king of all the Russian, Serbian, Rumanian, Syrian, Turkish, Bulgarian, German, and English gypsies in the whole of North America. When he is cold sober, however, and in a truthful mood he says that he is the king of exactly thirty-eight families of Russian gypsies—about two hundred and thirty men, women, and children, to all of whom he is related by blood or marriage. He refers to them as "my crowd." Officials of the Police and Welfare departments concede that Johnny has these families under his thumb, but they annoy him now and then by suggesting that he call himself spokesman rather than king. "To the Department of Welfare, I may not be no king," he recently told one of these officials, "and to the King of England, I may not be no king, but to those poor, persecuted gypsies that I run myself knock-kneed looking after their personal welfare, I am king."

Johnny does not know how many gypsies there are in the city, and neither does anyone else. Estimates range between seven and twelve thousand. Their forefathers came from every country in Europe, but the majority call themselves Russians, Serbians, or Rumanians. They are split into scores of vaguely hostile cliques, but they intermarry freely, speak practically the same dialect of Romany, the universal gypsy language, and are essentially alike. They are predominantly of the type that anthropologists call nomad gypsies; that is, unlike the Hungarian fiddler gypsies, for example, they never willingly become sedentary. They are contemptuous of the Hungarians, calling them house gypsies. In the past the nomads straggled from Maine to Mexico, spending only the winters in the city, but since the depression fewer and fewer have gone out on the road. Johnny has not been farther away than Atlantic City since 1934. At least two-thirds receive charity or relief of one sort or another. The gypsy kings are authorities on relief regulations; they know how to get their families on relief and keep them there. In the city, gypsies prefer to scatter out, but there are colonies of them on the lower East Side, on the Bowery, on the eastern fringe of Spanish Harlem, and on Varet Street in the Williamsburg neighborhood of Brooklyn. They rent the cheapest flats in the shabbiest tenements on the worst blocks. Three or four families often share one flat. They move on the spur of the moment; in the last two years one family has given seventeen addresses to the Department of Welfare. In the summer, like all slum people, they bring chairs to the sidewalks in front of their houses and sit in the sun. They nurse their babies in public. They have nothing at all to do with *gajo* neighbors. Even the kids are aloof; they play stick- and stoopball, but only with each other. The children are dirty, flea-ridden, intelligent, and beautiful; one rarely sees a homely gypsy child. They are not particularly healthy, but they have the splendid gutter hardihood of English sparrows. Practically all the adults are illiterate and only a few of the children have spent much time in public school. Johnny says he has never heard of a gypsy who went through high school. Both parents and children are opposed to education and they fight hysterically with truant officers. Not long ago one truant officer said that the very word "gypsy" made him shudder. All are able to speak slum English as well as Romany. Among themselves they use Romany exclusively. Some of the older ones are multilingual. Johnny can carry on conversations, volubly, in Russian, Rumanian, Romany, and English. They believe in child marriage; most gypsy brides and grooms are in their early teens. Brides have a price. Johnny sold his daughter, Rosie, to a Chicago gypsy in 1934 for $875. Each person has two first names, a travelling or *gajo* name, and a home or gypsy name. Johnny's home name is Lazillia. Wives use their husbands' first names; Dovie, say, becomes Dovie Steve, Annie becomes Annie Mike.

The older men are able coppersmiths and horse-traders, but their skills are anachronous. Some occasionally make a little money repairing copper stockpots for restaurants and hotels. Almost all of the younger men are good automobile mechanics. They repair their own ramshackle automobiles with odds and ends picked up in junk yards, but they are too temperamental to hold down garage jobs. A few are itinerant saloon musicians; they go from joint to joint on the lower East Side, taking up a collection after entertaining for a half-hour or so. The men pick guitars and the women learn to sing popular songs they have heard on the radio. "Amapola" is one of their favorites. The children, particularly the girls, are gifted beggars. Wearing the castoff clothes of their parents, grimy, and hungry-eyed, a pair of them will dart into a saloon, tap-dance and sing furiously for a few minutes, and then go from drunk to drunk with appealing looks and outstretched palms. When they get home, long after dark, their pockets are crammed with pretzels, potato chips, and small change.

The women are the real breadwinners. All of them are *dukkerers,* or fortune-tellers. They foretell the future by the interpretation of dreams and by the location of moles on the body, lines in the palm, and bumps on the head. This occupation is illegal in the city and they operate furtively. Each woman keeps on hand a stock of a paper-bound book called "Old Gipsy Nan's Fortune Teller and Dream Book." They buy this in bulk from Wehman Brothers, a wholesaler of cheap dream, astrology, sex-education, and joke books, at 712 Broadway, and give one to each client. Then, in case they are arrested, they are able to swear to the magistrate that they did not take money for telling a fortune, that instead they merely sold a book and taught the buyer how to use it. Practically all the *dukkerers* are thieves of one sort or another, and they give the Pickpocket Squad a lot of trouble. One member of the squad, Detective John J. Sheehan, has worked exclusively on gypsy crime for the last nine years. He has learned some Romany and has developed an admiration for gypsies. They call him Mr. Sheeny, and are quite frank with him. They invite him to weddings and he has often been asked to stand as godfather. He says that most victims of gypsy swindles are ignorant, worried, middle-aged women.

"There are thousands upon thousands of old sisters in the city so thick that any gypsy woman can con them out of their lifetime savings without half trying," Detective Sheehan says. "Women that want to know if their husbands are cheating on them, women that think they're about to die with some strange disease, superstitious old German chambermaids—the like of that. If I didn't see it every day, I wouldn't believe it." The detective says that a woman who acts and talks sensibly gets her fortune told when she visits a gypsy, and that's the end of it. "But," he says, "when one of those thick babies comes along, the *dukkerer* gets down to work. Most of them use a swindle that's old as the hills. We call it the gypsy-switch or the wallet-switch and they call it the *hokkano baro*, the big trick. First of all the gypsy convinces the victim there's something wrong with her insides; usually they say it's cancer. This may take several visits. Pretty soon the victim is so upset she'll do just about anything; when gypsies set their minds to it, they can be more scary than the stuff you'll see in the movies—Boris Karloff, the like of that. Then the gypsy says that money's what's wrong, that the money the victim has been saving for years is unclean, unholy, got the black mark on it. So the victim trots to the bank and withdraws her savings, every red cent, and gives it to the gypsy to be cleaned, or blessed. The gypsy rolls up the bills, sews them inside a little cloth bag, lights some dime-store candles, and blesses the bag with a lot of hocus-pocus. All the time the gypsy has another bag up her sleeve and this has a roll of blank paper in it. After a while she switches bags, and she sews the phony bag securely to the inside of the victim's dress over her heart, and she tells her to wear it that way seven days before opening it. At night she's supposed to put the dress with the bag on it under her pillow. That will make her well. And soon as the victim is out of sight the gypsy family packs up and moves. And a week later the victim runs howling to the police. When I arrest the gypsy, nine times out of ten the victim won't go to court to testify. Too scared. Not long ago I had a woman who had been conned out of eighteen hundred bucks, the head of a big beauty parlor, and she wouldn't go to court, not by any means. She kept saying, 'The old gypsy lady will put a curse on me and I'll die in my sleep.'"

Detective Sheehan says that now and then a man gets stung. "A gypsy girl stands in a tenement window and beckons to some man passing in the street," he says, "and the foolish fellow trots right in. He thinks he's going to have some kind of sexy adventure. The gypsy girl turns on the radio and dances around with him a few minutes, just to get his mind occupied, and while they're dancing she picks his pocket. He's so excited he doesn't know what's taking place. And then she sends him on his way. That's all that ever happens, just a dance. If he comes back looking for his money, one of the men gypsies appears and chases him off. Some of the girls are fair pickpockets, nothing to brag about. It seems to take a real one hundred per cent white man to be a good pickpocket. And all that stuff about loose, passionate gypsy girls that they have in stories is a myth. I've been hanging around gypsies nine long years and I've yet to see a real gypsy tramp. As a class, they're the straightest women in the city so far as sex is concerned. Good wives, good mothers. So far as general crookedness is concerned, they'd barbecue their grandmother for fifty cents. I guess they can't help it. I guess it's their nature."

Johnny's thirty-eight families live on Suffolk, Ridge, Pitt, Sheriff, Columbia, and Cannon streets, on the lower East Side. They usually haughtily refer to themselves as Russians, but all are American citizens, less than a dozen speak Russian, and only three families—the Nikanovs, the Sigilovs, and the Petrovs—still have Russian names. The others have long since translated their Russian names into English equivalents; among them are Smiths, Costellos, Thompsons, Mitchells, Johnsons, Stanleys, and Stevensons. Stefanovitch, for example, became Stevenson. Johnny says that his gypsies are the poorest in the United States. "If you was to turn them all upside down and give them a good shaking," he says, "you couldn't buy a quart of gin with what fell out." They are almost morbidly suspicious of American officialdom, and they send for Johnny whenever they have trouble with policemen, truant officers, relief investigators, health inspectors, clinic doctors, and landlords; he interprets and advises. They have great faith in Johnny's ability to deal shrewdly with gajos. Johnny is a passionate speechmaker, and he always presides at weddings, wakes, and parties. "I am the master of ceremony at everything," he says. "That's mainly what a gypsy king is for. It's a job, I tell you, because gypsies are serious about parties. You take the average gypsy, the main thing he wants out of life is a big, drunk party in his honor. Most of our parties don't amount to much. They are just *diwanos,* what we call tongue meetings. That is, we sit around and talk. I lead the talk. A *diwano* is an empty-belly affair. Other kinds are better, such as *pomanas,* where we eat and get drunk in honor of somebody that died, and *slavas,* where we eat and get drunk because somebody had a birthday, and *patchivs,* where we eat and get drunk because there don't seem to be anything better to do. Sometimes we hire a hall on Suffolk Street for big parties, but most any home will do. I guess that's one reason land-lords hate the sight of us. If you want to hear some noise, you get a crowd of gypsies full of wine, you'll hear some noise."

Whenever there is a death in his crowd, Johnny goes from home to home and takes up a collection. He hires the undertaker and makes arrangements for the funeral with Father Alexander Chechila of the Church of St. Peter and St. Paul, a small, poor Russian Orthodox Catholic church on Seventh Street, between First Avenue and Avenue A. It is the mother church of all the Russian gypsies in the East and is used by those of other nationalities; in 1941 Father Alexander preached thirty gypsy funerals. "Mr. Chechila is the only preacher I ever saw that gypsies don't make him nervous," Johnny says. "You take the average church, the preacher gets beside hisself when a gypsy comes in. He's afraid the gypsy might steal the bell right out of the steeple. The most of them they won't touch a gypsy funeral. But Mr. Chechila pitches right in. He speaks the words at the church and then he climbs into one of our dirty old cars and goes along to Jersey and speaks the words at the grave. All the New York gypsies bury in a graveyard in Linden, New Jersey. It's cheap. We used to bury in Paterson, but Paterson got too dear. At a gypsy funeral everybody gets full of wine and throws their head back and wails. Sometimes it seems to get on Mr. Chechila's nerves. I guess we treat him real mean. We never go to church except for Easter and for funerals. We just ain't godly people. Here a while back he told me to make my people go to church, and I said to him, 'Mr. Chechila, please excuse me, I don't mean no disrespect, but the only kind of gypsy that needs a preacher is a corpse gypsy.' "

Johnny's gypsies bicker a lot and he often has to act as peacemaker. If a dispute is serious, he holds a Romany *kris,* or gypsy trial, in his home; each disputant and each witness is permitted to speak as fully as he wishes so long as he doesn't bore Johnny, who presides as judge. Wine is drunk at these trials and they invariably end in an oratorical carousal. "Down at the bottom of every gypsy trial is womenfolks or five dollars," Johnny says. "I never yet heard a gypsy claim another one owed him three dollars or eighteen dollars. It's always five. They five-dollar me to death." When any of Johnny's people, whether a man, woman or child, does not show up for supper, it is taken for granted that he or she is in the hands of the police. In such cases Johnny puts on his black hat, picks up his copper-headed cane, and goes over to the Police Headquarters annex for a talk with Detective Sheehan. If the missing gypsy is under arrest, Johnny finds out the nature of the charge and the name of the jail; then he trudges wearily to get a lawyer. Johnny is abler at handling such matters than any of his rivals because he can read and write; he claims that he is the only gypsy king in the United States who can read well enough to dial a number on the telephone. He says he picked up his learning, out of boredom, from a cellmate in a Michigan jail where, sometime in his youth, he spent two and a half years for stealing a horse; he has never been inside a school-room. "I can read just enough to make out the carnival news in the *Billboard* magazine, and I can handwrite just enough to fill out a money order, but that's a whole lot better than the average gypsy can do," he says. "My grandmamma had a saying that fits me to a T. 'In the country of the blind,' she used to say, 'the man that can see out of one eye is king.' "

Johnny seldom gets any money from his subjects. The position of gypsy king pays off not in money but in prestige. He is supported by his wife, Mrs. Looba Johnny Nikanov, who is one of the best *dukkerers* in the city. Looba is tall, gaunt, sad-eyed, and austere; in profile she looks exactly like the old Indian on Indian-head nickels.

She goes to sleep at sundown and seldom gets up before 10 A.M., but she is constantly yawning, stretching, and grunting. Looba smokes a pipe. She is extremely irritable. Johnny says that she rarely refers to him by name; instead, using Romany, she calls him a ratbite, a sick toad, a blue-bellied eel, a black-yolked egg, a goat, a bat, a policeman, a *gajo,* and various other loathsome things. He doesn't mind. "A gypsy woman that don't scream half the time, something is wrong with her," he says. "Screaming is their hobby." Johnny and Looba live in a red-brick tenement on Sheriff Street, between Rivington and Delancey, paying $14 a month for two small rooms and a kitchen. They have the parlor front. Like all gypsies of their generation, they sleep on the floor between two thick, goosefeather-stuffed quilts, called *perrinas.* Many younger, city-born gypsies have taken to beds, but the old ones, who spent their youths in tents, prefer the floor. "I don't feel natural in a bed," Johnny says. "I feel like a fool." During the day the *perrinas* are rolled up and stacked in a corner and Johnny uses the bedroom for his headquarters. It is a sparsely furnished room. In it are an old wooden trunk, a wicker settee with a sprung bottom, and a table, on which there is a copper candlestick and a radio. The candlestick is usually surrounded by a mound of tallow drippings. The flat is wired for electricity, of course, and Johnny owns one bulb. He rarely screws it in, however. He feels that a candle throws sufficient illumination, even for a *kris* or a *patchiv.* There are no chairs. Tacked over the door is an ikon. The walls are covered with blankets and tent carpets and with a large canvas phrenological chart—a crude drawing of a human head divided into sections—that Looba once used in fortune-telling tents. Attached to the borders of the chart are a number of photographs of race horses torn out of newspapers. A dirty blanket hangs over the door. Gypsies try to make their flats look as much like the inside of a tent as possible.

Most afternoons Johnny's room is crowded with his subjects, who squat along the walls, sitting on their heels. Johnny reclines, barefooted and serene, on the wicker settee. Lying there, half asleep, he gossips, listens to the radio, and drinks popskull or tea. He drinks a lot of tea, taking it Russian fashion, in a tumbler. Looba has the exclusive use of the parlor; she calls it her *ofisa*, or office. It looks out on Sheriff Street and she sits at the window with a lapful of sewing and beckons to passers-by who look dopey enough to her to be interested in a fortune-telling. She has a rather high opinion of human intelligence; she beckons to about two passers-by in ten. Most *dukkerers* speak of themselves as Egyptians, doubtless feeling that this identifies them with mystery. The custom had its origin in the belief, once generally held, that gypsies sprang from Egypt; anthropologists now are pretty certain that they came from northern India, leaving it for good about a thousand years ago. Looba is known professionally as Madame Johnson and she has printed cards which read, "MADAME JOHNSON. REAL EGYPTIAN FROM EGYPT. YOUR HEAD IS LIKE AN OPEN BOOK TO ME. IF YOU HAVE TROUBLES OF A LOVE OR MONEY NATURE GIVE ME A TRY." She has been arrested nine times in the last five years for wallet-switching.

Like most gypsy women, Looba is skillful with the needle. She sews all her own clothes, using extravagantly colored curtain and drapery material, some of which she shoplifts from the mill-remnants stores on First Avenue. Her costume, winter and summer, consists of a silk kerchief, a loose, low-cut blouse, and four or five skirts, the newest on the outside. The kerchief, called a *diklo*, signifies that she is married; no gypsy virgin would ever put one on. She also wears eight rings, a pair of earrings, ten copper bracelets shaped like snakes and lizards, which Johnny hammered for her years ago, and a necklace of old coins from half a dozen European countries. Clients are often inquisitive about the coin necklace, and she usually tells them that it is worth $11,300 but that she will sell it for $23 with a fortune-telling thrown in. She has never had an offer. Looba wears high-heeled shoes on the street but goes barefooted indoors. She does not spend much time in the kitchen. There is always a pot of stew on the stove and she and Johnny eat whenever they feel hungry. They may eat five meals a day, or one.

It is customary for gypsy parents to let their married children live in the same flat with them, but Johnny and Looba do not. "I may be peculiar," Johnny says, "but I like to have room enough to turn around in." They have four sons and a daughter, all married.

The sons, with their families, twenty-two persons in all, live on one floor of a ratty tenement on Cannon Street, two blocks from Johnny's house. All of them have been on and off relief since early in the depression. In 1941 each of the sons was forced by relief officials to take a job on a WPA pick-and-shovel project, and each fainted shortly after showing up for work. "Gypsy men ain't built like ordinary men," Johnny says solemnly. "They ain't fitted for shovel work. They're high-strung and they rupture easy. The relief people just can't somehow seem to understand that. It ain't that they don't want to do shovel work. Why, they would be glad to, but they got to think about their health." Igor, the oldest son, was once assigned to a downtown curb-repairing project. According to Johnny, who snickers when he tells about it, Igor began to moan as soon as he was handed a shovel; after working for about ten minutes, he mumbled, "I just can't stand it," and fainted so overwhelmingly that he frightened the foreman, who had him taken to Gouverneur Hospital in a taxicab. The daughter, Mrs. Rosie Luke Stankovitch, is, like Looba, a real Egyptian from Egypt. She is known professionally as Madame Stanley. In the winter she has an *ofisa* on Halsted Street in Chicago. In the summer she operates a mitt joint, or fortune-telling tent, for the J. B. Jericho Kentucky Wonder Exposition, a small Southern carnival. When she was a kid Johnny made her go to P. S. 4, at Rivington and Pitt, and she is fairly literate. Johnny is proud of her. He gets a postcard from her about once a month and he carries it around in his wallet and shows it to *gajo* friends. "Rosie is probably the smartest gypsy girl in the entire U.S.," he says. A recent card from Rosie was mailed in Valdosta, Georgia. It said:

DEAR PA:
   This place sure stinks. We are eating and that is about the size of it. People too smart know it all don't trust gypsies. Sure wish I could send you a M.O. but will not be able to do so at this time. Hope the Japs doesn't drop some bums on my tent. If I half to die I sure hope it don't half to be in Valdosta, Ga. Take care yourself. Kiss ma.                                    ROSIE

A good deal of Johnny's jauntiness deserted him after we entered the war. The last time I visited him he was deeply dejected. When I pushed aside the door blanket and stepped into his room he was alone, sitting on the edge of the settee with his elbows on his knees and his head in his hands. He lifted his head an inch or so and glanced at me, and there was an utter lack of interest in his eyes. "Hello," he said halfheartedly. He was barefoot, his eyes were bloodshot, and he needed a shave. I tore the wrapping paper off a quart of gin I had brought along as a present and he suddenly scrambled to his feet. "Gimme that," he said. He impatiently unscrewed the cap, took a couple of finger-marked glasses off the table, and slopped some gin into them. He took the gin in his glass in two gulps. He shuddered and his teeth chattered for a few moments. "First today," he said when he had his breath. "It ain't the liquor that hurts. It's the doing without that hurts. The old woman wouldn't come across with my gin money this morning and we had an awful fight. It wore me out. I been sitting here two, three hours trying to get up enough strength to go in and fight some more." He sank back on the settee, holding the bottle in one hand and the glass in the other. I went over and sat on the window sill.

"I feel sad," Johnny said, "real blue-sad."

"What seems to be the matter?" I asked.

"The same thing that seems to be the matter with the rest of the world," he said. "The war. By the time this war's over there just won't be no travelling gypsies left in the U.S. There might not be no gypsies of any kind. The most of us, we been bottled up in cities since the depression, and that there gas-rationing business put the stopper in the bottle. The families out on the highways, one by one they're going to get rid of their cars and fall back on the buses and the railroad trains. And before long the ticket agents won't be so free about selling them tickets, and when that time comes New York's going to crawl with gypsies. All the other cities where the cops are halfway decent to us, it'll be the same—cities like Philly, Baltimore, Paterson, Chicago, New Orleans, Mexico City, Los Angeles, and Frisco. When a war hits the world the most sensible thing a gypsy can do is head for the nearest slum and hole up. And hope for the best. What gets me, some of our coppersmiths could do real fine shipyard work, but they won't give them a chance. Four of the coppersmiths in my crowd were taken on by a Brooklyn Navy Yard contractor, but along about noon the foreman found out they wasn't Greek fellers, like he thought, but gypsies, and he fired them. He was afraid they'd steal the tools."

Johnny sighed and slopped some more gin into his glass. "Things have been getting worse and worse for gypsies ever since the automobile was put on the market," he said. "When I was a little knee-high boy the U.S. was gypsy heaven. Everybody was real ignorant and believed in fortune-telling. You could take their money so easy they just about gave it to you. And horses to trade. And every woman had some pots with holes in them, and if she couldn't pay you to tinker, why, a dozen fresh eggs was just as good. And our wagons was red and yellow, and we had bells on the harness, and there wasn't no motorcycle cops, and you could camp anywhere. Private property wasn't even heard of. Nowadays, if gypsies was to make a camp out in the middle of some far desert a hundred and fifty miles from nowhere, about the time they got all settled down for the night a old farmer with a shotgun would come a-running and he'd say, 'Private property. You get right off my private property or I'll shoot you dead.' The entire country is overrun with private property. Some of them farmers, I'm surprised they let the airplanes fly over their goddam private property.

"But when I was a little boy any place would do. The air would be clean, no stinking automobiles around, and we'd camp under some green shade trees near a stream of cooking water. And we'd put the horses on long halters and leave them feed theirselves. And we'd go fishing and fry the fish right off the hook. And firewood was free. And there was a violin in every family—at least a guitar— and you didn't have to get drunk to feel like dancing. And the little kids would run around strip, stark naked. And the girls and womenfolks would go down the stream a piece and take a bath, and you would hear them through the trees a-giggling and a-hollering. And the yellow gypsy dogs that we don't even have no more, they would lie down under the wagons and scratch their fleas. These *gajo* dogs you see in New York that the women practically nurse them, I despise those dogs. When they bark, yah-yah, they don't even sound mad. They sound sick. A yellow gypsy dog, even a baby one, when he barked he sounded like a old bear. And the womenfolks would spread out and *dukker* at all the farms for miles around, and on the way back, after the sun went down, they would pick up a hen here and a cabbage there, and if they come across some clothes on a line, they would take the shirts and dresses. They never bothered the overalls. We didn't have no use for overalls. When I think of the whole armfuls of roasting ear corn we used to steal, and the watermelons, and now and then a little grunty pig, why, it hurts my heart to think of it. When I was a little boy we almost always had enough to eat. You never saw no skinny gypsies."

Johnny was interrupted by one of his daughters-in-law, a tall, haughty gypsy girl who came striding into the room, her heels clicking and her head held high. She went over to Johnny's trunk, threw the lid back, and took out a number of copies of "Old Gipsy Nan." Johnny keeps a supply on hand and sells them to the women in his families. "I took six," the girl said, slamming the lid shut. She offered Johnny a five-dollar bill, and he grunted angrily. "Don't bother me," he said. "Go get that changed and bring me sixty cents." She strode out of the room and Johnny's eyes followed her.

"I don't mean no disrespect," he said after the girl had gone, "but gypsy women have got it all over civilize women. They got such a springy walk on them. No corset, no girdle, no brassy, none of them *gajo* inventions to weight them down. When you look at a gypsy woman you not looking at a corset, you looking at a woman. Most *gajo* women, I bet they carry more harness than a dray horse."

Johnny kept working on the gin. Every few minutes he downed a drink and shuddered.

"Yes, sir," he said, "years back gypsies lived high. But along about the time I got grown up, whenever that was, the bottom fell out. Automobiles spread and spread. No more horses to trade. Then came aluminum and cheap kitchen pots. Aluminum was a severe blow to gypsies, but when they took to selling pots in the five-and-dime they should of held the gypsy funeral right then and there. Women got so they wouldn't have nothing tinkered; a pot got a hole in it, what the hell, pitch it out the window and get a brand-new one from the five-and-dime. Also, with only horses to feed, you could travel cheap. But when we took to cars we had to have gas and tire money. So we looked for big jobs. For a while we did fine. People don't generally know it, but gypsies handled some real big tinker jobs. Back in 1921, in one fall and winter, a crowd of gypsy coppersmiths I and six of my families was travelling with, old King Steve Kaslov's crowd, we did sixteen thousand dollars' worth of copper and tin work for the Arlington Mills at Lawrence, Massachusetts. Not long after we did ten thousand dollars' worth for the Waltham Bleachery and Dye Works at Waltham, Massachusetts. Bunged-up dye vats and dry cans, that kind of stuff. And Paterson, New Jersey, them big dye works out there, we handled the biggest kind of tinker jobs. We'd take the job right out of the factory and truck it to our camp in the woods. We'd leave gold coins on deposit, so the factory would trust us to bring the job back. We worked together in the woods like bees, with the old gypsy coppersmith secret that was handed down from centuries ago. We can shape a pipe sleeve so accurate it fits like a grape hull on a grape, and just use our fingers to measure by. A *gajo* coppersmith with a shopful of machinery, he can't do no better. Then came the depression, and the union fellers began to grab off all the copper work. In 1930 we handled a big job for a bleachery in Worcester, Massachusetts. After that the union fellers took everything. We was washed up."

Johnny rested his head in his hands and stared at the floor for a minute or two. "Well, we still had our gold," he said after a while. "It's hard to make people believe it nowadays, but gypsy women used to be loaded down with gold. They was our banks. In 1933 I and Looba had six thousand bucks in gold coins and she carried the most of it around sewed up in her skirts. And, compared to some gypsies, we was poor. What happened? President Roosevelt. Except he made everybody turn in their gold, I wouldn't say a word against him. Us gypsies, we had gold coins from damn near every country in the world. Some of it had been toted around for centuries.

We used to change all our money into gold. And the cops came to our camps and made us take it to the banks and turn it in. Orders from Washington, D.C. And the banks gave us paper money in exchange. What the hell good is paper money? It went like wine at a wedding. We all bought new cars—who wants a Ford? Give us a Packard. Make it two, one for Ma, one for Pa, ride in style, honk, honk! And along about that time, I don't know why, but the whole entire country turned against gypsies. Them motorcycle cops would chase us across one state line and then some more cops would chase us across another state line. Pretty soon we didn't know where the hell we was at. Whole sections of the country had to be dodged or they'd put us on the chain gang, or try to. Even the carnivals turned against us. Use to, up to the depression, every spring the carnivals and little circuses would put ads in the *Billboard* magazine, rounding up the attractions. And all of them would advertise for a gypsy mitt joint, split half and half with the carnival. And the amusement parks and beaches all up and down the Atlantic Coast would advertise for gypsies. Nowadays, you look at the carnival ads in *Billboard* and it says, 'No gypsies wanted.' Or it says, 'American palmistry only.' *Gajo* women *dukkering* for carnivals. It's sunk to that!

"So we began heading for New York, Chicago, big cities where there's slums to live in. And rent to pay. The fundamental thing a gypsy is opposed to is rent. Use to we was healthy. But now the babies get the rickets and the old folks get the itch. And colds, and t.b. And right after they're weaned the babies start eating hot dogs. And the steam heat, it's paralyzing us. It's drying us up. It takes us all summer to get over the steam heat. It makes our hair fall out. It gives us the dropsy. You take a gypsy woman, out on the road she'd have a baby every year. Let her spend a solid winter in a steam-heat room, she quits having babies. And the relief people, always wanting to know where at was you born. Now, how would a gypsy know that? You're born in a tent beside the road someplace and a week later you're in another state and there ain't nobody got time to keep track of where at you was born. Who cares? And birth certificates! Why, we never heard of birth certificates until we hit the relief. I don't have the slightest idea where I was born. All I know it was in the U.S. someplace. I'm alive, ain't I? I must of been born."

Johnny had worked himself into a frenzy. He lurched to his feet, and started to say something more to me, and then stuttered and stopped, and I could see that the gin was beginning to take hold. At this moment the tall, haughty gypsy girl returned, bringing the money for the books she had taken. She stood at his elbow and tried to give him some coins, but he disregarded her.

"And let me tell you something," he said finally, waving his hand at me with an oratorical gesture. "I just can't wait for the blowup."

"The blowup of what?" I asked.

"The blowup of the whole entire world, that's what," said Johnny. "It's going to bust wide open any day now, ask any gypsy, and I don't give a D-double-damn if it does."

"That's no way to talk," I said.

"And if it was left to me," continued Johnny, paying no attention to my remark, "I'd sure fix things up. The very first thing I'd do, I'd unlock the insane asylums all over the world and let them people out. I'd leave them run things. I'd hunt up the insanest feller of all and I'd say to him, 'Sir, you got any notion how to run the world?' And he'd say to me, 'Yes, *indeed!*' 'O.K., pal,' I'd say to him, 'take charge. You can't possibly do no worse than them that's been had charge.' And if the crazy fellers couldn't somehow straighten things out, why, I'd call on the gypsies. I'd put everything in their hands."

The gypsy girl snickered and made what I thought was a sound observation. "Uh oh!" she said.

(1942)

# The Gypsy Women

*I*N THE EARLY THIRTIES, I covered Police Headquarters at night for a newspaper, and I often ate in a restaurant named the Grotta Azzurra, which is only a block over, at the southwest corner of Broome and Mulberry, and stays open until two. I still go down there every now and then. The Grotta Azzurra is a classical downtown New York South Italian restaurant: it is a family enterprise, it is in the basement of a tenement, it has marble steps, it displays in a row of bowls propped up on a table dry samples of all the kinds of *pasta* it serves, its kitchen is open to view through an arch, and it has scenes of the Bay of Naples painted on its walls. Among its specialties is striped bass cooked in clam broth with clams, mussels, shrimp, and squid, and it may be possible to find a better fish-and-shellfish dish in one of the great restaurants of the world, but I doubt it. I had a late dinner in the Grotta Azzurra one Sunday night recently, and then sat and talked for a while with two of the waiters at a table in back. We talked about the upheavals in the Police Department under Commissioner Adams; a good many police officials eat in the Grotta Azzurra, and the waiters take an interest in police affairs. I left around midnight and walked west on Broome, heading for the subway. At the northeast corner of Broome and Cleveland Place, just across Broome from Headquarters, there is an eight-story brick building that is called Police Headquarters Annex. It is a dingy old box of a building; it was originally a factory, a Loft candy factory. It houses the Narcotics Squad, the Pickpocket and Confidence Squad, the Missing Persons Bureau, the Bureau of Criminal Information, and a number of other specialized squads and bureaus. I was about halfway up the block when a middle-aged man carrying a briefcase came out of the Annex and started across the street, and as he passed under a street lamp I saw that he was a detective I used to know quite well named Daniel J. Campion. I was surprised that he should be coming out of the Annex at that hour, particularly on a Sunday night, for some months earlier I had heard in the Grotta Azzurra that he had retired from the Police Department on a pension of thirty-five hundred dollars a year and had gone to work for the Pinkertons, the big private-detective agency. He was an Acting Captain when he retired, and the commanding officer of the Pickpocket and Confidence Squad. He had been a member of this squad for over twenty-five years, and had long been considered the best authority in the United States on pickpockets, confidence-game operators, and swindlers. He was also the Department's expert on gypsies. He had become curious about gypsies when he was a young patrolman on a beat and first arrested one, and had spent a great deal of time through the years seeking them out and talking with them, not only in New York City but in cities all over the country that he visited on police business. He sought them out on his own time as well as on Department time, and he always made notes on the information that he picked up from them. He made these notes on yellow legal scratch-paper, and kept them in some file folders, on the flaps of which he had pasted detailed labels, such as "Notes in re the gypsy confidence game known as doing, making, or pulling off a *bajour* (also pronounced *bahjo, boojoo,* and *boorjo*)," "Notes in re individual techniques of Bronka, Saveta, Matrona, Lizaveta, Zorka, Looba, Kaisha, Linka, Dunya, and certain other *bajour* women in the gypsy bands that frequent New York City," and "Notes in re various different spellings of gypsy given names and family names as shown on the tombstones of gypsies in two cemeteries in New Jersey." I became acquainted with Captain Campion while I was covering Headquarters. Afterwards, during the late thirties and up through the middle forties, I used to drop into his office in the Annex whenever I was down around Headquarters and had time to spare. If he also had time to spare, he would send out for a carton of coffee and we would sit at his desk and talk, almost always about gypsies. If he was busy, he would let me take his gypsy file folders out to a table in an anteroom and go through them and read his latest notes. In recent years, I hadn't seen much of him. I called out to Captain Campion and he stopped, and I hurried up the street to him.

"I bet I know where you've been," he said as we shook hands. "Over in the Grotta Azzurra, eating striped bass."

"Yes," I said, "and if it's all right to ask, what in the world are you doing down here at this hour of the night, and a Sunday night at that? I heard you had left the Department and gone to the Pinkerton Agency."

"I was attending to some unfinished business," he said. "Six months or so before I retired, somebody over at Headquarters spoke to me about two young detectives out in precinct squads who sounded like they might be good material for Pickpocket and Confidence. I had thirty-three detectives in the squad at the time, seventeen men and sixteen women, but two of my best men were about to be transferred to Narcotics because of certain skills they had. So I looked up these two young detectives, and I was impressed by them, and I asked them would they like to work in Pickpocket and Confidence. At first, they weren't so sure, but after I explained the nature of the squad to them in some detail they came to the conclusion they would. So I put in for their transfer. Well, these things take forever. Months went by. Then I got this offer to work in the private-detective field. I hadn't intended to retire from the Department for years yet, but this offer appealed to me, and I decided to go ahead and retire. And the way things happen, the very morning of the day I was due to leave, notification came through that the transfer of these two young detectives had been approved. So I got in touch with them and told them the situation—I wouldn't be able to break them in—but I told them I would call them as soon as I got settled in my new job and would meet them and sit down with them and tell them all I possibly could about pickpockets and confidence-game operators and swindlers, give them the benefit of my experience. I felt I had a moral obligation to do so. I called them the other day and asked if they still wanted me to talk to them, and they said they did, so we agreed to meet in the squad office on Sunday night—it would be quiet then and we'd have it pretty much to ourselves. And that's what I've been doing. I talked about four hours tonight, talked and answered questions, and I hardly got started, so we decided to meet two or three more Sunday nights. And where I'm going now, I thought I'd drop in at Headquarters for a minute and say hello to the lieutenant on the main desk and find out what's new since I retired. Come on, walk me around to the back door."

We turned in to Centre Market Place, a narrow, ominous, brightly lit, block-long street that runs behind Police Headquarters.

"What about the gypsies?" I asked. "Do you still see any of them?"

"I was waiting for you to ask me that," Captain Campion said. "Sure I do. Only the night before last I drove over to Brooklyn and had a talk with an old *bajour* queen from the West Coast named Paraskiva Miller. She's a Machvanka—that is, a female member of the Machwaya tribe of Serbian gypsies—and she's seventy-five. She calls herself Madame Miller. She's been telling fortunes and pulling off *bajours* since 1898, 1899, or 1900, somewhere around there, mainly in California, and I'm pretty sure she's one of the richest gypsies in the country. According to gypsy gossip, she believes that money will be worthless before long, something she saw in a dream, and she puts her money in diamonds and keeps them sewed up in her skirts and petticoats; one of these days some gypsy from another tribe is going to strip her down to her bones. I heard about her first in San Francisco in the summer of 1945. The New York Police Department and the police departments in several other cities around the country have an arrangement by which they lend detectives to each other on certain occasions, and I was loaned to San Francisco that summer. An international conference was going on out there, the one at which the United Nations was organized, and the city was crowded, and I was supposed to watch out for criminals from the East. When I had any time to myself, I looked up the local gypsies. Paraskiva and one of her daughters were running an *ofisa* in

San Francisco then—a fortune-telling joint in a store—and I tried several times to see her, but her daughter always came out and said Madame Miller wasn't in, which meant she was sitting behind the curtains and had peeped out at me and didn't like my looks. I got word here recently that she had come East to visit one of her granddaughters, Sabinka Uwanawich, who runs an *ofisa* on Atlantic Avenue in Brooklyn. I know Sabinka quite well; I've arrested her I think it's five times. So I went out to her *ofisa* the other night. When I walked in, Sabinka began to scream insults at me, the usual gypsy-woman insults—I was a rat, I was a stinking rat, she'd like to pull my guts out through my ears, all that stuff—but she knew I had left the Police Department and was curious what I wanted, and when I told her I just wanted to ask her grandmother some questions about gypsies on the West Coast in the old days, she quieted down and took me in the back room. Paraskiva turned out to be one of those stout, dark, gold-toothed, big-eyed, Hindu-looking gypsies. She was the bouncy kind. I've seen her kind over and over among the Serbian gypsy women; they're top-heavy—they're nine-tenths bosom—but they hold themselves erect and they're quick on their feet and they walk with a strut. As old and stout as she was, she had on high-heeled shoes and lipstick and rouge. She wasn't well. She had a cough, a persistent cough, and she said she had had t.b. some years ago and was afraid it had come back on her, but she talked to me an hour or more, and I got some odds and ends of information out of her that I couldn't have got anywhere else. She didn't tell me a whole lot, but what she told me fitted in with what I already knew."

One side of Centre Market Place is lined with red brick tenements whose street floors are occupied by gunsmiths, police tailors, and police-equipment stores. An old, black, and obese cat was sitting in the show window of one of the police-equipment stores, in the middle of a display of cartridge belts. "She's the biggest store cat in the neighborhood," Captain Campion said. "I've stopped and watched her many a night on my way past here. One night I saw her catch and eat a rat." We paused and stood in front of the show window. While Captain Campion continued to talk, he and I watched the cat, and the cat stared fixedly at us and slowly waved her tail.

"You remember I used to say the more I studied gypsies the less I knew about them," Captain Campion said. "Well, I've changed my tune. After all these years, I really believe I've got to the bottom of a good many gypsy matters. To tell you the truth, I found out more about some aspects of gypsy life the last few years than I did in all the years that went before. For one thing, there was an unusual amount of informing going on. During 1951, '52, and '53, the *bajour* women in three or four of the bands that hang out in the city had a run of luck pulling off *bajours* on mental cases. A high percentage of the women who go to gypsies for advice are off balance to some degree, and the gypsies would starve to death if they weren't, but what I'm talking about now are serious mental cases, advanced mental cases—women who should be in institutions or they already have been and shouldn't have been let out. As a rule, gypsies are leery of such cases. When women are that far gone, they're a good deal harder to swindle than you might think. Some of them are much more suspicious than normal people, they suspect everything and everybody, and some of them their minds are off in space and they don't retain and the gypsy can work on one of them a week and still be right where she started, and some of them are so shaky they're liable to throw a leaping, scratching, screaming hysterical fit at any moment and create a disturbance and attract the whole neighborhood into the *ofisa*. And the very best of them, when the gypsy tries to worm the facts out of them concerning do they have any money put away and they let drop they do have, it may be true and it may be a complete delusion. All the same, around 1951 the *bajour* women in the bands I'm speaking of got to be very good at handling serious mental cases and began concentrating on them. They learned how to detect which ones were safe enough to work on, and how to see things their way, and how to calm them down and reason with them and plant ideas in their minds.

"One of their victims was an Italian woman of fifty-four, a widow. She had been a widow around two years, and she and a son-in-law ran a bakery that her husband had left her, a small bakery in an

Italian neighborhood on the lower East Side. She hadn't been herself since she lost her husband—she would stay in her room for days at a time and lie in there with the bedclothes pulled up over her and refuse to speak, and about the only time she went out in the streets was to go to church. A pair of *bajour* women opened an *ofisa* in an old store in the neighborhood, and one day this Italian woman was passing by on her way to church and they stopped her and talked to her and said they could see something was bothering her, why didn't she come in and visit them, maybe they could help her. She visited them several times, and they wormed out of her that she had a total of seventeen thousand six hundred dollars in two savings banks, and then they planted the idea in her mind this money had a curse on it and that was what was making her feel bad. So she went to the banks one morning and drew it out, every cent of it, and carried it to the *ofisa* and asked the gypsies to take the curse off it. They said to leave it with them and they would work over it all night and do their best. She returned to the *ofisa* the following morning and naturally the *ofisa* was empty and the gypsies were gone, and her reaction was she went on home and didn't say a word. This was in the latter part of October. Four months went by, and then one day early in March the son-in-law was filling out her income-tax return and she was lying in bed that day refusing to speak and he got her bankbooks out of her bureau drawer to see how much interest he should report, and both books had 'CAN-CELLED' cut in them, perforated in them, the way savings banks do when an account is closed, and he was shocked, and he dragged her out of bed and forced her to explain to him and the rest of the family what in the name of God had happened. And when she finally did so, he took her to the police station in the neighborhood, and the detectives there sent them to the Annex to see me, and I did the usual thing—I got out the file of photographs of *bajour* women and started showing them to her. She just kind of glanced at the first one I showed her and saw it was a gypsy, and then she bent over and put her head in her hands and wouldn't look at any more. She wouldn't reply to questions or make any further response. I asked the son-in-law to step out in the hall with me, and I urged him to take her to a psychiatrist, which he said he would. And some days later he phoned me that the psychiatrist said she was suffering from involutional melancholia in an advanced state.

"Another victim was a forty-two-year-old blonde, a member of a prominent family in Brooklyn. She's had three husbands, all well-to-do, and three divorces, and she has a daughter by her first husband that the husband has the full custody of; she isn't even allowed to visit her. She has a small income of some kind, and she lives alone. She hits the bottle and she picks up men who beat her up, but what's really wrong with her, she's a schizo and she's subject to auditory hallucinations. She'll be all right for a year, a year and a half, sometimes longer, and then she'll start hearing voices and she'll wander in the streets and scream and moan and run right in front of cars, trying to get away from the voices, and she'll wind up in the psychopathic division at Kings County Hospital; it's happened over and over. She spent three or four evenings in an *ofisa* in a store on Flatbush Avenue Extension, telling her troubles to the gypsies, and the gypsies sympathized with her from the bottom of their hearts and took twelve thousand dollars from her—twelve thousand three hundred and fifty, to be exact. It was part of the settlement from one of her divorces, and for some reason of her own she had been keeping it in cash in a safe-deposit box.

"They made several touches almost as big as these, and touches amounting to a couple of thousand, a thousand, five hundred, two hundred and fifty, and the like of that were just routine. The men in these bands began driving big brand-new cars instead of used cars and drinking whiskey instead of wine, and they began throwing their weight around at gypsy parties and talking out of turn and showing entirely too much interest in the women in the other bands. The men in the other bands got sick and tired of this, and certain ones of them decided to do some informing, and instead of just getting on the phone and refusing to give their names and jabbering a minute or two and hanging up, the way gypsy informers usually do, they came right into my office and sat down and put their hats on their laps and talked and talked, and much to my surprise about twenty per cent of what they told turned out to be true. In addition to straightening me out on who did various *bajours,* they gave me a lot of incidental information on gypsy customs."

The obese cat stirred herself and jumped clumsily out of the show window and waddled into the darkness in the rear of the store. Captain Campion and I resumed our walk.

"Another good source of information on gypsy customs I had in recent years," he said, "was an investigator in the Department of Welfare named Harry Brunner. In April, 1951, the Department of Welfare put all the gypsy relief cases in the entire city into one center, the Non-Residence Welfare Center, and started weeding them out. They had had trouble with gypsy families who were using several sets of names and several addresses and getting relief from several centers at the same time, and they shouldn't have been on relief in the first place. Such as a family that owned a new Buick Roadmaster with about a thousand dollars' worth of accessories and extra equipment on it—it was practically a rolling auto-supplies store—and they were getting relief from a center in Queens and a center in the Bronx, and were also on relief over in Newark. Brunner was assigned to the Non-Residence Center, and he got in behind the gypsies. He's a big, quiet, gloomy-looking fellow from Brooklyn. He's six feet two, and he's absolutely fearless and absolutely honest. His mother taught in public schools in Brooklyn for thirty-five years. She taught ungraded children—children with psychological problems—and Brunner must've learned from her how to get along with people. In a short while, he threw dozens upon dozens of gypsy families off relief, but for some reason I've never been able to figure out, instead of hating him, the gypsies liked him and respected him. They called him Bruno, and invited him to parties and weddings and funerals. He ate gypsy goulash with them and drank gypsy tea with them, and sat up all night talking with them, and they told him things right off the bat that it took me years to learn. Gypsies ordinarily don't like it a bit when people try to find out what's the gypsy word for this, what's the gypsy word for that, but all Brunner had to do was ask; they gave him hundreds of words. I had hopes that he would become a real gypsy scholar, which is something we need in this country—when I read about

American professors studying strange tribes of people in the far corners of the earth, it burns me up; you'd think at least one of them would study a strange tribe that's right under their noses. However, he disappointed me. He was a college man—he had a B.S. in psychology from Long Island University—but he wanted to work with his hands. In August, 1952, right out of a clear sky, he quit the Department of Welfare and went down to Fort Worth, Texas—he was married to a Texas girl—and the next thing I knew, I had a postcard from him saying he had become a structural steelworker.

"Another thing I might mention that happened in recent years was an experience we had with a *bajour* woman named Pearsa. Pearsa belongs to two of the biggest gypsy families in North and South America, the Nicholases and the Demetros. Her father was George Nicholas, a Serbian gypsy, and her mother was Sabinka Demetro, a Russian gypsy, and she was born in Buenos Aires in 1907. She was brought to the United States when she was a little girl, and she was married when she was fourteen. She's married to Steve Bimbo, who's the oldest son of old man Tene Bimbo, who's the head of the Bimbo family, which is another big gypsy family. Her main stamping grounds are New York City, Baltimore, Chicago, Detroit, Buffalo, and Boston, and the record we have on her dates back to 1926 and shows thirty-two arrests in eleven cities, but that's not as bad as it sounds. There's quite a few gypsy women with a hundred or more arrests on their records. Men, too. Old man Tene Bimbo himself, he's rolled up a hundred and forty arrests for everything from murder in the first degree to stealing an automobile jack. Still and all, you can just imagine how much she's paid to lawyers and bail bondsmen. Pearsa's a red-haired gypsy, the only one I've ever seen, and she used to be extremely good-looking in a wild and woolly sort of way. She's been a big money-maker, and other *bajour* women talk about her with the greatest respect, but she's had thirteen children and her back bothers her and she's developed sinus trouble and her nerves are all shot and she and Steve fight like cats and dogs and she doesn't have much patience any more and she's begun to take chances she wouldn't've dreamed of taking when she was in better command of herself. Well, in February, 1952, with the help of the District Attorney's office, we managed to plant a certain mechanical device in an *ofisa* that Pearsa was running in a flat above a store on East Broadway, and we listened to her actual words while she worked on a victim during the final stages of a *bajour*. It was the first time we'd ever been able to use such a device on a gypsy, and it was a very educational experience. When did I see you last? It must've been around four years ago."

"It was around that," I said. "I ran into you in Grand Central and we went and had some coffee."

"I remember," Captain Campion said. "Then I've never had a chance to tell you about the devil's head. Every so often, all through the years, we'd hear from a *bajour* victim about a little devil's head that the gypsy used on her to convince her she had cancer, which only the gypsy could cure, but we couldn't seem to find one. Every time we arrested a *bajour* woman, we'd search her right down to the seams in her skirts, and every time we made a raid on gypsy premises we'd turn everything upside down, and we came across a good many queer things, but a devil's head just never showed up. Well, in the summer of 1952 we finally found one, and it was a nasty thing. It was carved out of ivory, and it was about the size of a hazelnut, and it was grinning, and it had human hair glued on it—coarse, black gypsy hair. On January 3, 1953, we found another one."

We reached the back door of Headquarters.

"What did you do with them?" I asked. "I'd like to see one."

"The District Attorney's office has the last one we found," Captain Campion said. "It'll be put in evidence when the gypsy woman who was using it's case comes up in General Sessions, if it ever does—she jumped bail, and I suspect she went to Mexico City, which is where they generally go when they jump bail. The other one belongs to me—the gypsy we took it from died before *her* case came up; she was burned to death in a tenement fire in Coney Island. I've got it home. If you'd really like to see it, I tell you what I'll do. I was going to talk to the young detectives about gypsies sooner or later, and if you want to come down to the Annex next Sunday night, I'll devote the entire session to gypsies, and you can sit in on it, and I'll bring along the devil's head."

"What time should I come?" I asked.

"Meet me in the squad office in the Annex a little after eight," Captain Campion said.

CAPTAIN CAMPION is fifty-one years old. He is blue-eyed and black-haired, and he has a calm, ruddy, observant, handsome, strong-jawed, Irish face. He is five feet ten, and he weighs around a hundred and fifty. He was born on Fifty-eighth Street between Ninth and Tenth, in Hell's Kitchen, and he grew up on Twentieth Street between Second and Third, in the old Gashouse District. He went through the second year of high school. He was an amateur fighter. He fought in four weights, beginning as a flyweight and ending as a lightweight, and he had fifty-four fights and won forty-nine. He entered the Police Department in January, 1927. It soon became apparent that he was unusually intelligent, and that he had a re-markably accurate memory for faces, names, conversations, and sequences of actions, and that he was deeply curious about human behavior, and after two years as a patrolman he was transferred to the Detective Division and assigned to the Pickpocket and Confi-dence Squad. He was an exceedingly hard-working detective; he made over two thousand arrests, and was cited for bravery nine times. He is serious by nature, but friendly, and he has a cheerful, youthful smile. People talk to him willingly, and he is a good listener; he is one of those who believe very little of what they hear but always look and act as if they believe every word. He is a self-taught linguist. He can speak rough-and-ready Italian, German, and Yiddish, he can speak a little Romany, the gypsy language, and he is studying Spanish. He keeps a paper-backed Spanish-self-taught manual and a Spanish-English, English-Spanish dictionary in his pockets and studies them on the subway. He is religious, and he often reflects on death. For over ten years he was a member of a committee in the Society of St. Vincent de Paul that was composed of detectives and patrolmen and that went to Welfare Island every Sunday and called on terminal patients in the City Home and the old cancer hospital and talked or listened to them, whichever they seemed to want, and brought them cigarettes and magazines and playing cards and flowers. He goes to fights and horse races. He and his wife, Gertrude Campion, live in an apartment in Flushing. They have two sons, one of whom is a graduate of Fordham and both of whom are in the Air Force.

The next Sunday night, I went down to the Annex and took the elevator to the seventh floor, where the Pickpocket and Confidence Squad is quartered. When I stepped off the elevator, I found that Captain Campion was standing in the hall, waiting for me. "We won't be able to use the squad office tonight," he said. "The ex-girl friend of a confidence man came in just now and stated she wanted to give some information concerning him, and a couple of detectives are questioning her in there. She's telling everything she knows, and enjoying it to the full, and she'll be hours, so we're going to use the private office of the commanding officer of the squad. In other words, my old office." I followed Captain Campion down the hall and into his old office. I remembered it as being about as plainly furnished as it could be, and I saw that his successor had not made any changes in it. A battered old golden-oak desk stood in the center. In back of the desk was a swivel chair and facing it were three straight chairs. On one wall was one of those maps of the city that can be rolled up and down like a shade. In one corner was a coat tree. There was one window, at which two young men were standing looking out, each with one foot resting on the sill. "These are the young detectives I told you about," Captain Campion said. "I explained to them that the text for tonight is gypsies." They came over, and Captain Campion introduced us. One was Detective Joe Kane, and he was thickset and solemn, and the other was Detective Al Gore, and he was thin and solemn. They appeared to be in their middle twenties. Captain Campion's briefcase was on the desk, and he unbuckled it and took out some file folders. "Well, gentlemen," he said, "let's be seated." He sat in the swivel chair and put on spectacles and opened one of the folders, disclosing a rat's nest of notes. The young detectives and I sat in the straight chairs.

"In Pickpocket and Confidence," Captain Campion began, peering at us over his spectacles, "you run into two breeds of gypsies, the nomad coppersmith gypsies and the Boyasch. The nomads are by far the most numerous. They're the ones we're mainly concerned with, and I'll describe them in detail, but first I want to say a few words about the Boyasch and get them out of the way. The Boyasch are what you might call Serbo-Rumanian gypsies. Serbia was the last country they lived in before they came here, and back before that they lived for many generations in Rumania. Among themselves, they usually speak Rumanian or Hrvatski, which is the Serbo-Croatian language. They claim they can't speak a word of gypsy, and I guess it is dying out among them, but I've heard some of the old ones speaking it a mile a minute. They're small and dark and strange, and if you saw some on the street you'd notice them but it probably wouldn't occur to you they were gypsies. They're cleaner and neater than the nomads, and their women don't dress gypsy style any more, although a few of the real old ones still wear gold-coin necklaces. At the same time, they're tougher-looking. I guess hard is more the word. They look hard. It's something in their eyes. They have curious cold, hard eyes, and they watch you every second, and they rarely ever smile. They look like they've thought a lot about the way life is, they and their forefathers before them, and they don't see anything funny in it. That's how they look to me, but I remember hearing one of the women detectives in the squad describing them, and the way *she* described them, she said they look like they carry knives. I don't know what Boyasch means. The nomads say it's just an old gypsy word meaning gold-washer, but I've never been able to get a satisfactory explanation out of them what a gold-washer is. The nomads and the Boyasch don't get along. The nomad women call the Boyasch women the dirty, sneaking Boyaschutza, and make contemptuous remarks about them, such as they say they'll tell fortunes for a quarter and do both palms, and the Boyaschutza call the nomad women rag-heads. In the East, the Boyasch hang out in New York City and vicinity and Philadelphia and vicinity. In the Middle West, Chicago is their headquarters. They don't travel anywhere near as much as the nomads; they sometimes stay put for years. The ones here mostly live in tenements in Williamsburg and Greenpoint, out in Brooklyn. The nomads spy on them, and a nomad informer told me recently that there are eighteen families in Brooklyn at present, and two or three in Queens and two in Harlem and six or seven more in Newark and Paterson. The principal Boyasch family names are Ivanovich, Lazarovich, Lucas, Magill, Mitchell, Morgan, Mort, Peterson, Petrovich, Stanley, and Stevens. These are typical American gypsy family names; there are nomad families with the same names.

"The Boyasch men work. Some are automobile mechanics, and some work in factories that make tents and awnings and hammocks; they used to travel with circuses and carnivals and take care of the tents. The men don't give us much trouble, it's the women. When they're young, the Boyaschutza stay home and keep house like ordinary women, but as they grow older the gypsy in them seems to grow stronger and stronger, and when they reach middle age some of them become fortune-tellers and swindlers. They don't run fortune-telling joints. Instead of sitting and waiting for victims, they go out and hunt for them. They usually work in pairs. They lug around shopping bags containing a stock of dead and dried-up specimens of a peculiar kind of plant called the resurrection plant, and they go from house to house in working-class, home-owning neighborhoods out in Brooklyn, Queens, and Staten Island, and over in Jersey, and up in the Bronx and Westchester, and ring doorbells and try to sell these plants to housewives. 'If your husband doesn't show as much interest in you as he used to,' they tell the housewives, 'buy one of these plants and sit it in a saucer of water and put it under your bed, if you and your husband sleep in the same bed, and if you don't, put it under his bed, and leave it there, and you'll soon notice a change for the better.' They're terrifying fast-talkers, and after they get inside a house and demonstrate how to sit the plant in water, they offer to tell the woman's fortune. Usually, that's as far as they go, but now and then they hit a woman who responds to their superstitious talk and who they can feel in their bones has some money hid away in the house, and they go to work on her and swindle her. They use a swindle called the *bajour,* the same as the nomad women. I'll explain this swindle, or confidence game, in a few minutes. The resurrection plant is just a means of getting the door open, and they've been using it for this purpose in and around the city for twenty years, to my knowledge. They know what they're doing—when they hold one up in front of a woman, no matter how bright she is, or suspicious, she usually takes a good look at it and starts asking questions. A couple of months before I left the Department, we apprehended a pair of Boyaschutza who were wanted for a *bajour,* and they had a hundred and sixty resurrection plants in their possession. After the case was disposed of, I took some of the plants home, and I brought one along tonight for you to see. If you stay in the Pickpocket and Confidence Squad, it won't be the last one you'll see."

Captain Campion reached into his briefcase and brought out a paper bag. He held the bag over the desk and shook it, and out dropped a dead plant whose stems and leaves were tightly curled into a dusty, mossy, lopsided ball. In size and shape, it roughly resembled a woman's clenched hand. From it hung a tuft of hairy roots.

"It's a weed that grows down in the lower parts of Texas, and over in Mexico," Captain Campion said. "It's also called Mary's hand, Our Lady's rose, and bird's-nest moss, and it belongs to the genus *Selaginella.* The reason I know, some years ago I took one out to the Brooklyn Botanic Garden and had it identified. According to the nomads, the Boyasch learned about the resurrection plant back in the days they used to travel with circuses and they have some connection down in Texas that keeps them supplied. In dry weather, the resurrection plant tightens up into a ball the same as you see here. If it gets damp, if some dew falls on it, or a little sprinkle of rain, it opens up. Even if it's dead, it opens up. This one here is as dead as a brickbat, but if you sit it in a saucer of water the roots will absorb the water and the stems will turn from gray to green and slowly uncurl and expand and stiffen up and straighten out."

"Why don't we try it?" asked Detective Kane. There was a glass ashtray on the desk and he picked it up. "I could take this out to the water cooler and run some water in it."

"I'd rather you'd wait until I get through talking," Captain Campion said. "Please don't interrupt me now."

He opened the bulkiest of his file folders. "So much for the

Boyasch," he said. "Now we come to another breed of cat." He took off his spectacles and lit a cigarette and leaned back in the swivel chair. "When people talk about gypsies," he said, "it's usually the nomad coppersmith gypsies they're talking about. The great majority of the gypsies that frequent New York City are nomads. In fact, the great majority of the gypsies in Canada, the United States, Mexico, and South America are nomads. There doesn't seem to be any way to find out when they first started coming to the United States—according to immigration statistics and census reports, there's no such thing as gypsies—but from what I've been able to piece together, I'm pretty sure the biggest migrations took place in the late seventies, the eighties, and the nineties. They came from many parts of Europe, but mostly from Russia and Serbia and the countries surrounding Serbia, and it didn't take them long to get acquainted with the country. Some bands roamed the North, some roamed the South, some roamed the Middle West, a few roamed the West, and some roamed up and down and across and all over. In the early days, in the South and Middle West, the principal occupation of the men was horse trading and horse doctoring, and coppersmith work and tinkering came second. Then the horse business gradually died out, and tinkering came first. It was about the same out West. In the North, in most of the bands, coppersmith work and tinkering always came first. And in all the bands, wherever they roamed, the women told fortunes and swindled and stole. Just about anything they saw lying around loose, if it could be eaten or worn or sold or swapped or pawned or played with, and if nobody was watching it, and if they could lift it and carry it, they'd steal it. Why I say played with, an old gypsy once told me his favorite plaything when he was a little boy was a doctor's stethoscope his mother had stolen. And while I'm on the subject, you'll never understand gypsies until you understand how they feel about stealing. It's simple: they believe they're born with the right to steal, and the reason they give, they tell the blasphemous story there was a gypsy in the crowd that followed Jesus up the hill, and on the way this gypsy did his best to steal four nails that the Roman soldiers had brought with them to nail Jesus to the Cross—two for His hands, one for His feet, and one that was extra long for His head or His heart, whichever they decided to drive it through— but the gypsy succeeded in stealing only one, and it was the one that was extra long, and when the soldiers got ready to use it and couldn't find it they suspected the gypsy and beat him bloody trying to make him tell where he had put it, but he wouldn't, and while Jesus was dying He spoke to the gypsy from the Cross and said that from then on gypsies had the right to wander the earth and steal."

"Do they really believe that?" asked Detective Kane.

"They believe it as much as they believe anything," Captain Campion said, "and they bring their children up to believe it. They like to tell it; you can't stop them; they seem to feel they're slapping you in the face with it. I must've heard it fifty times. Now, as I said, coppersmith work and tinkering always came first in most of the bands that roamed the North, and some of these bands became quite prosperous. They followed fairly regular routes through Pennsylvania, New Jersey, New York, Connecticut, Rhode Island, and Massachusetts. They'd stay a day or two in some places and a week or two in others. The men would repair and re-tin copper utensils and fixtures, mainly for hotels, restaurants, hospitals, bakeries, canneries, laundries, and cloth-dyeing factories, and the women would circulate around and tell fortunes and keep their eyes open. The men picked up jobs that ordinary American metalworkers wouldn't touch—a dye vat with so many holes eaten in it it should've been junked, a broken piece of equipment in a contagious-disease hospital, an old restaurant soup kettle so caked with grease they'd have to burn the grease off it with a blowtorch before they could mend it, jobs like that. Then the depression struck, and in a little while there weren't any jobs that American metalworkers wouldn't touch. Instead of which, no matter what the job was, they'd fight and scratch each other to get it, let alone leave it to the gypsies. By the end of 1932, in most localities, the money gypsies were able to make from tinkering wasn't enough to pay for their gasoline, and they began to leave the roads and hole up in tenements in big cities. This demoralized the men, but it didn't the women. One thing you want to keep in mind about gypsies: it would take ten of the men to make one of the women. The women talked to other women in the tenements about relief, which was just getting going then. After they learned some of the ins and outs of the relief regulations, they took off their good clothes and put on rags, and they hid their gold-coin necklaces, and they told the men to sell the automobiles or stop parking them in the neighborhood, where a relief investigator might see them and notice the licenses on them from other states and put two and two together who they belonged to. Then they went into the relief offices with their children following along behind and broke down and cried and said they were starving to death, and if that didn't impress the relief officials to the proper extent they screeched and screamed and fell on the floor and fainted and used foul and abusive language and swept papers off desks and stood in doors and wouldn't let people pass and brought everything in general to a standstill. They pretty soon got their families on relief. And after they had that attended to, they began to go shares with each other and rent stores and open fortune-telling joints—what the old ones call *ofisas* and the young ones call locations—and right from the start, even with the overhead, most of them made far more than they ever had out on the road. Any period where people are uneasy is good for fortune-tellers. The depression was good for them, and then came the war and things got even better, and then came the A-bomb and the H-bomb and the possibility the whole world may be blown out like a light any moment now, either that or you'll die of cancer from smoking cigarettes, and things got even better still, the best yet. Nowadays, in most gypsy families, I think I can safely say the women bring in ninety per cent of the money. A few of the young men in the bands around here work as parkers in parking lots—they're crazy about automobiles and they're un-usually skillful drivers. And a few have become fender-bangers—they canvass garages and get jobs now and then at cut rates ham-mering dents out of automobile bodies. And a few of the older men, once in a while the spirit moves them, or some dim memory the way things used to be, and they go out with their hammers and tongs and files and soldering irons and try to pick up jobs mending pots and pans for restaurants. But the majority of the men, young and old, they don't do anything. If it's unusually nice and sunny, they may go up to the automobile showrooms around Columbus Circle and spend the whole day lifting hoods and kicking tires and comparing prices, but they just sit around home most of the time and stare at each other and drink tea and spit on the floor and grumble. The main thing they grumble about is the women. They look down on the women, and they beat and bang them around. Of course, some of the women know how to return the compliment. A gypsy woman, the situation she's in, she's in between her husband and the police. If she becomes too cautious and lets chances go by, her husband beats her, and if she takes chances and gets arrested, then he really beats her. And as far as gratitude, if she pulls off a *bajour* running into the thousands, the way her husband feels about it, it's only what she should do, the same as she should wash the dishes, but if *he* brings in a few dollars, that's a different matter; that shows brains. I heard a gypsy talking one day whose wife promises women who come into her *ofisa* it'll cost them only fifty cents to have their fortunes told and she's so slick they hardly ever get out without paying her anywhere from a couple of dollars to fifteen or twenty, and she's made several big *bajours*; she's made at least one ten-thousand-dollar *bajour*. This gypsy was drunk, and he was bragging, but he wasn't by any means bragging about his wife, he was bragging about himself. 'When it comes to stealing,' he said, 'I believe in letting the women do it, but if I happen to feel like it, I can go into any grocery store in the United States and stand around and get in the way and ask the price of this and the price of that, and before you know it four or five cans of sardines will jump into my pockets.'

"The fundamental thing that identifies the nomad gypsies is the way the women dress. They wear head scarves, and loose, low-cut blouses, and long, full, flashy skirts. That's their basic outfit, and if one of them took it in her head to dress some other way, she'd soon regret it. The other women would call her a *kurwa,* a whore, and spit at her; I've known it to happen. That is, of course, unless she was doing it temporarily to evade the police or confuse a victim.

They buy the brightest pieces of cloth they can find for their head scarves; these scarves are what the Boyaschutza are referring to when they call the nomad women rag-heads. They take a lot of pride in their skirts. They make them themselves, and they sometimes use very expensive material, and they wear old ones underneath new ones for petticoats. When they're dressed up, nine out of ten wear Spanish shawls, or that's what they were called when I was young and they were quite the style—the kind with big red roses all over them, red or yellow, and a row of tassels on each end. There must be a factory somewhere that turns them out especially for gypsies. They generally wear cheap fur coats. They seldom wear stockings. They wear the highest-heeled shoes they can find, and I've seen them many a time knocking around the streets in broad daylight in old scuffed-up gold or silver evening slippers. When it comes to jewelry, jewelry is their be-all and end-all, the breath of life, and I've seen everything on them from dime-store junk to a stolen diamond lavaliere worth fifteen thousand dollars, but what they like best is gypsy jewelry—gold coins rigged to gold chains and worn as necklaces and bracelets and earrings. When I first started working on gypsies, the women wore quite a few foreign coins, some old, some new, and I'd see certain coins over and over, such as an Austrian four-ducat with Emperor Franz Josef's head on it that many of them used for earrings—it's a big coin but unusually thin and light. However, what I mostly saw were United States gold coins. For necklaces, they used eagles and double eagles—that is, ten- and twenty-dollar gold pieces. For bracelets and earrings, they used quarter eagles and half eagles—that is, two-fifty and five-dollar gold pieces. Then, in 1933, the government ordered everybody to exchange their domestic gold money for silver or paper, and what I think happened, I think the gypsies found some way to swap the bulk of their United States gold coins for Mexican gold coins, because ever since then that's mainly what I've seen the women wearing. They wear them and they hoard them. It isn't a bit unusual for women detectives or police matrons searching gypsy women to find dozens of Mexican gold coins sewed up in tucks running around the insides of their skirts. Every gypsy woman in the country, if she's got anything at all, she's got a few, and if she's a smart old woman who's made some big *bajours* in her time, she's liable to have a trunkful. There's no law against owning them, and the gold in them is purer even than the gold in United States gold coins, and you can pawn them anywhere or take them to a money dealer and get a good price. They come in several denominations, and the most popular among the gypsies is the fifty pesos. It's thick and heavy—it's worth sixty dollars in New York City at present—and it's just right for necklaces. I looked in on a gypsy wedding in a hall on the lower East Side one night last summer—Beethoven Hall, on East Fifth Street—and I observed a woman who was wearing three necklaces of fifty-pesos coins. She had nineteen on the top necklace, and twenty-one on the middle one, and twenty-three on the bottom one, and they overlapped on her bosom. She was a big, stout woman and she had some wine in her and it was hot in the hall and she was breathing heavily, and every time her bosom rose and fell the gold coins shifted their positions and glinted and gleamed."

CAPTAIN CAMPION got to his feet. "Before I go any further," he said, "there's something I'll just have to explain, or try to, and that's the divisions and subdivisions among these gypsies." He took a rolled-up paper from his briefcase and unrolled it and smoothed it out on the desk. It was a piece of wrapping paper about a yard long, and it was wrinkled and dog-eared and coffee-spotted, and drawn on it in ink was a chart consisting of lists of names enclosed in boxes. The boxes varied in size, and were arranged in groups, and lines linked some boxes to others. It was an untidy chart; scores of interlinear corrections had been made in the lists of names, and a number of corrections had been pasted on. In one place, a pasted-on correction had been crossed out and an arrow ran from it to a new correction, on the margin. Captain Campion studied the chart for several minutes, refreshing his memory. "This is the third one of these things I've drawn up," he remarked. "I wore out the others, correcting them and adding new information. Sometimes I wish I'd never heard the word gypsy." He sat back down.

"To continue," he said, "the nomad coppersmith gypsies are

pretty much alike in appearance, they speak the same dialect of the gypsy language, and they have the same general customs and beliefs, but during the years they've been in the United States they've gradually divided themselves into tribes. The principal tribes, and they're all represented here in the city, are the Russians, the Serbians, the Kalderash, the Argentines, the Argentinos, the Mexicans, the Machwaya, and the Greeks. Don't take some of these names at face value. As I told you, the nomads came mostly from Russia and Serbia. The Argentines are Serbians that roamed in Spain and South America before coming here. The Argentinos are also Serbians. After they left Serbia, and they'll give you twenty dates when that was, they went to Brazil and then came to the United States and then went to Argentina and then came back to the United States. The Mexicans are Russians and Serbians that go back and forth between Mexico and the United States. Their stamping grounds are Mexico City, three or four Texas cities, Philadelphia, New York City, and Boston. Like the Argentines and the Argentinos, they not only speak gypsy and English and a little Serbian and a little Russian but they also speak Spanish, and up around here, in recent years, they've specialized in skinning Puerto Ricans. The Kalderash are Russians and Serbians—in gypsy a *kalderash* is a coppersmith. The Machwaya are Serbians. They take their name from a region in West Serbia named Machva, where they roamed for generations upon generations before coming here. The Greeks are Russians who came here via Greece.

"Those are the tribes, but that's not the end of it. The tribes are subdivided into bands, or what we call bands—the gypsies call them *vitsas*. They pronounce it several ways—*vitsa, veetsa, witsa, weetsa*. In most cases, the *vitsa* is more important than the tribe. Some *vitsas* are small and compact. They consist of a few families that are closely related and that always travel together, and they generally have one leader. Other *vitsas* are big and loose and split up. Their members travel in families or in groups of families that are really *vitsas* within a *vitsa,* and about the only time the *vitsa* gathers together in anything like its full strength is when some prominent old gypsy dies and his or her family decides to hold a big funeral. The families in a *vitsa* may be scattered from Mexico City to some small town in Michigan, and it always surprises me how fast they spread the word around that So-and-So is dead and a big funeral is going to be held and when and where, but there's really nothing mysterious about it. One family knows where another family is, and gets word to it, even if they have to phone the mayor of the town or the chief of police and talk him into relaying the information, and that family knows where a couple of other families are, and gets word to them, and in a day or so, all over everywhere, everybody has been notified and everybody that can is on the way. In the big *vitsas,* there are generally several leaders, one of whom is the head leader, or king. Some *vitsas* hate other *vitsas,* and all of them are suspicious of each other; they trust each other about as much as they trust the police. If a woman in one *vitsa* pulls off a big *bajour* and the leader of a rival *vitsa* finds out about it, he's likely to walk in and demand a cut, else he'll inform, but don't worry, sooner or later, it may take years, the leader of the woman's *vitsa* will even matters up. Also, all of them are snobbish and superior; the people in each and every *vitsa* look down on the people in all the other *vitsas.* At the same time, all of them intermarry. The way gypsy marriages are arranged, a boy's parents have to buy him a wife, and they buy him the smartest girl they can afford, no matter what *vitsa* she's in. They may buy a girl from a family in another *vitsa* in their own tribe or from a family in a *vitsa* in some other tribe. The price depends on how good a money-maker the girl promises to be. If she can probably support a family telling fortunes but obviously doesn't have the nerve and the initiative to pull off *bajours,* she'll cost only a few hundred dollars; if she's cold-blooded and sharp and greedy, and if her mother and her aunts are good *bajour* women, she'll cost from two to five thousand.

"A few *vitsas* have descriptive names, such as the Saporeschti, or the Snakes; the Cuneschti, or the Knifers; and the Foosoo Yarri, or the Bean Eaters. But the majority are named after highly respected old gypsies in the past, patriarchs and matriarchs, all of whom, the way the gypsies tell it, were twice or three times as big as ordinary people and very rich and very wise and lived to be at least a hundred.

The biggest of the *vitsas* that hang out in New York City is a Russian *vitsa,* the Frinkuleschti, and it's named after Frinka, or Frinkulo, Mikhailovich. I once asked one of the leaders of the Frinkuleschti, a skinny little fellow with stomach ulcers named Frank Ranko, what did he know about Frinka, who was he. 'All I know,' Frank said, 'he was my father's grandfather or great-grandfather, and my father told me his father told him he was the biggest gypsy in Russia. He was seven feet three, and one time when he was quite an old man, up around a hundred and ten, they put him on some scales in a hay market and he weighed four hundred and sixty.' There've been twenty-five or thirty Frinkuleschti families holed up in the city ever since the depression, and a good many others come and go. You'll always find some in Brooklyn, usually in Red Hook, the Navy Yard district, or Williamsburg, but they mostly live within twenty blocks of each other in a section of the lower East Side that's the gypsiest section in the city. This section is bounded by Houston Street, the Bowery, Canal Street, Pike Street, and the river, and families belonging to a dozen or more *vitsas* live in there. The Frinkuleschti are poor gypsies. They can't spend much on wives for their sons, and every generation they get poorer. Sometimes a family gets down to the point where they're feeding the children on bread soaked in tea. The women tell fortunes but they're no good at *bajours*; they're just too clumsy. And the men are so clumsy I've known them to get in trouble stealing canned goods in supermarkets. The next-biggest *vitsa* is the Mineschti, another Russian *vitsa.* It's named after a woman, Mina Demetro. Mina lived to be a hundred and twenty. I've never heard the exact figures on how big she was, but I've heard she had thirty children, the last one when she was sixty-five. Some say she died in the far-distant past, centuries ago, and some say she died around 1880; some say she died in Russia and some say Serbia and some say Poland; every old gypsy in the Mineschti will give you a different story. Anyway, four brothers who were direct descendants of hers left Russia with their families in the late eighties and came to the United States via Canada and spread out and multiplied. Their names were Zlatcho, Groffo, Bortchi, and Wasso, and I've arrested children of theirs, and grandchildren, and

great-grandchildren. The richest of the *vitsas* is one named the Koleschti, only the people in it don't use that name much any more.
They prefer to use their tribe name. They belong to the Machwaya
tribe, and they're very proud of it. The Machwaya are West Coast
gypsies primarily, but in recent years they've been extending their
range and showing up in Reno, Las Vegas, the big cities in Texas,
the Florida resort cities, Atlantic City, and New York City. Their
women, the Machvankas, are the best-looking gypsy women in the
country, and the sharpest. The Machwaya are big-car gypsies. They
drive Cadillacs and Packards and Lincolns. The other gypsies have
a saying that if a Machwaya had to choose between a brand-new
Ford and an old wreck of a Cadillac that you'd have trouble even
getting it to start, he'd choose the Cadillac. There's usually at least
a dozen families of them in the city. They run *ofisas* the same as the
others, and they also run gypsy tearooms—not those places where
when a woman finishes her sandwiches and tea some woman dressed
up like a gypsy comes over and stares at the leaves in the bottom
of the cup and reels off some fortune-telling talk that she thinks
sounds like gypsy talk and then she gets a tip, but ratty little second-
floor-front places on side streets in the theatrical district and along
Eighth Avenue and Sixth Avenue and Third Avenue that look like
tearooms but don't make any real pretense of being tearooms beyond
they'll bring out one cup of tea solely for the purposes of tea-leaf
reading, and when the Machvanka finishes with the tea-leaf nonsense
she really starts talking to the woman, and if the woman listens and
keeps on listening and gets involved and comes back a time or two
the Machvanka will take everything she has but her back teeth
maybe and her corset and her eyeballs.

"I don't know how many gypsies there are in the United States.
The gypsies themselves certainly don't know, although gypsy leaders
are always willing to give you a figure, the first big round figure
that pops in their minds. I've seen a wide variety of estimates, but
it was all too obvious they were based on the wildest kind of
guesswork. The fact is nobody knows, and not only that, nobody
is capable of making a good guess. I don't even know how many
there are in New York City. There may be two hundred families

in the city tonight, or there may be less; there may be six hundred, or there may be more. Some families stay here years at a time, but they move so often from borough to borough and neighborhood to neighborhood that you couldn't begin to keep up with them; a family that was up some side street in the upper Bronx last week may be down on the lower end of Staten Island this week, down in Tottenville, or it may be over in Long Island City, or then again, it may be out in Akron, Ohio. Some families spend the winter here, or part of it, and some spend the summer, or part of it, and some come in and go out several times a year, and some might show up once in five years. Even to give the loosest kind of approximate figure how many are here at any one particular time, I'd just about as soon try to estimate how many English sparrows were sitting in a certain bush in Central Park at high noon last Tuesday. Furthermore, I'm not at all sure how many *vitsas* there are in the United States, and I'll confine my remarks to the ones I'm closely acquainted with. I'm closely acquainted with twenty-three, and that's because all or most or many or some of the families that belong to them either hang out in New York City a good part of the time or show up here fairly often. I'll give you the names of these *vitsas,* and the names of their principal families. Seven are Russian *vitsas*—the Frinkuleschti, the Mineschti, the Mitteleschti, the Gooneschti, the Goneschti, the Chookooriah, and the Lydakurschti, and the names of the principal families in them are Thompson, Demetro, Ranko, Ufie, Siganoff, Vladochakowski, Vlado, Costello, Mikhailovich, Mitchell, Magill, Mittilo, Merchon, Marko, Martino, Nicholas, Stokes, Guy, Petro, and Bimbo. Some of these names are Anglicized versions of Russian, Serbian, and gypsy names—after the Mikhailovich family got to be very big and branched out, for example, one branch changed Mikhail into Mitchell and another branch changed it into Magill. A number of names, such as Nicholas and Costello, are used by families in the *vitsas* of several tribes. Also, another thing, it's hard to make a flat statement about gypsies; you have to qualify practically everything you say, and I better mention that the families in two or three of the big *vitsas,* particularly the Mineschti, don't all belong to the same tribe, or claim they don't; some families in the Mineschti claim they are Russian and some claim they are Kalderash. As I said, sometimes I wish I'd never heard the word gypsy. We'll take up the Kalderash next. Six of the twenty-three *vitsas* are Kalderash—the Risturschti, the Jaikurschti, the Macholeschti, the Wankurschti, the Gureschti, and the Yotzurschti—and the names of the principal families in them are Stevens, Stevenson, Thompson, Ristick, Johnson, Marks, Evans, Wanko, Eli, Stanley, Demetro, Urich, Costello, Ephraim, and Morgan. Three are Serbian—the Lameschti, the Tooteschti, and the Rishtoni—and their principal family names are Evans, Lee, Stevens, Uwanawich, Miller, Marino, and Marinko. Three are Mexican—the Bokurschti, the Chokurschti, and the Yonkurschti—and their principal family names are Flores, Spiro, Costello, Yonko, Steve, and John. One is Machwaya—the Koleschti—and the principal family names in it are Adams, Uwanawich, Marks, Williams, Lee, Yankovich, Stevens, Miller, and George. One is Greek—the Poopeschti. It takes its name from an old hellcat of a fortune-teller named Poopa. It's a small *vitsa,* and its principal family name is Kaslov. One is Argentine— the Cuneschti—and the names of the principal families in it are Montez, George, and Miller. One is Argentino, but it doesn't have a *vitsa* name; the families in it simply call themselves the Argentinos. Their names are Christo, Miller, Toney, and Nicholas.

"When it comes to first names, most of these gypsies have two. A man may be Joe this or John that when he's dealing with *gajos,* or non-gypsies, but when he's among his own he's Uwano or Mitya or Spirako, or some such. Likewise, a woman who may be known to the police in sixteen cities as Annie this or Rosie that, when she's home she's Repanka or Troka or Pavlena. To complicate matters, a good many have gypsy nicknames. Take a man we've often had dealings with whose *gajo* name is George Adams. I don't know his proper gypsy name, and he himself, if he was asked, he'd probably have to stop and think. He's always Bongo Nock, or Broken Nose, and if you'll look up his photograph in the gallery in the squad office—look under Male Gypsies, File 1, Tray 1—you'll see why. To further complicate matters, most of the women and many of the men have a string of aliases—*gajo* aliases and gypsy aliases.

"Now I want to give you a few details concerning the way gypsies live in the city, and then I'll describe the *bajour,* and then we'll go get some coffee. The first thing to remember, you'll almost always find gypsies living close to the street. They prefer to live in old stores, or in first-floor-front flats in tenements, or in parlor-front flats in brownstones. I've very seldom found them above the second floor. I used to think they wanted to be as close as possible to Mother Earth, but all it is, they want to be where people passing by can see them who might be interested in having their fortunes told. It's a form of advertising. More often than not, two or three families live together and operate an *ofisa* on shares. If they're prosperous, they may have the *ofisa* at one address and live at another, but in most cases they live right in the *ofisa,* back behind the curtained-off fortune-telling booths. If it's a store, they do their best to conceal this; it's illegal to live in a store. When a family or two or three families travelling together arrive in the city, they pile in with other families in their *vitsa,* if any are here, and stay with them until they can rent a place of their own, and if none are here, they ride around during the day looking at old stores with 'FOR RENT' signs on them and sleep in their cars at night. It's sometimes very hard for them to find a place; most landlords have to be tricked into renting to them. They like a location that's conspicuous but not too conspicuous; they're well aware that women don't want to be seen entering or leaving a gypsy place. What they like best is a low-rent store in a run-down block right off a busy crosstown street, such as Fourteenth or Twenty-third. I've known a Machwaya family to pay six hundred a month for a good location, but that's unusual, even for them, and the others won't pay anywhere near that. When they find a store that suits them, the man gypsy among them who looks least like a gypsy goes to the landlord or the renting agent and says he wants to open a rug store in the place, or sometimes it's a mill-remnants store or a lampshade store or a toy store. If they can come to terms, the gypsy puts down a month's rent and gets a receipt and a key. Next morning, two or three cars with trunks and bedrolls strapped on top of them park in front of the store, or maybe it's two or three station wagons, and what at first glance looks like a thousand gypsies get out and start carrying things in. They're systematic. First they bring in some folding chairs and some folding tables and some *gonyas*. A *gonya* is a pair of capacious big canvas bags joined with a strap that fits over the shoulder, and they hold a surprising amount; if a gypsy woman was determined to, she could stuff most of Macy's into one of them. The women do two-thirds of the work. They stand on the chairs and hammer nails in the walls and run wires from the nails. Then they take some curtains and draperies from the *gonyas,* yards and yards and yards of them, and hang them on the wires, dividing the store into a maze of rooms and booths. They may decorate the walls up front with some of those fake tapestries that auction joints sell on boardwalks, or they may tack up one of those pictures that they have sign painters paint for them on oilcloth—a giant human palm, or a phrenological head, or a zodiac, or a crescent and star. Next they take out a stack of moldy old paper-backed palmistry, horoscope and dream books that they've been carrying around for years, and arrange them in the front window. That's a form of camouflage. Fortune-telling is illegal in the city, and when gypsies are brought into court for it, it's their practice to screech and scream and swear to God they didn't tell the woman's fortune, far from it, they just sold her a book and showed her how to use it, if she thought she was having her fortune told she must be crazy. They work fast. They can have an *ofisa* rigged up and ready for business in an hour, and later on, if they pull off a *bajour* and have to get out in a hurry, they can unrig it down in much less time than that. They sometimes buy a couple of overstuffed chairs from a junk store and put them up front to sit on while waiting for customers, but they always leave them behind when they move on. The last things they carry in are their trunks and bedrolls—that is, if they're going to live in the *ofisa*. The bedrolls are quilts stuffed with feathers; they spread them on the floor at night and sleep between them, and in the morning they roll them up and pile them in a corner. Quite often, in one corner, they put up something, it's like a little shrine. They put a box in the corner, a box or an orange crate, and they stand a photograph on it of the last person in the family group who died.

The photograph is in a frame with a prop in back. It generally shows the person lying in state in his or her coffin. Gypsies go in for such photographs—they hire photographers to come to the funeral parlor and make them; they have them made in color, or tinted. They stand icons on both sides of the photograph—pictures of saints, Orthodox Catholic saints. And they stand a candle in front of it, usually it's a big, thick candle trimmed down at the base and fitted into the mouth of a quart milk bottle, and on certain days connected with the dead person they light the candle. For cooking facilities, if there isn't a gas stove in the place, they plug in a pair of hot plates, one for the goulash pot and one to boil water on for tea. That's the backbone of their diet—goulash and tea. That, and candy bars. They spend a good part of their time sitting around drinking tea. They make good tea, good and hot and strong, and then they spoil it. They drink it from glasses, and they not only put slices of lemon in it, they put slices of orange or apple or peach or pear in it, or most any other fruit that's in season. I've seen them take a ripe plum, one of those big purple plums, and poke holes in it with a fork until the juice was dripping out and drop it in a glass of tea. I've seen them drop strawberries in and press them against the side of the glass with the spoon until the tea was red. I've seen them put jam in their tea, spoonfuls of jam. And the amount of sugar they put in, it's a wonder they have any teeth at all, instead of which they have beautiful, strong, shiny white teeth; their teeth are far and away the healthiest things about them. If the women are making money, the men eat out quite a lot. Oh, sometimes they take the women along. They mainly eat in two kinds of places. They eat in Jewish restaurants on the lower East Side, the kind that have a sign in the window saying 'RUMANIAN BROILINGS,' and they eat in Italian restaurants, not the kind of Italian restaurants Americans know anything about but places in Italian neighborhoods, mostly in basements, called *capozzelle* places, where they specialize in sheepsheads, or *capozzelle,* that they buy in slaughterhouses for next to nothing and saw in two and broil, and various inner organs, such as lungs and tripe.

"Out on the road, for all I know, gypsies may be happy-go-lucky, rolling along, not a care in the world, the way gypsies are supposed to be, but here in the city, my experience with them, they're not happy-go-lucky. They're always complaining about the way they feel, and they've always got something; if it isn't pinkeye, it's the itch. One thing you'll always notice in the trash that gypsies leave behind anyplace they've been living is a lot of empty patent-medicine bottles. They're afraid of doctors, and they're always running to the drugstore and asking the druggist to give them something to settle their stomachs, or their nerves—they've got a pain here, a pain there, what's good for it. And one reason they understand super-stitious people, they're about as superstitious as they can be them-selves. They see signs everywhere, signs and warnings, especially the women. Every so often gypsy women have dreams that terrify them, the way they interpret them, and next day they keep the whole family in—nobody's allowed to go out and nobody's allowed to come in; you can knock and knock, and you can see them moving around in there, but they won't come to the door. Sometimes one of them has a premonition, and the family suddenly packs up and moves. And one thing you're always sure to find when you search a gypsy is a good-luck charm of some kind. There's an old building on the Bowery just below Canal, 42 Bowery, that's had a dozen *ofisas* in it in the last six or seven years, and they've all been run by women in the Bimbo family—some of old man Tene Bimbo's daughters and daughters-in-law and granddaughters; he's got an army of them. A pair of Bimbos will open an *ofisa* in there and run it awhile and all of a sudden they're gone, and it'll be empty a few weeks or months, and then another pair of Bimbos will turn up and take it over. They draw most of their customers from the Italian neighborhood down around here, the Mulberry Street neighborhood. They always keep a couple of cardboard signs in the window, and if you go in and they suspect you're a detective, they'll snatch them out and tear them up. One says, 'DREAM BOOKS. LADY FROM JE-RUSALEM. SPEAKS SEVEN LANGUAGES.' The other is in Italian, and it says, 'VIENI QUI CHE DIVINA LA FORTUNA,' which means 'Come here that I may tell your fortune.' There's an old Italian woman down here who peddles evil-eye charms. She has a little satchel that hangs from her neck and opens up into a tray, and at night she makes the rounds of the Grotta Azzurra and the Villa Penza and the Antica Roma and the Nuova Napoli and Angelo's and the other restaurants in the neighborhood that attract people from uptown, and goes from table to table showing the charms; people buy them for ornaments or souvenirs. One night I was standing in a doorway on Mulberry Street, working on a job that had nothing to do with gypsies. I was back in the shadows, watching the street, and I saw two women approaching each other over on the opposite side. One was the old charm woman making the rounds with her tray, and the other was one of the gypsy women from the *ofisa* on the Bowery, one of the Bimbos. Just as they were about to go past each other, the gypsy woman stopped the old charm woman and bent over and looked in her tray, and the two of them stood there several minutes with their heads close together, talking very seriously, and then the gypsy picked out a charm and paid for it, and I thought to myself, 'I've seen everything now.'"

"Taking in each other's washing," said Detective Kane.

"Either that," said Captain Campion, "or the blind leading the blind. One reason they're so superstitious, they're gypsies, it's the atmosphere they live in, and another reason, they're illiterate. They don't believe in education, and they won't send their children to school unless they're forced to. I've had them tell me that going to school is all right for *gajos,* they've been going for hundreds of years and they're used to it, but gypsies aren't used to it and the strain it puts on their minds is liable to lead to epileptic fits. I doubt if more than one out of ten of them knows how to read and write, but arithmetic is something else again; all of them seem to know enough arithmetic to take care of themselves, it's a mystery to me how they learn it.

"As far as religion, the great majority of them are Russian Orthodox or Serbian Orthodox. The Russians go to two small churches in Russian neighborhoods—St. Peter and St. Paul, which is on Seventh Street, over between First Avenue and Avenue A, and Carpatho-Russian Holy Trinity, which is on Fourth Street, over near the East River. The Serbians go to St. Sava's, which is on West

Twenty-sixth Street; it's the Serbian Orthodox cathedral. I've given up trying to understand how gypsies feel about religion. It seems to be a matter each one makes up his own rules. Some get married by a priest, and some don't. Some have their children baptized, and some don't. Very few ever go to confession. The Orthodox people bring bottles to church on the Feast of Saint John the Baptist— old medicine bottles, old whiskey bottles, old bottles of every description—and the priest fills them with holy water and the people take them home, and a good many gypsies show up that day, the most that ever do, only where the ordinary person brings one bottle, the gypsy brings two or three. A good many also show up on Easter Eve and Easter. And now and then a gypsy woman shows up and buys a candle and lights it before some particular icon. Otherwise, the bulk of them, the principal contact they have with religion is at funerals. Gypsies have the regulation Orthodox funeral services, but the heart of their funerals is at the grave. They open the coffin at the grave, even if they've already had it open at the services, and all of them crowd around it to take a last look, and then they begin to cry out in the gypsy language and moan and wail, the men and the women. The women sometimes let themselves go to such an extent it's pitiful; I've seen them run over and fall on their knees and butt their heads against tombstones, and when they stood up they'd be so dazed they'd walk around in circles and stumble into each other. And before they close the coffin for good, they drop coins in it. And after it's been lowered into the grave and the gravediggers start shovelling the dirt in, they throw coins into the grave. One of the wildest sights I've ever seen, it was in a cemetery over in New Jersey late one afternoon in February, and it was bitter cold and windy, and two gravediggers were working on one side of a gypsy grave, shovelling the dirt in, and the gypsies were crowded together on the other side, moaning and crying out, some with babies in their arms, and an old man among them was leaning over pouring wine into the grave from a gallon jug that was resting on his shoulder, cheap red wine, and one moment the wind blew some of the wine on the gravediggers and the next moment it blew some on the gypsies. After a grave has been filled, they usually spread a cloth on the ground nearby and have a funeral feast. If the family is prosperous, they'll have cold turkeys and hams and legs of lamb; if they're poor, they'll have cold cuts. And if it rains, they'll put up a tent.

"Back around 1900, gypsies started burying in Evergreen Cemetery in Elizabeth, New Jersey, and some still do, but during the thirties the Linden Cemetery in Linden, New Jersey, became more popular, and now it's used by gypsies all over the East. Evergreen is a beautiful old cemetery; it's like the deep woods, it has so many big old trees in it, and that appeals to gypsies. Linden doesn't have as many trees, but it's easier to get to; U.S. 1 passes right by it. The burial of a prominent gypsy will draw a couple of hundred cars loaded with gypsies to Linden, and the cars will have licenses on them from a dozen states. Steve Kaslov is buried over there, the old king of the Poopeschti. He's lying in a two-thousand-dollar coffin, and he's got a red granite tombstone on top of him that cost six hundred dollars, and a photograph of him covered with some kind of plastic material that you can see through is cemented to the tombstone; he's got a grin on his face. And Uwano Ufie, who was better known as Cockeye Johnny Nikanov, is buried over there. Cockeye Johnny was one of the Frinkuleschti kings, and he was quite powerful during the depression. He could read a little, and he learned the relief regulations inside out, and he was the scourge of the Welfare Department; there wasn't a regulation in the book that he couldn't get around. It was his dream to attract all the gypsies in North and South America to New York City and get them on relief, and then he'd become the supreme ruler of the whole lot of them, the Emperor of the Gypsies. He died during a heat wave in the summer of 1944; he overexerted himself carrying a heavy watermelon home to his grandchildren and had a heart attack. And Marta Evans is buried over there, who used to be the queen of the gypsies in Philadelphia. And Little Nina Marks is buried over there, the most beautiful gypsy girl I ever saw. Little Nina was an Argentino married to a Kalderash. She was one of the best of the gypsy pickpockets, and she was very good at what the gypsies call winking at a man. If a man stopped in front of her *ofisa* and stood there, peering in, she'd size him up, and if he looked as if he could be taken, she'd get up from her chair and bend over very low and rearrange the books in the show window and let the man get a good look at her and then she'd give him a wink and he'd come right in and she'd lead him into one of the booths and they'd start wrestling around and while they were wrestling she'd pick his pockets and then she'd scream rape and her husband would rush in with a knife and start slashing the air, just barely missing the man, and the man would leap out of the booth and run like a rat. She died of cancer of the breast in Memorial Hospital in 1952, when she was only twenty-seven, and she's buried on the side of a hill facing U.S. 1, under a horse-chestnut tree. And old Matrona Nicholas is over there, and Repanka Zlotkovich and Elaina Thompson and Sabinka Miller and Mary Demetro who grabbed my necktie in court one day and jerked the breath out of me and Birka Vlado who used to smoke a pipe, and dozens of other women that I spent a good part of the last twenty-five years tracking down and keeping under surveillance and apprehending and interrogating. Some of them, the first time I saw them, they were young women, young or just getting middle-aged, and they were walking around with their heads held high, wearing flashy skirts and switching their tails, and the last time I saw them, they were old and ugly and full of spite. Sometimes, on a Sunday afternoon, I drive over there and look at their graves and see if any new ones have turned up. There's women lying over there that I stood in doorways across the street from their *ofisas* many a cold night waiting and watching for the right moment to go in and nail them, and they despised me and I despised them, but I knew them very well, and I remember so many things about them, and when I look at their tombstones and read their names and dates, after all they're dead and gone, I must admit it makes me sad."

CAPTAIN CAMPION stood up again, and put the *vitsa* chart back in his briefcase. Then he sat down. "Now we come to the *bajour,*" he said. "The first thing I want to impress on you is that the majority of those who visit gypsies for any purpose at all—to have their fortunes told, to seek advice, to have a dream interpreted, to ask for a good number to play in the numbers game, just to have somebody to talk to, or just blind curiosity—are women. And the great majority of those who end up as *bajour* victims are women between the ages of forty and fifty-five, a high proportion of whom are in the change of life. After you've interrogated a few of these victims, and I've interrogated hundreds, you begin to realize that they have things in common. Most of them are unhappily married or they've never been married or they're divorced or they're widows. Most of them are deeply depressed, and they either don't know why, just everything in general, or they lay it to something in their past—it might be something very complicated, or it might be something as simple as they once had an illegitimate baby and let it be adopted and never saw it again. Most of them are worried about their health—the fact is most of them are more than halfway convinced they have cancer. Most of them have a passion to talk about themselves, a passion to confess—it's probably the strain they're under, and they probably don't know they're doing it, but they talk about themselves all the time, or all the time they can get anybody to listen; they just can't stop. And most of them, they may be smart in some ways, but they're fundamentally ignorant; if it's presented to them the right way, they'll believe anything. And a good many are the kind of women who if they go out at night to walk a dog they'll unerringly head for some vacant lot or some dark corner in a park, or if they have to be out late and go home alone they'll take shortcuts through blocks that the ordinary person wouldn't go through at that hour fully armed, or if they're sitting in a barroom and it gets late and some stranger on the next bar stool offers to see them home they'll go right along.

"The second thing I want to impress on you is that gypsy women are shrewd, really shrewd, and don't make any mistake about that. When they're tiny little girls, their mothers and grandmothers and aunts start drilling the facts of life into them, and as soon as they're old enough to keep quiet and be still they're allowed to hide behind the curtains and eavesdrop while *gajo* women tell their innermost secrets; that's part of their training. By the time they're twenty, they're well acquainted with the fears that lurk around in the minds of middle-aged women, and the crazy ideas, and by the time they're middle-aged themselves they can just look at a woman and observe the expression in her eyes and the set of her mouth and the sags and wrinkles in her face and the way she holds herself and find out a good deal about her past, particularly her past in relation to men.

"The third thing I want to impress on you is that gypsy women are very skillful at making ordinary, everyday objects seem highly mysterious. The *bajour* is a flexible confidence game, and it's up to the individual gypsy's imagination how she does it. However, in recent years, in and around New York City, the majority of the women have been doing it the same way. They've been doing it with an egg, an ordinary white egg.

"Usually, when a woman enters an *ofisa* for the first time, she's apprehensive. 'Come right in, dear,' the gypsy says, and talks soothingly to her and tells her what a pretty dress she has on, so becoming, and leads her back into one of the booths. There's two chairs in there, and a little table with a candle sticking up on it about a foot and a half long and as big around as your wrist, and that's all. Every picture of a gypsy fortune-teller I've ever seen, she was gazing into a crystal ball, but I've never once seen a crystal ball in an *ofisa*. The gypsy lights the candle, and she and the woman sit facing each other, and the gypsy takes the woman's right hand and opens it and gently strokes the palm, smoothing it out, and all this time the woman is talking, telling her troubles. The gypsy concentrates on the lines in the woman's palm and doesn't appear to be listening, but she's listening; she's trying to decide if the woman is worth working on, and if the woman slows down, she asks her a question or two that encourages her to talk some more. If the gypsy decides the woman has too much sense to fall for a *bajour* and all she can hope to get out of her is the fortune-telling fee, she doesn't waste much time on her. She studies her right palm, and her left one, too, if the woman is willing to double the fee, and then she gives her the age-old fortune-telling rigamarole: a little about the past, a little about the future; she should watch this, she should be careful about that, she shouldn't make any important decisions on Tuesdays. The gypsy may go through this procedure with a long succession of women, and months may go by, and then one day she's staring at a woman's palm and the woman is talking on and on—her husband died six weeks ago last Friday and now she's all alone, there isn't a single remaining soul who cares what happens to her; sometimes she sees him in a dream, and he's sitting up in his coffin and his eyes are wide open and he's looking straight at her; she wasn't as good to him as she should've been, and her heart is broken; she hasn't slept more than a couple of hours a night since he passed away, and she doesn't see how she lives on the little she eats; she wishes she could take back some of the things she said to him, but it's too late now; he was good to her, and she didn't appreciate it; he left her everything he had, and she doesn't deserve it, she doesn't deserve a penny of it—and suddenly the gypsy knows she has a victim. She looks up from the woman's palm, and interrupts her. 'Have you noticed any unusual pains lately, dear,' she says, 'any pains you never noticed before?' or 'Come a little closer, dear,' she says, 'and let me look at that mole on your cheek.' Then she goes back to studying the woman's palm. She studies it for five minutes or so. 'Let me see your other hand, dear,' she says. She studies the left palm awhile, and then she glances from one to the other, comparing the lines, and finally she looks up and says, 'I don't want to scare you, dear—we may be able to do something about it—but I see something bad in your hand. I see something very bad.' 'What is it?' 'It's a good thing you came in here today,' the gypsy says. 'The spirits must've sent you to me.' 'What did you see in my hand?' the woman asks. 'Tell me what you saw.' 'I can't tell you now,' the gypsy says. 'There's a certain other thing I have to look into, and then I'll tell you. I want you to go home now, and on your way home I want you to buy a fresh white egg, and tonight I want you to get out the three warmest blankets you have and put them on your bed, and then I want you to get undressed and get under the blankets and lie on your back, and then I want you to take the egg and hold it on your navel with both hands clasped over it, and I want you to lie there that way until the egg feels warm, real warm, and then I want you to wrap it in a white handkerchief, and tomorrow morning I want you to bring it to me. And I don't want you to pay me anything, now or ever; in cases like yours, we work in close connection with the spirits, and we don't take money. And I want to warn you, if you say one word about this to anybody, even a priest or a minister, you'll break my power so far as you're concerned and I won't be able to help you, and you better not let that happen, dear, because the spirits must've sent you to me, they must've meant for me to help you, and if they did, I'm the only one in the world that *can* help you. I'm your only hope.'

"If the gypsy has the woman sized up right, she's back at the *ofisa* bright and early next morning, and she has the egg with her, all wrapped up in a handkerchief. They go into the booth, and the woman tries to give the egg to the gypsy; she wants to get rid of it. 'Just a moment,' the gypsy says. 'I have to use a fresh candle for this.' She steps out of the booth and goes in back to get the candle, and while she's back there she hides a tiny little object between two of the fingers of her left hand. She returns to the booth and stands the candle up and lights it. Then she takes the egg from the woman. She unwraps the egg and holds it and gives the handkerchief back to the woman and tells her to spread it on the table, which the woman does. Then the gypsy breaks the egg and empties it on the handkerchief, and while she's doing so she executes some sleight of hand and the object between her fingers drops out, and when she takes her hands away it's lying on the yolk of the egg—sometimes it's a ball of tangled hair, sometimes it's a knotted-up piece of string with some kind of stringy green matter clinging to it, and sometimes it's a hairy little devil's head."

Captain Campion dug around in his briefcase and brought out a small cardboard box that had originally contained paper clips and opened it and placed it on the desk. "Such as this," he said. In the box, on a wad of cotton, lay a devil's head carved out of ivory. It was approximately an inch and a quarter long and three-quarters of an inch wide. The devil's horns were down-turned over his forehead, his eyes were shut, his cheeks were sunken, his mouth was fixed in an agonized grin, and he had a shock of bristly black hair. "When I first saw this thing," Captain Campion said, "I was pretty sure it wasn't carved by a gypsy, and I took it uptown and showed it to a pawnbroker who's an expert on queer jewelry and bric-a-brac, and he said it's a type of ivory miniature that was quite popular in Germany during the latter part of the last century. They turn up now and then in antique stores and curiosity shops and pawnshops. When a gypsy woman buys one, she cuts off some of her own hair and glues it on the top and the back. We found this one in the possession of a Kalderash *bajour* woman named Linka Stevens. That flaky stuff sticking to the hair is dried-up egg yolk. The last time Linka used it, she took seven thousand nine hundred dollars from an old Irish-woman, a hotel maid. The old woman had worked in cheap side-street hotels in New York City for over forty years, and it was her life's savings." Captain Campion closed the box and put it back in his briefcase.

"To continue," Captain Campion said, "the gypsy and the woman stand there a few moments and look at the little object on the yolk of the egg, and then the gypsy says, 'Let's sit down, dear.' They sit down, and the gypsy says, 'It's just as I thought, dear. You've got a curse on you. You've got something growing inside you.' 'Is it a tumor?' the woman asks. 'We won't talk about what it is,' the gypsy says, but the woman interrupts her. 'Is it cancer?' she asks. 'I told you we won't talk about what it is,' the gypsy says. 'We'll talk about what we're going to do about it. You've got some money in the bank, haven't you, dear?' The woman says she has. 'That may be where the curse is coming from,' the gypsy says. 'It usually is. Back before you put that money in the bank, you or your husband or whoever put it in, some of it might've passed through the hands of a man who ruined his own child, or some of it might've passed through the hands of Antichrist, or, the way it often happens, a man might've killed himself making it. The actual same money may not be in the bank any more, but the curse is there, waiting; it's in among all that dirty, filthy, stinking money piled up down there in the vaults of the bank, waiting. And it'll jump to any money that replaces the actual same money; it'll jump to any money that you draw out. I want you to go home now and get your bankbook, and then I want you to go to the bank and draw out a small bill—a five-dollar bill will do—and then I want you to buy another white egg and a white handkerchief, and then I want you to bring the five-dollar bill and the egg and the handkerchief back here to me.

While you're gone, I'm going to burn this handkerchief and the egg I broke and that thing that's on the egg. I'm going to put them in a bucket and pour kerosene on them and burn them.'

"When the woman returns, she opens her handbag and starts to give the bill and the egg and the handkerchief to the gypsy, but the gypsy backs away. 'Oh, no,' she says. 'I don't want to touch that money.' She leads the woman into the booth. 'Now, dear,' she says, 'I want you to wrap the five-dollar bill around the egg, and then I want you to wrap the handkerchief around it, and then I want you to lay it on the floor, over in the corner.' Which the woman does. 'I'm going to leave you in here by yourself a little while,' the gypsy says. 'Just sit there and be quiet until I come back.' Fifteen minutes go by, a half hour, an hour, and then the gypsy comes back. 'You can pick up the egg now, dear,' she says. 'Spread the handkerchief on the table, and put that five-dollar bill back in your handbag and give the egg to me.' The woman does as she's told, and the gypsy bends over the table and breaks the egg and empties it on the handkerchief, and once again there's that little object lying on the yolk of the egg. 'This is no surprise to me,' the gypsy says. 'The money you have in the bank has a curse on it, just as I expected, and it's responsible for that thing that's growing inside you, and there's only one thing you can do. You've got to go to the bank and draw out that money and bring it here, and I've got to hold it in my right hand and get in connection with the spirits and ask them to throw the curse off.' The woman comes to her senses for a moment. 'What will happen if I don't?' she asks. The gypsy shrugs her shoulders. 'Look, dear,' she says, 'I'm not getting anything out of this, and it doesn't make any difference to me what you do. The spirits are using me, and I'm doing my part. If you do your part, the spirits will throw the curse off the money and that thing that's growing inside you will dissolve and disappear. If you don't do your part, the spirits won't hold me responsible for what happens to you.' 'Do you know what will happen to me?' the woman asks. 'Yes, dear,' the gypsy says, 'I know. One morning before long you'll wake up and you'll notice you have a gumboil, that's the first thing you'll notice, and by and by you'll have dozens of gumboils, and then your gums will grow soft and your teeth will come loose and drop out two or three at a time, you'll spit them out like cherry pits, and then a goiter will grow on your neck and big, hairy moles will sprout out all over you, and then your bones will start to rot and clog your blood—if you were to cut your hand around this time and rub some of the blood between your fingers, it would feel gritty—and pretty soon you won't be able to sit in a chair, let alone stand on your feet, and you'll have to go to bed for good, and then your lungs will start drying up, and then one day your heart will race a few minutes and stop and race a few more minutes and stop again and suddenly a pain will plunge through you like a flash of lightning, and that will be the end.' 'Do I have to draw out all the money?' the woman asks. 'You have to draw out every cent of it,' the gypsy says. 'And if the man at the bank asks you any questions why you're drawing it out, tell him it's a confidential matter, you're investing in some real estate. And tell him to give it to you in large denominations, such as fifties and hundreds, so it won't be such a nuisance to handle.'

"There are several ways of bringing a *bajour* to a conclusion. The two most frequently used are the sew-up and the burn-up. If the gypsy isn't quite sure how much power she has over the woman and feels she'd better work fast, she does a sew-up. When the woman returns from the bank with her money, the gypsy takes her into the booth and tells her to sit down at the table. 'Don't worry, dear,' she says. 'You're doing the right thing, and it'll all be over in a few minutes.' Then she gets a needle and thread and a piece of coarse white cloth cut into the shape of paper money, only a little wider and a little longer. She tells the woman to lay the stack of bills flat on the cloth, and then she tells her to fold them over once, both the cloth and the bills, with the cloth on the outside, which the woman does, and then the gypsy sews up the three open sides of the cloth, enclosing the bills in a snug little bag. That's the basic meaning of the word 'bajour'—a little bag of money. The gypsies claim it's an old gypsy word, but I had a Serbian Orthodox priest tell me it's really a Serbian word, 'bozur,' that the gypsies borrowed and changed; 'bozur' means a beautiful flower, and it can be extended to mean anything unusually beautiful. The gypsy clutches the bag in her right hand and gets down on her knees on the floor. 'Kneel down beside me, dear,' she tells the woman, 'and hold my left hand and close your eyes. While I'm talking to the spirits, I want you to pray in your own way. I want you to pray that I get the right answer.' The woman joins the gypsy on the floor, and then the gypsy begins to jibber-jabber in the gypsy language. She talks, and then she chants, and then she talks, and then she chants, and it sounds as if she's begging and beseeching. The gypsy has two slit pockets in the right side of her skirt. One pocket is empty. While she's jibber-jabbering, she slips the money bag into this pocket. In the other pocket, she has an assortment of bags similar to the money bag, only they're phonies; they vary in thickness, and all they contain are pieces of crackly bond paper cut to paper-money size. She feels around in this pocket and picks out a phony bag that corresponds in thickness to the money bag, and she takes it out and holds on to it. She continues to talk to the spirits for a few minutes, and then she suddenly lets out a cry of joy and rises to her feet and pulls the woman up with her. 'Now, dear,' she says, 'I'll have to ask you to undo your dress, or take it off, so I can get at your underclothes.' The woman does as she's told, and the gypsy sews the phony bag to the woman's slip or whatever kind of underclothes she has on. 'Now, dear,' she says, 'I want you to go straight home and lie down, and as it begins to grow dark the curse will begin to leave you. It won't leave you all at once. It'll leave you gradually, and at midnight it'll be gone entirely. It'll take longer for the curse to leave the money. I want you to wear this slip with the bag on it every day for the next seven days, and I want you to sleep with it under your pillow. On the eighth day, the money will be clean, and you can take it out of the bag and put it back in the bank. Only I want to warn you, if you open the bag beforehand, or if you say one word about this matter to anybody, if you even hint at it, the money will turn to plain white paper and the curse will jump back on you.'

"That's the sew-up, and it's the easiest way. However, if the gypsy feels she has the woman completely in her power, she does it differently; she does a burn-up. It's more trouble, but it makes a deeper impression on the woman, and in the long run it's safer— it's very hard for us to get a conviction on a burn-up. In most cases, the victim won't go near the police unless some relative finds out what's happened and forces her to, and that's usually weeks later, and then, if we knock ourselves out and succeed in apprehending the gypsy, half the time the victim will back down at the last minute and refuse to go into court and testify. A burn-up takes longer than a sew-up. 'Look, dear,' the gypsy says when the woman returns from the bank, 'I've got to hold that money while I'm talking to the spirits, and there's always a danger the curse will jump from the money to me, and I don't want to touch it with my naked hand. I'm going to give you this handkerchief, and I want you to take that stack of bills and roll it up and lay it in the middle of the handkerchief, and then I want you to pull the corners of the hand-kerchief together and tie them in two good strong knots.' The woman starts to do this, but the gypsy isn't overlooking anything. 'Just a moment, dear,' she says. 'Open your handbag and get that five-dollar bill that you wrapped around the egg, and put it in the handkerchief, too.' The woman does as she's told. When she's finished, the gypsy clutches the knotted-up handkerchief in her right hand, and gets down on her knees. She chants awhile in gypsy, and then she goes into a kind of self-induced fit. I've heard dozens of victims describe this fit. The gypsy whimpers and moans. She grinds her teeth. She beats her forehead on the floor. She tears her blouse to rags. She scratches her face until it bleeds, and it's real blood; I've arrested gypsy women several days after a burn-up and I've seen the scratches. She throws her head back and rolls her eyes and shudders and gargles, as if she's choking. One moment she's walking on her hands and knees and quivering all over, and the next moment she's flat on the floor, thrashing around. And while she's thrashing around, she slips the handkerchief with the money in it into one of the slit pockets in her skirt, and she takes another knotted-up handkerchief from the other pocket. It's a phony, of course; it contains some more of those pieces of paper cut to paper-money size. Presently, she wears herself out, and lies face forward on the floor, gasping. Then she gets up, and she's dusty and dirty and sweaty, and her blouse is hanging down in rags, and her eyes are wild, and her face is all scratched and bloody. She totters over to her chair and sits down. 'I've got good news, dear,' she says, 'and I've got bad news. The spirits will draw the curse off you, but first you'll have to destroy the money. You'll have to burn it up.' This horrifies the woman, but the gypsy is ready for her. She reminds her about that thing that's growing inside her, and goes on from that to gumboils and big, hairy moles and rotting bones, and all the rest of it, and this time she uses her imagination to the utmost. Pretty soon the woman becomes reconciled. Whereupon the gypsy brings in a bucket about half full of splinters and coal, on which she sprinkles some kerosene. She starts a fire, and waits until it's burning good, and then she pours some kerosene on the phony knotted-up handkerchief. She saturates it with kerosene. Then she hands it to the woman, and tells her to throw it in the bucket. 'You have to do this part yourself,' the gypsy says. The woman throws it in, and it blazes up and starts burning. Then the gypsy tells the woman to kneel, and she kneels beside her. 'You pray your way,' she says, 'and I'll pray my way.' By and by the gypsy gets up and looks in the bucket. She makes sure the handkerchief and its contents have been destroyed, and then she pours some water on the fire. 'Now, dear,' she says, 'I want you to go straight home and lie down, and as it begins to grow dark the curse will begin to leave you. It'll leave you gradually, and at midnight it'll be gone entirely. Only I want to warn you, if you ever say anything to anybody about this matter the rest of your life, the split second the words are out of your mouth the curse will jump back on you and your bones will begin to rot.'

"Usually, at the conclusion of a *bajour,* whether it's been a sew-up or a burn-up, the woman is in a state of shock, she hardly knows where she is, and the gypsy has to take her by the arm and lead her to the door. The moment she leaves, the gypsies start packing. It doesn't take them long. In half an hour, or even less, they're out and gone."

(1955)

# The Deaf-Mutes Club

*T*HE UNION LEAGUE OF THE DEAF, Inc., is a social club
exclusively for deaf-mutes. It was founded in 1886 and has four
hundred members. A man I know, a linotype operator for a morning
newspaper, is a member. A couple of weeks ago he sent me a letter
of introduction to Mr. Samuel Frankenheim, the club's historian.
"Mr. Frankenheim is a retired Wall Street man and he kills a lot
of time around the Union League," the linotype operator wrote in
a note accompanying the letter. "If you'd be interested in writing
an article about the club, he would be glad to see you. Drop in
most any afternoon and he will be on hand. Take along a note pad,
as you will have to write out your questions to him. He will reply
the same way. In conversing with him, avoid the term 'deaf-mute'
as much as possible. I don't mind it, and he probably doesn't, but
many do. The club used to be called the Deaf-Mutes' Union League,
but five years ago the name was changed because of this. Nearly all
so-called deaf-mutes have normal vocal organs and can speak at
least a few words if given a chance, and it provokes them to be
considered 'mute' or 'dumb.' As a class, they prefer to be known
as 'the deaf.' The people generally referred to as 'deaf' (the people
you see with hearing aids attached to their heads) now insist on
being called 'hard of hearing.' The two classes pretty much keep to
themselves. As a rule, the hard of hearing do not belong to deaf
organizations, and vice versa. The address of the Union League is
711 Eighth Avenue, just below Forty-fifth. Go to the top floor. You
will see a door with two upraised hands painted on it. The hands

represent 'U' and 'L' in the manual alphabet. Don't knock, as naturally no one will hear. Go right in, find Mr. Frankenheim, and hand him my letter."

I visited the Union League on a Saturday afternoon. Its address turned out to be a three-floor, walkup taxpayer. Near the landing on the third floor I found the door with the hands on it. Before opening it, I got out my note pad and wrote, "I am looking for Mr. Frankenheim." Then I went inside. The room was spacious and sunny. In one corner stood a big, soft-drink slot machine. On the walls were a number of framed group photographs, a bulletin board, an American flag, and a cloth banner on which was printed in red, white, and blue letters, "GOD BLESS AMERICA. WE ARE PROUD TO BE AMERICANS." Along one wall was a row of straight-backed chairs. In one of them sat a small, thin, grizzled man in a brown tweed suit. His hands were limp in his lap, his chin was on his chest, and he appeared to be sound asleep. In disarray at his feet lay a *Wall Street Journal*. There were three billiard tables in the room. A man with a derby on the back of his head was hunched over the middle table, deliberating on a shot. After he made it, I went over and handed him my pad. He read what I had written on it and a look of annoyance came on his face. He took a pencil out of his vest pocket and swiftly wrote on the pad, "What do you want to see Mr. F. in reference to? No salesmen allowed in here." I wrote, "I am not selling anything. I have a letter for him." The billiard player read this, shrugged his shoulders, and pointed at the sleeping man. Then he took the pad again and wrote. "That is Mr. F. asleep. O.K. to wake him up."

I went over and touched Mr. Frankenheim on the shoulder, and he opened his eyes and yawned. I gave him the letter. After reading it, he motioned to me to sit down. Then he got out a loose-leaf notebook, rested it on a knee, and began writing. When he reached the bottom of the leaf, he tore it out and gave it to me. His handwriting was small and meticulous. "Glad to meet you," he had written. "Nice day, isn't it? Paper said rain! Always glad to tell hearing people about the U.L. Great club. Best of its kind in the entire U.S. I am one of the founders. Our rooms have been located here eight years. Had rooms in a building on West 125th Street for 31 years. Burnt out there. A fire. Loss to club $7,000. Severe loss. Accommodations here are real nice, if I do say so. This is the billiard room. Equipped with the best tables money can buy. Many good players in the U.L. Adjoining this room is the cardroom and the officers' room. Will show them to you later."

While I was reading this, Mr. Frankenheim paid no attention to me but continued to write in his notebook. Presently he tore out another leaf and gave it to me. "Down the hall," this note read, "we have an assembly room. Seating capacity 500. Only use it for membership meetings and Lit. Nights. Name dates back to days when we began having debates in sign language. Debates were considered refined and literary in those days. On Lit. Nights we have lectures, silent movies, and sometimes a debate, and then push the chairs back, switch on the radio, and have dancing. The deaf are A-1 dancers. None better. We don't hear, but when we dance on a wooden floor most of us feel the vibrations of the music. To watch us dancing, you'd never guess we didn't hear anything at all. Even have a few jitterbug dancers. Can't say I think much of jitterbugs myself. A nuisance to one and all. The U.L. is exclusively for men, but we always invite the ladies to our affairs. We have many lectures on worthy topics, sometimes by hearing people. A hearing lecturer gets up on the platform and talks same as he would anywhere else. A hearing man who knows sign language stands beside him and interprets for us. We open all meetings by 'singing' the 'Star-Spangled Banner' in sign language. All stand erect and go through the entire song with our hands. Do you find these facts interesting?"

After reading this, I started to write a reply, but Mr. Frankenheim motioned to me to wait. He took back one of the leaves he had given me and wrote a sentence on the back of it: "I am 72 years old." I knew what was expected of me. On my pad I wrote, "You certainly don't look it, Mr. Frankenheim." I held this up, and he read it, smiled proudly, and began writing again. "Never worry!" he wrote this time. "That's the secret. Been a busy man all my life, but did not worry. Spent 23 years with Lee Higginson Corp. selling stocks and bonds to the deaf throughout U.S. and Canada. Travelled extensively. Retired three years ago. Taking it easy now. It's great fun! We will take a look at the cardroom. The U.L. has some of the sharpest pinochle players you ever saw. I myself prefer whist."

Mr. Frankenheim got up and I followed him to the door of an adjoining room. The door had been pegged open, and we stood at the threshold and looked in. In the room, sitting around big, circular, old-fashioned card tables, were about two dozen men, most of whom were middle-aged. A few were reading, one was writing a letter, one was working out a crossword puzzle, and one was repairing a cigarette lighter with a nail file, but the majority were intent on card games. It was not quiet in the room—pinochle players grunted angrily at each other, decks of cards were noisily riffled and cut, chairs were occasionally scraped back, and a couple of kibitzers were wandering around. At the table nearest us, two men were studying racing papers. One had a *Daily Racing Form* and the other had a past-performance page out of a *Morning Telegraph*. Suddenly they looked up and began talking to each other in sign language. They were obviously at odds about something; they closed and unclosed their hands in the air, wriggled their fingers, and made complicated gestures. I wrote on my pad, "What are they arguing about?" Mr. Frankenheim watched them for a few moments and wrote, "Their conversation is in reference to a horse."

A man came up behind us and we stood aside to let him in. He was a shoeshine man. He slid his shine box under a table, pulled off his cap, and sat down. Then he took out a handful of change and began counting it. Mr. Frankenheim sensed that I was curious about the man and he wrote, "Gentleman who just came in is a member. Shines shoes along Eighth Avenue. Well known in the neighborhood and has made many hearing friends. The pursuits of U.L. members are varied from common laborer right on up to one member who owns a big printing business and sells insurance to the deaf as a sideline. In the club all members are equal, no matter what line they are in, or race, or religion, etc. This is not a Park Avenue club. No man blackballed because of race or class. Political and religious matters taboo at our meetings. Most of the members now in the cardroom are night workers who take their leisure in the afternoon. Now let us step into the officers' room, and I will write you out a brief history of the club."

THE OFFICERS' ROOM was unpretentious. It was furnished with a roll-top desk, an iron safe, a long table, and half a dozen chairs. On the walls were framed souvenir programs of Union League balls, a bathing-girl calendar, a faded tintype of a brownstone house, and a row of photographs of the club's past presidents. Mr. Frankenheim's photograph was among them. Two men were sitting at one end of the table. One was a prematurely bald young man who wore spectacles with lenses so thick they made his eyes look protuberant. A Leica camera, slung from his neck, rested on his chest. The other man was middle-aged; he was stout and red-haired and had an unmistakably Irish face. They were examining some negatives. When we came in both men looked up, and Mr. Frankenheim conversed with them for several minutes in sign language. Then he and I sat down at the other end of the table. He sharpened his pencil with a pearl-handled knife and began scribbling in his notebook. After a while, I got out a cigarette. The prematurely bald young man looked up and watched me light it. Presently he said, "Could I bum a cigarette? I have a pipe, but I forgot my pouch this morning." I had not expected him to speak, of course, and I was startled. His voice was without inflection and not much louder than a whisper. He spoke haltingly and with obvious difficulty.

"Certainly," I said, sliding the pack down the table. He took one and slid the pack back. I offered the pack to the red-haired man, but he shook his head.

"Much obliged," he said, "but I don't smoke." His voice was normal. The bald young man lit the cigarette and then said, "You were surprised to hear me talk, weren't you?" I said that I had been, and asked him if he was a member of the Union League.

"I'm a member," he said, "but my friend here isn't. He's a hearing man, but he knows sign language. He drops in occasionally to shoot pool. I'm totally deaf myself, but I can talk a little and I'm a lip reader. I went deaf when I was around twelve. I had the measles and lost my hearing, but I retained the ability to talk."

"That's very interesting," I said. He frowned and looked at me fixedly for a few moments.

"It may be very interesting to you," he said finally, "but it isn't to me."

I was embarrassed and changed the subject. "Are you a photographer?" I asked.

He shook his head. "Just an amateur," he said. "I'm a bookbinder by trade."

I wanted to ask more questions, but at this moment Mr. Frankenheim tore a leaf out of his notebook and handed it to me. He had covered both sides of it with his precise handwriting.

"Will now tell you how the good old U.L. was founded," this message began. "It was founded in the parlor of my boyhood home at 531 Lexington Avenue. The old brownstone in the tintype picture on the wall is the house. It was later torn down to make way for the Hotel Shelton. I and three other young men met in the parlor one Saturday afternoon in January, 1886. All were grads of the Institution for the Improved Instruction of Deaf-Mutes, now known as the Lexington School for the Deaf, and all were great chums. Decided to form a social club exclusively for deaf-mutes. Each became an officer—I was the first president—and each chipped in to establish a treasury. Then we passed two resolutions. One required every member to learn how to dance and the other authorized a draft on the treasury for the purpose of having our photograph made. Went to Mrs. C. A. N. Smith's Tintype Gallery at Broadway and Thirteenth, which was famous in its day. Remember it as well as yesterday. How times flies! By the fall of 1888, the year of the blizzard, the club had grown to such an extent we decided to hold a ball. Hired old Lyric Hall on Sixth Avenue and every member was required to wear a full dress suit or pay a fine of $2. Ball was a gratifying success and won a name for the U.L. in deaf-mute circles all over. So we made it an annual affair. Now hold our balls in big hotels, such as the Astor.

"Club gradually got to be of great importance in the lives of the members. Like when the Grim Reaper stalked into the ranks and claimed a member, the club took full charge of the funeral arrangements. Still do that quite often. Always send a wreath to the funeral of a prominent deaf person, even when not a member. U.L. members have always been men of sterling character. Did have to expel one back in 1893 for deserting his young wife. Can't have that sort of thing. In the early days of the club we didn't have any regular headquarters, but we grew in strength like the green bay tree of yore and got tired of meeting here today and there tomorrow. So we began to rent clubrooms. First we had rooms in an Elks' lodge hall, then in Jacob Ruppert's old Central Opera House, then in a Broadway office building, then for years on West 125th Street, then here. Improved ourselves with each jump. At present we are in A-1 financial condition. Let us knock wood. We have 400 members. Have around three dozen out-of-town members, mostly from Jersey. They make the U.L. their headquarters when in town. A few who live in distant points go to great trouble and expense to come to Lit. Nights, just for the companionship, etc. Members good about helping each other find employment. Club gives freely to charities for the needy deaf. Has equipped many deaf athletic teams. I could sit here and write until far in the night, but have given you the main facts, and my fingers are tired, and you will have to excuse me. Pleased to have met you."

After I had finished reading this, I wrote a note to Mr. Frankenheim, thanking him, and then we shook hands. I got my hat and started to leave, but he grabbed my elbow and escorted me to the soft-drink machine in the billiard room. We had Coca-Colas and shook hands all over again. Then I left. The red-haired man followed me out of the room. In the hall he asked me, "Was Mr. Frankenheim telling you about the Union League?"

I said, "That's right."

"Are you interested in the deaf?" he asked.

I told him that I planned to write an article about the club.

"Well," he said, "the Union League is a wonderful organization, but it isn't the only deaf club in the city by any means. It's the biggest, but there are dozens of others. If you're interested, I could tell you about some of them." I suggested that we go somewhere and have a drink, and he said, "Downstairs in this building there's a place called Larry's Café. We could go there."

WE WENT DOWNSTAIRS to Larry's, which was a typical Eighth Avenue saloon, stood at the bar, and ordered Tom Collinses.

"My name is Jack Fitzsimmons," said the red-haired man. "I'm a proofreader. I work in a big job-printing plant in Brooklyn. I have a lot of deaf friends and I'm a sign-language interpreter. That's my hobby. My parents were deaf and I learned the signs from them. Practically all deaf clubs have honorary hearing members who know the signs and act as interpreters. I hold honorary membership in a small deaf club in Brooklyn, but I'll tell you about that later. If a deaf person has to go to court, or is called to the income-tax bureau, or wants to take out citizenship papers or a marriage license, or the like of that, he usually asks his organization's interpreter to go along and help him out. Like myself, most of these interpreters picked up the signs from their parents. The children of deaf parents are an interesting group in themselves. Helen Menken, the actress, is one. I don't know if she can sign, but I do know she does a lot of good propaganda work for the National Association of the Deaf, which has a chapter in the city. It isn't a social organization. It fights laws which interfere with the rights of the deaf to drive automobiles, and it has an impostor bureau, which investigates beggars who claim to be deaf and often aren't, and it has a nomenclature committee, which writes to newspapers when they use unpleasant phrases like 'deaf and dumb,' and it acquaints employers with the special capabilities of deaf workers, and it does a lot of things like that. By the way, how do you like this saloon?"

I said that I liked it all right.

"Nothing unusual about it," he said, "except that it's a hangout for the deaf. Gets more deaf trade than any other saloon in the city. On Union League meeting nights it's crowded. The owner is a fellow named Laurence Blau. He takes an interest in the deaf. He has a son named Sheldon, who tends bar at night. Sheldon knows finger spelling. I guess he's the only bartender in town who does. When you were upstairs in the club, did you happen to notice a shoeshine man?"

"Yes, I saw him," I said.

"Well, his name is Hughie Schmidt. To amuse himself, Hughie teaches hearing people how to converse with the deaf. He taught Sheldon. He also taught one of the cops on the beat, Henry O'Connor of the West Fifty-fourth Street station. When the Union League runs a big affair, the arrangements committee always gets in touch with the station house and asks that O'Connor be detailed to keep order. Not that they really need a cop. The deaf are very orderly and there aren't many drunks among them. It's just a custom. O'Connor is a patient man, and Hughie was able to teach him quite a little sign language, as well as finger spelling."

"What is the difference?" I asked.

"In the manual alphabet," Fitzsimmons said, "the letters are represented by the positions of the fingers of the hand, and talking with it is called finger spelling. It's tedious. The sign language is a great body of gestures which has been passed down from one generation to the next, each adding to it. If I put my right hand to my chin and pretend to pull an imaginary beard, which is a sign for 'old,' and then point my index finger at a deaf person a couple of times, he will understand that I'm asking 'How old are you?' Many deaf signs are used by the general public, and thousands of them are exactly like the signs used by the Plains Indians. An example is the sign for 'crazy.' You touch the forehead with the index finger and then move the finger in a circle over the forehead two or three times. In many conversations both signs and finger spelling are used. Unfamiliar names, for example, are always finger-spelled. Some signs require great skill in pantomime. No one person knows all the signs. Some are expert, others know just enough for simple conversations."

"How many deaf persons are there in the city?" I asked.

"In the five boroughs," Fitzsimmons said, "there are between five and six thousand so-called deaf-mutes. By and large, they live in a restricted world, a world of their own. They prefer their own company because most hearing people have a tendency to look upon them as peculiar, or mysterious, or unnatural. When they converse with each other in sign language out in public, they are stared at as if they had escaped from the zoo. On the street or in subways, no one takes them for granted; they are always stared at. Because of this, they like to go about in groups. Even the phrases used to describe them, particularly 'deaf and dumb,' show a lack of understanding. There is nothing wrong with the vocal organs or the intelligence of the average deaf person. One learns to speak by imitation, and the deaf child can't speak, simply because he can't hear. He doesn't know what speech is. It's like expecting a blind child to visualize a color.

"Only about thirty-five per cent of the deaf were born that way, and they are called the congenitally deaf. The bulk of the others lost their hearing during babyhood or childhood after having the measles, influenza, diphtheria, scarlet fever, meningitis, or some such disease, and they are called the adventitiously deaf. The vocal organs of practically all the people in both groups are normal, and it is possible to teach many of them to speak intelligibly, but it takes almost superhuman patience. This effort is made in most of the deaf schools in New York State. Finger spelling and the signs aren't permitted in classrooms in these schools. Instead, the pupils are taught to speak and lip-read. Some become proficient, particularly those who had talking experience before they went deaf, but others manage to learn only a few phrases. However, the speech of just about all deaf persons sounds queer to those unaccustomed to it. Hearing people complain that it is too guttural, or that it lacks modulations, or that it sounds animal-like. In any case, for one reason or another, it seems to make most of them ill at ease. If they don't understand a deaf person right off the bat, they motion to him to write out what he has to say. And they always stare. You see how it is. If the deaf use signs, they are stared at. If they speak, they are stared at. Upstairs a while ago you jumped when my friend asked you for a cigarette. Was his speech that unpleasant?"

"I'm very sorry. It wasn't that his speech was unpleasant," I said. "Mr. Frankenheim spoke to both of you in sign language when we came into the room, and I took it for granted all of you were deaf. When your friend suddenly spoke, I was startled."

Fitzsimmons shrugged his shoulders.

"The chief characteristic of the deaf is their clannishness," he said, abruptly changing the subject. "I don't mean to imply that they are embittered. Most of them are happy enough as humans go, but for understanding and companionship they have to depend almost entirely on each other. For this reason there is a slew of clubs, societies, leagues, lodges, federations, and associations exclusively for them. The majority are little informal groups or cliques. The club in which I hold honorary membership is one of these. It has fourteen members. They all come from Brooklyn. Our members are above the average in intelligence. They are great readers. One has an A.B. from Gallaudet College, the old National Deaf-Mute College, which is the only one of its kind in the world. It's in Washington. During the winter we meet above a cafeteria near Borough Hall. The cafeteria is owned by a relative of a member and he lets us use a vacant room on the second floor. We sit around and talk and smoke and drink beer until late at night. The deaf prefer cafeterias, by the way, particularly Automats. I know a deaf woman who has eaten in an Automat regularly for twelve years without ever uttering a single word. Every Sunday during the summer our club goes down to Coney. We always meet at the Brighton Beach Baths, which for some reason is popular with the deaf. Several clubs go there. On winter Sundays the club often goes in a body to the Metropolitan Museum, which has free lectures for lip readers. The deaf are great for museums. We have a couple of members who damned near live in the Metropolitan. We had a wedding in the club not long ago—a girl from our club and a fellow who belongs to the Union League. The deaf almost always marry the deaf. Look here, I'm tired of standing. Let's get a seat somewhere."

WE ORDERED ANOTHER ROUND of drinks and sat down in a booth in the back room.

"Our group is quite informal," Fitzsimmons continued. "We have officers and dues and we call ourselves the Borough Hall Ephphatha Society. 'Ephphatha' is a word that Jesus spoke when he healed a deaf man. You'll find it in St. Mark. It means 'Be opened.' It has been picked for a name by many Protestant and Catholic deaf clubs.

We seldom use it. Usually we just say 'the crowd' or 'the gang.' Once in a while we have a regular meeting with parliamentary order and everything, but mostly we just sit around and talk. That's the way it is with most of the small clubs. Then there are larger, better-organized groups who have religious affiliations and hold their meetings in churches. Four or five of these groups meet in the parish house of St. Ann's Church for Deaf-Mutes at 511 West 148th Street. This little church was the first of its kind in the world. The pastor is deaf, of course, and all services—sermons, weddings, funerals, christenings, everything—are conducted in sign language. During services the front of the chapel is flooded with light so the congregation won't have any trouble seeing the pastor's hands. It has a choir and the people in it sing hymns with their hands. St. Ann's is old. It was founded in 1852, and the building they're in now was put up in 1898.

"St. Ann's is Episcopal, but people of all religions go to it. The Catholics have many deaf organizations. The principal ones are the Knights and Ladies of De L'Epee Sick and Disability Association and the Ephphatha Society for the Catholic Deaf. Both are combined social and insurance organizations. They pay sick benefits, hold card parties and socials, and sponsor athletic teams. The De L'Epee Association meets in an office building in Brooklyn. It was named after an eighteenth-century French priest who founded what was probably the first deaf school. The Ephphatha Society meets at St. Francis Xavier's on West Sixteenth Street. Deaf athletic teams use the gym at this church for tournaments. Services in the sign language are held there the first Sunday of every month by an old Jesuit named Father Michael A. Purtell. He is a hearing man, now in his seventies, who has been working for the deaf since he was a young priest. He puts out a paper full of social notes about the deaf from all over the country, and it is widely read. It used to be called the *Catholic Deaf-Mute,* but not long ago he changed the name to *Ephphatha.* As a matter of fact, in the last ten or fifteen years almost every title with 'deaf and dumb' or 'deaf-mute' in it has been changed. Used to be that every school for the deaf had 'deaf and dumb' in its title."

"How do deaf Catholics confess?" I asked.

"There are a number of priests who know the signs, and they hear confession in sign language," Fitzsimmons said. "In Brooklyn, for example, you'll find them at St. Brigid's, St. Michael's, Transfiguration, St. Monica's, and Fourteen Holy Martyrs. Some of these priests had deaf parents. In membership, the Jewish organizations are next in size to the Catholic ones. The largest of these is the Society for the Welfare of Jewish Deaf, which rents space in a hall on West Eighty-fifth Street in Manhattan. It's a lively outfit. It gives classes in sign language. It has a dramatics group, which puts on plays and vaudeville in signs, a gym group, and several athletic teams. It has Friday-night religious services, in which an interpreter stands beside the rabbi and translates, and it has teas, lectures, movies, and Bingo parties. It even has a plot of its own in New Mount Carmel Cemetery in Brooklyn. Every so often, a delegation goes out and puts flowers on the graves of departed members. Also, this society has an employment service."

"I wanted to ask about that," I said. "How do the deaf go about finding jobs?"

"They have the devil of a time," Fitzsimmons said. "It is the thorniest problem they have to meet. There is one employment agency specifically for them. It is operated by an energetic young woman named Margarette Helmle, who used to be a personnel manager for General Motors, and it has office space in the New York State Employment Service building down on East Twenty-eighth Street. Miss Helmle is an expert signer. Her salary is paid by the three schools in which most of the deaf in the city are educated—the Lexington in Manhattan, St. Joseph's in the Bronx, and the New York School in White Plains. She tries to find jobs for all applicants, whether they come from these schools or not. She goes out and calls on the personnel managers of big corporations and talks up the deaf, and she averages twenty-two placements a month. The deaf are strongest in the printing trades. There are four in the job plant where I work, and you'll find two or three in most big newspaper plants. They can do any kind of work that doesn't absolutely require hearing. Employers usually write out orders to them. They make particularly good welders, power-machine operators, carpenters, and electricians."

WE HAD LONG SINCE FINISHED our drinks. Fitzsimmons appeared to be tired of talking and I suggested another round, but he refused. He said he thought he would go back upstairs to the Union League and play some pinochle. I left Larry's Café with him.

"This may interest you," he said, just before he started up the stairs. "The deaf, particularly lip readers, are suspicious of hearing people who begin sympathizing with them. They've learned that sooner or later these people will ask questions that are rather embarrassing. There is the type who right away wants to know exactly how it feels to live in a soundless world. One of the members of my club, the graduate of Gallaudet I told you about, has an answer. He got it out of some book or other, and all of our members have memorized it. It goes, 'The deaf live in a world of deadly silence. The singing of the birds, the inflections of the human voice, beautiful music, and the confusion of noises that proclaim life are lacking. Many things are in motion, but there is no sound.'

"Then there is a type of woman who has caused many a lip reader to think of murder. She will sigh and say, 'Sometimes I get so tired of the noise in the city, I think deafness would be a blessing.' All lip readers have had to put up with this remark scores of times. My friend upstairs, the fellow who asked you for a cigarette, is very meek and mild, but it always infuriates him. The last time a woman handed him this line, he gritted his teeth and said, 'Lady, please forgive me, but you sure are a god-damn fool.'"

(1941)

# Santa Claus Smith

$A$ RAGGED, WHITE-BEARDED OLD MAN who tells people he is John S. Smith of Riga, Latvia, Europe, began hitchhiking aimlessly on the highways of the United States early in 1934. He has been seen as far north as Clinton, Connecticut, but he spends most of his time in the South and Southwest. He wanders from Louisiana to California and back again about twice a year. He is approximately seventy years old. People who have had dealings with him say he has a kind, honest face, speaks broken English, smokes a pipe, wears an overcoat winter and summer, loves cats, and keeps a supply of brown wrapping paper, cut into oblong slips, in a pack he carries on his back. His behavior has puzzled waitresses, tourist-camp proprietors, and housewives in at least twenty-three states, and he is frequently a subject of conversation in highway lunchrooms at which drivers of cross-country trucks pull up for hamburgers and coffee.

On the night of October 23, 1936, for example, he strayed into a lunchroom on a highway near Columbus, Texas, told the waitress he had no money, and asked for a cup of coffee. She took him into the kitchen and gave him a bowl of stew, a jelly roll, and coffee. When he finished eating he took a grimy slip of brown paper out of his pack and scribbled on it with an indelible pencil. He slid the paper under his plate and hurried out into the night. When the waitress picked it up she found that it was an improvised check for $27,000, written on the Irving National Bank of New York and signed "John S. Smith of Riga, Latvia, Europe." On the back of the check was a note, "Fill your name in, send to bank." Four days later he turned up at a diner on the outskirts of Yuma, Arizona, and asked the counterman for coffee. After Smith departed, a similar check, for $2,000, was found beside his cup. On October 30th he was wandering along a highway near Indianola, Mississippi. He asked a farmer's wife for something to eat and was so pleased with the flapjacks and molasses she gave him that he handed her two checks, one for $25,000 and the other for $1,000. On November 9th he asked the proprietor of a tourist camp near Denver if he could come in out of the cold for a few minutes. He sat beside the stove and filled his pipe with tobacco salvaged from a handful of cigarette stubs he took from his overcoat pocket. The proprietor made him a present of a dime can of tobacco. He wrote a check for $16,000, handed it to the proprietor, and went on his way. Five days later a housewife in Baldwin Park, California, gave him some scrambled eggs; he left a check for $12,000 beside the plate. Next day he gave checks aggregating $52,000 to waitresses in two cafés in Los Angeles. A month later he was back in Texas. On December 12th, on a street in Fort Worth, he asked a young woman sitting in a parked automobile for a nickel. She gave him a dime. Using a fender for a desk, he wrote her a check for $950. She laughed and thanked him. Then he took the check back, tore it up, and wrote another for $26,000. "That's for your sweet smile," he said.

All these checks, like the one he gave the waitress in Columbus, Texas, were written on the Irving National Bank of New York. This bank went out of existence on January 6, 1923, eleven years before John S. Smith of Riga, Latvia, Europe, began writing checks on it. Mail addressed to the Irving National Bank is eventually delivered to its successor, the Irving Trust Company, and in the last six years two hundred and forty letters, most of them enclosing checks, have turned up at the Irving Trust from beneficiaries of John S. Smith's generosity.

THE OLD MAN WROTE HIS FIRST CHECK on the Irving National on January 15, 1934. He handed it to a housewife in Dallas who had given him coffee. It was for $2,000. The housewife kept the check a few days, wondering if "it was just an old man's fancy."

Then she mailed it to the Irving National, and the Post Office delivered it to the Irving Trust. The teller who got the letter was startled. He went into a vault in which the Irving National's books are still kept and searched through them, finding no trace of a Latvian Smith. There had been John S. Smiths among the depositors, but it did not take long to ascertain that none of them could be this one. The perplexed teller wrote the woman in Dallas, asking for more information about the unusual transaction. While he waited for her answer, a letter arrived from a housewife in Los Angeles, inquiring if Mr. John S. Smith of Riga, Latvia, Europe, had an account in the Irving National Bank of New York, N.Y. She wrote that after she gave him something to eat he left her a check for $3,700. "This old man may not have good sense," she added.

Since then hardly a week has gone by that the Irving Trust has not received a hopeful letter from someone who has given food, tobacco, transportation, lodging, small change, or a sweet smile to Mr. John S. Smith, getting a check for a substantial amount in return. The checks contained in the letters have ranged from $90 to $600,000. He handed the biggest check to a waitress in New Iberia, Louisiana, who had given him a hamburger sandwich. The $90 check was received by a minister's wife in Terre Haute who gave him what she describes as "a good hot lunch"; evidently he did not think much of her cooking. The checks are always written on slips of brown wrapping paper and many are spotted with grease. Occasionally the old man writes the name of the recipient on a check. He gave a farmer's wife a check for $8,000 bearing her name, and when she asked him how he knew it, he pointed to the R.F.D. mailbox in front of her house. Most often, however, he leaves a space on the check in which the recipient may write his or her name. He always misspells "thousand," writing it "tousand." His handwriting is vaguely Gothic and is often difficult to read. He decorates many of his checks with a symbol. It is a crude face with a smile on it. There are two pencil dots for eyes, a dot for a nose, and a line turned up at both ends for a mouth. This symbol, evidently his trademark, appears in the upper right-hand corner of some checks; on others it follows directly after the signature.

Just why he picked the Irving National Bank always has been a mystery. At first it was thought that he might once have worked for the bank as a janitor or guard, but personnel lists have been vainly checked for a clue. Tellers and stenographers at the Irving Trust have been put to a lot of trouble by the old man's check-writing, but the trust company has never attempted to have him arrested, since no forgery is involved. So far as can be learned, he has never tried to cash a check or purchase anything with one. Irving Trust officials believe that John S. Smith is a simple-minded, goodhearted old man who feels that he should reward those treating him with kindness. The bank people call him Santa Claus Smith and wish that he had millions of dollars on deposit. Sometimes, for amusement, an official will get out the file of letters and, from postmarks, trace the old man's crazy progress back and forth across the continent. However, the relationship between the old man and the bank has long since become a routine matter. The bank used to send lengthy replies to people who wrote letters, enclosing checks; now, when such a letter comes in, it is handed to a stenographer who types out this unvarying reply: "We are sorry we have to disillusion you, but we have no record that John S. Smith of Riga, Latvia, Europe, has ever maintained an account with the Irving Trust Company, or its predecessor, the Irving National Bank of New York. From numerous inquiries we have received from various sections of the country, it appears that this individual, in return for gratuitous meals or lodging, has given what purport to be drafts for large amounts drawn on the Irving National Bank. Sincerely yours, Irving Trust Company."

ONE AFTERNOON NOT LONG AGO an official of the bank gave me permission to go through the file of letters written by John S. Smith's deluded beneficiaries. The file is kept in the company's main office at 1 Wall Street. First, however, I had to promise that I would not mention any of the names signed to the letters; the official feared that such mention might in some cases expose the writers to ridicule.

The first letter I read was from a waitress in a café at a tourist camp on U.S. Highway 11, near Gadsden, Alabama. It was written in pencil on two sheets of ruled tablet paper and dated March 27, 1936. She wrote that a few nights ago she had given a ham-and-egg sandwich to "a raggedy old man in his sixties or seventies with a pack on his back." Just before he left he handed her two slips of paper. One was a check for $25,000 and the other was a check for $1,000. This combination of checks turned up often. Possibly the check for $1,000 was Santa Claus Smith's idea of a tip.

"I naturally thought the old man was a nut going through the country," the waitress wrote, "but I studied the matter over, and it got my curiosity up, and I want to know has he got any money in your bank. As you know, strange things happen. If these checks are O.K., please send the money as I sure can use it to advantage. If not, please return same, as I desire to keep them for souvenirs."

The next letter I pulled out of the file was from a farmer's wife on Route 1, Metamora, Indiana. She also enclosed a check for $25,000 and one for $1,000.

"Just a word of information please," she wrote. "Is there a man by the name of John S. Smith of Riga, Latvia, Europe, that has dealings with your bank? I will explain to you. Late one evening last July about the 18th [1935] there was an old man with a long beard and a very kind face turned in our lawn. He seemed to be a tramp. It was almost dusk. He asked if there was a chance to get a piece of bread. It has always been my custom to give to tramps if I have anything I can handy give. He was carrying a pack on his back so I told him to set down on the lawn. I had a nice warm supper cooked so I served him on the lawn. He seemed to be very hungry. I gave him a second serving. When he finished he took from his pack two checks copied on brown paper looked like they were cut from paper bags. He came forward and handed these to me with his plate. His face was so kind it is hard to believe he meant anything false."

A similar confidence in the old man was displayed by a farmer of Silsbee, Texas, who wrote, "I received these checks from an old gentleman who ate breakfast at our home and I asked the bank here to handle same for me, and they seemed to think they were no good. I am different. This man had no reason to give us these checks knowing they were no good. So I still believe he wanted us to have this amount of money and we sure need it. Wishing you a merry Christmas and a happy New Year." The letter was dated December 20, 1937.

THE MAJORITY OF THE LETTER-WRITERS, however, are not so confident. They are suspicious but hopeful. Their letters follow a pattern. First the writers indicate that they are far too worldly-wise to believe that the checks are good; then in the next sentence they give the bank explicit instructions for forwarding the money. A waitress in San Antonio sent in a check for $7,000 and wrote, "I know this is just a joke, but a girl friend dared me to send it to you, so here it is. If he has an account with you, please send me the money by registered mail." A rather snippety waitress in a truck-drivers' café in Muncie, Indiana, wrote, "Enclosed you will find one cheque for $1,000 given me by an uncouth beggar on your bank. If it has any value to it, open an account for me in your bank and deposit amount of check." A waitress in a restaurant on South Halsted Street, Chicago, was blunter. To a check for $270,000 she attached a note: "I guess the old nut who gave me this is fresh out of the nut house, but send me the money if true." A woman in Alabama City, Alabama, sent in a check for $21,000 via air mail and special delivery. Her letter contained an interesting description of old John S. "He was baldheaded wearing an overcoat and whiskers all over his face and I could not understand anything much he said, and he also had a walking stick," she wrote.

Some of the correspondents were not only suspicious of John S. Smith; they also showed that they did not entirely trust the Irving National Bank of New York. I found seven letters from people who sent photostatic copies of checks and said they would deposit the originals in their local banks if John S. Smith was sufficiently solvent. Also in the file were letters from banks in which people had tried to cash or deposit his checks. A bank in Kansas City wrote, "A customer of ours has high hopes that the enclosed paper is an order on your bank for the payment of $15,000. We have looked it over and our foreign-exchange teller has examined it, but none of us have quite figured it out. If you can throw any light on the matter, we will appreciate it."

John S. Smith is far more generous to waitresses and housewives than he is to the motorists and truck-drivers with whom he hitches daylong rides. Evidently he places little value on transportation. He has never given a check exceeding $1,000 for an automobile ride; for a hamburger he has gone as high as $600,000.

The old straggler is a cat-lover. On July 6, 1934, he went into a café in Groton, South Dakota, and asked the wife of the proprietor to care for a cat he was carrying. She said she would. Then he wrote out two checks. One, for $4,000, was made payable "to person who upkeep the black and white cat name Smiles from John S. Smith of Riga, Latvia, Europe." On the other, which was for $1,000, he wrote, "Pay to anyone assisting care of cat."

THE LETTERS DO NOT THROW MUCH LIGHT on the mystery of John S. Smith's past. He told a woman in Tuscaloosa, Alabama, that he left home in 1934 and began to wander because the depression got on his mind. This woman expressed a belief that "there is something wrong with the old man's head." "I think he got loose from an institution and has been lost ever since," she wrote. He built up a romantic picture of himself for a young woman in San Antonio. She wrote, "I befriended a poorly dressed man who insisted upon writing me the attached order for $6,000. I put this paper away and attached no importance to it until recently when it occurred to me that so many strange things do happen that this might possibly be another instance. He stated that he purposely wore ragged clothes and rewarded those who helped him when he asked for help only through such an instrument as the attached as arrangements had been made with your bank to honor these and no others."

For a few minutes on the morning of July 19, 1936, it looked as if the mystery might be solved. On that day a letter from John S. Smith was delivered to the Irving Trust. The official on whose desk it was placed became excited. The envelope was postmarked Wabash, Indiana. Inside there was a letter scribbled wildly on the backs of seven lunchroom menus. It began, "Irv. Nat. Bank of N.Y. Dear Sir," and then became illegible. The official was exasperated. He glanced through page after page and none of the writing made sense. The letter had been written with an indelible pencil and had come in contact with water; most of the words had beome ugly purple blots. Also, it was evident that John S. Smith had carried the letter around in his pocket for days before mailing it. The sheets were mottled with grease and there were tobacco crumbs in the folds. The official got a magnifying glass and he and a colleague went to work. After a considerable amount of agonizing labor, they isolated the following phrases: "listen those three waitress," "put something in that bank," "in USA for 26 yrs 30 yrs 22," "mortgage and now," "to see about cats," "waitress girl in that place in Ohio," and "all over USA." To make matters worse, two of his ubiquitous checks were pinned to the letter. Both were made payable to the Irv. Nat. Bank and both were written on the Irv. Nat. Bank. One was for $6,000, the other was for $15,000.

WHEN I FINISHED READING the letters in the file I realized that I did not have a clear impression of John S. Smith. At first he reminded me vaguely of W. C. Fields, but that impression soon disappeared; for one thing, I found no letters indicating that he had ever given checks to bartenders. For a day or so after I read the letters I thought of him as a benevolent old screwball. Then I began to be troubled by the memory of those crude, grinning faces with which he decorated so many of the checks. I began to think of the vain hopes he raised in the breasts of the waitresses who had graciously given him hundreds of meals and the truck-drivers who had hauled him over a hundred highways, and to feel that about John S. Smith of Riga, Latvia, Europe, there is something a little sinister.

(1940)

# The Don't-Swear Man

ONE DANK AFTERNOON I dropped into Shannon's, an Irish saloon on the southeast corner of Third Avenue and Seventy-sixth Street, and ordered a split of Guinness. "Fine pneumonia weather we're having," the bartender remarked. "Yes," I said, "it's one hell of a day." A portly old man standing a few feet up the bar gave a grunt, abruptly put down his beer glass, turned to me, and said, "My boy, a profane word never yet had any effect on the weather." The remark irritated me. I was in extremely low spirits; my shoes had been sopping wet all day and I felt certain that I was going to catch a cold and die. However, I nodded perfunctorily and said, "I guess that's right, Mister." "Oh, don't apologize," the old man said. Then he dug into a pocket of his coat and pulled out a small, pale-pink card. "Here," he said, "read this and think it over." The card said, "NEW HOPE FOR THE WORLD. GOD BLESS AMERICA AND OUR HOMES. HAVE NO SWEARING. BOYCOTT PROFANITY! PLEASE DO NOT SWEAR, NOR USE OBSCENE OR PROFANE LANGUAGE. THESE CARDS ARE FOR DISTRIBUTION. SEND FOR SOME—THEY ARE FREE. ANTI-PROFANITY LEAGUE. A. S. COLBORNE, PRES. 185 EAST SEVENTY-SIX STREET."

After reading this, I took a good look at the old man. He was over six feet tall and he had a double chin and a large paunch. His cheeks were ruddy and his eyes, behind steel-rimmed glasses, were clear and utterly honest. Instead of a vest, he wore a brown sweater. In the knot of his polka-dot tie there was a horseshoe stickpin. Three pencils and a fountain pen were clipped to his breast pocket.

He had placed his hat on the bar, upside down, to dry off. He had a white mustache and a fine head of white hair, several locks of which had been brushed down across his forehead, old bartender style. He looked, in fact, like a dignified, opinionated, old-fashioned bartender on his day off. I have always had a high regard for that kind of man, and I said, "If I offended you, sir, I'm sorry, only what makes you think 'hell' is a profane word?"

"Well, I tell you," he said gravely, "it might not be one-hundred-per-cent profanity, but it's a leader-on. You start out with 'hell,' 'devil take it,' 'Dad burn it,' 'Gee whizz,' and the like of that, and by and by you won't be able to open your trap without letting loose an awful, awful, blasphemous oath. It's like the cocaine dope habit. I know. I talked real rough myself when I was a young squirt, but I had the mother wit to quit. I haven't uttered a solitary profane word since a Sunday morning in the winter of 1886. I was running to catch a ferryboat and I got left, and let an oath out of me so awful I broke down and cried like a baby."

I was about to ask what the oath was, but thought better of it. Instead I said, "You remind me a lot of a man who used to work behind the bar at the Murray Hill Hotel. Are you a bartender?"

The old man did not answer me. He picked up his glass and finished his beer. Then, after a resounding smack of the lips, he said, "Profanity! Blasphemy! Evil tongues a-wagging and a-wagging! That's why the world is headed for wrack and ruin! Let me introduce myself. Name is Arthur Samuel Colborne. I'm the founder and head of the Anti-Profanity League. Founded 1901. An international organization. If the truth was known, I'm also the founder of the Safe and Sane Fourth of July movement. Founded 1908. On the Fourth I used to stand on the steps of City Hall and read the Declaration of Independence to all that would listen. People called me a crank, but I told them I wasn't crank enough to spend good money on firecrackers. Others took up the Safe and Sane, and I kept plugging away with the Anti-Profanity. I've spent the better part of forty years cleaning up profanity conditions. I and my members have passed out six million cards like the one I handed you. We call them profanity-exterminators. Six million. Think of it! I'm past seventy, but I'm a go-getter, fighting the evil on all fronts. Keeps me busy. I'm just after seeing a high official at City Hall. There's some Broadway plays so profane it's a wonder to me the tongues of the actors and the actresses don't wither up and come loose at the roots and drop to the ground, and I beseeched this high official to take action. Said he'd do what he could. Probably won't do a single, solitary thing. I wanted to have a chat with Mayor La Guardia, but they told me he'd just stepped out. That's what they always say. The Mayor's a pompish little fellow, as strutty as a duck. I've heard that he gets so profane when he loses his temper it's enough to make your head swim. You think that's true?"

"It wouldn't surprise me a bit," I said.

Mr. Colborne pursed his lips and sadly shook his head from side to side. "He ought to be ashamed of hisself," he said.

The bartender had poured my stout. I asked Mr. Colborne to have a drink with me. He drew out a thick gold watch, glanced at it, and said, "Much obliged, but I seldom take more than two, and I've had that. Nothing wrong in beer. Good for your nerves. I'd have another, but I want to get home in time for a radio program. Hillbilly singing. I'm a great believer in it. Very wholesome. I'm also a great believer in opera music, Hawaiian music, Kate Smith, and Charlie McCarthy. Here a while back, this Bergen feller had Charlie saying 'Doggone this' and 'Doggone that' on the radio, and I wrote him and attached an exterminator to the letter. 'Think it over, Mr. Bergen,' I said. Got a speedy reply. 'Won't happen again,' he said."

"Is 'doggone' a leader-on?" I asked.

"I'll say it is! One of the hardest to eradicate! Look here, my boy, I'd like to give you some exterminators to pass out to your friends, keep the ball rolling, but I'm cleaned out. Put a handful in my pocket this morning, but I gave some out on the subway, and I slipped a few into some cars that were parked in front of City Hall, including the Mayor's car, and I left a couple with the Mayor's secretary, and the one I handed you was the last of the lot. Drop into my headquarters sometime and I'll give you a supply. My address is printed on the exterminator."

"Thanks very much," I said.

He waved his hand deprecatingly. "Don't mention it," he said.

He put on his hat, paid for his beers, shook hands with me, and nodded to the bartender. Halfway to the door, he turned and came back to the bar. "Interesting case out in Chicago here a while back," he said to me. "Two big German butchers had been working at the same block in a slaughterhouse for eighteen years. One morning one butcher took up his cleaver and split the other butcher's head. Police asked him why he did it, and he said, 'I just couldn't stand his profanity any longer!'" I laughed, and Mr. Colborne gave an indignant snort. "Look here, my boy," he said, frowning at me, "first-degree murder's not a laughing matter. If you look at it the right way, there's a good lesson in that case. Think it over!" Then he left.

"Was the old gentleman kidding me?" I asked the bartender, who had been listening.

"Oh, no," the bartender said. "He's a big reformer. He's well known in the neighborhood. His headquarters are up the street half a block."

Mainly because he was the first beer-drinking reformer I had ever encountered, I resolved to visit Mr. Colborne. Several afternoons later I did. The address printed on the exterminator he had given me turned out to be an old, red-brick apartment house, on the front of which, just left of the stoop, was nailed a foot-square tin sign reading, "HEADQUARTERS ANTI-PROFANITY LEAGUE. CARDS THAT READ DO NOT SWEAR CAN BE HAD FREE." A woman with a poodle in her arms was standing on the stoop. She watched me read the sign, and when I walked up the steps she said, "If you're looking for the don't-swear man, he lives down in the basement." I rang the basement bell and Mr. Colborne let me in. Over his suit he had on a black, full-length apron, the kind printers wear. He held a frying pan in his left hand and a dish towel in this right. "Come in and make yourself at home," he said. "Take a seat, and I'll be with you soon as I finish washing up in the kitchen. This room here is the headquarters of the League. I sleep and eat in a couple of rooms in back. I'm a bachelor and I get my own meals. I'm a bit set in my ways, and I prefer the grub I cook for myself to the highest-class restaurant there is. Cleaner. While you're waiting, look at my scrapbook. You'll find it somewhere in that mess on my desk."

He went back to his kitchen and I took a look around the room. It was a long, narrow, low-ceilinged room. There were two windows, but not much light came through them. Both were shut, and there was a kitchen smell in the air. The floor was covered with linoleum. Running just below the ceiling were a couple of asbestos-sheathed steam-heat pipes. On the mantel stood a highly colored plaster statue of St. Michael trampling the Devil. The statue was wrapped in cellophane, doubtless to keep off dust. Along one wall were two tables and a small iron safe. There was a typewriter on one table, and on the other were a radio and a tall vase of artificial roses; dust was thick on the red petals of the roses. Two walls were hung with oil paintings from baseboard to ceiling. At least half were religious, many of them portraits of saints and of the Virgin; other subjects included a windmill in the moonlight, a mother sewing beside a cradle, a thatched cottage, and a Jersey cow standing belly-deep in a lush meadow. All were in gilded frames.

On Mr. Colborne's flat-topped desk were a coffee cup half filled with foreign stamps clipped from envelopes, a begonia plant and a geranium plant in little red pots, an alarm clock, and a great pile of correspondence, books, and religious magazines. There were also five neat stacks of exterminators. I found the scrapbook he had mentioned under some copies of a monthly magazine called the *Holy Name Journal*. Pasted in the scrapbook were scores of letters from publishers, politicians, actors, public officials, and moving-picture and radio-station executives, either replying to Mr. Colborne's complaints about "profanity conditions" or thanking him for sending them exterminators. Most of the letters were evasive, but all were extremely respectful. One, from William Randolph Hearst's secretary, said, "On behalf of Mr. Hearst, I want to thank you for the little cards you sent to him. It was very kind of you. Mr. Hearst is not in town, and therefore it is impossible to give them to him." I was about half through the book when Mr. Colborne returned, still wearing his black apron. He sat down, clasped his hands over his paunch, and yawned.

"I'm sort of sleepy," he said. "Sat up late last night studying over bar and grill profanity. Why, the women are worse than the men. And you can't talk to them! Why, they'll spit in your eye! I got a notion to revive the warnings I used to put up in saloons back before prohibition. In those days the liquor-dealing element cooperated with me. In 1916 I had posters tacked up in four thousand premises, bar and back room. I'll show you one." He ransacked a desk drawer and brought out a cardboard poster which said, "IN THE INTEREST OF CLEAN SPEECH AND COMMON DECENCY, PLEASE REFRAIN FROM THE OBJECTIONABLE USE OF PROFANE AND OBSCENE LANGUAGE AND EXPECTORATING IN PUBLIC PLACES. WOULD YOU USE SUCH LANGUAGE IN YOUR OWN HOME? RESPECT YOUR FELLOW MAN. ANTI-PROFANITY LEAGUE."

"Those warnings did a world of good," Mr. Colborne said. "They just about put a stop to saloon profanity, and then along came prohibition and tore down all my work. Looking at it from an anti-profanity standpoint, prohibition was an awful nuisance. Nowadays saloons don't even look like saloons, and I'm not sure they'll let me hang posters in them. In the old days saloonkeepers were generous friends of the League. They used to call me the Professor. Practically every place I put up posters, the boss would insist on making a contribution. I held them in high esteem. So much so that when Mayor Jimmy Walker, a fine man, was organizing his great beer parade up Fifth Avenue in May, 1932, I went to my most active members and I said, 'The liquor-dealing element was always nice to us, and now we should hit a lick for them. Let's have a delegation from the League in the beer parade.' The idea caught on, and during the morning of the parade we rounded up five hundred head of people and a brass band. That afternoon we marched right behind the Tammany Hall delegation. We carried tin growlers and shouted, 'We want beer!,' 'Down with profanity,' 'Beer for taxation,' 'Boycott profanity!,' and the like of that, and had a most enjoyable time. We wound up in a saloon and drank more beer than John saw."

Mr. Colborne was interrupted by the doorbell. He grunted and got up and opened the door. A thin, elderly woman came in. "I already passed out the exterminators you gave me last month," she said, with obvious pride. "You better let me have about two hundred this time." "Oh, my!" said Mr. Colborne. "That's good work. Keep at it, and one of these days you'll have the Bronx all cleaned up." He handed the woman a supply of cards held together with a rubber band and she dropped them in her handbag. "Mr. Colborne," she said, "do you think there's been an improvement over last year?" Mr. Colborne stood quite still for a few moments, deep in thought. "I've noticed a decline in street swearing," he said finally, "but there's an awful lot of work still to be done." "You never spoke a truer word," the woman said. "You know, it's disgusting to me the way the city's tearing down the elevated lines. There was always less swearing on the 'L' than on the dirty old subway. A lot less obscenity, too, if you ask me. It just means we'll have to redouble our efforts." "That's the spirit!" Mr. Colborne exclaimed. "We'll have to keep plugging away. Isn't that right?" The woman smacked her palms together. "That's right, Mr. Colborne!" she said emphatically. Then she left.

"She's a widow woman from the Bronx and one of our most active workers," Mr. Colborne said. "Look here, my boy, would you be interested in hearing how I came to start this work?"

I said that I would.

"Well, now," he said, "the history of the League and the story of my life are all wrapped up together, so I'll begin at the beginning, as the fellow said. I'm English-Irish by descent, born down on Avenue A and Fourteenth Street. I'm a Roman Catholic by religion, although some think I'm hooked up with the Salvation Army. Not that the Army isn't a fine thing. Some of those Salvation fellers are wonderful for passing out exterminators. By trade, I'm a picture-restorer, frame-maker, and gilder, the third generation in that line. I own a set of gilder's tools and a toolbox that was used by my grandfather and my father. I'm also a painter—not house but oil. I painted most of the pictures you see on the walls of this room. I went to work in the picture line when I was fresh out of knee britches and became a fine craftsman. Look at my hands, the hands of a man that knows his trade. In 1890, I took my savings and went over to Brooklyn and opened me up a store of my own, the Paris Art

Gallery, occupying an entire four-floor building at Broadway and Gates Avenue. Pictures, frames, gilding, and bric-a-brac. Did a big business.

"The Paris was the number-one thing in my life until on or about the middle of October, 1901, when I heard a sermon concerning the profanity evil that shook me up to such an extent I determined to go out in the highways and byways and do something about it. And I did, let me tell you! At first I would just step up to profane persons and reason with them, telling them that swearing was vile and vicious, out of place, uncalled for, and a snare and a delusion, signifying nothing. I would say, 'Your dear old mother never taught you to talk like that. Think it over!' Or I'd say, 'If you haven't got self-respect, please have some respect for the general public. Think it over!' Or I'd say, 'Now, aren't you ashamed of yourself, a grown man a-carrying on like that? Think it over!' But in those days I was a little bashful about talking to strangers, and one day the idea came to me: Why not let the printed word do the job? So I had a few thousand cards printed up requesting people to control their tongues. To make it look official, I had the printer put Anti-Profanity League down at the bottom.

"Then, when I had any spare time, I'd stuff my pockets full of cards and go out in search of profanity conditions. Like I would attend meetings in the union halls of the teamsters. They used to be bad for swearing, but not as bad as the truck-drivers of today. A teamster would just swear at his poor old nag, but a truck-driver will swear at anything, man or beast, quick or dead, going or coming. And when I saw a building in construction, I'd drop around at noon and ask the foreman for permission to address the bricklayers and hod-carriers. They would be squatting around eating their dinner out of buckets and I would give them a little oration. Some would laugh, but some would take heed. My, the fun we had! And I'd go to baseball parks and pass cards out right and left. Baseball is an incubator of profanity. And I'd go to prisons, to the Navy Yard district, to pool parlors, to saloons where longshoremen and the rowdy element hung out. Everywhere I went, subway, elevated, or streetcar, I passed out cards. Nobody rebuked me. In fact, in forty years of cleaning up profanity nobody has ever got their back up with me. Instead, they apologize. That's how I enrolled my first members. A man would say, 'You're dead right, Mister. What a fool a man is to swear!' Then I'd catch him up. I'd look him right in the eye and say, 'If you feel that way, my boy, take a few hundred cards and pass them out yourself.' Presently I had around three hundred and fifty card-passing members in the city. For some reason the city membership stays around that figure. Old ones drop out, new ones come in. Internationally, I just don't know how many members we have. It must run into thousands. I don't burden myself down with a lot of records."

I lit a cigarette, and Mr. Colborne sniffed the smoke wistfully.

"Used to be a great cigar-smoker, but the doctors made me cut it out," he said. "Nothing like a good cigar! Well, as I told you, my store in Brooklyn did a big business, but in 1905, after I had operated it for fifteen years, I lost interest. It was taking up too much of my time. I had saved up some money and I had no dependents. All my family is dead. Far's I know, I'm the last of the Colbornes. So I closed the store and retired from business. Friends tried to stop me, but I told them I didn't want to do anything but fight profanity. I became a world traveller. In fact, between 1905 and 1936, I crossed the ocean twenty-five times. Went to all the important cities of Europe, passing out exterminators and talking. On shipboard you can really talk to people. They can't get away. I had exterminators printed up in French, Italian, Spanish, and Hebrew. Here and there I'd meet a go-getter, and I'd prevail on him to establish a branch of the League in his home country. At present there's branches in Italy, Cuba, Australia, and Kingston, Jamaica. I always had great success in Rome. Pope Pius X and Pope Pius XI both wrote me letters, blessing my work. I wouldn't take a mint of money for those letters. I bought me an iron safe in a second-hand store just to keep them locked up in. In Rome, in 1926, I sent a note to King Victor Emmanuel on a League letterhead. I told him I represented a multitude of right-thinking Americans, and we had a chat that lasted all morning. I got him so stirred up he talked the matter over with old Mussolini, and next year the two of them passed drastic laws against profanity. They posted warnings everywhere, even in streetcars, and arrested hundreds. I figure I'm personally responsible for ridding Italy of the profanity evil."

"Did the money you saved between 1890 and 1905 keep you going all these years?" I asked.

"Oh, that money ran out a generation ago," Mr. Colborne said. "I live very economic, and I return to my trade when I run low. I restore paintings in big churches, including St. Patrick's Cathedral. Off and on, I do special frame-making and gilding jobs. Sometimes I'll keep a job for years. Between 1918 and 1926, I worked for the Hippodrome Theatre, repairing everything that got out of whack. Profanity conditions among those show people were past belief when I went to work for the Hippodrome, but I cleaned things up, let me tell you. When I was travelling all over the world, it didn't cost me much. I used to make most of my expenses guiding Americans. I know the big cities of Europe as well as I know this basement. I've guided many a party to the miraculous grotto in Lourdes, to Rome, and to the Holy Land. Anyhow, it doesn't take much to keep the League going. I can get a hundred thousand exterminators printed for fifty dollars. It's the postage that amounts up. The mail I get! It's a sight. I have to do a lot of pecking on my typewriter to answer all my mail."

Mr. Colborne suddenly chuckled and slapped his knee.

"I sure got upset here the other day," he said. "I had written a whole lot of letters and I went out to mail them. On the way I stopped at a grocery for a box of eggs, and I got to talking to the clerk about profanity. After a while I left the grocery, and I was crossing the street when I heard a cabdriver a-cussing at a truckdriver. I got out an exterminator and started over to the cabdriver, and just then the lights changed and he drove off, still a-cussing. He drove right past me and splashed some muddy water on my britches. It was very provoking! And when I got back to my door I found I had forgotten to mail my letters, and when I looked in my pocket for my keys I remembered I had left them on my desk. Well, I got so vexed I stomped my foot on the floor and the eggs fell down and broke all to pieces, and then I came right out and said it!"

Mr. Colborne slapped his knee again.

"What did you say?" I asked.

"I said, 'The dickens!' "

We both laughed. While we were laughing, the alarm clock on the desk began to ring.

"That's to remind me to turn on the radio," Mr. Colborne said. "There's a program due I don't want to miss. Hillbilly singing. Very wholesome."

I got up to go. Mr. Colborne counted out twenty-five exterminators and insisted that I take them and pass them out.

"I'm afraid that's too many," I said.

"Oh, you'll use them up in no time," he said.

At the door I asked him if he believed that there is less profanity now than in 1901, when he began his work.

"Oh, my goodness, yes!" he said. "Sooner or later we'll have it all eradicated. There was a story in the *Holy Name Journal* that has some bearing on your question. It seems that two big turtles and one little turtle went into a saloon and ordered beers. It began to rain and one big turtle said to the other big turtle, 'We should've brought our umbrellas. How about asking the little turtle to run home and get our umbrellas?' But the little turtle was listening and he said, 'I'll not go get your umbrellas, because when I'm gone you'll drink my beer.' The big turtles promised they wouldn't, so the little turtle started out. Two months later one of the big turtles said to the other, 'If that little turtle doesn't come back soon, I'm going to drink his beer.' And just then, at the end of the bar, a tiny voice said, 'If you do, I won't go get your umbrellas.' "

I laughed, but there must have been a puzzled expression on my face, because Mr. Colborne said, "You don't get the connection between those turtles and the total eradication of cussing, do you?"

"I'm afraid I don't," I said.

"Slow but sure!" Mr. Colborne said, laughing heartily and giving me a poke in the ribs with an index finger. "Slow but sure!"

(1941)

# Obituary of a Gin Mill

*I*T MAKES ME LONESOME to walk past the old yellow-brick building, just south of Washington Market, once occupied by Dick's Bar and Grill. The windows are so dusty and rain-streaked and plastered with "For Rent" stickers that you can't see inside, and there is a padlock growing rusty on the door. Dick's prospered as a speakeasy throughout prohibition; after repeal, as a licensed establishment, it was just about as lawless as ever. A year or so ago, however, when Dick moved up the street, things changed. In his new place he commenced obeying the New York State Liquor Authority's regulations: he refused to let his customers shake Indian dice on the bar for rounds of drinks; he refused to put drinks on the tab; he refused to sell liquor by the bottle late at night after the liquor stores had closed. In the old days Dick was an independent man. He was delighted when he got an opportunity to tell a customer to go to hell. He and his bartenders, in fact, usually acted as if they loathed their customers and the customers liked this because it made them feel at home; most of them were men who were made ill at ease by solicitude or service. When Dick started abiding by the liquor laws, however, a hunted look appeared on his fat, sad-eyed, Neapolitan face. He began to cringe and bow and shake hands with the customers, and he would even help them on with their coats. When they finished eating, he would go over, smile with effort, and ask, "Was the pot roast O.K.?" In the old days he never acted that way. If someone complained about a gristly steak or a baked potato raw in the middle, he would grunt and say, "If you don't like my

243

grub, you don't have to eat in here. I'd just as soon I never saw you again."

The change in Dick reflects the innovations in his new saloon, which is six blocks away from the old one—a big, classy place with a chromium and glass-brick front, a neon sign in four colors, a mahogany bar, a row of chromium bar stools with red-leather seats like those in the uptown cocktail lounges, a kitchen full of gleaming copper pots, a moody chef who once worked in Moneta's, a printed menu with French all over it, and seven new brands of Scotch. He told the bartenders they would have to shave every morning and made them put on starched white coats. For several days thereafter they looked clean and aloof, like people when they first get out of the hospital. The place was so stylish that Dick did not, for good luck, frame the first dollar bill passed across the bar; he framed the first five-dollar bill.

Dick's regular customers had always been clannish—hanging together two and three deep at the end of the bar near the greasy swinging door to the kitchen—and some of them began to congregate at the fancy bar in Dick's new place. Here they resented everything. They snickered at the French on the menu, they sneered at the bartenders in their starched white coats. One of them waved a menu in Dick's face. "What the hell does this mean," he demanded, "this here 'Country Sausage Gastronome'?" The question made Dick uncomfortable. "It means meat sauce," he said.

Before the night of the grand opening was half over, one of the customers, an amateur evangelist who used to deliver burlesque sermons regularly in the old place, climbed up on the shiny new bar and began to preach. He had given out his text for the evening and was shouting "Brothers and sisters! You full of sin! You full of gin! You and the Devil are real close kin! Are you ready for the Judgment Day? Where will you spend eternity? Ain't it awful?" when Dick came out of the kitchen and caught sight of him. "Oh, my God!" Dick screamed. "Do you want to ruin me? I can't have such monkey business in here. I got a big investment in here." There was so much genuine agony in his voice that the amateur evangelist jumped down from his pulpit and apologized. Thereupon the old customers felt sorry for Dick. Sitting behind his bar on a busy night in the old joint, Dick used to have the aplomb of a sow on her belly in a bog, but in the new place he soon became apprehensive and haggard. One night the kitchen door swung open and the old customers saw Dick bent over a big ledger, struggling with his cost accounting. From the look on his face they knew he was quite sick of the chromium stools and the French menu. "He don't like this joint, either," one of them said. From then on they would tone down anyone who started to holler and throw glasses when Dick insisted on obeying the letter and the spirit of one of the alcohol laws. "After all," they would say, "he's got a big investment in here. He don't want to lose his license." However, no matter how big the investment, I never felt the same about the new Dick's.

When he is asked why he moved, Dick grunts and mutters, "It was time to change the sheets," but I have learned that he opened the new place only because he wanted a bigger kitchen. Soon after he made up his mind to move, however, a salesman for a bar-fixtures concern got hold of him and sold him a bill of goods. I believe that bar-equipment salesmen have done more to destroy the independence and individuality of New York gin mills and their customers than prohibition or repeal; there is nothing that will make a gin mill look so cheap and spurious as a modernistic bar and a lot of chairs made of chromium tubing. Dick's old place was dirty and it smelled like the zoo, but it was genuine; his new place is as shiny and undistinguished as a two-dollar alarm clock. The bar-equipment salesman was so relentless that Dick, who merely wanted a bigger kitchen, ended up by keeping nothing from the old place but the big, greasy, iron safe and a framed and fly-specked photograph of Gallant Fox. He even threw away all the photographs of Lupe Velez, his favorite movie actress. He used to have about a dozen pictures of Miss Velez tacked up on the wall, and sometimes he would gaze at one of them, shake his head, and say, "I would crawl a mile over broken beer bottles just to get one look at her in the flesh."

Dick is proud of his new kitchen. Food always interested him more than alcohol. He used to say, "I keep an A-1 kitchen." Once I saw him stand at the bar and eat an eight-pound turkey the chef had cooked for the luncheon trade. Dick had intended to eat only a drumstick, but after he had satisfied himself there was nothing left but a plateful of bones. Maxie, the tub-bellied head bartender, watched admiringly as Dick dismantled the turkey. "The boss sure does have a passion for groceries," he said. Even in the old days Dick often put strange dishes on his mimeographed menu. He had a friend who worked in a soup cannery up the street and one day the friend gave him a bucket of turtle livers. Dick put them on the menu. A customer said, "Well, that's something I never et." He ordered them, and while he ate, Dick watched intently. When the man put down his fork Dick went over to his table.

"How were them turtle livers?" he asked.

The customer deliberated for a moment.

"Fact of the matter is," he said, "they were kind of unusual."

"Well," said Dick proudly, "I want you to know that you're the first man in New York to eat turtle livers, so far as I know."

The customer shuddered.

A few nights ago I saw turtle livers on the menu in the new place. They were listed as "Pâté de Foie de Tortue Verte." Until I saw those pretenious words I never fully realized how dead and gone were the days when Dick was the plain-spoken proprietor of a dirty, lawless, back-street gin mill. I am aware that it is childish, but sometimes, leaning against the spick-and-span new bar, I am overcome by nostalgia for the gutter; I long for a "cabaret night" in Dick's old place. Friday was pay day in many of the offices and factories in the neighborhood and Friday night was "cabaret night" in Dick's. A beery old saloon musician would show up with an accordion and a mob of maudlin rummies would surround him to sing hymns and Irish songs. The place would be full of hard-drinking, pretty stenographers from the financial district, and they would be dragged off the bar stools to dance on the tiled floor. The dancers would grind peanut hulls under their shoes, making a strange, scratchy noise.

Some of the drunks would try to push the bar over, putting their

shoulders to it and heaving-to as they hummed the "Volga Boat-
men." Dick often threatened to use a seltzer siphon on their heads.
"I'll knock some sense in your heads someday, you goats!" he would
yell at his straining customers. He once classified the nuts in his
place as the barwalkers, the firebugs, the weepers, and the Carusos.
The barwalker was a type of drunk who was not happy unless he
was up on the sagging bar, arms akimbo, dancing a Cossack dance
and kicking over glasses of beer. The most unusual barwalker was
the ordinarily dignified city editor of an afternoon newspaper. He
would crawl up and down the bar, making a peculiar, dreadful
screech. Dick was always fascinated by him. One night he stared
at him and said, "What in the hell is that noise you're making?"
The city editor stopped screeching for a moment. "I'm a tree frog,"
he said, happily. The firebugs were those who found it impossible
to spill whiskey on the bar without setting it afire. The bartenders
would come running and slap out the fitful blue flames with bar
towels. One drunk used to pour whole glasses of brandy on the bar
and ignite it just to hear Dick yell. Once Dick hit this firebug over
the head with a seltzer siphon. The blow would have fractured the
firebug's skull if he hadn't been wearing a derby.

On those lovely, irretrievable nights a kind of mass hysteria would
sweep through the establishment. The customers would tire of
singing and dancing and shaking dice. There would be a lull. Then,
all of a sudden, they would start bellowing and throwing their drinks
on the floor. Arguments would commence. Someone would shout,
"Take off your glasses!" One night an ambulance from Broad Street
Hospital had to come and get two men who had differed over which
had the more nourishment in it: buttermilk or beer. As in a comic
strip, the air on these occasions would be full of missiles. Once a
customer who had been standing moodily at the bar for hours
suddenly let go with a little, heavy-bottomed whiskey glass and
knocked a big, jagged hole in the mirror behind the bar. Maxie, the
bartender, dodged out of the way. Then he remembered that the
mirror cost fifty-five dollars. "Dick's going to dock me a week's
pay because I ducked," said Maxie, groaning.

On cabaret nights one customer, an oyster shucker from Washington Market, would go off in a corner by himself, smiling happily, and lead an invisible jazz band, using a swizzle stick for a baton and sometimes yelling at an invisible trombone player, "Get hot, you bum!" Another customer, a tall, emaciated accountant, would hold up whatever object he got his hands on first and shout, "How much am I offered? Going, going, gone! Sold to that big dope over there with a cigar in his mouth." The accountant's name was Peterson, but Dick always called him Mr. St. Peter because he was so thin and old. Mr. St. Peter lived in a furnished room and spent whole days and nights in Dick's. Dick used to say that he had a bar-rail foot, that his right foot had become twisted by resting on the rail so much. Dick would point at him proudly and say, "Look at old Mr. St. Peter. When he goes home he walks on one heel." Mr. St. Peter's principal failing was an inability to make up his mind. For years he complained about the rolls in Dick's, wanting the poppy-seed variety. Dick finally ordered some and at lunch Mr. St. Peter said, "These sure are fine rolls." A moment later he added, "And then again, they ain't."

When he got tired of imitating an auctioneer, Mr. St. Peter would sidle over to the coat rack and slip such objects as beer pads and salt shakers into people's overcoat pockets. In Dick's, the customers wandered in and out of the kitchen at will, and once Mr. St. Peter got a mackerel out of the icebox and slipped it into someone's pocket. One cabaret night Dick got suspicious of Mr. St. Peter and found that the thin, undernourished rummy had slipped enough food into his own pockets to last him several days. In the old man's ragged overcoat Dick found eight cans of sardines and a big hunk of Swiss cheese. Dick was not angry. He was amused. "Mr. St. Peter reminds me," he said, "of a squirrel storing away nuts for a rainy day." In one stage of drunkenness Mr. St. Peter would spray people with a Flit gun; once he took the fire extinguisher off the kitchen wall and came out with it going full blast. Mr. St. Peter showed up for the grand opening night in Dick's new place, but I never saw him there again.

It was dangerous to pass out in Dick's old gin mill on a cabaret night. His customers thought there was nothing quite so funny as an unconscious man. They would strip him of his clothes and outfit him in a waiter's uniform or whatever garments, including raincoats, they could find in the lockers in the kitchen. Then they would stuff his pockets full of cryptic notes and drag him up the block, depositing him in a doorway and forgetting all about him. When the man woke up he would begin to scream and would never be the same again. I kept some of the slips one victim found in his pockets. They include the following: "The Shadow called. Said for you to call back." "Well, old boy, I guess your number is up this time." "Thursday afternoon at three. Make haste. The F.B.I. knows all about it." One man woke up with a rope around his neck.

There are never any good fist fights among the dried-up, mannerly men and women who hang out in Dick's new place. In the old saloon people were always slugging away at each other. The only rule of behavior Dick ever tried to enforce was "No fights outside on the street. It don't look nice. I don't want my store to get a bad name." (Like many old-fashioned saloonkeepers, Dick always referred to his place as "the store.") When a particularly violent cabaret-night seizure struck the gin mill, Dick usually locked the doors, knowing from experience that each newcomer would be infected with the hysteria and join right in. Dick would yell, "Lock the doors! We're having a nervous breakdown in here! Lock the doors!" Maxie was never unnerved. He would sometimes grin at the antics of a customer, shake his head, and say, "This place is a regular Bellevue Island." Once, in the middle of a furious Thanksgiving Eve, I saw him hunched over the bar reading a sports section and peacefully singing a song he learned in public school: "Glow, little glowworm, glisten, glisten."

In the new place, dressed like a drug clerk, Maxie is often called a sourpuss, but he laughed a lot in the old days. Nothing amused him so much as a customer with a hangover. "Did the Brooklyn boys get you?" he would ask. He would sing, "Shut the door, they're coming through the window. Shut the window, they're coming through the door." The suffering customer would shudder and beseech him to stop, but Maxie would keep on singing. "My God," he would wind up, triumphantly, "they're coming through the floor!"

Dick's old place was isolated; at night the streets surrounding it were deserted. Consequently there was always the fear of a holdup. When Maxie had the late trick and things were dull, he would take the money out of the cash register, hide it under the bar in a trash bucket, stretch out on the bar, and go to sleep, using his rolled-up overcoat for a pillow. "Let the robbers come," he would say, yawning. If more customers arrived, they would have to put pieces of ice in his ears to arouse him.

You never hear any conversation worth listening to in Dick's new place. In the old gin mill, when the customers got tired of whooping and sat down to talk to each other, they really had something to say. I remember a conversation I heard between two men in Dick's.

"So this friend of yours died, you mean?"

"Sure, she was murdered."

"How do you know she was murdered?"

"If you're murdered, you die, don't you, for God's sake?"

For a moment the two men were quiet, thinking.

"I'm preparing evidence," said the friend of the dead woman.

"What you got to do with it?"

"I'm afraid they might suspect me."

"Why should they suspect you?"

"Well, I'm getting everything ready in case they do."

Obeying the law spoiled Dick. Now he is just another gloomy small businessman, the same one day as the next. In the old days he was unpredictable. One night he would be as generous as a happy idiot, next night he would be stingy, setting up no drinks on the house at all.

Usually, when a customer came in, Dick would be expansive. He would call the customer by his first name and inquire about his health. However, if the customer got short of cash and began to put drinks on the tab, Dick would become distant in manner. His hearing would seem to fail. Soon he would begin using the customer's last name and putting an emphatic *"Mister"* in front of it. After a while the customer would be a total stranger to Dick. Then all Dick's civility would vanish and he would call the customer "You bum" or "You goat." If the customer got angry and said, "I'll never come into this place again," Dick's fat face would harden and he would lean forward and ask, "Will you put that in writing?"

One time Dick got drunk. Ordinarily he was able to withstand an enormous amount of liquor, but this time he got drunk. He had mixed up a big tub of May wine on a warm day and had sampled the brew as he mixed it. He developed fits of laughter, as though he were a schoolgirl with her first drink. The customers who came in looked funny to him. He pointed at them, slapped a thigh, and shook with laughter. Somebody suggested that he should buy drinks for everybody if he felt that good and he sobered up immediately. However, even on his stingy nights, Dick always gave a quarter to the grim Salvation Army women who came into the place, half-heartedly shaking tambourines. And I always liked the way he treated the scrubwomen from the skyscrapers in the financial district who would come in the place late at night for beer. Dick used to give them gin and say, "This is on the house. Drink hearty." He knew the old women really wanted gin but could not afford it.

You had to respect Dick, too, when you saw the way he behaved when one of his customers died. He would order a big, expensive wreath. Just before the funeral he and Maxie and the other bartenders would take off their aprons and shave themselves carefully at the sink in the kitchen. Then they would put on dark suits, and with solemn looks on their faces, they would get into Dick's automobile and go to the funeral, leaving the gin mill in the hands of the cook. Sometimes, particularly on dull, rainy nights, Dick would close up early and take all the customers left in the place to a burlesque show or to a basement chow-mein restaurant in China-town. He would take along a couple of bottles of Scotch and pay all the bills.

In the old days Dick often took part in the incessant dice game. He was an intense gambler. "This ain't ping-pong," he would yell when an unsteady player rolled the dice off the uneven bar. In the old gin mill they used to gamble for drinks and for money every night, but around Thanksgiving and Christmas they would have pig and turkey pools. For a quarter, a customer would get three throws of the dice. The dice would be thrown into a soup dish. After a certain number of games the customer with the highest score would get a live turkey or a suckling pig. One Christmas Dick kept the suckling pig in the window of the gin mill. The man who won the pig lifted it out of the window and named it Dick. He took off his necktie and tied it around the pig's belly. Then he lost interest in the pig and it ran around the saloon for hours, squealing and sniffing at the customers' shoes. Late that night the customer took the pig home with him in a taxicab. The customer lived in a hotel, and he put the pig in his bathroom. Next morning his wife found the pig and telephoned the A.S.P.C.A. to come and take it away.

The customers in the old place were always playing jokes on Dick. One night a man left the saloon, ostensibly to buy some aspirin. Instead, he went up the street to a telephone booth and called Dick, posing as a gangster. Warning Dick that he would have to pay for protection in the future, the customer said that two of the boys would be around to collect and for Dick to have fifty dollars in five-dollar bills ready to hand over. Otherwise it would be just too bad. Dick came out of the telephone booth with a frightened look on his face. After a while two strangers *did* happen to come in. They ordered beers. Trembling, Dick served them with the utmost courtesy. He had the money ready to hand over. When they finished their beers, the strangers went out, leaving two dimes on the bar. Dick sighed with relief. Presently one of the customers said, "Say, Dick, have you heard about the trick a lot of drunks have been playing on bartenders? They call them up and pose as gangsters. They tell them they have to pay protection or it'll be just too bad."

"Is that right?" said Dick, his face brightening.

"Yes," said the customer. "It's going on all over town. I'm surprised they haven't tried it on you."

"I'm surprised, too," said Dick, laughing heartily.

His worried look vanished. He even bought a round of drinks.

"Say, Dick," said the customer, after a while, "what would you do if some gangsters really tried to shake you down, God forbid?"

"What would I do?"

"Yes."

"Oh, hell," said Dick, "I just wouldn't stand for it. I'd reach across the bar and grab them and crack their heads together. I'd jar their back teeth loose."

(1939)

# Houdini's Picnic

CALYPSO SONGS COME FROM TRINIDAD, a British West Indian island, six miles off the coast of Venezuela, which also provides the world with asphalt and Angostura Bitters. They are written and sung by a band of haughty, amoral, hard-drinking men who call themselves Calypsonians. The majority are Negroes. With guitars slung under their arms, they hang out in rumshops and Chinese cafés on Marine Square and Frederick Street in Port-of-Spain, the principal city of Trinidad, hunting for gossip around which they can construct a Calypso. Several brag truthfully that women fight to support them. Most of them are veterans of the island jails. To set themselves apart from lesser men, they do not use their legal names but live and sing under such adopted titles as the Growler, the Lord Executor, King Radio, Attila the Hun, the Lion, the Gorilla, the Caresser, the Senior Inventor, and Lord Ziegfeld. Some of their songs are based on sensational news stories—a bedroom murder, a switchblade fight between two prominent madams, the suicide of a concupiscent white Englishwoman. Other Calypso songs deal with abstract matters like love, honor, man's fall, the wisdom of marrying a woman uglier than you, or the question of which has the most ache in it, a rum hangover or a gin hangover. Others are character studies; one of these is called "They Talk about Nora's Badness." In it, Nora's frailty is defined in a recurring line: "She go to the old dance hall and drink alcohol with Peter and Paul."

Some Calypsonians sing in a patois which contains English, Spanish, French, and Hindu words and idioms, but the majority sing in

English with a peculiarly distorted British accent; in their mouths "parrot" becomes "pair-ott," "temperament" becomes "tem-pair-a-mint," and "hat" becomes "hot." They are fond of big words and their conversation is flamboyant. The Lion, for example, does not say "Hello"; he says, "I embrace the rotundity of conventionality and wish you good day." Many Calypso songs are considered obscene or subversive by the British colonial government; sometimes it bans a song and jails the singer. Just before the war, for what it said was a diplomatic reason, the government banned an arrogant Calypso called "Hitler Demands," in which the Growler sang, "Hitler, me lad, take things easily, otherwise we sure to run you out of Germany." By "we," the Growler meant the British Empire.

The most prolific of the Calypsonians is a Negro who calls himself Wilmoth Houdini. A few years ago he left Trinidad and worked his way to New York as a greaser on a freighter. Occasionally he goes back for a long visit, making expenses by singing in Port-of-Spain movie theatres under the billing of "The Calypso King of New York," but most of the time he lives in a furnished room on West 114th Street, in lower Harlem, where there is a large settlement of immigrants from Trinidad. His passport name is Edgar Leon Sinclair; in Harlem he is called Mr. Houdini. He took the name from a movie serial he saw in 1916 in which Houdini, the magician, was featured. He was the first Calypsonian to make recordings. He has turned out thousands of songs, and more than six hundred of them have been put on records. He is the author of many classics. They include "Old Man You Too Old, You Too Bold, in Fact You Too Cold," "I Like Bananas Because They Have No Bones," "Keep Your Money, Hot Daddy," and "Drunk and Disorderly." Houdini makes public appearances at "picnics" held in Harlem halls by an organization of convivial, homesick West Indians called the Trinidad Carnival Committee. He is the moving spirit of the Committee; other members are the manager of a beauty parlor, an ex-alderman, and a dentist. In Harlem there are two good hot West Indian bands, the Caribbean Serenaders and the Krazy Kats, and musicians selected from these bands are hired to supply the music at picnics. The Committee sends out folders bearing this proclamation: "Let us Dine and Dance!

People talk about Dance? Mister, look Dance! Madam, look Dance!"

One night I went to one of the Committee's picnics with Mr. Ralph Perez, a Puerto Rican of Spanish descent who works in the export department of Decca Records, Inc. He has been in the record business nearly twenty years, building up catalogues of Latin-American, Mexican, and West Indian music for several companies. Decca sends him to Port-of-Spain once each year. He arrives just before the pre-Lenten carnival, when Calypsonians set up palm-thatched "tents" in vacant lots and sing the pick of their newest songs. He rents a house, makes it soundproof, sobers up a few singers, and records a year's supply of Calypso.

The picnic Mr. Perez took me to was held in a long, narrow hall on the third floor of a seedy building on Lenox Avenue, just below 116th Street. When we arrived, at ten o'clock, only about fifty people were there. "Picnics are apt to start late and wind up at the break of day," Mr. Perez said. Against one wall there was a row of slat-backed chairs. A number of stout, middle-aged women were sitting on these chairs, smoking cigarettes and gossiping. A space had been roped off for the band. Beyond this space, in the far corner of the room, there was a short bar and five tables covered with white oilcloth. At these tables sat young Negro and Creole women in evening dresses, drinking. I saw one take a pint of whiskey out of her handbag. She poured some of the whiskey in a paper cup, drank it straight, and put the bottle back in her handbag. "They're waiting for their menfolks to arrive," Mr. Perez said. "The men in this neighborhood work late, most of them. The men you'll see here tonight will be elevator operators, barbers, hotel workers, musicians, and a few professional people." We went over and stood at the bar, which was tended by a buxom, smiling woman. Mr. Perez said she was Mrs. Lynch, a Committee member and manager of Isabel's Salon, a Harlem beauty parlor. Assisted by two solemn, pretty children, her daughters, Mrs. Lynch was transferring bottles of beer and pop to a washtub which was half full of cracked ice. Back of the bar was a sign: "PATTIES AND PAYLOU SERVED FREE AT THE BAR AT INTERMISSION. DRINKS WILL BE SOLD AT MODERATE PRICES." Mr. Perez said the favorite drink at a picnic is rye mixed with orange pop. "Most people bring their own whiskey," he said. When Mrs. Lynch finished putting the bottles on ice, she said, "I told Houdini to run out and get the whiskey we going to sell here tonight, and he's sure taking his time." Mrs. Lynch had white strings hanging from the lobes of her ears, and I asked her what they signified. "Just dental floss," she said. "I had my ears pierced for earrings, and the doc told me to keep the pierces open with floss. It may look unusual, but it don't hurt." I heard some noise on the stairs, and then the band arrived. It was made up of Gregory Felix and three members of his Krazy Kat band—a drummer, a violinist, and a piano-player. The piano-player was a girl named Wilhelmina Gale. "I'm the clarinet," said Mr. Felix, "and Houdini's going to play the shakers and the gin bottle. Consequently, we got a five-piece band." Miss Gale went to the upright piano and removed its front and top boards. Then, with no preliminaries at all, she and the others took their places and began playing a rumba. Almost immediately, as if by signal, people started coming up the stairs in droves. Soon there were more than two hundred Negroes in the little hall.

After the band had knocked off a couple of rumbas, a lean, gloomy-eyed man came up the stairs. There was a yellow rose in the lapel of his camel's-hair topcoat. Under one arm he had a bulky package, and under the other was a big roasting pan. The lid of the pan was tied on with a piece of heavy cord. "That's Houdini," Mr. Perez said. As Houdini walked jauntily past the band, he said, "I got whiskey and paylou, me lads." Mr. Perez said that paylou is joints of fowl cooked with rice and onions. (In Charleston it is spelled "pilau.") Houdini gave the pan of paylou to Mrs. Lynch. Mr. Perez introduced me to Houdini, and he said, "Please to make your acquaintance. Let's have a drink." He tore open his package and placed five quarts of whiskey on the bar. Then he went away for a moment and returned with a jug of a heavy, milky liquid. "Home-brewed ginger beer," he said. "This the drink that dominates alcohol. Whiskey can go to your feet when you got ginger beer inside you, but it can't go to your head because it's dominated." He poured some ginger beer into a paper cup and laced it heavily with rye. He drank it in one gulp. Then he said, "Where me shakers?"

Mrs. Lynch handed him a pair of maracas, which are gourds with shot inside. "First song's going to be 'Daddy, Turn on the Light,' " he said. He went inside the band enclosure, stood up on a chair, and yelled, "Now then, me lads!" The band livened up when he began shaking the maracas. Presently the hall was seething with Lindy-hop, Susy-Q, and shim-sham-shimmy dancers, and Houdini stuffed the maracas in the pockets of his jacket and picked up a megaphone. The dancers seemed to pay no attention as he sang, but the old women sitting stiffly on the slat-backs along the wall listened attentively with big smiles on their faces. The first verse was:

> *Please turn on the light, Dad-dee.*
> *Why you like to bite?*
> *Honey, don't squeeze me so tight.*
> *Act so you mean to kill me tonight.*

The song went on and on. It ended this way:

> *This is what I want you to know.*
> *It is indeed inescapably so.*
> *Daddy, don't treat me like that,*
> *You got to le' me go, le' me shake meself.*
> *By did de-dup, bick bick bickety buck,*
> *Le' me shake meself!*

When the song was finished, Houdini jumped off the chair and hurried to the bar. "Where me ginger beer?" he asked. Mrs. Lynch handed him the jug and he mixed drinks for the band. Men and women were standing three deep at the bar. Mrs. Lynch was kept busy measuring out rye at fifteen cents a jigger. Some held a bottle of orange pop in one hand and a jigger of rye in the other, following a gulp of rye with a long swallow of pop. A laughing, half-drunk girl got up on one of the tables opposite the bar and commenced to tap-dance. The table tilted and she screamed and leaped to the floor, ripping her dress in the rear. An older woman, evidently her mother, rushed to the girl and examined her dress. "Why don't you behave yourself, Miss Wriggle-Tail?" she said. "Now you've ruined your dress." "Oh, I don't care," the girl replied. "It was rump-sprung anyway." Houdini went behind the bar and got a spoon and a square green gin bottle. He showed the bottle to me. "I brought her from Trinidad," he said. "I beat out many a tune on her. I can make her palpitate. I call her Ol' Square Face." The bottle was a third full of water. The band struck up another rumba—whatever it played sounded like a rumba—and Houdini returned to the enclosure and got up on his chair. He began a rhythmic, tantalizing beat on the bottle with the spoon. Soon he was making more noise than all the other musicians. After a while, abruptly, he began to sing:

> I look for miser-ee
> Wherever I meet Johnnie.
> People, people, be sorry to see
> The grave for Johnnie, the gallows for me.

The old women along the wall began to smile again. "The name of this one is 'Johnnie Take My Wife,'" Mr. Perez said.

> This Mr. Johnnie must be ver-ee nice,
> For me wife called Johnnie in her sleep last night.
> But from today I intend to go
> On a hunt for Mr. Johnnie, that gigolo.
> I went in the house to get me gun,
> Me wife seen me coming and she starts to run.
> But let me tell you where I lose me head:
> Mr. Johnnie was hiding underneath the bed.
> Johnnie, you should never do a t'ing like that,
> To stab Papa Houdini in the back.
> The judge and jury going to see me face,
> For the thing going to end in a murder case.

Houdini's next number was also about unhappy love. It was excessively sentimental. At intervals he would quit singing and speak in an unknown tongue, "Bick bick bickety bong bong de dup." The chorus went, "But I'm sure you will pay for me love some good day, that is all what I have got to say." Only the old women along the wall listened to him. The men and women on the crowded dance floor minded their own business. Occasionally one of the expertly wanton dancers would shudder and let out a loud moan, and then all the others would laugh uproariously and scream, "Hold tight! Hold tight!" or "Peace, sister!" Mr. Perez looked at the sweating dancers and said, "There's a mixture of bloods in Trinidad. There's French, Spanish, Carib, Negro, Hindu, and Chinese. You can see it reflected in the faces here. You can see Hindu in the face of that big rumba-dancer. There are thousands of Hindus in Trinidad. The girl with him is a Creole." I looked at the Creole. Her face was lovely. She reminded me of Dolores Del Rio. Presently Houdini got tired and stepped off the chair. Mr. Perez asked him to sit with us and have a drink. He brought his jug of ginger beer to the table. I asked him how he became a Calypso singer, and he began to talk smoothly and rapidly, almost like a public speaker.

"I was inspired in 1916," he said. "Before that, I was just nobody. In the year 1916 a band were organized in Port-of-Spain by a distinguished girl named Maggie Otis. She was Queen of the band. I was King. It was called the African Millionaires. It had twenty-four men and girls. The men wore striped green silk shirts, flannel pants, and white shoes, and each had strung to him a camera, a stuffed crocodile, or a pair of field glasses. That was to ape the rich tourists who come to Trinidad. The girls dressed in a manner likewise. At Mardi Gras, which falls on the two days before Lent, the big stores and companies in Port-of-Spain give prizes of rum and money to the Calypsonian who improvises the best song about their merchandise. In 1916, with the African Millionaires in back of me, I entered the advertising competitions and won seven in one day, singing extemporaneously against men like the Senior Inventor and the Lord Executor. I collected the big prize from the Angostura Bitters people and the big prize from the Royal Extra Stout brewery people, and all like that. In those competitions you have to improvise a song on the spur of the moment, and it has to be in perfect time with the band. You must be inspired to do so.

"That night, in a tent, I had a war with some old Calypsonians. A tent is a bamboo shack with a palm roof. The Calypsonians sing in them during carnival and charge admission. A war is where three Calypsonians stand up on the platform in a tent and improvise in verse. One man begins in verse, telling about the ugly faces and impure morals of the other two. Then the next man picks up the song and proceeds with it. On and on it goes. If you falter when it comes your turn, you don't dare call yourself a Calypsonian. Most war songs are made up of insults. You give out your insults, and then the next man insults you. The man who gives out the biggest insults is the winner. I was so insulting in my first war the other men congratulated me. Since then I maintain my prestige and integrity as Houdini the Calypsonian. I got a brain that ticks like a clock. I can sing at any moment on any matter. If you say to me, 'Sing a song about that gentleman over there,' I swallow once and do so."

The lovely Creole came over to our table. She put a hand on Houdini's head and said, "Quit beating your gums together, Papa Houdini, and help me out with a drink." Houdini laughed and said, "The greatest pleasure, Madam!" He poured her a drink; she kissed him and walked away.

"Excuse the interruption," said Houdini, following the girl with his eyes. "As I say, I am a true Calypsonian, the only one in this country. Of course, I have to go back to Trinidad to renew me inspiration. It is like a door that has been shut a long time. The hinge get rusty. But the minute the rust fall off the hinge, the door come back supple again. I have to go back to Trinidad to drop off the rust on me. I have to go back and eat some calaloo. That's bluecrab soup. It's Sunday soup. I have to go back and drink some gin juleps. That's green-coconut water and gin. That builds up me vitamin and contributes to me inspiration. I tell you a most peculiar thing about me. I am born in Brooklyn. The year of 1902. Father was a steward, and the family were living in Brooklyn when I came. Of course, we return to Trinidad when I was two. I come from a wandering family.

"Houdini, come here!" Mrs. Lynch shouted.

"I be there in a minute," Houdini called. Then he took another drink and resumed the conversation. "I tell you," he said, "the thing I don't comprehend is why some big night club doesn't hire me to sing Calypso in it. It would be remarkable. It would be a rage. That will happen sooner or late. Whiskey don't murder me, Madison Square Garden is where I wind up.

"I am now in possession of a numerous amount of new compositions. They come to me at all hours, day and night. Last night I went to the Apollo Theatre and I ran home in the drizzling rain. So I decide to take a bath to keep off a cold. I was in the tub and a Calypso come to me. I beat on the side of the tub with me fingernails to get the tune. The name turned out to be 'From the Day of Birth I Been Told I Got Rhythm in My Soul.' Me trunk is so full of compositions I got no room for me suits. Pretty soon I think I make some new records. I used to get paid fifty dollars per record for me and the musicians, and a royalty of a penny per record. The royalties running thin, and I think I make some new ones. I am favorably known for suggestive Calypso, but I am a true Catholic and I have made many shouting Calypsos of a religious nature. One is a carol. It starts off like this: 'The Blessed Virgin had a baby boy. The baby came from the Kingdom and the name of the baby was Jesus.' "

He was interrupted again.

"You got to come help with the paylou!" Mrs. Lynch shouted. "It's intermission!"

"Everybody depend on me," Houdini said, getting up. "After a picnic I go to bed for a week."

He hurried to the bar and pulled the strands of cord off the roasting pan. He took off the lid and began dishing out the paylou, placing mounds of rice and joints of chicken on paper plates. Mrs. Lynch passed out the patties. They were small, herb-seasoned meat pies, wrapped in wax paper. Pretty soon Houdini sent a man to Mrs. Lynch's apartment for two more pans of paylou and patties. Each person who could show the stub of a fifty-cent admission ticket got a plate of paylou from Houdini and a patty from Mrs. Lynch. "I made those patties," Houdini said. "They got my signature on them." The people ate standing up. Presently the floor around the bar was strewn with paper plates and forks and empty pint bottles. An aged woman sat on a chair in a corner, peacefully sleeping with her mouth open, in the midst of the hubbub. "She sure did a good job of passing out," Houdini said. "If she don't wake up, she's going to miss out on the paylou." He went over and shook her awake and placed a plate of paylou on her lap. She blinked blearily and said, "I thank you. Now fetch me a fork." Intermission was over at two-thirty. Then the band went back to work. At three o'clock, Mr. Perez and I said goodbye to Mrs. Lynch and Houdini. After I turned to go downstairs, I looked back and saw Houdini climb up on his chair. He began beating out a tune on Ol' Square Face, the green gin bottle, and singing a Calypso called, Mr. Perez said, "Tiger Tom Kill Tiger Cat, Damblay Santapie and Rat." I asked him what the title meant. "I don't know," he said. "Something to do with a woman, I guess."

Downstairs Mr. Perez and I stopped in a fried-fish café for a cup of coffee. I asked him how Calypso originated, and he quoted a song written by the Lord Executor:

> Would you like to know what is Calypso?
> It was sung by the Creoles years ago.
> It was danced by the African drums in a bamboo tent
> And sung in patois for amusement.
> Now it is played in tone
> On a gramophone.

Mr. Perez said that Calypso is probably an old patois word meaning "work song." There seems to be no connection between Calypso songs and the Calypso of the "Odyssey." Historians on the island believe the institution had its origin when slaves, recently from Africa, would divide into competitive groups and sing ribald songs of derision at each other as they worked in the fields. In their huts at night, however, they directed the songs against their masters. A few Calypsonians still sing in this tradition. When Sir Alfred Claud

Hollis, once governor for the Crown in Trinidad, returned to England, a Calypsonian sang:

> *I must be very frank and say*
> *I was glad when Sir Hollis went away.*
> *He cared only for his own enjoyment*
> *And did nothing to help us find employment.*

The Growler and Attila the Hun have often been jailed for criticism of the colonial administration. The Crown officials evidently have mixed feelings about Calypso; at Mardi Gras they put up $500 in prizes for the best songs, yet they exercise a strict and sometimes stifling censorship over the singers. Mr. Perez must submit any song he wishes to record to the Colonial Secretary. Many of the most inspired songs are turned down because they are considered indecent, sacrilegious, or "detrimental to the Government." Some Calypsonians get in trouble with the administration by writing blackmail songs. Such a singer will learn an embarrassing fact about a prominent Trinidadian and write a song around it; then he will go to the man and offer to forget the song for a few dollars. Sometimes, after he has been paid off, he will sing it in the cafés and rumshops anyway, just for the hell of it.

The principal benefactor of the Calypsonians is a Portuguese businessman named Edward Sa Gomes, who operates a chain of music stores on Trinidad and Tobago, a nearby island. He lends them money, bails them out when they land in jail, and arbitrates their incessant disputes. He helps Mr. Perez round them up to make records. Mr. Perez pays the Calypsonians ten dollars a song and royalties. On one trip he recorded three hundred. When the singers get paid, they promptly spend their money for clothes and liquor. They are constantly fighting with each other, sometimes for a sly business reason. For example, Houdini once made an insulting record called "Executor, the Homeless Man." The Lord Executor answered with an equally insulting record, "My Reply to Houdini." People in Trinidad bought both records, just to see whose reputation was damaged more. The Lord Executor is dean of the Calypsonians. He is old and wizened and touchy. He walks the streets mumbling to himself. He says he is composing, but his colleagues say, "The Executor's got a mumbling jag on." His songs are all gloomy, such as "Seven Skeletons Found in the Yard" and "I Don't Know How the Young Men Living."

Few of the Calypsonians can read or write, but they are able to keep hundreds of songs in their heads. Even so, no Calypsonian ever sings a song the same way twice; that would bore him. They are contemptuous of each other. The hungrier they get the haughtier they get. It is characteristic of a Calypsonian to sing about his colleagues like this:

> *Walking with a toothpick between their teeth,*
> *Making people understand they just done eat,*
> *Crediting beds from the stores in town,*
> *But the agents coming and unmount them down.*

The Calypsonian is highly ethical in his own fashion. He will steal a bottle of rum from a colleague, or a pair of shoes, or a girl, but never a song. "The Executor would damn near cut his throat before he would sing one of Houdini's songs, and vice versa," Mr. Perez said. All Calypsonians believe that women are powerless to resist them. King Radio, a small, one-eyed man who wears dark glasses, boasts that he is supported by fifty women. Mr. Perez quoted one of Radio's songs:

> *They can't find a lover like me again.*
> *I'm the only lover in Port-of-Spain.*
> *Fifty women now supporting me*
> *And all of them belong to high society.*
> *I even got a boy to tend the phone*
> *In case you should ring me up at home.*

Many of Radio's songs contain advice about women. One song is "Man Smart, Woman Smarter." Another begins:

*If you want to be happy and live a king's life,*
*Never make a pretty woman your wife.*
*That's from a logical point of view,*
*Always love a woman uglier than you.*

The best-selling Calypso records in the United States are those based on the adventures of Nettie, Nora, Lizzie, and other loose girls. Those concerning the womanly qualities of Mrs. Simpson and the abdication of King Edward VIII also sell well. The abdication was the most popular subject in the history of Calypso; every singer had a go at it. It is generally conceded that the Caresser did the best job. He had an idea that "old Baldwin" kept the King imprisoned in England, preventing him from crossing the sea and marrying Mrs. Simpson in New York. This is the chorus of the Caresser's song:

*It's love, it's love alone*
*That cause King Edward to leave the throne.*

Some of the verses are:

*Oh, what a sad disappointment*
*Was endured by the British Government.*
*On the tenth of December we heard the talk*
*That he gave the throne to the Duke of York.*

*Am sorry my mother is going to grieve,*
*But I cannot help, I am bound to leave.*
*I got the money, I got the talk,*
*And the fancy walk just to suit New York.*

*And if I can't get a boat to set me free*
*I'll walk to Miss Simpson across the sea.*
*He said my robes and crown is upon my mind,*
*But I cannot leave Miss Simpson behind.*

*If you see Miss Simpson walk down the street,*
*She could fall an angel with the body beat.*
*Let the organ roll, let the church bell ring,*
*Good luck to our second bachelor King.*

The Gorilla, in his abdication song, was more defiant. He sang:

*Believe me, friends, if I were King,*
*I'd marry any woman and give her a ring.*
*I wouldn't give a damn what the people say*
*So long as she can wash, cook, and dingo-lay.*

(1939)

# The Mohawks in High Steel

*T*HE MOST FOOTLOOSE INDIANS in North America are a band of mixed-blood Mohawks whose home, the Caughnawaga Reservation, is on the St. Lawrence River in Quebec. They are generally called the Caughnawagas. In times past, they were called the Christian Mohawks or the Praying Mohawks. There are three thousand of them, at least six hundred and fifty of whom spend more time in cities and towns all over the United States than they do on the reservation. Some are as restless as gypsies. It is not unusual for a family to lock up its house, leave the key with a neighbor, get into an automobile, and go away for years. There are colonies of Caughnawagas in Brooklyn, Buffalo, and Detroit. The biggest colony is in Brooklyn, out in the North Gowanus neighborhood. It was started in the late twenties, there are approximately four hundred men, women, and children in it, it is growing, and it shows signs of permanence. A few families have bought houses. The pastor of one of the churches in the neighborhood, the Cuyler Presbyterian, has learned the Mohawk dialect of the Iroquois language and holds a service in it once a month, and the church has elected a Caughnawaga to its board of deacons. There have been marriages between Caughnawagas and members of other groups in the neighborhood. The Caughnawaga women once had trouble in finding a brand of corn meal (Quaker White Enriched and Degerminated) that they like to use in making *ka-na-ta-rok,* or Indian boiled bread; all the grocery stores in North Gowanus, even the little Italian ones, now carry it. One saloon, the Nevins Bar & Grill, has become a Caughnawaga hangout and is referred to in the neighborhood as the Indian Bank; on weekend nights, two-thirds of its customers are Caughnawagas; to encourage their patronage, it stocks one Montreal ale and two Montreal beers. A saying in the band is that Brooklyn is the downtown of Caughnawaga.

Caughnawaga Reservation is on the south shore of the St. Lawrence, just above Lachine Rapids. It is nine miles upriver from Montreal, which is on the north shore. By bus, it is half an hour from Dominion Square, the center of Montreal. It is a small reservation. It is a tract of farmland, swamp, and scrub timber that is shaped like a half-moon; it parallels the river for eight miles and is four miles wide at its widest point. On the river side, about midway, there is a sprawled-out village, also named Caughnawaga. Only a few of the Caughnawagas are farmers. The majority live in the village and rent their farmland to French Canadians and speak of the rest of the reservation as "the bush." The Montreal-to-Malone, New York, highway goes through Caughnawaga village. It is the main street. On it are about fifty commonplace frame dwellings, the office of the Agent of the Indian Affairs Branch of the Canadian government, the Protestant church (it is of the United Church of Canada denomination), the Protestant school, and several Indian-owned grocery stores and filling stations. The stores are the gathering places of the old men of the village. In each store is a cluster of chairs, boxes, and nail kegs on which old men sit throughout the day, smoking and playing blackjack and eating candy bars and mumbling a few words now and then, usually in Mohawk. In the front yards of half a dozen of the dwellings are ramshackly booths displaying souvenirs—papoose dolls, moccasins, sweet-grass baskets, beadwork handbags, beadwork belts, beadwork wristwatch straps, and pincushions on which beads spell out "Mother Dear," "Home Sweet Home," "I Love U," and similar legends. In one yard, between two totem poles, is a huge, elm-bark tepee with a sign on it that reads, "Stop! & Pow Wow With Me. Chief White Eagle. Indian Medicine Man. *Herbages Indiens.*" Except on ceremonial occasions and for show purposes, when they put on fringed and beaded buckskins and feather headdresses of the Plains Indian type, Caughnawagas dress as other Canadians do, and if it were not for these front-yard establishments, most motorists would be unaware that they were passing through an Indian village. A scattering of Caughnawagas look as Indian as can be; they have high cheekbones and jut noses, their eyes are sad, shrewd, and dark brown, their hair is straight and coal black, their skin is smooth and coppery, and they have the same beautiful, erect, chin-lifted, haughty walk that gypsies have. White blood, however, has blurred the Indianness of the majority; some look dimly but unmistakably Indian, some look Indian only after one has searched their faces for Indian characteristics, and some do not look Indian at all. They run to two physical types; one type, the commoner, is thickset, fleshy, and broad-faced, and the other is tall, bony, and longheaded. Some of the younger Caughnawagas have studied a little of the Indian past in school and they disapprove of the front-yard establishments. They particularly disapprove of Chief White Eagle's establishment; they feel that it gives visitors a highly erroneous impression of Caughnawaga right off the bat. First of all, the old Mohawks did not live in tepees but in log-and-bark communal houses called longhouses, and they did not make totem poles. Also, there haven't been any chiefs in Caughnawaga, except self-appointed ones, since 1890. Furthermore, while all Caughnawagas have Indian names, some much fancier than White Eagle, few go under them outside their own circles, and those who do almost invariably run them together and preface them with a white given name; John Goodleaf, Tom Tworivers, and Dominick Twoax are examples. Caughnawagas discovered long ago that whites are inclined to look upon Indian names, translated or untranslated, as humorous. In dealing with whites, ninety-five per cent of them go under white names, and have for many generations. Most of these names are ordinary English, Scotch, Irish, or French ones, a number of which date back to intermarriages with early settlers. The names of the oldest and biggest Caughnawaga families are Jacobs, Williams, Rice, McComber, Tarbell, Stacey, Diabo (originally D'Ailleboust), Montour, De Lisle, Beauvais, and Lahache. The most frequent given names are Joe, John, and Angus, and Mary, Annie, and Josie.

On each side of the highway there is a labyrinth of lanes, some dirt, some gravel, and some paved. Some are straight and some are snaky. The dwellings on them are much older than those on the highway, and they range from log cabins to big field-stone houses with frame wings and lean-tos; members of three and even four generations of a family may live in one house. In the yards are gardens and apple trees and sugar-maple trees and piles of automobile junk and groups of outbuildings, usually a garage, a privy, a chicken coop, and a stable. Large families keep a cow or two and a plug horse; the French Canadians who rent the reservation farmland sell all their worn-out horses to the villagers. The dwellings in Caughnawaga are wired for electricity, just about every family has a radio and a few have telephones, but there is no waterworks system. Water for drinking and cooking is obtained from public pumps—the old-fashioned boxed-up, long-handled kind—situated here and there on the lanes. Water for washing clothes and for bathing is carted up from the river in barrels, and the horses are used for this. They are also used for carting firewood, and the children ride them. Most mornings, the cows and horses are driven to unfenced pastures on the skirts of the village. A few always mosey back during the day and wander at will.

The busiest of the lanes is one that runs beside the river. On it are the reservation post office, the Catholic church, the Catholic schools, a parish hall named Kateri Hall, and a small Catholic hospital. The post office occupies the parlor in the home of Frank McDonald Jacobs, the patriarch of the band. A daughter of his, Veronica Jacobs, is postmistress. The church, St. Francis Xavier's, is the biggest building in the village. It is a hundred years old, it is made of cut stone of a multiplicity of shades of silver and gray, and the cross on its steeple is surmounted by a gilded weathercock. It is a Jesuit mission church; at its altar, by an old privilege, masses are said in Mohawk. In the summer, sightseeing buses from Montreal stop regularly at St. Francis Xavier's and a Jesuit scholastic guides the sightseers through it and shows them its treasures, the most precious of which are some of the bones of Kateri Tekakwitha, an Indian virgin called the Lily of the Mohawks who died at Caughnawaga in 1680. The old bones lie on a watered-silk cushion in a glass-topped chest. Sick and afflicted people make pilgrimages to the church and pray before them. In a booklet put out by the church, it is claimed that sufferers from many diseases, including cancer, have been healed through Kateri's intercession. Kateri is venerated because of the bitter penances she imposed upon herself; according to the memoirs of missionaries who knew her, she wore iron chains, lay upon thorns, whipped herself until she bled, plunged into icy water, went about barefoot on the snow, and fasted almost continuously.

On a hill in the southern part of the village are two weedy graveyards. One is for Catholics, and it is by far the bigger. The other is for Protestants and pagans. At one time, all the Caughnawagas were Catholics. Since the early twenties, a few have gone over to other faiths every year. Now, according to a Canadian government census, 2,682 are Catholics, 251 belong to Protestant denominations, and 77 are pagans. The so-called pagans—they do not like the term and prefer to be known as the longhouse people— belong to an Indian religion called the Old Way or the Handsome Lake Revelation. Their prophet, Handsome Lake, was a Seneca who in 1799, after many years of drunkenness, had a vision in which the spirits up above spoke to him. He reformed and spent his last fifteen years as a roving preacher in Indian villages in upstate New York. In his sermons, he recited some stories and warnings and precepts that he said the spirits had revealed to him. Many of these have been handed down by word of mouth and they constitute the gospel of the religion; a few men in each generation—they are called "the good-message-keepers"—memorize them. The precepts are simply stated. An example is a brief one from a series concerning the sins of parents: "It often happens that parents hold angry disputes in the hearing of their infant child. The infant hears and comprehends their angry words. It feels lost and lonely. It can see for itself no happiness in prospect. This is a great sin." During the nineteenth century, Handsome Lake's religion spread to every Iroquois reservation in the United States and Canada except Caughnawaga. It reached Caughnawaga right after the First World War and, despite the opposition of Catholics and Protestants, began to be practiced openly in 1927. Handsome Lake's followers meet in ceremonial structures that they call longhouses. The Caughnawaga longhouse is on the graveyard hill. It resembles a country schoolhouse. It is a plain, one-room, frame building surrounded by a barbed-wire fence. Several times a year, on dates determined by the phases of the moon or the rising of sap in the sugar maples or the ripening of fruits and vegetables, the longhouse people get together and hold thanks-giving festivals, among which are a Midwinter Festival, a Thanks-to-the-Maple Festival, a Strawberry Festival, and a String Bean Festival. In the course of the festivals, they burn little heaps of sacred tobacco leaves, eat a dish called corn soup, make public confessions of their sins, and chant and dance to the music of rattles and drums. The smoke from the tobacco fires is supposed to ascend to the spirits. The sacred tobacco is not store-bought. It is a kind of tobacco known as Red Rose, an intensely acrid species that grows wild in parts of the United States and Canada. The longhouse people grow it in their gardens from wild seed and cure the leaves in the sun. The longhouse rattles are gourds or snapping-turtle shells with kernels of corn inside them, and the drums are wooden pails that barn paint came in with rawhide or old inner tubes stretched over their mouths. The Catholics and Protestants complain that for several days after a longhouse festival everyone on the reservation is moody.

The Caughnawagas are among the oldest reservation Indians. The band had its origin in the latter half of the seventeenth century, when French Jesuit missionaries converted somewhere between fifty and a hundred Iroquois families in a dozen longhouse villages in what is now western and northern New York and persuaded them to go up to Quebec and settle in a mission outpost. This outpost was on the St. Lawrence, down below Lachine Rapids. The converts began arriving there in 1668. Among them were members of all the tribes in the Iroquois Confederacy—Mohawks, Oneidas, Onondagas, Cayugas, and Senecas. There were also a few Hurons, Eries, and Ottawas who had been captured and adopted by the Iroquois and had been living with them in the longhouse villages. Mohawks greatly predominated, and Mohawk customs and the Mohawk dialect of

Iroquois eventually became the customs and speech of the whole group. In 1676, accompanied by two Jesuits, they left the outpost and went up the river to the foot of the rapids and staked out a village of their own, naming it Ka-na-wá-ke, which is Mohawk for "at the rapids"; Caughnawaga is a latter-day spelling. They moved the village three times, a few miles at a time and always upriver. With each move, they added to their lands. The final move, to the present site of Caughnawaga village, was made in 1719. Until 1830, the Caughnawaga lands were mission lands. In that year, the Canadian government took control of the bulk of them and turned them into a tax-free reservation, parcelling out a homestead to each family and setting aside other pieces, called the Commons, for the use of future generations. Through the years, grants of Commons land have grown smaller and smaller; there are only about five hundred acres of it left; according to present policy, a male member of the band, after reaching his eighteenth birthday, may be granted exactly one-fourth of an acre if he promises to build upon it. A Caughnawaga is allowed to rent his land to anybody, but he may sell or give it only to another member of the band. Unlike many reservation Indians, the Caughnawagas have always had considerable say-so in their own affairs, at first through chiefs, each representing several families, who would go to the Indian Agent with requests or grievances, and then through an annually elected tribal council. The council has twelve members, it meets once a month in the parish hall, and it considers such matters as the granting of Commons land, the relief of the needy, and the upkeep of lanes and pumps. Its decisions, when approved by the Indian Affairs Branch in Ottawa, are automatically carried out by the Agent.

IN THE EARLY YEARS at Caughnawaga, the men clung to their old, aboriginal Iroquois ways of making a living. The Jesuits tried to get them to become farmers, but they would not. In the summer, while the women farmed, they fished. In the fall and winter, they hunted in a body in woods all over Quebec, returning to the village now and then with canoeloads of smoked deer meat, moose meat, and bear meat. Then, around 1700, a few of the youths of the first generation born at Caughnawaga went down to Montreal and took jobs in the French fur trade. They became canoemen in the great fleets of canoes that carried trading goods to remote depots on the St. Lawrence and its tributaries and brought back bales of furs. They liked this work—it was hard but hazardous—and they recruited others. Thereafter, for almost a century and a half, practically every youth in the band took a job in a freight canoe as soon as he got his strength, usually around the age of seventeen. In the eighteen-thirties, forties, and fifties, as the fur trade declined in Lower Canada, the Caughnawaga men were forced to find other things to do. Some switched to the St. Lawrence timber-rafting industry and became famous on the river for their skill in running immense rafts of oak and pine over Lachine Rapids. Some broke down and became farmers. Some made moccasins and snowshoes and sold them to jobbers in Montreal. A few who were still good at the old Mohawk dances came down to the United States and travelled with circuses; Caughnawagas were among the first circus Indians. A few bought horses and buggies and went from farmhouse to farmhouse in New England in the summer, peddling medicines—tonics, purges, liniments, and remedies for female ills—that the old women brewed from herbs and roots and seeds. A good many became depressed and shiftless; these hung out in Montreal and did odd jobs and drank cheap brandy.

In 1886, the life at Caughnawaga changed abruptly. In the spring of that year, the Dominion Bridge Company began the construction of a cantilever railroad bridge across the St. Lawrence for the Canadian Pacific Railroad, crossing from the French-Canadian village of Lachine on the north shore to a point just below Caughnawaga village on the south shore. The D.B.C. is the biggest erector of iron and steel structures in Canada; it corresponds to the Bethlehem Steel Company in the United States. In obtaining the right to use reservation land for the bridge abutment, the Canadian Pacific and the D.B.C. promised that Caughnawagas would be employed on the job wherever possible.

"The records of the company for this bridge show that it was our understanding that we would employ these Indians as ordinary day laborers unloading materials," an official of the D.B.C. wrote recently in a letter. "They were dissatisfied with this arrangement and would come out on the bridge itself every chance they got. It was quite impossible to keep them off. As the work progressed, it became apparent to all concerned that these Indians were very odd in that they did not have any fear of heights. If not watched, they would climb up into the spans and walk around up there as cool and collected as the toughest of our riveters, most of whom at that period were old sailing-ship men especially picked for their experience in working aloft. These Indians were as agile as goats. They would walk a narrow beam high up in the air with nothing below them but the river, which is rough there and ugly to look down on, and it wouldn't mean any more to them than walking on the solid ground. They seemed immune to the noise of the riveting, which goes right through you and is often enough in itself to make newcomers to construction feel sick and dizzy. They were inquisitive about the riveting and were continually bothering our foremen by requesting that they be allowed to take a crack at it. This happens to be the most dangerous work in all construction, and the highest-paid. Men who want to do it are rare and men who can do it are even rarer, and in good construction years there are sometimes not enough of them to go around. We decided it would be mutually advantageous to see what these Indians could do, so we picked out some and gave them a little training, and it turned out that putting riveting tools in their hands was like putting ham with eggs. In other words, they were natural-born bridgemen. Our records do not show how many we trained on this bridge. There is a tradition in the company that we trained twelve, or enough to form three riveting gangs."

In the erection of steel structures, whether bridge or building, there are three main divisions of workers—raising gangs, fitting-up gangs, and riveting gangs. The steel comes to a job already cut and built up into various kinds of columns and beams and girders; the columns are the perpendicular pieces and the beams and girders are the horizontal ones. Each piece has two or more groups of holes bored through it to receive bolts and rivets, and each piece has a code mark chalked or painted on it, indicating where it should go in the structure. Using a crane or a derrick, the men in the raising gang hoist the pieces up and set them in position and join them by running bolts through a few of the holes in them; these bolts are temporary. Then the men in the fitting-up gang come along; they are divided into plumbers and bolters. The plumbers tighten up the pieces with guy wires and turnbuckles and make sure that they are in plumb. The bolters put in some more temporary bolts. Then the riveting gangs come along; one raising gang and one fitting-up gang will keep several riveting gangs busy. There are four men in a riveting gang—a heater, a sticker-in, a bucker-up, and a riveter. The heater lays some wooden planks across a couple of beams, making a platform for the portable, coal-burning forge in which he heats the rivets. The three other men hang a plank scaffold by ropes from the steel on which they are going to work. There are usually six two-by-ten planks in a scaffold, three on each side of the steel, affording just room enough to work; one false step and it's goodbye Charlie. The three men climb down with their tools and take their positions on the scaffold; most often the sticker-in and the bucker-up stand on one side and the riveter stands or kneels on the other. The heater, on his platform, picks a red-hot rivet off the coals in his forge with tongs and tosses it to the sticker-in, who catches it in a metal can. At this stage, the rivet is shaped like a mushroom; it has a buttonhead and a stem. Meanwhile, the bucker-up has unscrewed and pulled out one of the temporary bolts joining two pieces of steel, leaving the hole empty. The sticker-in picks the rivet out of his can with tongs and sticks it in the hole and pushes it in until the buttonhead is flush with the steel on his side and the stem protrudes from the other side, the riveter's side. The sticker-in steps out of the way. The bucker-up fits a tool called a dolly bar over the buttonhead and holds it there, bracing the rivet. Then the riveter presses the cupped head of his pneumatic hammer against the protruding stem end of the rivet, which is still red-hot and malleable, and turns on the power and forms a buttonhead on it. This operation is repeated until every hole that can be got at from the scaffold is riveted up.

Then the scaffold is moved. The heater's platform stays in one place until all the work within a rivet-tossing radius of thirty to forty feet is completed. The men on the scaffold know each other's jobs and are interchangeable; the riveter's job is bone-shaking and nerve-racking, and every so often one of the others swaps with him for a while. In the days before pneumatic hammers, the riveter used two tools, a cupped die and an iron maul; he placed the die over the stem end of the red-hot rivet and beat on it with the maul until he squashed the stem end into a buttonhead.

After the D.B.C. completed the Canadian Pacific Bridge, it began work on a jackknife bridge now known as the Soo Bridge, which crosses two canals and a river and connects the twin cities of Sault Ste. Marie, Ontario, and Sault Ste. Marie, Michigan. This job took two years. Old Mr. Jacobs, the patriarch of the band, says that the Caughnawaga riveting gangs went straight from the Canadian Pacific job to the Soo job and that each gang took along an apprentice. Mr. Jacobs is in his eighties. In his youth, he was a member of a riveting gang; in his middle age, he was, successively, a commercial traveller for a wholesale grocer in Montreal, a schoolteacher on the reservation, and a campaigner for compulsory education for Indians. "The Indian boys turned the Soo Bridge into a college for them-selves," he says. "The way they worked it, as soon as one apprentice was trained, they'd send back to the reservation for another one. By and by, there'd be enough men for a new Indian gang. When the new gang was organized, there'd be a shuffle-up—a couple of men from the old gangs would go into the new gang and a couple of the new men would go into the old gangs; the old would balance the new." This proliferation continued on subsequent jobs, and by 1907 there were over seventy skilled bridgemen in the Caughnawaga band. On August 29, 1907, during the erection of the Quebec Bridge, which crosses the St. Lawrence nine miles above Quebec City, a span collapsed, killing ninety-six men, of whom thirty-five were Caughnawagas. In the band, this is always spoken of as "the disaster."

"People thought the disaster would scare the Indians away from high steel for good," Mr. Jacobs says. "Instead of which, the general effect it had, it made high steel much more interesting to them. It made them take pride in themselves that they could do such dangerous work. Up to then, the majority of them, they didn't consider it any more dangerous than timber-rafting. Also, it made them the most looked-up-to men on the reservation. The little boys in Caughnawaga used to look up to the men that went out with circuses in the summer and danced and war-whooped all over the States and came back to the reservation in the winter and holed up and sat by the stove and drank whiskey and bragged. That's what they wanted to do. Either that, or work on the timber rafts. After the disaster, they changed their minds—they all wanted to go into high steel. The disaster was a terrible blow to the women. The first thing they did, they got together a sum of money for a life-size crucifix to hang over the main altar in St. Francis Xavier's. They did that to show their Christian resignation. The next thing they did, they got in behind the men and made them split up and scatter out. That is, they wouldn't allow all the gangs to work together on one bridge any more, which, if something went wrong, it might widow half the young women on the reservation. A few gangs would go to this bridge and a few would go to that. Pretty soon, there weren't enough bridge jobs, and the gangs began working on all types of high steel—factories, office buildings, department stores, hospitals, hotels, apartment houses, schools, breweries, distilleries, powerhouses, piers, railroad stations, grain elevators, anything and everything. In a few years, every steel structure of any size that went up in Canada, there were Indians on it. Then Canada got too small and they began crossing the border. They began going down to Buffalo and Cleveland and Detroit."

Sometime in 1915 or 1916, a Caughnawaga bridgeman named John Diabo came down to New York City and got a job on Hell Gate Bridge. He was a curiosity and was called Indian Joe; two old foremen still remember him. After he had worked for some months as bucker-up in an Irish gang, three other Caughnawagas joined him and they formed a gang of their own. They had worked together only a few weeks when Diabo stepped off a scaffold and dropped into the river and was drowned. He was highly skilled and his misstep was freakish; recently, in trying to explain it, a Caughnawaga said, "It must've been one of those cases, he got in the way of himself." The other Caughnawagas went back to the reservation with his body and did not return. As well as the old men in the band can recollect, no other Caughnawagas worked here until the twenties. In 1926, attracted by the building boom, three or four Caughnawaga gangs came down. The old men say that these gangs worked first on the Fred F. French Building, the Graybar Building, and One Fifth Avenue. In 1928, three more gangs came down. They worked first on the George Washington Bridge. In the thirties, when Rockefeller Center was the biggest steel job in the country, at least seven additional Caughnawaga gangs came down. Upon arriving here, the men in all these gangs enrolled in the Brooklyn local of the high-steel union, the International Association of Bridge, Structural, and Ornamental Iron Workers, American Federation of Labor. Why they enrolled in the Brooklyn instead of the Manhattan local, no one now seems able to remember. The hall of the Brooklyn local is on Atlantic Avenue, in the block between Times Plaza and Third Avenue, and the Caughnawagas got lodgings in furnished-room houses and cheap hotels in the North Gowanus neighborhood, a couple of blocks up Atlantic from the hall. In the early thirties, they began sending for their families and moving into tenements and apartment houses in the same neighborhood. During the war, Caughnawagas continued to come down. Many of these enrolled in the Manhattan local, but all of them settled in North Gowanus.

At present, there are eighty-three Caughnawagas in the Brooklyn local and forty-two in the Manhattan local. Less than a third of them work steadily in the city. The others keep their families in North Gowanus and work here intermittently but spend much of their time in other cities. They roam from coast to coast, usually by automobile, seeking rush jobs that offer unlimited overtime work at double pay; in New York City, the steel-erecting companies use as little overtime as possible. A gang may work in half a dozen widely separated cities in a single year. Occasionally, between jobs, they return to Brooklyn to see their families. Now and then, after long jobs, they pick up their families and go up to the reservation for a vacation; some go up every summer. A few men sometimes take their families along on trips to jobs and send them back to Brooklyn by bus or train. Several foremen who have had years of experience with Caughnawagas believe that they roam because they can't help doing so, it is a passion, and that their search for overtime is only an excuse. A veteran foreman for the American Bridge Company says he has seen Caughnawagas leave jobs that offered all the overtime they could handle. When they are making up their minds to move on, he says, they become erratic. "Everything will be going along fine on a job," he says. "Good working conditions. Plenty of overtime. A nice city. Then the news will come over the grapevine about some big new job opening up somewhere; it might be a thousand miles away. That kind of news always causes a lot of talk, what we call water-bucket talk, but the Indians don't talk; they know what's in each other's mind. For a couple of days, they're tensed up and edgy. They look a little wild in the eyes. They've heard the call. Then, all of a sudden, they turn in their tools, and they're gone. Can't wait another minute. They'll quit at lunchtime, in the middle of the week. They won't even wait for their pay. Some other gang will collect their money and hold it until a postcard comes back telling where to send it." George C. Lane, manager of erections in the New York district for the Bethlehem Steel Company, once said that the movements of a Caughnawaga gang are as impossible to foresee as the movements of a flock of sparrows. "In the summer of 1936," Mr. Lane said, "we finished a job here in the city and the very next day we were starting in on a job exactly three blocks away. I heard one of our foremen trying his best to persuade an Indian gang to go on the new job. They had got word about a job in Hartford and wanted to go up there. The foreman told them the rate of pay was the same; there wouldn't be any more overtime up there than here; their families were here; they'd have travelling expenses; they'd have to root around Hartford for lodgings. Oh, no; it was Hartford or nothing. A year or so later I ran into this gang on a job in Newark, and I asked the heater how they made out in Hartford that time. He said they didn't go to Hartford. 'We went to San Francisco, California,' he said. 'We went out and worked on the Golden Gate Bridge.'"

In New York City, the Caughnawagas work mostly for the big companies—Bethlehem, American Bridge, the Lehigh Structural Steel Company, and the Harris Structural Steel Company. Among the structures in and around the city on which they worked in numbers are the R.C.A. Building, the Cities Service Building, the Empire State Building, the Daily News Building, the Chanin Building, the Bank of the Manhattan Company Building, the City Bank Farmers Trust Building, the George Washington Bridge, the Bayonne Bridge, the Passaic River Bridge, the Triborough Bridge, the Henry Hudson Bridge, the Little Hell Gate Bridge, the Bronx-Whitestone Bridge, the Marine Parkway Bridge, the Pulaski Skyway, the West Side Highway, the Waldorf-Astoria, London Terrace, and Knickerbocker Village.

NORTH GOWANUS IS AN OLD, sleepy, shabby neighborhood that lies between the head of the Gowanus Canal and the Borough Hall shopping district. There are factories in it, and coal tipples and junk yards, but it is primarily residential, and red-brick tenements and brownstone apartment houses are most numerous. The Caughnawagas all live within ten blocks of each other, in an area bounded by Court Street on the west, Schermerhorn Street on the north, Fourth Avenue on the east, and Warren Street on the south. They live in the best houses on the best blocks. As a rule, Caughnawaga women are good housekeepers and keep their apartments Dutch-clean. Most of them decorate a mantel or a wall with heirlooms brought down from the reservation—a drum, a set of rattles, a mask, a cradleboard. Otherwise, their apartments look much the same as those of their white neighbors. A typical family group consists of husband and wife and a couple of children and a female relative or two. After they get through school on the reservation, many Caughnawaga girls come down to North Gowanus and work in factories. Some work for the Fred Goat Company, a metal-stamping factory in the neighborhood, and some work for the Gem Safety Razor Corporation, whose factory is within walking distance. Quite a few of these girls have married whites; several have broken all ties with the band and the reservation. In the last ten years, Caughnawaga girls have married Filipinos, Germans, Italians, Jews, Norwegians, and Puerto Ricans. Many North Gowanus families often have relatives visiting them for long periods; when there is a new baby in a family, a grandmother or an aunt almost always comes down from the reservation and helps out. Caughnawagas are allowed to cross the border freely. However, each is required to carry a card, to which a photograph is attached, certifying that he or she is a member of the band. These cards are issued by the Indian Affairs Branch; the Caughnawagas refer to them as "passports." More than half of the North Gowanus housewives spend their spare time making souvenirs. They make a lot of them. They specialize in dolls, hand-bags, and belts, which they ornament with colored beads, using variations of ancient Iroquois designs such as the sky dome, the night sun, the day sun, the fern head, the ever-growing tree, the world turtle, and the council fire. Every fall, a few of the most Indian-looking of the men take vacations from structural steel for a month or so and go out with automobile loads of these souvenirs and sell them on the midways of state, county, and community fairs in New York, Connecticut, New Jersey, and Pennsylvania. The men wear buckskins and feathers on these trips and sleep in canvas tepees pitched on fairgrounds. Occasionally, on midways, to attract atten-tion, they let out self-conscious wahoos and do fragments of the Duel Dance, the Dove Dance, the Falseface Dance, and other old half-forgotten Mohawk dances. The women obtain the raw materials for souvenirs from the Plume Trading & Sales Company, at 155 Lexington Avenue, in Manhattan, a concern that sells beads, deer-skin, imitation eagle feathers, and similar merchandise to Indian handicraftsmen all over the United States and Canada. There are approximately fifty children of school age in the colony. Two-thirds go to Public School 47, on Pacific Street, and the others go to parochial schools—St. Paul's, St. Agnes's, and St. Charles Borro-meo's. Caughnawaga children read comic books, listen to the radio while doing their homework, sit twice through double features, and play stick ball in vacant lots the same as the other children in the neighborhood; teachers say that they differ from the others mainly in that they are more reserved and polite. They have unusual manual dexterity; by the age of three, most of them are able to tie their shoelaces. The adult Caughnawagas are multilingual; all speak Mohawk, all speak English, and all speak or understand at least a little French. In homes where both parents are Caughnawagas, Mohawk is spoken almost exclusively, and the children pick it up. In homes where the mother is non-Indian and the father is away a good deal, a situation that is becoming more and more frequent, the children sometimes fail to learn the language, and this causes much sadness.

The Caughnawagas are churchgoers. The majority of the Catholics go to St. Paul's Church, at Court and Congress streets, and the majority of the Protestants go to Cuyler Presbyterian Church, on Pacific Street. Dr. David Munroe Cory, the pastor at Cuyler, is a man of incongruous interests. He is an amateur wrestler; he is vice-president of the Iceberg Athletic Club, a group that swims in the ocean at Coney Island throughout the winter; he once ran for Borough President of Brooklyn on the Socialist ticket; he is an authority on Faustus Socinus, the sixteenth-century Italian religious thinker; he studies languages for pleasure and knows eight, among them Hebrew, Greek, and Gaelic. A few Caughnawagas started turning up at Cuyler Church in the middle thirties, and Dr. Cory decided to learn Mohawk and see if he could attract more of them. He has not achieved fluency in Mohawk, but Caughnawagas say that he speaks it better than other white men, mostly anthropologists and priests, who have studied it. He holds a complete service in Mohawk the first Sunday evening in each month, after the English service, and twenty or thirty Caughnawagas usually attend. Twenty-five have joined the church. Michael Diabo, a retired riveter, was recently elected a deacon. Steven M. Schmidt, an Austrian-American who is married to Mrs. Josephine Skye Schmidt, a Caughnawaga woman, is an elder. Mr. Schmidt works in the compensation-claim department of an insurance company. Under Dr. Cory's guidance, two Caughnawaga women, Mrs. Schmidt and Mrs. Margaret La-hache, translated a group of hymns into Mohawk and compiled a hymnal, *The Caughnawaga Hymnal,* which is used in Cuyler and in the Protestant church on the reservation. Dr. Cory himself translated the Gospel According to Luke into Mohawk. Dr. Cory is quiet and serious, his sermons are free of cant, he has an intuitive understanding of Indian conversational taboos, and he is the only white person who is liked and trusted by the whole colony. Caughnawagas who are not members of his congregation, even some Catholics and longhouse people, go to him for advice.

OCCASIONALLY, IN A SALOON or at a wedding or a wake, Caughnawagas become vivacious and talkative. Ordinarily, however, they are rather dour and don't talk much. There is only one person in the North Gowanus colony who has a reputation for garrulity. He is a man of fifty-four whose white name is Orvis Diabo and whose Indian name is O-ron-ia-ke-te, or He Carries the Sky. Mr. Diabo is squat and barrel-chested. He has small, sharp eyes and a round, swarthy, double-chinned, piratical face. Unlike most other Caughnawagas, he does not deny or even minimize his white blood. "My mother was half Scotch and half Indian," he says. "My grandmother on my father's side was Scotch-Irish. Somewhere along the line, I forget just where, some French immigrant and some full Irish crept in. If you were to take my blood and strain it, God only knows what you'd find." He was born a Catholic; in young manhood, he became a Presbyterian; he now thinks of himself as "a kind of a free-thinker." Mr. Diabo started working in riveting gangs when he was nineteen and quit a year and a half ago. He had to quit because of crippling attacks of arthritis. He was a heater and worked on bridges and buildings in seventeen states. "I heated a million rivets," he says. "When they talk about the men that built this country, one of the men they mean is me." Mr. Diabo owns a house and thirty-three acres of farmland on the reservation. He inherited the farmland and rents it to a French Canadian. Soon after he quit work, his wife, who had lived in North Gowanus off and on for almost twenty years but had never liked it, went back to the reservation. She tried to get him to go along, but he decided to stay on awhile and rented a room in the apartment of a cousin. "I enjoy New York," he says. "The people are as high-strung as rats and the air is too gritty, but I enjoy it." Mr. Diabo reads a lot. Some years ago, in a Western magazine, he came across an advertisement of the Haldeman-Julius Company, a mail-order publishing house in Girard, Kansas, that puts out over eighteen hundred paperbound books, most of them dealing with religion, health, sex, history, or popular science. They are called Little Blue Books and cost a dime apiece. "I sent away for a dollar's worth of Little Blue Books," Mr. Diabo says, "and they opened my eyes to what an ignorant man I was. Ignorant and superstitious. Didn't know beans from back up. Since then, I've become a great reader. I've read dozens upon dozens of Little Blue Books, and I've improved my mind to the extent that I'm far beyond most of the people I associate with. When you come right down to it, I'm an educated man." Mr. Diabo has five favorite Little Blue Books—*Absurdities of the Bible,* by Clarence Darrow; *Seven Infidel U.S. Presidents,* by Joseph McCabe; *Queer Facts about Lost Civilizations,* by Charles J. Finger; *Why I Do Not Fear Death,* by E. Haldeman-Julius; and *Is Our Civilization Over-Sexed?,* by Theodore Dreiser. He carries them around in his pockets and reads them over and over. Mr. Diabo stays in bed until noon. Then, using a cane, he hobbles over to a neighborhood saloon, the Nevins Bar & Grill, at 75 Nevins Street, and sits in a booth. If there is someone around who will sit still and listen, he talks. If not, he reads a Little Blue Book. The Nevins is the social center of the Caughnawaga colony. The men in the gangs that work in the city customarily stop there for an hour or so on the way home. On weekend nights, they go there with their wives and drink Montreal ale and look at the television. When gangs come in from out-of-town jobs, they go on sprees there. When a Caughnawaga high-steel man is killed on the job, a collection is taken up in the Nevins for the immediate expenses of his family; these collections rarely run less than two hundred dollars; pasted on the bar mirror are several notes of thanks from widows. The Nevins is small and snug and plain and old. It is one of the oldest saloons in Brooklyn. It was opened in 1888, when North Gowanus was an Irishtown, and it was originally called Connelly's Abbey. Irish customers still call it the Abbey. Its present owners are Artie Rose and Bunny Davis. Davis is married to a Caughnawaga girl, the former Mavis Rice.

One afternoon a while back, I sat down with Mr. Diabo in his booth in the Nevins. He almost always drinks ale. This day he was drinking gin.

"I feel very low in my mind," he said. "I've got to go back to the reservation. I've run out of excuses and I can't put it off much longer. I got a letter from my wife today and she's disgusted with me. 'I'm sick and tired of begging you to come home,' she said. 'You can sit in Brooklyn until your tail takes root.' The trouble is, I don't want to go. That is, I do and I don't. I'll try to explain what I mean. An Indian high-steel man, when he first leaves the reservation to work in the States, the homesickness just about kills him. The first few years, he goes back as often as he can. Every time he finishes a job, unless he's thousands of miles away, he goes back. If he's working in New York, he drives up weekends, and it's a twelve-hour drive. After a while, he gets married and brings his wife down and starts a family, and he doesn't go back so often. Oh, he most likely takes the wife and children up for the summer, but he doesn't stay with them. After three or four days, the reservation gets on his nerves and he highballs it back to the States. He gets used to the States. The years go by. He gets to be my age, maybe a little older, maybe a little younger, and one fine morning he comes to the conclusion he's a little too damned stiff in the joints to be walking a naked beam five hundred feet up in the air. Either that, or some foreman notices he hasn't got a sure step any longer and takes him aside and tells him a few home truths. He gives up high-steel work and he packs his belongings and he takes his money out of the bank or the postal savings, what little he's been able to squirrel away, and he goes on back to the reservation for good. And it's hard on him. He's used to danger, and reservation life is very slow; the biggest thing that ever happens is a funeral. He's used to jumping around from job to job, and reservation life boxes him in. He's used to having a drink, and it's against the law to traffic in liquor on the reservation; he has to buy a bottle in some French-Canadian town across the river and smuggle it in like a high-school boy, and that annoys the hell out of him.

"There's not much he can do to occupy the time. He can sit on the highway and watch the cars go by, or he can sit on the riverbank and fish for eels and watch the boats go by, or he can weed the garden, or he can go to church, or he can congregate in the grocery stores with the other old retired high-steel men and play cards and talk. That is, if he can stand it. You'd think those old men would talk about the cities they worked in, the sprees they went on, the girls that follow construction all over the country that they knew, the skyscrapers and bridges they put up—only they don't. After they been sitting around the reservation five years, six years, seven years, they seem to turn against their high-steel days. Some of them, they get to be as Indian as all hell; they won't even speak English any more; they make out they can't understand it. And some of them, they get to be soreheads, the kind of old men that can chew nails and spit rust. When they do talk, they talk gloomy. They like to talk about family fights. There's families on the reservation that got on the outs with each other generations ago and they're still on the outs; maybe it started with a land dispute, maybe it started with a mixed-marriage dispute, maybe it started when some woman accused another woman of meeting her husband in the bushes in the graveyard. Even down here in Brooklyn, there's certain Indians that won't work in gangs with certain other Indians because of bad blood between their families; their wives, when they meet on Atlantic Avenue, they look right through each other. The old men like to bring up such matters and refresh their recollections on some of the details. Also, they like to talk about religion. A miraculous cure they heard about, something the priest said—they'll harp on it for weeks. They're all amateur priests, or preachers. They've all got some religious notion lurking around in their minds.

"And they like to talk about reservation matters. The last time I was home, I sat down with the bunch in a store and I tried to tell them about something I'd been studying up on that interested me very much—Mongolian spots. They're dark-purple spots that occur on the skin on the backs of Japanese and other Mongolians. Every now and then, a full-blood American Indian is born with them. The old men didn't want to hear about Mongolian spots. They were too busy discussing the matter of street names for Caughnawaga village. The electric-light company that supplies the village had been trying and trying to get the Indians to name the streets and lanes. The meter-readers are always getting balled up, and the company had offered to put up street signs and house numbers free of charge. The old men didn't want street names; they were raising holy hell about it. It wouldn't be Indian. And they were discussing the pros and cons of a waterworks system. They're eternally discussing that. Some want a waterworks, but the majority don't. The majority of them, they'd a whole lot rather get behind a poor old horse that his next step might be his last and cart their water up from the river by the barrel. It's more Indian. Sometimes, the way an Indian reasons, there's no rhyme or reason to it. Electric lights are all right and the biggest second-hand car they can find, and radios that the only time they turn them off is when they're changing the tubes, and seventy-five-dollar baby carriages, and four-hundred-dollar coffins, but street names and tap water—oh, Jesus, no! That's going entirely too damned far.

"On the other hand, there's things I look forward to. I look forward to eating real Indian grub again. Such as *o-nen-sto,* or corn soup. That's the Mohawk national dish. Some of the women make it down here in Brooklyn, but they use Quaker corn meal. The good old women up on the reservation, they make it the hard way, the way the Mohawks were making it five hundred years ago. They shell some corn, and they put it in a pot with a handful of maple ashes and boil it. The lye in the ashes skins the hulls off the kernels, and the kernels swell up into big fat pearls. Then they wash off the lye. Then they put in some red kidney beans. Then they put in a pig's head; in the old days, it was a bear's head. Then they cook it until it's as thick as mud. And when it's cooking, it smells so good. If you were breathing your last, if you had the rattle in your throat, and the wind blew you a faint suggestion of a smell of it, you'd rise and walk. And I look forward to eating some Indian bread that's made with the same kind of corn. Down here, the women always use Quaker meal. Indian bread is boiled, and it's shaped like a hamburger, and it's got kidney beans sprinkled through it. On the reservation, according to an old-time custom, we have steak for breakfast every Sunday morning, whether we can afford it or not, and we pour the steak gravy on the Indian bread.

"And another thing I look forward to, if I can manage it—I want to attend a longhouse festival. If I have to join to do so, I'll join. One night, the last time I was home, the longhousers were having a festival. I decided I'd go up to the Catholic graveyard that's right below the longhouse and hide in the bushes and listen to the music. So I snuck up there and waded through the thistles and the twitch grass and the Queen Anne's lace, and I sat down on a flat stone on the grave of an uncle of mine, Miles Diabo, who was a warwhooper with the Miller Brothers 101 Ranch Wild West Show and died with the pneumonia in Wheeling, West Virginia, in 1916. Uncle Miles was one of the last of the Caughnawaga circus Indians. My mother is in that graveyard, and my father, old Nazareth Diabo that I hardly even knew. They called him Nazzry. He was a pioneer high-steel Indian. He was away from home the majority of the time, and he was killed in the disaster—when the Quebec Bridge went down. There's hundreds of high-steel men buried in there. The ones that were killed on the job, they don't have stones; their graves are marked with lengths of steel girders made into crosses. There's a forest of girder crosses in there. So I was sitting on Uncle Miles's stone, thinking of the way things go in life, and suddenly the people in the longhouse began to sing and dance and drum on their drums. They were singing Mohawk chants that came down from the old, old red-Indian times. I could hear men's voices and women's voices and children's voices. The Mohawk language, when it's sung, it's beautiful to hear. Oh, it takes your breath away. A feeling ran through me that made me tremble; I had to take a deep breath to quiet my heart, it was beating so fast. I felt very sad; at the same time, I felt very peaceful. I thought I was all alone in the graveyard, and then who loomed up out of the dark and sat down beside me but an old high-steel man I had been talking with in a store that afternoon, one of the soreheads, an old man that fights every improvement that's suggested on the reservation, whatever it is, on the grounds it isn't Indian—this isn't Indian, that isn't Indian. So he said to me, 'You're not alone up here. Look over there.' I looked where he pointed, and I saw a white shirt in among the bushes. And he said, 'Look over there,' and I saw a cigarette gleaming in the dark. 'The bushes are full of Catholics and Protestants,' he said.

'Every night there's a longhouse festival, they creep up here and listen to the singing. It draws them like flies.' So I said, 'The longhouse music is beautiful to hear, isn't it?' And he remarked it ought to be, it was the old Indian music. So I said the longhouse religion appealed to me. 'One of these days,' I said, 'I might possibly join.' I asked him how he felt about it. He said he was a Catholic and it was out of the question. 'If I was to join the longhouse,' he said, 'I'd be excommunicated, and I couldn't be buried in holy ground, and I'd burn in Hell.' I said to him, 'Hell isn't Indian.' It was the wrong thing to say. He didn't reply to me. He sat there awhile—I guess he was thinking it over—and then he got up and walked away."

(1949)

# All You Can Hold for Five Bucks

*T*HE NEW YORK STEAK DINNER, or "beefsteak," is a form of gluttony as stylized and regional as the riverbank fish fry, the hot-rock clambake, or the Texas barbecue. Some old chefs believe it had its origin sixty or seventy years ago, when butchers from the slaughterhouses on the East River would sneak choice loin cuts into the kitchens of nearby saloons, grill them over charcoal, and feast on them during their Saturday-night sprees. In any case, the institution was essentially masculine until 1920, when it was debased by the Eighteenth and Nineteenth Amendments to the Constitution of the United States. The Eighteenth Amendment brought about mixed drinking; a year and a half after it went into effect, the salutation "We Greet Our Better Halves" began to appear on the souvenir menus of beefsteaks thrown by bowling, fishing, and chowder clubs and lodges and labor unions. The big, exuberant beefsteaks thrown by Tammany and Republican district clubs always had been strictly stag, but not long after the Nineteenth Amendment gave women the suffrage, politicians decided it would be nice to invite females over voting age to clubhouse beefsteaks. "Womenfolks didn't know what a beefsteak was until they got the right to vote," an old chef once said.

It didn't take women long to corrupt the beefsteak. They forced the addition of such things as Manhattan cocktails, fruit cups, and fancy salads to the traditional menu of slices of ripened steaks, double lamb chops, kidneys, and beer by the pitcher. They insisted on dance orchestras instead of brassy German bands. The life of the party at a beefsteak used to be the man who let out the most ecstatic grunts, drank the most beer, ate the most steak, and got the most grease on his ears, but women do not esteem a glutton, and at a contemporary beefsteak it is unusual for a man to do away with more than six pounds of meat and thirty glasses of beer. Until around 1920, beefsteak etiquette was rigid. Knives, forks, napkins, and tablecloths never had been permitted; a man was supposed to eat with his hands. When beefsteaks became bisexual, the etiquette changed. For generations men had worn their second-best suits because of the inevitability of grease spots; tuxedos and women appeared simultaneously. Most beefsteaks degenerated into polite banquets at which open-face sandwiches of grilled steak happened to be the principal dish. However, despite the frills introduced by women, two schools of traditional steak-dinner devotees still flourish. They may conveniently be called the East Side and West Side schools. They disagree over matters of menu and etiquette, and both claim that their beefsteaks are the more classical or old-fashioned.

The headquarters of the East Side school is the meat market of William Wertheimer & Son, at First Avenue and Nineteenth Street. It is situated in a tenement neighborhood, but that is misleading; scores of epicures regularly order steaks, chops, and capons from Wertheimer's. The moving spirit of the East Side school is Sidney Wertheimer, the "Son" of the firm. A dozen old, slow-moving, temperamental Germans, each of whom customarily carries his own collection of knives in an oilcloth kit, are the chefs. Mr. Wertheimer is not a chef. He selects, cuts, and sells the meat used at the majority of the old-fashioned beefsteaks thrown in East Side halls, like the Central Opera House, the Grand Street Boys' clubhouse, the Manhattan Odd Fellows' Hall, and Webster Hall. The caterers for these halls get an unusual amount of service when they order meat from Mr. Wertheimer. If the caterer wishes, Mr. Wertheimer will engage a couple of the old Germans to go to the hall and broil the meat. He will also engage a crew of experienced beefsteak waiters. He owns a collection of beefsteak-cooking utensils and does not mind lending it out. The chefs and waiters telephone or stop in at Wertheimer's about once a week and are given assignments. Most of them work in breakfast and luncheon places in the financial district, taking on beefsteaks at night as a sideline. For engaging them, Mr. Wertheimer collects no fee; he just does it to be obliging. In addition, for no charge, he will go to the hall and supervise the kitchen. He is extremely proud of the meat he cuts and likes to make sure it is cooked properly. He succeeded old "Beefsteak Tom" McGowan as the East Side's most important beefsteak functionary. Mr. McGowan was a foreman in the Department of Water Supply who arranged beefsteaks as a hobby. He was an obscure person, but in 1924 his hearse was followed by more than a thousand sorrowful members of Tammany clubs.

Mr. Wertheimer had almost finished cutting the meat for a beefsteak the last time I went to see him. Approximately three hundred and fifty men and women were expected that night, and he had carved steaks off thirty-five steer shells and had cut up four hundred and fifty double-rib lamb chops. In his icebox, four hundred and fifty lamb kidneys were soaking in a wooden tub. The steaks and chops were piled up in baskets, ready to be delivered to the uptown hall in which the beefsteak was to be thrown. (Technically, a beefsteak is never "given" or "held"; it is "thrown" or "run.") Mr. Wertheimer, a pink-cheeked, well-nourished man, looked proudly at the abundantly loaded baskets and said, "The foundation of a good beefsteak is an overflowing amount of meat and beer. The tickets usually cost five bucks, and the rule is 'All you can hold for five bucks.' If you're able to hold a little more when you start home, you haven't been to a beefsteak, you've been to a banquet that they called a beefsteak."

Classical beefsteak meat is carved off the shell, a section of the hindquarter of a steer; it is called "short loin without the fillet." To order a cut of it, a housewife would ask for a thick Delmonico. "You don't always get it at a beefsteak," Mr. Wertheimer said. "Sometimes they give you bull fillets. They're no good. Not enough juice in them, and they cook out black." While I watched, Mr. Wertheimer took a shell off a hook in his icebox and laid it on a big, maple block. It had been hung for eight weeks and was blanketed with blue mold. The mold was an inch thick. He cut off the mold.

Then he boned the shell and cut it into six chunks. Then he sliced off all the fat. Little strips of lean ran through the discarded fat, and he deftly carved them out and made a mound of them on the block. "These trimmings, along with the tails of the steaks, will be ground up and served as appetizers," he said. "We'll use four hundred tonight. People call them hamburgers, and that's an insult. Sometimes they're laid on top of a slice of Bermuda onion and served on bread." When he finished with the shell, six huge steaks, boneless and fatless, averaging three inches thick and ten inches long, lay on the block. They made a beautiful still life. "After they've been broiled, the steaks are sliced up, and each steak makes about ten slices," he said. "The slices are what you get at a beefsteak." Mr. Wertheimer said the baskets of meat he had prepared would be used that night at a beefsteak in the Odd Fellows' Hall on East 106th Street; the Republican Club of the Twentieth Assembly District was running it. He invited me to go along.

"How's your appetite?" he asked.

I said there was nothing wrong with it.

"I hope not," he said. "When you go to a beefsteak, you got to figure on eating until it comes out of your ears. Otherwise it would be bad manners."

That night I rode up to Odd Fellows' Hall with Mr. Wertheimer, and on the way I asked him to describe a pre-prohibition stag beefsteak.

"Oh, they were amazing functions," he said. "The men wore butcher aprons and chef hats. They used the skirt of the apron to wipe the grease off their faces. Napkins were not allowed. The name of the organization that was running the beefsteak would be printed across the bib, and the men took the aprons home for souvenirs. We still wear aprons, but now they're rented from linen-supply houses. They're numbered, and you turn them in at the hat-check table when you get your hat and coat. Drunks, of course, always refuse to turn theirs in.

"In the old days they didn't even use tables and chairs. They sat on beer crates and ate off the tops of beer barrels. You'd be surprised how much fun that was. Somehow it made old men feel young again. And they'd drink beer out of cans, or growlers. Those beef-steaks were run in halls or the cellars or back rooms of big saloons. There was always sawdust on the floor. Sometimes they had one in a bowling alley. They would cover the alleys with tarpaulin and set the boxes and barrels in the aisles. The men ate with their fingers. They never served potatoes in those days. Too filling. They take up room that rightfully belongs to meat and beer. A lot of those beefsteaks were testimonials. A politician would get elected to some-thing and his friends would throw him a beefsteak. Cops ran a lot of them, too. Like when a cop became captain or inspector, he got a beefsteak. Theatrical people were always fond of throwing beef-steaks. Sophie Tucker got a great big one at Mecca Temple in 1934, and Bill Robinson got a great big one at the Grand Street Boys' clubhouse in 1938. Both of those were knockouts. The political clubs always gave the finest, but when Tammany Hall gets a setback, beefsteaks get a setback. For example, the Anawanda Club, over in my neighborhood, used to give a famous beefsteak every Thanks-giving Eve. Since La Guardia got in the Anawanda's beefsteaks have been so skimpy it makes me sad.

"At the old beefsteaks they almost always had storytellers, men who would entertain with stories in Irish and German dialect. And when the people got tired of eating and drinking, they would harmonize. You could hear them harmonizing blocks away. They would harmonize 'My Wild Irish Rose' until they got their appetite back. It was the custom to hold beefsteaks on Saturday nights or the eve of holidays, so the men would have time to recover before going to work. They used to give some fine ones in Coney Island restaurants. Webster Hall has always been a good place. Local 638 of the Steamfitters holds its beefsteaks there. They're good ones. A lot of private beefsteaks are thrown in homes. A man will invite some friends to his cellar and cook the steaks himself. I have a number of good amateur beefsteak chefs among my customers. Once, during the racing season, a big bookmaker telephoned us he wanted to throw a beefsteak, so we sent a chef and all the makings to Saratoga. The chef had a wonderful time. They made a hero out of him."

When we reached the hall, we went directly to the kitchen. Two of Mr. Wertheimer's chefs were working at a row of tremendous gas ranges. One had a pipe in his mouth; the other was smoking a cigar. There was a pitcher of beer on a nearby table and at intervals the chefs would back away from the ranges and have some beer. They were cooking the four hundred high-class hamburgers. The air was heavy with the fragrance of the meat. The steaks, chops, and kidneys were racked up, ready for the broilers. A strip of bacon had been pinned to each kidney with a toothpick. I asked a chef how many minutes the steaks were kept on the fire. "It's all according," he said. "Twelve on one side, ten on the other is about the average. Before they go in, we roll them in salt which has been mixed with pepper. The salt creates a crust that holds the juice in." In a corner, waiters were stacking up cardboard platters on each of which a dozen half-slices of trimmed bread had been placed. "This is day-old bread," one of them said. "The steak slices are laid on it just before we take them out to the tables. Day-old bread is neutral. When you lay steak on toast, you taste the toast as much as the steak."

In a little while I went out to the ballroom. The Republicans were arriving. Most of them were substantial, middle-aged people. They all seemed to know each other. At the hat-check booth, everybody, men and women, put on cloth butcher's aprons and paper chef's hats. This made them look a lot like members of the Ku Klux Klan. The hats had mottoes on them, such as "It's Hell When Your Wife Is a Widow" and "Prohibition Was Good for Some. Others It Put on the Bum." Before sitting down, most couples went from table to table, shaking hands and gossiping. After shaking hands, they would say, "Let's see what it says on your hat." After they read the mottoes on each other's hats, they would laugh heartily. On each table there were plates of celery and radishes, beer glasses, salt shakers, and some balloons and noisemakers. Later, a spavined old waiter told me that liquor companies send balloons and noisemakers to many beefsteaks as an advertisement. "In the old days they didn't need noisemakers," he said contemptuously. "If a man wanted some noise, he would just open his trap and howl."

While couples were still moving from table to table, a banquet photographer got up on the bandstand and asked everybody to keep still. I went over and watched him work. When he was through we talked for a while, and he said, "In an hour or so I'll bring back a sample photograph and take orders. At a beefsteak I usually take the picture at the start of the party. If I took it later on, when they get full of beer, the picture would show a lot of people with goggle eyes and their mouths gapped open."

As the photographer was lugging his equipment out, waiters streamed into the ballroom with pitchers of beer. When they caught sight of the sloshing beer, the people took seats. I joined Mr. Wertheimer, who was standing at the kitchen door surveying the scene. As soon as there was a pitcher of beer in the middle of every table, the waiters brought in platters of hamburgers. A moment later, a stout, frowning woman walked up to Mr. Wertheimer and said, "Say, listen. Who the hell ever heard of hamburgers at a beefsteak?" Mr. Wertheimer smiled. "Just be patient, lady," he said. "In a minute you'll get all the steak you can hold." "O.K.," she said, "but what about the ketchup? There's no ketchup at our table." Mr. Wertheimer said he would tell a waiter to get some. When she left, he said, "Ketchup! I bet she'd put ketchup on chocolate cake." After they had finished with their hamburgers some of the diners began inflating and exploding balloons.

I heard one of the chefs back in the kitchen yell out "Steaks ready to go!" and I went inside. One chef was slicing the big steaks with a knife that resembled a cavalry sabre and the other was dipping the slices into a pan of rich, hot sauce. "That's the best beefsteak sauce in the world," Mr. Wertheimer said. "It's melted butter, juice and drippings from the steak, and a little Worcestershire." The waiters lined up beside the slicing table. Each waiter had a couple of the cardboard platters on which bread had been arranged. As he went by the table, he held out the platters and the chef dropped a slice of the rare, dripping steak on each piece of bread. Then the waiter hurried off.

I went to the kitchen door and looked out. A waiter would go to a table and lay a loaded platter in the middle of it. Hands would reach out and the platter would be emptied. A few minutes later another platter would arrive and eager, greasy hands would reach out again. At beefsteaks, waiters are required to keep on bringing platters until every gullet is satisfied; on some beefsteak menus there is a notice: "2nd, 3rd, 4th, etc., portions permitted and invited." Every three trips or so the waiter would bring a pitcher of beer. And every time they finished a platter, the people would rub their hands on their aprons. Sometimes a man would pour a little beer in one palm and rub his hands together briskly. At a table near the kitchen door I heard a woman say to another, "Here, don't be bashful. Have a steak." "I just et six," her friend replied. The first woman said, "Wasn't you hungry? Why, you eat like a bird." Then they threw their heads back and laughed. It was pleasant to watch the happy, unrestrained beefsteak-eaters. While the platters kept coming they did little talking except to urge each other to eat more.

"Geez," said a man. "These steaks are like peanuts. Eat one, and you can't stop. Have another." Presently the waiters began to tote out platters of thick lamb chops.

Then a man stepped up to the microphone and introduced a number of politicians. Each time he said, "I'm about to introduce a man that is known and loved by each and every one of you," a beaming politician would stand and bow and the constituents would bang the tables with their noisemakers. There were no speeches. A politician would have to be extraordinarily courageous to make a speech at a beefsteak. When all the Republican statesmen of the Twentieth A.D. had been introduced, a band went into action and two singers stepped out on the dance floor and began singing numbers from "Show Boat." By the time they got to "Ol' Man River," the four hundred and fifty double lamb chops were gone and the waiters were bringing out the kidneys. "I'm so full I'm about to pop," a man said. "Push those kidneys a little nearer, if you don't mind." Then the lights were dimmed. Here and there a couple got up, grunting, and went out on the dance floor. The band played waltzes. Done by aproned, middle-aged people, ponderous with beefsteak and beer, the waltz is an appalling spectacle. The waiters continued to bring out kidneys and steak to many tables. There was no dessert and no coffee. Such things are not orthodox. "Black coffee is sometimes served to straighten people out," Mr. Wertheimer said, "but I don't believe in it."

When the Republicans began dancing in earnest, the activity in the kitchen slackened, and some of the waiters gathered around the slicing table and commenced eating. While they ate, they talked shop. "You know," said one, "a fat woman don't eat so much. It's those little skinny things; you wonder where they put it." Another said, "It's the Cat'lics who can eat. I was to a beefsteak in Brooklyn last Thursday night. All good Cat'lics. So it got to be eleven-fifty, and they stopped the clock. Cat'lics can't eat meat on Friday." The two weary chefs sat down together at the other side of the room from the waiters and had a breathing spell. They had not finished a glass of beer apiece, however, before a waiter hurried in and said, "My table wants some more steak," and the chefs had to get up and put their weight on their feet again. Just before I left, at midnight, I took a last look at the ballroom. The dance floor was packed and clouds of cigar smoke floated above the paper hats of the dancers, but at nine tables people were still stowing away meat and beer. On the stairs to the balcony, five men were harmonizing. Their faces were shiny with grease. One held a pitcher of beer in his hands and occasionally he would drink from it, spilling as much as he drank. The song was, of course, "Sweet Adeline."

The West Side school of beefsteak devotees frequents the Terminal Hotel, a for-gentlemen-only establishment at Eleventh Avenue and Twenty-third Street. Its chef is Bob Ellis, an aged, truculent Negro, whose opinion of all other beefsteak chefs is low. Of them he says, "What they call a beefsteak ain't no beefsteak; it's just a goddamn mess." Mr. Ellis is also a talented clambake and green-turtle chef and used to make trips as far west as Chicago to supervise one meal. His most unusual accomplishment, however, is the ability to speak Japanese. He once worked on freighters that went to the Orient, and he sometimes reminds people who hang out around the belly-shaped Terminal bar that he has a wonderful command of the Japanese language. When someone is skeptical and says, "Well, let's hear some," he always says haughtily, "What in hell would be the use of talking Jap to you? You wouldn't comprehend a word I was saying."

Among the groups of rough-and-ready gourmands for whom Mr. Ellis is official chef are the I.D.K. ("I Don't Know") Bowling Club, a hoary outfit from Chelsea, and the Old Hoboken Turtle Club. This club was founded in 1796, and Alexander Hamilton and Aaron Burr were charter members; now it is an exclusive association of West Side and Jersey butchers, brewers, saloonkeepers, boss stevedores, and businessmen. Most of the members are elderly. Mr. Ellis has cooked for them since 1879. In 1929 they gave him a badge with a green turtle and a diamond on it and made him a Brother Turtle. The Turtles and the I.D.K.'s and many similar West Side organizations always hold their beefsteaks in the Terminal cellar, which is called the Hollings Beefsteak Keller after John Hollings, a former owner of the hotel, who sold out in disgust and moved to Weehawken when prohibition was voted in. He used to store his coal in the cellar. Mr. Ellis refuses to call it a *Keller*; he calls it "my dungeon."

"In the old days all steak cellars were called dungeons," he told me. "To me they're still dungeons."

The dungeon has a steel door on which is printed the initials "O.I.C.U.R.M.T." That is a good sample of beefsteak humor. Also on the door is a sign: "WHEN YOU ENTER THIS KELLER YOU FIND A GOOD FELLER." The dungeon has a cement floor, over which sawdust has been scattered. The ceiling is low. On the trellised walls are yellowed beefsteak photographs ranging from an 1898 view of the M. E. Blankmeyer Clam Bake Club to a picture of a beefsteak thrown in 1932 by the New York Post Office Holy Name Society. Over the light switch is a warning: "HANDS OFF THE THIRD RAIL." In one corner is a piano and a platform for a German band. The dungeon will hold a hundred and twenty-five persons. "When a hundred and twenty-five big, heavy men get full of beer, it does seem a little crowded in here," Mr. Ellis said. Beer crates and barrels were once used, but now people sit on slat-backed chairs and eat off small, individual tables. Down a subterranean hall from the dungeon is the ancient brick oven, over which Mr. Ellis presides with great dignity.

"I'm not one of these hit-or-miss beefsteak chefs," he said. "I grill my steaks on hickory embers. The efflorescence of seasoned hardwood is in the steak when you eat it. My beefsteaks are genuine old-fashioned. I'll give you the official lineup. First we lay out celery, radishes, olives, and scallions. Then we lay out crabmeat cocktails. Some people say that's not old-fashioned. I'm getting close to ninety years old, and I ought to know what's old-fashioned. Then we lay out some skewered kidney shells. Lamb or pig—what's the difference?

"Then comes the resistance—cuts of seasoned loin of beef on hot toast with butter gravy. Sure, I use toast. None of this day-old-bread stuff for me. I know what I'm doing. Then we lay out some baked Idahoes. I let them have paper forks for the crabmeat and the Idahoes; everything else should be attended to with fingers. A man who don't like to eat with his fingers hasn't got any business at a beefsteak. Then we lay out the broiled duplex lamb chops. All during the beefsteak we are laying out pitchers of refreshment. By that I mean beer."

Old Mr. Ellis lives in the Bronx. He spends most of his time at home in a rocking chair with his shoes off, reading the Bible or a weekly trade paper called "The Butcher's Advocate." Whenever Herman Von Twistern, the proprietor of the Terminal, books a beefsteak, he gets Mr. Ellis on the telephone and gives him the date. Usually he also telephones Charles V. Havican, a portly ex–vaudeville actor, who calls himself "the Senator from Hoboken." He took the title during prohibition, when everything connected with Hoboken was considered funny. Mr. Havican is a celebrated beefsteak entertainer. Most often he sits down with the guests and impersonates a windy, drunken senator. He also tells dialect stories and gives recitations. In his repertoire are "The Kid's Last Fight," "Christmas Day in the Workhouse," "The Gambler's Wife," and "Please Don't Sell My Father Rum."

"If I am not previously known to people at a beefsteak, I sometimes impersonate a dumb waiter," Mr. Havican told me, listing his accomplishments. "I spill beer on people, bump into them, step on their feet, and hit them in the face with my elbows. All the time I look dumb. It is a very funny act to people with a keen sense of humor. Of course, some people just don't have a keen sense of humor."

"What do they think of your act?" I asked.

"Well, I tell you," said Mr. Havican, "look at this scar on my forehead. And I guess you noticed that I walk with a limp."

(1939)

# A Mess of Clams

*P*RACTICALLY ALL THE LITTLENECK and cherrystone clams
served on the half shell in New York restaurants come out of the
black mud of the Long Island bays. They are the saltiest, cleanest,
and biggest-bellied clams in the world. The most abundant beds are
in Great South Bay and are owned by the towns of Islip and Babylon.
Right after dawn every weekday about seventy licensed clammers
from these towns go out on the Bay in a fleet of dilapidated sloops
and catboats and spread out over the beds. They work over the
sides of their anchored boats, using long-handled tongs and rakes;
the clams are bedded in bottoms which lie under eight to ten feet
of water. At noon the buy-boats of two clam-shipping firms—Still
& Clock of Bay Shore, and G. Vander Borgh & Son of West Say-
ville—go out and anchor near the fleet, and from then until 4 P.M.
the clammers bring their catches to the buy-boats in bushel bags
and sell them over the rail for cash.

One muggy June day I made a trip to the South Bay beds with
Captain Archie M. Clock, who commands the Still & Clock buy-
boat. This boat is the *Jennie Tucker,* a battered, stripped-down, 38-
foot sloop powered with a motor the Captain took out of an old
Chrysler. Captain Clock and his partner, Louis Still, are members
of families which have fished, oyster-farmed, and clammed on the
South Shore since the middle of the eighteenth century. I arrived
at their weather-beaten clam shed on Homan Avenue Creek in Bay
Shore at ten in the morning and found Captain Clock on the narrow
wharf at the rear. He was sitting on an overturned clam bucket,

smoking his pipe. A man I know who runs a wholesale shellfish business in Fulton Fish Market had written me a note of introduction to the Captain, and I handed it to him. He read it, grunted, and said, "You picked a good day to see the beds. We're going out a little early." He motioned toward a bucket with the stem of his pipe. "Have a seat and make yourself at home," he said. "Do you care much for clams?"

I sat down on the bucket and told him that one Sunday afternoon in August, 1937, I placed third in a clam-eating tournament at a Block Island clambake, eating eighty-four cherries. I told him that I regard this as one of the few worth-while achievements of my life.

"Well, you can eat yourself a bellyful today," he said. "I feel like having a few myself. They tell me brewers sometimes get so they hate beer, and sometimes I get so I can't stand the sight of a clam, but I'm real hungry this morning."

The *Jennie Tucker* was lying alongside the wharf, and the mate, a muscular young man named Charlie Bollinger, was sloshing down her decks with buckets of water. "Give her plenty of water, Charlie," the Captain told him. He turned to me and said, "You have to be extra clean when you're handling clams. Let a few dead clams lie around and you'll breed up a smell that'll make a strong man weak, a smell that'll knock your hat off, unravel the knot in your necktie, and tear holes in your shirt." He stood up, yawned, spat, and went into a little office in the shed. When he returned he carried an armful of gear which included a lunch bucket, a tattered old ledger, and a green metal box. Later I learned that this box contained the cash with which he would buy the day's load.

"Everything O.K., Charlie?" he asked.

"She's clean as a whistle, Archie," said the mate.

"Let's get going then," he said. We went aboard and the Captain stowed his gear in the sloop's tiny cabin. The Captain was stocky, slow-moving, and sleepy-eyed. He was deeply tanned, but he had smeared some white salve on his nose and ears to guard against sunburn. He was roughly dressed; he wore patched pants, a blue work shirt, and a long-visored swordfisherman's cap. He took the tiller, which he handled expertly, until we were well out in the Bay. Then he turned it over to Bollinger, got his ledger, and sat down beside me on the hatch. "The beds they're clamming lie about four miles down the Bay," he said, motioning with his head in the direction of Babylon. He opened the ledger and got a new page ready, writing down the names of the clammers. The wind from the ocean ruffled the pages as he worked. Most of the names he wrote down were old Long Island ones like Doxsee, Ricketts, Baldwin, Crowell, and Tooker.

"Most of the clammers come from families that have been around this bay so many generations they long since lost track," he said. "The bulk of them are of English descent or Holland Dutch, and there's quite a few squareheads. They know the bottom of the Bay like they know their wife's face. Clamming is back-breaking, but a man can get a living if his muscle holds out. I looked through this ledger last night and figured I paid one clammer eighty-some-odd dollars last week, but that's unusual. Most of them average between five and ten bucks a day. It's all according to how good a man can handle the tongs."

He laid his ledger on the hatch, stretched his arms, and yawned. The morning had been cloudy, but the sun came out soon after we left the wharf and now it was burning off the haze on the Bay. After it had been shining fifteen minutes, we could see the striped Fire Island lighthouse and the long, glistening dunes on Oak and Captree islands. I asked the Captain if any bayman can go out to the beds and clam.

"He cannot," the Captain said. "He has to get a Conservation Department license that costs two and a half, and he has to be a resident of the town that owns the beds he works. A Babylon man can't clam in Islip water, and vice versa. In fact, they're always fussing among themselves about the division line. That's a fuss that'll go on as long as there's a clam left in the mud."

"How much do you pay for a bushel?" I asked.

"The price is based on the size of the clam and the demand in Fulton Market," the Captain said. "Prices may fluctuate as much as a dollar in a single season, but right now I'm paying the boys two dollars a bushel for littlenecks and a dollar and a half for cherrystones. That's for the half-shell trade. For the big ones— what we call chowders—I pay a dollar a bushel.

"The bulk of the clams in South Bay are hard-shells—they're called quahogs in New England. There's a few soft-shells, or steamers, around the shores of the Bay, but we don't bother with them. Most of the steam clams you see in the city come from New England. The hard-shell is the king of the clams. He can be baked, fried, steamed, put into chowder, or served on the half shell. I *will* say that the best chowder is made with a mixture of softs and hards. Out here we believe in Manhattan-style chowder, a couple of tomatoes to every quart of shucked clams. Our chowder clams are around four years old, a couple of years older than littlenecks. We truck our necks and cherries to dealers in Fulton Market and to restaurants in Manhattan and Brooklyn, and we truck the chowders to the Campbell's soup factory in Camden, New Jersey. They take around fifteen hundred bushels of chowders off us every week." He turned to the mate. "I'll take her now, Charlie," he said.

Soon after Captain Clock took the tiller, we approached the fleet. The little boats were laying with the wind and the tide about two miles southeast of Babylon. Captain Clock said the majority of the boats were anchored near the imaginary line dividing the beds, and that some were hugging it. "Human nature," he said. "The boys from Islip just itch to work the Babylon water, and the Babylon boys think they could tong up twice as many if they could get over on the Islip territory." A few of the boats carried two clammers, one for each side, but one man to a boat seemed to be the rule. When we were about fifty yards from the nearest clammer, the Captain ducked into the cabin and cut off the motor. Bollinger hurried to the bow and threw out the anchor.

"Now I'll show you how to clam," said Captain Clock. "We'll tong up a few pecks for us to eat."

He rolled up his shirtsleeves and picked up a pair of tongs, an implement with two sets of teeth fixed to the ends of two fourteen-foot handles. He lowered the tongs into the water, which was nine feet deep, and pushed the opened teeth into the mud; then he

brought the handles together scissors-fashion, closing the teeth. Just
before hauling the tongs over the rail, he doused the closed teeth
in the water several times, washing out the mud. He opened the
teeth on the deck and out dropped a dazed spider crab, two bunches
of scarlet oyster sponge, a handful of empty shells, and twelve
beautiful clams. The shells of the clams were steel blue, the color
of the Bay water.

"A good haul," he said. "I got four cherries, two necks, two
chowders and four peanuts." He said that a state law forbids the
sale of clams less than an inch thick and that such undersized clams
are called peanuts. He tossed the peanuts and the crab back into
the water. Then he put the tongs overboard again. He sent the teeth
into the mud seven times and brought up forty-three clams. Then
he laid aside the tongs and got two clam knives off a shelf in the
cabin. He gave me one and we squatted on the deck and went to
work opening the cherries. When the valves were pried apart, the
rich clam liquor dribbled out. The flesh of the cherries was a delicate
pink. On the cups of some of the shells were splotches of deep
purple; Indians used to hack such splotches out of clamshells for
wampum. Fresh from the coal black mud and uncontaminated by
ketchup or sauce, they were the best clams I had ever eaten. The
mate sat on the hatch and watched us.

"Aren't you going to have any?" I asked.

"I wouldn't put one of them goddamn things in my mouth if I
was perishing to death," he said. "I'm working on this buy-boat
ten years and I'm yet to eat a clam."

He scornfully watched us eat for a few moments; then he went
into the cabin and came out with a portable radio, which he placed
on the cabin roof, and tuned in on a news broadcast. While the
Captain and I opened and ate clams we looked out at the fleet and
watched the clammers. The Captain said that a clammer works both
sides of his boat until the tongs start coming up empty; then he
lets out slack in his anchor cable and drifts into unworked territory.
"Most of them are patient," he said, "but some will be lifting and
dropping their anchors all day long. When a man does that we say
he's got the runs." The fleet was made up largely of catboats stripped

of their rigs and powered with old automobile motors. The majority of the men were tonging, but here and there a man worked with a rake. The Captain said that rakes are used only on stretches of soft bottom. "The handle of a rake is twenty-two feet long," he said, "and it takes a Joe Louis to pull it." Some of the clammers were stripped to their belts, but most of them worked in their undershirts. Occasionally a man would lay aside his tongs or rake and squat in the bottom of the boat and bag up his clams. Captain Clock said it is customary for the clammers to sell their catches in the early-afternoon hours, so the shippers will have time to cull and barrel the clams for trucking in the evening.

The Captain and I were finishing the last of the forty-three clams when a whistle in Babylon blew for noon. "We better eat dinner, Archie," Bollinger said. "They'll start bringing their loads over pretty soon now." Intent on his last clam, the Captain nodded. Bollinger brought out their lunch buckets and a thermos jug of iced tea. I had bought a couple of sandwiches in Bay Shore and I got them out of my raincoat. Bollinger tuned in on a program of waltzes broadcast from a Manhattan hotel. We sat on peck baskets in the hot sun and ate and listened to the waltzes. We were drinking tea out of tin cups when the first of the clammers came alongside. Bollinger jumped up, tossed the clammer a rope, and helped him make fast to the *Jennie Tucker*. The clammer was a small, spry old man in hip boots.

"What you got?" Captain Clock asked him.

"Nothing to speak of," he said. "Just a mess of clams. I been scratch-raking off Grass Island. I got two bushels of cherries, a bushel of necks, and two bushels of chowders." Gripping the bags by their ears, he passed them to Bollinger. Captain Clock took a five and two ones out of his cashbox and handed them to the clammer, who carefully placed them in an old-fashioned snap purse. Then he picked up two conches from the bottom of his boat and tossed them to Bollinger.

"I was about to forget your konks," he said. He threw aside the ropes, pushed off, and started his engine.

"Be good," yelled Captain Clock.

"I'm getting so old," the clammer said, "I can't be anything else."

Bollinger deposited the conches in a rusty wire basket. "Konks are my racket," he said. "They get caught in the tongs and the boys save them for me instead of throwing them back. One of the truck-drivers takes them in and sells them to Italian clam stands in down-town New York and we divvy up. It's just cigarette money. The Italians boil the konks and make something called *scungili.*"

We drank some more tea, and then another clammer, a gloomy-eyed, sunburned young man, pulled alongside. He was in a catboat that had been patched with tin in a dozen places.

"Hello, Tarzan," said Bollinger. "Didn't that old eelpot sink yet? How many clams you got?"

"I been croshaying the mud for six hours and I barely took enough to bait a hook," the young man said. "They was thin where I was tonging."

"Quit bellyaching," said Bollinger. "If it was to rain clams, you wouldn't be satisfied." The young man passed over a bushel of necks, two bushels of cherries, a scanty peck of chowders, and three conches. Captain Clock handed him five ones and twenty cents. He folded the bills into a wad and stuffed it in his watch pocket. "Another day, another dollar," he said. "My back feels like it was run over by a load of bricks." He cranked his engine and moved off, heading for Babylon. "He'll get drunk tonight," Captain Clock said. "I can tell by the way he was talking." The Captain bent over a bag of cherries. He scooped a double handful out of the mouth of the bag and spread them on the deck. "Beauties," he said. "Uniform as peas in a pod. The shells are blue now, but they'll turn gray or white before we get them to town." He opened a cherry and balanced it on his palm. He looked at it admiringly. "A spawner," he said. "Now, that's the beauty of a clam. He doesn't make a bit of fuss about spawning. An oyster's just the opposite. He spawns from May through August—the months without an 'r' in them—and he gets so milky you can't eat him on the half shell. You can fry him, but you can't eat him raw. A clam is better behaved. He never gets milky enough to notice and he's just as good in the midsummer months, when he's spawning, as he is on the coldest day of the winter."

Captain Clock said that once a year the town of Islip buys a couple of truckloads of hardshells from Massachusetts or New Jersey to scatter on its beds. "Foreign clams put new life in the natives," he said. "They improve the breed. The spawn mixes and we get a better set. Hey, Charlie, hand me a knife. I'm going to try some of these chowders." The Captain opened a dozen chowders and arranged them in a semicircle on the hatch. We were eating them when Bollinger suddenly shouted, "Here come the cops!" He pointed in the direction of Babylon, and I saw a launch flying a green flag. In a minute it cut the water just off our bow, heading for the fleet. The clammers stopped work and commenced yelling. "They're warning each other," Bollinger said. "That's the police boat from Babylon. The cops go through the beds every day or so. You never know when they'll show up. If they spy an Islip man in Babylon water, they give him a ticket and he has to go to court and get fined." The clammers leaned on their tong and rake handles while the police boat slowly picked its way through the fleet. It did not halt; evidently the clammers were behaving themselves.

Presently another clammer called it a day and came alongside. He was a gaunt, stooped man, who silently handed over four bushels of necks, three bushels of cherries, and a bushel and a peck of chowders. He collected thirteen dollars and seventy-five cents, bit a chew of tobacco off a plug he took from his hip pocket, mumbled "Good night, Cap," and pushed off. "He's one of the best clammers on Long Island," said Captain Clock. "I bet he's got ten thousand dollars in the bank, and he's so saving he gets his wife to cut his hair." The gaunt clammer's departure from the beds appeared to be a signal to the others. Soon after he left, they began moving toward the buy-boat in twos and threes. In twenty minutes the *Jennie Tucker* was surrounded by loaded boats, waiting their turns to come alongside. "They all have to come at once," Bollinger said indignantly. Captain Clock stood at the stern, hunched over his ledger, which he had placed on the cabin roof. Bollinger helped the clammers heft their bags over the rail. He piled the chowders aft, the cherries on the hatch, and the necks forward. When a boat finished unloading he would call out the number of bushels, and the Captain would make a notation in his ledger and then pay off the clammer.

To get out of Bollinger's way, I went to the bow and sat on a bale of empty bags. Standing in their boats, the waiting clammers smoked cigarettes and shouted insults at each other. I couldn't tell if the insults were good-natured or genuine. "If I was you, I'd take that old cement-mixer home and set fire to it," one yelled at his neighbor. "I wouldn't be caught dead in that dirty old boat." "Well, it's paid for," said the master of the cement-mixer, "and that's more'n you can say." "Paid for!" screamed the first man. "You mean you stole it off the beach. Nothing's safe when you're around. Why, by God, you'd steal a tick off a widow's belly!" Most of the clammers seemed to be irritable. "Hello, Pop," a young clammer said to the man in an adjoining boat, a sullen old man in wet overalls, "how's your hammer hanging?" "Shut up!" said the old man. The young clammer snickered and said, "Didn't get your share of clams today, did you, Pop?" "Shut up!" said the old man. "Why, hell," said the young clammer, "I was just passing the time of day." "Shut up!" said the old man.

At a quarter after four the last clammer finished unloading, cast off, and made for home. The Captain snapped his cashbox shut and we sat down and drained the iced tea in the thermos jug. Then Bollinger hoisted the anchor, started the motor, and pointed the *Jennie Tucker* for her wharf. The decks were piled high. "A regular floating clam mountain," said Bollinger. The Captain rearranged some bags on the hatch, clearing away a space to sit. He lit his pipe and added up the row of figures in his ledger.

"We took a hundred and forty-five bushels," he said. "One day I took two hundred bushels. I emptied my cashbox for that load. The stern was awash on the trip in." He pointed toward Oak Island. "See those boats over there? Some of the boys are still out, but they don't sell over the rail like the others. They have bigger boats and they stay out until late in the afternoon and bring their loads right to our shed. We buy every clam that's offered, no matter if there's a glut in New York or a big demand. Some days we buy more clams than we can get rid of, and we take the surplus out to some lots of water we lease from the town of Islip and shovel them overboard. In the last five weeks we've planted thirteen hundred bushels of cherries and five hundred bushels of necks in those lots.

When we need them, we go out and tong them up. No waste that way. In the old days, when clams were very dear, we used to have clam pirates. They would steal up at night and tong our lots, but not any more. We keep a watchman, just in case."

At five o'clock, the *Jennie Tucker* puttered up to her wharf. Mr. Still, the senior partner of the firm, was standing in the back doorway of the shed, waiting. He looks after the office end of the business. He is a shellfish expert and belongs to the family which once ran Still's, a renowned sea-food restaurant and hangout for Tammany gluttons on Third Avenue, and which still runs a thriving oyster business in a scow anchored in Pike Slip, beneath Manhattan Bridge. When the *Jennie Tucker* scraped against the wharf, Mr. Still shouted, "Here she is," and four men came out of the shed. The moment the buy-boat was tied up, two of these men leaped aboard and began lifting the bags to the wharf. The others placed them on handtrucks and wheeled them into the culling room. This was a long, cool room, which smelled like a clean cellar. There the clams were poured in great heaps on tables built against the walls. The tables and the cement floor had recently been hosed down and they were wet and immaculate. Captain Clock, Mr. Still, and Bollinger took places at the tables and culled the clams, tossing aside those with broken shells or gapped-open lips.

After they had been culled, the clams were poured into woven-wire baskets and dipped in a tank of tap water in which an antiseptic solution had been poured. Then some were emptied into great, three-bushel barrels and others into tubs holding three pecks. Soon the room was crowded with loaded barrels, and Mr. Still got a hammer out of the roll-top desk in the little office adjoining the culling room. He tacked tags on the heads of the barrels, addressing them to various restaurants and Fulton Market dealers. Then they were wheeled into one of the company's three trucks. At seven o'clock, this truck contained sixty-five barrels and twenty-two tubs. "She's ready to roll," said Mr. Still. "If you're a mind to, you can ride into the city with this load." He introduced me to Paul Boice, the driver, and I climbed into the cab of the truck. It was one of those massive, aluminum-painted trucks.

We took the Sunrise Highway. At Valley Stream, we stopped at a diner for hamburgers and coffee. The counterman knew Boice. "Care for some clams tonight, Paul?" he asked, grinning. "How about a dozen nice clams for supper?" The driver laughed perfunctorily. Evidently it was an old joke. "When I want clams for supper," he said, "I'll notify you. Fix me a hamburger." We did not tarry long in the diner. In Brooklyn the driver deftly guided the heavy truck through a maze of side streets. "I've been hauling clams over this route eight years and I know every short cut there is," he said. "Clams are nowhere near as perishable as oysters, but I don't like to dawdle." When we rolled off Manhattan Bridge he glanced at his watch. "Took less than two hours," he said. "That's good time."

He made his first delivery at Vincent's Clam Bar, at Mott and Hester streets, unloading three clam tubs and the basket of *scungili* conches Bollinger had gathered during the day. The proprietor brought Boice a goblet of red wine. "I get a drink on the house every time I hit this place," he said. He drove down Mott Street, passing slowly through Chinatown. Entering South Street, he had to climb out of the cab and drag a sleeping drunk out of the road. "Truck-drivers have to slow-poke through here just because of drunks," he said. "I drag one out of my way at least once a week." The Fulton Market sheds were dark, deserted, and locked up when we arrived. "I make four deliveries in the Market," Boice said, "and then I head uptown and make stops at big restaurants in the theatrical district." He backed the truck up to the door of a shellfish wholesaler and we climbed out of the cab. We looked up and down the street and did not see a soul. "There's a night watchman down here who helps me unload," Boice said, "and I always have to wait for him to show up." We sat down on the steps of the wholesale house and lit cigarettes. Across the street, on top of a pile of broken lobster barrels, three overfed fishhouse cats were screeching at each other. We sat for fifteen minutes, watching the cats screech and fight, and then I said goodbye. "If you order clams or chowder tomorrow," Boice said, peering up the dark street for the night watchman, "like as not you'll eat some of the ones we hauled in tonight."

(1939)

# The Same as Monkey Glands

Returning from a late vacation, I stopped off in Savannah, Georgia, and made a pilgrimage to Mr. Will Barbee's diamondback-terrapin farm on the Isle of Hope, a small, lush island nine miles below Savannah. I was there on the first day of autumn, when he starts shipping live terrapin to Northern hotels, clubs, seafood dealers, and luxury restaurants, and was in time to see his Negro foreman barrel up three dozen nine-year-old cows, or females; this, the first shipment of the season, was dispatched to a dealer in Fulton Fish Market. The diamondback is a handsome reptile, whose meat, when properly stewed, is tender and gelatinous. Gastronomically, it is by far the finest of the North American turtles, and terrapin stew is our costliest native delicacy. Three styles of stew—Philadelphia, Maryland, and Southern—are made in bulk by a man in Fulton Market and sold to families and clubs; what he calls Maryland style, in which dry sherry and thick cream are used, costs $10 a quart. In Manhattan hotels the price is never less than $3.50 a plate. A live terrapin in New York City brings from $3.50 to $7 retail, according to the length of its belly shell. For the last decade, under the protection of conservation laws, the diamondback has been slowly increasing in numbers in brackish sloughs all along the Eastern seaboard, but it still is scarce enough to make the fecundity of Mr. Barbee's farm of the utmost importance to chefs in New York, Baltimore, Philadelphia, Washington, and New Orleans, the cities in which the stew is most respected. Mr. Barbee is the country's largest shipper; in one year he shipped three hundred dozen live terrapin at an average price of $30 a dozen. He also put up four thousand cans of stew meat. In addition, on the porch of a rustic dance pavilion which he operates as a sideline, he sold terrapin dinners to hundreds of Yankee yachtsmen who stopped at the farm on their way to Florida through the Inland Waterway, which skirts the Isle of Hope. His wife, Rose, who looks after the cooking, is revered by yachtsmen, and her terrapin stew, Southern style, is famous from Cape Cod to Key West.

My train arrived at Union Station in Savannah at 9:30 the morning of the day I visited the farm, and an unselfish cab-driver I consulted advised me to check my bag and take a streetcar to the Isle of Hope. "I could drive you there," he said, "but if you want to see some old-fashioned yellow-fever country, you better take the street-car." I am thankful I followed his advice. The Isle of Hope line is a single-track interurban railroad; in its steam-engine days it bore the stirring title Savannah, Thunderbolt & Isle of Hope Railroad. I recommend a trip on it to lovers of Americana. There were only three passengers on the car I boarded. We rattled through Savannah and its suburbs and plunged into a swampy forest of live oaks whose great limbs dripped with a parasite plant called gray moss. Occasionally we crossed tracks over marshes in which rice was once grown with slave labor, and we passed through a number of small farms whose door-yard bushes were heavy with ripe, crimson pomegranates, the autumn fruit of the South. About five miles out of Savannah, the streetcar rounded a curve and the motorman suddenly put on his brake. A fat milk cow was on the track, grazing on nut grass that grew between the ties. The motorman pulled his whistle cord, but the cow did not budge. Some Gullah Negroes were digging yams in a patch beside the track; one hurried over and kicked the cow and she ambled off. The motorman, who was laughing, stuck his head out and said, "I give you fair warning. Next time she gets on my right of way I'm going to climb out and milk her." The Negro, also laughing, said, "Help yourself, Captain. She's got enough for the both of us."

A short while later we crossed a bridge spanning one of the rice marshes and reached the Isle of Hope. The streetcar line came to an end directly in front of several weatherbeaten frame buildings, on one of which there was a sign: "ALEXANDER M. BARBEE'S SON. DANCE PAVILION. OPERATING THE ONLY DIAMONDBACK TERRAPIN FARM IN THE WORLD. OYSTERS, SHRIMP, FANCY CRABMEAT. YOU ARE WELCOME." This building extended out over the water on piles, and two battered shrimp sloops were tied to the wharf abutting it; later I learned that this water was the Skidaway, a tidal river. I entered the building and found Mr. Barbee behind a counter, opening bottles of Coca-Cola for some shrimp fishermen. I recognized him from a description given by a Northern yachtsman who told me about the farm just before I went on vacation; he said Mr. Barbee looked "like an easygoing country storekeeper." I introduced myself and told him I was from New York and wanted to see his terrapin farm.

"Well, sir," he said, "I'm glad to see you. I'll show you the whole works, and I'll see that you get all the terrapin stew you can hold. We're going to barrel up a few terrapin for the New York trade today. The season opens up North around the second week of October, and we commence shipping on the first day of autumn. I've got forty-five hundred in my fattening pen ready to go and I want you to see them, but first we'll go up to the breeding farm. It's up the road a ways." He took off his apron and called to his wife, who was upstairs. "We keep house on the second floor of the pavilion," he told me. His wife came downstairs and he introduced us, saying, "Rose, I've invited this gentleman to have dinner with us. Make sure he gets a bait of terrapin." Mrs. Barbee, a pretty, red-cheeked young woman, smiled and said, "Mighty glad to have you."

I followed Mr. Barbee out on the front porch of the pavilion. "Right off the bat," he said, "I better tell you that the most important thing about terrapin meat is its tonic quality. It fills you full of fuss, fight, and gumption. Eat enough of it, it'll make an old rooster out of you. Why do you think so many rich old men eat terrapin? Well, sir, I'll tell you why. A terrapin is loaded down with a rich, nourishing jelly, and this jelly makes you feel young again. To be frank, it's the same as monkey glands. If you were to take and feed terrapin stew to all the people of this country, the birth rate would jump like a flash of lightning. There was a time when the coastal marshes were so full of terrapin they fed the meat to plantation slaves. It was cheaper than sowbelly. Well, I was up to City Hall in Savannah one day and a man there showed me some old papers he had dug out that said the plantation owners of Chatham County were forced to quit feeding terrapin to slaves because it made them breed too much. They wanted them to breed, of course, but they didn't want them to breed that much. Why, they spent all their time breeding. After all, there's a limit to everything."

We started up an oyster-shell lane that ran beside the river, and I said, "It must be convenient to have the streetcar line end right in front of your pavilion."

"To tell you the truth," Mr. Barbee said, "that's no accident. In a way, that's how the terrapin farm began. My daddy, Alexander Barbee, was a conductor on that road back in steam-engine days. He was French descent, and he liked to eat. He used to buy terrapin the colored people along the railroad would capture in the marshes. At first he just bought a mess now and then for his own table, but in time he took to trading in them, shipping them up to Maryland by the barrel.

"Well, around 1895, diamondbacks got so scarce the price shot up. They had been fished-out. When an old millionaire up North got ready to throw a banquet, he sometimes had to send men up and down the coast to get a supply. So in 1898 it came to pass that my daddy decided to make a stab at raising terrapin in captivity during his off hours from the railroad. Some Yankee scientists he wrote to said it was a foolish idea, absolutely impossible, but he went out at night with the colored people and bogged around in the salt marshes and got so he understood terrapin better than any man in history. When he got ready to buy land for his terrapin farm, he naturally thought of the end of the railroad line. The land there had always looked good to him. It was the most beautiful scene in the world; when he reached it he could knock off and have a cigar. So he bought a few swampy acres, built a shed, and stocked it with terrapin. Every time he got to the end of the run he would jump out and tend to them. He got them in a breeding mood, and by 1912 they were breeding to such an extent he quit his job on the railroad. From time to time he bought more land down here. He was an unusual man. He played the cornet in a band up in Savannah and he had a high opinion of fun, so he built a dance pavilion down here. The pavilion isn't any gold mine, but we still keep it going. I sort of like it. People come out from Savannah on hot nights to smell the ocean and cool themselves off, and you know how it is—you like to see them."

We reached the end of the oyster-shell lane and came upon a long, rather dilapidated shed in an oak grove. Green moss was growing on the shingled roof and the whitewash on the clapboards was peeling. There was a big padlock on the door. "This shed is the breeding farm," Mr. Barbee said. "They're born in here, and they stay here until they're around nine summers old. At the beginning of the ninth summer they're put in the fattening pen and allowed to eat their heads off. In the autumn, after they've been fattened for four or five months, they're sent to market. You can eat a terrapin when it's five years old, but I think they taste better around nine. Also, it's wasteful to eat young terrapin, when you consider it takes two nine-year-olds to produce a good pint of clear meat." He unlocked the door but did not open it. Instead, as if he had suddenly changed his mind, he turned around on the steps of the shed and resumed the story of his father.

"Daddy passed away ten years ago and I took charge," he said. "He was quite a man, if I do say so. That white house we passed up there at the bend in the lane was his home. His room is just the way he left it. It's called the Barbee Musical Room, because everything in it plays a tune. Touch the bed, and a music box in the mattress plays a tune. Hang your hat on the rack, and the same thing happens. Pick up anything on the table from a dice cup to a hair-brush, and you get a tune. Why, there's one hundred and fifty objects in that room that'll play a tune if you just touch them. There's a rubberneck wagon up in Savannah that brings tourists down here to the island just to see it, and we employ a colored girl to stay in the room and answer questions. I bet half the yachtsmen that go to Florida in the winter have visited it.

"Three things Daddy truly admired were diamondbacks, music boxes, and William Jennings Bryan. In 1911, just before he quit the railroad, he put a clutch of terrapin eggs in his grip and went up to Washington and called on Mr. Bryan at his hotel. He had one egg that needed only a few minutes to hatch, and he said to Mr. Bryan, 'Sir, I have long been an admirer of yours and I want to ask you a slight favor. I want you to hold this here terrapin egg in your hand until it hatches out.' Mr. Bryan leaped out of his chair and said, 'I never heard of such a fool idea. Get away from me with that nasty thing.' But Daddy was known for having his own way. People said he could argue his way through a brick wall. They said he could argue the tail off a dog. So he argued Mr. Bryan into holding the egg, and in about twenty minutes a little bull terrapin hatched out right in Mr. Bryan's fist. Daddy thanked him and said he was going to name the little fellow William Jennings Bryan, but Mr. Bryan begged him to have mercy on him and call it something else. So Daddy named it Toby. He kept that Toby terrapin for years and years. He would carry it in his coat pocket everywhere he went. He had it trained so it would wink its right eye whenever he said, 'See here, Toby, ain't it about time for a drink?' "

Mr. Barbee laughed. "Yes, siree," he said, "Daddy was a sight." He swung the shed door open. A rickety catwalk extended the length of the shed, and on each side of it were nine stalls whose floors swarmed with thousands of terrapin of all ages. Some were the size of a thumbnail and some were as big as a man's hand. There was a musky but not unpleasant smell in the shed. The diamondback is a lovely creature. On both sides of its protruding, distinctly snakelike head are pretty, multi-colored lines and splotches. The hard shell in which it is boxed glints like worn leather. On the top shell, or carapace, are thirteen diamond-shaped designs, which may be pale gold, silvery, or almost black. Sometimes a terrapin shows up with fourteen diamonds on its shell; Mr. Barbee said that people on the Isle of Hope save these rare shells for good luck. The belly shell, or plastron, is the color of the keys of an old piano. "We measure them by placing a steel ruler on the belly shell," Mr. Barbee said, bending over and lifting a terrapin out of a stall. The creature opened its sinister little jaws, darted its head from left to right, and fought with its claws. "This cow will measure six and a half inches, which means she's around eight years of age. Next year she'll be ready for the stewpot. The price a terrapin brings at retail is largely based on shell length. In New York you'd pay between three and a half and five dollars for a seven-inch cow. An eight-inch one might bring seven dollars." Mr. Barbee noticed that I was watching the terrapin's jaws. "Oh, they never bite," he said.

"Are bull terrapin used in stews?" I asked.

"A bull's meat is tougher but just as palatable," he said. "A bull doesn't grow as big as a cow. You seldom see one longer than five inches. Also, from eggs hatched in captivity we get eighteen cows to every bull. That's a fact I can't explain. The bulls have a tendency to get a little overexcited at breeding time, and to keep them from working themselves to death we always put some wild bulls in the pens to help them out. This strengthens the herd. We employ hunters to go out and capture wild terrapin in the winter, when they hibernate. Wild terrapin don't eat a thing from frost until around March. They burrow in the marsh mud and sleep through the winter. They always leave an air hole in the mud, and that's what hunters look for. Some hunters use dogs called terrapin hounds, which are trained to recognize these holes. When a hound finds a hole he bays, and the hunter digs the terrapin out. We buy wild terrapin and ship them right along with our home-grown stock. My terrapin are raised so naturally they taste exactly like wild ones just pulled out of the mud. The difference is impossible to detect."

Mr. Barbee returned the terrapin he had been holding to its stall, and she crawled off. He said that, just as in the wild state, captive cows begin laying eggs in the late spring, nesting in shallow holes which they dig with their hind claws in sand on the stall floors. A cow may lay twice in a season, depositing a total of twenty eggs. The eggs are about the size of pecans and are elastic; they do not crack under pressure. In the tidal marshes the eggs hatch in from two to three months; on the farm they are stolen from the nests and incubated. Just how this is done, Mr. Barbee flatly declined to tell. "That's the Barbee family secret," he said.

An old Negro came into the shed. "Looky, looky, here comes Cooky," he said. He was carrying a bucket. "Jesse Beach, my foreman," Mr. Barbee said. "His bucket is full of crab legs and chopped-up oysters." The old man went down the catwalk, tossing a handful of food into each stall. I had noticed that the moment he entered the shed, the terrapin commenced crawling toward the front of their stalls. "They know Jesse," Mr. Barbee said. The terrapin converged on the food, shouldering each other out of the way, just as puppies do. They ate greedily. "Diamondbacks make wonderful pets," Mr. Barbee said. "I sell a lot of babies for that purpose. They are much more interesting than the dumb little turtles they sell in pet shops."

We followed the old Negro out of the shed and Mr. Barbee locked the door. "We'll take a look at the fattening pen now," he said. We went to one of the shacks alongside the pavilion. It housed a crabmeat cannery, another of the thrifty Mr. Barbee's enterprises. Between the shack and the riverbank, half in the water and half in the shore mud, was a board corral. The shallow, muddy water in it seethed with forty-five hundred full-grown terrapin. "This is a terrapin heaven," Mr. Barbee said. On one side of the corral was a cement walk, and when we stepped on it our shadows fell athwart the water and the terrapin sunning themselves on the surface promptly dived to the bottom. The tips of their inquisitive heads reappeared immediately and I could see hundreds of pairs of beady eyes staring up. "They're fat and sassy," Mr. Barbee said. "There's a pipe leading from the shucking table in the crab cannery right into the pen, and the legs and discarded flesh from the shucked crabs drop right into the water. The terrapin hang around the spout of the pipe and gobble up everything that comes along. Sooner or later those terrapin down there will appear on the finest tables in the country. God knows they're expensive, but that can't be helped. I feed a terrapin nine years before I sell it, and when you think of all the crabmeat and good Georgia oysters those fellows have put away, you can understand why a little-bitty bowl of terrapin stew costs three dollars and a half." While we stood there gazing down into a muddy pool containing more than $11,000 worth of sleek reptiles, the Negro foreman walked up toting an empty barrel and a basket of tree moss. After dousing some of the moss in the river, he made a bed with it on the bottom of the barrel. The barrel had air holes cut in it. Then he reached in the pool and grabbed six terrapin. He scrubbed them off with a stiff brush and placed them on the wet moss. Then he covered them with moss and placed six more on this layer, continuing the sandwiching process until the barrel contained three dozen. While he was putting the head on the barrel, Mrs. Barbee came to a window of the pavilion and called, "Come to dinner."

The table was laid on the back porch of the pavilion, overlooking the Skidaway, and there was a bottle of amontillado on it. Mr. Barbee and I had a glass of it, and then Mrs. Barbee brought out three bowls of terrapin stew, Southern style, so hot it was bubbling. The three of us sat down, and while we ate, Mrs. Barbee gave me a list of the things in the stew. She said it contained the meat, hearts, and livers of two diamondbacks killed early that day, eight yolks of hard-boiled eggs that had been pounded up and passed through a sieve, a half pound of yellow country butter, two pints of thick cream, a little flour, a pinch of salt, a dash of nutmeg, and a glass and a half of amontillado. The meat came off the terrapins' tiny bones with a touch of the spoon, and it tasted like delicate baby mushrooms. I had a second and a third helping. The day was clear and cool, and sitting there, drinking dry sherry and eating terrapin, I looked at the scarlet leaves on the sweet gums and swamp maples on the riverbank, and at the sandpipers running stiff-legged on the sand, and at the people sitting in the sun on the decks of the yachts anchored in the Skidaway, and I decided that I was about as happy as a human can be in this day and time. After the stew we had croquettes made of crabmeat and a salad of little Georgia shrimp. Then we had some Carolina whiting that had been pulled out of the Atlantic at the mouth of the Skidaway early that morning. With the sweet, tender whiting, we had butter beans and ears of late corn that were jerked off the stalk only a few minutes before they were dropped in the pot. We began eating at one o'clock; at four we had coffee.

Three afternoons later, back in Manhattan, I visited the terrapin market of New York, which is located in three ancient buildings near the corner of Beekman and Front streets, in Fulton Market. The largest of these is occupied by Moore & Co., an old black-bean, turtle-soup, and terrapin-stew firm now owned by a gourmet named Francesco Castelli. Each winter it sells around two thousand quarts of diamondback stew. In Mr. Castelli's establishment I saw the barrel of terrapin I had watched Mr. Barbee's foreman pack on the Isle of Hope. "I order a lot of Barbee's stuff and I ordered it from his father before him," Mr. Castelli said. "I also use terrapin from the Chesapeake Bay area, from the Cape Hatteras area of North Carolina, from New Jersey, and Long Island." Mr. Castelli believes that turtle and terrapin meat is the most healthful in the world and likes to tell about a fox terrier which lived in his factory and ate nothing but turtle meat until he died in 1921, aged twenty-five. He uses all his terrapin in his stewpots and sells no live ones.

Live ones are sold by a rather sharp-spoken old Irishman on Front Street named D. R. Quinn, who has been in the business most of his life and has not developed a taste for the meat, and by Walter T. Smith, Inc., also on Front Street. Smith's is sixty-two years old and is one of the largest turtle firms in the world; its cable address, Turtling, is known to many European chefs. It sells all kinds of edible turtles, including treacherous snappers and great 150-pound green turtles out of the Caribbean, from which most turtle soup is made. Snappers, prized for soup in Philadelphia, are not popular here. They can knock a man off his feet with their alligatorlike tails and have been known to snap off the fingers of fishermen; few New York chefs are hardy enough to handle them. I had a talk with Mr. Kurt W. Freund, manager of the firm, and he took me up the sagging stairs to the room in which his tanks are kept and showed me diamondbacks from every state on the Eastern seaboard except Maine. A few were from sloughs on Long Island. He said that in the local trade all terrapin caught from Maryland north are called Long Islands. He said that in the North, terrapin hunting is a fisherman's sideline and that few hunters north of Maryland catch more than a couple of dozen a year.

"I imagine you're under the impression that millionaires buy most of our terrapin," Mr. Freund said. "If so, you're mistaken. The terrapin business was hard hit by prohibition, and it never has got on its feet again, and for years the poor Chinese laundryman has been the backbone of our trade. I'd say that seventy per cent of the sixteen thousand live diamondbacks sold on this street last year were bought by old Chinese. Come look out this window and see my sign." Hanging from the second-floor window was a red-and-white wooden signboard smeared with Chinese characters. Mr. Freund said the characters were pronounced "gim ten guoy" and meant "diamondback terrapin." He said that each autumn he hires a Chinese to write form letters quoting terrapin prices, which are distributed by the hundred in Chinatown.

"An old Chinese doesn't run to the doctor or the drugstore when he feels bad," Mr. Freund said. "He saves his pennies and buys himself a terrapin. He cooks it with medicinal herbs and rice whiskey. Usually he puts so much whiskey in it he has himself a spree as well as a tonic. In the autumn and in the spring crowds of old Chinese come in and bargain with me. They balance terrapin on their palms and stare at them and deliberate an hour sometimes before making a selection. They tell me that the turtle has been worshipped in China for centuries. It's supposed to be a kind of holy reptile. Most of my steady Chinese customers are old laundrymen, and I know that some of them are practically penniless, but they think terrapin meat will do them more good than a month in the hospital, and they're willing to pay the price."

I told Mr. Freund that Mr. Barbee professed to believe that the consumption of terrapin meat is better than monkey glands for regaining youthfulness.

"Seriously," I said, "do you think there's anything to it?"

"I've been around terrapin for years and years, and I eat the meat myself, and I've talked the matter over with dozens of old Chinese fellows," Mr. Freund said, "and I wouldn't be the least bit surprised."

(1939)

# · II ·

# Goodbye, Shirley Temple

*I*'VE BEEN GOING TO MADAME VISAGGI'S Third Avenue spaghetti house off and on since speakeasy days, and I know all the old customers. Madame Visaggi calls them "the regulars." Peggy is one. She is an Irish girl, around thirty-five, who works in the office of a wholesale butcher on First Avenue. She is in Madame Visaggi's practically every night. Most often she is full of brandy when she leaves, but her apartment is only a few blocks away, in Tudor City, and she always gets home all right. The butcher is her uncle and doesn't say anything if she shows up late for work. Peggy is an attractive girl despite a large birthmark on her left cheek, which makes her self-conscious. When she comes in, usually between five-thirty and six, she is always tense. She says, "I got the inside shakes." Then she sits in one of the booths across from the bar, orders a brandy, and opens an afternoon newspaper. By the time she has finished with the newspaper, she has had two or three drinks and has conquered her self-consciousness. Then she doesn't mind if one of the other regulars comes over and sits in the booth with her. She knows many bitter Irish stories, she uses profanity that is fierce and imaginative, and people like to listen to her. All the regulars are familiar with the fact that Eddie, the bartender, has been in love with her for several years. Eddie has an interest in the restaurant. He is big, cheerful, and dumb. He is always begging Peggy not to drink so much and asking her to go out with him. Once Madame Visaggi sat down with Peggy and said, "Say, Peggy, sweetheart, what's the matter you don't like Eddie? He's such a nice boy."

Peggy snorted and said, "The back of my hand to Eddie." Then she laughed and said, "Oh, Eddie's O.K."

Another one of the regulars is Mike Hill. He works in an office around the corner, on Lexington, and usually drops in for a couple of drinks before going down to Grand Central to get his train. Each Wednesday night his wife comes into town, and they have dinner in Madame Visaggi's and go to the theatre. One Wednesday night they brought their little girl in to show her to Madame Visaggi. Mrs. Hill said she had been shopping most of the afternoon, and she looked tired, but the little girl was full of life. She appeared to be about five and she had curls. Madame Visaggi lifted her up, kissed her on both cheeks, and sat her on the bar. "Hello, Shirley Temple," she said. Eddie took a little white horse off the neck of a whiskey bottle and gave it to the child. Then Madame Visaggi told Eddie to take a bottle of champagne out of the refrigerator. "On the house," she said. She turned to Mrs. Hill and said, "We'll have dinner together tonight. Special. On the house." They had Martinis at the bar and then they went into the dining room in the rear. At the door, Madame Visaggi turned and said, "Send in a bottle of ginger ale for Shirley Temple, Eddie."

In a little while the child came back into the bar. "Hello, young lady," said an old man standing at the bar. "Hello," said the child. The old man said, "How do you like this place?" The child said, "I like it," and the people along the bar laughed. This pleased the child. She said, "I have a riddle. Do you know Boo?" The old man thought a moment, and then asked. "Boo who?" "Please don't cry," the child said. Then she laughed and ran back into the dining room. In a minute or two she was back again. This time she walked along the row of booths, looking into each. I was sitting in one of the middle booths with Peggy and a girl named Estelle, a friend of Peggy's. The child looked at us and smiled. Peggy said, "Hello there." "Hello," said the child. She started to leave, and then Peggy asked, "What's your name?" The child said, "My name is Margaret." "Why, that's my name, too," Peggy said. Estelle lifted the child into the booth and put an arm around her. The child stared across the table at Peggy and said, "What's that on your face?"

Peggy hesitated a moment. Then she said, "It's something God put there, Margaret."

"Won't it come off?" the child asked.

Estelle interrupted. "Do you go to school?" she asked.

"No," said the child. She looked at Peggy again and said, "Why did God put it there?"

"Because I was a bad girl," Peggy said.

"What did you do?"

Peggy asked Estelle for a cigarette. While Peggy was lighting it, the child gazed at her.

"What did you do?" she asked again.

"I shot off my father's head and cut out his heart and ate it," Peggy said.

"When?"

Estelle interrupted again.

"How old are you, sweetheart?" she asked.

"Five and a half," said the child.

She looked at Peggy and said, "Can I touch it?"

Peggy said, "Sure." She bent over and the child touched her left cheek. Then Madame Visaggi came out of the dining room, looking for the child. She picked her up. "You've got to come eat your soup, so you'll be a big girl," she said.

"Goodbye," the child said to Peggy.

"Goodbye, Shirley Temple," Peggy said.

Everything was quiet in the booth for a few minutes. I was afraid to say anything. Then Estelle asked Peggy to go with her to a movie at Loew's Lexington.

"It'll do you good," Estelle said.

"The hell with it," Peggy said.

A game of Indian dice started at the bar, and Estelle and I went over and got in it. Peggy said she wasn't interested. There were six in the game, playing for drinks. The second time the dice went down the bar, I glanced at Peggy, thinking I would ask her if she wanted a drink; Mike Hill's little girl was back again. She was standing just outside Peggy's booth. I saw Peggy lean over and speak to her. The child stared at Peggy, fascinated. When Peggy stopped talking, the child walked backward a few steps, retreating. Then she turned and ran headlong into the dining room. It was a long dice game with two ties, and we played one-tie-all-tie. I got stuck. I paid for the round, and Estelle and I went back and sat down with Peggy.

"I see the kid came back to see you," I said.

Peggy laughed.

"I sent Shirley Temple back to her mamma," she said.

Every twenty minutes or so, Estelle and I would go over to the bar and shake for drinks with the others. Every time we came back to the booth, we brought Peggy a brandy. We tried to get her to talk, but she wouldn't pay any attention to us. She was morose and silent.

At ten o'clock, Mrs. Hill came out of the dining room with Madame Visaggi. "Thanks for everything," Mrs. Hill said. "It was a wonderful dinner, and thank you so much for the champagne." "No, no, no," said Madame Visaggi. "It was nothing." Then Mike came out. He had the little girl in his arms. She looked sleepy now. They said good night to Eddie and started for the door. When they approached the booth in which we were sitting, the little girl began to kick and scream hysterically. Mike sat her down on a bar stool and said, "What in the world is the matter, baby doll?" The child continued to scream. "She's all tired out and nervous," Mrs. Hill said. "The day was too much for her. Here, let me take her." Suddenly Peggy said, "Damn it to hell." She got up abruptly and hurried toward the door. We thought she was going out of the restaurant and I got up to follow her, but at the front end of the bar she turned left and went into the ladies' room. As soon as Peggy was out of sight, the child calmed down. "She should've been in bed hours ago," Mrs. Hill said. Then they said thanks and goodbye to Madame Visaggi all over again, and left.

After a while another dice game began. While we were shaking, Peggy returned. She didn't go back to the booth. She came and stood next to me and put her elbows on the bar. I could see that she had been crying. Eddie automatically poured her a brandy.

"How's it, Peggy?" he asked.

Peggy didn't answer. She drank the brandy. Then she said, "You want to take me home, Eddie?"

"You kidding?" Eddie asked.

"No," Peggy said.

"You drunk?"

"I certainly am not," Peggy said.

"Look," Eddie said, "I'm not supposed to knock off until midnight, but I'll ask Madame to put one of the waiters behind the bar."

"O.K., Eddie," Peggy said.

(1939)

# On the Wagon

*I*T HAD BEEN SIX WEEKS, but Mike couldn't get used to it. "A month and a half," he said, "and I've just got started. Sooner or later I'll get used to it. I got to get used to it."

Half past five was quitting time in the office, and that was the hardest part of the day. He would walk it off. He would leave as if in a hurry to get home, and then walk eighteen blocks to his furnished room. He would wash up and go over to a diner on Third Avenue. While he ate, he would try to look preoccupied. Mike was embarrassed by his loneliness; he didn't want anybody, not even a counterman in a diner, to guess that he was lonesome. Like many lonesome people, he felt there was something shameful about it. Some nights after dinner he couldn't force himself to go back to his furnished room, and he would go for a ride on the Third Avenue "L." It would please him to see the four enormous, beautifully polished copper kettles in the windows of Ruppert's brewery, and it would please him to smell the wet hops, a lovely smell that blew into the car as it rattled past. He would get off the "L" at the Hanover Square station, light a cigarette, and walk back and forth on the cement plaza in front of the Cotton Exchange. He found it comforting to walk there in the dark and listen to the whistles of the tugs in the East River. The best job he ever had had been in a coffee warehouse a block from Hanover Square. That had been four years ago, and since then he had lost three other jobs, all because of drinking. After a while he would leave the plaza and get back on the "L." And all the way uptown he would stare down into the street, watching for the cheerful, flickering neons over the entrances of barrooms. "Six weeks on the wagon," he would say. "Six weeks and not even a beer!" Whenever the "L" got on his nerves, he would get out and walk until he was so tired he could sleep. Sometimes, walking at night, he saw things that made him feel better because they took his mind off himself—a street fight, an automobile wreck, a boat unloading dripping bushels of mackerel at a Fulton Market pier. He seldom stopped to look at such things, however; his purpose in walking was to tire himself out.

The hardest part of the day for Mike, certainly, was the moment he put on his coat and hat and left the wholesale drug company where, for three weeks, he had been assistant bookkeeper. But lunchtime was almost as bad. The others in the office, even Miss O'Brien, the fussy file clerk, ate across the street in the bar and grill, but he always went up the street to the coffeepot. After work, Mr. Schmidt, the bookkeeper, and Clancy, the head shipping clerk, would go across the street for beers. Once Mr. Schmidt, getting into his coat, turned to Mike and said, "I never see you across the street, Thompson. Why don't you drop in and have a beer with me and Clancy?" Mike said, "My liver isn't all it should be," and Mr. Schmidt had said, "That's tough. Take care of yourself." There was nothing wrong with Mike's liver. Mike loathed the coffeepot, but he was afraid to go across the street. He would make up his mind to have lunch in the bar and grill with the others and then he would get to thinking, and he would say to himself, "I better go up to the coffeepot. Like Betty said, unless I stay on the wagon I'll never be able to hold down a job. I'm thirty-nine and I'm not getting any younger. I had an awful time getting this job and I got to hold on to it."

He dreaded Sunday. The Sunday which marked the beginning of his seventh week on the wagon was cold and clear. He spent the afternoon in his furnished room, reading a newspaper. Late in the day he pulled his chair to the window and sat there. Acres of tenement roofs stretched out beneath his window; on one roof a pigeon-keeper was waving a bamboo pole and frightening his birds aloft. Each time they were driven off their coop the birds flew into the air, wheeled around, and settled immediately a couple of roofs away on chimneys decorated with the yellow-paint signs of the New York Frame & Picture Co. They perched on the chimneys a few tentative moments and then flew back to their coop and were driven aloft again. Mike was amused by the game. After a while the pigeon-keeper locked the birds in their coop, took a paper bag out of his pocket, and tossed some corn into each pen. Then he left the roof, and Mike felt deserted. While he sat at the window, leaning forward, with his elbows on the sill, it became dark and he began to feel bad. He had slept little the night before. A hot bath had done no good and aspirin had made him even more shaky. He had been too jittery and too lonesome to sleep. Staring out over the dark roofs, he tried to get control of himself, but it was no use. He began to cry. He took off his glasses and rubbed his eyes. His eyes were strained by sleeplessness and the tears made them smart. Mike had got so he talked to himself. "I cry as easy as an old maid in the dark at a movie," he said. "I got to hold on to myself somehow." He walked up and down in the shabby room. When he could bear it no longer he stretched out on the bed, face downward. After a while he sat up. He reached into a pocket of his coat, which hung on the back of a chair, and got his cigarettes. He sat on the edge of the bed, smoking in the dark. When he had finished the cigarette he put on his coat, got his hat, and felt in the dark for the doorknob. He didn't want to turn on the light and see, on the bureau, the photograph of Betty. As he walked downstairs, Mike thought, "I can't blame her much for leaving me. I can't blame anybody but myself." On the street he felt that people looked away when they saw his strained face.

He walked down the street, hunting for a new place to eat. For six weeks he had eaten in places that did not sell liquor—diners, coffeepots, cafeterias, and chow-mein joints. He was hungry. After he had sent the weekly money order to Betty Saturday afternoon and paid the rent on the furnished room, he had fourteen dollars left. In the old days he had spent twice that on a Saturday night, making a round of barrooms, and had thought nothing of it. "I'm sick of the junky grub in those cafeterias," he said. "I'm going someplace and get a decent meal." He stared into the neon-lit window of a bar and grill. There was a row of booths parallel with the bar. The place was not crowded. He could eat in peace. Mike went in. He ordered a steak. An old man and a young man were standing at the bar, hunched over beers. The old man was quiet, but the young man hummed a song. He would hum a few moments, absent-mindedly, and then he would break out into a verse.

" 'Oh,' " he sang, " 'the wheel flew off the hearse, and the coffin rolled out in the road. The widow got out of her carriage and she said—' "

The bartender came out of the kitchen and gave the young man a stern look; he quit singing in the middle of the verse.

"Don't look at me like that," the young man said, frowning at the bartender. "I know I'm a nuisance. I know I'm a no-good bum. No good to myself, no good to nobody. Day I was born, I wish they'd dropped me in a tub, like I was a cat. Let me have a beer. 'Oh, the wheel flew off the hearse, and the coffin rolled out in the road.' What's the matter with you? Did you have a stroke? Let's have that beer."

"Keep your pants on," said the bartender.

"None of your lip," said the young man. "Let's have that beer."

"I think he wants a beer," said the old man, not looking up.

The bartender took the empty glass and went reluctantly to the spigot.

"I never saw a man could drink so much beer," he said angrily. "It ain't human."

"I drink so much beer," said the young man, winking at his companion, "because I'm afraid if I was to drink whiskey, it would make me drunk. They say whiskey makes you drunk. I sure wouldn't want that to happen to me."

The old man snickered.

Eating his steak and potatoes, Mike felt at ease. The atmosphere of the barroom, the bickering of the men at the bar, the beer smell comforted him. It was a small barroom, a neighborhood joint. Over the bar was a poster advertising a Monster Bingo Party at the Catholic church around the corner. When he had finished his coffee,

Mike got up and walked over to the bar and stood there. The bartender was out in the kitchen. Mike stood at the bar, one foot on the rail, with his right hand in a pocket of his trousers. He rubbed coins together in his pocket and his palm was sweating. Suddenly he realized he hadn't left a tip for the waitress. He went back to the table and put fifteen cents beside his coffee cup. Then the bartender came out and Mike handed him his check and a dollar bill. "Eighty-fi' cents," said the bartender, ringing up Mike's bill. He gave Mike his change and Mike put on his overcoat and started for the door. He glanced at the clock on the wall; it was eight-thirty. He remembered the furnished room with the unshaded electric light hanging from the middle of the splotched ceiling and his heart sank, and he thought, "I just can't stand it any longer." At the door he paused. He turned and walked over to the cigarette machine. "Six weeks," Mike thought, "and not even a beer." Opening the package of cigarettes, he walked back to the bar. The bartender came and stood in front of him.

"What'll it be?" he asked.

Mike stared nervously at the bottles behind the bar and noticed a blue Bromo-Seltzer bottle, upended in its rack.

"Fix me a Bromo," Mike sid.

The bartender mixed the Bromo in two beer glasses. Mike drank the violently bubbly mixture.

"Good for what ails you," the bartender said, smiling.

The young man looked at Mike.

"You got a hangover, too?" he asked.

"Well, not exactly," Mike said.

"I got a hangover would kill a horse, damn near," said the young man.

"Hell," said the old man, "you don't know what a hangover is."

The young man grunted.

"Once I had a job in a liquor store," said the old man. "Some mornings I'd come in with a hangover and I'd have to stand there all day with thousands of bottles of the stuff staring me in the face. I'd have to say, 'Yes, sir, that's an A-1 grade of Scotch. Best we have in stock,' when just to look at it made me rock back on my heels. It was worse than a bartender with a hangover, because he can sneak a drink to brace himself, but I worked in that store six months and I never saw a cork pulled out of a bottle."

"Geez," said the young man.

"Talk about a hangover," said the old man, hunched over his beer. "You don't know what a hangover is."

Mike laughed. He thought, "A beer or two won't hurt me. A couple of beers, and I'll go home. I'll have a couple of beers and maybe I can get some sleep. I got to get some sleep. A man can't live without sleep." The bartender saw Mike looking at the rack of bottles behind the bar.

"You want something?" he asked.

Mike heard himself say, "A beer."

The bartender spanked the foam off the beer with his black paddle. Then he held the glass under the spigot an instant longer. He set the glass in front of Mike and Mike put a dime on the wet bar.

"First in six weeks," said Mike. "I been on the wagon six weeks now."

The bartender did not seem impressed.

"It don't hurt nobody to leave the stuff alone for a while," he said. "Once I was on the wagon eight months."

"Yeah?" said Mike.

"Yeah," said the bartender. "I was in a hospital."

They both laughed.

"St. Vincent's," said the bartender. "Auto accident."

Mike took a deep drink of the beer. In a little while the old man and the young man finished their beers and walked toward the door. "Pleasant dreams," the bartender called out, and took their glasses away. Left alone, Mike suddenly felt desolate. He finished his beer and lit a cigarette. He had made up his mind to leave when two women came in and sat down on bar stools at the end of the bar, next to the cigarette machine. They knew the bartender. "How's it, Tommy?" said one. "Never better," said the bartender. "What'll it be, two Manhattans?" "How'd you guess?" asked the woman, smiling. Mike felt cheerful again. When he had finished with the women, the bartender looked at Mike's empty glass.

"Fill her up?" he asked.

"Fill her up," said Mike.

A man came in with a *Daily News*. He stood at the bar and looked through a comic strip in the back of the paper. He did not order, but the bartender automatically placed a bottle of rye, a whiskey glass, and a glass of water on the bar in front of him. When he finished the comic strip, the man laughed.

"Hey, Tommy," he called to the bartender, "don't miss Moon Mullins. Kayo certainly pulled a fast one on Lord Plushbottom."

Mike smiled. On his way home he would pick up the *News* and see what had happened to Lord Plushbottom. He would get a *News* and a *Mirror* and read himself to sleep. His glass was empty again.

"I tell you," he said to the bartender, "let's have a rye this time. Beer chaser."

"O.K.," said the bartender. "Rye and a small beer."

He placed the bottle of rye in front of Mike.

"It looks the same," said Mike, filling his glass.

(1939)

# The Kind Old Blonde

*I* WAS IN SHINE'S, an Irish restaurant near the Pennsylvania Station, eating bluefish. A man and a woman came in and took the table opposite mine. While they were getting settled at the table, the man told the waiter they had just come in from the Belmont track. The waiter seemed pleased to see them. The man was bald and red-faced and substantial. He looked like a contractor, or maybe he had something to do with the horses. The woman was a big, sound, well-dressed blonde. She might have been the co-leader of a Tammany club, or an old vaudeville actress who had saved her money or perhaps married well. The waiter passed out menus and the man began to study his at once, but the woman ordered an Old-Fashioned before she opened hers. The man kept running a finger under his stiff blue collar and twisting his head from side to side. When the waiter placed the cocktail in front of the woman, the man looked at it sullenly.

"That's the only way I know to get ten cents for a little piece of orange peel," he said, staring at the cocktail. "Same amount of whiskey you get in a quarter drink. They stick in a strip of orange peel and charge you thirty-fi' cents."

"I like it," said the blonde.

"Rather take mine straight," he said.

She was considering clams and planked shad. He said he thought he would have some spaghetti. He spoke without enthusiasm.

"I'm going to have another cocktail before I order," she said.

"Go right ahead," said the man.

The way he said it made her look up from her menu. She closed it and looked at him.

"You not drinking, Jim?"

"No."

"That why you been so gloomy all day?"

"I guess so. I'm sorry."

"Is there something wrong, Jim?"

"I don't know. I haven't had a drink for three days. I went up to see my doctor, Doctor Phillips. I got orders to lay off the stuff. He told me I been digging my grave with cigars and booze. I been worried. It worried me."

The waiter came and the woman told him she wanted another cocktail and a dozen clams. She reached in her handbag and took out her cigarettes. The man held a match for her. She took a deep breath; then she let the smoke out through her nostrils.

"Had a friend used to like spaghetti," said the blonde, settling her fat elbows on the tablecloth. "I bet he weighed three hundred pounds. Big as a horse. He was a handicapper. Used to kill a quart a day, and in the summer he'd take ten, fifteen beers at one sitting."

The man grunted.

"He was an Eyetalian fellow, name of Al," said the blonde, "but he never drank wine. One fall he got shooting pains. Doctor told him he better lay off the booze. He wasn't no good after that; had to quit operating. He was up to my place for dinner one night and I told him, 'Al,' I said, 'your system's like a machine. It's got to have erl to operate. You taking the erl away and it's killing you.' I was right. Year and a half later I was to his funeral. Been here now if he'd a gone ahead and drank with some moderation. In my humble opinion he was murdered by the doctor."

"I guess it was a shock to his heart," said the man.

"What I told him," said the blonde. "I said to him, 'Al, it's a strain on your heart. Your heart can't stand it.' "

"How old a man was he?"

"He was fifty-some-odd, Jim. He was about your age, Jim. He thought he'd live to be ninety if he gave up the booze. He said all the men in his family lived to hit ninety. Poor old Al. In a year and a half he was dead and gone. Died broke. Left hardly enough to take care of the funeral."

They were silent for a little while, and then the man sat up in his chair.

"Well, it just goes to show," he said.

The waiter brought the woman's second cocktail and the plate of clams. She looked at them critically.

"If you don't mind," she said to the waiter, "these clams are mighty small. I'd like to have the cherrystones. If you don't mind."

The waiter picked up the plate of littlenecks.

"Jim, please," she said to the man. "If I was you, I'd have a drink."

When the waiter was about six steps from the kitchen the man called him back.

"I want a drink of rye," he said. "Let me have a drink of rye."

"You want soda or ginger ale?"

"Rye and plain water," said the man.


WHEN THE WAITER brought the cherrystones, the blonde looked at them and said, "Now, that's more like it." She picked up the little fork and went to work on the clams. The man poured the rye into the plain water and stirred it. Drinking it, he took his time.

"Tell you what," he said to the blonde, "I think I'll change my mind. Think I'll have some shad roe and bacon. Before you know it the season for shad roe will be over and gone."

She had a cherrystone halfway to her mouth.

"Personally, Jim, I always liked the shad better than the roe," she said, smiling at him. "You feel better now, don't you, darling?"

(1938)

# I Couldn't Dope It Out

*T*HERE IS AN EATING PLACE on River Street in Hoboken, across from the piers and a couple of blocks from the Lackawanna ferry shed, called the My Blue Heaven Italian Restaurant. One summer I came back from Copenhagen on a Hog Island freighter and the food was bad, and when the freighter finally docked in Hoboken the first place to eat that I saw was the My Blue Heaven, and I went directly to it with my suitcase in my hand. I sat down and the waiter handed me a menu, but before I started looking at it he said that the combination that day was risotto and calamari and that he recommended it. "It's rice," he said, "and squid." At that time I had never eaten risotto, let alone calamari, but I ordered the combination, impulsively, and I found it to be extraordinarily appetizing. Since then I have gone back to the My Blue Heaven really quite often, considering that I live in Greenwich Village and have to cross the river on the ferry to get to it, which, of course, is part of the fun. I have got to know the people who run the place and some of the regular customers. (I have never asked about the name, and I guess it is because I sense that there is something sentimental or even cute about it, and I have such a good opinion of the place and the people who run it that I would just as soon not know.)

One Sunday not long ago I woke up in the middle of the morning. It was a beautiful day and I decided to take a ferry over to Hoboken and have lunch in the My Blue Heaven.

When I arrived at the place around noon, Paulie, the bartender, was sleepily polishing glasses. A grouchy dock superintendent named Chris, who hangs out there, was sitting at a front table drinking Dutch beer and reading a Newark Sunday paper. Udo, the cook, and a waiter named Vinnie were at a table in the rear, opposite the door to the kitchen. Udo was drinking coffee and Vinnie was feeding free-lunch liverwurst to the kitchen cat. I sat down with Chris. While I had lunch, he scornfully read aloud a story in the Newark paper speculating on a fight between Joe Louis and "Two Ton" Tony Galento, the fat, eccentric New Jersey heavyweight. Paulie stopped polishing glasses and came over to our table and we got into a discussion about Galento.

While we were talking, a man and a woman came in. I would say they were in their late forties. She was small and red-haired and quite good-looking in a scrawny, slapdash way. I remember that she had on a green dress that was very becoming. The man was heavyset and his face was double-chinned and gloomy. The main thing I remember about him is that he was wearing a blue serge suit that seemed to be too tight, as if he had been putting on weight. In the front of the My Blue Heaven are two small tables pushed close together so the sun coming in through the window will strike them. Chris, Paulie, and I were sitting at one of them. The newcomers sat down right across from us at the other sunny table.

Vinnie came out of the kitchen, bringing them menus and glasses of water. Without looking at the menu or at Vinnie, the man ordered a hot roast-beef sandwich. He had a *Herald Tribune* and he slipped out the news and sports and tossed the other sections on a stand back of his chair, on which stacks of napkins are kept. He didn't pay any attention to the woman, but let her order for herself. She studied the menu quite a while before she made up her mind.

"Charlie," she said when the waiter had gone, "I want to see the magazine section, please."

He was reading the sports. He didn't look up when she spoke, but motioned with his head in the direction of the napkin stand behind him. She stared at him, waiting to see if he would get the paper for her. Then she stood up, walked around to the stand, and got it herself. At our table we resumed the discussion about Galento.

"Galento won't take things serious," Paulie said. "He thinks it's funny to train on beer and hot dogs. If he'd quit boozing around and really train, he could take Joe Louis."

"Nuts!" said Chris. "It would be like dropping a safe on his head. It would be murder."

There were two big photographs of Louis and Galento in the Newark paper. Chris had the page spread out on the table. Paulie bent over and studied the photograph of Galento.

"He looks like a tough man to shave," he said.

"He just *looks* tough," said Chris. "There wouldn't be any sense to a fight like that. It would be first-degree murder. Tony couldn't take Joe if Joe was tied up hands and feet and Tony was fighting with a baseball bat."

The man with the woman stopped reading. He turned around in his chair and looked at Chris. He appeared to be annoyed.

"What makes you so sure about everything?" he asked Chris.

"Beg your pardon?" said Chris, surprised.

"What makes you so sure it would be murder?" he asked. "Are you a big fight expert or something?"

The woman grabbed him by the wrist.

"Charlie," she said. "Please, for my sake."

"Shut up, stupid," he said.

He pulled his hand away and turned again to Chris. "You think you're an expert?" he asked.

"My friend," said Chris, "I think Galento is a bum. If it's anything to you."

"An expert," said the man.

"My friend," said Chris, "do you happen to know what Tommy Loughran said to the referee? What he said when Sharkey got through with him that time?"

"What?"

"He said, 'Could I please sit down some place?' "

"So what?"

"So I'm just making a prediction."

At that moment Vinnie came up, bringing the woman some

tomato juice. The man turned around in his chair. "Another one of those Jersey experts," he said, returning to his sports section. Chris shrugged his shoulders. He told Paulie he wanted a beer and Paulie hurried off to draw it. There was no more conversation at our table. I drank my coffee and Chris turned back to his paper and his beer. Presently the man at the other table stopped reading, stretched his arms, and yawned.

"I'm tired," he said to the woman.

"Tired?" said the woman. Her face was strained.

"Yeah," he said. "Tired. Ever hear of it?"

VINNIE BROUGHT THEIR ORDERS. The woman had an omelet and Udo had fixed the man a big roast-beef sandwich. When they finished eating, the woman said, "How was the sandwich, Charlie?"

"Worst roast-beef sandwich I ever had," he said. "I think it'll stunt me for life."

"My omelet was very good," she said.

"What about a drink?" the man said. "Maybe it would improve your disposition."

"*My* disposition!" she said, opening her eyes in amazement. "What's the matter with my disposition?"

"Nothing," he said, "except you haven't cracked a smile since Christ left Cleveland."

The woman laughed nervously.

"No," she said, "I don't care for a drink."

The tables were so close together Chris and I could hear everything they said, and it made us ill at ease. I tried to reopen the prizefighting discussion, but Chris had become sullen. He wouldn't answer me.

"It's a lovely day, isn't it, Charlie?" the woman said.

He didn't answer her. A moment later he said, "Didn't I tell you you should go see the dentist?" The woman nodded.

"I know, Charlie," she said hastily. "I know."

"I never saw such crooked teeth," he said. "You got to have some work done on your teeth. You look like you been in a wreck.

Didn't you promise me a dozen times you'd go see the dentist?"

Her lips trembled. Vinnie came up to clear the dishes away, and while he was at the table she was smiling. It was a strained, painful smile. When Vinnie left, she got a handkerchief out of her purse, not looking down at the purse in her lap but searching in it blindly. Her eyes were full of tears. Chris and I stared out of the window.

We could hear the man angrily rattling his paper. Then he got up and went to the washroom. A minute later the woman walked over to the slot-machine phonograph at the end of the bar. She selected a record and slipped a nickel in the slot. It was "Night and Day," a Frances Langford record. The music sounded a little hysterical. While she stood there, bent over the titles in the glass front of the phonograph, he came out of the washroom and sat down. She did not return to the table until the record was finished.

"What did you put that on for?" he asked when she sat down.

"I don't know," she said nervously. "I just did."

" 'In the silence of my lonely room,' " he sang, nasally mocking the song, " 'I think of you.' "

"Let's go, Charlie," she said.

"It was your idea," he said scornfully, "a ferryboat ride."

"I thought it would be fun, like a fool," she said. "Let's go, Charlie."

Vinnie put a check on their table. The man paid Paulie and they walked out.

"Gee," said Paulie, as soon as they reached the street, "what a nasty guy!"

"I shoulda bopped him one," said Chris. "He wasn't even drunk."

"The way he treated that woman!" said Paulie indignantly. "Gee, that's no way to treat a woman."


I STAYED IN THE MY BLUE HEAVEN until about two. Then I walked up River Street. At the head of the street I went down the hill and walked out on the Gdynia American pier. I killed most of the afternoon on the pier, sitting on a stringpiece in the sun and watching the traffic out in the river. Late in the afternoon I climbed the hill, turned back into River Street, and headed for the Lacka-wanna ferry shed. On the cement plaza in front of the shed a crowd was watching a man feed the flock of pigeons that haunts the Hoboken piers. It was the man I had seen in the My Blue Heaven, the nasty guy. He was tossing peanuts to the pigeons. The woman was standing beside him, holding a bag of peanuts. They were having a good time. The man was kneeling. He would reach up and get some peanuts out of the bag, shell them, and fling them out. The arrogant pigeons would hurry across the cement, shouldering each other out of the way and walking across the shoes of the onlookers, and the woman would laugh. When she laughed she was very attractive. I remember I thought, "I bet he's poisoning the pigeons."

I went into the ferry shed and got a cup of coffee at the lunch stand. After a while the gates to the ferry slid back and I went aboard. I walked to the front of the ferry and stood at the rail. While the ferry was moving out of the slip the man and woman walked out on the deck, arm in arm. They walked up and put their elbows on the rail. The woman stood right beside me. They were talking. He said something to the woman that I didn't hear, and she laughed and said, "You wouldn't kid me, would you?" I didn't hear his answer. Then the woman, laughing happily, said, "I bet you tell that to all the girls." They were talking that way, laughing and talking, all the way across the river. I couldn't dope it out.

(1938)

# · III ·

# The Downfall of Fascism in Black Ankle County

*E*VERY TIME I SEE MUSSOLINI shooting off his mouth in a newsreel or Göring goose-stepping in a rotogravure, I am reminded of Mr. Catfish Giddy and my first encounter with Fascism. In 1923, when I was in the ninth grade in Stonewall, North Carolina, Mr. Giddy and Mr. Spuddy Ransom organized a branch of the Knights of the Ku Klux Klan, or the Invisible Empire, which spread terror through Black Ankle County for several months. All the kids in town had seen "The Birth of a Nation," and they were fascinated by the white robes and hoods worn by the local Klansmen, and by the fiery crosses they burned at midnight on Saturdays in the vacant lot beside the Charleston, Pee Dee, and Northern depot. On Tuesday and Friday, the Klan's meeting nights, the kids would hide in the patch of Jerusalem-oak weeds in the rear of the Planters Bank & Trust Company and watch the Klansmen go up the back stairs to their meeting hall above the bank. Sometimes they reappeared in a few minutes, dressed in flowing white robes, and drove off mysteriously. I spent so many nights hiding in the weed patch that I failed my final examinations in algebra, the history of North Carolina, English composition, and French, and was not promoted, which I did not mind, as I had already spent two years in the ninth grade and felt at home there.

Now, when I look back on that period and reflect on the qualities of Mr. Giddy, Mr. Ransom, and their followers, I wonder why the people of Black Ankle County, particularly the people of Stonewall, stood for the Ku Klux Klan as long as they did. Traditionally, the

346

people of Stonewall are sturdy and self-reliant. In fact, the town was named General Stonewall Jackson, North Carolina, when it was founded right after the Civil War; later the name was shortened to Stonewall. There was certainly nothing frightening about Mr. Giddy, the Führer of the local Klan. His full name was J. Raymond Giddy, but he had a mustache on his plump face which he treated with beeswax and which stuck out sharply on both sides, and consequently he was almost always referred to as Mr. Catfish Giddy, even in the columns of the weekly *Stonewall News*. He was rather proud of the nickname. He used to say, "I may not be the richest man in Black Ankle County, but I sure am the ugliest; you can't take that away from me." Mr. Giddy was a frustrated big businessman. Before he got interested in the Klan, he had organized the Stonewall Boosters and a Stonewall Chamber of Commerce, both of which died after a few meetings. He was always making speeches about big business, but he was never much of a big businessman himself. At the time he and Mr. Ransom organized the Klan he was a travelling salesman for a chewing-tobacco concern. When he returned from a trip he would never brag about how many boxes of cut plug he had sold. Instead, he would brag that the cut plug manufactured in North Carolina in one year, if laid end to end, would damn near reach to Egypt, or Australia, or the moon, or some other distant place.

"In the manufacture of chewing tobacco, my friends," he would boast, "the Tarheel State leads the whole civilized world."

He was the town orator and the town drunk. In his cups, he would walk up and down Main Street, singing. He had a bass voice and his favorite songs were "Old Uncle Bud," new verses for which he would make up as he went along, and a song about Lydia Pinkham's vegetable compound and its effect on the human race, a song he had learned when he was a young man attending a business college in Atlanta. The high-school boys and girls, drinking Coca-Colas in the Stonewall Drug Company, would run to the door and stare and giggle when Mr. Giddy got drunk and marched up Main Street. "Old Uncle Bud," he would sing, "is the jelly-roll king. Got a hump on his back from shaking that thing."

Mr. Ransom was far more frightening than Mr. Giddy. He was

a gaunt, wild-eyed farmer. He was a religious fanatic, always screaming about wickedness. Even when he was dressed in his Ku Klux
Klan outfit, he could easily be identified because he walked with a
peculiar, hobbledehoy gait. He was a deacon in the Stonewall Jackson
Baptist Church, the church I went to, and he used to ring the bell
before services until he got a little too impassioned one Sunday
morning and pulled the rope so hard the bell came unscrewed and
fell out of the loft, giving a glancing blow to his left shoulder as it
fell. After that accident he always walked as if his next step would
be his last. Like Mr. Giddy, he had a nickname. He was christened
John Knox Ransom, but he was called Mr. Spuddy because he
habitually argued that the Southern farmer should quit planting
cotton and tobacco and plant Irish potatoes. "Something you can
eat," he would argue, smacking his palms together for emphasis.
"Goodness gracious, my friends, if you can't sell your crop, you can
put it on the table and eat it." One winter he tried to live on Irish
potatoes and got so thin his belt wouldn't hold his pants up. His
worried wife would urge him to eat some meat to get his strength
back, and he would shout, "Is a mule strong? Does a mule eat
meat?" His wife, who was a sensible woman, would ask meekly,
"Does a mule eat Irish potatoes?"

I don't think Mr. Giddy, the drunken drummer, and Mr. Ransom,
the fanatical deacon, thought very highly of each other until Mr.
Giddy returned from a selling trip in the winter of 1923 with some
booklets about the Klan he had picked up in Atlanta. Mr. Giddy
discreetly distributed the booklets among some of the loafers in
Stonewall, and Mr. Ransom got one. After reading it, he came to
the conclusion that the best way to fight wickedness, the best way
to drive corn-whiskey distillers, loose women, gypsy mule traders
and fortune tellers, chautauquas, and Holy Roller preachers out of
Black Ankle County was to organize the Klan there.

He and Mr. Giddy got together, hired the hall over the bank,
painted the windows black for the sake of secrecy, and enrolled
seventeen men in the Klan. They included a tobacco auctioneer, an
undertaker, a grocery clerk, an indolent house painter, and a number
of farmers. The farmers were all like Mr. Ransom in that they spent

less time in their fields than they did around the pot-bellied stove of the Stonewall Hardware & General Merchandise Company, arguing about religion and politics. Most of the men joined the Klan because it gave them an excuse to get away from their wives at night and because it seemed to them to have even more mystery and ceremony than the Masons or the Woodmen of the World. The undertaker and Mr. Ransom were the only "respectable" men in it; most of the others, according to the standards of Stonewall, were either "common" or "sorry." Some were both—the house painter, for example. I once heard him summed up by an old woman in Stonewall, who said, "He's common. Fishes in the summer and hunts in the winter, and when it rains he sits by the stove and plays checkers. He sure is one sorry man."

The fathers of some of my friends joined the Klan and gradually I learned many of the Klan secrets. I learned that the initiation fee was ten dollars and that the robe and hood cost six-fifty. A friend of mine swiped his father's Klan books. One was called "The Platform of the Invisible Empire." I persuaded him to let me have it in exchange for Zane Grey's "Riders of the Purple Sage." I still have it. On the cover is this declaration: "The Ku Klux Klan stands on a platform of 100-per-cent Americanism, white supremacy in the South, deportation of aliens, purity of womanhood, and eradication of the chain store." In the book are a number of denunciations of Catholics, Jews, Negroes, and labor unions. The kids in Stonewall spied on the Klan much as kids now play G-men and gangsters; it was a game. We were frightened by the Klansmen, but not too frightened to hide in the weed patch and watch them come and go. I remember one kid, lying beside me in the weeds, pointing to a robed figure and hoarsely whispering, "There goes Pa."

Mules are used almost exclusively instead of horses in the tobacco and cotton fields of Black Ankle County, and during the first weeks of the Klan's existence in Stonewall the members rode plough mules on their night rides about the countryside. They preferred to ride cross-country, probably because that made them feel invincible, and they couldn't use automobiles because they would quickly bog down in the sticky mud of the bottom fields and the sloblands, the black

mud which gives the county its name. The mules were supplied by
Mr. Ransom and by other members who were farmers. That lasted
until Mr. Giddy and Mr. Ransom, as the leaders, sent to Klan
headquarters in Atlanta for some white horse-robes. They draped
the robes over their mules one dark night and rode out to a sawmill
in a swamp to keep a rendezvous with their followers. When they
galloped up on their shrouded steeds the mules of the other Klansmen got frightened; they let out angry neighs, reared back on their
heels, and stampeded into the swamp with their riders. One Klans-
man was thrown from his mule and suffered a broken leg and three
fractured ribs. After that the Klansmen gave up cross-country riding.
They stuck to the highways and used automobiles. Fat Mr. Giddy
undoubtedly felt out of place on the sharp back of a plough mule,
anyway.

The Klansmen began their terrorism by burning fiery crosses,
huge crosses made of fence rails sprinkled with kerosene, in the
yards of all the Negro churches in the lower part of the county.
Then they kidnapped an aged, irritable blacksmith who was celebrated for his profanity. They covered him with tar. They sprinkled
chicken feathers over the tar. Then they tossed him into Bearcat
Millpond. I have heard that the old blacksmith crawled out of the
millpond with ten brand-new oaths. A few nights later the Klansmen
went after a mentally defective woman who used to wander about
the county with her fatherless children, sleeping in tobacco barns
and haylofts. They flogged her, clipped her hair close to her scalp,
and branded a "K" on her head. Next day a rural policeman found
the bleeding, frantic woman on a ditch bank beside a country road
and took her to a hospital. Later she was sent to an asylum. One
night, a few weeks later, they broke into a chain grocery in Stonewall,
the A. & P., and wrecked it. The same night they went to a Negro
café in the Back Alley, the Negro section of Stonewall, and smashed
a big, loud Edison phonograph, which the proprietor of the café
had mortgaged her home to buy. Then they began threatening a
quiet, lonesome Jew who lived above his dry-goods store on Main
Street. Some of the members of the Klan had charge accounts, long
unpaid, at his store. At the post office one night, waiting around

for the evening mail to be sorted, I heard Mr. Giddy talking about him. He said, "He sits up there all night long, reading books. No telling what he's plotting." The dry-goods merchant went to the hardware store one morning at a time when some of the Klan members were sitting around the stove and bought a double-barrelled shotgun and three boxes of twelve-gauge shells. He was not threatened any more.

Late that spring it was rumored in Stonewall that the Klan had decided to do something about the corn-whiskey-distilling situation. The biggest distiller was Mr. Sledge MacKellar; he employed four men at his copper still in Pocahontas Swamp. We knew he was immune from the Klan because he was Mr. Giddy's personal bootlegger, because he was fabulously expert with a shotgun, and because he had publicly served notice on the Klan. Mr. MacKellar came out of the swamp one afternoon and said he was prepared for "the Bed-Sheets." By that time Klansmen were called "the Bed-Sheets." He said, "I'm a Democrat and I got my rights. The first time one of them Bed-Sheets sticks his head in my front gate, I'm going to take his head right off. I got a shotgun and I got it loaded and I'm just aching to pull the trigger."

We knew the distillers the Klan had in mind were the Kidney boys, and we were not surprised when we heard that a date had been set on which they were to be tarred and feathered. The Kidney boys were three drunken Irish brothers who lived in a house about two and a half miles out from Stonewall and operated a still in Big Cherokee Swamp, behind their house. Their names were Patrick, Pinky, and Francis. They drank about half the whiskey they manufactured. When they came to town that week for supplies, the clerks in the stores kidded them. "I hear the Bed-Sheets are going to call on you boys for a pot of tea Friday night," one clerk said.

The Kidney boys had a hired man, an aged Negro named Uncle Bowleg, who later worked for a relative of mine. One time Uncle Bowleg told me how the Kidney boys brought about the downfall of the Invisible Empire in Black Ankle County. There were three entrances to the Kidney house—a front door, a back door, and a side door. When they heard the Klan was planning a call on Friday night, the brothers rented three dynamite outfits from a man who made his living blasting out tree stumps. They swapped him a gallon of charcoal-cured corn whiskey for the use of the outfits. They buried three great charges of dynamite in the yard, under the three paths leading to the entrances of the house. Wires led from the buried dynamite to batteries, to which switches were attached. The Kidney boys placed the batteries in the house, beneath three windows where they could sit and watch for approaching Klansmen. They planned to throw a switch the moment the Klansmen walked up one of the paths.

That night the Kidney boys turned off all the lights and took places at the windows with the dynamite batteries and switches in their laps. Uncle Bowleg was in the house with them. The Kidneys soon got tired of staring out into the yard, waiting for Klansmen, and ordered Uncle Bowleg to fetch them a jug of whiskey and a pitcher of water. Uncle Bowleg said he was kept busy running from one Kidney to another with the whiskey. The whiskey made them happy and they began to talk, speculating on how much noise their blasts would make. "We'll blow those Bed-Sheets to Kingdom Come," said Pinky.

About ten o'clock, when the moon was high, Francis Kidney, who was guarding the side door, decided he could wait no longer. The whiskey had given him an irresistible desire to throw the switch on his battery.

"Get ready!" he shouted suddenly. "I just can't wait no longer. I'm going to test this dynamite. The Bed-Sheets won't come in by the side door, anyway."

He threw the switch and there was a blast that shook the entire lower half of Black Ankle County. It caused people to leap out of their beds. We heard the blast in my home, and I remember that my grandmother said she thought that Judgment Day or the Second Coming was at hand.

Uncle Bowleg said the blast tore up a massive longleaf pine tree in the yard of the Kidney house and threw it into the highway. Uncle Bowleg was so frightened he jumped under a bed and hid. The Kidneys ran to the front porch and looked at the great tree lying in the highway. It pleased them. They laughed and slapped each other's shoulders. They came in and poured themselves some drinks. Then Patrick and Pinky took their places again, but Francis had thrown his switch, so he lost interest and went to sleep in his chair. In about half an hour, Patrick Kidney, who was guarding the rear door, heard a rustle out in back of the house. He knew it was the wind rustling the leaves on the chinquapin bushes, but all he wanted was an excuse to throw his switch.

"I think I hear them coming!" he shouted to Pinky, who was sitting at the front door with his hand on his switch. "Get ready. I'm going to let go."

Pinky needed some excitement, too. "Throw the switch!" he yelled.

Patrick threw his switch. The blast rattled Pinky and he threw his switch, too. The blasts were almost simultaneous. The slats fell out of the bed under which Uncle Bowleg was hiding and bruised him all over. A big framed picture of the mother of the Kidney brothers fell off the wall and hit Francis on the head. The legs dropped off the kitchen range and it fell apart. The entire back porch was torn loose from the house. The blast blew up the chicken house and a barrel in which the two hounds slept. All the chickens were killed, except an old rooster, and he never crowed again. Next morning there were six dead hens on the roof of the house and dead hens and ducks were scattered all over the yard. The South Carolina line runs near the rear of the Kidney house, and Uncle Bowleg swears that the hounds landed in South Carolina and were so shocked and outraged they never crossed back into North Carolina again. The mule's stall fell in.

"The roof fell down on that old plug," Uncle Bowleg told me, "and he bolted out into the road with the roof on his back like a saddle and galloped two miles before he felt safe enough to slow down and look around. And there was a rocking chair on the back porch and the dynamite set it to rocking. Next morning it was still rocking."

When the noise died down that night, and when things stopped falling apart, the Kidney brothers looked at each other. They were shamefaced. Suddenly they felt frightened. Without their dynamite, they felt naked and defenseless. "If the Bed-Sheets come now, we're sure done for," Francis said. His mother's picture was raising a bump on his head. All of a sudden the Kidney boys ran out of the house and made a dash for Big Cherokee Swamp, with Uncle Bowleg following. Early next morning Uncle Bowleg got hungry and went back to the house for something to eat but the Kidney boys stayed in the swamp until noon.

As a matter of fact, they would have been just as safe in their wrecked house as they were in the swamp, because the Ku Klux Klan never did show up. The Klan had postponed its scheduled call because Mr. Giddy had arrived at the hall over the bank too drunk to take any interest in Klan matters. However, while the Kidneys were still snoring in the swamp, Mr. Ransom, who hadn't been able to get any sleep because of the three strange blasts, drove into Stonewall in his Ford and picked up Mr. Giddy. Mr. Ransom was sleepy and irritable and Mr. Giddy had a bad hangover, and they were not a happy pair. They drove out to the Kidney house to see what had happened during the night. When they arrived, Uncle Bowleg was sitting in the rocking chair on the front porch, eating a plate of corn bread and molasses. Mr. Giddy and Mr. Ransom walked into the yard and looked into the three gaping holes. Uncle Bowleg watched them like a hawk.

"Spuddy," said Mr. Giddy as he peered into the hole out of which the longleaf pine had come, "that sure is a damned big hole. I sure am glad I wasn't around when those holes were dug."

"Catfish," said Mr. Ransom in a frightened voice, "somebody might of got murdered last night. It's a good thing the Klan didn't ride last night."

Uncle Bowleg said they both stared into the holes and shuddered. Then they got into the Ford and drove away rapidly. During the day all the members of the Invisible Empire took occasion to drive by the Kidney house. They also shuddered when they saw the dynamite pits.

Late that afternoon Mr. Giddy showed up on Main Street. He was drunk again. He walked down Main Street, but he didn't sing.

He stopped each person he met and said, "Friend, I have resigned." "Resigned from what, Mr. Catfish?" people asked. "Don't make no difference what I resigned from," he answered. "I just want you to know I resigned." The Ku Klux Klan never held another meeting in Stonewall. In a week or two the black paint was scraped off the windows in the hall above the bank and a "For Rent" sign was hung out. One woman ripped up her husband's Klan robe and made a pillowcase out of the cloth. Others heard about it and did the same. Mrs. Catfish Giddy ripped up her husband's robe and told her friends he was so fat she found enough material in it for two pillowcases, an apron, and a tablecloth.

(1939)

# I Blame It All on Mamma

*M*RS. COPENHAGEN CALHOUN, who lives on a riverbank watermelon farm in Black Ankle County, about a mile from the town of Stonewall, is the only termagant I have ever admired. She has no fondness for authority and is opposed to all public officials, elected or appointed. Once a distinguished senator came to Stonewall and spoke in the high-school auditorium; just after he finished telling how he made it a practice to walk in the footsteps of Thomas Jefferson, she stood up and said, "Senator, you sure are getting too big for your britches." A mayor of Stonewall once tried to get her fired from her job as cook in the station restaurant of the Charleston, Pee Dee & Northern Railroad. A woman who got drunk in public, he said, was a disgrace to the town. She kept her mouth shut until he came up for reelection; then she went up and down Main Street making speeches which helped defeat him. "Why, the stuck-up old hypocrite!" she said in one of her speeches. "He goes to the country club on Saturday night and gets as drunk as a goose on ice, and Sunday morning he stands up in the Methodist choir and sings so loud the whole church echoes for a week." She believes that public officials are inclined to overlook the fact that Americans are free, and when she is brought into court for disturbing the peace she invariably begins her address to the judge by stating, "This is a free country, by God, and I got my rights." She has a long tongue, and Judge Elisha Mullet once said she could argue the legs off an iron pot. She has many bad qualities, in fact, and her husband often complains that she has made his life a hell on earth, but when I go back to Stonewall for a visit and find that she is still insisting on her rights, I always feel better about the vigor of democracy.

I was in the tenth grade when I became one of her admirers. At that time, in 1924, she was unmarried and had just come up from Charleston to cook in the station restaurant. It was the only restaurant in Stonewall; railroad men ate there, and so did people from the sawmill, the cotton gin, and the chewing-tobacco factory. After school I used to hang around the station. I would sit on a bench beside the track and watch the Negro freight hands load boxcars with bales of cotton. Some afternoons she would come out of the kitchen and sit on the bench beside me. She was a handsome, big-hipped woman with coal-black hair and a nice grin, and the station agent must have liked her, because he let her behave pretty much as she pleased. She cooked in her bare feet and did not bother to put shoes on when she came out for a breath of fresh air. "I had an aunt," she told me, "who got the dropsy from wearing shoes in a hot kitchen." Once I asked her how she came to be named Copenhagen. "Mamma named all her babies after big towns," she said. "It was one of her fancy habits. Her first was a boy and she named him New Orleans. Then my sister came along and she named her Chattanooga. Mamma was real fond of snuff, and every payday Pa would buy her a big brown bladder of Copenhagen snuff. That's where she got my name."

One Friday night, after Miss Copey had been working at the restaurant a couple of months, the station agent wrote her a pass and she went down to Charleston to see her family. When she returned Monday on the 3:30, she was so drunk the conductor had to grab her elbows and help her down the train steps. She paid no attention to him but sang "Work, for the Night Is Coming." She bustled into the kitchen, kicked off her shoes, and began throwing things. She would pick up a pot and beat time with it while she sang a verse of the hymn, and then she would throw it. "Work till the last beam fad-eth, fad-eth to shine no more," she would sing, and then a stewpot would go sailing across the room. I stood at a window and stared. She was the first drunken woman I had ever seen and the spectacle did not disappoint me; I thought she was wonderful. Finally the chief of police, who was called Old Blunderbuss by the kids in town, came and put her under arrest. Next day she was back at work. In the afternoon she came out to sit in the sun for a few minutes, and I asked her how it felt to get drunk. She gave me a slap that almost knocked me off the bench. "Why, you little shirttail boy," she said, "What do you mean asking me such a question?" I rubbed my jaw and said, "I'm sorry, Miss Copey. I didn't mean any harm."

She leaned forward and held her head in her hands like a mourner and sat that way a few minutes. Then she straightened up and said, "I'm sorry I slapped you, son, but that was a hell of a question to ask a lady. Drinking is a sad, sad thing, and I hate to talk about it. I was a liquor-head sot before I got past the third grade, and I blame it all on Mamma. I had the colic real often when I was a little girl, and to ease the pain Mamma would take Pa's jug and measure out half a cup of liquor and sweeten it with molasses and dose me with it, and I got an everlasting taste for the awful stuff. If I knew then what I know now, I would've got up from my sickbed and knocked that liquor outa my mamma's hand." She sighed and stood up. "Still and all," she said, and a broad smile came on her face, "I got to admit that it sure cured my colic."

Miss Copey had not worked at the restaurant long before she got acquainted with Mr. Thunderbolt Calhoun. He has a watermelon farm on the bank of Shad Roe River in a section of the county called Egypt. He is so sleepy and slow he has been known as Thunderbolt ever since he was a boy; his true name is Rutherford Calhoun. He is shiftless and most of his farm work is done by a Negro hired boy named Mister. (When this boy was born his mother said, "White people claim they won't mister a Negro. Well, by God, son, they'll mister you!") Mr. Thunderbolt's fifteen-acre farm is fertile and it grows the finest Cuban Queen, Black Gipsy, and Irish Gray watermelons I have ever seen. The farm is just a sideline, however; his principal interest in life is a copper still hidden on the bank of a bay in the river swamp. In this still he produces a vehement kind of whiskey known as tanglefoot. "I depend on watermelons to pay the taxes and feed me and my mule," he says. "The whiskey is pure profit." Experts say that his tanglefoot is as good as good Kentucky bourbon, and he claims that laziness makes it so. "You have to be patient to make good whiskey," he says, yawning, "and I'm an uncommonly patient man."

After Miss Copey began buying her whiskey from him, she went on sprees more often; his whiskey did not give her hangovers or what she called "the dismals." At least once a month, usually on a Saturday afternoon, she would leave her kitchen and walk barefooted down Main Street, singing a hymn at the top of her voice, and she seldom got below Main and Jefferson before she was under arrest. Most of the town drunks meekly paid the usual fine of seven dollars and costs or went to jail, but Miss Copey always took advantage of the question "What have you got to say for yourself?" First she would claim that the right to get drunk is guaranteed by the Constitution, and then she would accuse the judge of being a hypocrite.

"I got a right to let loose a hymn when I feel like it," she would say. "That don't harm nobody. Suppose I do make a little noise? Do they put 'em in jail for blowing the whistle at the sawmill? And anyhow, I don't drink in secret. There's nothing so low-down sorry as a man that drinks in secret. You're a secret sot, Judge Mullet, and don't try to deny it."

"I like a drop now and then, to be sure," the Judge would reply, "but that don't give me the right to run up and down the highways and byways in my bare feet."

"Now you're trying to tell me there's one law for a judge and another for a railroad cook," Miss Copey would say triumphantly. "That's a hell of a way for a judge to talk."

Miss Copey had been cooking in the station restaurant about two years when a stovepipe crumpled up and fell down on her head, stunning her. It made her so angry she quit her job and threatened to sue the railroad for a thousand dollars. She settled out of court, however, when a claim agent offered her a check for seventy-five. "I haven't got the patience to fight a railroad," she said. She cashed the check, insisting on having the sum in one-dollar bills, and hurried out to Mr. Thunderbolt's to buy a Mason jar of tanglefoot. When he saw her roll of bills he said he felt they ought to celebrate. He

359

drew some whiskey out of a charred-oak keg that had been buried in the swamp for five years, and they sat in rocking chairs on the front porch and began to drink to each other. After an hour or so, Mr. Thunderbolt told her he was a lonesome man and that he had grown mighty damned tired of Mister's cooking. He wound up by asking her to be his wife. Miss Copey broke down and sobbed. Then she said, "I'll make you a good wife, Thunderbolt. We better hurry to town before the courthouse closes. If we wait until you're sober, I'm afraid you'll change your mind." Mister drove them to Stonewall in Mr. Thunderbolt's old Ford truck. They stopped at Miss Copey's rooming house and picked up her trunk; then they went over to the courthouse and were married. Judge Mullet was surprised by the marriage but said he guessed Mr. Thunderbolt's star customer wanted to get closer to the source of supply. For a week the bride and groom went fishing in Shad Roe River in the morning, got drunk in the afternoon, and rode about the country in the Ford truck at night. Then, Saturday morning, Miss Copey woke up, looked out a window, and saw that the figs were ripe on the door-yard bushes; she shook her husband awake and said, "The honeymoon's over, Thunderbolt. I got to get busy and can them figs before they drop on the ground."

For a couple of months, Miss Copey was a model wife. That autumn I hunted squirrels practically every afternoon in the swamp that runs alongside Mr. Thunderbolt's farm, and I used to stop by and see her. She showed me scores of jars of watermelon-rind pickles and fig preserves she had canned and arranged on the cellar shelves. She had spaded a pit in the back yard for barbecues, and in the corncrib she had a big barrel of scuppernong grapes in ferment. She had bought four Rhode Island Red hens and four settings of eggs, and she had a yardful of biddies. She proudly told me that every night when Mr. Thunderbolt came home from the swamp, worn out after a day of squatting beside his still, he found a plate of fried chicken and a sweet-potato pie on the kitchen table waiting for him.

After a while, however, she began to get bored. "It's too damned still around here," she told me one evening. "I need some human company. Sometimes a whole day goes past and I don't get a single word out of Thunderbolt. He lived by himself so long he almost lost the use of his tongue." There is a Baptist church a half mile up the river, and one lonesome Sunday she attended a service there. She picked an unfortunate time, because there was a fight in progress in the congregation. In fact, at that period, which was the autumn of 1926, there was dissension in many rural Baptist churches in the South over the ceremony of immersion. One group believed a convert should be immersed three times face forward in the still water of a pond and the other favored a single immersion in the running water of a river. The opposing groups were called the Trine Forwardites and the Running Riverites. Miss Copey became a churchgoer merely because she wanted to sing some hymns, but she soon got mixed up in this theological wrangle. The second Sunday she attended services she was sitting in a back pew when a man got up and advocated changing the name of the church from Egypt Baptist to Still Water Trine Forward Baptist. He said any sensible person knew that a calm pond was more spiritual than the troubled waters of a river. This did not seem right to Miss Copey; she arose and interrupted him. "Jordan wa'n't no pond," she said. "It was a running river. On that rock I stand." "That's right, sister!" exclaimed a man up front. "You hit the nail on the head." He went back and asked Miss Copey to come forward and sit with the Running River faction. "Why, I'll gladly do so," Miss Copey said. "What's this all about, anyhow?"

Presently the argument between the factions grew bitter, and Miss Copey arose again and suggested singing "On Jordan's Stormy Banks," a revival hymn. The leader of her faction said, "Let's march out of this church as we sing that hymn." Thereupon seven men and women marched up the aisle. Miss Copey got up and followed them. In the yard outside, they held a meeting and decided to organize a new church and call it the Running River One Immersion Baptist. "You can meet at my house until you locate a more suitable place," Miss Copey suggested. "Let's go there now and sit on the porch and do some singing. I feel like letting loose a few hymns." The Running Riverites were pleased by this suggestion. With Miss

Copey leading, they marched down the road singing "There Is a Green Hill Far Away." When Mr. Thunderbolt saw them heading up the lane, he was sitting on the porch, playing his harmonica. He leaped off the porch and fled to the swamp. Miss Copey arranged chairs on the porch and announced that her favorite hymns were "There Is a Fountain Filled with Blood" and "The Old Time Religion Is Good Enough for Me." All afternoon they sang these hymns over and over. At sundown Miss Copey said, "If you're a mind to, we'll meet here again next Sunday. We'll show those Trine Forwardite heathens!" Then the meeting ended. Late that night Mr. Thunderbolt came in, raging drunk. "Listen, you old hoot owl!" he shouted. "If you bring them hymn-singers to this house again, I'll leave you and never come back!" "Don't threaten me, you drunk old sinner," Miss Copey said. "You start threatening me, I'll pull a slat out of the bed and fracture your skull."

Next Sunday afternoon the hymn-singers held another meeting on Miss Copey's porch, and that night Mr. Thunderbolt did not come home at all. Monday night he was still missing. Early Tuesday morning, Miss Copey went down to Mister's cabin and found that he was missing too. She looked in the barn and found that the Ford truck was gone. On my way home from the swamp that afternoon I stopped by to see her, and she was sitting on the front steps, moaning. There was a carving knife in her lap. "I'll cut his black heart out," she said. "I'll put my trademark on him. The wife-deserter!" I sat down and tried to comfort her. Presently two of the hymn-singers came up the lane. "How are you this fine fall day, sister?" one called out. Miss Copey ran out to meet them. "You come another step closer, you old hymn-singers," she said, "and I'll throw you in the river! You've turned a man against his wife! You've broke up a happy home!" After a while we went in the house and she made some coffee. We were sitting on the back porch drinking it when Mister drove up in the Ford truck. "Hey there, Miss Copey!" he yelled. "They got Mr. Thunderbolt in jail down in Charleston." "Why, bless his heart," said Miss Copey. She ran in the house and got her hat and her purse. "Get back in that truck," she said to Mister, "and take me to him." The three of us climbed in the seat.

In Charleston, the jailer let us go in and see Mr. Thunderbolt. He was lying in his cell playing his harmonica. He was in fine spirits. He told us the hymn-singing had made him so angry he had ordered Mister to drive him to Charleston. There was a moving-picture theatre near the place they parked the truck, and Monday night he decided to go in and see a show; he had never seen a moving picture. Mary Pickford was in it, he said, and he became so absorbed in her troubles that he crouched way forward in his seat and got a cramp in his left leg. At first he tried not to notice it, but when he could bear it no longer he decided to try the old-fashioned remedy of kicking the cramp out. He got out in the aisle, held on to an end seat, and began kicking backward, like a mule that is being shod. All the time he kept his eyes on the picture. "I didn't want to miss a thing," he said. People began to yell for him to sit down, he said, and an usher hurried up and told him to stop kicking. "Please go away and don't bother me," he told the usher. The usher got the manager and together they grabbed him. "I couldn't properly defend myself," Mr. Thunderbolt told us. "I couldn't fight them two busy-bodies and keep up with what was happening to Miss Mary Pickford and kick the cramp out of my foot all at the same time. It was more than any one human could do." The usher and the manager hustled him to the lobby, and when he realized he wouldn't be able to see the rest of the picture, he put all his attention on self-defense and knocked the two men flat. Then a policeman came and arrested him for disorderly conduct.

"Why, it's a damned outrage, honey," Miss Copey said. "I'm going right down and bail you out."

"Just a minute," Mr. Thunderbolt said. "You're not going to bail me out until I get your solemn promise to leave them hymn-singers alone. It's real quiet in this jail."

"Oh, hell, Thunderbolt!" said Miss Copey. "I threw them hymn-singers in the river before I left home."

(1940)

# Uncle Dockery and the Independent Bull

*I*OFTEN FIND IT COMFORTING to think of Uncle Dockery Fitzsimmons, a serene old bright-leaf tobacco farmer who lives in Black Ankle County, about six miles from Stonewall. He is the only man I have ever known who has absolutely no respect for the mechanical genius of Western civilization. One day, when I was about fifteen, we were fishing Little Rump River for blue bream and a motorboat chugged by, scaring all the fish to the bed of the river, and Uncle Dockery said, "Son, the only inventions that make sense to me are the shotgun, the two-horse wagon, the butter churn, and the frying pan. Sooner or later such contraptions as the motorboat will drive the whole human race into Dix Hill." Dix Hill is a suburb of Raleigh, where the North Carolina State Asylum for the Insane is located.

Uncle Dockery is still opposed to the automobile. "I don't want to go nowhere," he used to say, "that a mule can't take me." His hatred of automobiles embraces people who ride in them. One summer afternoon we were sitting on his veranda, eating a watermelon, when a neighbor ran up the road and said, "There's been a terrible auto accident up on the highway, Mr. Fitzsimmons." The news pleased Uncle Dockery. He placed his rasher of watermelon on the rail of the veranda, smiled broadly, and asked, "How many killed?" "Four," said the neighbor. "Well, that's just fine," said Uncle Dockery. "Where were they going in such a rush?" "They were going to the beach for a swim," said the neighbor. Uncle Dockery nodded with satisfaction and said, "I guess they figured the Atlantic Ocean wouldn't wait."

Uncle Dockery did not often leave his farm, but once, during a series of revival meetings at the General Stonewall Jackson Baptist Church, he spent the night in Stonewall at the home of his married daughter. In the middle of the night there was a frightful uproar in his room, and his daughter and her husband ran in to rescue him. They thought someone was trying to murder him. They found he had got out of bed to get a drink of water and had pulled the electric-light cord loose from the ceiling. He said, "I tried to turn the damned thing on, but I couldn't somehow seem to make it work. I thought maybe if I grabbed hold of it and gave it a jerk, the light would come on." He was so maddened by his mistake that he wouldn't spend the balance of the night in the room. He asked his daughter to take some blankets and spread a pallet for him outside on the porch. In the morning he denounced her for having electric lights installed in her house. "A fat-pine knot or a kerosene lamp was good enough for Grandpa, and it was good enough for Pa, and it was good enough for Ma, and by God, Miss Priss, it's good enough for me," Uncle Dockery told her.

Although I always called him Uncle Dockery, we are not related. Most of the families in Black Ankle County have been there since the time of the Lords Proprietors, most of them are Scotch-Irish, and most of them *are* related. (There are, however, no aristocrats in the county; in fact, the first mint julep I ever saw was in Lundy's seafood restaurant in Sheepshead Bay in the summer of 1934.) Because almost everybody in the county is at least a cousin by marriage of everybody else, it is natural for young people to use the word "Uncle" for old men they like. People in the county seem to take it for granted that everybody is kin to them.

I remember an incident which illustrates this. There is a ragged, epileptic old Cherokee Indian in Stonewall. He wears a rooster feather in the band of his hat and his beard comes down level with his belt buckle and he looks like Henry Wadsworth Longfellow. People call him Uncle John. He goes from house to house saying, "Have you please got something for poor old Uncle John?" and housewives customarily give him a nickel. One time an aunt from South Carolina was visiting us and she went to the door when Uncle John knocked. She was rather frightened by him. The old Indian bowed and said, "I don't think you know me. I'm Uncle John." My aunt said, "Goodness gracious! Which side of the family are you on?"

I spent a lot of time at Uncle Dockery's when I was a boy. I liked him, and I liked Aunt Dolly, his wife. When I was fourteen, I was given a horse and I used to ride out in the country after school and I often stopped at his farm. Most people in Stonewall disliked him. They used to say, "That old man would just as soon shoot you as tell you howdy-do." He always went out of his way to be sarcastic, and they considered him a public nuisance. On his rare trips to Stonewall he would walk down Main Street grinning to himself, as if he had a private joke on the human race. Once he saw a display of electric fans in the show window of the Stonewall Hardware & General Merchandise Co. and commenced to laugh. He went in and said, "Sell many of them things?" The clerk said, "Selling quite a few." Uncle Dockery said, "Be damned if the whole town don't belong in Dix Hill. A man that'd pay out good money for a breeze shouldn't be allowed to run loose." One time he visited the Black Ankle County Fair and stood around in front of a game-of-skill tent until the barker yelled at him, "Why don't you try your luck, old man?" Then Uncle Dockery pointed to the shabby merchandise offered as prizes and said, "Hell, Mister, I'm afraid I might win something." Uncle Dockery was particularly disliked by Senator C. B. McAdoo, the wealthiest man in Stonewall. Uncle Dockery knew a disgraceful story about him, and told it every time he got a chance. "C.B. hasn't spoken to me in Lord knows when," Uncle Dockery used to say, "but I knew him real well when we were boys. He was raised on a farm right down the road a piece from me, and we grew up together. He was every bit as stingy then as he is now. One summer when we were boys there was a big celebration in Stonewall. They had just finished laying the tracks for the Charleston, Pee Dee, and Northern Railroad, and the first train was due to come through, and the whole town was going to take a holiday and celebrate. All the country people for miles around drove in, and the streets were crowded. A peddler came up from Charleston and set up a lemonade tent night near the depot. He brought some ice packed in sawdust in a barrel. Ice in summer was a highly unusual sight in those days, and the people stood around and watched him crack it up. And lemons were unusual, too. The peddler squeezed out his lemons and made a big tubful of lemonade, and then he hollered out, 'Made in the shade, stirred with a spade, come buy my lemonade.' Well, C.B. walked up with his girl, Sarah Ann Barnes. C.B. was a big, overgrown country boy, and he was all dressed up. He had garters around his shirtsleeves and his hair was slicked back with tallow. He and his girl went up to the lemonade tent. C.B. reached away down in his britches and drew out a nickel, and he put the nickel on the table, got a glass of lemonade, took a swallow, and smacked his lips. Then he turned to his girl and he said, 'Mighty good stuff, Sarah Ann. Better buy yourself some.' "

I learned a lot from Uncle Dockery. He taught me how to bait a hook for blue and red-breast bream, how to use a shotgun, how to tell the age of a mule by examining his teeth, how to set a hen, how to dress partridges for the skillet, how to thump a watermelon to tell if it is green or ripe, and how to chew tobacco. He was what is called a "target chewer." He would light a candle and stick it up on a stump; then he would take up a stance five yards away and extinguish the flame without upsetting the candle. I admired this trick and he tried his best to teach it to me. He advised me to practice on pigeons, saying, "It's always best to practice on a moving target." There were pigeons all over the front yard and he would point to one and make me aim at it. He told me I might get a job with a circus when I grew up if I became a good shot. If I had been blessed with perseverance, I might be travelling about the country right now with Ringling Brothers and Barnum & Bailey.

Sometimes when I rode out, Uncle Dockery would be busy, and I would turn my horse loose in the mule lot and go fishing in Briar Berry Swamp with Little Dock. When Uncle Dockery was almost sixty, he and Aunt Dolly had a son. Aunt Dolly always referred to her husband as Old Man Dock, and their son came to be known as Little Dock. Their other children had grown up, married, and left home, and the old people were extremely fond of Little Dock; Aunt Dolly used to say, "He was mighty slow getting here, but he's the best of the lot." He was a wild, strange boy. When people in the village wanted to be polite about him, they said, "The poor boy isn't quite bright." Otherwise they said, "He's crazy as a bedbug. Takes after his Pa." I was three years older, but I liked to fish with him. He was a wonderful fisherman, except that he talked all the time. He would strike up a conversation with anything, animate or inanimate. He would talk to a fence post. He would catch a fish and say, "Hello, little sun perch, quit flopping around. You're going to make a nice supper for Little Dock."

He took a great interest in religion, but Uncle Dockery wouldn't let him go to Sunday school in Stonewall because he was afraid the town boys would make fun of him. Little Dock was always asking his father about Jesus. One day the three of us were sitting under the shed of the tobacco barn, and Little Dock said, "Pa, where is Jesus located, anyhow? Is he located up in Raleigh, or in Washington, or where?" Uncle Dockery, who was, in his own way, a deeply religious man, told him Jesus was everywhere—in the air, in the sky, in the water. Little Dock smiled, as if he didn't altogether believe the explanation. Later that afternoon, however, he pointed excitedly toward the top of a wild plum tree and said, "There goes Jesus! Lord God, how he can fly!" Uncle Dockery said, "Son, you musta got Jesus confused with a jay bird. I don't see nothing up there but some old blue jays." Little Dock said, "Oh, I saw him all right. He waved to me when he flew over the plum tree." I have always admired Uncle Dockery's behavior on that occasion. He patted the boy on the shoulder and said, "Son, I'm proud of you. It ain't everybody that's got such good eyesight." Anyone who joked about Little Dock's peculiarities in Uncle Dockery's presence made an enemy for life.

Little Dock aped his father. They talked alike. Uncle Dockery often spoke of himself in the third person. He would say, "Dockery went fishing this morning and brought back a trout big as a ham." Little Dock often spoke in the same manner. Once he told me, "Little Dock tried to harness the mule and got the hell kicked out of him. Little Dock sure does hate that mule." Uncle Dockery and Little Dock got a lot of pleasure out of talking to each other. And sometimes, on autumn afternoons, they would sit on kegs in the corncrib and drink sour persimmon beer and sing together. They sang "By and By We're Going Up to See the King," "The Hell Bound Train," and "If You Don't Like My Peaches, Please Quit Shaking My Tree." Their favorite, however, was a minstrel-show song called "Just the Same." I remember two verses of it:

> *"White girl wears a high-heel shoe.*
> *Yellow girl does the same.*
> *Black girl wears no shoe at all,*
> *But she gets there just the same.*
>
> *"White girl lives in a big brick house.*
> *Yellow girl does the same.*
> *Black girl lives in the county jail,*
> *But it's a brick house just the same."*

Uncle Dockery had his bad points. He was too stubborn and contrary for his own good. One bleak January his two mules got sick and died of something the veterinarian called vesicular stomatitis, or horsepox. Uncle Dockery was so indignant he refused to buy new mules. He owned a big bull and he decided he would force it to take the place of both mules. "I'll make a work bull out of him if it kills me," he said. A few mornings later, a bitter-cold morning with snow all over the ground, he woke up and found there was no firewood in the house. It was so cold the water in the pigpen trough had frozen solid. Aunt Dolly had no stovewood with which to cook breakfast. Uncle Dockery had some firewood cut and piled in the swamp but nothing he could use to haul it up to the house except a two-horse wagon, and he didn't think the bull could pull it without help. He called Aunt Dolly out of her cold kitchen and said, "Dockery is going to harness himself and the bull to that two-horse wagon and haul some wood." Alarmed, Aunt Dolly begged him to go borrow a mule from a neighbor to work beside the bull, but he said, "I ain't the borrowing kind." He took the heavy mule collar off a harness, tightened it up, and put it around his neck; then he strung some leather traces from the collar to the whiffletree of the wagon. Then he hitched himself securely to one side of the wagon tongue. When that was done, he ordered Aunt Dolly to harness the bull to the other side of the tongue. He said, "Dockery and the bull make a fine team, better than any two mules I ever saw." When everything was ready, he reached over and gave the bull a kick and said, "Let's go, bull." The bull, made frisky by the cold day and the unaccustomed snow, hurtled forward, pulling the wagon and Uncle Dockery with him. The driverless wagon rattled and bounced. The bull kept circling the house with a head-long lope and it was all Uncle Dockery could do to keep up with him. Although the harness restricted him, Uncle Dockery took high, nimble steps, because he knew if he stumbled once, he would fall down and the bull would drag him across the frozen ground. Aunt Dolly stood in the front yard, moaning. Every time the bull and Uncle Dockery clattered past, she waved her apron, which frightened the bull and made matters worse. Finally the bull got tired and he and Uncle Dockery slowed down simultaneously to a walk. Aunt Dolly ran to her husband's aid. She rushed up and started to take his harness off. Uncle Dockery was frantic; he was afraid the bull would start away again. He caught his breath and said, "Dolly, don't bother with me." He pushed her away and said, "Take out the bull. Dockery will stand." That afternoon he limped into Stonewall and bought a span of mules. When he got home, he and Little Dock butchered the bull for winter meat. Uncle Dockery said, "On a farm, it's teamwork that counts, and I can't stand a bull that won't cooperate."

(1939)

# Old Mr. Flood

# Author's Note

THESE STORIES OF FISH-EATING, whiskey, death, and rebirth first appeared in *The New Yorker*. Mr. Flood is not one man; combined in him are aspects of several old men who work or hang out in Fulton Fish Market, or who did in the past. I wanted these stories to be truthful rather than factual, but they are solidly based on facts. I am obliged to half the people in the market for helping me get these facts. I am much obliged to the following:

Mrs. James Donald, proprietor; James Donald, head bartender; and Gus Trein, manager, of the Hartford House, 309 Pearl Street.

Louis Morino, proprietor of Sloppy Louie's Restaurant, 92 South Street.

Drew Radel, president of the Andrew Radel Oyster Company, South Norwalk, Connecticut.

The late Amos Chesebro, one of the founders of Chesebro Brothers, Robbins & Graham, Stalls 1, 2, and 3, Fulton Fish Market, and the late Matthew J. Graham, of the same firm. Mr. Chesebro died in December, 1946, lacking a few weeks of reaching the age of ninety-three.

Joe Cantalupo, president of the Cantalupo Carting Company, 140 Beekman Street. Mr. Cantalupo is an antiquarian; he collects prints and photographs of old buildings in the fish-market district and environs. His company, which was founded by his father, Pasquale Cantalupo, sweeps and hoses down the market and carts the market trash—broken barrels and boxes, gurry, and discarded fish—to the city incinerators. His trucks are decorated with this sign:

"A LOAD ON THIS TRUCK
IS A LOAD OFF YOUR MIND."

F. Nelson Blount, president of the Narragansett Bay Packing Company, Warren, Rhode Island. Mr. Blount dredges black clams.

# Old Mr. Flood

*A* TOUGH SCOTCH-IRISHMAN I KNOW, Mr. Hugh G. Flood, a retired house-wrecking contractor, aged ninety-three, often tells people that he is dead set and determined to live until the afternoon of July 27, 1965, when he will be a hundred and fifteen years old. "I don't ask much here below," he says. "I just want to hit a hundred and fifteen. That'll hold me." Mr. Flood is small and wizened. His eyes are watchful and icy-blue, and his face is red, bony, and clean-shaven. He is old-fashioned in appearance. As a rule, he wears a high, stiff collar, a candy-striped shirt, a serge suit, and a derby. A silver watch-chain hangs across his vest. He keeps a flower in his lapel. When I am in the Fulton Fish Market neighborhood, I always drop into the Hartford House, a drowsy waterfront hotel at 309 Pearl Street, where he has a room, to see if he is still alive.

Many aged people reconcile themselves to the certainty of death and become tranquil; Mr. Flood is unreconcilable. There are three reasons for this. First, he deeply enjoys living. Second, he comes of a long line of Baptists and has a nagging fear of the hereafter, complicated by the fact that the descriptions of heaven in the Bible are as forbidding to him as those of hell. "I don't really want to go to either one of those places," he says. He broods about religion and reads a chapter of the Bible practically every day. Even so, he goes to church only on Easter. On that day he has several drinks of Scotch for breakfast and then gets in a cab and goes to a Baptist church in Chelsea. For at least a week thereafter he is gloomy and silent. "I'm a God-fearing man," he says, "and I believe in Jesus Christ crucified, risen, and coming again, but one sermon a year is all I can stand." Third, he is a diet theorist—he calls himself a seafoodetarian—and feels obliged to reach a spectacular age in order to prove his theory. He is convinced that the eating of meat and vegetables shortens life and he maintains that the only sensible food for man, particularly for a man who wants to hit a hundred and fifteen, is fish.

To Mr. Flood, the flesh of finfish and shellfish is not only good to eat, it is an elixir. "When I get through tearing a lobster apart, or one of those tender West Coast octopuses," he says, "I feel like I had a drink from the fountain of youth." He eats with relish every kind of seafood, including sea-urchin eggs, blowfish tails, winkles, ink squids, and barn-door skates. He especially likes an ancient Boston breakfast dish—fried cod tongues, cheeks, and sounds, sounds being the gelatinous air bladders along the cod's backbone. The more unusual a dish, the better he likes it. It makes him feel superior to eat something that most people would edge away from. He insists, however, on the plainest of cooking. In his opinion, there are only four first-class fish restaurants in the city—Sweet's and Libby's on Fulton Street, Gage & Tollner's in Brooklyn, and Lundy's in Sheepshead Bay—and even these, he says, are disinclined to let well enough alone. Consequently, he takes most of his meals in Sloppy Louie Morino's a busy-bee on South Street frequented almost entirely by wholesale fishmongers from Fulton Market, which is across the street. Customarily, when Mr. Flood is ready for lunch, he goes to the stall of one of the big wholesalers, a friend of his, and browses among the bins for half an hour or so. Finally he picks out a fish, or an eel, or a crab, or the wing of a skate, or whatever looks best that day, buys it, carries it unwrapped to Louie's, and tells the chef precisely how he wants it cooked. Mr. Flood and the chef, a surly old Genoese, are close friends. "I've made quite a study of fish cooks," Mr. Flood says, "and I've decided that old Italians are best. Then comes old colored men, then old mean Yankees, and then old drunk Irishmen. They have to be old; it takes almost a lifetime to learn how to do a thing simply. Even the stove has to be old. If the cook is an awful drunk, so much the better. I don't think a teetotaler could cook a fish. Oh, if he was a mean old tobacco-chewing teetotaler, he might."

Mr. Flood's attitude toward seafood is not altogether mystical. "Fish," he says, "is the only grub left that the scientists haven't been able to get their hands on and improve. The flounder you eat today hasn't got any more damned vitamins in it than the flounder your great-great-granddaddy ate, and it tastes the same. Everything else has been improved *and* improved *and* improved to such an extent that it ain't fit to eat. Consider the egg. When I was a boy on Staten Island, hens ate grit and grasshoppers and scraps from the table and whatever they could scratch out of the ground, and a platter of scrambled eggs was a delight. Then the scientists developed a special egg-laying mash made of old corncobs and sterilized buttermilk, and nowadays you order scrambled eggs and you get a platter of yellow glue. Consider the apple. Years ago you could enjoy an apple. Then the scientists took hold and invented chemical fertilizers especially for apple trees, and apples got big and red and shiny and beautiful and absolutely tasteless. As for vegetables, vegetables have been improved until they're downright poisonous. Two-thirds of the population has the stomach jumps, and no wonder."

Except for bread and butter, sauces, onions, and baked potatoes, Mr. Flood himself has rarely eaten anything but seafood since 1885 and he is in sound shape. For a man past ninety who worked hard in the wet and the wind from boyhood until the age of eighty, he is, in fact, a phenomenon; he has his own teeth, he hears all right, he doesn't wear glasses, his mind seldom wanders, and his appetite is so good that immediately after lunch he begins speculating about what he will have for dinner. He walks cautiously and a little feebly, it is true, but without a stick unless there is snow on the sidewalks. "All I dread is accidents," he said recently. "A broken bone would most likely wind things up for me. Aside from that, I don't fret about my health. I'm immune to the average germ; don't even catch colds; haven't had a cold since 1912. Only reason I caught that one, I went on a toot and it was a pouring-down rainy night in the dead of winter and my shoes were cracked and they let the damp in and

I lost my balance a time or two and sloshed around in the gutter and somewhere along the line I mislaid my hat and I'd just had a haircut and I stood in a draft in one saloon an hour or more and there was a poor fellow next to me sneezing his head off and when I got home I crawled into a bed that was beside an open window like a fool and passed out with my wet clothes on, shoes and all. Also, I'd spent the night before sitting up on a train and hadn't slept a wink and my resistance was low. If the good Lord can just see His way clear to protect me from accidents, no stumbling on the stairs, no hell-fired automobiles bearing down on me in the dark, no broken bones, I'll hit a hundred and fifteen easy."

Mr. Flood doesn't think much of doctors and never goes near one. He passes many evenings in a comfortable old spindle-back chair in the barroom of the Hartford House, drinking Scotch and tap water and arguing, and sometimes late at night he unaccountably switches to brandy and wakes up next morning with an overwhelming hangover—what he calls a katzenjammer. On these occasions he goes over to S. A. Brown's, at 28 Fulton Street, a highly aromatic little drugstore which was opened during President Thomas Jefferson's second term and which specializes in outfitting medicine chests for fishing boats, and buys a bottle of Dr. Brown's Next Morning, a proprietary greatly respected in the fish market. For all other ailments, physical or mental, he eats raw oysters. Once, in the Hartford barroom, a trembly fellow in his seventies, another tenant of the hotel, turned to Mr. Flood and said, "Flood, I had a birthday last week. I'm getting on. I'm not long for this world."

Mr. Flood snorted angrily. "Well, by God, *I* am," he said. "I just got started."

The trembly fellow sighed and said, "I'm all out of whack. I'm going uptown and see my doctor."

Mr. Flood snorted again. "Oh, shut up," he said. "Damn your doctor! I tell you what you do. You get right out of here and go over to Libby's oyster house and tell the man you want to eat some of his big oysters. Don't sit down. Stand up at that fine marble bar they got over there, where you can watch the man knife them open. And tell him you intend to drink the oyster liquor; he'll knife them on the cup shell, so the liquor won't spill. And be sure you get the big ones. Get them so big you'll have to rear back to swallow, the size that most restaurants use for fries and stews; God forgive them, they don't know any better. Ask for Robbins Islands, Mattitucks, Cape Cods, or Saddle Rocks. And don't put any of that red sauce on them, that cocktail sauce, that mess, that gurry. Ask the man for half a lemon, poke it a time or two to free the juice, and squeeze it over the oysters. And the first one he knifes, pick it up and smell it, the way you'd smell a rose, or a shot of brandy. That briny, seaweedy fragrance will clear your head; it'll make your blood run faster. And don't just eat six; take your time and eat a dozen, eat two dozen, eat three dozen, eat four dozen. And then leave the man a generous tip and go buy yourself a fifty-cent cigar and put your hat on the side of your head and take a walk down to Bowling Green. Look at the sky! Isn't it blue? And look at the girls a-tap-tap-tapping past on their pretty little feet! Aren't they just the finest girls you ever saw, the bounciest, the rumpiest, the laughingest? Aren't you ashamed of yourself for even thinking about spending good money on a damned doctor? And along about here, you better be careful. You're apt to feel so bucked-up you'll slap strangers on the back, or kick a window in, or fight a cop, or jump on the tailboard of a truck and steal a ride."

MR. FLOOD SOLD HIS HOUSE-WRECKING BUSINESS, the H. G. Flood Demolition & Salvage Co., Inc., a prosperous enterprise, in 1930, when he was eighty. A year and a half later, Mrs. Flood, his second wife, died. Directly after the funeral he gave up his apartment in Chelsea, put his furniture in storage, and moved into the Hartford, a hotel he had known and admired for many years as a truly peaceful place. "I was sadly in need of peace and quiet when I moved into here," he once said. "I had a saintly wife, God rest her. She was opposed to anything and everything in the line of fun. Use to, when I showed up with a load on, she'd persecute me. She never offered to hit me. She just stood in the door with her head thrown back and howled. She used both lungs and it didn't seem possible for all that racket to come out of one human mouth. Some nights I was afraid my eardrums wouldn't stand the strain. Once I said to her, 'Mary, dear, I'm thankful to God you ain't a drinking woman. If you can make that much noise cold sober, just think what you could do on a little gin.' "

The Hartford stands on the southwest corner of the junction of Pearl Street, Ferry Street, and Peck Slip, down in the old city. The South Ferry branch of the Third Avenue elevated line goes past it, on Pearl Street. The fish market is a couple of blocks to the south of it, and The Swamp, the tannery district, is one block north. Rooms run from three-fifty to four-fifty a week. Mr. Flood took one of the four-fifty rooms, and he has been happy in it. "You take an old retired widower crock like me," he says, "the perfect place for him is some back-alley hotel where he can be among his own kind, the rough element. I've got a married daughter by my first wife, and she begged me to go live with her. Praise the Lord I didn't! Like I said to her, 'Louise, in a month you'd hate the sight of me, and vice versa. You couldn't help it. That's nature. You'd be wanting me to die and get out of the way, and I'd probably go ahead and die, just to be accommodating.' " Mr. Flood is well off and could undoubtedly afford the Waldorf-Astoria, but newness depresses him. Like most old people, he feels best when he is around things that have lasted a long time. The Hartford is the oldest hotel in continuous operation in the city, and it just suits him. It was opened in 1836 as the Eastern Pearl Street House; the name was changed in the late sixties, when steamboats from Hartford and other New England ports docked nearby in Peck Slip. It is a shoebox-shaped building of five stories, it is surrounded by factories and hide and spice warehouses, and at night the friendly light in its combined lobby, barroom, and dining room is the only light that can be seen for blocks around. A flower-basket design is cut in the thick glass of the front door, across from the bar is a row of rickety spindle-backs, the bill of fare is scribbled in chalk on a big slate on the dining-room wall, and at the foot of the stairs is an oak rack on which the tenants hook their keys when they come down in the morning. The keys are heavy and each is attached to a serrated brass fob nearly the size of a saucer. There is no elevator. On the back-bar shelf are several photographs of the hotel. One, taken in 1901, shows Buffalo Bill and some Indians in fringed buckskins eating lobsters at a family table in the dining room. Around the margin, in a crabbed hand, someone has written, "Col. Buffalo Bill and 1 doz. red Indians just off the Boston boat, stayed three days, big eaters, lobster every meal, up all night, took the place."

The Hartford has about forty-five tenants right now, most of them elderly mariners who have retired on savings or pensions. Some of them do not budge out of the place, even to take a turn around the block, for weeks on end. Six were merchant-ship officers, four were Hudson River bargemen, two worked on scallop dredges, one owned a pair of harbor tugs, one operated three rows of shad nets in the Hudson off Edgewater, New Jersey, one had a bait barge in Sheepshead Bay, and one was captain of a seiner in the old Long Island Sound gurry-fleet that caught moss-bunkers for fertilizer factories. A few are grim and withdrawn and still unused to idleness after years of it. These stay quietly in their rooms much of the time. About a dozen are beery and wildly imaginative mythomaniacs, and Mr. Flood is often in their company. These get up at dawn, bustle downstairs to the barroom, and start talking big during breakfast; at closing time, around midnight, they are still there and still talking big. Before the night bartender goes home, he usually has to help two or three up the stairs and put them to bed; he considers this one of his duties. Some are cranks, but the proprietor, Mrs. James Donald, does not mind that. She says she has noticed that day in and day out it is easier to do business with a cranky man than with one who has forever got a grin on his face. Mrs. Donald is a handsome, friendly woman of Huguenot and German ancestry. She inherited the Hartford from her first husband, Diedrich Bloete, who had owned it since 1901. A brother of hers, Gus Trein, is manager. Her present husband, a retired policeman, is head bartender.

Mr. Flood's room is on the top floor. Its furnishings remind him pleasantly of years gone by; there is a brass bed, a washstand with pitcher and bowl, a wicker rocking chair, and a marble-top table. "The furniture in here goes back about as far as I do," he said one day. He has decorated one wall with a set of cardboard posters designed for display in retail fish stores, which he picked up in the office of the Fishery Council, the market's chamber of commerce. Among them are the following:

CRABS FROM THE BAY
ARE A TREAT ANY DAY.


FRESH MACKEREL IS IN SEASON
AT A COST WITHIN REASON.


BE OF GOOD CHEER
OYSTERS R HERE.

On another wall, just above the head of the bed, Mr. Flood has tacked up a map of Staten Island. He was born there. Once I asked him a question about his youth. He frowned and said, "My boy, I like to talk, but I don't much like to talk about my past. It's a sure sign of second childhood." On another occasion, however, he said, "I'm a third-generation Staten Islander. I'm from Pleasant Plains, a village on the south shore. My grandfather and my father before me were carpenters. I had an uncle in Brooklyn who was a general contractor—dwellings and small factories—and I went to work for him when I was a boy. Let me give you some advice: never work for your own flesh and blood. My uncle was a big-hearted man. Once I saw him chip in with a five-dollar bill to assist the family of a poor fellow who had been his bookkeeper for thirty-five years and died without funeral money. I worked for him I think it was sixteen years and then I got wise to myself and quit and became a house-wrecking contractor. I think I got into that line out of spite."

Mr. Flood's room has one window, and from it, looking south, he can see the gilded bluefish on the weathervane atop the great gray shed of the Fulton Market Fishmongers Association, a sight of which he is fond. Mr. Flood is tidy about his person; he goes to the barber every day, he keeps his suits pressed, and his derby is seldom dusty. His room, however, is extraordinarily untidy. He rarely lets the maid clean it. Above the washstand hangs a water-splotched calendar for 1932 on which the month pad, even the leaf for January, is still intact. On the marble-top table are four grape baskets filled with sea shells and river shells. He is a shell collector. One of his most prized possessions is a group of fresh-water mussel shells. They were given to him by a dealer in live carp in Peck Slip who got them, on a buying trip, from some Tennessee River carp fishermen who dredge mussels for the pearl-button trade as a sideline. Mr. Flood has shells of nine species. Each has, in addition to its Latin name, a name that is used in the trade. "I've got a pig toe, a pistol grip, a heel splitter, a warty back, a maple leaf, a monkey face, a rose bud, a rabbit's foot, and a butterfly," he says with pride. "I *had* a washboard, a lady finger, and a mule ear, but I came home one night in poor order and I was reeling around and I couldn't find the light cord and they were on the floor and I stepped on them." The floor around Mr. Flood's rocking chair is always cluttered. Scattered every which way about it the last time I visited him were a wooden shrimp scoop that he knocks his cigar ashes into, a kind of fish knife known as a ripper, a whiskbroom, a Bible, two volumes of Mark Twain (he owns a ten-volume, large-type set), a scrapbook filled with yellowing clippings of Heywood Broun's column in the *World-Telegram,* a copy of the *War Cry,* the magazine that Salvation Army women hawk on street corners, and an old, beautifully written United States Bureau of Fisheries reference book, "Fishes of the Gulf of Maine," which he ordered years ago from the Government Printing Office and which he reads over and over. He knows the habits and ranges of hundreds of fishes, mollusks, and crustaceans; he has even memorized the Latin names of many of them. Twain and Broun are Mr. Flood's favorite writers. "If I get to heaven," he once said, "the first Saturday night I'm up there, if it's O.K. with the management, I'm going to get hold of a bottle of good whiskey and look up Mr. Twain and Mr. Broun. And if they're not up there, I'll ask to be sent down to the other place." A moment later he added uneasily, "Of course, I don't really mean that. I'm just talking to hear myself talk."

Mr. Flood visits the fish market every weekday morning. He rises at five, has a cup of black coffee in the Hartford dining room, lights a cigar, and begins a leisurely tour of the fish stalls, the oyster sheds, the flounder-filleting houses, the smoking lofts, and the piers. When he reaches Fulton Street, the pandemonium in the market invigorates him. He throws his shoulders back, sniffs the salty air, and rubs his palms together. To him, the reek of the fish houses is not unpleasant. "I'll tell you a valuable secret," he once said. "The Fulton Fish Market smell will cure a cold within twenty minutes. Nobody that works in the market ever has a cold. They don't know what a cold is. The fishmongers are afraid the general public will find this out. It's too crowded around here as it is, and if the public took to coming down here to cure their colds there wouldn't be room enough to turn around in." When making his tour, he dresses like a boss fishmonger, wearing a full-length white apron and knee-high rubber boots. The streets down there, as well as the floors of the stalls, are constantly being hosed down, and he believes in heeding the old market proverb, "Keep your feet dry and you'll never die." He goes first to the piers and looks on as the trawlers, draggers, and scallop dredges are unloaded. The fishermen treat him with respect and answer all his questions. They seem to think that he is an official of some kind. They call him Pop or Commissioner. One morning I was standing on the Fulton Street pier with Edmond Irwin, supervisor of the Fishery Council, when Mr. Flood came poking along. He looked down into an unloading trawler from New Bedford and yelled, "Hey, Captain, step over here!" The captain stopped what he was doing, obediently crossed his deck, and peered up at Mr. Flood, who asked, "What you got today, Captain?"

"Nothing to speak of, sir," the captain said. "Just a load of flounders—blackbacks and yellowtails."

"Fine, fine, Captain," said Mr. Flood. "You got enough filly of sole in that load for five thousand dinners. Where'd you go this trip?"

"We was up north of Brown's Bank."

"Up in The Gully?"

"That's right. We was up in The Gully."

"Fine, fine, Captain!" said Mr. Flood, beaming and rubbing his hands. "That's just fine!"

Mr. Flood moved on down the pier. The captain stared after him for a moment, obviously puzzled, and then turned to Mr. Irwin and said, "Ed, who in hell is that man, anyway? Does he work for the government, or what?"

"It's hard to say," Mr. Irwin said. "All I know he's an old boy who's trying to live to be a hundred and fifteen years old by eating fish."

"God bless us!" said the captain. "How far along is he?"

"He's way past ninety," Mr. Irwin said.

"I declare to Jesus!" the captain said. "Well, we live and learn. Maybe I ought to start eating fish."

After Mr. Flood has inspected the boats, he goes into the shed of the Fishmongers Association. He listens to the blasphemous haggling between the fishmongers and the buyers from the retail fish stores, asks scores of questions, peers into bins, hefts and admires a striped bass here and a red snapper there, and carries market gossip from one stall to the next. He has so much curiosity that a few of the fishmongers look the other way when they see him coming, but the others treat him considerately and sometimes introduce him to visitors as the Mayor of the Fish Market. Presently he leaves the shed and steps into one of the filleting houses on South Street and helps himself to a bucket of gurry, or fish scraps, with which to feed some one-legged gulls that he has adopted. The fish market supports a flock of several hundred gulls and there are always a few crippled ones among them. "This condition," Mr. Flood says, "is due to the fact that sea gulls don't understand traffic lights. There's a stretch of South Street running through the market that's paved with Belgian blocks. And every so often during the morning rush a fish or two and sometimes a whole slew of them drop off a truck and are ground up by the wheels and packed down tight into the cracks between the blocks. The gulls go wild when they see this. They wait until traffic gets halted by a red light, and then they drop out of the sky like bats out of hell and try to worry the fish from between the cracks with their beaks and claws. They're stubborn birds. They get so interested they don't notice when the light changes and all of a sudden, wham bang, the heavy truck traffic is right on top of them. Some get killed outright. Some get broken wings and flop off and hide somewhere and starve to death. Those that lose only one leg are able to keep going, but the other gulls peck them and claw them and treat them as outcasts and they have a hard, hard time." The crippled gulls are extremely distrustful, but Mr. Flood has been able to make friends with a few of them. When he strides onto a pier toting a bucket of gurry they circle down and surround him. One or two will eat from his hands.

Mr. Flood finishes feeding his gulls around nine o'clock. Then he is ready for his first drink of the day. He is opposed to drinking alone—he says it leads to the mumbles—so he proceeds along South Street, hunting for company. He often goes to the fresh-water branch of the market, in Peck Slip, and invites Mrs. Birdy Treppel, a veteran fishwife, to step into a bar and grill near her stand and have one. "I *do* need a little something," she usually says, "to thaw me out." Mr. Flood and Mrs. Treppel are old friends. She fascinates him because she is always cold. Mrs. Treppel handles a variety of fresh-water fish, including carp, whitefish, pike, buffaloes, and red horses, and her stand, a three-bin affair partly on the sidewalk under a tarpaulin shelter and partly in the gutter, is in Peck Slip, just below Water Street, right in the path of the wind from the harbor. "I am beautifully situated," she says, "on the corner of Influenza Street and Pneumonia Slip." In the wintertime, Mrs. Treppel lets an assistant handle the bulk of her trade, while she keeps a fire jumping in an old oil drum beside her stand, feeding it with barrel staves and discarded fish boxes. She says that it doesn't do much good. She hovers near the fire, shivering, with her arms in her apron, which she rolls up and uses as a muff. She has a nervous habit of hopping up and down and stamping her feet. She does this in the heat of summer as well as in the winter; she can't seem to stop. She appears to be unusually corpulent, but she says that this is misleading. "I'm really a thin little thing, nothing but skin and bones," she says, "but I got on twelve layers of clothes— thirteen, counting my shimmy. If you was to see me undressed, you wouldn't know me." One morning I was going through the market with Mr. Flood. We paused beside Mrs. Treppel's fire and he said, "Birdy, tell the man how cold it gets in Peck Slip." "Well, son, I tell you," she said, hopping up and down as she talked, "if you went up to the North Pole in the dead of December and stripped to the drawers and picked out the biggest iceberg up there and dug a hole right down to the heart of it and crawled in that hole and put a handful of snow under each arm and sat on a block of ice and et a dish of ice cream, why, you wouldn't be nowhere near as cold as you'd be in Peck Slip in a sheepskin coat with a box fire in the gutter."

Another fish-market notable with whom Mr. Flood occasionally takes a first-today drink is Mr. Ah Got Um, a high-spirited Savannah Negro who operates a retail fish store on Lenox Avenue in Harlem and who attends the market two mornings a week to do his buying. If he feels good, he chants as he walks through the stalls:

> *Ah got pompanos!*
> *Ah got buffaloes!*
> *Ah got these!*
> *Ah got those!*
> *Ah got um!*
> *Ah got um!*
> *Ah'm the ah-got-um man!*

Around eleven o'clock, Mr. Flood shows up for lunch at Sloppy Louie's. The last time I visited him, we had lunch together. He had decided on a blue-black sea bass that day, and while the chef was broiling it we sat at a table up front, talking. A young fishmonger in an Army uniform, on furlough and looking up his colleagues in the market, came in. Mr. Flood hadn't seen him in a year or so. "Why, hello, Pop," the soldier said. "Are *you* still alive?" Mr. Flood's face fell. "Look here, son," he said. "That's a rather personal question." He became gloomy and didn't say anything for a while. When the chef brought his fish in, however, he started talking again. "You're damned right I'm still alive," he said, opening his fish and deftly removing its spine and fin bones. "Fact of the matter is, I feel the best I've felt in years. I et four dozen oysters last night and I felt so good I almost had an oyster fit." He stared at me for a moment. "Did you ever see anybody have an oyster fit?" he asked.

"No, sir," I said.

"My boy," Mr. Flood said, "people who are unaccustomed to oysters sometimes behave real queer after putting away a few dozen. I've witnessed many seizures of this nature. I'll tell you about one. My daughter Louise lives up in South Norwalk, Connecticut, and I visit her once a year, the first week in September, when the oysters come back in season. I've got a good friend in South Norwalk, Mr. Drew Radel, president of the Andrew Radel Oyster Company. Drew owns twenty-two thousand acres of oyster beds in the Sound and he produces the biggest oyster in the United States, the Robbins Island. Some get as big as omelettes. His main dock is located on the Norwalk River, and when I'm visiting my daughter I walk down there every day and Drew and I sit around and talk and eat oysters.

"Well, back in September, 1934, during the depression, Drew and I were on the dock, talking, and up walked three fellows said they were from Brooklyn. They took off their hats and asked for deckhand jobs on one of Drew's dredge boats. They were weevily fellows, pale, stoop-shouldered, and clerky-looking, three runts, no life in them at all. I don't believe a one of them had cracked a smile in months. Drew took pity on them and hired them. And before they went out to bring in a load of oysters, he took the captain aside and told him to let those Brooklyn boys eat all the oysters they could hold as soon as the dredge got out on the beds. 'Let them stuff themselves,' Drew said. 'It might possibly put some life into them.'

"Well, when the dredge came back the first time, I noticed that those Brooklyn boys were whistling. When it came back the second time, I noticed that they were singing. Late in the afternoon, Drew and I were sitting in his office on the dock when the dredge came back the third time. Shortly after it tied up, I heard a hullabaloo on the dock and I went to the window. Those Brooklyn boys were laughing and shouting and wrestling and throwing each other's hats in the water. They were flinging themselves head over heels. The air was full of Brooklyn boys. One picked up a tin bucket and began to bang on it with a stick—a-rumpatiddy-rumpatiddy-rump-atump. He marched up the dock, drumming on the bucket and yodelling, stepping high, a regular one-man band. Another one turned a double somerset and stood on his head right on the edge of the dock. He got up, shook himself, and began to sing a song called 'Tiptoe Through the Tulips with Me.' 'Uh-oh!' I said to Drew. 'The oysters have caught up with them.'

"In a little while they came trooping into Drew's office, whistling. Drew was dictating an important letter and he frowned at them. 'Boys,' he said, 'what in the hell do you want in here?' One of them, the littlest, snickered and said, 'We want to throw you off the dock.' 'At the present moment,' Drew said, 'I'm far too busy. You'll have to excuse me.' 'Well, then,' this fellow said, 'we'll box you.' Drew told them he didn't have time right then to do any boxing, and this fellow said, 'In that case, we'll go up the street and find somebody else to box. Will that be all right?' 'Why, yes indeed,' Drew said, 'that'll be all right.' In about half an hour the phone rang and I answered it. It was the sergeant at the police station in South Norwalk, and he said he'd just locked up two men who claimed they worked for the Radel Company. 'That's funny,' I said. 'There should be three of them.' 'Hold the phone a minute,' the sergeant said. 'There's a dreadful racket out in the street.' I held the phone and presently the sergeant came back. 'Everything's O.K.,' he said. 'They're bringing the third man in now, and it's taking four patrolmen, three detectives, and a couple of civilians to do it.' "

Mr. Flood cackled. "Drew and I were so proud of those Brooklyn boys," he said, "we went right over and bailed them out."

(1944)

# The Black Clams

$O$NE NOVEMBER MORNING I got a letter from Mr. Flood, inviting me to come down to the Hartford House and help him eat a bushel of black clams. "Hope this finds you well and enjoying life to the full," he wrote. "I am well, can't complain. On Friday the next I'll have something down here I want to show you, something highly unusual in the eating line, a bushel of black clams, the mysterious *Arctica islandica*. It's also known as the ocean, or deep-sea, quahog. I doubt you ever even heard of the beast. Until here lately only a few people in the world had seen one, let alone eaten one. Now and then a fisherman would find a nest of empty black clam shells in the belly of a cod or a haddock (these fishes root them off the bottom of the ocean and swallow them whole and naturally the shells don't digest), and every year or so along certain stretches of the New England coast a hurricane or a freaky storm with an onshore wind would tear a small quantity off the bottom somewhere and wash them ashore. A few would be undamaged, and people who picked these up and ate them always spoke highly of their flavor, better than bay quahogs, or steamers, or skimmers, or razor-shells, better than cockles, or winkles, or scallops, or whelks, better than mussels, better than most oysters you get nowadays. All up and down the coast from Boston to Sheepshead Bay the oystermen and clammers tried their best for generations to find out where the black clams come from. They dredged here and they dredged there, but they couldn't locate a bed anywhere at all. It was one of the secrets of the old briny. Now at last they have succeeded. In fact, they have succeeded beyond their wildest dreams. They have just discovered thirteen beds out in the open ocean off Point Judith, Rhode Island. As far as the financial end is concerned, it is like they brought in an oil well. The beds are whoppers. One bed is about as big as R.I. itself, tons of clams, mountains of clams, millions upon millions, untold boatloads, a bellyful of clams for EVERYBODY, glory be to God. One of the fishmongers down here got hold of some last week and we ate them on the half shell. No fault to find. A friend of mine in Warren, R.I., is going to get me a bushel of them on Thursday the next and put them on The Round-Up, the fish train that the N.Y., New Haven & H. runs down five nights a week from Boston. I will pick them up in the market Friday A.M. Come down around noon and meet me in the lobby of the H. H. and we will eat some clams and drink some whiskey and tell some lies and sing the One-eyed Riley. I remain, yrs. very truly, H. G. Flood."

I wrote Mr. Flood that I would meet him at noon on Friday. I showed up in the combined lobby, barroom, and dining room of the Hartford exactly at noon on that day, but he wasn't around. Three of the old men who live in the hotel were sitting on stools at one end of the bar. They had a map spread out and they were hunched over it, each with pencil, probably dividing up Europe to suit themselves. I knew one of them, to speak to, Mr. P. J. Mooney, who used to be part owner of a pair of big harbor tugs, the *Nora T.* and the *Linda Lane*. He is a raucous old man with mournful eyes and a paunch so enormous that he says it embarrasses him. (Mr. Flood once told me that Mr. Mooney, who is a wrestling fan, has a recurring nightmare in which he becomes separated from his paunch, which assumes the shape of a headless wrestler and advances on him. They square off and then they lunge at each other and wrestle for what seems like hours to Mr. Mooney. "Some nights the paunch throws P. J.," Mr. Flood said, "and some nights P. J. throws the paunch. I told P. J. he had a gold mine there. 'Put that match on in Madison Square Garden,' I said to him, 'and you'll go down in history, the both of you. Anyway,' I said, 'you shouldn't fret so much about that paunch. In days to come, when you're too

old and feeble to get about at all, it'll keep you company.'") Gus
Trein, the manager of the Hartford, was behind the bar, spelling
the regular bartender, and he beckoned for me to come over. He
seemed worried.

"Mr. Flood telephoned just now," Mr. Trein said, "and asked
me to tell you to step over to Tom Maggiani's, the ship chandler
on Dover Street. He's waiting for you over there. What in the
world is he up to now?"

"All I know," I said, "he invited me to come down and eat some
black clams."

Mr. Trein looked at me suspiciously. "Some what did you say?"
he asked.

"Some black clams," I said. "They discovered some black clams
up in Rhode Island, and Mr. Flood ordered a bushel."

Mr. Trein glanced knowingly at Mr. Mooney and said, "Did you
hear that, P. J.?" Mr. Mooney nodded, and then he tapped his
forehead with his index finger and described a circle in the air. I
became uneasy. "How *is* Mr. Flood?" I asked.

Mr. Trein frowned. "To tell you the God's green truth," he said,
"I'm worried about him. He acted real peculiar this morning, didn't
he, P. J.?"

"He did," said Mr. Mooney. "He did, indeed. Black clams, be
Jesus! That's another delusion. The old boy's out of his head, no
doubt about it. When he came downstairs this morning, I was sitting
over there reading the paper and I said to him, 'Good morning,
Old Man Flood. How you feeling? You look a bit pale.' And he
stood and stared at me like he didn't recognize me, like he was
deathly afraid of me, and he shouted out, 'Shut up, Old Scratch!'
Then he commenced to stomp around the lobby and shake his fist
and carry on. 'You got to put a stop to it!' he yelled. 'Coffins!
Undertakers! Hearses! Funeral parlors! Cemeteries! Woodlawn! Cypress Hills! Fresh Pond Crematory! Calvary! Green-Wood! It starts
the day off wrong! It's more than a man can stand!' That's what
he yelled, word for word. Then he got ahold of himself and his
mind quit wandering and he looked me straight in the eye and
cursed me for a damned old pot-gutted fool. 'I'd be much obliged

if you'd keep your trap shut when I come down in the morning, P. J.,' he said to me, 'you damned old pot-gutted fool.' Then he walked about eight or nine feet out of his way and deliberately kicked a chair. I started to inquire what in hell was the matter, but he stomped right past me and went out the side door, mumbling to himself."

"Oh, well," said Mr. Trein, "he just probably got up on the wrong side. Either that or a hangover."

Mr. Mooney snorted. "No, no, no, Gus," he said. "I hate to say this, but Old Man Flood's not long for this world. It's his time to go. I've had my eye on him lately. He's failing, the poor man. He's failing fast. He'll drop off any day now."

I was taken aback by this conversation. I decided that Mr. Flood's gnawing fear of the hereafter had got the best of him and I made up my mind, with misgivings, that I would try to persuade him to go with me and have a talk with a doctor I know at Beekman Hospital, which is at Beekman and Water, on the rim of the fish-market district. I said goodbye to Mr. Trein and Mr. Mooney and started over to Maggiani's. I was quite depressed.

MAGGIANI'S IS A FISHING-BOAT chandlery. There are sixteen boats—ground-fish draggers and trawlers and sea-scallop dredges—that regularly make ten-day voyages from the Fulton Market piers to the banks in the Gulf of Maine, and Maggiani's "grubs" seven of them; that is, it equips them with meat, groceries, and galley gear. The fishermen, most of whom are Scandinavians or New-foundlanders, are clannish; they don't mix much with the fishmong-ers and Maggiani's is their favorite hangout in the market. It is also one of Mr. Flood's favorite hangouts. He sometimes behaves as if Maggiani had him on the payroll; he frequently answers the tele-phone and on busy days he pitches in and helps make up orders. It is hidden away in the rear half of the ground floor of a converted Revolutionary-period dwelling on Dover Street, a crooked alley that runs beneath the Brooklyn Bridge from Franklin Square to the river. This building is of a type that old-time Manhattan real-estate men call a humpback; it is box-square and three stories high, its tar-papered roof is as steep as an inverted V, it is made of salmon-colored bricks, and it looks proud and noble, ten times nobler than the Chrysler Building. There are several fine humpbacks in the market, a district that contains the oldest and the most patched-up commercial buildings in the city. Maggiani's is poorly illuminated, it is as cool as a cellar in summer and as warm as a kitchen in winter, it smells garlicky, and it is a pleasant place in which to sit and doze. Up front, surrounded by a collection of slat-back chairs and up-ended boxes, is an oblong coal stove with a cooking hob on it. Nearby is a deal table on which are some packs of cards, an accumulation of back numbers of the *Fishing Gazette,* and a greasy *World Almanac,* edition of 1936. There is a big brass spittoon. There is a cat hole in the door, and there are usually two or three burly fish-house cats roving about. Hanging on the walls are a lithograph of Franklin D. Roosevelt, a rusty swordfish harpoon, a photograph of the officers of the Fisherman's Union of the Atlantic, a finger-smudged Coast and Geodetic chart of the Nantucket Shoals, an oar with a mermaid crudely carved on the blade, and a sign which says, "LAUGH AND THE WORLD LAUGHS WITH YOU, WEEP AND YOU WEEP ALONE." In the middle of the tile floor, resting on its side and dominating the room, is a hogshead of molasses with "EXTRA FANCY BARBADOS" stencilled on the spigot end; fishing-boat cooks take along several gallons of high-grade molasses every voyage for flap-jacks and for beans and brown bread. On the days the boats are in, Maggiani's is packed. On such days, Tommaso Maggiani, the pro-prietor, a Palermitano, puts complimentary platters of cheese, sliced onions, and salami under fly screens on the counter, and he keeps a pot of coffee on the hob, and the loafing fishermen get up from their seats around the stove, yawn, and fix themselves snacks—what they call "mug-ups"—whenever the spirit moves them.

Mr. Flood was in Maggiani's, standing with his back to the stove. He and Mr. Maggiani, who was snoring in a swivel chair with his heels on his roll-top desk, were the only people in the place. As soon as I got a good look at Mr. Flood, I felt relieved. His eyes were alert, his face was ruddy, his shoulders were erect, he was smoking a big cigar, and he shook hands vigorously. As usual, like a boss fishmonger, he had on rubber boots and a stiff straw hat with holes cut in it, and over his blue serge suit he wore a full-length white apron. He had two loaves of Italian bread, wrapped in a piece of newspaper, under his left arm. I asked him how he felt.

"Well," he said, "there are days when I hate everybody in the world, fat, lean, and in between, and this started out to be one of those days, but I had a drop to drink, and now I love everybody."

"Yes," I said, "they told me up at the Hartford you didn't feel so good this morning."

Mr. Flood gave me a sharp look. "Were you talking to P. J. Mooney?" he asked.

"Yes," I said, "I was."

"I thought I could detect the track of his tongue," said Mr. Flood. "What did he tell you?"

"He seemed worried about you."

"What in hell did he tell you?"

"For one thing," I said, "he believes those black clams you wrote me about are a delusion. They're not, are they?"

"Are you trying to insult me? What else did he tell you?"

"He said you were failing fast and that he expects you to drop off any day."

Mr. Flood snickered. "Oh, he does, does he?" he said. "Oh, the fat old fool, the miserable, bilious old pot-gutted fool! He got my back up this morning. That's why I brought my clams into here. If I took them up to the Hartford, like I planned, I'd be obliged to offer him some. I used to have a high regard for P. J. Mooney; knows quite a bit about striped-bass fishing, but he's picked up a habit that's so queer—well, it's so queer, so ghouly, so disgusting, so low-down nasty that I don't even like to talk about it. I'll tell you about it later. Here, my boy, have a cigar." He handed me a cigar. It was a Bulldog Avenue, a perfecto cigar hand-rolled in Tampa that costs sixty-five cents apiece; he buys them by the box. He tossed his two loaves on the counter and went into Maggiani's coldroom, a cubicle in back in which sides of beef are hung to age.

In a few moments he came shuffling out with a bushel basket in his arms. The basket was heaped with little pitch-black clams. Grunting, he set it on the counter and tipped it and let about half the contents pour out, cornucopia fashion—an exuberance of clams. The noise awakened Mr. Maggiani, who shouted, "Stop! Stop! Don't you mess up my counter. I just laid new oilcloth on that counter." "Shut up, Tommy," said Mr. Flood, "and go back to sleep."

He strewed about two yards of the counter with clams, and then stepped back and looked at them gloatingly. They were so black they glinted, they were so plump they were almost globular, and they were beautiful. The lips of the shells were tightly shut, a sign of health and freshness—a clam out of water stays shut until it begins to die, and then the adductors, the two muscles that hold the shells together, relinquish their grip and the lips gape. In Fulton Market and on the Boston Fish Pier, quahogs are graded in three sizes—Little Necks, cherrystones, and chowders. These black quahogs were Little Necks, about an inch and three quarters from hinge to lip, and they were as uniform as silver dollars. Mr. Flood got out a knife he carries in a belt holster, a kind of fish knife known as a gut-blade, and shucked a clam for me. The meat was a rosy yellow, a lovely color, the color of the flesh next to the stone of a freestone peach. Bay quahogs have splotches of yellow in some seasons, but, with the exception of the liver and the siphons, all of this clam was yellow—the foot, the muscles, the gills, the intestines, even the mantle. I ate the clam and found that it was as tender and sweet-meated as a Little Neck out of Great South Bay, the finest bay clam on the whole coast. Then I drank the juice from the cup of the shell. It was rich, invigorating, and free of grit, but, surprisingly, not as briny as the juice of a bay quahog; that was the only fault I could find with the *Arctica islandica*.

Mr. Maggiani came over with a tray on which he had put three tumblers, a carafe of water, and a fifth of Scotch about half full. "Clams don't agree with me," he said, "but I think I'll eat six or seven dozen, just to be sociable." "Help yourself, Tommy," said Mr. Flood. "That's what they're here for." Mr. Maggiani fixed us each a drink. He poured an extra gollop in Mr. Flood's tumbler and Mr. Flood smiled. "Old age hasn't taught me a whole lot," he said, "but it's sure taught me the true value of a dollar, a kind word, and a drink of whiskey." We had our drinks. Mr. Flood took six lemons and six limes from the pockets of his apron and halved them with his gut-blade to squeeze on the clams. Then he began slicing one of the Italian loaves. Mr. Flood will not eat factory-made American bread; he calls it gurry, a word applied by fishmongers to the waste that is left after a fish has been dressed. "I doubt a hog would eat it," he says, "unless it was toasted and buttered and marmalade put on it and him about to perish to death." Every other morning Mr. Flood walks up to Mrs. Palumbo's *panetteria italiana*, a hole-in-the-wall bakery on Elizabeth Street, and buys a couple of loaves. He takes his meals in restaurants in the fish-market district— Sloppy Louie's, the Hartford dining room, Sweet's, and Libby's— and he always brings his own bread. Like most Sicilian neighborhood bakers, Mrs. Palumbo turns out loaves in a multitude of shapes, some of which are symbols that protect against the Evil Eye. The loaves that Mr. Flood had this day were long and whole-wheat and S-shaped and decorated with gashes.

Mr. Maggiani, watching Mr. Flood slice, said, "Hugh, do you know the name of that loaf?"

"I heard it once," Mr. Flood said, "but it's slipped my mind."

"It's called a *cosa minuta a zighizaghi,* a small thing with zigzags," Mr. Maggiani said. "The S stands for *sapienza*—wisdom."

Mr. Flood grunted, "Whatever to hell it's called," he said, "it's good. Mrs. Palumbo knows what she's doing. She don't take ads in the papers to tell big black lies about her vitamins, she don't have a radio program rooting and tooting about her enriched bread, she don't wrap in cellophane, she don't even have a telephone. She just goes ahead and bakes the way her great-great-granddaddy baked. Consequently, by God, lo and behold, her bread is fit to eat. I'm not against vitamins, whatever to hell they are, but God took care of that matter away back there in the hitherto—God and nature, and not some big scientist or other. Years back, bread was the staff of life. It looked good, it smelled good, it tasted good, and it had all the vitamins in it a man could stand. Then the bakers fiddled and fooled and improved their methods and got things down to such a fine point that a loaf of bread didn't have any more nourishment in it than a brickbat. Now they're putting the vitamins back in by scientific means—the way God did it don't suit them; it ain't complicated enough—and they've got the brass to get on the radio and brag about it; they should hide their heads in shame."

Mr. Maggiani hadn't been paying much attention to Mr. Flood's remarks; he only half listens to him. Now he pursed his lips and nodded his head a couple of times. "Science is a great thing," he said piously. "It's wonderful what they can do." Mr. Flood stared at him for a moment and then let the matter drop. We had another round of Scotch. Mr. Maggiani found a knife for me and one for himself, and the three of us got down to work on the clams.

"The bed this basket of clams came out of is called Bed Number Two," said Mr. Flood. He is one of those who can talk and eat at once. "It's located two and an eighth miles east-southeast of the whistling buoy off Point Judith, Rhode Island. The water out there is eighty to a hundred and twenty feet deep. That's why it took so long to find the blackies. The bottom of Number Two is muddy, what the Coast and Geodetic charts call sticky, and it's just about solid with clams. They're as thick as germs. Bay clams come from much shallower water. To give you an idea, the water over most of the quahog beds in Great South Bay is only twelve feet deep. The Rhode Island clammers are working the ocean beds with the same kind of dredge boats that oystermen use, except the cables are longer. They lower a dredge on a steel cable and drag it over the bottom. The dredge plows up the mud and the clams are thrown into a big chain-metal bag that's hung on the tail of the dredge. They drag for fifteen minutes, and then they haul up and unload the bag on the deck. The ocean clammers are making a ton of money. They're getting a dollar to a dollar and a half a bushel."

"That don't sound so good," said Mr. Maggiani. "The last I heard, bay clammers were getting two and a half to three."

"A dredge boat can take fifty bushels of bay clams a day," Mr. Flood said, "if the crew don't mind rupturing themselves. The same boat can take two hundred and fifty bushels of blackies a day and just coast along. That's the difference. I heard about one boat that took five hundred and thirty-eight bushels in six hours. Also, most of the beds are outside the three-mile limit and there's no restrictions on the length of the season and the size of the catch; you can dredge the year round and you can take all you can get. Blackies have one drawback, a merchandising drawback—they aren't suited for the raw trade, the half-shell trade. You can only eat the young ones on the half shell—that is, the Little Necks, like these here. Young blackies are the finest-flavored clams in the world, in my opinion, but when they grow to cherrystone size they coarsen up. In addition, they don't stand travel as good as bay clams; they're more perishable and their shells are brittle. All the clams in the bottom of this basket are probably broken and squashed. Blackies are perfect chowder clams—the old ones and the young ones—and that's what the Rhode Islanders are selling them for. The clam-packing plants in Warren and Bristol and East Greenwich are buying all that's brought to their docks, and they're shucking and canning the entire catch. They're putting them up in gallon cans and selling them to hotels and restaurants and soup factories. They aren't going to fool with the half-shell trade. If the general public wants some for half-shell eating, unless they've got a friend in the business, I'm afraid they'll have to go to the docks and buy them off the boats, and that's a shame. Tommy, quit eating a moment and tell me what you think of these clams."

"The only thing that's got them beat in the shellfish line," said Mr. Maggiani, "is bay scallops eaten out of the shell—the whole raw scallop, and not just that scallop muscle that they fry in res-taurants."

Mr. Flood was pleased. "I tell you, Tommy," he said, "it's been my experience that just about any animal that lives in a shell and comes out of salty water is good eating. Back in 1940 the oyster beds in Great Peconic Bay became infested with millions of gastropod pests called quarterdecks, a kind of limpet, the *Crepidula fornicata.* These pests fix themselves to oyster shells in great stacks and clusters, one on top of the other, and they smother the oysters to death. Around Christmas that winter I went out on the bay with a friend of mine, Drew Radel, whose family owns the Robbins Island beds. He fattens his stock in the North Race, a swift current of water between Great and Little Peconic, and they're the biggest, finest oysters in the United States. They're so big and fine that back before the war Drew used to ship hundreds of barrels by fast ocean liner to Paris, London, and Dublin, the chief oyster-eating cities of Europe. Drew took me to a ruined bed in the Race, a bed that had three thousand bushels of oysters in it, and thirteen thousand bushels of quarterdecks. It was enough to break your heart. I took a quarterdeck in my hand, an animal about an inch and a half long, and I thought to myself, 'I wonder how you taste.' I got my knife and I dug the meat out of one and I ate it, and Drew and the dredge-boat captain looked at me like I was an outcast from human society. I ate another, and I kept on eating, and I said to Drew, 'Drew, my boy,' I said, 'it's a sacrilegious thing to say, and I'm ashamed of myself, but the little buggers taste damned near as good as oysters.' He broke down and ate a few and he had to agree with me. Said they tasted to him like the tomalley of a lobster. I told him he should give them a French name and bribe the Waldorf-Astoria to put some on the menu at three dollars and a half a dozen. 'Create a demand for them,' I said, 'and you got the problem solved.' He said he wouldn't deal in the damned things for any amount of money. Anyhow, next year they vanished, the most of them. They come and go in cycles, like a good many pests.''

THE WIND OFF THE RIVER shook Maggiani's windows. Mr. Flood went over to the stove, punched the fire, threw in a shovelful of coal, and returned to the clams. He was quiet for a while, brooding. Then he began to talk again. "I promised to tell you about Mr. Mooney's queer habit, didn't I?" he said to me.

"Yes, sir," I said.

"This is something I got no business telling a young man," Mr. Flood said, "but the pleasantest news to any human being over seventy-five is the news that some other human being around that age just died. That's provided the deceased ain't related, and some-

400

times even if he is. You put on a long face, and you tell everybody how sad and sorrowful it makes you feel, but you think to yourself, 'Well, I outlived him. Thank the Lord it was him and not me.' You think to yourself, 'One less. More room for me.' I've made quite a study of the matter, and I'm yet to find any agy man or any agy woman that don't feel the same deep down inside. It cheers you up somehow, God forgive me for saying so. I used to be ashamed of myself, but the way I figure, you can't help yourself, it's just nature. There's about a dozen and a half old crocks around seventy-five to eighty-five up at the Hartford, and here a few months back, the way it happens sometimes, they all got blue at once. Everybody had been sour-faced for days and getting sourer by the minute; they were all talked out; they had got on each other's nerves; a man would order a beer and go away down to the end of the bar by himself and drink it; you would say something to a man and he wouldn't answer you. It had just about got to the point where they were spitting in each other's eye. One afternoon around four I walked in and they were all up at the bar, the whole, entire mob, buying each other drinks, whacking each other on the shoulder. Two or three had reached the singing stage. Everybody was friends again. I asked one what happened, and he said to me, 'Didn't you hear the news? Old Dan up the street dropped dead an hour ago, the poor man. In the middle of cutting a customer's hair he keeled over and passed away.' Old Dan was a barber on Fulton Street; had a two-chair shop down here for fifty years; all the Hartford crowd went to him; a highly dignified man; everybody liked him; not an enemy in the world. I thought to myself, 'You heathen monsters! A poor old soul drops dead on the floor and it cheers you up!' But I got to be honest. In a minute I was hanging on the bar with the rest of them, going on about how sad it was, and what a fine man Old Dan had been, and how he'd given me a shave and a shampoo only the day before, and drinking more than I could handle, and feeling the best I had in I don't know when.

"Well, Mr. P. J. Mooney has an awful, awful case of what I'm talking about, the worst by far I ever saw. He comes downstairs in the morning in a hell of a hurry, and he grabs the *Times* and opens it up to the obituaries and death notices. The *Times* has the best death notices, all the details. And he sits there, drinking his coffee, happy, humming a song, reading up on who died since yesterday. And he talks to himself. He says, 'Well, my friend,' he says, looking at the picture of some poor deceased or other, 'I outlived you. You may have been one of the biggest investment bankers of our time, you may have left a thirty-million estate, you may have been a leader in social and financial circles in New York and Palm Beach, but I outlived you. You're in the funeral parlor, you old s.o.b., you and your thirty million, and here I am, P. J. Mooney, esquire, eating a fine big plate of ham and eggs, and I'm not going to have two cups of coffee this morning, I'm going to have three.' All that used to tickle me somewhat. I'd come downstairs and I'd say to him, 'Any good ones this morning, P. J.?' And he'd answer back, real cheerful, 'The president of a big steel company, well along in years, eighty-seven, fell and broke his hip, and a big doctor, a stomach specialist, seventy-three, had a stroke. It's sad,' he'd say, 'real sad.' And he'd sit there and give you all the details, the name of the undertaker that had the job, the name of the cemetery, how long was the final illness, who survived, and the like of that.

"Here lately, the past month or so, in addition to studying the obituaries, P. J. has taken to studying the old men at the Hartford. I caught him several times staring at this one and that one, looking them over, eying them, and I knew for certain what he was doing; he was estimating how much longer they had to live. One day I caught him eying me. It gave me a turn. It made me uneasy. It upset me. And he's taken to inquiring about people's health; takes a great interest in how you feel. He says, 'Did you rest well last night?' And he says, 'You sure got the trembles. You can't drink nowhere near as much as you used to, can you?' And he says, 'Mr. Flood, it seems to me you're showing your age this morning. We're not getting any younger, none of us.' And last night he came out with a mighty upsetting question. 'Mr. Flood,' he said, 'if you were flat on your back with a serious illness and the doctor told you there was no hope left, what would you do?' And I said to him, 'Why, P. J., I would put on the God-damnedest exhibition that ever a dying man put on in the history of the human race. I would moan and groan and blubber and boohoo until the bricks came loose in the wall. I wouldn't remain in bed. I would get up from there and put me on a pair of striped pants and a box-back coat and I would grab the telephone and get in touch with preachers of all descriptions—preachers, priests, rabbis, the Salvation Army, the Mohammedans, Father Divine, any and all that would come, and I'd say to them, "Pray, brothers, pray! It can't do me no harm and it might possibly do me some good." And while they prayed I'd sit there and sing the "Rock of Ages" and drink all the liquor that the doctor would allow.' I thought that'd shut him up, but I was just wasting my breath. Next he wanted to know had I made my will, had I given much thought to what I wanted cut on my tombstone, did I have any favorite hymns I wanted sung at my funeral. 'Shut up,' I said to him, 'for the love of God, shut up!' And this morning I came downstairs, and I had a hangover to begin with, a katzen-jammer, and he had that estimating look in his eye, and he said to me, 'Good morning, Old Man Flood. How you feeling? You look a bit pale.' And I flew off the handle and danced around and made a holy show of myself. If he inquires about my health one more time, if he so much as says good morning, I'm going to answer him politely, like a gentleman, and I'm going to wait until he looks the other way, and then I'm going to pick up something heavy and lay him out."

"The way I look at it," said Mr. Maggiani, "those questions Mr. Mooney asks you, they're personal questions. I wouldn't stand for it."

"I'm not going to stand for it any longer," said Mr. Flood. "I'm going to put my foot down. All I want in this world is a little peace and quiet, and he gets me all raced up. Here a while back I heard a preacher talking on the radio about the peacefulness of the old, and I thought to myself, 'You ignorant man!' I'm ninety-four years old and I never yet had any peace, to speak of. My mind is just a turmoil of regrets. It's not what I did I regret, it's what I didn't do. Except for the bottle, I always walked the straight and narrow; a family man, a good provider, never cut up, never did ugly, and I regret it. In the summer of 1902 I came real close to getting in serious trouble with a married woman, but I had a fight with my conscience and my conscience won, and what's the result? I had two wives, good, Christian women, and I can't hardly remember what either of them looked like, but I can remember the face on that woman so clear it hurts, and there's never a day passes I don't think about her, and there's never a day passes I don't curse myself. 'What kind of a timid, dried-up, weevily fellow were you?' I say to myself. 'You should've said to hell with what's right and what's wrong, the devil take the hindmost. You'd have something to re-member, you'd be happier now.' She's out in Woodlawn, six feet under, and she's been there twenty-two years, God rest her, and here I am, just an old, old man with nothing left but a belly and a brain and a dollar or two."

"Life is sad," said Mr. Maggiani.

"And the older I get," continued Mr. Flood, "the more impatient I get. I got no time to waste on fools. There's a young Southern fellow drops into the Hartford barroom every night before he gets on the 'L'; comes from Alabama; works in one of those cotton offices on Hanover Square. Seemed to be a likable young fellow. I got in the habit of having a whiskey with him. He'd buy a round, I'd buy a round. Night before last, when he dropped in, I was sitting at a table with a colored man. When I was in the house-wrecking business, this colored man was my boss foreman. He was in my employ for thirty-six years; practically ran the business; one of the finest men I've ever known; raised eight children; one's a doctor. In the old days, when my second wife was still alive, he and his wife came to our house for dinner, and me and my wife went to his house for dinner; played cards, told stories, listened to the phonograph. When I sold the business, I gave him a pension, an annuity. He bought a little farm on Long Island, and whenever he's in town he pays me a visit and we talk about the days gone by. Tommy, you remember Peter Stetson. He's been in here with me."

"Sure," said Mr. Maggiani. "Fellow that runs the duck farm."

"That's right," said Mr. Flood. "Well, Pete and I finished our talk, and I walked to the door with him, and we shook hands, and he left. And I went over to the bar to have a drink with this young Southern fellow, and he says, 'That was a nigger you were sitting down with, wasn't it?' And I said, 'That was an old, old friend of mine.' And he began to talk some ugly talk about the colored people, and I shut him right up. 'I'm an old-time New Yorker,' I said to him, 'the melting-pot type, the Tammany type before Tammany went to seed, all for one, one for all, a man's race and color is his own business, and I be damned if I'll listen to that kind of talk.' And he says, 'You're a trouble-maker. What race do you belong to, anyhow?' 'The human race,' I said. 'I come from the womb and I'm bound for the tomb, the same as you, the same as King George the Six, the same as Johnny Squat. And furthermore,' I said, 'I'll never take another drink with you. It would be beneath me to do so.' Now that's a heathen kind of thing to happen in New York City. I'm going over and talk to the Mayor one of these days, tell him about a plan I have. I got a plan for a parade. The population is all split up; they don't even parade with each other. The Italians parade on Columbus Day, the Poles parade on Pulaski Day, the Irish parade on St. Patrick's Day, and all like that. My plan is to have a citywide Human Race Parade, an all-day, all-night parade up Fifth Avenue. The only qualification you'll need to march in this parade, you have to belong to the human race. The cops even, they won't stand and watch, they'll get right in and march. Tommy, how about you, would you march in the Human Race Parade?"

"It would depend on the weather," said Mr. Maggiani.

Mr. Flood sighed and tossed his gut-blade on the counter. "I'm full," he said. "I've had my bait of clams."

"Me, too," said Mr. Maggiani. "There's no law says we got to make pigs of ourselves."

Mr. Flood got a rag and a pan of water and cleaned off the oilcloth counter, and I gathered up the empty shells and put them in a trash bucket. Mr. Maggiani carried what was left of the basket of blackies back to the coldroom. Then the three of us sat down by the stove. Mr. Maggiani put a pot of coffee on the hob. We heard steps in the hall, the door opened, and in came a friend of Mr. Flood's, a grim old Yankee named Jack Murchison, who is a waiter in Libby's Oyster House. Libby's is one of the few New England restaurants in the city. It was established on Fulton Street in 1840 by Captain Oliver Libby of Wellfleet, Cape Cod. It is unpretentious, its chefs and waiters are despotic and opinionated but highly skilled, it broils or boils or poaches ninety-nine fish orders for every one it fries, it has Daniel Webster fish chowder on Wednesdays and Fridays, and it has New England clam chowder every day. On its menu is a statement of policy: "OPEN TO 8 P.M. NOT RESPONSIBLE FOR PERSONAL PROPERTY. NO MANHATTAN CLAM CHOWDER SERVED IN HERE."

"Been down to the river for a breath of air," Mr. Murchison said. "Sat on the stringpiece for fifteen minutes and I'm cold to the bone."

"Draw up a chair, Jack," said Mr. Flood, "and take the weight off your feet."

Mr. Murchison lifted the tails of his overcoat and stood with his back to the stove for a few minutes. Then he sat down and sighed with satisfaction. "Hugh," he said to Mr. Flood, "got something I want to show you." He took his wallet from a hip pocket, drew out a newspaper clipping, and gave it to me to pass over to Mr. Flood, who was sitting on the other side of the stove. It was a clipping of Lucius Beebe's column, "This New York," in the *Herald Tribune*.

Mr. Flood glanced at it and said, "Oh, God, what's this? Is he one of those ignorant fellows writes about restaurants in the papers, ohs and ahs about everything they put before him? Every paper nowadays has a fellow writing about restaurants, an expert giving his opinion, a fellow that if he was out of a job and went to a restaurant to get one, this expert on cooking, this Mr. Know-it-all, the practical knowledge he has, why, they wouldn't trust him to peel the potatoes for a stew."

"This gentleman is a goormy," said Mr. Murchison. "Go ahead and read what he says."

Mr. Flood read a paragraph or two. Then he groaned and handed the clipping to me. "God defend us, son," he said. "Read this."

In the column, Mr. Beebe described a dinner that had been "run

up" for him and a friend by Edmond Berger, the *chef de cuisine* of
the Colony Restaurant. He gave the menu in full. One item, the
fish course, was "Fillet de Sole en Bateau Beebe." "The sole, cour-
teously created in the name of this department by Chef Berger for
the occasion," Mr. Beebe wrote, "was a delicate fillet superimposed
on a half baked banana and a trick worth remembering."

"Good God A'mighty!" said Mr. Flood.

"Sounds nice, don't it?" asked Mr. Murchison. "A half baked
bananny with a delicate piece of flounder superimposed on the top
of it. While he was at it, why didn't he tie a red ribbon around
it?"

"Next they'll be putting a cherry on boiled codfish," said Mr.
Flood. "How would that be, a delicate piece of codfish with a cherry
superimposed on the top of it?"

The two old men cackled.

"Tell me the truth, Hugh," said Mr. Murchsion, "what in the
world do you think of a thing like that?"

"I tell you what I think," said Mr. Flood. "I got my money in
the Corn Exchange Bank. And if I was to go into some restaurant
and see the president of the Corn Exchange Bank eating a thing
like that, why, I would turn right around and walk out of there,
and I'd hightail it over to the Corn Exchange Bank and draw out
every red cent. It would destroy my confidence."

"President, hell," said Mr. Murchison. "If I was to see the janitor
of the Corn Exchange Bank eating a thing like that, I'd draw *my*
money out."

"Of course," said Mr. Flood, "you got to take into consideration
this fellow is a gourmet. A thing like that is just messy enough to
suit a gourmet. They got bellies like schoolgirls; they can eat anything, just so it's messy."

"We get a lot of goormies in Libby's," said Mr. Murchison. "I
can spot a goormy right off. Moment he sits down he wants to
know do we have any boolybooze."

"Bouillabaisse," said Mr. Flood.

"Yes," said Mr. Murchison, "and I tell him, 'Quit showing off!
We don't carry no boolybooze. Never did. There's a time and a

place for everything. If you was to go into a restaurant in France,' I ask him, 'would you call for some Daniel Webster fish chowder?' I love a hearty eater, but I do despise a goormy. All they know is boolybooze and pompano and something that's out of season, nothing else will do. And when they get through eating they don't settle their check and go on about their business. No, they sit there and deliver you a lecture on what they et, how good it was, how it was almost as good as a piece of fish they had in the Caffy dee lah Pooty-doo in Paris, France, on January 16, 1928; they remember every meal they ever et, or make out they do. And every goormy I ever saw is an expert on herbs. Herbs, herbs, herbs! If you let one get started on the subject of herbs he'll talk you deef, dumb, and blind. Way I feel about herbs, on any fish I ever saw, pepper and salt and a spoon of melted butter is herbs aplenty."

"Let's see that clipping again," Mr. Flood said. He took the Beebe column and read it slowly from start to finish. Then he handed it back to me. "Burn a rag," he said.

Mr. Maggiani lifted the pot of coffee off the hob and poured us each a mug. Then he stepped over to the counter and got his Scotch bottle. There was an ounce or two left in it, and he poured this into Mr. Murchison's coffee.

"Much obliged, Tommy," said Mr. Murchison. "It was cold out."

"I know it," said Mr. Maggiani. "I heard the wind whistling." Mr. Maggiani turned to Mr. Flood. "Hugh," he said, "there's something I was going to ask you. You've got enough money put away you could live high if you wanted to. Why in God's name do you live in a little box of a room in a back-street hotel and hang out in the fish market when you could go down to Miami, Florida, and sit in the sun?"

Mr. Flood bit the end off one of his sixty-five-cent cigars and spat it into the scuttle. He held a splinter in the stove until it caught fire, and then he lit the cigar. "Tommy, my boy," he said, "I don't know. Nobody knows why they do anything. I could give you one dozen reasons why I prefer the Fulton Fish Market to Miami, Florida, and most likely none would be the right one. The right reason is something obscure and way off and I probably don't even know it myself. It's like the old farmer who wouldn't tell the drummer the time of day."

"What are you talking about?" asked Mr. Maggiani.

"It's an old, old story," Mr. Flood said. "I've heard it told sixteen different ways. I even heard a muxed-up version one night years ago in a vaudeville show. I'll tell it the way my daddy used to tell it. There was an old farmer lived beside a little branch-line railroad in south Jersey, and every so often he'd get on the train and go over to Trenton and buy himself a crock of applejack. He'd buy it right at the distillery door, the old Bossert & Stockton Apple Brandy Distillery, and save himself a penny or two. One morning he went to Trenton and bought his crock, and that afternoon he got on the train for the trip home. Just as the train pulled out, he took his watch from his vest pocket, a fine gold watch in a fancy hunting case, and he looked at it, and then he snapped it shut and put it back in his pocket. And there was a drummer sitting across the aisle. This drummer leaned over and said, 'Friend, what time is it?' The farmer took a look at him and said, 'Won't tell you.' The drummer thought he was hard of hearing and spoke louder. 'Friend,' he shouted out, 'what time is it?' 'Won't tell you,' said the farmer. The drummer thought a moment and then he said, 'Friend, all I asked was the time of day. It don't cost anything to tell the time of day.' 'Won't tell you,' said the farmer. 'Well, look here, for the Lord's sake,' said the drummer, 'why won't you tell me the time of day?' 'If I was to tell you the time of day,' the farmer said, 'we'd get into a conversation, and I got a crock of spirits down on the floor between my feet, and in a minute I'm going to take a drink, and if we were having a conversation I'd ask you to take a drink with me, and you would, and presently I'd take another, and I'd ask you to do the same, and you would, and we'd get to drinking, and by and by the train'd pull up to the stop where I get off, and I'd ask you why don't you get off and spend the afternoon with me, and you would, and we'd walk up to my house and sit on the front porch and drink and sing, and along about dark my old lady would come out and ask you to take supper with us, and you would, and after supper I'd ask if you'd care to drink some more, and you would, and it'd get to be real late and I'd ask you to spend the night in the spare room, and you would, and along about two o'clock in the morning I'd get up to go to the pump, and I'd pass my daughter's room, and there you'd be, in there with my daughter, and I'd have to turn the bureau upside down and get out my pistol, and my old lady would have to get dressed and hitch up the horse and go down the road and get the preacher, and I don't want no God-damned son-in-law who don't own a watch.' "

(1944)

# Mr. Flood's Party

M<small>R.</small> FLOOD WAS NINETY-FIVE YEARS OLD on the twenty-seventh of July, 1945. Three evenings beforehand, on the twenty-fourth, he gave a birthday party in his room at the Hartford House. "I don't believe in birthday parties never did but some do and I will have one this time to suit myself if it kills me," he wrote on a penny postal, inviting me. "Will be obliged to have it on the 24th as I promised my daughter Louise in South Norwalk I would be with her and my grandchildren and great grandchildren on my birthday itself. Couldn't get out of it. And due to I can't seem to find any pure Scotch whiskey any more it has got so it takes me two or three days to get over a toot. Louise is deadset against whiskey talk talk talk and I know better than to show up in South Norwalk with a katzenjammer. I will expect you. It will not be a big party just a few windbags from the fish market. Also Tom Bethea. He is an old old friend of my family. He is an undertaker. The party will start around six and it is immaterial to me when it stops. I am well and trust you are the same."

I walked up Peck Slip around six-thirty on the evening of the twenty-fourth, and the peace and mystery of midnight was already over everything; work begins long before daybreak in the fish market and ends in the middle of the afternoon. There wasn't a human being in sight, or an automobile. The old pink-brick fish houses on both sides of the Slip had been shuttered and locked, the sidewalks had been flushed, and there were easily two hundred gulls from the harbor walking around in the gutters, hunting for fish scraps. The gulls came right up to the Hartford's stoop. They were big gulls and they were hungry and anxious and as dirty as buzzards. Also, in the quiet street, they were spooky. I stood on the stoop and watched them for a few minutes, and then I went into the hotel's combined lobby and barroom. Gus Trein, the manager, was back of the bar. There were no customers and he was working on his books; he had two ledgers and a spindle of bills before him. I asked if Mr. Flood was upstairs. "He is," said Mr. Trein, "what's left of him. Are you going to his party?" I said I was. "In that case," he said, "hold your hat. He was in and out all afternoon, toting things up to his room, and he had three bottles of whiskey one trip. The last time he came in, half an hour ago, Birdy Treppel was with him—the old fishwife from the Slip. He had a smoked eel about a yard long in one hand and a box of cigars in the other, and he was singing 'Down, Down Among the Dead Men,' and Birdy had him by the elbow, helping him up the stairs."

One of Mr. Flood's closest friends, Matthew T. Cusack, was sitting on the bottom of the stairs in the rear of the lobby. He had one shoe off and was prizing a tack out of it with his pocketknife. Mr. Cusack is a portly, white-haired old Irish-American, a retired New York City policeman. He is a watchman for the Fulton Market Fishmongers Association; he sits all night in a sprung swivel chair beside a window in a shack on the fish pier. In the last six or seven months, Mr. Cusack's personality has undergone an extraordinary change. He was once a hearty man. He laughed a lot and he was a big eater and straight-whiskey drinker. He had a habit of remarking to bartenders that he didn't see any sense in mixing whiskey with water, since the whiskey was already wet. At a clambake for marketmen and their families in East Islip, in the summer of 1944, he ate three hundred and sixty-six Great South Bay quahogs, one for every day in the year (it was a leap year), and put four rock-broiled lobsters on top of them. He has a deep chest and a good baritone, and at market gatherings he always stood up and sang "The Broken Home," "Frivolous Sal," and "Just Fill Me One Glass More." In recent months, however, he has been gloomy and irritable and pious; he is worried about his health and believes that he may have a heart attack at any moment and drop dead. He was in vigorous health until last Christmas, when the Fishery Council, the market's chamber of commerce, gave him a present, a radio for his shack. Aside from listening in barrooms to broadcasts of championship prizefights, Mr. Cusack had never before paid any attention to the radio, but he soon got to be a fan. He got so he would keep his radio on all night. A program he especially likes is sponsored by a company that sells a medicine for the acid indigestion. Around the middle of February, he developed the acid indigestion and began to take this medicine. Then, one morning in March, on his way home from the market, he was troubled by what he describes as "a general run-down feeling." At first he took it for granted that this was caused by the acid indigestion, but that night, while listening to a radio health chat, he came to the conclusion that he had a heart condition. He is fascinated by health chats; they make him uneasy, but he dials them in from stations all over the country. He got over the run-down feeling but continued to brood about his heart. He went to a specialist, who made a series of cardiograms and told him that he was in good shape for a man of his age and weight. He is still apprehensive. He says he suspects he has a rare condition that can't be detected by the cardiograph. He never smiles, he has a frightened stare, and his face is set and gray. He walks slowly, inching along with an almost effortless shuffle, to avoid straining his heart muscles. When he is not at work, he spends most of the time lying flat on his back in bed with his feet propped up higher than his head. He takes vitamin tablets, a kind that is activated *and* mineralized. Also, twice a day, he takes a medicine that is guaranteed to alkalize the system. The officials of the Council are sorry they gave him the radio. Edmond Irwin, the executive secretary, ran into him on the pier a while back and told him so. "Why, what in the world are you talking about?" Mr. Cusack asked. "That radio probably saved my life. If it wasn't for that radio, I might've dropped dead already. I didn't start taking care of myself until those health chats woke me up to the danger I was in."

I went on back to the rear of the lobby and spoke to Mr. Cusack, but he didn't look up or answer. He had the stairs blocked or I would have gone on past him. After he got the tack out of his shoe, he stood up and grunted. His face was heavy with worry. We shook hands, and I asked him if he was going to Mr. Flood's party or coming from it. "Going, God help me," he said, "and I dread it. I feel like I ought to pay my respects to Hugh, but I dread the stairs. A poor old man in my condition, it's taking my life in my hands." The Hartford is five floors high and it doesn't have an elevator. Mr. Flood's room is on the top floor. I stood aside and waited for Mr. Cusack to start up, but he said, "You go ahead. I'm going to take my time. It'll take me half an hour and when I get to the top I'll most likely drop dead."

MR. FLOOD HAS A CORNER ROOM, overlooking the Slip. The door was open. His room is usually in a mess and he had obviously had it straightened up for the party. There was a freshly ironed counterpane on his brass bed. His library had been neatly arranged on top of his tin, slatbound trunk; it consists of a Bible, a set of Mark Twain, and two thick United States Bureau of Fisheries reference books, "Fishes of the Gulf of Maine" and "Fishes of Chesapeake Bay." His collection of sea shells and river shells had been laid out on the hearth of the boarded-up fireplace. Ordinarily, his books and shells are scattered all over the floor. On the marble mantelpiece were three small cast-iron statues—a bare-knuckle pug with his fists cocked, a running horse with its mane streaming, and an American eagle. These came off one of the magnificent fire escapes on the Dover Street side of the old *Police Gazette* building, which is at Dover and Pearl, in the fish-market neighborhood. (Mr. Flood is sentimental about the stone and iron ornaments on many buildings down in the old city, and he thinks they should be preserved. He once wrote the Museum of the City of New York suggesting that the owners of the *Gazette* building be asked to donate the fire-escape ornaments to the Museum. "Suppose this bldg. is torn down," he wrote. "All that beautiful iron work will disappear into scrap. If the owners do not see fit to donate, I am a retired house-wrecker and I could go there in the dead of night with a monkey-wrench and blow-torch and use my own discretion.") Above the mantelpiece hung a lithograph of Franklin D. Roosevelt, a Thomas Rowlandson aquatint of some scuffling fishwives in Billingsgate that came off a calendar, and a framed beatitude: "BLESSED IS THE MAN WHO DOES NOT BELLYACHE—ELBERT HUBBARD." In the middle of the room stood an ugly old marble-top table, the kind that has legs shaped like the claws of a dragon, each claw grasping a glass ball. There was a clutter on the table—a bottle of Scotch, a pitcher of water, a bucket of ice, a box of cigars, a crock of pickled mussels, a jar of marinated herrings, a smoked eel, a wire basket of sea urchins, two loaves of Italian bread, some lemons, and a stack of plates. The sea urchins were wet and dripping.

There were four people sitting around the table—Mr. Flood, Mrs. Treppel, a salesman of fishing-boat hardware named Ben Fass, and an old man I had never seen before. Mrs. Treppel had Commodore, the Hartford's big black cat, on her lap; she had given it the head of the eel. Mrs. Treppel was still in her market clothes. She wore a full-length coat-apron over her dress and she had on knee boots and a man's stiff straw hat; this is the uniform of the boss fishmonger. The hat was on the side of her head. Mrs. Treppel is stout, red-cheeked, and good-natured. Even so, as a day wears on, she becomes quite quarrelsome; she says she quarrels just to keep her liver regulated. "Quarreling is the only exercise I take," she says. She is a widow in her late sixties, she has worked in the market since she was a young woman, and she is greatly respected, especially by the old-timers; to them, she is the very embodiment of the primary, basic, fundamental Fulton Fish Market virtue—the ability to look after Number One. "Birdy Treppel likes to run her mouth, and she sometimes sounds a little foolish," I once heard one old boss fishmonger say to another, "but don't ever underestimate her. She could buy or sell half the people down here, including me." Mrs. Treppel owns a couple of the old buildings on Peck Slip, she has money in a cooperage that builds boxes and barrels for the fish trade; she owns a share in a dragger, the *Betty Parker,* which runs out of Stonington, Connecticut; and she keeps a fresh-water stall on the Slip, dealing mainly in carp, whitefish, and pike, the species that are used in gefüllte fish. Mr. Fass is known in the market as Ben the Knifeman. He is slight, edgy, and sad-eyed, a disappointed man, and he blames all his troubles on cellophane. He says that he was ruined by cellophane, and he sometimes startles people by muttering, "Whoever he is, wherever he is, God damn the man that invented cellophane!" He once was a salesman for a sausage-casings broker in Gansevoort Market, selling sheep intestines to manufacturers of frankfurters. He enjoyed this work. Ten years ago many manufacturers began using cellophane instead of intestines for casings, calling their product "skinless" frankfurters, and in 1937 Mr. Fass was laid off. He became an outside man for a Water Street fishing-boat supply house, which is owned by an uncle of his. Carrying samples in a suitcase, he goes aboard trawlers and draggers at the pier and sits down with the captains and takes orders for knives, honing steels, scalers, bait grinders, swordfish darts, fog bells, and similar hardware.

Mr. Fass and Mr. Flood are good friends, which is puzzling. Mr. Fass has no interest in boats, he dislikes the fish market, and he despises fish. He is outspoken about it; not long ago he lost one of his best customers by remarking that he would rather have one thin cut off a tough rib roast than all the fish God ever made. Mr. Flood, on the other hand, believes that people would be much better off in mind and body if they ate meat on Fridays and fish all the rest of the week. I have known Mr. Flood for nine years, but I found out only recently how he arrived at this conclusion. From 1885 until 1930, when he retired, the offices of his firm, the H. G. Flood Demolition & Salvage Co., Inc., were on Franklin Square, a couple of blocks from the fish market. In the winter of 1885, soon after moving there, he observed that there was a predominance of elderly and aged men among the fishmongers. "I began to step up to these men and inquire about their ages," he told me. "There were scores in their eighties and dozens in their nineties and spry old crocks that had hit a hundred weren't rare at all. One morning I saw a fist fight between two men in their nineties. They slapped each other from one end of the pier to the other, and it was a better fight than many a fight I paid to see. Another morning I saw the fellows shaking hands with a man of eighty-seven and it turned out his wife had just had a baby boy. All these men were tough and happy and full of the old Adam, and all were big fish eaters, and I thought to myself, 'Flood, no doubt about it, you have hit on a secret.' " Since that winter he has seldom eaten anything but seafood.

When I came into the room, Mr. Flood had just begun a song. He has a bullfrog bass, and he sang loudly and away off key. He had a highball in his left hand and a cigar in his right, and he kept time with the cigar as he sang:

> *"Come, let us drink while we have breath,*
> *For there's no drinking after death*
> *And he that will this health deny,*
> *Down among the dead men,*
> *Down among the dead men——"*

I was quite sure that he would put in more "downs" than the song called for, and I counted them. There were eleven, and each was louder than the one before it:

> *"Down, down, down, down, down,*
> *down, down, down, down, down,*
> *Down among the dead men*
> *Let him lie!"*

Mr. Flood's guests banged on the marble-top with their glasses, and he beamed. He was looking well. His friendly, villainous eyes were bright and his face was so tanned that the liver freckles on his cheeks didn't show; he carries a blanket down to the pier and lies in the sun an hour or two on good afternoons. He had on a white linen suit and there was a red rosebud in his lapel. I tried to congratulate him on his birthday. He wouldn't let me. "Thanks, my boy," he said, "but it's too early for that. I just got started. Wait'll I hit a hundred." He turned to the stranger at the table. "This is Tom Bethea," he said. "Tom's an undertaker up in Chelsea, my old neighborhood. Tom's wife and my second wife were great friends.

We belong to the same Baptist church, only he goes and I don't."
Mr. Bethea was roly-poly, moon-faced, and bald. His eyes were
remarkably distrustful. He wore a blue serge suit that was so tight
it made me uncomfortable to look at him. He had a glass about a
third full of straight whiskey in one hand. With the other, he was
plucking mussels out of the crock and popping them into his mouth
as if they were peanuts. He seemed offended by Mr. Flood's introduction. "I'm *not* an undertaker," he said. "I'm an embalmer. I've
told you that time and time again, and I do wish you'd get it
straight."

"Whichever it is," said Mr. Flood. He turned to me and said,
"Pull up a chair and fix yourself a drink. I got something I want
to show you." He took a photograph out of his wallet and handed
it to me. It was a photograph of a horse, an old white sway-backed
horse. "Look at it and pass it around," he said. "I was going through
some papers in my trunk the other day and came across it. Thought
I'd lost it years ago. It's a snapshot of a horse named Sam. Sam was
a highly unusual horse and I want to tell about him. He was owned
by George Still, fellow that ran Still's Oyster and Chop House. Still's
was on Third Avenue, between Seventeenth and Eighteenth, middle
of the block, east side of the avenue. It opened in the eighteen-
fifties—1853, I think it was—and it closed in 1922 because of
prohibition, and it was the finest oyster house the country ever had.
It was a hangout for rich old goaty high-living men—Tammany
bosses and the like of that. Some of them could taste an oyster and
examine the shell and tell you what bed it came out of; I'm pretty
good at that myself. And it got crowds of out-of-towners, especially
people from Boston, Philadelphia, Baltimore, Norfolk, and New
Orleans, the big oyster-eating cities. Mr. Still handled a wider variety
of oysters than any restaurant or hotel in the world, before or since.
He had them out of dozens of beds. From New Jersey he had
Shrewsburys and Maurice River Coves. From Rhode Island he had
Narragansetts and Wickfords. From Massachusetts he had Cotuits
and Buzzards Bays and Cape Cods. From Virginia—they were very
fine—he had Chincoteagues and Lynnhavens and Pokomokes and
Mobjacks and Horn Harbors and York Rivers and Hampton Bars

and Rappahannocks. From Maryland he had Goose Creeks. From Delaware he had Bombay Hooks. From New York—the finest of all—he had Blue Points and Mattitucks and Saddle Rocks and Robbins Islands and Diamond Points and Fire Places and Montauks and Hog Necks and Millponds and Fire Island Salts and Rockaways and Shinnecocks. I love those good old oyster names. When I feel my age weighing me down, I recite them to myself and I feel better. Some of them don't exist any more. The beds were ruined. Cities grew up nearby and the water went bad. But there was a time when you could buy them all in Still's."

"Oh, God, Hughie," said Mrs. Treppel, "it *was* a wonderful place. I remember it well. It had a white marble bar for the half-shell trade, and there were barrels and barrels and barrels of oysters stood up behind this bar, and everything was nice and plain and solid— no piddling around, no music to frazzle your nerves, no French on the bill of fare; you got what you went for."

"I remember Still's, too," said Mr. Bethea. "Biggest lobster I ever saw, I saw it in there. Weighed thirty-four pounds. Took two men to hold it. It was a hen lobster. It wasn't much good—too coarse and stringy—but it was full of coral and tomalley and it scared the women and it was educational."

"That's right," said Mr. Flood. "That's the way it was." He poured himself a drink. "In addition to the restaurant," he continued, "Mr. Still did a wholesale oyster business in a triple-decked barge that was docked year in and year out at a pier at the foot of Pike Street, upriver from the fish market. The barge was his warehouse. In the old days all the wholesalers operated that way; they brought their stock in from the beds in schooners that'd come alongside the barges and unload. At the time I'm speaking of—in 1912—there were fourteen barges at Pike Street, all in a row and all painted as loud and bedizy and fancy-colored as possible, the same as gypsy wagons; that was the custom. George Still is dead, God rest him, but the business is there yet. His family runs it. It's one of the biggest shellfish concerns in the city, and it's right there in the old barge, head office and all—George M. Still, Incorporated, Planters of Diamond Point Oysters. Still's barge is the only one left, and it's a pretty one. It's painted green and yellow and it's got scroll-saw work all over the front of it.

"Back in 1912, Mr. Still delivered his oysters to hotels and restaurants and groceries with horse-drawn drays. He owned nine horses and he thought a lot of them. Every summer he gave them two weeks off on a farm he had in New Jersey. One of those horses was Sam. Sam was the oldest. In fact, he was twenty-two years old, and that's a ripe old advanced age for a horse. Sam was just about worn out. His head hung low, his eyes were sleepy and sad, and there wasn't hardly any life in him at all. If some horseflies lit on him, he didn't even have the energy to switch his tail and knock them off. He just poked along, making short hauls and waiting for the day to end. Mr. Still had made up his mind to retire Sam to New Jersey for good, but he was one of those that puts things off; tomorrow will do.

"Sam's driver was a man named Woodrow and he was attached to Sam. Sam was noted for his good disposition, but one morning in October, 1912, Woodrow went to put the harness on Sam and Sam kicked at him. It was the first time that ever happened. Next morning Sam was worse. Every single time Woodrow got near, Sam kicked. He was so old and awkward he always missed, but he kept on trying; he did his best. Every day that passed, Sam got more free and easy. He'd rear back in the shafts and tangle up the strappings on his harness, and sometimes Woodrow would tell him to whoa and he'd keep right on going until he was good and damn ready to whoa. He got a mean look in his eye and he kept his head up and he walked faster and faster. He'd toss his head to and fro and dance along like a yearling. One day, all of a sudden, up on Sixth Avenue, he started running after a bay mare that was hauling a laundry wagon. It was all Woodrow could do to pull him up. And Sam kept on doing this. Every day or so he'd catch sight of a mare somewhere up ahead and he'd whinny and whicker and break into a fast trot and Woodrow would have to brace himself against the footboard and seesaw on the lines and curse and carry on to stop him. Sometimes a crowd would collect and cheer Sam on. Woodrow worried about Sam, and so did Mr. Still, but they didn't know what to do. They couldn't figure him out.

"One of the places that Woodrow and Sam made a daily delivery was a chop house on Maiden Lane. Sam would stand at the curb and Woodrow would shoulder a barrel of oysters off the dray and roll it in. The cashier of this chop house was an old lady and every morning she'd step out to the curb and pat Sam's nose and coo at him and give him sugar. She'd been doing it for years. She was one of those old ladies that just can't leave horses alone. One morning she came out, cooing, and she put her hand out to pat Sam and Sam bit her. He bit her on the hand and he bit her on the wrist and he bit her on the arm. She was all skint up. As you might expect, a great deal of screeching took place. They sent for a doctor, but that didn't quiet the old lady. According to Woodrow, she kept screeching she didn't want a doctor, she wanted a lawyer.

"Woodrow led Sam back to the barge and broke the news to Mr. Still that he had a damage suit on his hands. Mr. Still called in a veterinarian to see could he find out what was the matter with Sam, what ailed the old fool. The veterinarian looked Sam over and he punched and he thumped and he put his head against Sam's belly and listened. He said he couldn't find anything wrong except extreme old age. Then he happened to look into Sam's feed bag, and what in hell and be damned was in there, mixed in with the oats, only some shucked oysters. They weren't little nubby oysters; they were great big Mattitucks. And what's more, Sam was eating them. He was eating them and enjoying them. The veterinarian stood there and he looked at Sam and he said, 'Well, I be good God damned!' He said he'd run into some odd and unusual horses in his practice but that Sam was certainly the first horse he'd run into that'd eat oysters.

"Mr. Still called his help together and inquired did anybody know who put the oysters in Sam's feed bag. Finally one of the oyster shuckers confessed he did it. Said he just wanted to see what would happen. Said he'd been slipping them in for about a month. Said he'd go out on the pier, where Sam was hitched between hauls, and he'd make believe he was petting Sam, and he'd slip the oysters into Sam's feed bag. Said he started with one oyster a day and worked up to where he was giving him four and five dozen a day. Mr. Still was put out; at the same time, somehow, he was proud of Sam. He decided to fire the shucker and send Sam to hell and gone to New Jersey, but he changed his mind. What he did, he cut Sam down to one dozen oysters a day. That worked out all right. It wasn't too few, it wasn't too many. It was just enough to keep Sam brisk and frisky, but it wasn't enough to make him cut up and do ugly. People would come from all over the market just to see Sam get his one dozen oysters. Everything was just fine until Christmas Eve. You know how it is on Christmas Eve; people get high-spirited. And you can just imagine how high-spirited they get around an oyster barge on Christmas Eve. When it came time to feed Sam, the fellows got generous and gave him six or seven dozen oysters, compliments of the season. And that night Woodrow was driving Sam back to the stable and Sam caught sight of a mare about three blocks up and he took out after her and there was ice on the street and he slipped and broke a leg and God knows they hated to do it, but they had to shoot him."

A glint came into Mr. Bethea's eyes. "Hugh," he said, "I was just thinking. Suppose you took and fed a race horse on oysters! I bet you could make a lot of money that way."

Mr. Flood snickered. "Tom," he said, "there's a certain race horse on the New York tracks right now that's an oyster eater. He's owned by an oysterman here in the market, but the way I understand it, just to throw people off that might possibly get thoughts in their head, he's registered in the name of a distant cousin of this oysterman's wife. He's not much of a horse—no looks, no style; he only cost eleven hundred dollars—but he wins every race they want him to win. They don't let him win every race he runs; that'd look peculiar."

I watched Mr. Flood's face. It was impassive.

"They pick a day," he continued, "and two days in advance they start feeding him raw oysters or raw clams, according to season. They experimented and found he runs about as fast on clams as he does on oysters. They give him five dozen the first day, eight dozen the second day, and one dozen the morning of the race. He always comes through; you just get a bet down and think no more about it. I don't know how many are in on it. I do know that this oysterman and all his friends are rolling in money. He was nice enough to let me and Birdy in on it. Whenever the horse is ready to run an oyster-fed race, we get notified, and naturally we've picked up a dollar or two ourselves."

"Hugh Griffin Flood!" said Mrs. Treppel. "I'm shocked and surprised at you. You were told about that horse in the strictest confidence. It's a highly confidential matter, and you know you shouldn't talk about it. Suppose it gets out. They'll be stuffing all the race horses full of oysters, and then where'll we be?"

"I know, Birdy, I know," said Mr. Flood. "I'm sorry. Anyhow, I didn't tell the name of the horse."

"You keep your big mouth shut from now on," said Mrs. Treppel.

"Speaking of the old days," said Mr. Bethea, "it seems to me businessmen were different in the old days. They had the milk of human kindness in them. Like George Still. Like the way he gave his dray horses a vacation."

"It's the truth, Tom," said Mr. Flood. "They weren't always and eternally thinking of the almighty dollar."

"I was doing business in the old days," said Mrs. Treppel, "and that's something I never noticed."

"You always remember the bad, Birdy," said Mr. Flood. "You never remember the good."

"I don't know about that," said Mrs. Treppel. "Take for example, were you acquainted with A. C. Lowry that they called the finnan-haddie king?"

"I was," said Mr. Flood. "Old Gus Lowry." He nodded his head. "Gus was a fine man," he said, "a fine man."

"He was like hell," said Mrs. Treppel. "He was the meanest man ever did business in this market. He was the lowest of the low."

"He was," said Mr. Flood, reversing his judgment without batting an eye. "He was indeed."

"What form did his meanness take?" asked Mr. Bethea.

"Well, to begin with," Mrs. Treppel said, "you couldn't trust him. You couldn't trust his weights or his invoices or the condition of his fish, not that that was so highly unusual down here and not that people necessarily looked down on him for that. After all, this isn't the New York Stock Exchange, where everybody is upright and honest and trustworthy, or so I have been told—this is the Fulton Fish Market. No, it wasn't his crookedness, it was the way he conducted himself in general that turned people against him. He was stingy. He believed everybody was stealing from him. He treated his help in such a way they didn't know if they were going or coming. And he grumbled about this and he complained about that from morning to night; everything he et disagreed with him. I worked for him once—he had a fresh-water branch on the Slip around 1916 and I had charge of it. I worked for him a year and a half and it aged me before my time; when I took that job I was just a girl and when I gave it up I was an old, old woman. Gus was into everything. He did a general salt-water business. He owned a trawler. He handled Staten Island oysters and guaranteed they came from Norfolk, Virginia. And he had the biggest smoking loft in the market—eels, haddies, kippers, and bloaters. He was an old bachelor. He had a nephew keeping books for him, Charlie Titus, his sister's son, and everybody was sorry for Charlie. It was understood that Charlie was to inherit the business, and God knows it was a good sound business, but the beating he took, we wondered if it was worth it. Charlie was real polite, Uncle this and Uncle that, but it didn't do no good. Three or four times a year, at least, Gus would get it in his head that Charlie was falsifying the books. He'd see something in Charlie's figures that didn't look just right and it'd make him happy. 'I've caught you now!' he'd say. 'I've caught you now!' Then he'd grab the telephone and call in a firm of certified public accountants. Those damned C.P.A.s were in and out of the office all the time. They'd go over Charlie's books and they'd try their best, but they couldn't ever find anything wrong, and it'd make Gus so mad he'd put his head down on the desk and cry. 'You low-down thief,' he'd say to Charlie, 'you're stealing from me, and I know you are. You got some secret way of doing it. My own flesh and blood, and you're stealing every cent I got.' Charlie would say, 'Now, Uncle Gus, that's just not so,' and Gus would say, 'Shut up!' And Charlie would shut up. I remember one morning Gus was having his coffee at the round table in Sweet's, and there was a crowd of us sitting there, four or five fishmongers and some of the shellfish gang, and Charlie came running up the stairs and asked Gus a question about a bill of lading, and Gus hauled off and shied a plate at him. 'Get out of here, you embezzler!' he said. 'When I want you,' he said, 'I'll send for you.' Right before everybody.

"Another thing about Gus, he tried to look poor. He tried to look like he didn't have a dime to his name. There's an old notion in Fulton Market: if you want to know a fishmonger's financial standing, don't bother Dun & Bradstreet, just look at him—if he looks like he's been rolling around in some gutter, his credit is good; if he's all dolled up, stay away from him. Gus Lowry carried that to an extreme. As soon as he got to his office in the morning, he'd hang his good suit in a locker and he'd put on a greasy old raggedy suit that was out at the elbow and patched in the seat and a coupla sizes too small for him to begin with, and he used a piece of rope he'd picked up somewhere for a belt, and he'd put on a pair of knee boots that always had fish scales sticking to them, and he'd slap on a hat that was so dirty you wouldn't carry bait in it. He wouldn't wear a necktie; some days he wouldn't even wear a shirt. He'd light a cigar, one of those cheap Italian cigars that they call rattails. He'd spit on the floor. Then he'd sit down at his desk, looking like something the cat dragged in, the King of the Bums, and he'd be ready for business.

"And if you had to do business with him, you just took it for granted you'd be skinned. He'd skin you alive and then he'd shake your hand and inquire about your family. Up on his office wall he had a sign which said, 'KEEP SMILING,' but *he* never smiled. And he had a sign which said, 'All that I am or hope to be I owe to my angel mother.' And he had poems about the flag stuck up there and friendship and only God can make a tree and let me live in a house by the side of the road and be a friend to man. He'd recite you one of those poems—you couldn't stop him—and he'd begin to cry. Gus liked to cry. He really enjoyed it. Next to doing something mean to somebody, he liked to cry. I went in his office many a time and found him sitting there with tears in his eyes. People said it was second childhood, but when it come to a dollar he wasn't in his second childhood. The strangest thing, when he was close to eighty he started going to see a woman that lived in a hotel up on Union Square, and everybody hoped and prayed she'd get him into a lot of trouble. She was an old busted-down actress of some kind, a singer. She'd sing and he'd cry; that was his idea of a high old time. He took me up there with him once to call on her. He wanted me to look her over and tell him what I thought of her, about like he'd ask my opinion on a consignment of jack shad. We hadn't hardly got in the door before she commenced to bang on the piano and sing. Oh, she was a noisy one. Gus asked her to sing 'I'll Take You Home Again, Kathleen,' and by the time she got to 'the ocean wild and wide' he was crying. He hung around her a year or more and then he quit. I guess maybe the poor old thing tried to borrow a dollar and seventy-five cents off him and it broke his heart.

"The summer of 1921, Gus took a trip to Havana, Cuba, doctor's orders, and one morning there came a cable he was dead. Bright's disease. As soon as the news got out it put everybody in a good humor. Some tried to act like they were sorry, but they couldn't keep a straight face, and pretty soon the fellows all over the market were slapping each other on the back and laughing and old Mr. Unger that kept the stall next to mine shouted out, 'Hooray for the Bright's disease!' Everybody was so glad for Charlie. Captain Oscar Doxsee had worked for Gus off and on for thirty years—he was captain of Gus's trawler—and I remember what he said when they told him Gus was dead. 'God is good,' he said. It was prohibition, but little Archie Ennis the scallop dealer had a quart of whiskey in his safe, bourbon, and he got it out and him and I and Captain Oscar and several others went over to Charlie's office to congratulate him. We figured a little celebration was in order. Well, what do you know? Charlie was sitting in there with his head in his hands. 'Ladies and gentlemen,' he said to us, 'this is the saddest day of my life.' *Oh, oh, oh,* we were disgusted! I've seen many and many a disgusting thing in my time, but that took the prize. 'Young man,' I thought to myself, 'the opinion your uncle had of you, he was right.' "

Mr. Bethea grunted. "Blood is thicker than water," he said.

"Yes," said Mrs. Treppel, "I guess that's one way of looking at it."

MR. CUSACK CAME SHUFFLING into the room. He'd finally made it.

"Well, look who's here," said Mrs. Treppel. "Old Drop-Dead Matty himself. Hello, Matty. Didn't you drop dead yet?"

Mr. Cusack disregarded her. "Happy birthday, Hugh," he said.

"Why, thank you, Matty," said Mr. Flood. "Matty, this is Tom Bethea. Tom's an embalmer."

"A what?" asked Mr. Cusack.

"I'm an embalmer," said Mr. Bethea. "I'm a trade embalmer."

Mr. Cusack stared at Mr. Bethea for a few moments. "How do you do, sir?" he said respectfully.

"Please to meet you," said Mr. Bethea. "I've heard Hugh speak of you. Sing us a song."

"Oh, no!" said Mr. Cusack. "I ain't in a singing mood."

"It was good of you to come, Matty," said Mr. Flood.

"Yes, it was," said Mr. Cusack. "I guess this is the last time I'll ever come. I can't stand those stairs no more. I've had some bad news. I was to the doctor for a checkup last Thursday and the way he diagnosed it, my heart's some better but I got the high blood pressure."

"I got the high blood pressure, too," said Mr. Fass.

"I got it, too," said Mr. Bethea. "Had it for years."

"Oh, for God's sake!" said Mrs. Treppel. She got to her feet and began to hop about the room. As she hopped, she sang a children's street song, a rope-skipping song—"Oh, I hurt, I hurt, I hurt all over. I got a toothache, a gum boil, a bellyache, a pain in my right side, a pain in my left side, a pimple on my nose."

"Shut up, Birdy, and behave yourself," said Mr. Flood. "Come over here, Matty, and sit down. What can I get you?"

"You can get me a glass of cold water," said Mr. Cusack. "I asked the doctor what about whiskey and he said it was the better part of wisdom to leave it alone. I haven't had a drink for six days. All I drink is water."

"If you was to drink a glass of water, Matty," said Mrs. Treppel, "it'd be weeks and weeks before your stomach got over the shock."

"Now look here, Birdy," Mr. Flood said, "don't talk to Matty that way. I won't have it. The high blood pressure is a serious matter." He got up from his wicker rocking chair. "Here, Matty," he said, "take this chair. How do you feel tonight? Do you feel any worse than usual?"

"I feel irritable," said Mr. Cusack. He slapped the pillow in the chair a time or two and sat down. "It makes me irritable to see people drinking and enjoying themselves," he said. "If I can't drink it, I don't want *nobody* to drink it. I wish they'd bring prohibition back and I wish they'd enforce it. I got so I don't approve of whiskey."

Mr. Flood fixed himself a drink—half Scotch, half water, no ice—and went over and stood with an elbow on the mantelpiece. "I'm the same," he said. "I love it and I depend on it, but I don't approve of it. When I think of all the trouble it's caused me, I feel like I ought to pick some distillery at random and sue it for sixty-five million dollars. Still and all, there've been times if it hadn't been for whiskey, I don't know what would've become of me. It was either get drunk or throw the rope over the rafter. I've thought a lot about this matter over the years and I've come to the conclusion there's two ways of looking at whiskey—it gives and it takes away, it lifts you up and it knocks you down, it hurts and it heals, it kills and it resurrects—but whichever way you look at it, I'm glad I'm not the man that invented it. That's one thing I wouldn't want on my soul." He suddenly snapped his fingers. "He's the one!" he said. "I was lying in bed the other night, couldn't go to sleep, and I got to thinking about death and sin and hell and God, the way you do, and a question occurred to me, 'I wonder what man committed the worst sin in the entire history of the human race.' The man that invented whiskey, he's the one. When you stop and think of the mess and the monkey business and the fractured skulls and the commotion and the calamity and the stomach distress and the wife

428

beating and the poor little children without any shoes and the howling and the hell raising *he's* been responsible for down through the centuries—why, good God A'mighty! Whoever he was, they've probably got him put away in a special brimstone pit, the deepest, red-hottest pit in hell, the one the preachers tell about, the one without any bottom." He took a long drink. "And then again," he continued, "just as likely, he might've gone to heaven."

"The man that invented cellophane," said Mr. Fass. "*He's* the one."

Mr. Cusack sighed. "I got to be careful what I eat, too," he said.

"Oh, Matty, Matty," said Mrs. Treppel, "please take a drink and cheer up."

"Leave me alone," said Mr. Cusack. He glanced at his wristwatch, and then he peered into every corner of the room. "Where's your radio, Hugh?" he asked. "There's a program coming on in five minutes I don't want to miss."

"I got no radio," said Mr. Flood.

Mr. Cusack looked disappointed. "You should get one," he said. "It'd do you a world of good. It'd be a comfort to you."

"It wouldn't be no comfort to me," said Mr. Flood. "I despise the radio. I can't endure it. All that idiotic talk and noise, it goes right through me; it jars my nerves. Son," he said to me, "you sit on the bed and let me have your chair. I'll open up some sea urchins and we'll have a snack."

He got out a fish knife he carries in a holster and began preparing the sea urchins. He had three or four dozen full-grown ones, the biggest of which was about the size of a man's clenched fist. Urchins are green, hemispherical marine animals. They are echinoderms; they are thickly covered with bristly prickles. They are gathered at low tide off rocky ledges on the southern Maine coast and shipped in bushel baskets. Fulton Market handles two hundred thousand pounds a summer, but they are rarely seen in restaurants. They are eaten in the home by Italians and Chinese; Italians call them *rizzi*, or sea eggs. Mr. Flood cut the tops off ten. He had trouble knifing through the leathery rinds and he muttered to himself as he worked. "Sorry damned knife," he muttered. "Stainless steel. They don't care if it's sharp or not, just so it's stainless, as if anybody gave a hoot about stains on a knife blade. I wish they'd leave knives alone, quit improving them. Look at it. Shiny. Stainless. Plastic handle. Only one thing wrong with it. It won't cut." Each urchin had a pocket of orange roe, from two to five tablespoonfuls. Mr. Flood spooned the roe out and spread it on slices of bread. Urchins are inexpensive, around fifty cents a dozen, but in Mr. Flood's opinion their roe is superior to caviar. He sprinkled lemon juice on the roe. Then he fixed six plates. On each he placed three open-faced roe sandwiches, a slice of eel, a herring, and a mound of pickled mussels. Mr. Fass refused his plate. "Drinking makes me hungry," he said, "but it don't make me that hungry."

ALL THE TIME MR. FLOOD had been preparing the urchins, Mr. Cusack had been staring at Mr. Bethea. Finally he spoke up. "I hope you won't think I'm prying into your affairs, Mr. Bethea," he said, "but there's two questions I'd like to ask you."

Mr. Bethea stopped eating for a moment. "It'll be a privilege to answer them, Mr. Cusack," he said, "if they ain't too personal."

"What I was wondering about is your line of work," Mr. Cusack said. "How in the world does a man ever come to take up that particular line of work?"

"Well, I tell you," said Mr. Bethea, "most of the embalmers of my generation started out as something else. Some were barbers and some were carpenters. I was a carpenter myself, a carpenter and cabinetmaker, and back in 1908 I took a job with Cantrell Brothers & Bishop, on Little West Twelfth Street. That was a coffin factory—what *we* call a casket factory. I built high-quality caskets for a year and a half, and you know how it is—an up-and-coming young man, you want to make something out of yourself. Every casket factory has a staff of embalmers, and I kept my eyes open when our staff was working and I asked questions and naturally I was handy with tools and the upshot was, I became an embalmer. I'm a trade embalmer, a free lance. We're the aristocrats of the trade—that is, the profession. All the overhead we have is a telephone. There's a multitude of undertaking parlors, little neighborhood affairs, that don't get enough cases to employ a steady embalmer. They just have a parlor with a desk and a pot of palms and a statue of an angel and a casket catalogue. Oh, some will have a sample casket or two on the premises. And there's seven or eight of these parlors, when they get a case, they telephone me. Wherever I go, I have to leave a number where I can be reached. And I get on the subway and I go and attend to the case and I collect my seventeen dollars—we got a union and that's the union rate—and I go on home. That's the end of the matter. I don't have to console the bereaved and I don't have to listen to the weeping and the wailing and I don't have to fuss with the floral offerings. Of course, these days, like everybody else, embalmers go to college. I went to college myself some years back, just to brush up on the latest scientific advances. There's two big colleges, the American Academy of Embalming and Mortuary Research on Lexington Avenue and the New York School of Embalming and Restorative Art on Fourth Avenue. They're the Harvard and the Yale of the embalming world. The past few years women have been flocking into the profession. You take the American Academy—a third of their students are women. I don't know. I may be old-timey, but the way I look at it, I just wouldn't have no confidence in a lady embalmer." He paused and glanced at Mrs. Treppel. "Present company excepted," he said.

Mrs. Treppel snorted. "If she puts her mind to it and works hard," she said, "I bet a woman can embalm as good as a man."

"I didn't mean to be rude," said Mr. Bethea. He took the Scotch bottle by the neck and poured a big gollop in his glass. "I'm a disappointed man, Mr. Cusack," he continued. "If I had it to do all over again, I don't know as I'd choose embalming as my life's work. You don't get the respect that's due you. A doctor gets respect, a dentist gets respect, a veterinarian gets respect, but the average man, if he's introduced to an embalmer, he giggles or he shudders, one or the other. Some of my brother embalmers don't like to tell their profession to strangers. They're close-mouthed. They keep to themselves. Not me. Deep down inside, I'm proud of my profession. I carry a kit, a satchel, my professional satchel, and it's always been my dream to have my name printed on it. I can just see it—'THOMAS FOSTER BETHEA, LICENSED EMBALMER.' But I can't do it. If I got on the subway, the people would edge away. I'd have the whole car to myself. The public don't like to be reminded of death. It's going on all around them—like the fellow said, it looks like it's here to stay—but they want to keep it hid. We have to work like a thief in the night. I daresay there's not a one of you that's ever seen a deceased moved out of a New York apartment house or hotel. No, and you never will. We got ways." He smiled. "Oh, well," he said, "no matter how the public feels about embalmers, in the end some embalmer gets them all."

"You needn't be so happy about it," said Mr. Flood. "In the end, some embalmer's going to get you, too."

"That's the truth," said Mr. Bethea. He sighed. "It's a peculiar thing. I'm a veteran in my line. If you took all the deceased I've attended to and stood them shoulder to shoulder, they'd make a picket fence from here to Pittsburgh, both sides of the road. With all that in back of me, you'd think I wouldn't mind death. Oh, but I do! Every time I think about it in connection with myself, I tremble all over. What was that other question you wanted to ask, Mr. Cusack?"

"I wanted to ask, do you believe in a reward beyond the grave," said Mr. Cusack. "By that, I mean heaven or hell."

"No, sir," said Mr. Bethea, "I can't say that I do."

"Well, then," said Mr. Flood, "what makes you go to church so steady? You're there every Sunday in the year, Sunday school *and* sermon."

"Hugh," said Mr. Bethea, "it don't pay to be too cock-sure."


THE TURN OF THE CONVERSATION made me restless and I went over and sat on the window sill, with my plate in my lap, and looked out over the rooftops of the market. It was a full-moon night. There was a wind from the harbor and it blew the heady, blood-quickening, sensual smell of the market into the room. The

Fulton Market smell is a commingling of smells. I tried to take it apart. I could distinguish the reek of the ancient fish and oyster houses, and the exhalations of the harbor. And I could distinguish the smell of tar, a smell that came from an attic on South Street, the net loft of a fishing-boat supply house, where trawler nets that have been dipped in tar vats are hung beside open windows to drain and dry. And I could distinguish the oakwoody smell of smoke from the stack of a loft on Beekman Street in which finnan haddies are cured; the furnace of this loft burns white-oak and hickory shavings and sawdust. And tangled in these smells were still other smells— the acrid smoke from the stacks of the row of coffee-roasting plants on Front Street, and the pungent smoke from the stack of the Purity Spice Mill on Dover Street, and the smell of rawhides from The Swamp, the tannery district, which adjoins the market on the north. Mr. Cusack came over and took a look out the window. He returned immediately to his chair.

"I'm thankful to God I'm not an officer walking the streets tonight," he said.

"Why's that, Matty?" asked Mr. Flood.

"It's a full-moon night," said Mr. Cusack. "There'll be peculiar things happening all over town. It's well known in the Police Department that a full-moon night stirs up trouble. It stirs up people's blood and brings out all the meanness and craziness in them, and it creates all manner of problems for policemen. A man or woman who's ordinarily twenty-five per cent batty, when the moon is full they're one hundred per cent batty. A full moon has a pull to it. Look at the tide; the tide is highest on a full moon. The moon pulls people this way and that way. With some, it's a feeble pull; they don't hardly notice it. Others just can't resist; they don't know what's got hold of them. They act peculiar. They act like bashi-bazouks. They pick on their wives and they get drunk and they insult people twice their size and they do their best to get into serious trouble. They look at black and say it's white, and if you don't agree it's white they hit you on the head. In the Department, we call such people full-mooners. It's been my experience that they're particularly numerous among the Irish and the Scandinavians and the people who come up here from the South. On a full-moon night the saloons are like magnets. The full-mooners try to walk past them and they get drawn right in."

"That explains a lot to me," said Mr. Flood. "I must be a full-mooner. I've started home many a night with no intention in the world of stopping off. It was the last thing in my mind. And four A.M. would come, and there I'd be, holding on to some bar, and I wouldn't half know how I got there."

"Exactly," said Mr. Cusack. "Some full-mooners get drunk and some get delusions. The Department is well aware of this. There's a glassed-in booth down in the lobby of Headquarters, the information booth. They have a calendar hanging in there, and they always have a red circle drawn around the date of the full moon. That's to remind the officer on duty what's ahead of him. I had an accident when I was in the Department, broke my leg, and I was a year and a half convalescing, and most of that time they had me on night duty in the information booth. And every full-moon night, I had visitors from all over. The full-mooners'd come trooping in. They'd step up and ask to see the Commissioner; nobody else would do. There was one who always came at midnight; he never missed. He'd ask for the Commissioner and I'd say, 'Lean over, sir, and whisper it to me. You can trust me.' And he'd lean over and whisper, 'They're after me!' And I'd get out my pad and pencil and ask for the details. And he'd talk on and on and on, and I'd take it all down. And I'd tell him, 'Rest assured the proper steps will be taken.' That'd satisfy him. He'd go away and I'd tear up whatever it was I took down and I'd throw it in the wastebasket." Mr. Cusack laughed. "Next full moon, he'd be back again."

"Mr. Cusack," said Mr. Bethea, "I recall a talk I had some years ago with an old gentlemen who works for one of the big cemeteries in Brooklyn, a foreman gravedigger. He said that a grave dug around the time of the new moon, the dirt that comes out of it won't fill it up. It'll have a sunk-in look. Whereas, a grave dug around the time of the full moon, there'll be plenty of dirt left over; you can make a nice mound on top. Another fact he told me, he said that women's bosoms get bigger during the time of the full moon. Did you know that?"

"No, I didn't, Mr. Bethea," said Mr. Cusack. "I'm glad you brought it up. While we're on the subject, I recall a case I was personally mixed-up in that might be of considerable interest to a man in your line."

"What was that?" asked Mr. Bethea.

"It happened in 1932, the year before I retired from the Department," said Mr. Cusack. "At that time I was attached to the First Precinct. One morning around four A.M. I was patrolling on South Street, proceeding east, and a radio car pulled up and the driver-officer informed me they were looking for two lads that stole an empty hearse. It seems this big black hearse had been parked in front of a garage on Third Avenue in the Sixties, the Nineteenth Precinct. The lads stole it and proceeded south on Third. Just ahead of them was a *Daily News* truck, delivering bundles of *Daily News*es to newsstands. You know the way they operate; they pull up to a corner where there's a stand and heave a bundle out on the sidewalk. At that hour a good many stands haven't opened, and the bundle lies there until the man that runs the stand comes to work. The lads in the hearse conceived the idea of collecting these bundles. The hearse would pull up and one lad would leap out, grab a bundle, and heave it in the hearse. They went from stand to stand, doing this. Headquarters was soon getting calls from all over, people that saw them, and it was put on the police radio. The hearse was last seen on lower Broadway, heading for the Battery. I told the driver-officer I hadn't observed no hearse, but I got on the running board and went along to help search the South Street docks. We hadn't gone three blocks before we ran into them. They had the hearse backed up to the river, right beside the Porto Rico Line dock, and they were heaving the bundles of *Daily News*es in the water."

"That was the right place for them," said Mr. Flood.

At this moment, Mr. Trein, the manager of the Hartford, began to shout up the stairwell. "Is Mr. T. F. Bethea up there?" he shouted.

Mr. Bethea went to the door. "That's me," he said.

"You're wanted on the telephone," said Mr. Trein.

"I'll be right down," said Mr. Bethea. Then he turned to Mr. Cusack. "Please go right ahead, Mr. Cusack," he said. "They'll hold on."

"I jumped off the running board of the radio car," continued Mr. Cusack, "and began to interrogate the lads. 'What are you lads doing?' I asked. One of them, the littlest, heaved another bundle in the drink, and he said to me, 'We're having some fun. What's it to you?' I asked them didn't they like newspapers, and they said they liked them all right. So I asked them what in hell was they heaving them bundles in the water for. They said they be damned if they knew. I asked was they drunk, and they said they wasn't. Maybe a beer or two. I asked was they narcotic addicts, and they said they wasn't. So I turned to the driver-officer, and I said, 'It looks to me they're Reds, or I.W.W.s, or Black Hands. All those radicals,' I said, 'are opposed to newspapers, the free press, and all like that.' And the driver-officer said to me, 'You sure are a thick one.' He jerked his thumb upwards, and I looked up and there was a full moon up there. It was as round as a basketball, and it was so full it was brimming over. It was very embarrassing. I just wasn't thinking. I should've known all along that those lads were full-mooners."

(1945)

# The Bottom of
# The Harbor

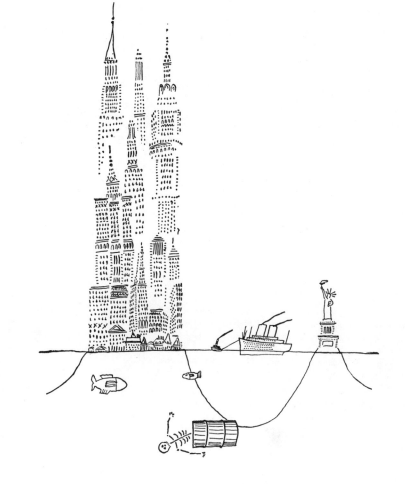

# Up in the Old Hotel

*E*VERY NOW AND THEN, seeking to rid my mind of thoughts of death and doom, I get up early and go down to Fulton Fish Market. I usually arrive around five-thirty, and take a walk through the two huge open-fronted market sheds, the Old Market and the New Market, whose fronts rest on South Street and whose backs rest on piles in the East River. At that time, a little while before the trading begins, the stands in the sheds are heaped high and spilling over with forty to sixty kinds of finfish and shellfish from the East Coast, the West Coast, the Gulf Coast, and half a dozen foreign countries. The smoky riverbank dawn, the racket the fish-mongers make, the seaweedy smell, and the sight of this plentifulness always give me a feeling of well-being, and sometimes they elate me. I wander among the stands for an hour or so. Then I go into a cheerful market restaurant named Sloppy Louie's and eat a big, inexpensive, invigorating breakfast—a kippered herring and scrambled eggs, or a shad-roe omelet, or split sea scallops and bacon, or some other breakfast specialty of the place.

Sloppy Louie's occupies the ground floor of an old building at 92 South Street, diagonally across the street from the sheds. This building faces the river and looks out on the slip between the Fulton Street fish pier and the Old Porto Rico Line dock. It is six floors high, and it has two windows to the floor. Like the majority of the older buildings in the market district, it is made of hand-molded Hudson River brick, a rosy-pink and relatively narrow kind that used to be turned out in Haverstraw and other kiln towns on the

439

Hudson and sent down to the city in barges. It has an ornamented tin cornice and a slate-covered mansard roof. It is one of those handsome, symmetrical old East River waterfront buildings that have been allowed to dilapidate. The windows of its four upper floors have been boarded over for many years, a rain pipe that runs down the front of it is riddled with rust holes, and there are gaps here and there on its mansard where slates have slipped off. In the afternoons, after two or three, when the trading is over and the stands begin to close, some of the slimy, overfed gulls that scavenge in the market roost along its cornice, hunched up and gazing downward.

I have been going to Sloppy Louie's for nine or ten years, and the proprietor and I are old friends. His name is Louis Morino, and he is a contemplative and generous and worldly-wise man in his middle sixties. Louie is a North Italian. He was born in Recco, a fishing and bathing-beach village thirteen miles southeast of Genoa, on the Eastern Riviera. Recco is ancient; it dates back to the third century. Families in Genoa and Milan and Turin own villas in and around it, and go there in the summer. Some seasons, a few English and Americans show up. According to a row of colored-postcard views of it Scotch-taped to a mirror on the wall in back of Louie's cash register, it is a village of steep streets and tall, square, whitewashed stone houses. The fronts of the houses are decorated with stenciled designs—madonnas, angels, flowers, fruit, and fish. The fish design is believed to protect against the evil eye and appears most often over doors and windows. Big, lush fig bushes grow in almost every yard. In the center of the village is an open-air market where fishermen and farmers sell their produce off plank-and-sawhorse counters. Louie's father was a fisherman. His name was Giuseppe Morino, and he was called, in Genoese dialect, Beppe du Russu, or Joe the Redhead. "My family was one of the old fishing families in Recco that the priest used to tell us had been fishing along that coast since Roman times," Louie says. "We lived on a street named the Vico Saporito that was paved with broken-up sea shells and wound in and out and led down to the water. My father did a kind of fishing that's called haul-seining over here, and he set lobster traps and jigged for squid and bobbed for octopuses. When the weather was right, he used to row out to an underwater cave he knew about and anchor over it and take a bob consisting of a long line with scraps of raw meat hung from it every foot or so and a stone on the end of it and drop it in the mouth of the cave, and the octopuses would shoot up out of the dark down there and swallow the meat scraps and that would hold them, and then my father would draw the bob up slow and steady and pull the octopuses loose from the meat scraps one by one and toss them in a tub in the boat. He'd bob up enough octopuses in a couple of hours to glut the market in Recco. This cave was full of octopuses; it was choked with them. He had found it, and he had the rights to it. The other fishermen didn't go near it; they called it Beppe du Russu's cave. In addition to fishing, he kept a rickety old bathhouse on the beach for the summer people. It stood on stilts, and I judge it had fifty to sixty rooms. We called it the Bagni Margherita. My mother ran a little buffet in connection with it."

Louie left Recco in 1905, when he was close to eighteen. "I loved my family," he says, "and it tore me in two to leave, but I have five brothers and two sisters, and all my brothers were younger than me, and there were already too many fishermen in Recco, and the bathhouse brought in just so much, and I had a fear kept persisting there might not be enough at home to go around in time to come, so I got passage from Genoa to New York scrubbing pots in the galley of a steamship and went straight from the dock to a chop-house on East 138th Street in the Bronx that was operated by a man named Capurro who came from Recco. Capurro knew my father when they both were boys." Capurro gave Louie a job washing dishes and taught him how to wait on tables. He stayed there two years. For the next twenty-three years, he worked as a waiter in restaurants all over Manhattan and Brooklyn. He has forgotten how many he worked in; he can recall the names of thirteen. Most of them were medium-size restaurants of the Steaks-&-Chops, We-Specialize-in-Seafood, Tables-for-Ladies type. In the winter of 1930, he decided to risk his savings and become his own boss. "At that time," he says, "the stock-market crash had shook everything up and the depression was setting in, and I knew of several restaurants in midtown that could be bought at a bargain—lease, furnishings, and good will. All were up-to-date places. Then I ran into a waiter I used to work with and he told me about this old run-down restaurant in an old run-down building in the fish market that was for sale, and I went and saw it, and I took it. The reason I did, Fulton Fish Market reminds me of Recco. There's a world of difference between them. At the same time, they're very much alike—the fish smell, the general gone-to-pot look, the trading that goes on in the streets, the roofs over the sidewalks, the cats in corners gnawing on fish heads, the gulls in the gutters, the way everybody's on to everybody else, the quarreling and the arguing. There's a boss fishmonger down here, a spry old hardheaded Italian man who's got a million dollars in the bank and dresses like he's on relief and walks up and down the fish pier snatching fish out of barrels by their heads or their tails and weighing them in his hands and figuring out in his mind to a fraction of a fraction how much they're worth and shouting and singing and enjoying life, and the face on him, the way he conducts himself, he reminds me so much of my father that sometimes, when I see him, it puts me in a good humor, and sometimes it breaks my heart."

Louie is five feet six, and stocky. He has an owl-like face—his nose is hooked, his eyebrows are tufted, and his eyes are large and brown and observant. He is white-haired. His complexion is reddish, and his face and the backs of his hands are speckled with freckles and liver spots. He wears glasses with flesh-colored frames. He is bandy-legged, and he carries his left shoulder lower than his right and walks with a shuffling, hipshot, head-up, old-waiter's walk. He dresses neatly. He has his suits made by a high-priced tailor in the insurance district, which adjoins the fish-market district. Starting work in the morning, he always puts on a fresh apron and a fresh brown linen jacket. He keeps a napkin folded over his left arm even when he is standing behind the cash register. He is a proud man, and somewhat stiff and formal by nature, but he unbends easily and he has great curiosity and he knows how to get along with people. During rush hours, he jokes and laughs with his customers and recommends his daily specials in extravagant terms and listens to fish-market gossip and passes it on; afterward, in repose, having a cup of coffee by himself at a table in the rear, he is grave.

Louie is a widower. His wife, Mrs. Victoria Piazza Morino, came from a village named Ruta that is only two and a half miles from Recco, but he first became acquainted with her in Brooklyn. They were married in 1928, and he was deeply devoted to her. She died in 1949. He has two daughters—Jacqueline, who is twenty-two and was recently graduated from the Mills College of Education, a school for nursery, kindergarten, and primary teachers on lower Fifth Avenue, and Lois, who is seventeen and was recently graduated from Fontbonne Hall, a high school on Shore Road in Brooklyn that is operated by the Sisters of St. Joseph. They are smart, bright, slim, vivid, dark-eyed girls. Louie has to be on hand in his restaurant in the early morning, and he usually gets up between four and five, but before leaving home he always squeezes orange juice and puts coffee on the stove for his daughters. Most days, he gets home before they do and cooks dinner.

Louie owns his home, a two-story brick house on a maple-bordered street in the predominantly Norwegian part of the Bay Ridge neighborhood in Brooklyn. There is a saying in Recco that people and fig bushes do best close to salt water; Louie's home is only a few blocks from the Narrows, and fifteen years ago he ordered three tiny fig bushes from a nursery in Virginia and set them out in his back yard, and they have flourished. In the late fall, he wraps an accumulation of worn-out suits and dresses and sweaters and sheets and blankets around their trunks and limbs. "All winter," he says, "when I look out the back window, it looks like I got three mummies stood up out there." At the first sign of spring, he takes the wrappings off. The bushes begin to bear the middle of July and bear abundantly during August. One bush bears small white figs, and the others bear plump black figs that split their skins down one side as they ripen and gape open and show their pink and violet flesh. Louie likes to gather the figs around dusk, when they are still warm from the heat of the day. Sometimes, bending beside a bush, he plunges his face into the leaves and breathes in the musky smell of the ripening figs, a smell that fills his mind with memories of Recco in midsummer.

LOUIE DOESN'T THINK MUCH of the name of his restaurant. It is an old restaurant with old furnishings that has had a succession of proprietors and a succession of names. Under the proprietor preceding Louie, John Barbagelata, it was named the Fulton Restaurant, and was sometimes called Sloppy John's. When Louie took it over, he changed the name to Louie's Restaurant. One of the fishmongers promptly started calling it Sloppy Louie's, and Louie made a mistake and remonstrated with him. He remonstrated with him on several occasions. As soon as the people in the market caught on to the fact that the name offended Louie, naturally most of them began using it. They got in the habit of using it. Louie brooded about the matter off and on for over three years, and then had a new swinging signboard erected above his door with SLOPPY LOUIE'S RESTAURANT on it in big red letters. He even changed his listing in the telephone book. "I couldn't beat them," he says, "so I joined them."

Sloppy Louie's is small and busy. It can seat eighty, and it crowds up and thins out six or seven times a day. It opens at five in the morning and closes at eight-thirty in the evening. It has a double door in front with a show window on each side. In one window are three sailing-ship models in whiskey bottles, a giant lobster claw with eyes and a mouth painted on it, a bulky oyster shell, and a small skull. Beside the shell is a card on which Louie has neatly written, "Shell of an Oyster dredged from the bottom of Great South Bay. Weighed two and a quarter pounds. Estimated to be fifteen years old. Said to be largest ever dredged in G.S.B." Beside the skull is a similar card, which says, "This is the skull of a Porpoise taken by a dragger off Long Beach, Long Island." In the other window is an old pie cupboard with glass sides. To the left, as you enter, is a combined cigar showcase and cashier's desk, and an iron safe with a cash register on top of it. There are mirrors all around the walls. Four lamps and three electric fans with wooden blades that resemble propellers hang from the stamped-tin ceiling. The tables in Louie's are communal, and there are exactly one dozen; six jut out from the wall on one side of the room and six jut out from the wall on the other side, and a broad aisle divides them. They are long tables, and solid and old and plain and built to last. They are made of black walnut; Louie once repaired a leg on one, and said it was like driving a nail in iron. Their tops have been seasoned by drippings and spillings from thousands upon thousands of platters of broiled fish, and their edges have been scratched and scarred by the hatchets and bale hooks that hang from frogs on fishmongers' belts. They are identical in size; some seat six, and some have a chair on the aisle end and seat seven. At the back of the room, hiding the door to the kitchen, is a huge floor mirror on which, each morning, using a piece of moistened chalk, Louie writes the menu for the day. It is sometimes a lengthy menu. A good many dishes are served in Louie's that are rarely served in other restaurants. One day, interspersed among the staple seafood-restaurant dishes, Louie listed cod cheeks, salmon cheeks, cod tongues, sturgeon liver, blue-shark steak, tuna steak, squid stew, and five kinds of roe— shad roe, cod roe, mackerel roe, herring roe, and yellow-pike roe. Cheeks are delectable morsels of flesh that are found in the heads of some species of fish, one on each side, inset in bone and cartilage. The men who dress fish in the fillet houses in the market cut out a few quarts of cheeks whenever they have the time to spare and sell them to Louie. Small shipments of them come down occasionally from the Boston Fish Pier, and the fishmongers, thinking of their own gullets, let Louie buy most of them. The fishmongers use Louie's as a testing kitchen. When anything unusual is shipped to the market, it is taken to Louie's and tried out. In the course of a year, Louie's undoubtedly serves a wider variety of seafood than any other restaurant in the country.

WHEN I GO TO SLOPPY LOUIE'S for breakfast, I always try to get a chair at one of the tables up front, and Louie generally comes out from behind the cash register and tells me what is best to order.

Some mornings, if there is a lull in the breakfast rush, he draws himself a cup of coffee and sits down with me. One morning a while back, he sat down, and I asked him how things were going, and he said he couldn't complain, he had about as much business as he could handle. "My breakfast trade still consists almost entirely of fishmongers and fish buyers," he said, "but my lunch trade has undergone a change. The last few years, a good many people in the districts up above the market have taken to walking down here occasionally for lunch—people from the insurance district, the financial district, and the coffee-roasting district. Some days, from noon to three, they outnumber the fishmongers. I hadn't realized myself how great a change had taken place until just the other day I happened to notice the mixed-up nature of a group of people sitting around one table. They were talking back and forth, the way people do in here that never even saw each other before, and passing the ketchup, and I'll tell you who they were. Sitting on one side was an insurance broker from Maiden Lane, and next to him was a fishmonger named Mr. Frank Wilkisson who's a member of a family that's had a stand in the Old Market three generations, and next to him was a young Southerner that you're doing good if you understand half what he says who drives one of those tremendous big refrigerator trucks that they call reefers and hits the market every four or five days with a load of shrimp from little shrimp ports in Florida and Georgia. Sitting on the other side was a lady who holds a responsible position in Continental Casualty up on William Street and comes in here for bouillabaisse, only we call it *ciuppin di pesce* and cook it the way it's cooked fishing-family style back in Recco, and next to her was an old gentleman who works in J. P. Morgan & Company's banking house and you'd think he'd order something expensive like pompano but he always orders cod cheeks and if we're out of that he orders cod roe and if we're out of that he orders broiled cod and God knows we're never out of that, and next to him was one of the bosses in Mooney's coffee-roasting plant at Fulton and Front. And sitting at the aisle end of the table was a man known all over as Cowhide Charlie who goes to slaughterhouses and buys green cowhides and sells them to fishing-boat captains to rig to the undersides of their drag nets to keep them from getting bottom-chafed and rock-cut and he's always bragging that right this very minute his hides are rubbing the bottom of every fishing bank from Nantucket Shoals to the Virginia Capes."

Louie said that some days, particularly Fridays, the place is jammed around one o'clock and latecomers crowd together just inside the door and stand and wait and stare, and he said that this gets on his nerves. He said he had come to the conclusion that he would have to go ahead and put in some tables on the second floor.

"I would've done it long ago," he said, "except I need the second floor for other things. This building doesn't have a cellar. South Street is old filled-in river swamp, and the cellars along here, what few there are, the East River leaks into them every high tide. The second floor is my cellar. I store supplies up there, and I keep my Deepfreeze up there, and the waiters change their clothes up there. I don't know what I'll do without it, only I got to make room someway."

"That ought to be easy," I said. "You've got four empty floors up above."

"You mean those boarded-up floors," Louie said. He hesitated a moment. "Didn't I ever tell you about the upstairs in here?" he asked. "Didn't I ever tell you about those boarded-up floors?"

"No," I said.

"They aren't empty," he said

"What's in them?" I asked.

"I don't know," he said. "I've heard this and I've heard that, but I don't know. I wish to God I did know. I've wondered about it enough. I've rented this building twenty-two years, and I've never been above the second floor. The reason being, that's as far as the stairs go. After that, you have to get in a queer old elevator and pull yourself up. It's an old-fashioned hand-power elevator, what they used to call a rope-pull. I wouldn't be surprised it's the last of its kind in the city. I don't understand the machinery of it, the balancing weights and the cables and all that, but the way it's operated, there's a big iron wheel at the top of the shaft and the wheel's got a groove in it, and there's a rope that hangs down one side of the cage to go up, and you pull on the part that hangs down the other side to go down. Like a dumbwaiter. It used to run from the ground floor to the top, but a long time ago some tenant must've decided he didn't have any further use for it and wanted it out of the way, so he had the shaft removed from the ground floor and the second floor. He had it cut off at the second-floor ceiling. In other words, the way it is now, the bottom of the shaft is level with the second-floor ceiling—the floor of the elevator cage acts as part of the ceiling. To get in the elevator, you have to climb a ladder that leads to a trap door that's cut in the floor of the cage. It's a big, roomy cage, bigger than the ones nowadays, but it doesn't have a roof on it—just this wooden floor and some iron-framework sides. I go up the ladder sometimes and push up the trap door and put my head and shoulders inside the cage and shine a flashlight up the shaft, but that's as far as I go. Oh, Jesus, it's dark and dusty in there. The cage is all furry with dust and there's mold and mildew on the walls of the shaft and the air is dead.

"The first day I came here, I wanted to get right in the elevator and go up to the upper floors and rummage around up there, see what I could see, but the man who rented the building ahead of me was with me, showing me over the place, and he warned me not to. He didn't trust the elevator. He said you couldn't pay him to get in it. 'Don't meddle with that thing,' he said. 'It's a rattlesnake. The rope might break, or that big iron wheel up at the top of the shaft that's eaten up with rust and hasn't been oiled for a generation might work loose and drop on your head.' Consequently, I've never even given the rope a pull. To pull the rope, you got to get inside the cage and stand up. You can't reach it otherwise. I've been tempted to many a time. It's a thick hemp rope. It's as thick as a hawser. It might be rotten, but it certainly looks strong. The way the cage is sitting now, I figure it'd only take a couple of pulls, a couple of turns of the wheel, and you'd be far enough up to where you could swing the cage door open and step out on the third floor. You can't open the cage door now; you got to draw the cage up just a little. A matter of inches. I reached into the cage once and tried to poke the door open with a boat hook I borrowed off one of the fishing boats, but it wouldn't budge. It's a highly irritating situation to me. I'd just like to know for certain what's up there. A year goes by sometimes and I hardly think about it, and then I get to wondering, and it has a tendency to prey on my mind. An old-timer in the market once told me that many years ago a fishmonger down here got a bug in his head and invented a patented returnable zinc-lined fish box for shipping fish on ice and had hundreds of them built, sunk everything he had in them, and they didn't catch on, and finally he got permission to store them up on the third and fourth floors of this building until he could come to some conclusion what to do with them. This was back before they tinkered with the elevator. Only he never came to any conclusion, and by and by he died. The old-timer said it was his belief the fish boxes are still up there. The man who rented the building ahead of me, he had a different story. He was never above the second floor either, but he told me that one of the men who rented it ahead of him told him is was *his* understanding there was a lot of miscellaneous old hotel junk stored up there—beds and bureaus, pitchers and bowls, chamber pots, mirrors, brass spittoons, odds and ends, old hotel registers that the rats chew on to get paper to line their nests with, God knows what all. That's what he said. I don't know. I've made quite a study of this building for one reason and another, and I've took all kinds of pains tracking things down, but there's a lot about it I still don't know. I do know there was a hotel in here years back. I know that beyond all doubt. It was one of those old steamship hotels that used to face the docks all along South Street."

"Why don't you get a mechanic to inspect the elevator?" I asked. "It might be perfectly safe."

"That would cost money," Louie said. "I'm curious, but I'm not that curious. To tell you the truth, I just don't want to get in that cage by myself. I got a feeling about it, and that's the fact of the matter. It makes me uneasy—all closed in, and all that furry dust. It makes me think of a coffin, the inside of a coffin. Either that or a cave, the mouth of a cave. If I could get somebody to go along with me, somebody to talk to, just so I wouldn't be all alone in there, I'd go; I'd crawl right in. A couple of times, it almost happened I did. The first time was back in 1938. The hurricane we had that fall damaged the roofs on a good many of the old South Street buildings, and the real-estate management company I rented this building from sent a man down here to see if my roof was all right. I asked the man why didn't he take the elevator up to the attic floor, there might be a door leading out on the roof. I told him I'd go along. He took one look inside the cage and said it would be more trouble than it was worth. What he did, he went up on the roof of the building next door and crossed over. Didn't find anything wrong. Six or seven months ago, I had another disappointment. I was talking with a customer of mine eats a fish lunch in here Fridays who's a contractor, and it happened I got on the subject of the upper floors, and he remarked he understood how I felt, my curiosity. He said he seldom passes an old boarded-up building without he wonders about it, wonders what it's like in there—all empty and hollow and dark and still, not a sound, only some rats maybe, racing around in the dark, or maybe some English sparrows flying around in there in the empty rooms that always get in if there's a crack in one of the boards over a broken windowpane, a crack or a knothole, and sometimes they can't find their way out and they keep on hopping and flying and hopping and flying until they starve to death. He said he had been in many such buildings in the course of his work, and had seen some peculiar things. The next time he came in for lunch, he brought along a couple of those helmets that they wear around construction work, those orange-colored helmets, and he said to me, 'Come on, Louie. Put on one of these, and let's go up and try out that elevator. If the rope breaks, which I don't think it will—what the hell, a little shaking up is good for the liver. If the wheel drops, maybe these helmets will save us.' But he's a big heavy man, and he's not as active as he used to be. He went up the ladder first, and when he got to the top he backed right down. He put it on the basis he had a business appointment that afternoon and didn't want to get all dusty and dirty. I kept the helmets. He wanted them back, but I held on to them. I don't intend to let that elevator stand in my way much longer. One of these days, I'm going to sit down awhile with a bottle of Strega, and then I'm going to stick one of those helmets on my head and climb in that cage and put that damned elevator back in commission. The very least, I'll pull the rope and see what happens. I do wish I could find somebody had enough curiosity to go along with me. I've asked my waiters, and I've tried to interest some of the people in the market, but they all had the same answer. 'Hell, no,' they said."

Louie suddenly leaned forward. "What about you?" he asked. "Maybe I could persuade you."

I thought it over a few moments, and was about to suggest that we go upstairs at any rate and climb in the cage and look at the elevator, but just then a fishmonger who had finished his breakfast and wanted to pay his check rapped a dictatorial rat-a-tat on the glass top of the cigar showcase with a coin. Louie frowned and clenched his teeth. "I wish they wouldn't do that," he said, getting up. "It goes right through me."

LOUIE WENT OVER and took the man's money and gave him his change. Two waiters were standing at a service table in the rear, filling salt shakers, and Louie gestured to one of them to come up front and take charge of the cash register. Then he got himself another cup of coffee and sat back down and started talking again. "When I bought this restaurant," he said, "I wasn't too enthusiastic about the building. I had it in mind to build up the restaurant and find a location somewhere else in the market and move, the trade would follow. Instead of which, after a while I got very closely attached to the building. Why I did is one of those matters, it really doesn't make much sense. It's all mixed up with the name of a street in Brooklyn, and it goes back to the last place I worked in before I came here. That was Joe's in Brooklyn, the old Nevins Street Joe's, Nevins just off Flatbush Avenue Extension. I was a waiter there seven years, and it was the best place I ever worked in. Joe's is part of a chain now, the Brass Rail chain. In my time, it was run by a very high-type Italian restaurant man named Joe

Sartori, and it was the biggest chophouse in Brooklyn—fifty waiters, a main floor, a balcony, a ladies' dining room, and a Roman Garden. Joe's was a hangout for Brooklyn political bosses and officeholders, and it got a class of trade we called the old Brooklyn family trade, the rich old intermarried families that made their money out of Brooklyn real estate and Brooklyn docks and Brooklyn streetcar lines and Brooklyn gasworks. They had their money sunk way down deep in Brooklyn. I don't know how it is now, they've probably all moved into apartment houses, but in those days a good many of them lived in steep-stoop, stain-glass mansions sitting up as solid as banks on Brooklyn Heights and Park Slope and over around Fort Greene Park. They were a big-eating class of people, and they believed in patronizing the good old Brooklyn restaurants. You'd see them in Joe's, and you'd seen them in Gage & Tollner's and Lundy's and Tappen's and Villepigue's. There was a high percentage of rich old independent women among them, widows and divorced ladies and maiden ladies. They were a class within a class. They wore clothes that hadn't been the style for years, and they wore the biggest hats I ever saw, and the ugliest. They all seemed to know each other since their childhood days, and they all had some peculiarity, and they all had one foot in the grave, and they all had big appetites. They had traveled widely, and they were good judges of food, and they knew how to order a meal. Some were poison, to say the least, and some were just as nice as they could be. On the whole, I liked them; they broke the monotony. Some always came to my station; if my tables were full, they'd sit in some leather chairs Mr. Sartori had up front and wait. One was a widow named Mrs. Frelinghuysen. She was very old and tiny and delicate, and she ate like a horse. She ate like she thought any meal might be her last meal. She was a little lame from rheumatism, and she used a walking stick that had a snake's head for a knob, a snake's head carved out of ivory. She had a pleasant voice, a beautiful voice, and she made the most surprising funny remarks. They were coarse remarks, the humor in them. She made some remarks on occasion that had me wondering did I hear right. Everybody liked her, the way she hung on to life, and everybody tried to do things for her.

I remember Mr. Sartori one night went out in the rain and got her a cab. 'She's such a thin little thing,' he said when he came back in. 'There's nothing to her,' he said, 'but six bones and one gut and a set of teeth and a big hat with a bird on it.' Her peculiarity was she always brought her own silver. It was old family silver. She'd have it wrapped up in a linen napkin in her handbag, and she'd get it out and set her own place. After she finished eating, I'd take it to the kitchen and wash it, and she'd stuff it back in her handbag. She'd always start off with one dozen oysters in winter or one dozen clams in summer, and she'd gobble them down and go on from there. She could get more out of a lobster than anybody I ever saw. You'd think she'd got everything she possibly could, and then she'd pull the little legs off that most people don't even bother with, and suck the juice out of them. Sometimes, if it was a slow night and I was just standing around, she'd call me over and talk to me while she ate. She'd talk about people and past times, and she knew a lot; she had kept her eyes open while she was going through life.

"My hours in Joe's were ten in the morning to nine at night. In the afternoons, I'd take a break from three to four-thirty. I saw so much rich food I usually didn't want any lunch, the way old waiters get—just a crust of bread, or some fruit. If it was a nice day, I'd step over to Albee Square and go into an old fancy-fruit store named Ecklebe & Guyer's and pick me out a piece of fruit—an orange or two, or a bunch of grapes, or one of those big red pomegranates that split open when they're ripe the same as figs and their juice is so strong and red it purifies the blood. Then I'd go over to Schermerhorn Street. Schermerhorn was a block and a half west of Joe's. There were some trees along Schermerhorn, and some benches under the trees. Young women would sit along there with their babies, and old men would sit along there the whole day through and read papers and play checkers and discuss matters. And I'd sit there the little time I had and rest my feet and eat my fruit and read the *New York Times*—my purpose reading the *New York Times*, I was trying to improve my English. Schermerhorn Street was a peaceful old backwater street, so nice and quiet, and I liked it. It did me good to sit down there and rest. One afternoon the thought occurred to me, 'Who the hell was Schermerhorn?' So that night it happened Mrs. Frelinghuysen was in, and I asked her who was Schermerhorn that the street's named for. She knew, all right. Oh, Jesus, she more than knew. She saw I was interested, and from then on that was one of the main subjects she talked to me about—Old New York street names and neighborhood names; Old New York this, Old New York that. She knew a great many facts and figures and skeletons in the closet that her mother and her grandmother and her aunts had passed on down to her relating to the old New York Dutch families that they call the Knickerbockers—those that dissipated too much and dissipated all their property away and died out and disappeared, and those that are still around. Holland Dutch, not German Dutch, the way I used to think it meant. The Schermerhorns are one of the oldest of the old Dutch families, according to her, and one of the best. They were big landowners in Dutch days, and they still are, and they go back so deep in Old New York that if you went any deeper you wouldn't find anything but Indians and bones and bears. Mrs. Frelinghuysen was well acquainted with the Schermerhorn family. She had been to Schermerhorn weddings and Schermerhorn funerals. I remember she told about a Schermerhorn girl she went to school with who belonged to the eighth generation, I think it was, in direct descent from old Jacob Schermerhorn who came here from Schermerhorn, Holland, in the sixteen-thirties, and this girl died and was buried in the Schermerhorn plot in Trinity Church cemetery up in Washington Heights, and one day many years later driving down from Connecticut Mrs. Frelinghuysen got to thinking about her and stopped off at the cemetery and looked around in there and located her grave and put some jonquils on it."

At this moment a fishmonger opened the door of the restaurant and put his head in and interrupted Louie. "Hey, Louie," he called out, "has Little Joe been in?"

"Little Joe that's a lumper on the pier," asked Louie, "or Little Joe that works for Chesebro, Robbins?"

"The lumper," said the fishmonger.

"He was in and out an hour ago," said Louie. "He snook in and got a cup of coffee and was out and gone the moment he finished it."

"If you see him," the fishmonger said, "tell him they want him on the pier. A couple of draggers just came in—the *Felicia* from New Bedford and the *Positive* from Gloucester—and the *Ann Elizabeth Kristin* from Stonington is out in the river, on her way in."

Louie nodded, and the fishmonger went away. "To continue about Mrs. Frelinghuysen," Louie said, "she died in 1927. The next year, I got married. The next year was the year the stock market crashed. The next year, I quit Joe's and came over here and bought this restaurant and rented this building. I rented it from a real-estate company, the Charles F. Noyes Company, and I paid my rent to them, and I took it for granted they owned it. One afternoon four years later, the early part of 1934, around in March, I was standing at the cash register in here and a long black limousine drove up out front and parked, and a uniform chauffeur got out and came in and said Mrs. Schermerhorn wanted to speak to me, and I looked at him and said, 'What do you mean—Mrs. Schermerhorn?' And he said, 'Mrs. Schermerhorn that owns this building.' So I went out on the sidewalk, and there was a lady sitting in the limousine, her appearance was quite beautiful, and she said she was Mrs. Arthur F. Schermerhorn and her husband had died in September the year before and she was taking a look at some of the buildings the estate owned and the Noyes company was the agent for. So she asked me some questions concerning what shape the building was in, and the like of that. Which I answered to the best of my ability. Then I told her I was certainly surprised for various reasons to hear this was Schermerhorn property. I told her, 'Frankly,' I said, 'I'm amazed to hear it.' I asked her did she know anything about the history of the building, how old it was, and she said she didn't, she hadn't ever even seen it before, it was just one of a number of properties that had come down to her husband from his father. Even her husband, she said, she doubted if he had known much about the building. I had a lot of questions I wanted to ask, and I asked her to get out and come in and have some coffee and take a look around, but I guess she figured the signboard SLOPPY LOUIE'S RESTAURANT meant what it said. She thanked me and said she had to be getting on, and she gave the chauffeur an address, and they drove off and I never saw her again.

"I went back inside and stood there and thought it over, and the effect it had on me, the simple fact my building was an old Schermerhorn building, it may sound foolish, but it pleased me very much. The feeling I had, it connected me with the past. It connected me with Old New York. It connected Sloppy Louie's Restaurant with Old New York. It made the building look much better to me. Instead of just an old run-down building in the fish market, the way it looked to me before, it had a history to it, connections going back, and I liked that. It stirred up my curiosity to know more. A day or so later, I went over and asked the people at the Noyes company would they mind telling me something about the history of the building, but they didn't know anything about it. They had only took over the management of it in 1929, the year before I rented it, and the company that had been the previous agent had gone out of business. They said to go to the City Department of Buildings in the Municipal Building. Which I did, but the man in there, he looked up my building and couldn't find any file on it, and he said it's hard to date a good many old buildings down in my part of town because a fire in the Building Department around 1890 destroyed some cases of papers relating to them—permits and specifications and all that. He advised me to go to the Hall of Records on Chambers Street, where deeds are recorded. I went over there, and they showed me the deed, but it wasn't any help. It described the lot, but all it said about the building, it said 'the building thereon,' and didn't give any date on it. So I gave up. Well, there's a nice old gentleman eats in here sometimes who works for the Title Guarantee & Trust Company, an old Yankee fish-eater, and we were talking one day, and it happened he told me that Title Guarantee has tons and tons of records on New York City property stored away in their vaults that they refer to when they're deciding whether or not the title to a piece of property is clear. 'Do me a favor,' I said, 'and look up the records on 92 South Street—nothing private or financial; just the history—and I'll treat you to the best broiled lobster you ever had. I'll treat you to broiled lobster six Fridays in a row,' I said, 'and I'll broil the lobsters myself.'

"The next time he came in, he said he had took a look in the Title Guarantee vaults for me, and had talked to a title searcher over there who's an expert on South Street property, and he read me off some notes he had made. It seems all this end of South Street used to be under water. The East River flowed over it. Then the city filled it in and divided it into lots. In February, 1804, a merchant by the name of Peter Schermerhorn, a descendant of Jacob Schermerhorn, was given grants to the lot my building now stands on—92 South—and the lot next to it—93 South, a corner lot, the corner of South and Fulton. Schermerhorn put up a four-story brick-and-frame building on each of these lots—stores on the street floors and flats above. In 1872, 1873, or 1874—my friend from Title Guarantee wasn't able to determine the exact year—the heirs and assigns of Peter Schermerhorn ripped these buildings down and put up two six-story brick buildings exactly alike side by side on 92 and 93. Those buildings are this one here and the one next door. The Schermerhorns put them up for hotel purposes, and they were designed so they could be used as one building—there's a party wall between them, and in those days there were sets of doors on each floor leading from one building to the other. This building had that old hand-pull elevator in it from bottom to top, and the other building had a wide staircase in it from bottom to top. The Schermerhorns didn't skimp on materials; they used heart pine for beams and they used hand-molded, air-dried, kiln-burned Hudson River brick. The Schermerhorns leased the buildings to two hotel men named Frederick and Henry Lemmermann, and the first lease on record is 1874. The name of the hotel was the Fulton Ferry Hotel. The hotel saloon occupied the whole bottom floor of the building next door, and the hotel restaurant was right in here, and they had a combined lobby and billiard room that occupied the second floor of both buildings, and they had a reading room in the front half of the third floor of this building and rooms in the rear half, and all the rest of the space in both buildings was single rooms and double rooms and suites. At that time, there were passenger-line steamship docks all along South Street, lines that went to every part of the world, and out-of-town people waiting for passage on the various steamers would stay at the Fulton Ferry Hotel. Also, the Brooklyn Bridge hadn't yet been built, and the Fulton Ferry was the principal ferry to Brooklyn, and the ferryhouse stood directly in front of the hotel. On account of the ferry, Fulton Street was like a funnel; damned near everything headed for Brooklyn went through it. It was full of foot traffic and horse-drawn traffic day and night, and South and Fulton was one of the most ideal saloon corners in the city.

"The Fulton Ferry Hotel lasted forty-five years, but it only had about twenty good years; the rest was downhill. The first bad blow was the bridges over the East River, beginning with the Brooklyn Bridge, that gradually drained off the heavy traffic on the Fulton Ferry that the hotel saloon got most of its trade from. And then, the worst blow of all, the passenger lines began leaving South Street and moving around to bigger, longer docks on the Hudson. Little by little, the Fulton Ferry Hotel got to be one of those waterfront hotels that rummies hole up in, and old men on pensions, and old nuts, and sailors on the beach. Steps going down. Around 1910, somewhere in there, the Lemmermanns gave up the part of the hotel that was in this building, and the Schermerhorn interests boarded up the windows on the four upper floors and bricked up the doors in the party wall connecting the two buildings. And the hotel restaurant, what they did with that, they rented it to a man named MacDonald who turned it into a quick lunch for the people in the fish market. MacDonald ran it awhile. Then a son of his took it over, according to some lease notations in the Title Guarantee records. Then a man named Jimmy Something-or-Other took it over. It was called Jimmy's while he had it. Then two Greek fellows took it over. Then a German fellow and his wife and sister and brother-in-law had it awhile. Then two brothers named Fortunato and Louie Barbagelata took it over. Then John Barbagelata took it over, a nephew of the other Barbagelatas, and eventually I came along and bought the lease and furnishings off of him. After the party wall was bricked up, the Lemmermanns held on to the building next door a few years more, and kept on calling it the Fulton Ferry Hotel, but all it amounted to, it was just a waterfront saloon with rooms for rent up above. They operated it until 1919, when the final blow hit them—prohibition. Those are the bare bones of the matter. If I could get upstairs just once in that damned old elevator and scratch around in those hotel registers up there and whatever to hell else is stored up there, it might be possible I'd find out a whole lot more."

"Look, Louie," I said, "I'll go up in the elevator with you."

"You think you would," Louie said, "but you'd just take a look at it, and then you'd back out."

"I'd like to see inside the cage, at least," I said.

Louie looked at me inquisitively. "You really want to go up there?" he asked.

"Yes," I said.

"The next time you come down here, put on the oldest clothes you got, so the dust don't make any difference," Louie said, "and we'll go up and try out the elevator."

"Oh, no," I said. "Now or never. If I think it over, I'll change my mind."

"It's your own risk," he said.

"Of course," I said.


LOUIE ABRUPTLY STOOD UP. "Let me speak to the waiter at the cash register," he said, "and I'll be with you."

He went over and spoke to the waiter. Then he opened the door of a cupboard in back of the cash register and took out two flashlights and the two construction-work helmets that his customer, the contractor, had brought in. He handed me one of the flashlights and one of the helmets. I put the helmet on and started over to a mirror to see how I looked. "Come on," Louie said, somewhat impatiently. We went up the stairs to the second floor. Along one wall, on this floor, were shelves stacked with restaurant supplies—canned goods and nests of bowls and plates and boxes of soap powder and boxes of paper napkins. Headed up against the wainscoting were half a dozen burlap bags of potatoes. A narrow, round-runged, wooden ladder stood at a slant in a corner up front, and Louie went directly to it. One end of the ladder was fixed to the floor, and the other end was fixed to the ceiling. At the top of the ladder, flush with the ceiling, was the bottom of the elevator cage with the trap door cut in it. The trap door was shut. Louie unbuttoned a shirt button and stuck his flashlight in the front of his shirt, and immediately started up the ladder. At the top, he paused and looked down at me for an instant. His face was set. Then he gave the trap door a shove, and it fell back, and a cloud of black dust burst out. Louie ducked his head and shook it and blew the dust out of his nose. He stood at the top of the ladder for about a minute, waiting for the dust to settle. Then, all of a sudden, he scrambled into the cage. "Oh, God in Heaven," he called out, "the dust in here! It's like somebody emptied a vacuum-cleaner bag in here." I climbed the ladder and entered the cage and closed the trap door. Louie pointed his flashlight up the shaft. "I thought there was only one wheel up there," he said, peering upward. "I see two." The dust had risen to the top of the shaft, and we couldn't see the wheels clearly. There was an iron strut over the top of the cage, and a cable extended from it to one of the wheels. Two thick hemp ropes hung down into the cage from the other wheel. "I'm going to risk it," Louie said. "I'm going to pull the rope. Take both flashlights, and shine one on me and shine the other up the shaft. If I can get the cage up about a foot, it'll be level with the third floor, and we can open the door."

Louie grasped one of the ropes and pulled on it, and dust sprang off it all the way to the top. The wheel screeched as the rope turned it, but the cage didn't move. "The rope feels loose," Louie said. "I don't think it has any grip on the wheel." He pulled again, and nothing happened.

"Maybe you've got the wrong rope," I said.

He disregarded me and pulled again, and the cage shook from side to side. Louie let go of the rope, and looked up the shaft. "That wheel acts all right," he said. He pulled the rope again, and this time the cage rose an inch or two. He pulled five or six times, and the cage rose an inch or two each time. Then we looked down and saw that the floor of the cage was almost even with the third floor. Louie pulled the rope once more. Then he stepped over and pushed on the grilled door of the cage and shook it, trying to swing it open; it rattled, and long, lacy flakes of rust fell off it, but it wouldn't open. I gave Louie the lights of both flashlights, and he examined the door. There were sets of hinges down it in two places. "I see," Louie said. "You're supposed to fold it back in." The hinges were stiff, and he got in a frenzy struggling with the door before he succeeded in folding it back far enough for us to get through. On the landing there was a kind of storm-door-like affair, a three-sided cubbyhole with a plain wooden door in the center side. "I guess they had that there to keep people from falling in the shaft," Louie said. "It'll be just our luck the door's locked on the other side. If it is, I'm not going to monkey around; I'm going to kick it in." He tried the knob, and it turned, and he opened the door, and we walked out and entered the front half of the third floor, the old reading room of the Fulton Ferry Hotel.

It was pitch-dark in the room. We stood still and played the lights of our flashlights across the floor and up and down the walls. Everything we saw was covered with dust. There was a thick, black mat of fleecy dust on the floor—dust and soot and grit and lint and slut's wool. Louie scuffed his shoes in it. "A-a-ah!" he said, and spat. His light fell on a roll-top desk, and he hurried over to it and rolled the top up. I stayed where I was, and continued to look around. The room was rectangular, and it had a stamped-tin ceiling, and tongue-and-groove wainscoting, and plaster walls the color of putty. The plaster had crumbled down to the laths in many places. There was a gas fixture on each wall. High up on one wall was a round hole that had once held a stove-pipe. Screwed to the door leading to the rear half of the floor were two framed signs. One said, "THIS READING ROOM WILL BE CLOSED AT 1 A.M. FULTON FERRY HOTEL." The other said, "ALL GAMBLING IN THIS READING ROOM STRICTLY PROHIBITED. BY ORDER OF THE PROPRIETORS. FULTON FERRY HOTEL. F. & H. LEMMERMANN, PROPRIETORS." Some bedsprings and some ugly white knobby iron bedsteads were stacked criss-cross in one corner. The stack was breast-high. Between the boarded-up windows, against the front wall, stood a marble-top table. On it were three seltzer bottles with corroded spouts, a tin water cooler painted to resemble brown marble, a cracked glass bell of the kind used to cover clocks and stuffed birds, and four sugar bowls whose metal flap lids had been eaten away from their hinges by rust. On the floor, beside the table, were an umbrella stand, two brass spittoons, and a wire basket filled to the brim with whiskey bottles of the flask type. I took the bottles out one by one. Dampness had destroyed the labels; pulpy scraps of paper with nothing legible on them were sticking to a few on the bottom. Lined up back to back in the middle of the room were six bureaus with mirrors on their tops. Still curious to see how I looked in the construction-work helmet, I went and peered in one of the mirrors.

Louie, who had been yanking drawers out of the roll-top desk, suddenly said, "God damn it! I thought I'd find those hotel registers in here. There's nothing in here, only rusty paper clips." He went over to the whiskey bottles I had strewn about and examined a few, and then he walked up behind me and looked in the mirror. His face was strained. He had rubbed one cheek with his dusty fingers, and it was streaked with dust. "We're the first faces to look in that mirror in years and years," he said. He held his flashlight with one hand and jerked open the top drawer of the bureau with the other. There were a few hairpins in the drawer, and some buttons, and a comb with several teeth missing, and a needle with a bit of black thread in its eye, and a scattering of worn playing cards; the design on the backs of the cards was a stag at bay. He opened the middle drawer, and it was empty. He opened the bottom drawer, and it was empty. He started in on the next bureau. In the top drawer, he found a square, clear-glass medicine bottle that contained two inches of colorless liquid and half an inch of black sediment. He wrenched the stopper out, and put the bottle to his nose and smelled the liquid. "It's gone dead," he said. "It doesn't smell like anything at all." He poured the liquid on the floor, and handed the bottle to me. Blown in one side of it was "Perry's Pharmacy. Open All Night. Popular Prices. World Building, New York." All at once, while looking at the old bottle, I became conscious of the noises of the market seemingly far below, and I stepped over to one of the boarded-up windows and tried to peep down at South Street through a split in a board, but it wasn't possible. Louie continued to go through the bureau drawers. "Here's something," he said. "Look at this." He handed me a foxed and yellowed photograph of a dark young woman with upswept hair who wore a lace shirtwaist and a long black skirt and sat in a fanciful fan-backed wicker chair. After a while, Louie reached the last drawer in the last bureau, and looked in it and snorted and slammed it shut. "Let's go in the rear part of the floor," he said.

Louie opened the door, and we entered a hall, along which was a row of single rooms. There were six rooms, and on their doors were little oval enameled number plates running from 12 to 17. We looked in Room 12. Two wooden coat hangers were lying on the floor. Room 13 was absolutely empty. Room 14 had evidently last been occupied by someone with a religious turn of mind. There was an old iron bedstead still standing in it, but without springs, and tacked on the wall above the head of the bed was a placard of the kind distributed by some evangelistic religious groups. It said, "The Wages of Sin is Death; but the Gift of God is Eternal Life through Jesus Christ our Lord." Tacked on the wall beside the bed was another religious placard: "Christ is the Head of this House, the Unseen Host at Every Meal, the Silent Listener to Every Conversation." We stared at the placards a few moments, and then Louie turned and started back up the hall.

"Louie," I called, following him, "where are you going?"

"Let's go on back downstairs," he said.

"I thought we were going on up to the floors above," I said. "Let's go up to the fourth floor, at least. We'll take turns pulling the rope."

"There's nothing up here," he said. "I don't want to stay up here another minute. Come on, let's go."

I followed him into the elevator cage. "I'll pull the rope going down," I said.

Louie said nothing, and I glanced at him. He was leaning against the side of the cage, and his shoulders were slumped and his eyes were tired. "I didn't learn much I didn't know before," he said.

"You learned that the wages of sin is death," I said, trying to say something cheerful.

"I knew that before," Louie said. A look of revulsion came on his face. "The wages of sin!" he said. "Sin, death, dust, old empty rooms, old empty whiskey bottles, old empty bureau drawers. Come on, pull the rope faster! Pull it faster! Let's get out of this."

(1952)

# The Bottom of the Harbor

*T*HE BULK OF THE WATER in New York Harbor is oily, dirty, and germy. Men on the mud suckers, the big harbor dredges, like to say that you could bottle it and sell it for poison. The bottom of the harbor is dirtier than the water. In most places, it is covered with a blanket of sludge that is composed of silt, sewage, industrial wastes, and clotted oil. The sludge is thickest in the slips along the Hudson, in the flats on the Jersey side of the Upper Bay, and in backwaters such as Newtown Creek, Wallabout Bay, and the Gowanus Canal. In such areas, where it isn't exposed to the full sweep of the tides, it accumulates rapidly. In Wallabout Bay, a nook in the East River that is part of the Brooklyn Navy Yard, it accumulates at the rate of a foot and half a year. The sludge rots in warm weather and from it gas-filled bubbles as big as basketballs continually surge to the surface. Dredgemen call them "sludge bubbles." Occasionally, a bubble upsurges so furiously that it brings a mass of sludge along with it. In midsummer, here and there in the harbor, the rising and breaking of sludge bubbles makes the water seethe and spit. People sometimes stand on the coal and lumber quays that line the Gowanus Canal and stare at the black, bubbly water.

Nevertheless, there is considerable marine life in the harbor water and on the harbor bottom. Under the paths of liners and tankers and ferries and tugs, fish school and oysters spawn and lobsters nest. There are clams on the sludgy bottom, and mussels and mud shrimp and conchs and crabs and sea worms and sea plants. Bedloe's Island, the Statue of Liberty island, is in a part of the harbor that is grossly polluted, but there is a sprinkling of soft-shell clams in the mud beneath the shallow water that surrounds it. The ebb of a spring tide always draws the water off a broad strip of this mud, and then flocks of gulls appear from all over the Upper Bay and light on it and thrash around and scratch for clams. They fly up with clams in their beaks and drop them on the concrete walk that runs along the top of the island's sea wall, and then they swoop down and pluck the meats out of the broken shells. Even in the Gowanus Canal, there are a few fish; the water is dead up at the head of it— only germs can live there—but from the crook at the Sixth Street Basin on down to the mouth there are cunners and tomcods and eels. The cunners nibble on the acorn barnacles on the piles under the old quays.

In the spring, summer, and fall, during the great coastwise and inshore and offshore migrations of fishes along the Middle Atlantic Coast, at least three dozen species enter the harbor. Only a few members of some species show up. Every spring, a few long, jaggy-backed sea sturgeon show up. Every summer, in the Lower Bay, dragger nets bring up a few small, weird, brightly colored strays from Southern waters, such as porcupine fish, scorpion fish, triggerfish, lookdowns, halfbeaks, hairtails, and goggle-eyed scad. Every fall, a few tuna show up. Other species show up in the hundreds of thousands or in the millions. Among these are shad, cod, whiting, porgy, blackback flounder, summer herring, alewife, sea bass, ling, mackerel, butterfish, and blackfish. Some years, one species, the mossbunker, shows up in the hundreds of millions. The mossbunker is a kind of herring that weighs around a pound when full-grown. It migrates in enormous schools and is caught in greater quantity than any other fish on the Atlantic Coast, but it is unfamiliar to the general public because it isn't a good table fish; it is too oily and bony. It is a factory fish; it is converted into an oil that is used in making soaps, paints, and printing inks (which is why some newspapers have a fishy smell on damp days), and into a meal that is fed to pigs and poultry. In the summer and fall, scores of schools of mossbunkers are hemmed in and caught in the Lower Bay, Sandy Hook Bay, and Raritan Bay by fleets of purse seiners with Negro crews that work out of little fishing ports in North Carolina, Virginia, Delaware, New Jersey, and Long Island and rove up and down the coast, following the schools.

The migratory fishes enter the harbor to spawn or to feed. Some mill around in the bays and river mouths for a few days and leave; some stay for months. Only one fish, the eel, is present in great numbers in all seasons. Eels are nocturnal scavengers, and they thrive in the harbor. They live on the bottom, and it makes no difference to them how deep or dirty it is. They live in ninety feet of water in the cable area of the Narrows and they live in a foot of water in tide ditches in the Staten Island marshes; they live in clean blue water in Sandy Hook Bay and they live around the outfalls of sewers in the East River. There are eight or nine hundred old hulks in the harbor. A few are out in the bays, deeply submerged, but most of them lie half sunk behind the pierhead line in the Jersey Flats and the flats along the Arthur Kill and the Kill van Kull—old scows and barges, old boxcar floats, old tugs, old ferryboats, old sidewheel excursion steamers, old sailing ships. They were towed into the flats and left to rot. They are full of holes; the water in the hulls of many of them rises and falls with the tides. Some are choked with sea lettuce and sea slime. In the summer, multitudes of eels lay up in the hulks during the day and wriggle out at night to feed. In the winter, they bed down in the hulks and hibernate. When they begin to hibernate, usually around the middle of December, they are at their best; they are fleshy then, and tender and sweet. At that time, Italian-Americans and German-Americans from every part of Staten Island go to certain old scows in the flats along the kills and spear so many eels that they bring them home in washtubs and potato sacks. The harbor eels—that is, the eels that live in the harbor the year round—are all males, or bucks. The females, or roes, until they become mature, live in rivers and creeks and ponds, up in fresh water. They become mature after they have spent from seven to thirteen years in fresh water. Every fall, thousands upon thousands of mature females run down the rivers that empty into the harbor— the Hudson, the Hackensack, the Passaic, the Elizabeth, the Rahway, and the Raritan. When they reach salt water, they lie still awhile and rest. They may rest for a few hours or a few days. Divers say that some days in October and November it is impossible to move about anywhere on the harbor bottom without stirring up throngs of big, fat, silver-bellied female eels. After resting, the females congregate with the mature harbor males, and they go out to sea together to spawn.

Hard-shell clams, or quahogs, the kind that appear on menus as littlenecks and cherrystones, are extraordinarily abundant in the harbor. Sanitary engineers classify the water in a number of stretches of the Lower Bay and Jamaica Bay as "moderately polluted." In these stretches, on thinly sludge-coated bottoms, under water that ranges in depth from one to thirty-five feet, are several vast, pullulating, mazy networks of hard-shell-clam beds. On some beds, the clams are crowded as tightly together as cobblestones. They are lovely clams—the inner lips of their shells have a lustrous violet border, and their meats are as pink and plump as rosebuds—but they are unsafe; they sometimes contain the germs of a variety of human diseases, among them bacillary and protozoal dysentery and typhoid fever, that they collect in their systems while straining nourishment out of the dirty water. The polluted beds have been condemned for over thirty years, and are guarded against poachers by the city Department of Health and the state Conservation Department. Quite a few people in waterfront neighborhoods in Staten Island, Brooklyn, and Queens have never been fully convinced that the clams are unsafe. On moonless nights and foggy days, they slip out, usually in rowboats, and raid the beds. In the course of a year, they take tons of clams. They eat them in chowders and stews, and they eat them raw. Every once in a while, whole families get horribly sick.

Just west of the mouth of the harbor, between Sandy Hook and the south shore of Staten Island, there is an area so out-of-the-way that anchorage grounds have long been set aside in it for ships and barges loaded with dynamite and other explosives. In this area, there are three small tracts of clean, sparkling, steel-blue water, about fifteen square miles in all. This is the only unpolluted water in the harbor. One tract of about five square miles, in Raritan Bay, belongs to the State of New York; the others, partly in Raritan Bay and partly in Sandy Hook Bay, belong to New Jersey. The bottoms of these tracts are free of sludge, and there are some uncontaminated hard-shell-clam beds on them. They are public beds; after taking out a license, residents of the state in whose waters they lie may harvest and sell clams from them. The New York beds are clammed by about a hundred and fifty Staten Islanders, most of whom live in or near the sleepy little south-shore ports of Prince's Bay and Great Kills. Some do seasonal work in shipyards, on fishing boats, or on truck farms, and clam in slack times, and some—thirty or so, mostly older men—clam steadily. They go out at dawn in sea skiffs and in rowboats equipped with outboard motors. When they reach the beds, they scatter widely and anchor. They lean over the sides of their boats and rake the bottom with clumsy rakes, called Shinnecock rakes, that have twenty-four-foot handles and long, inturned teeth. Last year, they raked up eighteen thousand bushels. A soup factory in New Jersey bought about half of these, and the rest went to fish stores and hotels and restaurants, mainly in New York City. Every New Yorker who frequently eats clams on the half shell has most likely eaten at least a few that came out of the harbor.

IN DUTCH AND ENGLISH DAYS, immense beds of oysters grew in the harbor. They bordered the shores of Brooklyn and Queens, and they encircled Manhattan, Staten Island, and the islands in the Upper Bay; to the Dutch, Ellis Island was Oyster Island and Bedloe's Island was Great Oyster Island. One chain of beds extended from Sandy Hook straight across the harbor and up the Hudson to Ossining. The Dutch and the English were, as they still are, gluttonous oyster eaters. By the end of the eighteenth century, all but the deepest of the beds had been stripped. Oysters, until then among the cheapest of foods, gradually became expensive. In the eighteen-twenties, a group of Staten Island shipowners began to buy immature oysters by the schooner-load in other localities and bring them to New York and bed them in the harbor until they got their growth, when they were tonged up and shipped to the wholesale oyster market in Manhattan, to cities in the Middle West, and to London, where they were prized. This business was known as bedding. The bedders obtained most of their seed stock in Chesapeake Bay and in several New Jersey and Long Island bays. Some bought three-year-olds and put them down for only six or seven months, and some bought younger oysters and put them down for longer periods. At first, the bedders used the shoals in the Kill van Kull, but by and by they found that the best bottoms lay along the seaward side of Staten Island, in the Lower Bay and Raritan Bay. Back then, the inshore water in these bays was rich in diatoms and protozoa, the tiny plants and animals on which oysters feed. Spread out in this water, on clean bottoms, at depths averaging around thirteen feet, oysters matured and fattened much faster than they did crowded together on their shell-cluttered spawning grounds; a thousand bushels of three-year-olds from Chesapeake Bay, put down in April in a favorable season, might amount to fourteen hundred bushels when taken up in October. Bedding was highly profitable in good years and many fortunes were made in it. It was dominated by old-settler Staten Island families—the Tottens, the Winants, the De Harts, the Deckers, the Manees, the Mersereaus, the Van Wyks, the Van Duzers, the Latourettes, the Housmans, the Bedells, and the Depews. It lasted for almost a century, during which, at one time or another, five Staten Island ports—Mariner's Harbor, Port Richmond, Great Kills, Prince's Bay, and Tottenville—had oyster docks and fleets of schooners, sloops, and tonging skiffs. Prince's Bay had the biggest fleet and the longest period of prosperity; on menus in New York and London, harbor oysters were often called Prince's Bays. Approximately nine thousand acres of harbor bottom, split up into plots varying from a fraction of an acre to four hundred acres, were used for beds. The plots were leased from the state and were staked with a forest of hemlock poles; nowadays, in deepening and widening Ambrose Channel, Chapel Hill Channel, Swash Channel, and other ship channels in the Lower Bay, dredges occasionally dig up the tube-worm-incrusted stumps of old boundary poles. Bedding was most prosperous in the thirty years between 1860 and 1890. In good

years in that period, as many as fifteen hundred men were employed
on the beds and as many as five hundred thousand bushels of oysters
were marketed. Some years, as much as a third of the crop was
shipped to Billingsgate, the London fish market. For a while, the
principal bedders were the richest men on Staten Island. They put
their money in waterfront real estate, they named streets after
themselves, and they built big, showy wooden mansions. A half
dozen of these mansions still stand in a blighted neighborhood in
Mariner's Harbor, in among refineries and coal tipples and junk
yards. One has a widow's walk, two have tall fluted columns, all
have oddly shaped gables, and all are decorated with scroll-saw
work. They overlook one of the oiliest and gummiest stretches of
the Kill van Kull. On the south shore, in the sassafras barrens west
of Prince's Bay, there are three more of these mansions, all empty.
Their fanlights are broken, their shutters swag, and their yards are
a tangle of weeds and vines and overturned birdbaths and dead pear
trees.

After 1900, as more and more of the harbor became polluted,
people began to grow suspicious of harbor oysters, and the bedding
business declined. In the summer of 1916, a number of cases of
typhoid fever were traced beyond all doubt to the eating of oysters
that had been bedded on West Bank Shoal, in the Lower Bay, and
it was found that sewage from a huge New Jersey trunk sewer
whose outfall is at the confluence of the Kill van Kull and the Upper
Bay was being swept through the Narrows and over the beds by
the tides. The Department of Health thereupon condemned the beds
and banned the business. The bedders were allowed to take up the
oysters they had down and rebed them in clean water in various
Long Island bays. They didn't get them all, of course. A few were
missed and left behind on every bed. Some of these propagated,
and now their descendants are sprinkled over shoaly areas in all the
bays below the Narrows. They are found on West Bank Shoal, East
Bank Shoal, Old Orchard Shoal, Round Shoal, Flynns Knoll, and
Romer Shoal. They live in clumps and patches; a clump may have
several dozen oysters in it and a patch may have several hundred.
Divers and dredgemen call them wild oysters. It is against state and

city laws to "dig, rake, tong, or otherwise remove" these oysters from the water. A few elderly men who once were bedders are still living in the old Staten Island oyster ports, and many sons and grandsons of bedders. They have a proprietary feeling about harbor oysters, and every so often, in cold weather, despite the laws, some of them go out to the old, ruined beds and poach a mess. They know what they are doing; they watch the temperature of the water to make sure the oysters are "sleeping," or hibernating, before they eat any. Oysters shut their shells and quit feeding and begin to hibernate when the temperature of the water in which they lie goes down to forty-one degrees; in three or four days, they free themselves of whatever germs they may have taken in, and then they are clean and safe.

There is a physician in his late fifties in St. George whose father and grandfather were bedders. On a wall of his waiting room hangs an heirloom, a chart of oyster plots on West Bank Shoal that was made in 1886 by a marine surveyor for the state; it is wrinkled and finger-smudged and salt-water-spotted, and his grandfather's plot, which later became his father's—a hundred and two acres on the outer rim of the shoal, down below Swinburne Island—is bounded on it in red ink. The physician keeps a sea skiff in one of the south-shore ports and goes fishing every decent Sunday. He stores a pair of pole-handled tongs in the skiff and sometimes spends a couple of hours hunting for clumps of harbor oysters. One foggy Sunday afternoon last March, he got in his skiff, with a companion, and remarked to the people on the dock that he was going codfishing on the Scallop Ridge, off Rockaway Beach. Instead, picking his way through the fog, he went up to the West Bank and dropped anchor on one of his father's old beds and began tonging. He made over two dozen grabs and moved the skiff four times before he located a clump. It was a big clump, and he tonged up all the oysters in it; there were exactly sixty. All were mature, all were speckled with little holes made by boring sponges, and all were wedge-shaped. Sea hair, a marine weed, grew thickly on their shells. One was much bigger than the others, and the physician picked it up and smoothed aside its mat of coarse, black, curly sea hair and counted the ridges on its upper shell and said that it was at least fourteen years old. "It's too big to eat on the half shell," he told his companion. He bent over the gunnel of the skiff and gently put it back in the water. Then he selected a dozen that ranged in age from four to seven years and opened them. Their meats were well developed and gray-green and glossy. He ate one with relish. "Every time I eat harbor oysters," he said, "my childhood comes floating up from the bottom of my mind." He reflected for a few moments. "They have a high iodine content," he continued, "and they have a characteristic taste. When I was a boy in Prince's Bay, the old bedders used to say that they tasted like almonds. Since the water went bad, that taste has become more pronounced. It's become coppery and bitter. If you've ever tasted the little nut that's inside the pit of a peach, the kernel, that's how they taste."

THE FISH AND SHELLFISH in the harbor and in the ocean just outside provide all or part of a living for about fifteen hundred men who call themselves baymen. They work out of bays and inlets and inlets within inlets along the coasts of Staten Island, Brooklyn, and Queens. Some baymen clam on the public beds. Some baymen set eelpots. Some baymen set pound nets, or fish traps. Pound nets are strung from labyrinths of stakes in shoal areas, out of the way of the harbor traffic. Last year, during the shad, summer herring, and mossbunker migrations, forty-one of them were set off the Staten Island coast, between Midland Beach and Great Kills, in an old oyster-bedding area. Some baymen go out in draggers, or small trawlers, of which there are two fleets in the harbor. One fleet has sixteen boats, and ties up at two shaky piers on Plumb Beach Channel, an inlet just east of Sheepshead Bay, on the Brooklyn coast. The other has nine boats, and ties up alongside a quay on the west branch of Mill Basin, a three-branched inlet in the bulrush marshes in the Flatlands neighborhood of Brooklyn. The majority of the men in both fleets are Italian-Americans, a few of whom in their youth fished out of the Sicilian ports of Palermo and Castellammare del Golfo. Some of them tack saints' pictures and miraculous medals and scapular medals and little evil-eye amulets on the walls of their pilothouses. The amulets are in the shape of hunchbacks, goat horns, fists with two fingers upraised, and opened scissors; they come from stores on Mulberry Street and are made of plastic. The harbor draggers range from thirty to fifty feet and carry two to five men. According to the weather and the season, they drag their baglike nets in the Lower Bay or in a fishing ground called the Mud Hole, which lies south of Scotland and Ambrose lightships and is about fifteen miles long and five to ten miles wide. The Mud Hole is the upper part of the Old Hudson River Canyon, which was the bed of the river twenty thousand years ago, when the river flowed a hundred and twenty-five miles past what is now Sandy Hook before it reached the ocean. The draggers catch lower-depth and bottom feeders, chiefly whiting, butterfish, ling, cod, porgy, fluke, and floun-der. They go out around 4 A.M. and return around 4 P.M., and their catches are picked up by trucks and taken to Fulton Market.

Some baymen set lines of lobster pots. In days gone by, there was a bountiful stock of lobsters in the harbor. Between 1915 and 1920, owing to pollution and overfishing and the bootlegging of berries, which are egg-carrying lobsters, and shorts and crickets, which are undersized lobsters, the stock began dwindling at a rapid rate. As late as 1920, forty-five lobstermen were still working the Upper Bay, the Narrows, and the Lower Bay. They ran out of seven inlets in Brooklyn and Staten Island, and their buoys dipped and danced all the way from the Statue of Liberty to the Hook. Every year in the twenties, a few of them either dropped out for good or bought bigger boats and forsook the bays and started setting pots out beyond the three-mile limit, in the harbor approaches. By 1930, only one lobsterman of any importance, Sandy Cuthbert, of Prince's Bay, continued to work the bays. In the fall of that year, at the close of the season, Mr. Cuthbert took up his pots—he had two hundred and fifty—and stacked them on the bank of Lemon Creek, an inlet of Prince's Bay, and went into the rowboat-renting and fish-bait business. His pots are still there, rotting; generations of morning-glory and wild-hop vines are raveled in their slats and hold them together. During the thirties and forties, the lobsters began

474

coming back, and divers say that now there are quite a few nests in the Upper Bay and many nests in the Lower Bay. However, they are still too scarce and scattered to be profitable. Sometimes, while repairing cables or pipelines on the bottom in parts of the Lower Bay where the water is clear and the visiblity is good, divers turn over rocks and pieces of waterlogged driftwood and lobsters scuttle out and the divers pick them up and put them in the tool sacks hooked to their belts.

At present, there are nine lobster boats working out of the harbor—six out of Plumb Beach; two out of Ulmer Park, on Gravesend Bay; and one out of Coney Island Creek. They are of the sea-skiff type. They range from twenty-six to twenty-eight feet, they are equipped with gasoline engines that are strong enough for much bigger boats, and, except for canvas spray hoods, they are open to the weather. The men on these boats are Scandinavians and Italians. They set their pots in a section of the Mud Hole southeast of Ambrose Lightship where the water in most places is over a hundred feet deep. They use the trawl method, in which the pots are hung at intervals from thick, tarred lines half a mile long; as a rule, thirty-five pots are hung from each line. The lines are buoyed at both ends with bundles of old, discarded ferryboat life preservers, which the lobstermen buy from a ship chandler in Fulton Market, who buys them from the Department of Marine and Aviation. Once a day, the lines are lifted, and each pot is pulled up and emptied of lobsters and chewed-up bait and stray crabs and fish, and rebaited with three or four dead mossbunkers. The coastwise and South American shipping lanes cross the lobster grounds in the Mud Hole, and every now and then a ship plows into a line and tears it loose from its buoys. Dump scows with rubbish from the city sometimes unload on the grounds and foul the lines and bury the pots. Mud Hole lobsters are as good as Maine lobsters; they can't be told apart. Some are sold to knowledgeable Brooklyn housewives who drive down to the piers in the middle of the afternoon, when the boats come in, and take their pick, but most are sold to Brooklyn restaurants. A boat working seven lines, which is the average, often comes in with around two hundred and fifty pounds.

A good many baymen work on public fishing boats that take sports fishermen out to fishing grounds in the harbor, in the harbor approaches, and along the Jersey coast. These boats are of two types—charter and party. Charter boats are cabin cruisers that may be hired on a daily or weekly basis. They are used for going after roaming surface feeders, big and small. Most of them are equipped with fighting chairs, fish hoists, and other contrivances for big-game fishing. They go out in the Lower Bay, Sandy Hook Bay, and Raritan Bay for striped bass, bluefish, and mackerel, and they go out to the Mud Hole and the Jersey grounds for tuna, albacore, bonito, and skipjack. They carry a captain and a mate, who baits and gaffs. Great Kills, which has fifteen boats, and Prince's Bay, which has eight, are the principal charter-boat ports in the harbor.

Party boats, also called open boats, are bigger boats, which operate on regular schedules and are open to anyone who has the fare; it varies from three and a half to five dollars a day. Sheepshead Bay is the principal party-boat port. It has over fifty boats. All of them leave from Emmons Avenue, which many people consider the most attractive waterfront street in the city. Emmons is a wide street, with a row of fluttery-leaved plane trees down the middle of it, that runs along the north shore of the bay. It smells of the sea, and of beer and broiled fish. On one side of it, for a dozen blocks, are bar-and-grills, seafood restaurants, clam stands, diners, pizza parlors, tackle and boat-gear stores, and fish markets, one of which has a cynical sign in its show window that says, "CATCH YOUR FISH ON THE NEVER-FAIL BANKS. USE A SILVER HOOK." The party-boat piers— there are ten of them, and they are long and roomy—jut out diagonally from the other side. Retired men from all over Brooklyn come down to the piers by bus and subway on sunny days and sit on the stringpieces and watch the boats go out, and rejuvenate their lungs with the brine in the air, and fish for blue-claw crabs with collapsible wirework traps, and quarrel with each other over the gulls; some bring paper bags of table scraps from home and feed the gulls and coo at them, and some despise the gulls and shoo them away and would wring their necks if they could get their hands on them. Among the boats in the Sheepshead Bay fleet are stripped-down draggers, converted yachts, and converted subchasers from both World Wars. The majority carry a captain and a mate and take around thirty passengers; the old subchasers carry a captain, a mate, an engineer, a cook, and a deckhand and take up to a hundred and ten passengers. Some have battered iceboxes on their decks and sell beer and pop and sandwiches, and some have galleys and sell hot meals. Some have conventional fishing-boat names, such as the *Sea Pigeon,* the *Dorothy B,* and the *Carrie D II,* and some have strutty names, such as the *Atomic,* the *Rocket,* and the *Glory.* Most of them leave at 5, 6, 7, 8, 9, or 10 A.M. and stay out the better part of the day. The passengers bring their own tackle, and fish over the rails. Bait is supplied by the boats; it is included in the fare. In most seasons, for most species, shucked and cut-up skimmer clams are used. These are big, coarse, golden-meated ocean clams. Cut-up fish, live fish, fiddler crabs, calico crabs, sand worms, and blood worms are also used. There are two dozen baymen in Sheepshead Bay who dig, dredge, net, and trap bait. They deliver it to three bait barges moored in the bay, and the bargekeepers put it into shape and sell it to the party boats by the tubful. For five weeks or so in the spring and for five weeks or so in the fall, during the mackerel migrations, the party boats go out and find schools of mackerel and anchor in the midst of them. The rest of the year, they go out and anchor over wrecks, reefs, scow dumps, and shellfish beds, where cod, ling, porgy, fluke, flounder, sea bass, blackfish, and other bottom feeders congregate.

There are many wrecks—maybe a hundred, maybe twice that; no one knows how many—lying on the bottom in the harbor approaches. Some are intact and some are broken up. Some are out in the Old Hudson River Canyon, with over two hundred feet of water on top of them. Some are close to shore, in depths of only twenty to thirty feet; around noon, on unusually clear, sunny fall days, when there is not much plankton in the water and the turbidity is low, it is possible to see these and see schools of sea bass streaming in and out of holes in their hulls. The wrecks furnish shelter for fish. Furthermore, they are coated, inside and out, with a lush, furry growth made up of algae, sea moss, tube worms, barnacles, horse mussels, sea anemones, sea squirts, sea mice, sea snails, and scores of other organisms, all of which are food for fish. The most popular party boats are those whose captains can locate the fishiest wrecks and bridle them. Bridling is a maneuver in which, say the wreck lies north and south, the party boat goes in athwart it and drops one anchor to the east of it and another to the west of it, so that party boat and wreck lie crisscross. Held thus, the party boat can't be skewed about by the wind and tide, and the passengers fishing over both rails can always be sure that they are dropping their bait on the wreck, or inside it. Good party-boat captains, by taking bearings on landmarks and lightships and buoys, can locate and bridle anywhere from ten to thirty wrecks. A number of the wrecks are quite old; they disintegrate slowly. Three old ones, all sailing ships, lie close to each other near the riprap jetty at Rockaway Point, in the mouth of the harbor. The oldest of the three, the *Black Warrior* Wreck, which shelters tons of sea bass from June until November, went down in 1859. The name of the next oldest has been forgotten and she is called the Snow Wreck; a snow is a kind of square-rigged ship similar to a brig; she sank in 1886, or 1887. The third one is an Italian ship that sank in 1890 with a cargo of marble slabs; her name has also been forgotten and she is called the Tombstone Wreck, the Granite Wreck, or the Italian Wreck. Over to the east, off the Rockaways, there is another group of old ones. In this group, all within five miles of shore, are the steamship *Iberia,* which sank in a snowstorm in 1889, after colliding with the steamship *Umbria;* the Wire Wreck, a sailing ship that sank around 1895 while outbound with a cargo of bedsprings and other wire products; the *Boyle* Wreck, a tug that sank around 1900; and the East Wreck, three coal barges that snapped their tow in a storm in 1917 and settled on the bottom in an equilateral triangle. Several of these wrecks have been fished steadily for generations, and party-boat captains like to say that they would be worth salvaging just to get the metal in the hooks and sinkers that have been snagged on them.

There are stretches of reefy bottom in the harbor approaches that are almost as productive of fish as the wrecks, and for the same reasons. These stretches are easier to locate than the wrecks, and much easier to fish. All have been named. Some are natural rock ledges, and among these are the Shrewsbury Rocks, the Buoy Four Grounds, the Cholera Bank, the Klondike Banks, the Seventeen Fathoms, and the Farms. Some are artificial ledges, consisting of debris from excavations and torn-down buildings that was transported from the city in scows and dumped. One such is the Subway Rocks, a ridge of underwater hills beginning four miles south of Ambrose Lightship and running south for several miles, that was made of rocks, bricks, concrete, asphalt, and earth excavated during the construction of the Eighth Avenue Subway. Another such is the New Grounds, or Doorknob Grounds, a stretch of bottom in the northwest corner of the Mud Hole that is used as a dump for slum-clearance projects. There are bricks and brownstone blocks and plaster and broken glass from hundreds upon hundreds of condemned tenements in the New Grounds. The ruins of the somber old red-brick houses in the Lung Block, which were torn down to make way for Knickerbocker Village, lie there. In the first half of the nineteenth century, these houses were occupied by well-to-do families; from around 1890 until around 1905, most of them were brothels for sailors; from around 1905 until they were torn down, in 1933, they were rented to the poorest of the poor, and the tuberculosis death rate was higher in that block than in any other block in the city. All the organisms that grow on wrecks grow on the hills of rubble and rubbish in the Subway Rocks and the New Grounds.

THE COMINGS AND GOINGS of the baymen are watched by a member of the staff of the Bureau of Marine Fisheries of the State Conservation Department. His name is Andrew E. Zimmer, his title is Shellfish Protector, and his job is to enforce the conservation laws relating to marine shellfish and finfish. Mr. Zimmer is a Staten Islander of German descent. He is muscular and barrel-chested and a bit above medium height. He is bald and he is getting jowly. The department issues him a uniform that closely resembles a state trooper's uniform, but he seldom wears it. On duty, he wears old, knockabout clothes, the same as a bayman. He carries a pair of binoculars and a .38 revolver. He is called Happy Zimmer by the baymen, some of whom grew up with him. He is a serious man, a good many things puzzle him, and he usually has a preoccupied look on his face; his nickname dates from boyhood and he has outgrown it. He was born in 1901 on a farm in New Springville, a truck-farming community on the inland edge of the tide marshes that lie along the Arthur Kill, on the western side of Staten Island. In the front yard of the farmhouse, his father ran a combined saloon and German-home-cooking restaurant, named Zimmer's, that attracted people from the villages around and about and from some of the Jersey towns across the kill. Picnics and clambakes and lodge outings were held in a willow grove on the farm. His father had been a vaudeville ventriloquist, and often performed at these affairs. Specialties of the restaurant were jellied eels, clam broth with butter in it, and pear conchs from the Lower Bay boiled and then pickled in a mixture of vinegar and spices and herbs. As a boy, Mr. Zimmer supplied the restaurant with eels he speared in eel holes in the marshes and with soft-shell clams that he dug in the flats along the kill. Until 1916, when the harbor beds were condemned, Prince's Bay oysters were sold from the barrel in the saloon side of the restaurant. Friday afternoons, he and his father would drive down to the Oyster Dock in Prince's Bay in the farm wagon and bring back three or four barrels of selects for the week-end trade. In 1915, after completing the eighth grade, Mr. Zimmer quit school to help his father in the restaurant. In 1924, he took charge of it. In his spare time, mainly by observation in the marshes, he became a good amateur naturalist. In 1930, he gave up the restaurant and went to work for the Conservation Department.

Mr. Zimmer patrols the harbor in a lumbering, rumbly old twenty-eight-foot sea skiff. It has no flag or markings and looks like any old lobster boat, but the baymen can spot it from a distance; they call it the State Boat. Some of Mr. Zimmer's duties are seasonal. From March 15th to June 15th, when pound-netting is allowed, he makes frequent visits to the nets at pull-up time and sees to it that the fishermen are keeping only the species they are licensed for.

When the mossbunker seiners come into the harbor, he boards them and looks into their holds and satisfies himself that they are not taking food fishes along with the mossbunkers. Now and then during the lobstering season, he draws up alongside the lobster boats inbound from the grounds and inspects their catches for shorts. Several times a year, he bottles samples of the water in various parts of the harbor and sends them to the department's laboratory. His principal year-round duty is to patrol the shellfish beds. He runs down and arrests poachers on the polluted beds, and he keeps an eye on the clammers who work the legal beds in Raritan Bay. It is against the law to do any kind of clamming between sundown and sunup, and he spends many nights out on the beds. He is a self-sufficient man. He can anchor his skiff in the shadow of a cattail hassock in Jamaica Bay and, without ever getting especially bored, sit there the whole night through with an old blanket over his shoulders, listening and watching for poachers and looking at the stars and the off-and-on lights on airplanes and drinking coffee out of a thermos jug. The legal beds in New Jersey territory in the harbor have been overworked and are not as fertile as the legal beds in New York territory. In recent years, allured by high clam prices, some of the Jersey clammers have become pirates. They tantalize Mr. Zimmer. On dark nights, using Chris Craft cruisers, they cross the state line, which bisects Raritan Bay, and poach on the New York beds. When they hear the rumble of Mr. Zimmer's skiff, they flee for Jersey. Mr. Zimmer opens his throttle and goes after them, shouting at them to halt and sometimes firing his revolver over their heads, but their cruisers draw less water than his skiff and at the end of the chase they are usually able to shoot up into one of the shallow tide creeks between South Amboy and the Hook and lose him. Mr. Zimmer keeps his skiff in Prince's Bay. Prince's Bay has gone down as a port since his boyhood. Not a trace of the oyster-bedding business is left there. It has a clam dock, a charter-boat pier, and two boatyards, and it has Sandy Cuthbert's rowboat livery and bait station, but its chief source of income is a factory that makes tools for dentists; the factory is on Dental Avenue. The old Prince's Bay Lighthouse still stands on a bluff above the village, but it is now a part of Mount

Loretto, a Catholic home for children; it is used as a residence by the Monsignor and priests who run the home. The light has been taken down and supplanted by a life-size statue of the Virgin Mary. The Virgin's back is to the sea.

Once in a while, Mr. Zimmer spends a day patrolling the Staten Island tide marshes on foot. He feels drawn to the marshes and enjoys this part of his job most of all. A good many people wander about in the marshes and in the meadows and little woods with which they are studded. He is acquainted with scores of marsh wanderers. In the fall, old Italians come and get down on all fours and scrabble in the leaves and rot beneath the blackjack oaks, hunting for mushrooms. In the spring, they come again and pick dandelion sprouts for salads. In midsummer, they come again, this time with scap nets, and scoop tiny mud shrimp out of the tide ditches; they use them in a fried fish-and-shellfish dish called *frittura di pesce*. On summer afternoons, old women from the south-shore villages come to the fringes of the marshes. They pick herbs, they pick wild flowers, they pick wild grapes for jelly, and in the fresh-water creeks that empty into the salt-water creeks they pick watercress. In the fall, truck farmers come with scythes and cut salt hay. When the hay dries, they pack it around their cold frames to keep the frost out. Bird watchers and Indian-relic collectors come in all seasons. The relic collectors sift the mud on the banks of the tide ditches. Mr. Zimmer himself sometimes finds arrowheads and stone net-sinkers on the ditchbanks. Once, he found several old English coins. In September or October, the rabbis and elders come. On Hoshanna Rabbah, the seventh day of the Festival of Succoth, an ancient fertility rite is still observed in a number of orthodox synagogues in the city. The worshipers who take part in the rite are given bunches of willow twigs; each bunch has seven twigs and each twig has seven leaves. After marching in procession seven times around the altar, chanting a litany, the worshipers shake the bunches or strike them against the altar until the leaves fall to the floor. The twigs must be cut from willows that grow beside water, the buds on the ends of the twigs must be unblemished, and the leaves must be green and flawless. For generations, most of the willow bunches have come from black willows and weeping willows in the Staten Island tide marshes. In the two or three days preceding Hoshanna Rabbah— it usually falls in the last week of September or the first or second week of October—rabbis and trusted elders go up and down the ditchbanks, most often in pairs, the rabbi scrutinizing twigs and cutting those that pass the test, and the elder trimming and bunching them and stowing them gently in brown-paper shopping bags.

There is much resident and migratory wildlife in the marshes. The most plentiful resident species are pheasants, crows, marsh hawks, black snakes, muskrats, opossums, rabbits, rats, and field mice. There is no open season on the pheasants, and they have become so bold that the truck farmers look upon them as pests. One can walk through the pokeweed and sumac and blue-bent grass on any of the meadow islands at any time and put up pair after pair of pheasants. At the head of a snaky creek in one of the loneliest of the marshes, there is an old rickamarack of a dock that was built by rum-runners during prohibition. One morning, hiding behind this dock, waiting for some soft-shell-clam poachers to appear, Mr. Zimmer saw a hen pheasant walk across a strip of tide flat, followed by a brood of seventeen. At times, out in the marshes, Mr. Zimmer becomes depressed. The marshes are doomed. The city has begun to dump garbage on them. It has already filled in hundreds of acres with garbage. Eventually, it will fill in the whole area, and then the Department of Parks will undoubtedly build some proper parks out there, and put in some concrete highways and scatter some concrete benches about. The old south-shore secessionists—they want Staten Island to secede from New York and join New Jersey, and there are many of them—can sit on these benches and meditate and store up bile.

MR. ZIMMER is a friend of mine, and I sometimes go out on patrols with him. One cold, windy, spitty morning, we made a patrol of the polluted skimmer-clam beds in the ocean off Rockaway Beach. On the way back to Staten Island, he suggested that we stop in Sheepshead Bay and get some oyster stew to warm us up. We turned in to the bay and tied the skiff to the Harbor Police float and went across the street to Lundy's, the biggest and best of the Emmons Avenue seafood restaurants. We went into the oyster-bar side and took a table, and each of us ordered a double stew. Mr. Zimmer caught sight of a bayman named Leroy Poole, who was standing at the bar, bent over some oysters on the half shell. Mr. Poole is captain and owner of the party boat *Chinquapin*. Mr. Zimmer went over to the bar, and he and Mr. Poole shook hands and talked for a minute or two. When he returned, he said that Mr. Poole would join us as soon as he'd finished his oysters. He told the waiter to set another place and add another double stew to the order. "Do you know Roy?" Mr. Zimmer asked me. I said that I had often seen him around the party-boat piers but that I knew him only to speak to.

"Roy's a south-shore boy," Mr. Zimmer said. "His father was one of the biggest oyster-bedders in Prince's Bay—lost everything when they condemned the beds, and took a bookkeeping job in Fulton Market and died of a stroke in less than a year; died on the Staten Island ferry, on the way to work. After Roy finished grade school, one of his father's friends got him a job in the market, and he became a fish butcher. When the carcass of a three- or four-hundred-pound swordfish is cut into pieces that the retail trade can handle, it's about the same as dressing a steer, and Roy had a knack for that type of work. He got to be an expert. When he cut up a swordfish, or a tuna, or a sturgeon, or a big West Coast halibut, he didn't waste a pound. Also, he was a good fillet man, and he could bone a shad quicker and cleaner than any man in the market. He made good money, but he wasn't happy. Every now and then, he'd quit the market for a year or so and work on one of the government dredges that dredge the sludge out of the ship channels in the harbor. He generally worked on a dredge named the *Goethals*. He made better pay in the market, but he liked to be out in the harbor. He switched back and forth between the market and the *Goethals* for years and years. Somewhere along the line, he got himself tattooed. He's got an oyster tattooed on the muscle of his right arm. That is, an oyster shell. On his left arm, he's got one of those tombstone tattoos—a tombstone with his initials on it and under his initials the date of his birth and under that a big blue question mark. Six or seven years ago, he turned up in Sheepshead Bay and bought the *Chinquapin*. Roy's a good captain, and a good man, but he's a little odd. He says so himself. He's a harbor nut. Most of the baymen, when they're standing around talking, they often talk about the bottom of the harbor, what's down there, but that's *all* Roy talks about. He's got the bottom of the harbor on the brain."

The waiter brought in the stews, and a moment later Mr. Poole came over and sat down. He is a paunchy, red-haired, freckled man. His hair is thinning and the freckles on his scalp show through. He has drooping eyelids; they make his eyes look sleepy and sad. He remarked on the weather; he said he expected snow. Then he tasted his stew. It was too hot for him, and he put his spoon down. "I didn't rest so good last night," he said. "I had a dream. In this dream, a great earthquake had shook the world and had upset the sea level, and New York Harbor had been drained as dry as a bathtub when the plug is pulled. I was down on the bottom, poking around, looking things over. There were hundreds of ships of all kinds lying on their sides in the mud, and among them were some wormy old wrecks that went down long years ago, and there were rusty anchors down there and dunnage and driftwood and old hawsers and tugboat bumpers and baling wire and tin cans and bottles and stranded eels and a skeleton standing waist-deep in a barrel of cement that the barrel had rotted off of. The rats had left the piers and were down on the bottom, eating the eels, and the gulls were flopping about, jerking eels away from the rats. I came across an old wooden wreck all grown over with seaweed, an old, old Dutch wreck. She had a hole in her, and I pulled the seaweed away and looked in and I saw some chests in there that had money spilling out of them, and I tried my best to crawl in. The dream was so strong that I crawled up under the headboard of the bed, trying to get my hands on the Dutch money, and I damn near scraped an ear off."

"Eat your stew, Roy," Mr. Zimmer said, "before it gets cold."

"Pass me the salt," said Mr. Poole. We ate in silence. It isn't easy to carry on a conversation while eating oyster stew. Mr. Poole finished first. He tilted his bowl and worked the last spoonful of the stew into his spoon. He swallowed it, and then he said, "Happy, you've studied the harbor charts a lot in your time. Where would you say is the deepest spot in the harbor?"

"Offhand," said Mr. Zimmer, "I just don't know."

"One of the deepest spots I know is a hole in the bed of the Hudson a little bit south of the George Washington Bridge," said Mr. Poole. "On the dredges, we called it the Gut. It's half full of miscellaneous junk. The city used to dump bargeloads of boulders in there, and any kind of heavy junk that wasn't worth salvaging. Private concerns dumped in there, too, years back, but it's against the harbor regulations now. During the worst part of the last war, when the dredges cleaned sludge out of the ship channel in the Hudson, they had the right to dump it in the Gut—save them from taking it out to sea. The old-timers say the Gut used to go down a hundred and eighty feet. The last sounding I heard, it was around ninety feet. I know where the shallowest spot in the harbor is. I've sounded it myself with a boat hook. It's a spot on Romer Shoal, out in the middle of the Lower Bay, that's only four feet deep at low tide."

"Oh, yes," said Mr. Zimmer. "I've seen it on the charts. It's called a lump."

"It's right on the edge of Ambrose Channel, the channel that the big liners use," continued Mr. Poole. "I told my mate I want him to take me out there someday when the *Queen Mary* is due to come upchannel, and leave me standing there with a flag in my hand."

"What in hell would you do that for?" asked Mr. Zimmer.

"I'd just like to," said Mr. Poole. "I'd like to wave the flag and make the people on the *Queen Mary* wonder what I was standing on—shoulder-deep, out there in the middle of the Lower Bay. I'd wear a top hat, and I'd smoke a big cigar. I'd like to see what would happen."

"I'll tell you what would happen," said Mr. Zimmer. "The wash from the *Queen Mary* would drown you. Did you think of that?"

"I thought of it," said Mr. Poole. "I didn't do it, did I?" He crumpled up his napkin and tossed it on the table. "Another queer spot in the harbor," he said, "is Potter's Field. It's in the East River, in between Williamsburg Bridge and Manhattan Bridge. The river makes a sharp bend there, an elbow. On an ebb tide, there's an eddy in the elbow that picks up anything loose coming downriver, afloat or submerged, and sweeps it into a stretch of backwater on the Brooklyn side. This backwater is called Wallabout Bay on charts; the men on the dredges call it Potter's Field. The eddy sweeps driftwood into the backwater. Also, it sweeps drownded bodies into there. As a rule, people that drown in the harbor in winter stay down until spring. When the water begins to get warm, gas forms in them and that makes them buoyant and they rise to the surface. Every year, without fail, on or about the fifteenth of April, bodies start showing up, and more of them show up in Potter's Field than any other place. In a couple of weeks or so, the Harbor Police always finds ten to two dozen over there—suicides, bastard babies, old barge captains that lost their balance out on a sleety night attending to towropes, now and then some gangster or other. The police launch that runs out of Pier A on the Battery—Launch One—goes over and takes them out of the water with a kind of dip-net contraption that the Police Department blacksmith made out of tire chains. I ride the Staten Island ferry a good deal, and I'm forever hearing the tourists remark how beautiful the harbor is, and I always wish they could see Potter's Field some mornings in April—either that or the Gowanus Canal in August, when the sludge bubbles are popping like whips; they'd get a brand-new idea how beautiful the harbor is."

"Oh, I don't know, Roy," said Mr. Zimmer. "They've stopped dumping garbage out in the harbor approaches, where the tide washes it right back, and they're putting in a lot of sewage-disposal plants. The water's getting cleaner every year."

"I've read that," said Mr. Poole, "and I've heard it. Only I don't believe it. Did you eat any shad last spring—Staten Island shad *or* Hudson River shad? They've still got that kerosene taste. It was worse last spring than it ever was. Also, have you been up the Gowanus Canal lately? On the dredges, they used to say that the smell in the Gowanus would make the flag on a mast hang limp in a high wind. They used to tell about a tug that was freshly painted yellow and made a run up the Gowanus and came out painted green. I was up there last summer, and I didn't notice any change."

"Seriously, Roy," said Mr. Zimmer, "don't you think the water's getting cleaner?"

"Of course it isn't," said Mr. Poole. "It's getting worse and worse. *Every*thing is getting worse *every*where. When I was young, I used to dream the time would come when we could bed oysters in the harbor again. Now I'm satisfied that that time will never come. I don't even worry about the pollution any more. My only hope, I hope they don't pollute the harbor with something a million times worse than pollution."

"Let's don't get on that subject," said Mr. Zimmer.

"Sometimes I'm walking along the street," continued Mr. Poole, "and I wonder why the people don't just stand still and throw their heads back and open their mouths and howl."

"Why?" asked Mr. Zimmer.

"I'll tell you why," said Mr. Poole. "On account of the God-damned craziness of everything."

"Oh, well," said Mr. Zimmer, glancing at the empty stew bowls, "we can still eat."

Mr. Poole grunted. He looked at his wristwatch. "Well," he said, "this ain't making me any money." He got up and put on his hat. "Thanks for the stew," he said. "I enjoyed it. My treat next time. Take care, all."

"That's right, Roy," said Mr. Zimmer. "You take care of yourself."

"Thanks again," said Mr. Poole. "Give my regards home. Take care. Take care. Take care."

(1951)

# The Rats on the Waterfront

*I*N NEW YORK CITY, as in all great seaports, rats abound. One is occasionally in their presence without being aware of it. In the whole city relatively few blocks are entirely free of them. They have diminished greatly in the last twenty-five years, but there still are millions here; some authorities believe that in the five boroughs there is a rat for every human being. During wars, the rat populations of seaports and ships always shoot up. A steady increase in shipboard rats began to be noticed in New York Harbor in the summer of 1940, less than a year after the war started in Europe. Rats and rat fleas in many foreign ports are at times infected with the plague, an extraordinarily ugly disease that occurs in several forms, of which the bubonic, the Black Death of the Middle Ages, is the most common. Consequently, all ships that enter the harbor after touching at a foreign port are examined for rats or for signs of rat infestation by officials of the United States Public Health Service, who go out in cutters from a quarantine station on the Staten Island bank of the Narrows. If a ship appears to be excessively infested, it is anchored in one of the bays, its crew is taken off, and its holds and cabins are fumigated with a gas so poisonous that a whiff or two will quickly kill a man, let alone a rat. In 1939 the average number of rats killed in a fumigation was 12.4. In 1940 the average rose abruptly to 21, and two years later it reached 32.1. In 1943, furthermore, rats infected with the plague bacteria, *Pasteurella pestis,* were discovered in the harbor for the first time since 1900. They were taken out of an old French tramp, the *Wyoming,* in from

Casablanca, where the Black Death has been intermittent for centuries.

The biggest rat colonies in the city are found in run-down structures on or near the waterfront, especially in tenements, live-poultry markets, wholesale produce markets, slaughterhouses, warehouses, stables, and garages. They also turn up in more surprising places. Department of Health inspectors have found their claw and tail tracks in the basements of some of the best restaurants in the city. A few weeks ago, in the basement and sub-basement of a good old hotel in the East Forties, a crew of exterminators trapped two hundred and thirty-six in three nights. Many live in crannies in the subways; in the early-morning hours, during the long lulls between trains, they climb to the platforms and forage among the candy-bar wrappers and peanut hulls. There are old rat paths beneath the benches in at least two ferry sheds. In the spring and summer, multitudes of one species, the brown rat, live in twisting, many-chambered burrows in vacant lots and parks. There are great colonies of this kind of rat in Central Park. After the first cold snap they begin to migrate, hunting for warm basements. Packs have been seen on autumn nights scuttering across the boulevards and transverses in the Park and across Fifth Avenue and across Central Park West. All through October and November, exterminating firms get frantic calls from the superintendents of many of the older apartment houses on the avenues and streets adjacent to the Park; the majority of the newer houses were ratproofed when built. The rats come out by twos and threes in some side streets in the theatrical district practically every morning around four-thirty. The scow-shaped trucks that collect kitchen scraps from restaurants, night clubs, and saloons all over Manhattan for pig farms and soap factories in New Jersey roll into these streets at that time. Shortly after the trucks have made their pick-ups, if no people are stirring, the rats appear and search for dropped scraps; they seem to pop out of the air.

The rats of New York are quicker-witted than those on farms, and they can outthink any man who has not made a study of their habits. Even so, they spend most of their lives in a state of extreme anxiety, the black rats dreading the brown and both species dreading human beings. Away from their nests, they are usually on the edge of hysteria. They will bite babies (now and then, they bite one to death), and they will bite sleeping adults, but ordinarily they flee from people. If hemmed in, and sometimes if too suddenly come upon, they will attack. They fight savagely and blindly, in the manner of mad dogs; they bare their teeth and leap about every which way, snarling and snapping and clawing the air. A full-grown black rat, when desperate, can jump three feet horizontally and make a vertical leap of two feet two inches, and a brown rat is nearly as spry. They are greatly feared by firemen. One of the hazards of fighting a fire in a junk shop or in an old warehouse is the crazed rats. It is dangerous to poke at them. They are able to run right up a cane or a broomstick and inflict deep, gashlike bites on their assailant's hands. A month or so ago, in broad daylight, on the street in front of a riding academy on the West Side, a stableboy tried to kill a rat with a mop; it darted up the mop handle and tore the thumbnail off the boy's left hand. This happening was unusual chiefly in that the rat was foraging in the open in the daytime. As a rule, New York rats are nocturnal. They rove in the streets in many neighborhoods, but only after the sun has set. They steal along as quietly as spooks in the shadows close to the building line, or in the gutters, peering this way and that, sniffing, quivering, conscious every moment of all that is going on around them. They are least cautious in the two or three hours before dawn, and they are encountered most often by milkmen, night watchmen, scrubwomen, policemen, and other people who are regularly abroad in those hours. The average person rarely sees one. When he does, it is a disquieting experience. Anyone who has been confronted by a rat in the bleakness of a Manhattan dawn and has seen it whirl and slink away, its claws rasping against the pavement, thereafter understands fully why this beast has been for centuries a symbol of the Judas and the stool pigeon, of soullessness in general. Veteran exterminators say that even they are unable to be calm around rats. "I've been in this business thirty-one years and I must've seen fifty thousand rats, but I've never got accustomed to the look of them," one elderly exterminator said recently. "Every time I see one my heart sinks and

I get the belly flutters." In alcoholic wards the rat is the animal that most frequently appears in the visual hallucinations of patients with delirium tremens. In these wards, in fact, the D.T.'s are often referred to as "seeing the rat."

There are three kinds of rats in the city—the brown (*Rattus norvegicus*), which is also known as the house, gray, sewer, or Norway rat; the black (*Rattus rattus*), which is also known as the ship or English rat; and the Alexandrian (*Rattus rattus alexandrinus*), which is also known as the roof or Egyptian rat and is a variety of the black rat. In recent years they have been killed here in the approximate proportion of ninety brown to nine black and one Alexandrian. The brown is hostile to the other kinds; it usually attacks them on sight. It kills them by biting their throats or by clawing them to pieces, and, if hungry, it eats them.

The behavior and some of the characteristics of the three kinds are dissimilar, but all are exceedingly destructive, all are hard to exterminate, all are monstrously procreative, all are badly flea-bitten, and all are able to carry a number of agonizing diseases. Among these diseases, in addition to the plague, are a form of typhus fever called Brill's disease, which is quite common in several ratty ports in the South; spirochetal jaundice, rat-bite fever, trichinosis, and tularemia. The plague is the worst. Human beings develop it in from two to five days after they have been bitten by a flea that has fed on the blood of a plague-infected rat. The onset is sudden, and the classic symptoms are complete exhaustion, mental confusion, and black, intensely painful swellings (called buboes) of the lymph glands in the groin and under the arms. The mortality is high. The rats of New York are all ridden with a flea, the *Xenopsylla cheopis,* which is by far the most frequent transmitting agent of the plague. Several surveys of the prevalence in the city of the *cheopis* have been made by Benjamin E. Holsendorf, a consultant on the staff of the Department of Health. Mr. Holsendorf, an elderly Virginian, is a retired Passed Assistant Pharmacist in the Public Health Service and an international authority on the ratproofing of ships and buildings. He recently supervised the trapping of many thousands of rats in the area between Thirty-third Street and the bottom of Manhattan, and found that these rats had an average of eight *cheopis* fleas on them.

"Some of these rats had three fleas, some had fifteen, and some had forty," Mr. Holsendorf says, "and one old rat had hundreds on him; his left hind leg was missing—probably lost it in a trap, probably gnawed it off himself—and he'd take a tumble every time he tried to scratch. However, the average was eight. None of these fleas were plague-infected, of course. I don't care to generalize about this, but I will say that if just one plague-infested rat got ashore from a ship at a New York dock and roamed for only a few hours among our local, uninfected rats, the resulting situation might be, to say the least, quite sinister."

Rats are almost as fecund as germs. In New York, under fair conditions, they bear from three to five times a year, in litters of from five to twenty-two. There is a record of seven litters in seven months from a single captured pair. The period of gestation is between twenty-one and twenty-five days. They grow rapidly and are able to breed when four months old. They live to be three or four years old, although now and then one may live somewhat longer; a rat at four is older than a man at ninety. "Rats that survive to the age of four are the wisest and the most cynical beasts on earth," one exterminator says. "A trap means nothing to them, no matter how skillfully set. They just kick it around until it snaps; then they eat the bait. And they can detect poisoned bait a yard off. I believe some of them can read." In fighting the rat, exterminating companies use a wide variety of traps, gases, and poisons. There are about three hundred of these companies in the city, ranging in size from hole-in-the-wall, boss-and-a-helper outfits to corporations with whole floors in midtown office buildings, large laboratories, and staffs of carefully trained employees, many of whom have scientific degrees. One of the largest is the Guarantee Exterminating Company ("America's Pied Piper"), at 500 Fifth Avenue. Among its clients are hospitals, steamship lines, railroad terminals, department stores, office buildings, hotels, and apartment houses. Its head is E. R. Jennings, a second-generation exterminator; his father started the business in Chicago, in 1888. Mr. Jennings says that the most effective rat traps are the old-fashioned snap or break-back ones and a thing called the glueboard.

"We swear by the glueboard," he says. "It's simply a composition shingle smeared on one side with a thick, strong, black glue. We developed this glue twenty-five years ago and it's probably the stickiest stuff known to man. It has been widely copied in the trade and is used all over. The shingle is pliable. It can be laid flat on the floor or bent around a pipe. We place them on rat runs—the paths rats customarily travel on—and that's where skill comes in; you have to be an expert to locate the rat runs. We lay bait around the boards. If any part of the animal touches a board, he's done for. When he tries to pull away, he gets himself firmly caught in the glue. The more he struggles, the more firmly he's caught. Next morning the rat, glueboard and all, is picked up with tongs and burned. We used to bait with ground beef, canned salmon, and cheese, but we did some experimenting with many other foods and discovered that peanut butter is an extremely effective rat bait. Rats have to be trapped, poisoned, or gassed. Cats, if they're hungry enough, will kill rats, but you can't really depend on them—in many cases, they're able to keep the number of rats down, but they're seldom able to exterminate them.

"Insects, particularly cockroaches and bedbugs, are the Number One exterminating problem in New York. Rats come next. Then mice. Perhaps I shouldn't tell this, but most good exterminators despise rat jobs because they know that exterminating by itself is ineffective. You can kill all the rats in a building on a Monday and come back on a Wednesday and find it crawling with them. The only way rats can be kept out is to ratproof the building from sub-basement to skylight. It's an architectural problem; you have to build them out. Killing them off periodically is a waste of time. We refuse to take a rat job unless the owner or tenant promises to stop up every hole and crack through which rats can get in, and seal up or eliminate any spaces inside the building in which they can nest. That may sound like cutting our own throats, but don't worry: insects are here to stay and we'll always have more work than we can do. Twenty-five years ago there were easily two rats for every human being in the city. They gradually decreased to half that, for many reasons. Better sanitary conditions in general is one reason. Fewer horses and fewer stables is another. The improved packaging of foods helped a lot. An increase in the power of the Department of Health is an important reason. Nowadays, if a health inspector finds rat tracks in a grocery or a restaurant, all he has to do is issue a warning; if things aren't cleaned up in a hurry, he can slap on a violation and make it stick. The most important reason, however, is the modern construction of buildings and the widespread use of concrete. It's almost impossible for a rat to get inside some of the newer apartment houses and office buildings in the city. If he gets in, there's no place for him to hide and breed."

NONE OF THE RATS in New York are indigenous to this country. The black rat has been here longest. Its homeland is India. It spread to Europe in the Middle Ages along trade routes, and historians are quite sure that it was brought to America by the first ships that came here. It is found in every seaport in the United States, and inland chiefly in the Gulf States. It has bluish-black fur, a pointed nose, and big ears. It is cleaner and not as fierce as the brown rat but more suspicious and harder to trap. It is an acrobatic beast. It can rapidly climb a drapery, a perpendicular drain or steam-heat pipe, an elevator cable, or a telephone or electric wire. It can gnaw a hole in a ceiling while clinging to an electric wire. It can run fleetly on a taut wire, or on a rope whether slack or taut. It uses its tail, which is slightly longer than its body, to maintain balance. It nests in attics, ceilings, and hollow walls, and in the superstructures of piers, away from its enemy, the ground-loving brown rat. Not all piers are infested; a few of the newer ones, which are made of concrete, have none at all. It keeps close to the waterfront, and until recently was rarely come across in the interior of the city. Whenever possible, it goes aboard ships to live. While docked here, all ships are required to keep three-foot metal disks, called rat guards, set on their hawsers and mooring cables. These guards sometimes get out of whack—a strong wind may tilt them, for example— and then a black or an Alexandrian can easily clamber over them. Occasionally a rat will walk right up or down a gangplank. It is almost impossible to keep a ship entirely free of them. Some famous ships are notoriously ratty. One beautiful liner—it was in the round-the-world cruise service before the war—once came in with two hundred and fifty aboard. Public Health Service officials look upon a medium-sized ship with twenty as excessively infested. The record for New York Harbor is held by a freighter that came in from an Oriental port with six hundred, all blacks and Alexandrians. The black and the Alexandrian are very much alike, and the untrained eye cannot tell them apart. The Alexandrian is frequently found on ships from Mediterranean ports. It is a native of Egypt, and no one seems to know, even approximately, when it first appeared in this country. It has never been able to get more than a toehold in New York, but it is abundant in some Southern and Gulf ports.

The brown rat, the *R. norvegicus,* originated somewhere in Central Asia, began to migrate westward early in the eighteenth century, and reached England around 1730. Most authorities believe that it got to this country during the Revolutionary War. From ports all along the coast it went inland, hot on the heels of the early settlers, and now it thrives in every community and on practically every farm in the United States. Its spread was slowest in the high and dry regions of the West; it didn't reach Wyoming until 1919 and Montana until 1923. Its nose is blunt, and its ears are small and alert, and its eyes are sharp and shiny and joyless and resentful and accusing. Its fur is most often a grimy brown, but it may vary from a pepper-and-salt gray to nearly black. Partial albinos occasionally show up; the tame white rat, which is used as a laboratory animal and sometimes kept as a pet, is a sport derived from the brown.

In addition to being the most numerous, the brown rat is the dirtiest, the fiercest, and the biggest. "The untrained observer," a Public Health Service doctor remarked not long ago, "invariably spreads his hands wide apart when reporting the size of a rat he has seen, indicating that it was somewhat smaller than a stud horse but a whole lot bigger than a bulldog. They are big enough, God protect us, without exaggerating." The average length of adult brown rats is ten inches, not counting the tail, which averages seven inches. The average weight is three-quarters of a pound. Once in a while a much heavier one is trapped. One that weighed a pound and a half and measured twenty and a half inches overall (that is, counting the tail) was recently clubbed to death in a Manhattan brewery; brewery and distillery rats feed on mash and many become obese and clumsy. Some exterminators have maintained for years that the biggest rats in the country, perhaps in the world, are found in New York City, but biologists believe that this is just a notion, that they don't get any bigger in one city than they do in another. The black and the Alexandrian are about two-thirds the size of the brown.

The brown rat is distributed all over the five boroughs. It customarily nests at or below street level—under floors, in rubbishy basements, and in burrows. There are many brownstones and red-bricks, as well as many commercial structures, in the city that have basements or sub-basements with dirt floors; these places are rat heavens. The brown rat can burrow into the hardest soil, even tightly packed clay, and it can tunnel through the kind of cheap mortar that is made of sand and lime. To get from one basement to another, it tunnels under party walls; slum-clearance workers frequently uncover a network of rat tunnels that link all the tenements in a block. Like the magpie, it steals and hoards small gadgets and coins. In nest chambers in a system of tunnels under a Chelsea tenement, workers recently found an empty lipstick tube, a religious medal, a skate key, a celluloid teething ring, a belt buckle, a shoehorn, a penny, a dime, and three quarters. Paper money is sometimes found. When the Civic Repertory Theatre was torn down, a nest constructed solely of dollar bills, seventeen in all, was discovered in a burrow. Exterminators believe that a high percentage of the fires that are classified as "of undetermined origin" are started by the brown rat. It starts them chiefly by gnawing the insulation off electric wires, causing short circuits. It often uses highly inflammable material in building nests. The majority of the nests in the neighborhood of a big garage, for example, will invariably be built of oily cotton rags.

The brown rat is as supple as rubber and it can squeeze and contort itself through openings half its size. It has strong jaws and long, curved incisors with sharp cutting edges. It can gnaw a notch big enough to accommodate its body in an oak plank, a slate shingle, or a sun-dried brick. Attracted by the sound of running water, it will gnaw into lead pipe. It cannot climb as skillfully as the black and the Alexandrian, it cannot jump as far, and it is not as fleet, but it is, for its size, a remarkable swimmer. A Harbor Police launch once came upon three brown rats, undoubtedly from New Jersey, in the middle of the Hudson; in an hour and twenty-five minutes, swimming against the wind in tossing water, they reached the pilings of one of the Barclay Street ferry slips, where the policemen shot them. The brown rat is an omnivorous scavenger, and it doesn't seem to care at all whether its food is fresh or spoiled. It will eat soap, oil paints, shoe leather, the bone of a bone-handled knife, the glue in a book binding, and the rubber in the insulation of telephone and electric wires. It can go for days without food, and it can obtain sufficient water by licking condensed moisture off metallic surfaces. All rats are vandals, but the brown is the most ruthless. It destroys far more than it actually consumes. Instead of completely eating a few potatoes, it takes a bite or two out of dozens. It will methodically ruin all the apples and pears in a grocery in a night. To get a small quantity of nesting material, it will cut great quantities of garments, rugs, upholstery, and books to tatters. In warehouses, it sometimes goes berserk. In a few hours a pack will rip holes in hundreds of sacks of flour, grain, coffee, and other foodstuffs, spilling and fouling the contents and making an overwhelming mess. Now and then, in live-poultry markets, a lust for blood seems to take hold of the brown rat. One night, in the poultry part of old Gansevoort Market, alongside the Hudson, a burrow of them bit the throats of over three hundred broilers and ate less than a dozen. Before this part of the market was abandoned, in 1942, the rats practically had charge of it. Some of them nested in the drawers of desks. When the drawers were pulled open, they leaped out, snarling.

SO FAR, IN THE UNITED STATES, the bubonic plague has been only a menace. From 1898 to 1923, 10,822,331 deaths caused by the plague were recorded in India alone; in the United States, in this period, there were fewer than three hundred deaths. The plague first occurred in this country in 1900, in the Chinatown of San Francisco. It is generally believed that the bacteria were brought in by infected rats that climbed to the docks from an old ship in the Far Eastern trade that caught afire while being unloaded. This epidemic killed a hundred and thirteen people and lasted until the end of 1903. The plague broke out again in 1907, a year after the earthquake. In the same year there was an epidemic in Seattle. There have been two epidemics in New Orleans—one in 1914 and one in 1919 and 1920—and there was one in Los Angeles in 1924 and 1925. Since then there have been only sporadic cases. However, there is a vast and ominous reservoir of plague infection in the rural rodents of the West. During the first epidemic in San Francisco, many rats fled the city and infected field rodents, chiefly ground squirrels, in the suburbs. In 1934, thirty years later, Public Health Service biologists turned up the fact that the plague had slowly spread among burrowing animals—ground squirrels, prairie dogs, chipmunks, and others—as far east as New Mexico and Wyoming. Late last year it appeared fifty miles inside the western border of North Dakota. Public Health Service officials say that there is no reason to assume that the infection will not infiltrate into rodents of the Great Plains, cross the Mississippi, and show up in the East. Most of the diseased rodents inhabit thinly settled sections and come in contact with human beings infrequently. Even so, every year several people, usually hunters, are bitten by infected rodent fleas and come down with the plague. There is an ever-present possibility that a few infected rodents may stray from rural areas and communicate the disease to town and city rats. If the disease ever gets loose among city rats, epidemics among human beings are apt to follow.

There has never been an outbreak of the plague in New York. There have, however, been two narrow escapes. In 1900, plague-infected rats were found in ships in the harbor of New York, as well as in the harbors of San Francisco and Port Townsend, Washington. They got ashore only in San Francisco, causing the first Black Death epidemic in North America. Plague rats were found in New York Harbor for the second time early in January of 1943. Among themselves, health officials refer to this discovery as "the *Wyoming* matter." The history of the *Wyoming* matter was told to me in 1944 by Dr. Robert Olesen, medical director of the New York Quarantine Station of the Public Health Service. Mr. Holsendorf sent me to see Dr. Olesen; they were colleagues years ago in the Public Health Service and are old friends. I saw Dr. Olesen in his office in an old, red-brick building overlooking the Narrows, in Rosebank, on Staten Island.

"The *Wyoming* matter has been one of the best-kept secrets in the history of the Public Health Service, and I'm proud of that," Dr. Olesen said, "but I agree with what Ben Holsendorf has been saying lately—there's no reason at all to keep it secret any longer. I'll tell you about it.

"First of all, I'd better explain how we inspect ships. Every ship in foreign trade that comes into the harbor is boarded by a party made up of a customs officer, an immigration officer, a plant-quarantine man from the Department of Agriculture, a Public Health doctor, and a sanitary inspector, whose main job is to determine the degree of rat infestation aboard. While the doctor is examining the crew and passengers for quarantinable diseases, the sanitary inspector goes through the ship looking for rat tracks, gnawings, droppings, and nests. Rats have a smell that is as distinctive as the smell of cats, although not as rank, and an experienced inspector can detect their presence that way. The inspector pays particular attention to ships that have touched at plague ports. There are quite a few of these ports right now; Suez had an outbreak the other day and was put on the list. After he's made his search, he reports to the doctor, who orders a fumigation if things look bad. If infestation is slight and if the ship comes from a clean port, the doctor probably won't insist on a fumigation. I won't give you any wartime figures, but in one peacetime month, for example, we inspected five hundred and sixty ships, found that a hundred and thirty-two were infested to some degree, and fumigated twenty-four, recovering eight hundred and ten rats.

"We've been short-handed since the war began, and most of our fumigating is done by a group of twenty-two Coast Guardsmen.

They were assigned to us early in the war and we trained them to make rat inspections and fumigations. We use hydrocyanic gas, which is one of the most lethal of poisons. An infested ship is anchored and a fumigation party of four or five Coast Guardsmen goes aboard. First, they send the entire crew ashore, carefully checking them off one by one. Then one of the Coast Guardsmen goes through the ship, shouting, banging on bulkheads with a wrench, and making as much racket as possible. He shouts, 'Danger! Fumigation! Poison gas!' Then the Coast Guardsmen put on gas masks and toss some tear-gas bombs into the holds. That's to fetch out any stowaways who might be aboard. During the first months we used hydrocyanic, we killed a number of stowaways. A few weeks ago, in the hold of a South American freighter, the tear gas brought out eight weeping stowaways who had been hiding in an empty water tank. Two fellows in the crew had smuggled them aboard in Buenos Aires and had been feeding them. These fellows had kept their mouths shut and gone ashore, leaving the stowaways to be killed, for all they cared. When the Coast Guardsmen are satisfied a ship is empty of human beings, they seal the holds and cabins and open cans of hydrocyanic, liberating the gas. They even fumigate the lifeboats; rats often hide in them. After a certain number of hours—ten for a medium-sized ship—the holds are opened and aired out, and the Coast Guardsmen go below and search for dead rats. The rats are dropped in wax-paper bags and brought to a laboratory in the basement here. They are combed for fleas. The fleas are pounded in a mortar, put into a solution, and injected into guinea pigs. Then the rats are autopsied, and bits of livers and spleens are snipped out and pounded up. These are also put into a solution and injected into guinea pigs. If the fleas or the rats are infected, the pigs sicken and die. We began this work in 1921, and for twenty-two years we injected scores of generations of pigs with the fleas and livers and spleens of rats from practically every port in the world without turning up a single Black Death germ. We didn't want to find any, to be sure, but there *were* days when we couldn't help but look upon our work as routine and futile.

"Now then, late in the evening of January 10, 1943, the French freighter *Wyoming* arrived from Casablanca, North Africa, with a miscellaneous cargo, mainly wine and tobacco. A big convoy came in that evening, sixty or seventy ships, and we didn't get to the *Wyoming* until next day. Casablanca was on the plague list at that time; there had been an outbreak in December, shortly before the *Wyoming* sailed. The crew was carefully examined. No sign of illness. Then the captain brought out a deratization certificate stating that the ship had recently been fumigated—in Casablanca, if I remember correctly—and was free of rats; looking back, I feel sure the official who signed this certificate had been bribed. She was allowed to dock at Pier 34, Brooklyn, where she discharged some bags of mail. Next day she proceeded to Pier 84, Hudson River, and began discharging her cargo. Some rats were seen in her by longshoremen, and on January 13th we went over her and found evidence of infestation. She was allowed to continue unloading. On January 18th we fumigated her right at her dock and found twenty rats. We combed and autopsied the rats, and inoculated a guinea pig. Four days later the pig sickened and died. An autopsy indicated plague infection and cultures from its heart blood showed an oval organism which had all the characteristics of *Pasteurella pestis.* We made a broth of tissue from this pig and inoculated a second pig. It sickened and died. It was the Black Death, no doubt about it. We had found it in the harbor for the first time in forty-three years.

"In the meantime, the *Wyoming* had moved from the Hudson to Pier 25, Staten Island, for repairs. On January 29th we went aboard her, removed all excess dunnage and gear to the decks, and ripped open all the enclosed spaces in the holds; we were afraid the hydrocyanic hadn't penetrated to these spaces. Then we refumigated. Twelve more dead rats were found. On the same day we got in touch with Dr. Stebbins, the Commissioner of Health for the city, and told him about the situation. We were terribly apprehensive. The *Wyoming* had touched at piers in rat-infested sections in three boroughs and there was, of course, a distinct possibility that infected rats had got ashore and were at that moment wandering around the waterfront, coming in contact with local rats and exchanging fleas. Mr. Holsendorf, in his capacity as the Health Department's rat consultant, quickly got together some crews of trappers and put them to work setting break-back traps on the Brooklyn pier, the Manhattan pier, and the Staten Island pier, and in buildings in the vicinity of each pier. The trapping was done unobtrusively; we were afraid a newspaper might learn of the matter and start a plague scare. Early in February the first batch of rats was sent for autopsies to the laboratory of the Willard Parker Hospital, a hospital for contagious diseases, on the East River at Fifteenth Street. We sent them there, rather than bring them way down here to our laboratory, in order to get a report on them as quickly as possible. We waited for the report with considerable anxiety. It was negative on every rat, and we began to breathe easier. Mr. Holsendorf and his crews trapped from the end of January to the middle of May and the reports continued to come in negative. At the end of May we concluded that no *Wyoming* rats had got ashore, and that the city was safe."

(1944)

# Mr. Hunter's Grave

W HEN THINGS GET TOO MUCH for me, I put a wild-flower
book and a couple of sandwiches in my pockets and go down to
the South Shore of Staten Island and wander around awhile in one
of the old cemeteries down there. I go to the cemetery of the
Woodrow Methodist Church on Woodrow Road in the Woodrow
community, or to the cemetery of St. Luke's Episcopal Church on
the Arthur Kill Road in the Rossville community, or to one on the
Arthur Kill Road on the outskirts of Rossville that isn't used any
longer and is known as the old Rossville burying ground. The South
Shore is the most rural part of the island, and all of these cemeteries
are bordered on at least two sides by woods. Scrub trees grow on
some of the graves, and weeds and wild flowers grow on many of
them. Here and there, in order to see the design on a gravestone,
it is necessary to pull aside a tangle of vines. The older gravestones
are made of slate, brownstone, and marble, and the designs on
them—death's-heads, angels, hourglasses, hands pointing upward,
recumbent lambs, anchors, lilies, weeping willows, and roses on
broken stems—are beautifully carved. The names on the gravestones
are mainly Dutch, such as Winant, Housman, Woglom, Decker,
and Van Name, or Huguenot, such as Dissosway, Seguine, De Hart,
Manee, and Sharrott, or English, such as Ross, Drake, Bush, Cole,
and Clay. All of the old South Shore farming and oyster-planting
families are represented, and members of half a dozen generations
of some families lie side by side. In St. Luke's cemetery there is a
huge old apple tree that drops a sprinkling of small, wormy, lopsided
apples on the graves beneath it every September, and in the Wood-

row Methodist cemetery there is a patch of wild strawberries. Invariably, for some reason I don't know and don't want to know,
after I have spent an hour or so in one of these cemeteries, looking
at gravestone designs and reading inscriptions and identifying wild
flowers and scaring rabbits out of the weeds and reflecting on the
end that awaits me and awaits us all, my spirits lift, I become quite
cheerful, and then I go for a long walk. Sometimes I walk along
the Arthur Kill, the tidal creek that separates Staten Island from
New Jersey; to oldtime Staten Islanders, this is "the inside shore."
Sometimes I go over on the ocean side, and walk along Raritan Bay;
this is "the outside shore." The interior of the South Shore is
crisscrossed with back roads, and sometimes I walk along one of
them, leaving it now and then to explore an old field or a swamp
or a stretch of woods or a clay pit or an abandoned farmhouse.

The back road that I know best is Bloomingdale Road. It is an
old oystershell road that has been thinly paved with asphalt; the
asphalt is cracked and pocked and rutted. It starts at the Arthur
Kill, just below Rossville, runs inland for two and a half miles, gently
uphill most of the way, and ends at Amboy Road in the Pleasant
Plains community. In times past, it was lined with small farms that
grew vegetables, berries, and fruit for Washington Market. During
the depression, some of the farmers got discouraged and quit. Then,
during the war, acid fumes from the stacks of smelting plants on
the New Jersey side of the kill began to drift across and ruin crops,
and others got discouraged and quit. Only three farms are left, and
one of these is a goat farm. Many of the old fields have been taken
over by sassafras, gray birch, blackjack oak, sumac, and other waste-
land trees, and by reed grass, blue-bent grass, and poison ivy. In
several fields, in the midst of this growth, are old woodpecker-
ringed apple and pear trees, the remnants of orchards. I have great
admiration for one of these trees, a pear of some old-fashioned
variety whose name none of the remaining farmers can remember,
and every time I go up Bloomingdale Road I jump a ditch and pick
my way through a thicket of poison ivy and visit it. Its trunk is
hollow and its bark is matted with lichens and it has only three live
limbs, but in favorable years it still brings forth a few pears.

In the space of less than a quarter of a mile, midway in its length,

Bloomingdale Road is joined at right angles by three other back roads—Woodrow Road, Clay Pit Road, and Sharrott's Road. Around the junctions of these roads, and on lanes leading off them, is a community that was something of a mystery to me until quite recently. It is a Negro community, and it consists of forty or fifty Southern-looking frame dwellings and a frame church. The church is painted white, and it has purple, green, and amber windowpanes. A sign over the door says, "AFRICAN METHODIST EPISCOPAL ZION." On one side of the church steps is a mock-orange bush, and on the other side is a Southern dooryard plant called Spanish bayonet, a kind of yucca. Five cedar trees grow in the churchyard. The majority of the dwellings appear to be between fifty and a hundred years old. Some are long and narrow, with a chimney at each end and a low porch across the front, and some are big and rambling, with wings and ells and lean-tos and front porches and side porches. Good pine lumber and good plain carpentry went into them, and it is obvious that attempts have been made to keep them up. Nevertheless, all but a few are beginning to look dilapidated. Some of the roofs sag, and banisters are missing on some of the porches, and a good many rotted-out clapboards have been replaced with new boards that don't match, or with strips of tin. The odd thing about the community is it usually has an empty look, as if everybody had locked up and gone off somewhere. In the summer, I have occasionally seen an old man or an old woman sitting on a porch, and I have occasionally seen children playing in a back yard, but I have seldom seen any young or middle-aged men or women sitting around, and I have often walked through the main part of the community, the part that is on Bloomingdale Road, without seeing a single soul.

For years, I kept intending to find out something about this community, and one afternoon several weeks ago, in St. Luke's cemetery in Rossville, an opportunity to do so presented itself.

I had been in the cemetery a couple of hours and was getting ready to leave when a weed caught my eye. It was a stringy weed, about a foot high, and it had small, lanceolate leaves and tiny white flowers and tiny seed pods, and it was growing on the grave of

Rachel Dissosway, who died on April 7, 1802, "in the 27th Yr of her Age." I consulted my wild-flower book, and came to the conclusion that it was peppergrass (*Lepidium virginicum*), and squatted down to take a closer look at it. "One of the characteristics of peppergrass," the wild-flower book said, "is that its seed pods are as hot as pepper when chewed." I deliberated on this for a minute or two, and then curiosity got the better of me and I stripped off some of the seed pods and started to put them in my mouth, and at just that moment I heard footsteps on the cemetery path and looked up and saw a man approaching, a middle-aged man in a black suit and a clerical collar. He came over to the grave and looked down at me.

"What in the world are you doing?" he asked.

I tossed the seed pods on the grave and got to my feet. "I'm studying wild flowers, I guess you might call it," I said. I introduced myself, and we shook hands, and he said that he was the rector of St. Luke's and that his name was Raymond E. Brock.

"I was trying to decide if the weed on this grave is peppergrass," I said.

Mr. Brock glanced at the weed and nodded. "Peppergrass," he said. "A very common weed in some parts of Staten Island."

"To tell you the truth," I said, "I like to look at wild flowers, and I've been studying them off and on for years, but I don't know much about them. I'm only just beginning to be able to identify them. It's mostly an excuse to get out and wander around."

"I've seen you from a distance several times wandering around over here in the cemetery," Mr. Brock said.

"I hope you don't mind," I said. "In New York City, the best places to look for wild flowers are old cemeteries and old churchyards."

"Oh, yes," said Mr. Brock, "I'm aware of that. In fact, I'll give you a tip. Are you familiar with the Negro community over on Bloomingdale Road?"

I said that I had walked through it many times, and had often wondered about it.

"The name of it is Sandy Ground," said Mr. Brock, "and it's a relic of the old Staten Island oyster-planting business. It was founded back before the Civil War by some free Negroes who came up here from the Eastern Shore of Maryland to work on the Staten Island oyster beds, and it used to be a flourishing community, a garden spot. Most of the people who live there now are descendants of the original free-Negro families, and most of them are related to each other by blood or marriage. Quite a few live in houses that were built by their grandfathers or great-grandfathers. On the outskirts of Sandy Ground, there's a dirt lane running off Bloomingdale Road that's called Crabtree Avenue, and down near the end of this lane is an old cemetery. It covers an acre and a half, maybe two acres, and it's owned by the African Methodist church in Sandy Ground, and the Sandy Ground families have been burying in it for a hundred years. In recent generations, the Sandy Grounders have had a tendency to kind of let things slip, and one of the things they've let slip is the cemetery. They haven't cleaned it off for years and years, and it's choked with weeds and scrub. Most of the gravestones are hidden. It's surrounded by woods and old fields, and you can't always tell where the cemetery ends and the woods begin. Part of it is sandy and part of it is loamy, part of it is dry and part of it is damp, some of it is shady and some of it gets the sun all day, and I'm pretty sure you can find just about every wild flower that grows on the South Shore somewhere in it. Not to speak of shrubs and herbs and ferns and vines. If I were you, I'd take a look at it."

A man carrying a long-handled shovel in one hand and a short-handled shovel in the other came into the cemetery and started up the main path. Mr. Brock waved at him, and called out, "Here I am, Joe. Stay where you are. I'll be with you in a minute." The man dropped his shovels.

"That's Mr. Damato, our gravedigger," said Mr. Brock. "We're having a burial in here tomorrow, and I came over to show him where to dig the grave. You'll have to excuse me now. If you do decide to visit the cemetery in Sandy Ground, you should ask for permission. They might not want strangers wandering around in it. The man to speak to is Mr. George H. Hunter. He's chairman of the board of trustees of the African Methodist church. I know Mr. Hunter. He's eighty-seven years old, and he's one of those strong, self-contained old men you don't see much any more. He was a hard worker, and he retired only a few years ago, and he's fairly well-to-do. He's a widower, and he lives by himself and does his own cooking. He's got quite a reputation as a cook. His church used to put on clambakes to raise money, and they were such good clambakes they attracted people from all over this part of Staten Island, and he always had charge of them. On some matters, such as drinking and smoking, he's very disapproving and strict and stern, but he doesn't feel that way about eating; he approves of eating. He's a great Bible reader. He's read the Bible from cover to cover, time and time again. His health is good, and his memory is unusually good. He remembers the golden age of the oyster business on the South Shore, and he remembers its decline and fall, and he can look at any old field or tumble-down house between Rossville and Tottenville and tell you who owns it now and who owned it fifty years ago, and he knows who the people were who are buried out in the Sandy Ground cemetery—how they lived and how they died, how much they left, and how their children turned out. Not that he'll necessarily tell you what he knows, or even a small part of it. If you can get him to go to the cemetery with you, ask him the local names of the weeds and wild flowers. He can tell you. His house is on Bloomingdale Road, right across from the church. It's the house with the lightning rods on it. Or you could call him on the phone. He's in the book."

I thanked Mr. Brock, and went straightway to a filling station on the Arthur Kill Road and telephoned Mr. Hunter. I told him I wanted to visit the Sandy Ground cemetery and look for wild flowers in it. "Go right ahead," he said. "Nobody'll stop you." I told him I also wanted to talk to him about Sandy Ground. "I can't see you today," he said. "I'm just leaving the house. An old lady I know is sick in bed, and I made her a lemon-mcringue pie, and I'm going over and take it to her. Sit with her awhile. See if I can't cheer her up. You'll have to make it some other time, and you'd better make it soon. That cemetery is a disgrace, but it isn't going to be that way much longer. The board of trustees had a contractor look it over and make us a price how much he'd charge to go in there with a bulldozer and tear all that mess out by the roots. Clean it up good, and build us a road all the way through, with a turn-around at the farther end. The way it is now, there's a road in there, but it's a narrow little road and it only goes halfway in, and sometimes the pallbearers have to carry the coffin quite a distance from the hearse to the grave. Also, it comes to a dead end, and the hearse has to back out, and if the driver isn't careful he's liable to back into a gravestone, or run against the bushes and briars and scratch up the paint on his hearse. As I said, a disgrace. The price the contractor made us was pretty steep, but we put it up to the congregation, and if he's willing to let us pay a reasonable amount down and the balance in installments, I think we're going ahead with it. Are you busy this coming Saturday afternoon?" I said that I didn't expect to be. "All right," he said, "I tell you what you do. If it's a nice day, come on down, and I'll walk over to the cemetery with you. Come around one o'clock. I've got some things to attend to Saturday morning, and I ought to be through by then."

SATURDAY TURNED OUT TO BE NICE and sunny, and I went across on the ferry and took the Tottenville bus and got off in Rossville and walked up Bloomingdale Road to Sandy Ground. Remembering Mr. Brock's instructions, I looked for a house with lightning rods on it, and I had no trouble finding it. Mr. Hunter's house is fully equipped with lightning rods, the tips of which are ornamented with glass balls and metal arrows. It is a trim, square, shingle-sided, two-story-and-attic house. It has a front porch and a back porch, both screened. The front porch is shaded by a rambler rose growing on a trellis. I knocked on the frame of the screen door, and a bespectacled, elderly Negro man appeared in the hall. He had on a chef's apron, and his sleeves were rolled up. He was slightly below medium height, and lean and bald. Except for a wide, humorous mouth, his face was austere and a little forbidding, and his eyes were sad. I opened the door and asked, "Are you Mr.

Hunter?" "Yes, yes, yes," he said. "Come on in, and close the door. Don't stand there and let the flies in. I hate flies. I despise them. I can't endure them." I followed him down the hall, past the parlor, past the dining room, and into the kitchen. There were three cake layers and a bowl of chocolate icing on the kitchen table.

"Sit down and make yourself at home," he said. "Let me put the icing on this cake, and then we'll walk over to the cemetery. Icing or frosting. I never knew which was right. I looked up icing in the dictionary one day, and it said 'Frosting for a cake.' So I looked up frosting, and it said 'Icing for a cake.' 'Ha!' I said. 'The dictionary man don't know, either.' The preacher at our church is a part-time preacher, and he doesn't live in Sandy Ground. He lives in Asbury Park, and runs a tailor shop during the week, and drives over here on Sundays. Reverend J. C. Ramsey, a Southern man, comes from Wadesboro, North Carolina. Most Sundays, he and his wife take Sunday dinner with me, and I always try to have something nice for them. After dinner, we sit around the table and drink Postum and discuss the Bible, and that's something I do enjoy. We discuss the prophecies in the Bible, and the warnings, and the promises—the promises of eternal life. And we discuss what I call the mysterious verses, the ones that if you could just understand them they might explain everything—why we're put here, why we're taken away—but they go down too deep; you study them over and over, and you go down as deep as you can, and you still don't touch bottom. 'Do you remember that verse in Relevation,' I say to Reverend Ramsey, 'where it says such and such?' And we discuss that awhile. And then he says to me, 'Do you remember that verse in Second Thessalonians, where it says so and so?' And we discuss that awhile. This Sunday, in addition to the preacher and his wife, I've got some other company coming. A gospel chorus from down South is going to sing at the church Sunday morning, a group of men and women from in and around Norfolk, Virginia, that call themselves the Union Gospel Chorus. They sing old hymns. Reverend Ramsey heard about them, and got into some correspondence with them. There's seven of them, and they're coming up on the bus today, and they'll spend the night in Asbury Park, and tomorrow, after they sing, they're coming to my house for Sunday dinner. That'll be ten for dinner, including the preacher and his wife and me, and that's nothing. I have twenty to dinner sometimes, like at Thanksgiving, and do it all myself, and it doesn't bother me a bit. I'm going to give them chicken fricassee and dumplings for the main course. Soon as I finish this cake, I'll take you in the dining room and show you what else I'm going to give them. Did you have your lunch?"

"I had a sandwich and some coffee on the ferryboat coming over," I said.

"Now, you know, I like to do that," Mr. Hunter said. "I never go cross on the ferryboat without I step up to the lunch counter and buy a little something—a sandwich, or a piece of raisin cake. And then I sit by the window and eat it, and look at the tugboats go by, and the big boats, and the sea gulls, and the Statue of Liberty. Oh, my! It's such a pleasure to eat on a boat. Years and years ago, I was cook on a boat. When I was growing up in Sandy Ground, the mothers taught the boys to cook the same as the girls. The way they looked at it—you never know, it might come in handy. My mother was an unusually good cook, and she taught me the fundamentals, and I was just naturally good at it, and when I was seventeen or eighteen there was a fleet of fishing boats on Staten Island that went to Montauk and up around there and fished the codfish grounds, and I got a job cooking on one of them. It was a small boat, only five in the crew, and the galley was just big enough for two pots and a pan and a stirring spoon and me. I was clumsy at first. Reach for something with my right hand and knock something else over with my left elbow. After a while, though, I got so good the captain of the biggest boat in the fleet heard about my cooking and tried to hire me away, but the men on my boat said if I left they'd leave, and my captain had been good to me, so I stayed. I was a fishing-boat cook for a year and a half, and then I quit and took up a different line of work altogether. I'll be through with this cake in just a minute. I make my icing thicker than most people do, and I put more on. Frosting. Speaking of wild flowers, do you know pokeweed when you see it?"

"Yes," I said.

"Did you ever eat it?"

"No," I said. "Isn't it supposed to be poisonous?"

"It's the root that's poisonous, the root and the berries. In the spring, when it first comes up, the young shoots above the root are good to eat. They taste like asparagus. The old women in Sandy Ground used to believe in eating pokeweed shoots, the old Southern women. They said it renewed your blood. My mother believed it. Every spring, she used to send me out in the woods to pick pokeweed shoots. And I believe it. So every spring, if I think about it, I go pick some and cook them. It's not that I like them so much—in fact, they give me gas—but they remind me of the days gone by, they remind me of my mother. Now, away down here in the woods in this part of Staten Island, you might think you were fifteen miles on the other side of nowhere, but just a little ways up Arthur Kill Road, up near Arden Avenue, there's a bend in the road where you can sometimes see the tops of the skyscrapers in New York. Just the tallest skyscrapers, and just the tops of them. It has to be an extremely clear day. Even then, you might be able to see them one moment and the next moment they're gone. Right beside this bend in the road there's a little swamp, and the edge of this swamp is the best place I know to pick pokeweed. I went up there one morning this spring to pick some, but we had a late spring, if you remember, and the pokeweed hadn't come up. The fiddleheads were up, and golden club, and spring beauty, and skunk cabbage, and bluets, but no pokeweed. So I was looking here and looking there, and not noticing where I was stepping, and I made a misstep, and the next thing I knew I was up to my knees in mud. I floundered around in the mud a minute, getting my bearings, and then I happened to raise my head and look up, and suddenly I saw, away off in the distance, miles and miles away, the tops of the skyscrapers in New York shining in the morning sun. I wasn't expecting it, and it was amazing. It was like a vision in the Bible."

Mr. Hunter smoothed the icing on top of the cake with a table knife, and stepped back and looked at it. "Well," he said, "I guess that does it." He placed a cover on the cake, and took off his apron.

"I better wash my hands," he said. "If you want to see something pretty, step in the dining room and look on the sideboard." There was a walnut sideboard in the dining room, and it had been polished until it glinted. On it were two lemon-meringue pies, two coconut-custard pies, a pound cake, a marble cake, and a devil's-food cake. "Four pies and four cakes, counting the one I just finished," Mr. Hunter called out. "I made them all this morning. I also got some corn muffins put away, to eat with the chicken fricassee. That ought to hold them." Above the dining-room table, hanging from the ceiling, was an old-fashioned lampshade. It was as big as a parasol, and made of pink silk, and fringed and tasseled. On one wall, in a row, were three religious placards. They were printed in ornamental type, and they had floral borders. The first said "JESUS NEVER FAILS." The second said "NOT MY WILL BUT THINE BE DONE." The third said "THE HOUR IS COMING IN WHICH ALL THAT ARE IN THE GRAVES SHALL HEAR HIS VOICE, AND SHALL COME FORTH; THEY THAT HAVE DONE GOOD, UNTO THE RESURRECTION OF LIFE AND THEY THAT HAVE DONE EVIL, UNTO THE RESURRECTION OF DAMNATION." On another wall was a framed certificate stating that George Henry Hunter was a life member of St. John's Lodge No. 29 of the Most Worshipful Prince Hall Grand Lodge of Free and Accepted Masons. While I was looking at this, Mr. Hunter came into the room. "I'm proud of that," he said. "There's several Negro Mason organizations, but Prince Hall is the biggest, and I've been a member since 1906. I joined the Masons the same year I built this house. Did you notice my floors?" I looked down. The floor boards were wide and made of some kind of honey-colored wood, and they were waxed and polished. "Virgin spruce," he said. "Six inches wide. Tongue and groove. Built to last. In my time, that was the idea, but in this day and time, that's not the idea. They've got more things nowadays—things, things, things; kitchen stoves you could put in the parlor just to look at, refrigerators so big they're all out of reason, cars that reach from here to Rossville—but they aren't built to last, they're built to wear out. And that's the way the people want it. It's immaterial to them how long a thing lasts. In fact, if it don't wear out quick enough, they beat it and bang it and kick it and jump up and down on it, so they can get a new one. Most of what you buy nowadays, the outside is everything, the inside don't matter. Like those tomatoes you buy at the store, and they look so nice and shiny and red, and half the time, when you get them home and slice them, all that's inside is mush, red mush. And the people are the same. You hardly ever see a son any more as good as his father. Oh, he might be taller and stronger and thicker in the shoulders, playing games at school and all, but he can't stand as much. If he tried to lift and pull the way the men of my generation used to lift and pull, he'd be ruptured by noon—they'd be making arrangements to operate. How'd I get started talking this way? I'm tired, that's why. I been on my feet all morning, and I better sit down a few minutes." He took a tablecloth from a drawer of the sideboard and shook it out and laid it gently over the cakes and pies. "Let's go on the back porch," he said.

THERE WERE TWO WICKER ROCKING CHAIRS on the back porch, and we sat down. Mr. Hunter yawned and closed his eyes and slowly lowered his chin to his chest. I looked at his back yard, in which there were several rows of sweet potatoes, a row of tomatoes, a weeping willow, and a feeding table for birds. Mr. Hunter dozed for about five minutes, and then some blue jays flew into the yard, shrieking, and they aroused him. Pressing his elbows against the chair, he sat up, and followed the jays with his eyes as they swooped and swirled about the yard. When they flew away, he laughed. "I enjoy birds," he said. "I enjoy their colors. I enjoy the noise they make, and the commotion. Even blue jays. Most mornings, I get up real early and go out in the yard and scatter bread crumbs and sunflower seeds on the feeding table, and then I sit up here on the porch and watch. Oh, it's nice out here in the early morning! Everything is so fresh. As my mother used to say, 'Every morning, the world anew.' Some mornings, I see a dozen different kinds of birds. There were redbirds all over the yard this morning, and a surprising number of brown thrashers and red-winged blackbirds. I see a good many I don't recognize; I do wish I knew their names.

Every so often, a pair of pheasants land on the feeding table. Some of the old fields around here are full of them. I was picking some tomatoes the other day, and a pair of pheasants scuttled out from under the tomato bushes and flew up right in my face. Whoosh! Up goes the cock bird. A second later—whoosh! Up goes the hen bird. One of her wings brushed against me. I had my mind on something else, or I could've caught her. I better not get on the subject of birds, or I'll talk your ears off. You said on the phone you wanted to know something about Sandy Ground. What do you want to know? How it began?"

"Yes, sir," I said.

"Oysters!" said Mr. Hunter. "That's how it began." There was a fly swatter on the floor beside Mr. Hunter's chair, and a few feet in front of his chair was an old kitchen table with a chipped enamel top. He suddenly reached down and grabbed the swatter and stood up and took a step toward the table, on which a fly had lit. His shadow fell on the fly, and the fly flew away. Mr. Hunter stared wildly into space for several moments, looking for the fly and muttering angrily, and then he sat back down, still holding the swatter.

"It's hard to believe nowadays, the water's so dirty," he continued, "but up until about the year 1800 there were tremendous big beds of natural-growth oysters all around Staten Island—in the Lower Bay, in the Arthur Kill, in the Kill van Kull. Some of the richest beds of oysters in the entire country were out in the lower part of the Lower Bay, the part known as Raritan Bay. Most of them were on shoals, under ten to twenty feet of water. They were supposed to be public beds, open to anybody, but they were mainly worked by Staten Islanders, and the Staten Islanders considered they owned them. Between 1800 and 1820, all but the very deepest of these beds gradually petered out. They had been raked and scraped until they weren't worth working any more. But the Staten Islanders didn't give up. What they did, they began to bring immature oysters from other localities and put them on the best of the old beds and leave them there until they reached market size, which took from one to four years, all according to how mature the oysters were to begin with. Then they'd rake them up, or tong them up, and load them on boats, and send them up the bay to the wholesalers in New York. They took great pains with these oysters. They cleaned the empty shells and bottom trash off the beds that they put them on, and they spread them out as evenly as possible. Handled this way, oysters grew faster than they did all scrouged together on natural beds. Also, they grew more uniform in size and shape. Also, they had a better flavor. Also, they brought higher prices, premium prices. The center of the business was the little town of Prince's Bay, over on the outside shore.

"At first, the Staten Islanders used sloops and bought their seed stock close by, in bays in New Jersey and Long Island, but the business grew very fast, and in a few years a good many of them were using schooners that could hold five thousand bushels and were making regular trips to Maryland and Virginia. Some went into inlets along the ocean side of the Eastern Shore, and some went into Chesapeake Bay. They bought from local oystermen who worked natural beds in the public domain, and they usually had to visit a whole string of little ports and landings before they got a load. At that time, there were quite a few free Negroes among the oystermen on the Eastern Shore, especially in Worcester County, Maryland, on the upper part of Chincoteague Bay, and the Staten Island captains occasionally hired gangs of them to make the trip North and help distribute the oysters on the beds. Now and then, a few would stay behind on Staten Island for a season or two and work on empty beds, cleaning them off and getting them ready for new seed stock. Late in the eighteen-thirties or early in the eighteen-forties, a number of these men left their homes in and around Snow Hill, Maryland, the county seat of Worcester County, and came up to Staten Island to live. They brought their families, and they settled over here in the Sandy Ground section. The land was cheap in Sandy Ground, and it was in easy walking distance of Prince's Bay, and a couple of Negro families were already living over here, a family named Jackson and a family named Henry. The records of our church go back to 1850, and they show the names of most of the original men from Snow Hill. Three of them were Purnells—

Isaac Purnell, George Purnell, and Littleton Purnell. Two were Lambdens, spelled L-a-m-b-d-e-n, only their descendants changed the spelling to L-a-n-d-i-n—Landin. One was a Robbins, and one was a Bishop, and one was a Henman. The Robbins family died out or moved away many years ago, but Purnells, Landins, Bishops, and Henmans still live in Sandy Ground. They've always been the main Sandy Ground families. There's a man from Sandy Ground who works for a trucking concern in New York, drives trailer trucks, and he's driven through Maryland many times, and stopped in Snow Hill, and he says there's still people down there with these names, plenty of them, white and Negro. Especially Purnells and Bishops. Every second person you run into in Snow Hill, just about, he says, is either a Purnell or a Bishop, and there's one little crossroad town near Snow Hill that's named Bishop and another one that's named Bishopville. Through the years, other Negro families came to Sandy Ground and settled down and intermarried with the families from Snow Hill. Some came from the South, but the majority came from New York and New Jersey and other places in the North. Such as the Harris family, the Mangin family, the Fish family, the Williams family, the Finney family, and the Roach family."

All of a sudden, Mr. Hunter leaned forward in his chair as far as he could go and brought the fly swatter down on the table. This time, he killed the fly.

"I wasn't born in Sandy Ground myself," he continued. "I came here when I was a boy. My mother and my stepfather brought me here. Two or three of the original men from Snow Hill were still around then, and I knew them. They were old, old men. They were as old as I am now. And the widows of several others were still around. Two of those old widows lived near us, and they used to come to see my mother and sit by the kitchen range and talk and talk, and I used to like to listen to them. The main thing they talked about was the early days in Sandy Ground—how poor everybody had been, and how hard everybody had had to work, the men and the women. The men all worked by the day for the white oystermen in Prince's Bay. They went out in skiffs and anchored over the beds and stood up in the skiffs from sunup to sundown, raking oysters off the bottom with big old clawtoothed rakes that were made of iron and weighed fourteen pounds and had handles on them twenty-four feet long. The women all washed. They washed for white women in Prince's Bay and Rossville and Tottenville. And there wasn't a real house in the whole of Sandy Ground. Most of the families lived in one-room shacks with lean-tos for the children. In the summer, they ate what they grew in their gardens. In the winter, they ate oysters until they couldn't stand the sight of them.

"When I came here, early in the eighteen-eighties, that had all changed. By that time, Sandy Ground was really quite a prosperous little place. Most of the men were still breaking their backs raking oysters by the day, but several of them had saved their money and worked up to where they owned and operated pretty good-sized oyster sloops and didn't take orders from anybody. Old Mr. Dawson Landin was the first to own a sloop. He owned a forty-footer named the *Pacific*. He was the richest man in the settlement, and he took the lead in everything. Still and all, people liked him and looked up to him; most of us called him Uncle Daws. His brother, Robert Landin, owned a thirty-footer named the *Independence,* and Mr. Robert's son-in-law, Francis Henry, also owned a thirty-footer. His was named the *Fanny Fern*. And a few others owned sloops. There were still some places here and there in the Arthur Kill and the Kill van Kull where you could rake up natural-growth seed oysters if you spliced two rake handles together and went down deep enough, and that's what these men did. They sold the seed to the white oystermen, and they made out all right. In those days, the oyster business used oak baskets by the thousands, and some of the Sandy Ground men had got to be good basket-makers. They went into the woods around here and cut white-oak saplings and split them into strips and soaked the strips in water and wove them into bushel baskets that would last for years. Also, several of the men had become blacksmiths. They made oyster rakes and repaired them, and did all kinds of ironwork for the boats.

"The population of Sandy Ground was bigger then than it is now, and the houses were newer and nicer-looking. Every family owned the house they lived in, and a little bit of land. Not much—an acre and a half, two acres, three acres. I guess Uncle Daws had the most, and he only had three and three-quarter acres. But what they had, they made every inch of it count. They raised a few pigs and chickens, and kept a cow, and had some fruit trees and grapevines, and planted a garden. They planted a lot of Southern stuff, such as butter beans and okra and sweet potatoes and mustard greens and collards and Jerusalem artichokes. There were flowers in every yard, and rose-bushes, and the old women exchanged seeds and bulbs and cuttings with each other. Back then, this was a big strawberry section. The soil in Sandy Ground is ideal for strawberries. All the white farmers along Bloomingdale Road grew them, and the people in Sandy Ground took it up; you can grow a lot of strawberries on an acre. In those days, a river steamer left New Brunswick, New Jersey, every morning, and came down the Raritan River and entered the Arthur Kill and made stops at Rossville and five or six other little towns on the kill, and then went on up to the city and docked at the foot of Barclay Street, right across from Washington Market. And early every morning during strawberry season the people would box up their strawberries and take them down to Rossville and put them on a steamer and send them off to market. They'd lay a couple of grape leaves on top of each box, and that would bring out the beauty of the berries, the green against the red. Staten Island straw-berries had the reputation of being unusually good, the best on the market, and they brought fancy prices. Most of them went to the big New York hotels. Some of the families in Sandy Ground, straw-berries were about as important to them as oysters. And every family put up a lot of stuff, not only garden stuff, but wild stuff—wild-grape jelly, and wild-plum jelly, and huckleberries. If it was a good huckleberry year, they'd put up enough huckleberries to make deep-dish pies all winter. And when they killed their hogs, they made link sausages and liver pudding and lard. Some of the old women even made soap. People looked after things in those days. They patched and mended and made do, and they kept their yards clean, and they burned their trash. And they taught their children how to conduct themselves. And they held their heads up; they were as good as anybody, and better than some. And they got along with each other; they knew each other's peculiarities and took them into consideration. Of course, this was an oyster town, and there was always an element that drank and carried on and didn't have any more moderation than the cats up the alley, but the great majority were good Christians who walked in the way of the Lord, and loved Him, and trusted Him, and kept His commandments. Everything in Sandy Ground revolved around the church. Every summer, we put up a tent in the churchyard and held a big camp meeting, a revival. We owned the tent. We could get three or four hundred people under it, sitting on sawhorse benches. We'd have visiting preachers, famous old-time African Methodist preachers, and they'd preach every night for a week. We'd invite the white oystermen to come and bring their families, and a lot of them would. Everybody was welcome. And once a year, to raise money for church upkeep, we'd put on an ox roast, what they call a barbecue nowadays. A Southern man named Steve Davis would do the roasting. There were tricks to it that only he knew. He'd dig a pit in the churchyard, and then a little off to one side he'd burn a pile of hickory logs until he had a big bed of red-hot coals, and then he'd fill the pit about half full of coals, and then he'd set some iron rods across the pit, and then he'd lay a couple of sides of beef on the rods and let them roast. Every now and then, he'd shovel some more coals into the pit, and then he'd turn the sides of beef and baste them with pepper sauce, or whatever it was he had in that bottle of his, and the beef would drip and sputter and sizzle, and the smoke from the hickory coals would flavor it to perfection. People all over the South Shore would set aside that day and come to the African Methodist ox roast. All the big oyster captains in Prince's Bay would come. Captain Phil De Waters would come, and Captain Abraham Manee and Captain William Haughwout and Captain Peter Polworth and good old Captain George Newbury, and a dozen others. And we'd eat and laugh and joke with each other over who could hold the most.

"All through the eighties, and all through the nineties, and right on up to around 1910, that's the way it was in Sandy Ground. Then the water went bad. The oystermen had known for a long time that the water in the Lower Bay was getting dirty, and they used to talk about it, and worry about it, but they didn't have any idea how bad it was until around 1910, when reports began to circulate that cases of typhoid fever had been traced to the eating of Staten Island oysters. The oyster wholesalers in New York were the unseen powers in the Staten Island oyster business; they advanced the money to build boats and buy Southern seed stock. When the typhoid talk got started, most of them decided they didn't want to risk their money any more, and the business went into a decline, and then, in 1916, the Department of Health stepped in and condemned the beds, and that was that. The men in Sandy Ground had to scratch around and look for something else to do, and it wasn't easy. Mr. George Ed Henman got a job working on a garbage wagon for the city, and Mr. James McCoy became the janitor of a public school, and Mr. Jacob Finney went to work as a porter on Ellis Island, and one did this and one did that. A lot of the life went out of the settlement, and a kind of don't-care attitude set in. The church was especially hard hit. Many of the young men and women moved away, and several whole families, and the membership went down. The men who owned oyster sloops had been the main support of the church, and they began to give dimes where they used to give dollars. Steve Davis died, and it turned out nobody else knew how to roast an ox, so we had to give up the ox roasts. For some years, we put on clambakes instead, and then clams got too dear, and we had to give up the clambakes.

"The way it is now, Sandy Ground is just a ghost of its former self. There's a disproportionate number of old people. A good many of the big old rambling houses that used to be full of children, there's only old men and old women living in them now. And you hardly ever see them. People don't sit on their porches in Sandy Ground as much as they used to, even old people, and they don't do much visiting. They sit inside, and keep to themselves, and listen to the radio or look at television. Also, in most of the families in Sandy Ground where the husband and wife are young or middle-aged, both of them go off to work. If there's children, a grandmother or an old aunt or some other relative stays home and looks after them. And they have to travel good long distances to get to their work. The women mainly work in hospitals, such as Sea View, the big t.b. hospital way up in the middle of the island, and I hate to think of the time they put in riding those rattly old Staten Island buses and standing at bus stops in all kinds of weather. The men mainly work in construction, or in factories across the kill in New Jersey. You hear their cars starting up early in the morning, and you hear them coming in late at night. They make eighty, ninety, a hundred a week, and they take all the overtime work they can get; they have to, to pay for those big cars and refrigerators and television sets. Whenever something new comes out, if one family gets one, the others can't rest until they get one too. And the only thing they pay cash for is candy bars. For all I know, they even buy them on the installment plan. It'll all end in a mess one of these days. The church has gone way down. People say come Sunday they're just too tired to stir. Most of the time, only a handful of the old reliables show up for Sunday-morning services, and we've completely given up Sunday-evening services. Oh, sometimes a wedding or a funeral will draw a crowd. As far as gardens, nobody in Sandy Ground plants a garden any more beyond some old woman might set out a few tomato plants and half the time she forgets about them and lets them wilt. As far as wild stuff, there's plenty of huckleberries in the woods around here, high-bush and low-bush, and oceans of blackberries, and I even know where there's some beach plums, but do you think anybody bothers with them? Oh, no!"

MR. HUNTER STOOD UP. "I've rested long enough," he said. "Let's go on over to the cemetery." He went down the back steps, and I followed him. He looked under the porch and brought out a grub hoe and handed it to me. "We may need this," he said. "You take it, if you don't mind, and go on around to the front of the house. I'll go back inside and lock up, and I'll meet you out front in just a minute."

I went around to the front, and looked at the roses on the trellised bush beside the porch. They were lush pink roses. It was a hot afternoon, and when Mr. Hunter came out, I was surprised to see that he had put on a jacket, and a double-breasted jacket at that. He had also put on a black necktie and a black felt hat. They were undoubtedly his Sunday clothes, and he looked stiff and solemn in them.

"I was admiring your rosebush," I said.

"It does all right," said Mr. Hunter. "It's an old bush. When it was getting a start, I buried bones from the table around the roots of it, the way the old Southern women used to do. Bones are the best fertilizer in the world for rosebushes." He took the hoe and put it across his shoulder, and we started up Bloomingdale Road. We walked in the road; there are no sidewalks in Sandy Ground.

A little way up the road, we overtook an old man hobbling along on a cane. He and Mr. Hunter spoke to each other, and Mr. Hunter introduced me to him. "This is Mr. William E. Brown," Mr. Hunter said. "He's one of the old Sandy Ground oystermen. He's in his eighties, but he's younger than me. How are you, Mr. Brown?"

"I'm just hanging by a thread," said Mr. Brown.

"Is it as bad as that?" asked Mr. Hunter

"Oh, I'm all right," said Mr. Brown, "only for this numbness in my legs, and I've got cataracts and can't half see, and I had a dentist make me a set of teeth and he says they fit, but they don't, they slip, and I had double pneumonia last winter and the doctor gave me some drugs that addled me. And I'm still addled."

"This is the first I've seen you in quite a while," said Mr. Hunter.

"I stay to myself," said Mr. Brown. "I was never one to go to people's houses. They talk and talk, and you listen, you bound to listen, and half of it ain't true, and the next time they tell it, they say you said it."

"Well, nice to see you, Mr. Brown," said Mr. Hunter.

"Nice to see you, Mr. Hunter," said Mr. Brown. "Where you going?"

"Just taking a walk over to the cemetery," said Mr. Hunter.

"Well, you won't get in any trouble over there," said Mr. Brown. We resumed our walk.

"Mr. Brown came to Sandy Ground when he was a boy, the same as I did," Mr. Hunter said. "He was born in Brooklyn, but his people were from the South."

"Were you born in the South, Mr. Hunter?" I asked.

"No, I wasn't," he said.

His face became grave, and we walked past three or four houses before he said any more.

"I wasn't," he finally said. "My mother was. To tell you the truth, my mother was born in slavery. Her name was Martha, Martha Jennings, and she was born in the year 1849. Jennings was the name of the man who owned her. He was a big farmer in the Shenandoah Valley in Virginia. He also owned my mother's mother, but he sold her when my mother was five years old, and my mother never saw or heard of her again. Her name was Hettie. We couldn't ever get much out of my mother about slavery days. She didn't like to talk about it, and she didn't like for us to talk about it. 'Let the dead bury the dead,' she used to say. Just before the Civil War, when my mother was eleven or twelve, the wife of the man who owned her went to Alexandria, Virginia, to spend the summer, and she took my mother along to attend to her children. Somehow or other, my mother got in with some people in Alexandria who helped her run away. Some antislavery people. She never said so in so many words, but I guess they put her on the Underground Railroad. Anyway, she wound up in what's now Ossining, New York, only then it was called the village of Sing Sing, and by and by she married my father. His name was Henry Hunter, and he was a hired man on an apple farm just outside Sing Sing. She had fifteen children by him, but only three—me, my brother William, and a girl named Hettie—lived past the age of fourteen; most of them died when they were babies. My father died around 1879, 1880, somewhere in there. A few months after he died, a man named Ephraim Purnell rented a room in our house. Purnell was an oysterman from Sandy Ground. He was a son of old man Littleton Purnell, one of the original men from Snow Hill. He had got into some trouble in Prince's Bay connected with stealing, and had been sent to Sing Sing Prison. After he served out his sentence, he decided he'd see if he could get a job in Sing Sing village and live there. My mother tried to help him, and ended up marrying him. He couldn't get a job up there, nobody would have him, so he brought my mother and me and William and Hettie down here to Sandy Ground and he went back to oystering."

We turned off Bloomingdale Road and entered Crabtree Avenue, which is a narrow dirt road lined on one side with sassafras trees and on the other with a straggly privet hedge.

"I didn't like my stepfather," Mr. Hunter continued. "I not only didn't like him, I despised him. He was a drunkard, a sot, and he mistreated my mother. From the time we landed in Sandy Ground, as small as I was, my main object in life was to support myself. I didn't want him supporting me. And I didn't want to go into the oyster business, because he was in it. I worked for a farmer down the road a few years—one of the Sharrotts that Sharrott's Road is named for. Then I cooked on a fishing boat. Then I became a hod carrier. Then something got into me, and I began to drink. I turned into a sot myself. After I had been drinking several years, I was standing in a grocery store in Rossville one day, and I saw my mother walk past outside on the street. I just caught a glimpse of her face through the store window as she walked past, and she didn't know anybody was looking at her, and she had a horrible hopeless look on her face. A week or so later, I knocked off work in the middle of the day and bought a bottle of whiskey, the way I sometimes did, and I went out in the woods between Rossville and Sandy Ground and sat down on a rock, and I was about as low in my mind as a man can be; I knew what whiskey was doing to me, and yet I couldn't stop drinking it. I tore the stamp off the bottle and pulled out the cork, and got ready to take a drink, and then I remembered the look on my mother's face, and a peculiar thing happened. The best way I can explain it, my gorge rose. I got mad at myself, and I got mad at the world. Instead of taking a drink, I poured the whiskey on the ground and smashed the bottle on the rock, and stood up and walked out of the woods. And I never drank another drop. I wanted to many a time, many and many a time, but I tightened my jaw against myself, and I stood it off. When I look back, I don't know how I did it, but I stood it off, I stood it off."

We walked on in silence for a few minutes, and then Mr. Hunter sighed and said, "Ah, well!"

"From being a hod carrier, I became a bricklayer," he continued, "but that wasn't as good as it sounds; bricklayers didn't make much in those days. And in 1896, when I was twenty-seven, I got married to my first wife. Her name was Celia Ann Finney, and she was the daughter of Mr. Jacob Finney, one of the oystermen. She was considered the prettiest girl in Sandy Ground, and the situation I was in, she had turned down a well-to-do young oysterman to marry me, a fellow with a sloop, and I knew everybody thought she had made a big mistake and would live to regret it, and I vowed and determined I was going to give her more than he could've given her. I was a good bricklayer, and I was especially good at arching and vaulting, and when a contractor or a boss mason had a cesspool to be built, he usually put me to work on it. We didn't have sewers down in this part of Staten Island, and still don't, and there were plenty of cesspools to be built. So, in 1899 I borrrowed some money and went into business for myself, the business of building and cleaning cesspools. I made it my lifework. And I made good money, for around here. I built a good house for my wife, and I dressed her in the latest styles. I went up to New York once and bought her a dress for Easter that cost one hundred and six dollars; the six dollars was for alterations. And one Christmas I bought her a sealskin coat. And I bought pretty hats for her—velvet hats, straw hats, hats with feathers, hats with birds, hats with veils. And she appreciated everything I bought for her. 'Oh, George,' she'd say, 'you've gone too far this time. You've got to take it back.' 'Take it back, nothing!' I'd say. When Victrolas came out, I bought her the biggest one in the store. And I think I can safely say we set the best table in Sandy Ground. I lived in peace and harmony with her for thirty-two years, and they were the best years of my life. She died in 1928. Cancer. Two years later I married a widow named Mrs. Edith S. Cook. She died in 1938. They told me it was tumors, but it was cancer."

We came to a break in the privet hedge. Through the break I saw the white shapes of gravestones half-hidden in vines and scrub, and realized that we were at the entrance to the cemetery. "Here we are," said Mr. Hunter. He stopped, and leaned on the handle of the hoe, and continued to talk.

"I had one son by my first wife," he said. "We named him William Francis Hunter, and we called him Billy. When he grew up, Billy went into the business with me. I never urged him to, but he seemed to want to, it was his decision, and I remember how proud I was the first time I put it in the telephone book—George H. Hunter & Son. Billy did the best he could, I guess, but things never worked out right for him. He got married, but he lived apart from his wife, and he drank. When he first began to drink, I remembered my own troubles along that line, and I tried not to see it. I just looked the other way, and hoped and prayed he'd get hold of himself, but there came a time I couldn't look the other way any more. I asked him to stop, and I begged him to stop, and I did all I could, went to doctors for advice, tried this, tried that, but he wouldn't stop. It wasn't exactly he wouldn't stop, he couldn't stop. A few years ago, his stomach began to bother him. He thought he had an ulcer, and he started drinking more than ever—said whiskey dulled the pain. I finally got him to go to the hospital, and it wasn't any ulcer, it was cancer."

Mr. Hunter took a wallet from his hip pocket. It was a large, old-fashioned wallet, the kind that fastens with a strap slipped through a loop. He opened it and brought out a folded white silk ribbon.

"Billy died last summer," he continued. "After I had made the funeral arrangements, I went to the florist in Tottenville and ordered a floral wreath and picked out a nice wreath-ribbon to go on it. The florist knew me, and he knew Billy, and he made a very pretty wreath. The Sunday after Billy was buried, I walked over here to the cemetery to look at his grave, and the flowers on the wreath were all wilted and dead, but the ribbon was as pretty as ever, and I couldn't bear to let it lay out in the rain and rot, so I took it off and saved it." He unfolded the ribbon and held it up. Across it, in gold letters, were two words. "BELOVED SON," they said.

MR. HUNTER REFOLDED THE RIBBON and returned it to his wallet. Then he put the hoe back on his shoulder, and we entered the cemetery. A little road went halfway into the cemetery, and a number of paths branched off from it, and both the road and the paths were hip-deep in broom sedge. Here and there in the sedge were patches of Queen Anne's lace and a weed that I didn't recognize. I pointed it out to Mr. Hunter.

"What is that weed in among the broom sedge and the Queen Anne's lace?" I asked.

"We call it red root around here," he said, "and what you call broom sedge we call beard grass, and what you call Queen Anne's lace we call wild carrot."

We started up the road, but Mr. Hunter almost immediately turned in to one of the paths and stopped in front of a tall marble gravestone, around which several kinds of vines and climbing plants were intertwined. I counted them, and there were exactly ten kinds—cat brier, trumpet creeper, wild hop, blackberry, morning glory, climbing false buckwheat, partridgeberry, fox grape, poison ivy, and one that I couldn't identify, nor could Mr. Hunter. "This is Uncle Daws Landin's grave," Mr. Hunter said. "I'm going to chop down some of this mess, so we can read the dates on his stone." He lifted the hoe high in the air and brought it down with great vigor, and I got out of his way. I went back into the road, and looked around me. The older graves were covered with trees and shrubs. Sassafras and honey locust and wild black cherry were the tallest, and they were predominant, and beneath them were chokeberry, bayberry, sumac, Hercules' club, spice bush, sheep laurel, hawthorn, and witch hazel. A scattering of the newer graves were fairly clean, but most of them were thickly covered with weeds and wild flowers and ferns. There were scores of kinds. The majority were the common kinds that grow in waste places and in dumps and in vacant lots and in old fields and beside roads and ditches and railroad tracks, and I could recognize them at a glance. Among these were milkweed, knotweed, ragweed, Jimson weed, pavement weed, catchfly, Jerusalem oak, bedstraw, goldenrod, cocklebur, butter-and-eggs, dandelion, bouncing Bet, mullein, partridge pea, beggar's-lice, sandspur, wild garlic, wild mustard, wild geranium, rabbit tobacco, old-field cinquefoil, bracken, New York fern, cinnamon fern, and lady fern. A good many of the others were unfamiliar to me, and I broke off the heads and upper branches of a number of these and stowed them in the pockets of my jacket, to look at later under a magnifying glass. Some of the graves had rusty iron-pipe fences around them. Many were unmarked, but were outlined with sea shells or bricks or round stones painted white or flowerpots turned upside down. Several had fieldstones at the head and foot. Several had wooden stakes at the head and foot. Several had Spanish bayonets growing on them. The Spanish bayonets were in full bloom, and little flocks of white moths were fluttering around their white, waxy, fleshy, bell-shaped, pendulous blossoms.

"Hey, there!" Mr. Hunter called out. "I've got it so we can see to read it now." I went back up the path, and we stood among the wrecked vines and looked at the inscription on the stone. It read:

DAWSON LANDIN
DEC. 18, 1828
FEB. 21, 1899
ASLEEP IN JESUS

"I remember him well," said Mr. Hunter. "He was a smart old man and a good old man—big and stout, very religious, passed the plate in church, chewed tobacco, took the New York *Herald,* wore a captain's cap, wore suspenders *and* a belt, had a peach orchard. I even remember the kind of peach he had in his orchard. It was a freestone peach, a late bearer, and the name of it was Stump the World."

We walked a few steps up the path, and came to a smaller gravestone. The inscription on it read:

SUSAN A. WALKER
MAR. 10, 1855
MAR. 25, 1912
A FAITHFUL FRIEND

"Born in March, died in March," said Mr. Hunter. "Fifty-seven years and fifteen days, as well as I can figure it out in my head. 'A Faithful Friend.' That hardly seems the proper thing to pick out and mention on a gravestone. Susan Walker was one of Uncle Daws Landin's daughters, and she was a good Christian woman. She did more for the church than any other woman in the history of Sandy Ground. Now, that's strange. I don't remember a thing about Uncle Daws Landin's funeral, and he must've had a big one, but I remember Susan Walker's funeral very well. There used to be a white man named Charlie Bogardus who ran a store at the corner of Woodrow Road and Bloomingdale Road, a general store, and he also had an icehouse, and he was also an undertaker. He was the undertaker for most of the country people around here, and he got some of the Rossville business and some of the Pleasant Plains business. He had a handsome old horse-drawn hearse. It had windows on both sides, so you could see the coffin, and it had silver fittings. Bogardus handled Susan Walker's funeral. I can still remember his two big black hearse-horses drawing the hearse up Bloomingdale Road, stepping just as slow, the way they were trained to do, and turning in to Crabtree Avenue, and proceeding on down to the cemetery. The horses had black plumes on their harnesses. Funerals were much sadder when they had horse-drawn hearses. Charlie Bogardus had a son named Charlie Junior, and Charlie Junior had a son named Willie, and when automobile hearses started coming in, Willie mounted the old hearse on an automobile chassis. It didn't look fish, fowl, or fox, but the Bogarduses kept on using it until they finally gave up the store and the icehouse and the undertaking business and moved away."

We left Susan Walker's grave and returned to the road and entered another path and stopped before one of the newer graves. The inscription on its stone read:

FREDERICK ROACH
1891–1955
REST IN PEACE

"Freddie Roach was a taxi-driver," Mr. Hunter said. "He drove a taxi in Pleasant Plains for many years. He was Mrs. Addie Roach's son, and she made her home with him. After he died, she moved in with one of her daughters. Mrs. Addie Roach is the oldest woman in Sandy Ground. She's the widow of Reverend Lewis Roach, who was an oysterman and a part-time preacher, and she's ninety-two years old. When I first came to Sandy Ground, she was still in her teens, and she was a nice, bright, pretty girl. I've known her all these years, and I think the world of her. Every now and then, I make her a lemon-meringue pie and take it to her, and sit with her awhile. There's a white man in Prince's Bay who's a year or so older than Mrs. Roach. He's ninety-three, and he'll soon be ninety-four. His name is Mr. George E. Sprague, and he comes from a prominent old South Shore family, and I believe he's the last of the old Prince's Bay oyster captains. I hadn't seen him for several years until just the other day I was over in Prince's Bay, and I was going past his house on Amboy Road, and I saw him sitting on the porch. I went up and spoke to him, and we talked awhile, and when I was leaving he said, 'Is Mrs. Addie Roach still alive over in Sandy Ground?' 'She is,' I said. 'That is,' I said, 'she's alive as you or I.' 'Well,' he said, 'Mrs. Roach and I go way back. When she was a young woman, her mother used to wash for my mother, and she used to come along sometimes and help, and she was such a cheerful, pretty person my mother always said it made the day nicer when she came, and that was over seventy years ago.' 'That wasn't her mother that washed for your mother and she came along to help,' I said. 'That was her husband's mother. That was old Mrs. Matilda Roach.' 'Is that so?' said Mr. Sprague. 'I always thought it was her mother. Well,' he said, 'when you see her, tell her I asked for her.' "

We stepped back into the road, and walked slowly up it.

"Several men from Sandy Ground fought in the Civil War," Mr. Hunter said, "and one of them was Samuel Fish. That's his grave over there with the ant hill on it. He got a little pension. Down at the end of this row are some Bishop graves, Bishops and Mangins, and there's Purnells in the next row, and there's Henmans in those big plots over there. This is James McCoy's grave. He came from

Norfolk, Virginia. He had six fingers on his right hand. Those graves over there all grown up in cockleburs are Jackson graves, Jacksons and Henrys and Landins. Most of the people lying in here were related to each other, some by blood, some by marriage, some close, some distant. If you started in at the gate and ran an imaginary line all the way through, showing who was related to who, the line would zigzag all over the cemetery. Do you see that row of big expensive stones standing up over there? They're all Cooleys. The Cooleys were free-Negro oystermen from Gloucester County, Virginia, and they came to Staten Island around the same time as the people from Snow Hill. They lived in Tottenville, but they belonged to the church in Sandy Ground. They were quite well-to-do. One of them, Joel Cooley, owned a forty-foot sloop. When the oyster beds were condemned, he retired on his savings and raised dahlias. He was a member of the Staten Island Horticultural Society, and his dahlias won medals at flower shows in Madison Square Garden. I've heard it said he was the first man on Staten Island to raise figs, and now there's fig bushes in back yards from one end of the island to the other. Joel Cooley had a brother named Obed Cooley who was very smart in school, and the Cooleys got together and sent him to college. They sent him to the University of Michigan, and he became a doctor. He practiced in Lexington, Kentucky, and he died in 1937, and he left a hundred thousand dollars. There used to be a lot of those old-fashioned names around here, Bible names. There was a Joel and an Obed and an Eben in the Cooley family, and there was an Ishmael and an Isaac and an Israel in the Purnell family. Speaking of names, come over here and look at this stone."

We stopped before a stone whose inscription read:

THOMAS WILLIAMS

AL MAJOR

1862–1928

"There used to be a rich old family down here named the Butlers," Mr. Hunter said. "They were old, old Staten Islanders, and they had a big estate over on the outside shore, between Prince's Bay and Tottenville, that they called Butler Manor. They even had a private race track. The last of the Butlers was Mr. Elmer T. Butler. Now, this fellow Thomas Williams was a Sandy Ground man who quit the oyster business and went to work for Mr. Elmer T. Butler. He worked for him many years, worked on the grounds, and Mr. Butler thought a lot of him. For some reason I never understood, Mr. Butler called him Al Major, a kind of nickname. And pretty soon everybody called him Al Major. In fact, as time went on and he got older, young people coming up took it for granted Al Major was his real name and called him Mr. Major. When he died, Mr. Butler buried him. And when he ordered the gravestone, he told the monument company to put both names on it, so there wouldn't be any confusion. Of course, in a few years he'll pass out of people's memory under both names—Thomas Williams, Al Major, it'll all be the same. To tell you the truth, I'm no great believer in grave-stones. To a large extent, I think they come under the heading of what the old preacher called vanity—'vanity of vanities, all is vanity'—and by the old preacher I mean Ecclesiastes. There's stones in here that've only been up forty or fifty years, and you can't read a thing it says on them, and what difference does it make? God keeps His eye on those that are dead and buried the same as He does on those that are alive and walking. When the time comes the dead are raised, He won't need any directions where they're lying. Their bones may be turned to dust, and weeds may be growing out of their dust, but they aren't lost. He knows where they are; He knows the exact whereabouts of every speck of dust of every one of them. Stones rot the same as bones rot, and nothing endures but the spirit."

Mr. Hunter turned and looked back over the rows of graves.

"It's a small cemetery," he said, "and we've been burying in it a long time, and it's getting crowded, and there's generations to come, and it worries me. Since I'm the chairman of the board of trustees, I'm in charge of selling graves in here, graves and plots, and I always try to encourage families to bury two to a grave. That's perfectly legal, and a good many cemeteries are doing it nowadays. All the law says, it specifies that the top of the box containing the coffin shall be at least three feet below the level of the ground. To speak plainly, you dig the grave eight feet down, instead of six feet down, and that leaves room to lay a second coffin on top of the first. Let's go to the end of this path, and I'll show you my plot."

Mr. Hunter's plot was in the last row, next to the woods. There were only a few weeds on it. It was the cleanest plot in the cemetery.

"My mother's buried in the first grave," he said. "I never put up a stone for her. My first wife's father, Jacob Finney, is buried in this one, and I didn't put up a stone for him, either. He didn't own a grave, so we buried him in our plot. My son Billy is buried in this grave. And this is my first wife's grave. I put up a stone for her."

The stone was small and plain, and the inscription on it read:

HUNTER
1877 CELIA 1928

"I should've had her full name put on it—Celia Ann," Mr. Hunter said. "She was a little woman, and she had a low voice. She had the prettiest little hands; she wore size five-and-a-half gloves. She was little, but you'd be surprised at the work she done. Now, my second wife is buried over here, and I put up a stone for her, too. And I had my name carved on it, along with hers."

This stone was the same size and shape as the other, and the inscription on it read:

HUNTER
1877 EDITH 1938
1869 GEORGE

"It was my plan to be buried in the same grave with my second wife," Mr. Hunter said. "When she died, I was sick in bed, and the doctor wouldn't let me get up, even to go to the funeral, and I couldn't attend to things the way I wanted to. At that time, we had a gravedigger here named John Henman. He was an old man, an old oysterman. He's dead now himself. I called John Henman to

535

my bedside, and I specifically told him to dig the grave eight feet down. I told him I wanted to be buried in the same grave. 'Go eight feet down,' I said to him, 'and that'll leave room for me, when the time comes.' And he promised to do so. And when I got well, and was up and about again, I ordered this stone and had it put up. Below my wife's name and dates I had them put my name and my birth year. When it came time, all they'd have to put on it would be my death year, and everything would be in order. Well, one day about a year later I was talking to John Henman, and something told me he hadn't done what he had promised to do, so I had another man come over here and sound the grave with a metal rod, and just as I had suspected, John Henman had crossed me up; he had only gone six feet down. He was a contrary old man, and set in his ways, and he had done the way he wanted, not the way I wanted. He had always dug graves six feet down, and he couldn't change. That didn't please me at all. It outraged me. So, I've got my name on the stone on this grave, and it'll look like I'm buried in this grave."

He took two long steps, and stood on the next grave in the plot.

"Instead of which," he said, "I'll be buried over here in this grave."

He stooped down, and pulled up a weed. Then he stood up, and shook the dirt off the roots of the weed, and tossed it aside.

"Ah, well," he said, "it won't make any difference."

(1956)

# Dragger Captain

*T*HE BIGGEST FISHING FLEET in the vicinity of New York
City is a fleet of thirty wooden draggers that works out of Stonington,
Connecticut. Stonington is four local stops beyond New London on
the New York, New Haven & Hartford. In the winter, when the
trees are bare, a corner of its harbor can be glimpsed from a train.
It covers a rocky jut in the mouth of Fishers Island Sound, it is
close to fertile flounder grounds, it has two fish docks, and its
harbor, protected by three riprap breakwaters, is an unusually safe
one. Its population is approximately two thousand. There are elms
on its sidewalks. On four of its narrow streets—Water, Main,
Church, and Elm—are eight clapboard houses that were built in
the eighteenth century. The gardens in back yards are fenced with
discarded fish nets; some gardeners put seaweed under their tomatoes and skates and sculpin and other trash fishes under their
rosebushes. It is an old port, once rich and busy, that has declined;
from the Colonial period until the Civil War, it had shipyards, sail
lofts, a ropewalk, a forge that made harpoons, a ship-biscuit bakery,
and a whaling fleet, and it had a sealing fleet from around 1790
until around 1895. In the eighteen-seventies, this fleet brought in a
hundred thousand sealskins a year for coats and lap robes. Nathaniel
Brown Palmer, who discovered the Antarctic Continent, according
to one school of geographers, and for whom Palmer Land in the
Antarctic was named, and Edmund Fanning, who discovered the
Fanning Islands in the Pacific, were Stonington sealing captains; they
were looking for new seal rocks. Many of the draggermen are

descendants of whalers and sealers. One Stonington sealer, Mr. Ben Chesebrough, is still around. There is a drafty shack adjacent to Johnny Bindloss's fish dock, at the foot of a lane off Water Street, in which the draggermen kill time when it is too rough or foggy to go out on the grounds. They sit on upended lobster traps and read the *Atlantic Fisherman* and drink coffee and play poker and sharpen knives and grumble. On such days, Mr. Ben sometimes drops in and talks about his experiences as a seal skinner long ago in the Antarctic. In the early summer, herds of seals would come up on the beaches of islands in the Antarctic to breed and while they were breeding the skinners would creep out from behind rocks and brain them by the dozens as cleanly as possible with clubs made of polished Connecticut oak; bullets would have marred the skins.

Stonington and Fulton Fish Market are closely linked. Several of the oldest commission firms in the market were founded by fishermen who came down from Stonington to handle shipments from relatives and friends and then branched out. Sam and Amos Chesebro (originally Chesebrough; they dropped the last three letters to save ink and time), who founded Chesebro Brothers, Robbins & Graham, were Stonington men. This firm occupies Stall 1 and is the biggest firm down there. Sam and Amos had long lives. Sam was approaching ninety when he died. Amos died a few years after him, in December, 1946, lacking a month of reaching ninety-three. He spent his last fifteen years reading and meditating and dozing in a sunny apartment on an upper floor of a house in Brooklyn Heights, directly across the East River from the market; on clear mornings he sat at a living-room window with a glass of whiskey and water at his elbow and, as if looking back through time at his youth, peacefully watched through binoculars the turmoil on the market piers. Others from Stonington or close by who came down and founded firms, or became partners in ones already founded, were Hiram Burnett, Frank Noyes, A. E. Potter, George Moon, the Haley brothers, Caleb and Seabury, the Gates brothers, Stanton and Gurdon, and the Keeney brothers, Frank, Gideon, and George. The Stonington draggers catch twenty million pounds a year for Fulton Market. They go out primarily for flounders and they bring in five species—flukes, blackbacks, yellowtails, witches, and windowpanes—all of which differ in looks and flavor and all of which dishonestly appear on menus under the catchall culinary term "fillet of sole"; none of them belong to the sole family. Another species, the Baptist flounder, is caught in abundance but thrown back; it goes bad shortly after it comes out of the water, whence its name.

The Stonington draggers range from thirty to seventy feet. They are built wide for their length and about as close to the water as tugs. Half have gasoline engines, and the other half, the newer ones, have Diesels. Each has a cramped pilothouse. Each has a combined cabin and galley containing from two to six bunks, an oilcloth-covered table, two benches, and a coal cookstove, on which there is always a big, sooty pot of coffee. Each has a mast and a boom, from which the towropes to the net depend. Each has a winch for hoisting the loaded net aboard. Each has a fish hold and an ice bin. The Stonington draggers are well made and sturdy and are frequently overhauled. Even so, lined up at the docks, with their seaweedy nets hanging every which way from their booms to dry and with the harbor gulls fluttering down to snatch fish scraps off their decks, they always look gone to pot. They cost from ten to forty thousand dollars. A few are owned by absentees, but the majority are owned by their captains, or by their captains and crews, who are Portuguese, Italians, and old-stock Yankees. They fish off eastern Connecticut and western Rhode Island and on the coastal shelf south of Block Island in grounds known as the Mouth, the Yellow Bank, the Hell Hole, and the Mussel Bed, working chiefly in depths between sixty and a hundred and sixty feet. The crews prefer to stay on the grounds only one day at a time. They go out before dawn, weather permitting, and drag steadily all day, sorting and icing and barreling one haul while dragging for the next. They return at sundown and land their barrels, some at Bindloss's dock—once known as the Hancock dock, which dates back deep into sealing days—and the others at Tony Longo's dock, the old Steamboat Pier, which was used in times long past by the Stonington Line, whose side-wheel steamers ran daily between Stonington and New York. The barrels are loaded on trailer trucks owned by the proprietors of the docks and transported during the night to the stalls in Fulton Market. Occasionally, a dragger that has picked up an exceptionally heavy load does not go to its dock but makes an overnight run down Long Island Sound straight to the market. Stonington fish are among the freshest we get.

A dragger is a small trawler. The principal difference between the Stonington draggers and the trawlers that work out of Gloucester and Boston and New Bedford and stay on the Nova Scotian banks a week a trip is size. Trawlers are two and three times the size of draggers. Both use otter trawls, which are heavy, clumsy, wide-mouthed, cone-shaped nets that are slowly dragged over the bottom and take in all the fish in their paths. The otter trawl towed by a medium-sized Stonington dragger, a fifty-footer, is a hundred and ten feet long. The mouth is eighty feet wide but puckers up to half that width when fishing; it is kept open by two doors, or otter boards, which are about as big as house doors and are rigged at such an angle, one on each side, that the pressure of the water flares them out. Towing this net at two miles an hour, a dragger can strip the fish off ten acres of bottom in an hour. Otter trawls snag easily on obstructions, and a snagged trawl usually has to be abandoned. They are expensive; the smallest, even when rigged with homemade doors, costs a hundred dollars. A Stonington captain once snagged three in one morning; he went home and got in bed and stayed there until Sunday, when he showed up in church for the first time in years, exclaiming brokenly, as he walked up the aisle, "Pray for me! Pray for me!"

There are a great many shipwrecks, clumps of rocks, and other obstructions on the Stonington bottoms. The Hell Hole is the dirtiest. It is a ground of approximately six square miles in Block Island Sound, it is crisscrossed by coastwise shipping lanes, and there are two dozen wrecks lying in it, some of which always have rotting otter trawls hanging on them. Every now and then, after a gale or a hurricane has opened up a wreck and washed it out, a haul made in the Hell Hole is dumped on the deck of a dragger, and human bones—most often a skull or a pelvic bone; they seem to last the longest in salt water—are found among the fish. On the bottom of the Mussel Bed, a ground in the open ocean off Block Island, there is a group of immense beds of horse mussels, the lips of whose shells point upward and are jagged and sharp. Dragger captains must know the locations of these beds and keep acquainted with their endlessly changing contours, and they must take great pains to skirt them; a net that even grazes one will come up with scores of holes cut and chafed in its underside, through which the fish have escaped. This ground also contains some wrecks. One is a collier, the *Black Point,* which was torpedoed by a German submarine in May, 1945, in the last week of the European war. The submarine lies nearby; it was depth-bombed by a destroyer as it tried to get away. The Yellow Bank is a narrow ground that runs along the Rhode Island coast from the lighthouse at Watch Hill to Weekapaug Point, a distance of six miles, and its bottom is broken here and there by beds of sponges—elephant flop sponge, which grows in slippery yellow lumps the size of cabbages, and a limp, tentacular species called dead man's fingers. Both of them are worthless. These animals do not damage nets, but they clog them, and they have to be sorted out of hauls, one by one, and thrown back, a time-wasting task. Some time ago, a net that had been dragged into a sponge bed came up bearing two and a half barrels of fish messily mixed in among approximately fifteen barrels of sponges. In the Mouth, a ground at the mouth of the Thames River, below New London, there are rank patches of seaweed, predominantly bladder wrack, the black, bulby kind on which live lobsters are displayed in the windows of seafood restaurants, and these have to be dodged for the same reason. All these grounds except the Mouth were entered a number of times during the war by enemy submarines, and Army and Navy aircraft dropped hundreds of aerial depth bombs in them, particularly in the Mussel Bed. Some of the heavier bombs, mostly six-hundred-and-fifty-pounders, stuck in the mud and did not explode, and are lying there still. They will be a menace for years, like the German mines in French farm land. There are suspect areas in the Hell Hole and the Mussel Bed that are shunned by draggermen and spoken of as the bomb beds. In the old days, when a winch creaked and backfired as it began to hoist a net off the bottom, indicating an exceptionally heavy haul, crews were elated and someone always shouted, "Money in the bank!," but nowadays the noise of a straining winch makes them uneasy; the net might be heavy with flounders or it might have a bomb in it. Five draggers—the Carl F., the George A. Arthur, the Gertrude, the Marise, and the Nathaniel B. Palmer—have brought up bombs in their nets. The first four had their nets on deck before the bombs in them, hidden by fish, were discovered. Rather than attempt to dump them back, each went cautiously to the nearest dock, to which Navy bomb-disposal officers were summoned. The bomb caught by the fifth dragger, the Palmer, was plainly visible, but it exploded shortly after the net hove out of the water, while the crew stood staring at it, wondering what to do. It blasted the dragger and three of the four men in the crew to pieces; the fourth man was freakishly thrown clear.

Because of these hazards—rocks, wrecks, mussel beds, sponge beds, bladder wrack, and bombs—it is necessary for a dragger captain to have a picture in his mind of what lies beneath every possible foot of water in the grounds he works. A captain's standing among his colleagues and the amount of ice and oil he can get on credit from the dock proprietor are based on his knowledge of the bottoms and his thriftiness with gear, and not on the quantity of fish he catches. A raw captain may drag blindly and bring up huge hauls for a while, but sooner or later he will snag or mussel-cut so many nets that his overhead will eat up his profits. The most highly respected captain in the Stonington fleet is a sad-eyed, easygoing Connecticut Yankee named Ellery Franklin Thompson, a member of a family that has fished and clammed and crabbed and attended to lobster traps in these waters for three hundred years.

ELLERY—HE SAYS HE IS CALLED Captain Thompson or Mr. Thompson only by people who want to get something out of him— is captain and owner of the gasoline dragger Eleanor, which usually carries a crew of three, including himself. Ellery is forty-seven years old and has been a draggerman for thirty years. He has worked out of five Connecticut ports—New London, Groton, Noank, Mystic,

and Stonington, all of which are close together—and out of two
Rhode Island ports, Newport and Point Judith. Stonington has been
his home port since 1930. He keeps the *Eleanor* at Bindloss's dock,
but he lives in New London, fourteen miles away, and drives an
automobile to and fro. He lives in a four-gabled, shingle-sided, two-
story house on Crystal Avenue. His widowed mother, Mrs. Florence
Thompson, keeps house for him. He used to sleep in a woven-wire
bunk aboard the *Eleanor* and do his own cooking year in and year
out, going home only for Sundays, but in recent years, because of
rheumatism, he has got so he rests better in a bed. He says he has
discovered that home life has one disadvantage. He is a self-taught
B-flat-trumpet player. While living on the *Eleanor,* he spent many
evenings in the cabin by himself practicing hymns and patriotic
music. Sometimes, out on the grounds, if he had a few minutes to
kill, he would go below and practice. One afternoon, blundering
around the Hell Hole in a thick summer fog, he grew tired of
cranking the foghorn and got out his trumpet and stood on deck
and played "The Star-Spangled Banner" over and over, alarming
the crews of other draggers fogbound in the area, who thought an
excursion boat was bearing down on them. After he went back to
sleeping at home, he continued to practice in the evenings, but he
had to give it up before long because of its effect on his mother's
health. "At that time," he says, "I was working hard on three
hymns—'Up from the Grave He Arose,' 'There Is a Fountain Filled
with Blood,' and 'What a Friend We Have in Jesus.' I had 'What
a Friend' just about where I wanted it. One evening after supper,
I went in the parlor as usual and Ma was sitting on the settee reading
the *Ladies' Home Journal* and I took the easy chair and went to work
on 'What a Friend.' I was running through it the second or third
time when, all of a sudden, Ma bust out crying. I laid my trumpet
down and I asked her what in the world was the matter. 'That
trumpet's what's the matter,' Ma said. 'It makes me sad.' She said
it made her so sad she was having nightmares and losing weight.
Under the circumstances, I decided whatever trumpet practice I
did in the future, I would do it four or five miles out at sea."

Ellery is five feet nine. He is thin and rather frail. Aboard the

*Eleanor,* he wears knee boots, trousers that are leathery with fish blood and slime, a heavy plaid woolen shirt, a pea jacket, and a misshapen old flop-brim hat that always has some toothpicks and pencil stubs stuck in its band. He walks with a pronounced stoop, favoring his left shoulder, where the rheumatism has settled, and he takes his time. "If I start to hustle and bustle," he says, "everything I eat repeats and repeats." He abhors hurry; he thinks that humanity in general has got ahead of itself. He once threatened to fire a man in his crew because he worked too hard. Ellery's face is narrow and bony and, except for the sadness in his deep-set eyes, impassive. His ears stick out, he is long-nosed, and he has a mustache. His voice is nasal but pleasant, and his Adam's apple works when he talks. A woman in Stonington in her nineties, a town character, once told him that he had an old-fashioned face. "Men's faces nowadays are either empty or worried to death, like they're dreading something," she said. "You look the way the old Yankees around here looked when I was a girl."

"Don't fool yourself," Ellery said. "I guess I'm dreading something, too."

"What are you dreading, Ellery?" she asked.

Ellery shrugged his shoulders. "I don't know," he said. "I wish to God I did know."

Ellery is companionable but reserved. He often sits out a weathery day in the dock shack with other draggermen, listening with enjoyment to the trade gossip and the story-telling but saying little himself. When he does get into a talking mood, much of what he says is ironical. He is deeply skeptical. He once said that the older he gets the more he is inclined to believe that humanity is helpless. "I read the junk in the papers," he said, "and sometimes, like I'm eating in some eating joint and I can't help myself, I listen to the junk on the radio, and the way it looks to me, it's blind leading blind out of the frying pan into the fire, world without end. It's like me and Doc Clendening. There used to be a department in the New London *Day* called 'Diet and Health.' It was run by Dr. Logan Clendening, and he was always bright and cheerful. 'Keep smiling!' he'd say. 'Worry will kill you. A good hearty laugh,' he'd say, 'is the best medicine. If you've got high blood pressure, laugh! If you've got low blood pressure, laugh! The more you laugh, the longer you'll live.' When I was down in the dumps, I always enjoyed 'Diet and Health.' It was the first thing I'd turn to. It cheered me up. And then one day I picked up the paper and it said that 'Diet and Health' wouldn't appear no more because Dr. Clendening had cut his throat."

Two things are mainly responsible for Ellery's outlook: rheumatism and the depression. He is one of those who are unable to forget the depression. Fish prices were at rock bottom in the thirties, and draggermen had to take foolish risks and double and triple their production to barely get by. Ellery had one brother, Morris, six years younger, who was also a dragger captain. While working in a December gale off Newport in 1931, Morris was knocked senseless by a huge wave that broke on the deck of his dragger; the wave, receding, sucked him in, and he drowned. "He shouldn't have been out there," Ellery says, "but the poor boy had just started a family and prices were dropping and he was fighting hard to make a living." Ellery and his father and several friends of the family took the *Eleanor* out while the gale was still in progress and began to drag for Morris's body. On the morning of the third day, when they had almost decided to quit and go in, it came up in the net.

Ellery is about as self-sufficient as a man can be. He has no wife, no politics, and no religion. "I put off getting married until I got me a good big boat," he says. "When I got the boat and got it paid for, the depression struck. There's mighty few women that'll eat fish three times a day, and that's about all I had to offer. I kept putting it off until times got better. When times got better, I got the rheumatism. And a man in his middle forties with the chronic rheumatism, there's not much of the old Romeo left in him." Ellery is a member of only one organization. "I'm a Mason," he says. "Aside from that, the only thing I belong to is the human race." His father was a Republican and his mother is a Democrat; he says he has never put any dependence in either party and has never once voted for anybody. His family belongs to the Baptist Church; he says he has managed somehow to get along without it. "I enjoy hymns," he says. "I enjoy the old ones, the gloomy ones. I used to go to church just to hear the good old hymns, but the sermons finally drove me away."


ELLERY'S ANCESTORS on both sides—his mother was a Chapman—came from England in the sixteen-thirties and settled near the mouth of the Connecticut River, probably in the Saybrook Colony. Both families have stuck pretty close to the coast of eastern Connecticut, and the majority of the men have been fishermen, mariners, or shipwrights. Some were whalers and sealers. "I'm widely related," Ellery says, "but damn the benefit in that." Ellery was born in Mystic, which is five miles from Stonington. When he was around ten, the family moved to New London. He is one of four children, two of whom, Morris and an elder sister, Louise, are dead. Eleanor, a younger sister, is the wife of a switchman on the New Haven; the dragger *Eleanor* was named for her. Ellery's father, Frank Thompson, who died in 1936, was a fisherman, but he occasionally did other kinds of work. One year he was a quartermaster on a famous old Long Island Sound passenger steamer, the *City of Worcester;* another year he was a mate on an ocean-going tug, the Thames Tow Boat Company's *Minnie,* that towed coal barges from Norfolk, Virginia, to New London; during the Spanish-American War he was master of a patrol boat, the *Gypsy,* that guided ships through mine fields off the harbor of New London; and for a while he ran a ferry on the Thames, between Groton and New London; but he spent most of his life hand-lining and dragging in the Mouth. He was one of the first American fishermen to use the otter trawl, which is a British net. "Pa was a restless man, but a good man, a good provider," Ellery says. "He had one bad habit. He played the trombone. He could do nearly about as much damage with a trombone as I can with a trumpet."

Ellery's father kept his dragger, the *Florence,* a thirty-one-footer, which was named for Mrs. Thompson, at the Old Fish Dock in New London. "I spent the happiest days of my life on that dock," Ellery says. "It was a perfect place for a boy. It was right across the tracks from the New Haven station. If you got tired looking at boats, you could step over to the station and watch a freight highball through like a bat out of hell for Boston. I despised school. I don't mean I didn't like it. Oh, Jesus, I despised it. Whatever I learned in school, I learned a whole lot more down on the Old Fish Dock. Like Pa would drop a barrel in the water off the end of the dock and teach me how to harpoon a swordfish without getting my tail wound up in the line; the barrel would be the swordfish. Or some other man would teach me how to stick little wooden plugs in the hinges of lobsters' claws; that locks their claws, so they can't kill each other during shipment. I learned how to scale and gut, how to mend nets, how to read charts, how to cut a fishhook out of your hand, how to crate crabs, and how to tie all kinds of knots and bends and hitches and splices. There were some old, old fishermen on that dock. Some went down in the whale with Jonah, to hear them tell it. They didn't go out much any more. They mostly just sat around, hawking and spitting and God-damning everything in sight. They were full of old, handed-down secrets and sayings. I learned two things from them. I learned how to judge weather, and I learned how to take the good Lord's name in vain. Like all fish docks, this dock had a shack on it with a kerosene stove inside, and I learned how to make coffee. That's important. There's nobody so worthless as a fisherman who can't make a good, strong pot of coffee. In the summer, the Block Island steamer used one side of the fish dock. It met three trains a day. Back then, Block Island was a resort for the rich. If you weren't quite rich enough for Newport, you went to one of those big wooden hotels on Block Island. It was great fun to watch the people get on and off the steamer. Some days, like the Fourth, they'd have a band aboard. The first drunk woman I ever saw was an old sister they took off the Block Island steamer. She was white-haired, and she was so saturated she didn't know Jack from jump rope. Somebody's mother. It was a revelation to me. Around that time—I must've been eleven or twelve—there was a Greek café near the station and up above were rooms for rent, and sometimes I'd notice a woman sitting in the window of one of the rooms for rent; she'd crook a finger at some man passing below or give him a wink. I'd try my damnedest to figure that out. The facts of life. If the boats were out on the grounds and nothing doing on the dock, I'd sit in the shack and read Frank books. Oh, Jesus, I enjoyed Frank books. They were called the Gun Boat Series. There was 'Frank on a Gun Boat,' 'Frank Before Vicksburg,' 'Frank on the Lower Mississippi,' 'Frank in the Woods,' and 'Frank the Young Naturalist.' I've still got some Frank books on my dresser at home. Every so often, I get one down. You take 'Frank on the Lower Mississippi'—I bet I've read it thirty times. When I was sixteen, I got into first-year high school, but I couldn't stand it. I went to Pa and I told him, 'One more day of that mess—*amo, amas, amat*—just one more day, and I'll drown myself.' Pa said he guessed he'd sooner have an ignorant living son than a highly educated dead one, and next morning I went out on the grounds with him."

In 1920, after fishing with his father for several years, Ellery borrowed four thousand dollars from a firm of fish shippers in New London and bought a dragger of his own, the *Grace and Lucy*. He lived on flounders and coffee, cut corners, went out in foul and fair, and paid for her in a year and ten months. He had a lot of affection for her, but she was top-heavy and she rolled and pounded. In 1924, he sold her and bought another, which he named the *Louise*, after his sister. "The *Louise* was rolly, too," he says. "She was the *Grace and Lucy* all over again." These were small draggers; both were less than forty feet. At the end of 1926, Ellery decided to build a new one, a bigger one. "I didn't want a whore's dream," he says. "On the other hand, I didn't want a barge. I wanted a good, plain working boat that would squat down in the water and let the net know who was boss. I wanted to crowd everything I could up forward, engine and winch and cabin and pilot-house and life dory, so I'd have plenty of deck in the stern to empty my net on. I tried to explain this to some boatyard fellows, some professional designers, but they had ideas of their own. They tried to talk me into one of those boats with so much labor-saving gear on them you're so busy saving labor you can't get any work done. I decided I'd take a chance and design my own boat, about like a fellow up for some awful crime would decide to be his own lawyer." Ellery made a study of several draggers in the Noank and Stonington fleets whose behavior in rough water he admired, and he went to the boatyards and examined the designs from which they had been built. Then he sat down with some dime-store calipers and rulers and made inboard and deck-arrangement plans for a fifty-foot dragger to be called the *Eleanor.* He made them on the backs of two wrinkled Coast and Geodetic charts. He showed these plans to a friend named Ernest C. Daboll. Mr. Daboll was, as he still is, editor of the *New England Almanac and Farmer's Friend,* familiarly called "Daboll's Weather Book," which has been published in New London by the Daboll family almost continuously since 1772. Many old fishermen still have more respect for its weather predictions than for those broadcast on the radio. Mr. Daboll is also a surveyor and draftsman. He corrected Ellery's plans and had them blueprinted. Early in 1927, Ellery sold the *Louise,* withdrew his savings, borrowed some more money, and took these blueprints to the Rancocas boatyard, in Delanco, New Jersey, down near Camden. "The *Eleanor* was launched the middle of May," Ellery says. "Oh, Jesus, I was nervous. When I started up the coast with her, I took a quart of gin along, in case of disappointment, but I didn't even unscrew the cap. Much to my satisfaction, she turned out good. In fact, she turned out perfect." Ellery is disinclined to tell how much the *Eleanor* cost. "What she cost doesn't mean a thing," he says. "She's getting old and frazzly, but I wouldn't sell her for what she cost, or nowheres near. I wouldn't sell her for fifteen thousand dollars."

In his first two boats, Ellery was nomadic. If a rumor came down from Martha's Vineyard that there was a phenomenal run of cod off Gay Head, he would fill his gasoline tanks and go up there. If he heard that swordfish had been sighted foraging on mackerel off Montauk Point, he would sharpen some lily irons and go out and try to strike a few. One morning, in the *Louise,* working out of New London, he and his mate went on a scallop-dredging trip, fully intending to be back that night. Instead, for three weeks they strayed down the coast, dredging until nightfall and then putting in at the nearest port to express their scallops to Fulton Market. They reached

Sheepshead Bay before turning back. "If there was a speakeasy near the fish dock in those ports, and there usually was," Ellery says, "we'd hole up in it and hobnob with the riffraff. I remember one speakeasy down on Great South Bay that was run by three sisters. All were red-headed and all were widows. They were called the Three Merry Widows. It was a disgraceful way of life, and I sure did enjoy it." Ellery found that the *Eleanor* was much more of a responsibility than his other boats. Shortly after getting her, he quit wandering and began concentrating on the Mouth, the Yellow Bank, and the Hell Hole.

THERE ARE TWO KINDS OF DRAGGER CAPTAINS: those who go out every day the weather allows and drag all over everywhere, figuring if they cover enough bottom they are bound to run into fish sooner or later, and those who carefully pick their days and drag only in areas where they are pretty sure fish are congregating. In his youth, Ellery was of the first kind; he is now the best example in the Stonington fleet of the second kind. He has a vast memory of the way the six species of flounders inhabiting the Stonington grounds have behaved in all seasons under all sorts of weather conditions. Consequently, he can foretell their migrations, sometimes to the day. Blackbacks, for example, the sweetest-meated of the flounders, spend the summer in the cold water offshore. Some time in the late fall, they begin moving inshore by the millions to the shallows, where they spawn. The biggest hauls are made during this migration. Ellery is always ready for the blackbacks. He knows the routes they follow and the best places to intercept them. Frank Muise, his mate, and Charlie Brayman, his third man, profess to believe that he thinks like a flounder. "Ellery doesn't need much sleep," Brayman says. "He only sleeps four or five hours. The rest of the night, he lies in bed and imagines he's a big bull flounder out on the ocean floor. When the blackbacks get restless, he gets restless. One morning he shows up at the dock with an odd look in his eye and he says, 'The blackbacks commenced moving into the coves last night.' And I say, 'How the hell do you know?' And he says, 'Let's go out to the Hell Hole and try the fifteen-fathom curve off the Nebraska Shoal.' Or he says, 'Let's go up to the Mouth and drag in between Bartlett Reef and the North Dumpling.' He never misses. We go where he says and we always hit them where they're good and thick." Ellery has a simpler explanation. "I take a look at the weather," he says, "and I act accordingly."

Ellery is also an extraordinarily skillful wreck fisher. Fish forgather in great numbers around wrecks, some to feed on the mollusks, crustaceans, sea worms, and other organisms that they harbor, and some to feed on those that are feeding on these organisms. If pickings elsewhere are thin, a few of the more self-confident captains will risk their nets to get at such fish. By trial and error and by hearsay, Ellery long ago learned the location and shape and condition—whether sitting, lying on a side, or broken up—of every wreck in the Mouth and the Hell Hole. On calm, clear days, when he can take accurate ranges on rocks and buoys and on landmarks ashore, he goes out and methodically drags up close to a dozen or so of these. The others are so decayed and their pieces scattered about so treacherously that even he will not approach them. He usually starts with the *Larchmont,* a Providence-to-New York side-wheel passenger steamer that collided with the three-masted schooner *Harry Knowlton* during a snowstorm on the night of February 11, 1907, drowning over a hundred and thirty people, and ends with a coal barge that sank from a leak in May, 1944. He drags around the barge more for the coal that spills out of it during storms than for fish. He burns this coal in the *Eleanor*'s galley stove. Some nights, he fills the back seat of his automobile with Hell Hole coal and takes it home.

Ellery is an almost overly cautious captain, and he says that wreck fishing made him so. "Once I heard a contractor tell about cutting a ditch through a graveyard," he says. "It reminded me of wreck fishing. I've brought up bones in my net many and many a time, and I've brought up skulls or parts of skulls several times. Oh, Jesus! Once I brought up a jawbone with nine teeth left in it, and there was a gold filling in every tooth; some had middle fillings *and* side fillings. Whoever he was—him or her, I couldn't tell which—the poor soul sure God wasted a lot of time in the dentist chair. Once I was fishing with my brother Morris. I was below eating lunch and Morris was on deck sorting a haul and he found a skull in a bunch of seaweed. The roots of the seaweed had grown around the skull and had kept it intact—the lower jaw was still attached to it, and you could open and shut the jaws with your hands. Morris was standing there, looking at the skull and opening and shutting the jaws, when I came on deck munching on a big juicy peach. Morris looked at me, and then he looked at that toothy jaw, and then he took sick.

"All kinds of odds and ends come up in the net. One day a bucket of U.S. Navy paint came up, a five-gallon bucket of battleship gray. We prized the lid off and there wasn't a thing wrong with it I could see. Some sailor probably took a sudden dislike to it and heaved it in. We used it on the *Eleanor*. Another day, what came up only a woman's pink lace shimmy. Some woman on a summer yacht probably got a couple of whiskey sours in her and flung it off. Oh, it was a pretty thing. It had roses and butterflies on it. We tied it to a stay and flew it like a flag all that summer. Johnny Bindloss said no doubt some mermaid off Newport lost it. 'Over around Newport,' he said, 'even the mermaids wear pink lace shimmies.' Back during prohibition, there were some rum runners around eastern Connecticut. Some were Canucks and some were local boys. They used to buoy their booze in shoal water in the Hell Hole. They'd wrap the bottles in straw and sew them up in waterproof tarpaulin bags, twenty-four bottles to a bag. They were called buoy bags. Sometimes a storm'd part one from the buoy and it'd go wandering around on the bottom. One hot August afternoon, we emptied the net and out dropped a buoy bag. Twenty-four bottles of square-bottle Scotch. The crew wanted to pitch right in, but I could just visualize the consequences, so I argued and pleaded we ought to store it and use it in the winter for chills. So we stored it. Fifteen minutes later, the mate complained he had a chill. Then the third man's teeth began to chatter. Then I began to feel a little shivery myself. It was a week before things got back to normal. I don't mind buoy bags. It's the bones I mind. I had a mate once, a peculiar man, a Rhode Islander, and every time a bone came up, or anything else unusual, he'd squat down and study it. 'Throw that thing back where it came from,' I'd tell him. He'd study it some more, and he'd say, 'Ellery, there's many and many a secret buried out there in that Hell Hole.' And I'd say, 'Damn the secrets! Please do like I told you and throw that thing overboard.' Oh, I dread those bones. There but for the grace of God go I. Sometimes I take chances. Like a fog comes up, and I keep right on dragging. Then, all of a sudden, I think of those bones, and I don't fool around no more; I open her up and I head for the dock."

Although Ellery puts in an appearance at Bindloss's dock every weekday, usually before dawn, he seldom goes out on the grounds more than three days a week. Last year, he went out only a hundred and thirty days. Nevertheless, he shipped seventeen hundred and twenty-six barrels to Fulton Market, each holding approximately two hundred pounds of fish. There are boats that went out one-third again as many days and did not catch as much. Ellery ships to John Feeney, Inc., in Stall 13. Feeney's is the company that once employed Alfred E. Smith as a basket boy. Ellery is not the kind of man who will talk about how much he makes. "That's what's known as nobody's business," he says. On a fish dock, everybody knows everybody else's business, and three of Ellery's closest friends estimate he cleared six thousand dollars last year, maybe a thousand more, maybe a thousand less. His mate and his third man probably cleared between twenty-five hundred and three thousand each. Like all captain-owners in the Stonington fleet, Ellery works on shares with his crew under the forty-per-cent system; that is, at the end of each week, from the *Eleanor*'s earnings, less operating expenses (gasoline, oil, ice, and barrels), forty per cent is subtracted. This percentage, called the boat's share, goes to Ellery; out of it, he pays for nets and gear, repairs, drydocking, insurance, taxes, and so on. The balance is split equally among Ellery, Muise, and Brayman.

Young draggermen regard Ellery with awe because of his frugality with gear. He once went a year and seven months without snagging a net. Unlike most draggermen, he doesn't buy ready-made nets; he buys netting by the yard and makes his own. He gets the netting from George Wilcox, who runs a net loft on his farm in Quiambaug Cove, a crossroads village between Stonington and Mystic. There is a sign in this loft which reads, "NO CREDIT EXTENDED IN HERE UNLESS OVER 75 YRS OF AGE & ACCOMPANIED BY GRANDPARENTS." "I'm related to George," Ellery says. "I guess we're cousins. My grandmother on Pa's side was a Wilcox. They're a long-lived set of people. George is in his eighties and the Wilcoxes don't hardly consider him full-grown; he's got two brothers and a sister older than him. There was another brother, but he died some months ago. His name was Jess. Jess was ninety-three years old and getting on close to ninety-four, but he was still able to do a little light work around the farm. A few days before he died, he was breaking up some boulders with a sledge hammer, so he could use them in a stone fence. He had a blood blister on his left thumb he'd got shingling a roof and couldn't use his left hand at all and he was swinging the sledge hammer with one arm and the boulders were great big ones and the job was taking him twice as long as it ordinarily would and it aggravated him. A pouring-down rain came up and he wouldn't stop. He worked right through it and he got the pneumonia. The only reason he died, they took him to the hospital. Jess never slept good in a strange bed. Around midnight, he got up in the dark and put on his clothes, intending to slip downstairs and strike out for home, but he fell over something and broke his hip. The Wilcoxes used to operate a big fish-scrap factory on the Cove, the Wilcox Fertilizer Company. That's the reason they're so long-lived. The factory was just across the yard from the house and the prevailing wind blew the fish-scrap smell right into the house. This smell was so strong it killed all the germs in the air, and it was so rich it nourished you and preserved you. People in poor health for miles around learned about this and used to come in droves and sit all day on the porch, especially people with the asthma and the dropsy. Some days, there'd be so many sitting on the porch, getting the benefit of the smell, that it was quite a struggle for the Wilcoxes to get in and out of the house."

# The Bottom of the Harbor

ELLERY IS THE MOST SKILLFUL and the most respected of the captains in the Stonington fleet, and he is also the least ambitious. His knowledge of the behavior of flounders is so acute that he could double his production without straining himself, but he doesn't see any point in doing so. There are four reasons for this. First, he has rheumatism. Second, he is a self-taught oil painter. He prefers to paint when it is too stormy or foggy to drag, but if a painting looks as if it might turn out good, he will stay with it for days on end of perfect fishing weather. Third, he is an amateur oceanographer, a kind of unofficial member of the staff of the Bingham Oceanographic Laboratory at Yale University, and this takes up quite a lot of his time. Fourth, he lacks an itch for money. He makes a good living and considers that sufficient. He says he owns a boat, an automobile, a house and lot, seventy-five books, a trumpet, a straight razor, and a Sunday suit, and can't think of anything else he particularly wants.

The way Ellery disposes of the lobsters he picks up in his net exemplifies his attitude toward money. There are lobsters in all the grounds dragged by the Stonington fleet. They are thickest in the Hell Hole, where swarms of them live in, under, and around the old shipwrecks that lie there. In the summer and fall, a few are caught in every drag. Now and then, a couple of bushels come up in a single haul, in among the fish. They bring high prices. The majority wind up in New York seafood restaurants as choice Maine lobsters; in these restaurants all lobsters, even those from Sheepshead Bay, come from Maine. All the captains except Ellery ship the young, combative, bronzy blue-green ones to Fulton Market and keep the culls and jumbos for their own tables. (The culls are those that have recently molted and whose new shells have not yet hardened, and those with one or both claws snapped off in fights or while mating. The jumbos are the sluggish, barnacle-incrusted, stringy-meated giants—old ones, who can be captured only in nets, since they have grown too big to go through the mouths of traps; the record for the fleet is a cock lobster that weighted twenty-two pounds and was fit only for salads and Newburgs.) Ellery does just the opposite. He selects the finest he catches and sets them aside for himself and his crew and ships the rest. "Let the rich eat the culls," he says. The third man in a three-handed fishing crew is supposed to do the cooking, but Ellery attends to most of it on the *Eleanor;* he is one of those who believe that to get a thing done right you have to do it yourself. He is a matchless lobster chef. He boils and he broils and he makes lobster chowder, but most often he boils. He puts a tub of fresh sea water on the little coal stove in the cabin and heats it until it spits. He wraps his lobsters in seaweed and drops them in, half a dozen in a batch, and times them with a rusty alarm clock that hangs from a cup hook on the underside of a shelf above the stove; after exactly fifteen minutes, he dips them out. He lets them cool slowly, so that the meat won't shrink and become flavorless and rubbery, the common condition of cold boiled lobsters in restaurants, and then he heaps them on the cracked ice in the ice bin in the forward fish hold. He and his crew—Frank, the mate, and Charlie, the third man—reach in and get a lobster any time they feel like it. They eat them standing on deck. They smack them against the rail to crack the shells, pluck out the tail and claw meat, and chuck the rest overboard. One fall day, out on the Hell Hole, the three of them ate fourteen in between meals.

ELLERY BEGAN TO PAINT in the winter of 1930. At that time, he was sleeping aboard the *Eleanor,* at Bindloss's dock in Stonington, going home to New London to see his mother only on Sundays. In school, in her teens, Mrs. Thompson went to an art class, and several prim paintings of flowers she did still hang in her parlor. That winter, because she complained about being by herself so much, Ellery tried to reawaken this interest. In Brater's, a small art-supplies store in New London, he bought some stretched canvases and a set of paints and brushes. "Ma tried, but she couldn't somehow seem to pick up where she'd left off," Ellery says. "Her hands were too stiff. I had all that art gear laying around, and one Sunday afternoon I took a notion I'd paint me a picture. Ma gave me some directions and told me to start out with a rose, but I started out with the *Titanic* hitting the iceberg. I worked on it four Sundays. I didn't have much trouble with the *Titanic* or the iceberg, but the poor souls bobbing around in the water like to drove me crazy." He called the painting "Nearer My God to Thee." His mother admired it; she had it framed and hung it in the parlor between two of hers and called the neighbors in. "To tell the truth," Ellery says, "that made me proud." He took the art gear to Stonington and began to spend off hours scrutinizing objects around the dock, getting the look of them in his head, and then doing paintings of them—a battered tin bucket, a clam rake, a scallop dredge with fragments of scallop shells sticking to it, a capstan, an anchor. A lobster buoy is a block of wood, most often two feet long, which is attached by a tarred rope to a lobster trap and which floats above it, marking its position. Buoys are painstakingly and sometimes beautifully whittled into a variety of shapes and are brightly painted, usually in stripes in three colors; each lobsterman has a different set of colors; like racing silks, they denote ownership. Some discarded and barnacle-speckled buoys heaped any old way on the dock caught Ellery's eye and he did a painting of them. He did three paintings of animals—two fish-house cats hatefully eying each other at the mouth of an overturned bait barrel, a cormorant of a kind known locally as the black shag roosting on a mooring stake, a herd of rats scampering single file along the ridge of a breakwater in the moonlight. The breakwater rats are notorious around Stonington, and Ellery did a series of pencil sketches as well as the painting of them. They are wharf rats that migrated to the outer breakwater in Stonington harbor, where they nest in the riprap and grow enormous on dead fish washed up by the tide. Some draggermen keep a supply of rocks and brickbats aboard and, passing the breakwater on their way to and from the grounds, amuse themselves by harassing the rats. Presently, Ellery began using the *Eleanor* as his subject. He painted her in rough water with her net down, and he painted her with a haul of flounders dumped on her deck and a flock of gulls hovering above, and he painted her at Bindloss's dock with her net drying in the wind and a red sun going down behind her. He worked meticulously, putting in every detail he could find room for. One of the pilothouse windows has a zigzag crack across it; he always put this crack in, with the identical zigs and zags. "I like to show everything," he says. "If I had my way, I'd show the nailheads in the planks and the knots in the ropes and the stitches in the flag, but Ma thinks that makes a picture look tacky." In about a year, he did sixteen paintings of the *Eleanor*.

One Sunday morning in August, 1931, Ellery put his most recent paintings in his automobile to take home and show his mother. He stopped at a filling station near Groton on U.S. 1A for a tank of gas, and the proprietor, an old acquaintance, saw them on the back seat and looked them over and asked if he could put one in his window. " 'Why, hell yes,' I told him," Ellery says. "He picked one out, the biggest, and he figured there ought to be a price on it, make it look professional, so we cracked some jokes about that, and finally he stuck a sticker on it reading one hundred dollars. He laughed and I laughed. It wasn't more than an hour and a half later he phoned me there was a party down there wanted to buy it, a man from New York who was building a summer home at Groton Long Point. He was planning a marine room and wanted some boat pictures for it. He took my address and drove to the house—he surprised me; didn't look odd at all—and inquired did I have any others for sale. 'Why, hell yes,' I said, and hauled them out. He took five, including the one that was in the window—three big and two small—and wrote me out a check for four hundred dollars."

This windfall had a bad effect on Ellery. When he started his next painting, he found that he couldn't get anything to look right. Halfway through, he gave it up and started another. "I know now what was wrong," he says. "Instead of painting a picture for the fun of it, just something to show to Ma and the fellows on the dock, I was trying to paint a picture worth one hundred dollars." After a number of false starts, he lost his confidence. He wrapped his art gear in a blanket and stowed it in the *Eleanor*'s spare bunk and didn't paint any more for three years. In the summer of 1934, a Stonington captain bought a new dragger and asked Ellery to paint a picture of it. "What'll you give me?" Ellery asked. The captain offered a box of cigars. "Make it a quart of Scotch and throw in the cost of the canvas," Ellery told him, "and I'll see what I can do." The captain agreed. Ellery got out a stretched canvas and propped it against a lobster trap on the dock and sat on another trap and went to work. "I was real fumbly at first," he says, "but I soon got my nerve back. Everybody around the dock dropped what they were doing and came and stood in back of me and told me how to do it, but I finished it that afternoon and it turned out good. The dragger was fresh off the ways, hadn't even been shook down, but I put her out on the high seas, fighting a storm. That tickled the captain. When I got through, two other captains made arrangements with me to paint their boats."

Since then, Ellery has painted between fifty and sixty draggers, trawlers, mackerel seiners, and lobster boats, and his price has advanced from a quart of Scotch to thirty-five dollars if the client is a Stonington man or seventy-five if he is a stranger. "I'm proud of my painting," Ellery says. "On the other hand, I'm sorry I ever started it. It's hard to satisfy a fishing captain and it gets harder and harder. You not only have to paint his boat as accurate as a blueprint, you have to put it in a storm, a terrible storm. They all insist on that. Like a captain said the other day, 'It's a good painting, Ellery, only I wish you'd put in a bolt of lightning striking the mast.' Each wants a worse storm than the others. It's got so if I was to paint a boat that looked as if there was a remote possibility it might make port, the captain would take offense." Except for his own work, Ellery doesn't have much interest in painting. Once, when the *Eleanor* was laid up in Newport by engine trouble, he and Frank and Charlie spent an afternoon in Providence and visited the museum at the Rhode Island School of Design. They had on their fishing clothes and felt ill at ease and stayed only a few minutes. "We couldn't get out of there fast enough," Ellery says. He sometimes seems to feel that his success as a painter is a joke he has played on the world. "Nearly about every fishing captain from Point Jude to New London has one of my paintings hung up in his home," Ellery says, "and every now and then, when I'm driving past those homes at night, I can't help saying to myself, 'Good God A'mighty! What have I done?'" Other paintings by Ellery hang in net lofts, chandleries, dock offices, and dockside saloons in eastern Connecticut fishing ports. Most of these are of the *Eleanor*. Bindloss, the dock proprietor, owns six. There is a Thompson in Fulton Market. It is owned by Jim Coyne, general manager of John Feeney, Inc., the firm to which Ellery ships his fish, and it hangs in the Feeney stall in the old Fishmongers Association shed. Every summer, people from New York City, on vacation in and around Stonington, buy some of Ellery's work. They never fail to inform him that he is a primitive. This word used to anger him. He now understands its significance in relation to painting, but he pretends that he doesn't. Last summer, a woman from New York told him that she knew dozens of painters but he was the first primitive she'd ever met. "I'm not as primitive as I have been," Ellery said. "Nowheres near. Back before I got the rheumatism, I was without a doubt the most primitive man in eastern Connecticut."

THE LAST FEW YEARS, owing to the growth of his interest in oceanography, Ellery has been devoting less and less time to painting. He says he first heard of oceanography one Saturday afternoon in May, 1943. He and several other dragger captains had called it a week and were sitting in the sun on the stringpiece of Bindloss's dock, sharing a bottle, when two strangers walked up and introduced themselves: they were Daniel Merriman, director of the Bingham Oceanographic Laboratory at Yale, and Herbert E. Warfel, a research assistant. Mr. Merriman told the captains that the staff of the laboratory was about to begin work on a lengthy study of the fishes in the eastern Connecticut and western Rhode Island grounds, and he asked for their cooperation. He said that he and Mr. Warfel would be in charge of the study and that they wanted to drive over from New Haven once or twice a month and go out to the grounds on Stonington draggers and examine catches and make oceanographic observations. When Ellery heard this, he promptly left the group and went down the dock and stayed in the cabin of the *Eleanor* until the oceanographers had departed. Scientists of one sort or another—aquatic biologists from the United States Fish and Wildlife Service, ichthyologists from New England universities, and, in recent years, drug-company chemists assaying the vitamins in the liver oil of various fishes—frequently visit the Stonington docks, and Ellery had formed a low opinion of them. On three occasions, just to be accommodating, he had taken scientists out to the Hell Hole. "They were all alike," he says. "The first hour, while we were making a drag, they got in the way. You couldn't turn around without stepping on Dr. Somebody-or-Other. The second hour, while we were sorting a haul, they sat on their tails and watched us sort and disputed among themselves concerning what was the right Latin name for this fish and that fish, and somehow—up to our knees in fish and wet to the skin—all that Latin had a tendency to get on our nerves. The third hour, they ate sandwiches. The fourth hour, they threw up."

The other captains were more sympathetic. That same month, Mr. Merriman and Mr. Warfel went out with Captain S. W. Stenhouse on the *Nathaniel B. Palmer* and with Captain W. H. McLaughlin on the *Marise*. During the first week of June, they went out with Captain Roscoe Bacchiocchi on the *Baby II.* Mr. Merriman noticed that these captains replied to a good many of the questions he and Mr. Warfel asked them by saying that they didn't know but that Captain Thompson, on the *Eleanor,* probably did. Captain Bacchiocchi, for example, when asked if hogchoker flounders ever entered Block Island Sound, said that he wouldn't know a hogchoker if he caught one but that he thought he remembered hearing Ellery Thompson say something or other about catching some. Twice, seeing the *Eleanor* tied up at Bindloss's dock, Mr. Merriman went aboard her looking for Captain Thompson, but each time a man down in the cabin, who he later found out was Captain Thompson himself, shouted up the companionway that Captain Thompson had just knocked off and gone to the movies. Finally, on a Sunday night late in June, Mr. Merriman telephoned Ellery at his home. Their conversation was an odd one, and Mr. Merriman can recollect it. He told Ellery that he was eager to make a trip to the grounds with him and started to tell why, but Ellery interrupted and asked, "What do you call yourself—Doctor or Mister?" Mr. Merriman said that he was a Ph.D. but much preferred to be called Mister. Ellery said he would have to think the matter over. Then, abruptly making up his mind, he said, "Oh, hell, be down at the dock tomorrow morning at half past five and we'll take you out and get it over with." Mr. Merriman tried to thank him, but Ellery interrupted again and said, "Don't thank me. Just keep out of the way. And when you see we've got our hands full pulling in a net and the dogfish are swarming around and the gulls are screeching and the winch is backfiring and everything on deck is all balled up, don't you and the other professor pick that particular moment to butt in and ask questions. And don't bring sandwiches. If there's anything I despise, it's sandwiches. While you're on my boat, I'll feed you."

Mr. Merriman, having known many fishing captains and having long since concluded that they are the most plainspoken of men, took Ellery's bluntness for granted. Mr. Merriman is a friendly, adaptable, serious young scientist who has put in about as much time in the field as in the laboratory. In 1930, deciding that fish interested him more than the liberal arts, he quit Harvard, where he was a junior, and spent two years knocking around fishing ports in the United States and England, going to banks in the Gulf of Maine in trawlers out of Groton and to banks in the North Sea in trawlers and herring drifters out of the English ports of Grimsby and Lowestoft. Then he returned to school—not to Harvard but to the College of Fisheries in the University of Washington, in Seattle. After getting a Master's degree at Washington for a study of the effects of temperature on the development of the eggs and larvae of the cut-throat trout, he went to Yale, in 1935, as a graduate student in zoology. In 1938, he became an instructor in biology. In 1942, when he was thirty-four, he was raised to assistant professor of biology, curator of oceanography in the Peabody Museum, and director of the Oceanographic Laboratory. A paper he did on the striped bass is the standard work on that fish. He is a Bostonian and a member of an old New England teaching family. His father, the late Professor Roger Bigelow Merriman, taught history at Harvard for forty-three years. Charles W. Eliot, the Harvard president, was an uncle.

Mr. Warfel is an Indianian of Pennsylvania Dutch descent. He has studied fish, sometimes as a teacher and sometimes as a state fish-and-game-department biologist, in Colorado, North Dakota, Oklahoma, Massachusetts, New Hampshire, and Connecticut. He believes that the proper study of fish embraces the cooking and eating of them. He originated a squid chowder. He and some of his colleagues occasionally stay late in the laboratory and make a quart of caviar, using eggs of the longhorn sculpin—the common hacklehead, a trash fish whose only value ordinarily is as bait for lobster traps.

Mr. Merriman and Mr. Warfel went out to the Hell Hole with Ellery on the last Monday in June, 1943. "Frank and I got down to the dock at five-thirty, as usual," Ellery says, "and the professors were already on the *Eleanor,* sitting on the hatch, making themselves at home, but Charlie hadn't showed up. The professors were sleepy-eyed and they hadn't bothered to shave and they had their old clothes on, and I mean old clothes. Frank and I went below to start the engine, and Frank said they were the most un-professor-looking two damned professors ever he saw. It was a hot, drizzly morning and Frank was cranky, and so was I. We got things started, but still no Charlie. Finally, the landlady of a rooming house up on Water Street that Charlie roomed with at that time's little boy came poking down the dock and said Charlie sent word he wasn't able to get out of bed, his left knee was hurting him so. Charlie's got something chronic the matter with his left knee, and he has to quit work every so often and doctor it. It's a peculiar affliction. It hardly ever troubles him until Saturday. Along about noon Saturday, he starts to limp around and look blue and complain his left knee is swoll up, and Saturday night he starts taking something to bring the swelling down. Sometimes it's Tuesday or Wednesday before the swelling goes down sufficient for him to do a day's work. He's tried all kinds of patent medicines and salves and liniments, but the only thing that seems to give him any real relief is rye whiskey. He takes it internally. I asked him one day, 'Charlie, for the love of God,' I said, 'why don't you try rubbing it on?,' but he said it seems to do more good if he takes it internally.

"I didn't much want to go out to the grounds without Charlie.

We can work the *Eleanor* two-handed, but I don't like to; I'm one draggerman that aims to reach old age without wearing a truss. The professors spoke up and said they'd be glad to pitch in and help. I thought to myself, 'A lot of help you two'll be.' On the other hand, I wanted to keep my promise, so I told Frank to let's get going. I took her out past Watch Hill Light; then I gave Frank the wheel and I went below and got breakfast. I made some coffee and scrambled some eggs and I broiled four nice hen lobsters. As it happened, it was the first time the professors ever et lobsters for breakfast, but I didn't hear any complaints. We hit the Hell Hole and started to set the net and got in trouble right away. Frank shoved the bag of the net off the stern, the way he always does, but a wave caught it before it sank and gave it a throwing around, and that jerked the wings of the net sideways on the deck, and the bridle on one of the net doors got all snaked up. In other words, a damned mess. I was at the wheel and couldn't do anything about it. Frank ran back to try and fix it, but before he got there, Mr. Merriman leaped on the door and grabbed the bridle. I thought to myself, 'That's one young man that wasn't present when the brains was passed out,' and I yelled to him to stand back there. I fully expected to see him snatched into the middle of next week, but he seesawed the bridle back into working order as good as I could have done, or Frank, or any other draggerman, and he leaped off the door a second or two before it went overboard like a shot out of a gun. I called him over to the wheel and I inquired where in hell did he learn how to handle an otter trawl. I asked him did they teach that up at Yale. And he said he'd worked in fishing boats to some extent when he was younger. So, naturally, when I heard that, I had some respect for him.

"When we brought the net in and emptied it on deck, the professors helped us sort. They squatted down and took right hold. There was all the difference in the world between them and the other scientists. They worked as hard as us, except for stopping now and then to jot down a note. And they didn't throw any Latin around. They used fishermen's fish names. They didn't call a squirrel hake a *Hippogloppus hoppogloppus;* they called it a snot head, the same as we do. We got the haul sorted and barreled, and then we went below for a mug-up, and they started in asking me questions such as did I ever come across any hogchokers, and when was the last bluefish run and how did it compare with the big bluefish runs in the old days, the bluefish gluts, and what species did I consider were being fished out, and other questions like that. They must've asked me fifty questions.

"We made two one-hour drags, and then a drizzly fog set in, so we proceeded back to the dock. We unloaded, and it was only noon, so I asked the professors why didn't they stay for lunch, I'd broil them a fluke. While we were eating, I told them it was my time to be district attorney, I'd like to ask *them* a question. I told them there was a matter that had bothered me since childhood days, that I had turned it over in my head a hundred times without coming to a sensible conclusion—namely, 'How do lobsters mate? How in the world do they manage it?' I asked did they know. Well, they knew. They had the scientific facts, and they got out their note pads and drew some diagrams to show the ABCs of the matter. Frank was up on deck, airing out a net, and I yelled to him to come below; I didn't want him to miss it. And that led to the mating habits of whales. And then I asked what was their private theories on the eelgrass mystery. That's a grass that used to grow on the bottom of bays all over the North Atlantic coast, thousands upon thousands of acres of it. It had long, narrow blades that looked eely. It was highly beneficial to fishermen, because scallops lived in it; it was shelter for the scallops. During 1931, it all disappeared. One week there'd be a thick stand of eelgrass in a bay; next week you couldn't find a living blade of it. Bay scallops practically disappeared, too. That's why they're so dear. The old retired fishermen sitting on the docks thought up all kinds of theories at the time, the way they do. One old man, an old Baptist, it was his idea that God was punishing the fishermen for their misspent lives. 'The eelgrass is only the beginning,' he used to say. 'The fish'll go next.' The professors had the facts. A fungus had got into the tissues of the grass— one of those buggers that can't be seen with the naked eye—and had multiplied to a God-awful extent. They made some sketches of it, how it looks under the microscope, and they explained how it rotted the grass. And then we got on the subject of the grounds in the Sargasso Sea, where the eels go to spawn, the American eels bedding down together in one ground and the European eels in another. And then we discussed the tides and the moon and the Gulf Stream and the Continental Shelf and the Continental Slope and the deeps. We talked and drank coffee all afternoon. I answered their questions and they answered mine. I gave them the practical dope and they gave me the scientific dope. It was quite a discussion and I really enjoyed it. When they were leaving, they asked could they go out again on the *Eleanor,* and I told them, 'Why, hell yes.' And they asked could they bring some of their apparatus aboard next trip, and I told them I didn't see any reason why not, they were entirely welcome to do so. I told them they could make the *Eleanor* their headquarters."

EVER SINCE THEN, Mr. Merriman and Mr. Warfel have spent at least one day a month on the *Eleanor;* it has become their research vessel. Ellery has an old Yale pennant, a souvenir of a Yale-Harvard boat race at New London, that he flies when they are aboard. The oceanographers keep a number of reference books in the *Eleanor's* pilothouse. In addition, one shelf of the canned-goods cupboard in the cabin is crammed with books, most of which are about fish. These belong to Ellery; he is building a scientific library of his own. He started it with *Fishes of the Gulf of Maine,* by Henry B. Bigelow and William W. Welsh, an old United States Bureau of Fisheries reference work that is a classic of American ichthyology. Mr. Merriman and Mr. Warfel found a copy for Ellery in a secondhand bookstore in Boston and gave it to him for Christmas in 1944. Ellery has great respect for it. He has read and reread it, he lends it to other captains, and he frequently quotes from it. Mr. Warfel believes that Ellery is no longer hostile to Latin and is quite sure that he has memorized the Latin fish names in Bigelow & Welsh. Ellery profanely denies this. He slips up every so often, however. Two sharks appear in multitudes in the Stonington grounds at certain seasons, the spiny dogfish (*Squalus acanthias*) and the smooth dogfish (*Mustelus canis*). Not long ago, in conversation with Mr. Warfel, Ellery mentioned a big shark that swam up while the net was coming out of the water and tore a hole in it trying to get at the fish inside, and Mr. Warfel asked, "What was it—a spiny dog or a smooth dog?" "It was an *acanthias*," Ellery said.

Ellery and the oceanographers have become good friends. He calls them Dan and Herb. In between their trips to Stonington, he sends them logs, which are full of information about conditions on the grounds. He has collected many specimens for them. Whenever a Stonington draggerman notices a queer fish in a haul, such as one of the strays from tropical waters that work their way north in the Gulf Stream, he saves it and gives it to Ellery. Ellery writes the date and place of capture, and any other relevant facts the draggerman can supply, on a strip of rag paper, sticks this in the fish's mouth, and drops the fish in a five-gallon can of formaldehyde that the oceanographers keep in Bindloss's dock house for this purpose. The oceanographers have finished half a dozen monographs on phases of their study. In each of these, they acknowledged Ellery's assistance. For example, in a footnote in "The Spawning Habits, Eggs, and Larvae of the Sea Raven, *Hemitripterus americanus,* in Southern New England," they wrote, "The authors are greatly indebted to Captain Ellery Thompson of the vessel *Eleanor,* out of Stonington, Connecticut, whose cooperation has been invaluable in much of the work of this laboratory in recent years." Two of Ellery's paintings of the *Eleanor* have been acquired by the laboratory. Mr. Merriman and Mr. Warfel occasionally bring a colleague along on their trips to the grounds. Dr. Ernest Freeman Thompson, an international authority on the hermit crab, and Dr. Werner Bergmann, a chemistry professor who studies the taxonomy of marine invertebrates for fun, have made three trips each. Mr. Merriman's father once came down from Harvard and went out to the Mussel Bed with Ellery. All the way out, he stood by the wheel and told Ellery stories about Suleiman the Magnificent, of whom he had written a biography. Ellery liked him. When Professor Merriman died, in September of 1945, Ellery sent flowers. "He had a good head on him," Ellery says. After their monthly trip, Ellery always gives a supper for the oceanographers at his home in New London. At first, he just had cold cuts and beer, but his mother considered that inhospitable. Mrs. Thompson is a cook in the old American big-kitchen tradition, the kind of woman who will make a fruit or meringue pie that no pastry chef in New York City could equal and then apologize for it. She likes to cook and she likes to see people eat, and Ellery's suppers have developed into banquets. For a recent one, Mrs. Thompson stuffed a twenty-pound turkey with three dozen Robbins Island oysters and roasted it.

Mr. Merriman and Mr. Warfel drive over to Stonington in an old truck that the Oceanographic Laboratory shares with the geology department, and park it on Bindloss's dock. They bring two chests of apparatus—thermometers, silk plankton nets, Mason jars for small specimens, a measuring board, and a jug of formaldehyde. They set the chests up on the *Eleanor*'s aft hatch. During a drag, they bottle samples of sea water, surface and bottom; take the temperature of the air and of the water, surface and bottom; make weather notes; and collect samples of plankton, the microscopic floating plant and animal life that is the basic food of most fishes. When the net is brought aboard and emptied on deck, they examine a few members of each species of fish in the haul. Twenty-three species are encountered in numbers in the Stonington grounds. Commercially, they fall into three categories—regularly marketed, occasionally marketed, and trash. Eight species are regularly mar-keted—blackback flounders, yellowtail flounders, fluke flounders, witch flounders, cod, haddock, cunners, and porgies. Five species are occasionally marketed—windowpane flounders, whiting, Boston hake, squirrel hake, and ocean pout. Ten species are regarded as trash—Baptist flounders, longhorn sculpin, little skates, big skates, barn-door skates, goosefish, sea ravens, sea robins, spiny dogfish, and smooth dogfish. These are always sorted out and thrown back, a process that kills a large proportion of them. By accumulating data on the whole hauls of the *Eleanor* and of other draggers over a period of seven months, a project in which they were assisted by Ellery, Mr. Merriman and Mr. Warfel determined that approximately fifty-three per cent of the catch of the Stonington fleet is thrown back. They consider this an appalling waste. All these fish are edible, but Americans are prejudiced against them, mainly because of their appearance; with the exception of the Baptist flounder, which has four lovely circle-within-a-circle designs on its top side, they are remarkably grotesque. In flavor and texture, most of them are as good as those that are regularly marketed, and one, the barn-door skate, when properly cooked, is superior. Skates are esteemed in England, and *raie au beurre noir* is one of the great fish dishes of France. Other New England fleets ship trash fish in small quantities to Fulton Market, where they are sold to two dissimilar groups: buyers for luxury hotels and restaurants, and proprietors of little one- and two-bin fish stores in Italian, Spanish, and Chinese neighborhoods.

A hodgepodge of invertebrates comes up in every dragger haul— lobsters, squid, blue crabs, rock crabs, hermit crabs, surf clams, blood clams, bay scallops, sea scallops, cockles, mussels, moon snails, pear conchs, sand dollars, starfish, serpent stars, sea anemones, sea squirts, sea mice, sea urchins, and sponges. Except for the lobsters and scallops, and sometimes the squid and blue crabs, these are also thrown back or swept through the scuppers—another example of blind American waste. The ripe raw roe of sea urchins is finer than most of the caviar that reaches us. Pear conchs, or conks, shipped as a sideline by oystermen and clammers, are used in a hot Italian dish called *scungili;* there are basement restaurants on Mulberry Street that specialize in it and are referred to as *scungili* places. *Scungili* is similar in taste and texture to mushrooms. Also, like mushrooms, it has a musky, wet-earth smell. People who go often to Italian restaurants have probably eaten pear conchs and moon snails without knowing it; both are widely used in a sauce for spaghetti and other *pasta* dishes. The Chinese in Chinatown use pear conchs in a number of dishes.

On every trip on the *Eleanor,* Mr. Merriman and Mr. Warfel pick out one haul, usually the second of the day, and buy all the fish in it, marketable and trash, paying whatever prices are current in Fulton Market. These fish, unsorted, are barreled and iced and set aside in the hold; there may be anywhere from two to six barrels. At the end of the trip, they are loaded on the truck and taken to the laboratory. Next day, Mr. Merriman and Mr. Warfel and their colleagues assemble around cutting tables in a room in the basement of the laboratory called the "crud room" and weigh and measure and decipher the sex of every fish. Samples of each species are then put in cold storage and taken out one by one and dissected and examined in regard to age, stage of sexual maturity, stomach contents, and parasites—a job that takes several days. This laboratory data and the data collected on the grounds, when put together, like the parts of a puzzle, yield information about spawning and feeding habits, rates of growth, ages, natural and fishing mortalities, fish diseases, competition among fishes for food, and relationships between individuals and between species. An analysis of the causes of fluctuations in abundance in southern New England fishing grounds will be made on the basis of this information. That is the main purpose of the study. The oceanographers hope that they will eventually be able to estimate the tonnage of each species that draggermen can take in a season without dangerously depleting the stock.

FISHERMEN AND FISHMONGERS along the southern New England coast have given obscene names to a number of fishes. Some of these names are so imaginative, scornful, and apt that they are startling. Mr. Merriman and Mr. Warfel collect them. They also collect Block Island stories, or Block Islands. Block Island is nine miles out in the Atlantic, off Rhode Island, to which it belongs; it is small and shaped like an oyster shell and almost treeless. The tides around it are treacherous, and hundreds of ships have been wrecked on its reefs and sand bars. The islanders are cold to strangers and are hostile to fishermen from the mainland who drag in the grounds surrounding it, such as the Hell Hole and the Mussel Bed. In retaliation, the mainlanders for generations have made up stories about them, accusing them of stinginess and of depending upon wrecks for a living.

One midwinter afternoon, the *Eleanor,* with the oceanographers aboard, skirted Cow Cove, on the northern tip of Block Island, while returning from a trip to the Mussel Bed. It was a sunny, still afternoon, and the air was so clear that the lighthouse on Montauk Point, twenty miles to the southwest, was visible. Frank was at the wheel. Ellery and Mr. Merriman and Mr. Warfel were sitting on the aft hatch, eating boiled lobsters. Charlie was lying on his back in the life dory, staring at a photograph in a magazine called *Sunshine and Health,* which is the official organ of the American Sunbathing Association, a nudist group. Next to *Popular Mechanics,* it is his favorite magazine. Ellery suddenly snapped his fingers. "I was about to forget," he said. "I heard a Block Island the other day. Johnny Bindloss told it. Johnny had it years ago from his grandfather, old man William Park Bindloss. He was a stonemason who specialized in lighthouses. He built South East Light on Block Island, and he lived over there a year or two and got acquainted. In those days, according to the general talk, the islanders got the better part of their bread and butter salvaging off wrecks. There'd be wrecks on the reefs all during the winter, coasting vessels mostly, and the stuff in them would wash up on the beach. The islanders would stand on the beach all day and all night, hooking for the stuff with poles that had bent nails on the ends of them. They were called wreck hooks. Everybody would line up down there and hook—little children, great-grandmothers, *every*body that could walk. The competition got so thick that they all agreed on a standard-length hook. Everybody had to use the same length. Around that time, a preacher from the mainland came over and settled on the island to preach the word of God and make a living for himself. The islanders listened to him, but they didn't offer to pay him anything. Along about February, he got real lean and raggedy. He was nothing but skin and bones. The islanders didn't want him to starve to death over there. For one thing, they'd have to bury him. So they held a meeting and argued the matter back and forth. One man made a motion they should take up a collection for the preacher, but this man had a reputation for being simple and his motion was so idiotic they didn't even discuss it. Some wanted each family to give the preacher a peck of potatoes or a turnip or two, and some were for giving him a fish whenever there was a good big catch, a glut. They couldn't agree. They argued until late that night. Finally, they decided they'd let him have a wreck hook an inch and a half longer than all the rest. If he couldn't make a living with that, he could go ahead and starve to death."

"Take the wheel a few minutes, Ellery, if you don't mind," said Frank, "and I'll tell a Block Island."

Ellery got up and relieved Frank, who came over and sat on the hatch.

"There was a fisherman from Stonington named Tucker Seabury who used to go over to Block Island and fish for cod a month or two every fall," Frank said. "Did it for years and years. Tuck was an old bachelor, and sort of odd himself. He got to know the Block Islanders, and they got to know him. In fact, he and the Block Islanders gradually got to be quite friendly. Tuck was what you call an old hand-liner. He'd go out in a dory and kneel over the side and fish for cod with hand lines. They don't fish much that way any more. He mostly fished on the Ledge. That's a hidden reef that juts out from the island a considerable distance. There's a buoy anchored off the end of it. Tuck was out there on the reef one afternoon in his dory, the way he used to tell it, and the cod were running and he was busy as Billy be damned and after a while he happened to look up and he saw a schooner heading for the reef, a big coasting schooner. It was coming in between the buoy and the island, taking a shortcut. It was an insane sight. Tuck stood up in his dory and waved both arms and screamed. 'Reef!' he screamed. 'Reef! Reef! Reef! Good God A'mighty, you're heading for a reef!' The schooner turned aside and shot out past the buoy, just in time. A few yards more and there'd've been an awful, awful wreck. Tuck glanced toward the landing on the island and there was a crowd of Block Islanders standing there, men and women, watching. Tuck was quite pleased with himself. He figured the Block Islanders would praise him for the good deed he had done. On toward sundown, he rowed in. The crowd of Block Islanders was still on the landing, standing around. Tuck nodded and spoke, the same as he always did, but the Block Islanders didn't speak. They just stood and looked at him. There was an old man among them who had always been Tuck's best friend on the island. Finally, this old man gave Tuck a cold look and said, 'Why don't you mind your own business?' "

Charlie laid aside his *Sunshine and Health* and sat up in the life dory. "That must've been around the time old Christine was ruling the south end of the island," Charlie said. "Old Chrissy was an old rascal of a woman that was the head of a gang of wreckers. They lured ships in with false lights, and they killed the sailors and passengers, so there wouldn't be any tales told. Old Chrissy always took charge of the killing. She had a big club and she'd hist her skirt and wade out in the surf and clout the people on the head as they swam in or floated in. She called a wreck a wrack, the way the Block Islanders do. That's the way she pronounced it. One night, she and her gang lured a ship up on the reef, and the sailors were floating in, and old Chrissy was out there clouting them on their heads. One poor fellow floated up, and it was one of old Chrissy's sons, who'd left the island and gone to the mainland to be a sailor. He looked up at old Chrissy and said, 'Hello, Ma.' Old Chrissy didn't hesitate a moment. She lifted up her club and clouted him on the head. 'A son's a son,' she said, 'but a wrack's a wrack.' "

(1947)

# The Rivermen

*I*OFTEN FEEL DRAWN to the Hudson River, and I have spent a lot of time through the years poking around the part of it that flows past the city. I never get tired of looking at it; it hypnotizes me. I like to look at it in midsummer, when it is warm and dirty and drowsy, and I like to look at it in January, when it is carrying ice. I like to look at it when it is stirred up, when a northeast wind is blowing and a strong tide is running—a new-moon tide or a full-moon tide—and I like to look at it when it is slack. It is exciting to me on weekdays, when it is crowded with ocean craft, harbor craft, and river craft, but it is the river itself that draws me, and not the shipping, and I guess I like it best on Sundays, when there are lulls that sometimes last as long as half an hour, during which, all the way from the Battery to the George Washington Bridge, nothing moves upon it, not even a ferry, not even a tug, and it becomes as hushed and dark and secret and remote and unreal as a river in a dream. Once, in the course of such a lull, on a Sunday morning in April, 1950, I saw a sea sturgeon rise out of the water. I was on the New Jersey side of the river that morning, sitting in the sun on an Erie Railroad coal dock. I knew that every spring a few sturgeon still come in from the sea and go up the river to spawn, as hundreds of thousands of them once did, and I had heard tugboatmen talk about them, but this was the first one I had ever seen. It was six or seven feet long, a big, full-grown sturgeon. It rose twice, and cleared the water both times, and I plainly saw its bristly snout and its shiny little eyes and its white belly and its glistening, greenish-yellow, bony-plated, crocodilian back and sides, and it was a spooky sight.

I prefer to look at the river from the New Jersey side; it is hard to get close to it on the New York side, because of the wall of pier sheds. The best points of vantage are in the riverfront railroad yards in Jersey City, Hoboken, and Weehawken. I used to disregard the "DANGER" and "RAILROAD PROPERTY" and "NO TRESPASSING" signs and walk into these yards and wander around at will. I would go out to the end of one of the railroad piers and sit on the stringpiece and stare at the river for hours, and nobody ever bothered me. In recent years, however, the railroad police and pier watchmen have become more and more inquisitive. Judging from the questions they ask, they suspect every stranger hanging around the river of spying for Russia. They make me uneasy. Several years ago, I began going farther up the river, up to Edgewater, New Jersey, and I am glad I did, for I found a new world up there, a world I never knew existed, the world of the rivermen.

Edgewater is across the river from the upper West Side of Manhattan; it starts opposite Ninety-fourth Street and ends opposite 164th Street. It is an unusually narrow town. It occupies a strip of stony land between the river and the Palisades, and it is three and a half miles long and less than half a mile wide at its widest part. The Palisades tower over it, and overshadow it. One street, River Road, runs the entire length of it, keeping close to the river, and is the main street. The crosstown streets climb steeply from the bank of the river to the base of the Palisades, and are quite short. Most of them are only two blocks long, and most of them are not called streets but avenues or terraces or places or lanes. From these streets, there is a panoramic view of the river and the Manhattan skyline. It is a changeable view, and it is often spectacular. Every now and then—at daybreak, at sunset, during storms, on starry summer nights, on hazy Indian-summer afternoons, on blue, clear-cut, stereoscopic winter afternoons—it is astonishing.

The upper part of Edgewater is largely residential. This is the oldest part of town, and the narrowest, but it still isn't entirely built up. There are several stretches of trees and underbrush, and several bushy ravines running down to the river, and a number of vacant lots. The lots are grown up in weeds and vines, and some of them are divided by remnants of stone walls that once divided fields or pastures. The streets are lined with old trees, mostly sweet gums and sycamores and tulip trees. There are some wooden tenements and some small apartment houses and some big old blighted mansions that have been split up into apartments, but one-family houses predominate. The majority are two-story houses, many of them set back in good-sized yards. Families try to outdo each other in landscaping and ornamenting their yards, and bring home all sorts of odds and ends for the purpose; in yard after yard conventional garden ornaments such as sundials and birdbaths and wagon wheels painted white stand side by side with objects picked up around the riverfront or rescued during the demolition of old buildings. The metal deckhouse of an old Socony tanker barge is in the front yard of one house on River Road; it is now a garden shed. In the same yard are a pair of mooring bitts, a cracked stone eagle that must have once been on the façade of a public building or a bank, and five of those cast-iron stars that are set in the walls of old buildings to cap the ends of strengthening rods. In the center of a flower bed in one yard is a coalhole cover and in the center of a flower bed in an adjoining yard is a manhole cover. In other yards are old anchors and worm wheels and buoys and bollards and propellers. Edgewater used to be linked to Manhattan by a ferry, the Edgewater-125th Street ferry. Most of the captains, wheelsmen, and deckhands on the ferryboats were Edgewater men, and had been for generations, and the ferry was the pride of the town. It stopped running in 1950; it was ruined by the George Washington Bridge and the Lincoln Tunnel. There are relics of it in a dozen yards. In former Mayor Henry Wissel's yard, on Hilliard Avenue, there is a chain post that came off the vehicle gangway of the ferryboat *Shadyside,* and the *Shadyside*'s fog bell hangs beside his door. In former Fire Chief George Lasher's yard, on Undercliff Avenue, there is a hookup wheel that came off the landing stage of the old ferryhouse. It resembles a ship's wheel. Chief Lasher has painted it white, and has trained a climbing rose on it.

In the middle of Edgewater, around and about River Road and the foot of Dempsey Avenue, where the ferryhouse used to stand, there is a small business district. In addition, a few stores and a few neighborhood saloons of the type known in New Jersey as taverns are scattered along River Road in the upper and lower parts of town.

The lower part of Edgewater is called Shadyside; the ferryboat was named for it. It is a mixed residential and factory district. The majority of the factories are down close to the river, in a network of railroad sidings, and piers jut out from them. Among them are an Aluminum Company of America factory, a coffee-roasting plant, a factory that makes roofing materials, a factory that makes sulphuric acid, and a factory that makes a shortening named Spry. On the roof of the Spry factory is an enormous electric sign; the sign looms over the river, and on rainy, foggy nights its pulsating, endlessly repeated message, "SPRY FOR BAKING," "SPRY FOR BAKING," "SPRY FOR BAKING," seems to be a cryptic warning of some kind that New Jersey is desperately trying to get across to New York.

There are six or seven large factories in Shadyside and six or seven small ones. The Aluminum Company factory is by far the largest, and there is something odd about it. It is made up of a group of connecting buildings arranged in a U, with the prongs of the U pointed toward the river, and inside the U, covering a couple of acres, is an old cemetery. This is the Edgewater Cemetery. Most of the old families in Edgewater have plots in it, and some still have room in their plots and continue to bury there. The land on which Edgewater is situated and the land for some distance along the river above and below it was settled in the seventeenth century by Dutch and Huguenot farmers. Their names are on the older gravestones in the cemetery—Bourdettes and Vreelands and Bogerts and Van Zandts and Wandells and Dyckmans and Westervelts and Demarests. According to tradition, the Bourdette family came in the sixteen-thirties—1638 is the date that is usually specified—and was the first one there; the name is now spelled Burdette or Burdett. Some of the families came over from Manhattan and some from down around Hoboken. They grew grain on the slopes, and planted orchards in the shelter of the Palisades. In the spring, during the shad and sturgeon runs, they fished, and took a large part of their catch to the city. The section was hard to get to, except by water, and it was rural and secluded for a long time. In the early eighteen-hundreds, some bluestone quarries were opened, and new people, most of whom were English, began to come in and settle down and intermarry with the old farming and fishing families. They were followed by Germans, and then by Irish straight from Ireland. Building stones and paving blocks and curbing for New York City were cut in the quarries and carried to the city on barges—paving blocks from Edgewater are still in place, under layers of asphalt, on many downtown streets. Some of the new people worked in the quarries, some worked on the barges, some opened blacksmith shops and made and repaired gear for the quarries and the barges, some opened boatyards, and some opened stores. The names of dozens of families who were connected with these enterprises in one way or another are on gravestones in the newer part of the cemetery; Allison, Annett, Carlock, Cox, Egg, Forsyth, Gaul, Goetchius, Hawes, Hewitt, Jenkins, Stevens, Truax, and Winterburn are a few. Some of these families died out, some moved away, and some are still flourishing. The enterprises themselves disappeared during the first two decades of this century; they were succeeded by the Shadyside factories.

The land surrounding the Edgewater Cemetery was once part of a farm owned by the Vreeland family, and the Aluminum Company bought this land from descendants of a Winterburn who married a Vreeland. As a condition of the sale, the company had to agree to provide perpetual access to the cemetery. To reach it, funerals go through the truck gate of the factory and across a freight yard and up a cement ramp. It is a lush old cemetery, and peaceful, even though the throb of machinery can be felt in every corner of it. A part-time caretaker does a good deal of gardening in it, and he likes bright colors. For borders, he uses the same gay plants that are used in flower beds at race tracks and seaside hotels—cannas, blue hydrangeas, scarlet sage, and cockscomb. Old men and old women come in the spring, with hoes and rakes, and clean off their family plots and plant old-fashioned flowers on them. Hollyhocks are widespread. Asparagus has been planted here and there, for its feathery ferny sprays. One woman plants sunflowers. Coarse, knotty, densely tangled rosebushes grow on several plots, hiding graves and gravestones. The roses that they produce are small and fragile and extraordinarily fragrant, and have waxy red hips almost as big as crab apples. Once, walking through the cemetery, I stopped and talked with an old woman who was down on her knees in her family plot, setting out some bulbs at the foot of a grave, and she remarked on the age of the rosebushes. "I believe some of the ones in here now were in here when I was a young woman, and I am past eighty," she said. "My mother—this is her grave—used to say there were rosebushes just like these all over this section when she was a girl. Along the riverbank, beside the roads, in people's yards, on fences, in waste places. And she said *her* mother—that's her grave over there—told her she had heard from *her* mother that all of them were descended from one bush that some poor uprooted woman who came to this country back in the Dutch times potted up and brought along with her. There used to be a great many more in the cemetery than there are now—they overran everything—and every time my mother visited the cemetery she would stand and look at them and kind of laugh. She thought they were a nuisance. All the same, for some reason of her own, she admired them, and enjoyed looking at them. 'I know why they do so well in here,' she'd say. 'They've got good strong roots that go right down into the graves.'"

The water beside several of the factory piers in Shadyside has been deepened by dredging to depths ranging between twenty and thirty feet. Everywhere else along Edgewater the inshore water is shallow. Off the upper part of town are expanses of shoals that are called the Edgewater Flats. They are mucky, miry, silty, and oily. Stretches of them are exposed at low tide, or have only a foot or two of water over them. In some places, they go out two hundred yards before they reach a depth of six feet. For generations, the Edgewater Flats have been a dumping ground for wrecks. Out in them, lying every which way, as if strewn about long ago by a storm, are the ruins of scores of river vessels. Some of these vessels were replaced by newer vessels and laid up in the flats against a time that they might possibly be used again, and that time never came. Some got out of commission and weren't worth repairing, and were towed into the flats and stripped of their metal and abandoned. Some had leaks, some had fires, and some had collisions. At least once a day, usually when the tide is at or around dead ebb, flocks of harbor gulls suddenly appear and light on the wrecks and scavenge the refuse that has collected on them during the rise and fall of the tide, and for a little while they crawl with gulls, they become white and ghostly with gulls, and then the gulls leave as suddenly as they came. The hulks of three ferryboats are out in the flats—the *Shadyside,* the *George Washington,* and the old *Fort Lee.* Nothing is left of the *Shadyside* but a few of her ribs and part of her keel. There are old tugboats out there, and old dump scows, and old derrick lighters, and old car floats. There are sand-and-gravel barges, and brick barges, and stone barges, and coal barges, and slaughterhouse barges. There are five ice barges out there, the last of a fleet that used to bring natural ice down to New York City from the old icehouse section along the west shore of the river, between Saugerties and Coxsackie. They have been in the flats since 1910, they are waterlogged, and they sit like hippopotamuses in the silt.

Close to shore are some barges that are still being used. They are drawn up in a straggly row, facing the shore, and narrow, zigzaggy footwalks built on piles made of drift lumber go out to them. These are second-hand railroad barges. They were once owned by the Pennsylvania, the Erie, the New York Central, the Jersey Central, and other railroads that operate barge fleets in the harbor. Their bottoms are sound and their roofs are tight, but they got too old to be jerked this way and that by tugs in a hurry and bumped about and banged into (most of them are over forty years old, and several are over sixty), so they were discarded and sold. Some are owned by shadfishermen, who move them up or down the river at the start of the shad season and tie them up along the bank, each fisherman placing his barge as close as possible to his row of nets. The fishermen eat and sleep aboard them and use them as bases while the shad are running, and then return them to the flats and keep them there the rest of the year and store their equipment in them. Others are owned by boat clubs. There are seven boat clubs on the Edgewater riverfront, and four are quartered in secondhand railroad barges. One club, the Undercliff Motor Boat Club, owns two, but uses both for the winter storage of its boats, and has its quarters in an old queen of an oyster barge named the *G. M. Still.* The wholesale oyster companies in New York City used to carry on their businesses in specially built barges that were docked the year round at piers on the East River, just north of Fulton Fish Market. These barges had two or three decks, and could hold huge stocks of oysters. They were top-heavy but beautifully made. Some had balconies with banisters shaped like tenpins on their upper decks, and the offices in several had mahogany paneling; the reputation of an oyster company partly depended on the splendor of its barge. There were over a dozen oyster barges on the East River at one time, and all were painted a variety of colors and all had ostentatious black-and-gold nameboards across their fronts and all flew swallowtail pennants; people visited the waterfront just to see them. The *G. M. Still* was the last to go. It was owned by George M. Still, Inc., the planters of Diamond Point oysters, and its final East River location was at a pier at the foot of Pike Street, under the Manhattan Bridge; it was there for a generation. In 1949, the city took over this pier, and the Still company was unable to find another, so it moved ashore, and sold the barge to a dealer in old boats, who sold it to the boat club. The *G. M. Still* is almost eighty years old—it was built in 1880—and the recent years have been hard on it. Even so, not all the teardrops, icicles, scallops, and other scroll-saw curlicues that once ornamented it have disappeared, and its last coat of paint under the Still ownership—black, yellow, white, orange, and green—has not entirely faded, and the balcony on the bow end of its upper deck looks as regal as ever.

Although Edgewater is only a short ride by subway and bus from the heart of New York City, it has some of the characteristics of an isolated and ingrown old town in New England or the South. The population is approximately four thousand, and a large proportion of the people are natives and know each other, at least to speak to. A surprising number of them are related, some so distantly that they aren't at all sure just how. The elderly people take a deep interest in local history, a good deal of which has been handed down from generation to generation by word of mouth, and nearly all of them who are natives consider themselves authorities on the subject. When these elderly people were young, quite a few men and women bearing the names of the original Dutch and Huguenot families were still living in old family mansions along River Road—one old man or one old woman living alone, as often as not, or, in some cases, two old bachelor brothers or two old spinster sisters living together, or an old woman living with a bachelor son or a spinster daughter— and they remember them. They know in a general way how the present-day old families are interrelated, and how several of these families are related to the original families. They can fish around in their memories and bring up vital statistics and stray facts and rumors and old jokes and sayings concerning a multitude of people who have been dead and gone for a generation, and can point out where buildings stood that have been torn down for fifty years. Sometimes, in the manner of old people in old towns, unable to tell only a little when they know so much, they respond to a simple question with a labyrinthine answer. One day, shortly after I began going up to Edgewater, I became acquainted with an elderly native named Henry R. Gaul, and went for a walk with him. Mr. Gaul is a retired oil-company executive. For many years, the Valvoline Oil Company operated a refinery on the riverbank in Shadyside, and Mr. Gaul was chief clerk there. He is secretary of the Undercliff Motor Boat Club and, to have something to do, he looks after the club's winter-storage barges and its headquarters barge, the old *G. M. Still.* His friends call him Henny. Walking on River Road, Mr. Gaul and I came to an automobile that had broken down. It was alongside the curb, and two men in greasy overalls were working on it. One had the hood up, and was bent over the engine. The other was under-neath the automobile, flat on his back. As we were passing by, the man underneath thrust his head out, to say something to the man working on the engine. As he did so, he caught sight of Mr. Gaul. "Hello, Henny," he said.

Mr. Gaul was startled. He paused and turned and peered down at the man's face, and then said, "Oh, hello, Bill." "That was Bill Ingold," he said as we resumed our walk. "He runs the Edgewater Garage."

I was curious about the name; Mr. Gaul had referred to several names as old Edgewater names, and I asked him if Ingold was another one of them.

"Ingold?" he said. "Well, I should hope to think it is. It isn't one of the old Dutch names, but it's old enough, and Bill's got some of the old Dutch blood in him anyhow, through his mother's people. Knickerbocker Dutch. Not that he'd ever mention it. That's the way it is in Edgewater. There's a number of people over here who have old, old families back behind them—much older, I dare say, than the families back behind a high percentage of the people in the *Social Register* in New York—but you'd never find it out from them. Bill's mother was a Bishop, and *her* mother was a Carlock. The old Dutch blood came down to him through the Carlocks. The Carlocks were big people over here once, but they had a preponderance of daughters and the name died out. They owned land, and one branch of them ran a boatyard. The boatyard was torn down years and years ago, but I can tell you where it stood. Did you ever notice an ancient old clapboard building on the upper part of River Road with a saloon in it named Sulyma's Bar & Grill? Well, in the old days that building was a hotel named the Buena Vista Hotel, only we called it Walsch's, after the family that ran it. And just before you got to Walsch's, on the right, in between River Road and the river, was Carlock's Boatyard. Bill Ingold's father was also named Bill—William, that is, William F. He was in the Edgewater Fire Department. In fact, he was Fire Chief. He was a highly respected man, and I'll tell you a little story to illustrate that. There used to be an old gentleman in Edgewater named Frederick W. Winterburn. Mr. Winterburn was rich. He had inherited money, and he had married money, and he had made money. His wife was a Vreeland, and she was related to the Dyckmans *and* the Westervelts. Among other things, he owned practically the whole of Shadyside, and he lived down there. He lived in a big house overlooking the river, and he had a rose garden in front and an orchard in back.

On warm summer nights, walking along River Road, you could smell the roses in his garden. And you could smell the peaches in his orchard, all soft and ripe and still warm from the sun and a little breeze blowing across them. And you could smell the grapes hanging on a fence between the garden and the orchard. They were fox grapes, and they had a musky smell. I'd give anything to smell those grapes again. The garden had marble statues in it. Statues of women. Naked woman. Naked marble women. Goddesses, I guess you'd call them. In the moonlight, they looked real. It's all gone now, and there's a factory there. One piece of Mr. Winterburn's property surrounded the Edgewater Cemetery. His parents were buried in this cemetery, and his wife's people all the way back to the seventeenth century were buried in there, and he knew he was going to be buried in there, and he took a personal interest in it. In 1909 or 1910 or thereabouts—it might've been a few years earlier or a few years later—Mr. Winterburn was beginning to have a feeling that time was running out on him, he wouldn't be here much longer, although to tell you the truth he lived quite a few years more, and one day he asked five men to come to his house. All of them were from old Edgewater families and had people buried in the cemetery, and one of them was Bill Ingold's father, Fire Chief Ingold. 'Sit down, boys,' Mr. Winterburn said, 'I want to talk to you. Boys,' he said, 'my family owns much more space in the cemetery than it'll ever need or make use of, and I'm going to set aside a section of it for a poor plot. Any bona fide resident of Edgewater who dies a pauper can be buried in this plot, free of charge. And suicides that are turned away by other cemeteries can be buried in there, provided they're residents. And non-residents that drown in the river and wash up on the Edgewater riverfront and don't have any identification on them, the way it sometimes happens, it doesn't make any difference if it looks accidental or looks as if they threw themselves in, they can be buried in there. Furthermore, I'm going to set up a trust fund, and I'm going to fix it so the principal can't ever be touched, whereas the interest can be used in perpetuity to keep up the cemetery. And I want you boys to form a cemetery association and elect a president and a secretary and a treasurer, and the duties of these officers shall be to keep an eye on the cemetery and visit it every now and then and make a tour of inspection through it and hire a caretaker and see that he keeps the weeds cut and the leaves raked and whenever the occasion arises rule on who can be buried in the poor plot and who can't be.' So they put it to a vote, and Fire Chief Ingold was elected president without any discussion whatsoever. It was taken for granted. That's how respected he was. And after he died, Bill was elected president, and he's held the office ever since. Did I mention Bill's mother was a Bishop? Well, she was. The Bishops were. . . "

Some of the people in Edgewater commute to jobs in New York City, and some work in the river towns south of Edgewater, which are, in order, going south, North Bergen, Guttenberg, West New York, Weehawken, Hoboken, and Jersey City, but the majority work in the factories in Shadyside. A score or so of men are spoken of around town as rivermen. This word has a special shade of meaning in Edgewater: a riverman not only works on the river or kills a lot of time on it or near it, he is also emotionally attached to it—he can't stay away from it. Charles Allison is an example. Mr. Allison lives in Edgewater and works in North Bergen. He is a partner in the Baldwin & Allison Dry Dock Co., a firm that operates a drydock and calks and repairs barges and drives piles and builds docks and does marine surveying and supplies pumps for salvage work, but that is only one of the reasons he is looked upon as a riverman. The main reason is that the river has a hold on him. Most days he is on or around it from early in the morning until sunset. Nevertheless, he often goes down to it at night and walks beside it. Even on Sundays and holidays, he often goes down to it. The offices of the drydock company are in a superstructure built on the deck of an old railroad barge that is permanently docked at a pier in North Bergen, and Mr. Allison has had big wide windows put in three of the walls of his private office, so that he can sit at his desk and see up, down, and across the river. Every spring, he takes a leave of absence from the drydock, and spends from six weeks to two months living aboard a shad barge on the river and fishing two rows of shad nets with a crew of hired fishermen.

Some men work full time on the river—on ferries, tugs, or

barges—and are not considered rivermen; they are simply men who work on the river. Other men work only a part of the year on the river and make only a part of their living there but *are* considered rivermen. Mr. Ingold, the garage proprietor, is one of these. His garage is on River Road, facing the river. It is a typical small, drafty, one-story garage, except that hanging on its walls, in among the fan belts and the brake linings and the dented chromium hubcaps and the calendars with naked girls on them, are anchors and oars and hanks of netting and dozens of rusty old eelpots. Also, standing in a shallow box of sand in the middle of the floor is a stove of a kind that would be recognizable only to people who are familiar with harbor shipping; it is shaped like an oil drum and burns coke and is a kind that is used in barges and lighters to keep perishable freight from freezing. Mr. Ingold took it out of an old Erie Railroad fruit-and-vegetable barge. In the winter, a group of elderly Edgewater men, most of whom are retired, sit around it and gossip and argue; in the summer, they move their chairs up front to the door, where they can look out on the river and the Manhattan skyline. Mr. Ingold owns two shad barges and several shad boats, and keeps them at a landing a short walk up the river from the garage. Off and on during the winter, he and another riverman, Eustus R. Smith, stretch shad nets across the floor of the garage and put them in shape. They rig new nets, and mend and splice old ones. They are helped occasionally by Mr. Ingold's son, Willy, and by Mr. Smith's son, Charlie. In the spring, Mr. Ingold leaves the garage in the hands of two mechanics, and he and his son and Mr. Smith and his son go out on the river and become shadfishermen for a couple of months. In the late fall and early winter, when the eels in the river are at their best and bring the highest prices, Mr. Ingold and Willy set eelpots. They set sixty, and their favorite grounds are up around Spuyten Duyvil, where the Harlem River runs into the Hudson. Some nights during the eel season, after knocking off work in the garage, Mr. Ingold gets in an outboard and goes up to Spuyten Duyvil and attends to the pots, drawing them up hand over hand from the bottom and taking out the trapped eels and putting in fresh bait, and some nights Willy goes up. On dark nights, they wear miner's caps that have head lamps on them. Mr. Ingold has been dividing his time between the garage and the river for thirty-five years. Invariably, at the end of the shad season he is so tired he has to hole up in bed for a few days, and he always resolves to stay put in the garage from then on—no man can serve two masters—but when the eel season comes around he always finds himself back on the river again.

THE RIVERMAN I KNOW BEST is an old-timer named Harry Lyons. Harry is seventy-four, and has been around the river all his life. He lives with his wife, Mrs. Juel Lyons, in a two-story frame-and-fieldstone house backed up against the base of the Palisades, on Undercliff Avenue, in the upper part of Edgewater. He owns a shad barge and an assortment of boats, and keeps them anchored just off the riverbank, a few minutes' walk from his house. Harry is five feet six, and weighs a hundred and fifty. He is one of those short, hearty, robust men who hold themselves erect and swagger a little and are more imposing than many taller, larger men. He has an old-Roman face. It is strong-jawed and prominent-nosed and bushy-eyebrowed and friendly and reasonable and sagacious and elusively piratical. Ordinarily, down on the riverfront, he looks like a beachcomber: he wears old pants and a windbreaker and old shoes with slashes cut in them, and he goes bareheaded and his hair sticks straight up. One day, however, by chance, I ran into him on a River Road bus, and he was on his way to a funeral down in Weehawken, and he was wearing his Sunday clothes and his hair was brushed and his face was solemn, and I was surprised at how distinguished he looked; he looked worldly and cultivated and illustrious.

Harry spends a large part of his time wandering up and down the riverfront looking at the river, or sitting on his barge looking at the river, but he isn't lazy. He believes in first things first; if there is anything at home or on the barge that should be attended to, he goes ahead and attends to it, and then sits down. He is handy with tools, and has a variety of skills. He is a good fisherman, a good netmaker, a fairly good carpenter, a fairly good all-round mechanic, and an excellent fish cook. He is especially good at cooking shad, and is one of the few men left who know how to run an old-fashioned Hudson River shad bake. Shad bakes are gluttonous spring-time blowouts that are held in the middle or latter part of the shad season, generally under the trees on the riverbank, near a shad barge. They are given by lodges and labor unions, and by business, social, political, and religious organizations, and by individuals. Former Mayor Wissel—he was Mayor of Edgewater for thirty years—used to give one every year for the public officials in Edgewater and nearby towns.

When Harry is engaged to run a bake, he selects a sufficient number of roe shad from his own nets and dresses them himself and takes the roes out of them. He has a shad boner come up from Fulton Fish Market and bone them. Then, using zinc roofing nails, he nails them spread-eagle fashion to white-oak planks, one fish to a plank; the planks are two feet long, a foot and a half wide, and an inch thick, and have adjustable props fixed to their sides so that it is possible to stand them upright or tilt them backward. He nails two or three strips of bacon across each fish. When it is time to cook the fish—they aren't baked, they are broiled—he props the planks up, fish-side foremost, in a ring around a bed of charcoal that has been burning on the ground for hours and is red-hot and radiant. He places the planks only six inches or so from the coals, but he gradually moves them farther back, so that the fish will broil slowly and pick up the flavors of the bacon and the oak; they broil for almost an hour. Every so often, he takes a turn around the ring and thoroughly mops each fish with a cotton mop, which he keeps dipping into a pot of melted butter. While Harry looks after the shad, Mrs. Lyons looks after the roes, cooking them in butter in huge frying pans. Pickled beets and new potatoes boiled in their skins are usually served with the shad and the roe. Paper plates are used. The people eat on tables made of boards laid across sawhorses, and are encouraged to have several helpings. Cooked shad-bake style by an expert, shad is crusty on the outside and tender and rich and juicy on the inside (but not too rich, since a good deal of the oil has been broiled out of it), and fully justifies its scientific name,

*Alosa sapidissima,* the *"Alosa"* of which means "shad" and the *"sapidissima"* of which means "good to eat to a superlative degree." Shad bakes require a lot of work, and most of them are small affairs. Some years, the New Jersey Police Chiefs' Association gives a big one. Some years, a group of boss fishmongers in Fulton Market gives a big one. Some years, the Palisades Interstate Park Commission gives a big one. The biggest on the river is one that Harry and Mrs. Lyons have been giving for over twenty years for the benefit of the building fund of Mrs. Lyons' church. This bake is held on the riverbank a short distance above the George Washington Bridge, usually on the Sunday following Mother's Day Sunday, and every year around two hundred and fifty people come to it.

Mrs. Lyons is a handsome, soft-spoken blond woman, quite a few years younger than Harry. She is a native of Fort Lee, the next town on the river north of Edgewater. Her maiden name was Kotze, her parents were Swiss-German, and she was brought up a Roman Catholic. When she was a young woman, out of curiosity, while visiting a friend in Brooklyn, she attended a meeting of a congregation of the Reorganized Church of Jesus Christ of Latter Day Saints, which is the oldest and most widespread of several schismatic branches of the Mormon religion. A number of prophecies and warnings from the Book of Mormon, an apocalyptic Mormon scripture, were read at the meeting, and she was deeply impressed by them. She borrowed a copy of the Book and studied it for some weeks, whereupon she left the Catholic Church and joined the Reorganized Church. The congregation with which she is affiliated holds its services in a hall in the Masonic Temple in Lyndhurst, New Jersey. Harry was brought up an Episcopalian, but he doesn't feel strongly about denominations—one is as good as another to him—and since his marriage he has gone regularly to the Reorganized Church services. Harry and his wife have one daughter, Audrey. She is a member of the Reorganized Church, and went to Graceland College, a junior college sponsored by the church, in Lamoni, Iowa. She is married to John Maxcy, who is a Buick salesman in Englewood, New Jersey, and they have two children—Michele, who is sixteen, and Brian, who is eleven.

Harry is generally supposed to know more about the river than any of the other rivermen, and a great deal of what he knows was handed down to him; his family has lived beside the river for a long time, and many of his ancestors on both sides were rivermen. He has old Dutch blood and old English blood, and gravestones of ancestors of his are all over the Edgewater Cemetery. He is related to several of the oldest families in New York and New Jersey. Through his mother, who was a Truax, he is a descendant of Philippe du Trieux, one of the first settlers of New York City. Du Trieux was a Walloon who lived in Amsterdam and who came to New Amsterdam in 1624 and build a house either on a lane that is now Beaver Street or on a lane that is now Pearl Street—the historians aren't sure which. A scholarly study of his descendants—the name has been spelled Truex or Truax for generations—was published in installments in The *New York Genealogical and Biographical Record* in 1926, 1927, and 1928. In this study, Harry is listed in the tenth generation of descent from du Trieux.

Harry was born in the upper part of Edgewater, in May, 1884. The house in which he was born is still standing; it is just up the street from the house he lives in now. He went to school in what people of his generation in Edgewater refer to as "the old school-house." This was a wooden building on River Road, on a bluff above the river. It had only two rooms—one for the lower grades and one for the upper grades—and was torn down many years ago. I once heard several old-timers sitting around the barge stove in Ingold's garage get on the subject of the old schoolhouse. One of them, former Fire Chief Lasher, said that he had gone to it, and mentioned a number of men around town who had gone to it at the same time, among them Bill Ingold and Charlie Allison and Harry Lyons, and I asked him what kind of student Harry Lyons had been. "Oh, Harry was bright enough, but he was like the rest of us—he didn't apply himself," Chief Lasher said. "All he studied was the river. At recess, he'd race down to the river and fool around in the mud and attend to some old eelpot he had down there, or crab trap, or bait car, or whatever it was, and I've never in my life seen anybody get so muddy. He was famous for it. He'd get that sticky river mud all over him, and he wouldn't even try to get it off. Some days, when recess was over, he'd be so muddy the teacher wouldn't let him come back in—she'd send him home. I've been watching rivermen a long time, and they're all like that; they love the mud. Harry's nickname was Hotch. People in Edgewater used to have an expression, if they wanted to say that somebody or something was unusually muddy, they'd say that he or she or it was as muddy as Hotch Lyons. Once in a long while, you still hear somebody come out with that expression. I was standing in line in the A. & P. one day last summer and just ahead of me were two ladies my age. I went to school with them, and I remember them when they were little girls, and I remember them when they were young women, and I remember them when they were middle-aged women in the prime of life, and I imagine the same thought that crosses my mind when I look at them nowadays must also cross their minds when they look at me—How fast time flew! So we were standing there, and one of them turned to the other and said, 'The rain this morning beat down my tomato bushes, and I went out and tried to straighten them up, and I got as muddy as Hotch Lyons,' and all three of us burst out laughing. It brought back the old times."

Harry's father, William Masters Lyons, was an engineer on the Edgewater ferry. Harry was never as close to him as he was to his maternal grandfather, Isaac Truax, who was a riverman. "My father had a good disposition, but he was serious," Harry says. "My grandfather Truax would say things that were funny—at least, to me. He would mimic people and say awful things about them. When I was just a little tiny boy, I began to eat most of my meals at his house and follow him around. He was a great one for going out on the river in the wind and the rain and all kinds of weather, and I'd go along. And then, on a nice sunshiny day, when he should've been out on the river, he'd sit on the porch and read. He didn't have much education, and he didn't even think much of schools, but he had three books that he liked—two books of Shakespeare's writings that had come down to him from his father, and a big Bible with pictures in it that would lift the hair on your head—and he'd sometimes read things to me and explain them, or try to."

Mr. Truax shadfished, and set fykes. A fyke is a long, tunnel-like net that is set on or close to the bottom. It is held open by a series of wooden hoops; a pair of wings flaring out from its mouth guide fish into it; and it catches a little of everything. The spring when Harry was fifteen, Mr. Truax made an unusually large fyke and set it in an inshore channel of the river, off Fort Lee, and Harry quit school to help him operate it. "I decided it was about time for me to graduate from school," Harry says, "so I graduated out the back door." Once or twice a week, if fish prices were good in the city, Mr. Truax and Harry would empty the fyke and row or sail their catch down to one of the riverfront markets in lower Manhattan. Sometimes they would go to Gansevoort Market or Washington Market, on the Hudson, and sometimes they would keep on and go around the Battery to Fulton Market, on the East River. Mr. Truax owned a horse and wagon. If prices were poor, he and Harry would drive out in the country and sell their fish at farmhouses. "My grandfather knew all the fish-eating country people in this part of Bergen County," Harry says, "and they liked to see him coming down the road. If they didn't have any money to spend he'd swap them fish for anything they had, and we'd go home with a wide variety of country produce in the wagon—sausage meat and head-cheese and blood pudding and hard cider and buttermilk and duck eggs and those good old heavy yellow-fleshed strong turnipy-tasting turnips that they call rutabagas, and stuff like that. One day, we drove up in a man's yard, and he had just cut down a bee tree in the woods in back of his house, and we swapped him a bucket of live eels for a quart of wild honey."

When Harry was nineteen, Mr. Truax gave up fishing with fykes and began to depend entirely on what he made from shadfishing. For ten years or so, Harry helped him fish a couple of rows of shad nets in the spring, and worked the rest of the year at jobs he picked up on or around the river. He worked mostly as a deckhand on tugboats. He worked on two of the Valvoline Oil Company's tugs, the *Magnet* and the *Magic Safety,* and on several of the tugs in the New York, New Haven & Hartford's fleet. Mr. Truax died in 1913, aged eighty-four. For three years thereafter, Harry fished a row of shad nets of his own and set a fyke of his own. In 1915, he got married, and began to worry about money for the first time in his life. In 1916, a fireman's job became open in the Edgewater Fire Department, and he took it. Edgewater has three firehouses. Firehouse No. 1, in which Harry was stationed, is on River Road, a few yards north of the site of the old schoolhouse. It faces the river, and it has a wooden bench in front of it. "Before I joined the Fire Department," Harry once said, "my main occupation was sitting down looking at the river. After I joined the department, that continued to be my main occupation, only I got paid for it." He was a fireman for twenty-six years, and was allowed to take a leave of absence every spring and fish a row of shad nets. He became eligible for a pension in 1942. On April 1st of that year, at the start of the shad season, he retired, and resumed his life as a full-time riverman.

In the spring, Harry sets shad nets. In the fall, he sets eelpots. Some days, he goes crabbing. Now and then, in every season, not for money but for fun and for the table, he fishes with a hand line or a bamboo pole or a rod and reel. He is an accomplished baitcaster, and it is a pleasure to watch him stand on the bank and cast a knot of bloodworms to the outer edge of the flats, out past the wrecks, and bring in a striped bass. He isn't a striped-bass snob, however, and he often joins the old men and women who come down to the river on sunny afternoons and pole-fish from the bank for anything at all that will bite. Many of the old men and women are opinionated and idiosyncratic, and he enjoys listening to them, and observing the odd rigs that they devise and the imaginative baits that they use. Around Edgewater, catfish and tomcod and lafayettes and eels are about the only fish that can be caught close to the bank, but that is all right with Harry; he doesn't look down on any of these fish. In common with most of the rivermen, he has a great liking for catfish; he likes to catch them and he likes to eat them. In the spring and early summer, large numbers of catfish show up in the lower Hudson; the spring freshets bring them down from fresh water. Some are enormous. In 1953, one was caught near the George Washington Bridge that weighed over thirty pounds, and every year a few are caught around Edgewater that weigh between ten and twenty pounds. One Saturday afternoon last spring, an old Negro woman fishing a short distance up the bank from Harry caught two big ones, one right after the other. Harry and several other fishermen went over to look at them, and one of the fishermen, who had a hand scale, weighed them; the first weighed seventeen pounds and the second weighed twelve. Harry asked the old woman what kind of bait she had been using. "Chicken guts," she said. Harry also has a great liking for tomcod. The tomcod is a greedy little inshore fish that belongs to the cod family and resembles the deep-sea codfish in every respect but size—it seldom gets much longer that seven inches or weighs more than half a pound, and it gives the appearance of being a midget codfish. It comes into the waters around the city to feed and to spawn, and it is almost as ubiquitous as the eel. There are a few tomcod in every part of the harbor every month of the year. In the late fall and early winter, during their spawning runs, they are abundant, and some days thousands upon thousands of them are caught from piers and sea walls and bulkheads and jetties all the way from Rockaway Point to the Battery, and from the banks of the Hudson and the East River and the Harlem River and the Arthur Kill and the Kill van Kull. They are eaten mainly in the homes of the people who catch them; I have rarely seen them in fish stores, and have never seen them on a menu. Harry thinks the tomcod is greatly undervalued; it is what he calls a sweet-meated fish, and he considers it the best fish, next to shad and snapper bluefish, that enters the river. "There's only one thing wrong with tommycods," he once said. "It takes seventeen of them to make a dozen." On sunny, crystal-clear mornings in the fall, when it is possible to see into the water, he gets in one of his boats and rows out into the flats and catches some river shrimp. River shrimp—they are also called harbor shrimp and mud shrimp, and are really prawns—are tiny; they are only about an inch and a quarter long, including the head. There are sometimes dense swarms of them in the slues between the barges. Harry catches them with a dip net and empties them into a bucket. When he has a supply, he rows farther out into the flats and ties up to one of the old wrecks and sits there and fishes for tomcod, using a hand line and baiting the hook with the shrimp. Occasionally, he pops some of the shrimp into his mouth—he eats them raw and spits out the shells. By noon, as a rule, he has all the tomcod he can use; he has often caught a hundred and fifty in a morning.

Every so often during January, February, and March, Harry gets up early and puts some sandwiches in his pockets and goes down to his barge and starts a fire in one of the stoves in it and spends the day working on his shadfishing gear. While the river wind hisses and purrs and pipes and whistles through cracks and knotholes in the sides of the barge, he paints an anchor, or overhauls an outboard motor, or makes one net out of the strongest parts of two or three old ones. He works in a leisurely fashion, and keeps a pot of coffee on the stove. Sometimes he goes over and sits beside a window and watches the traffic on the river for an hour or so. Quite often, in the afternoon, one of the other rivermen comes in and helps himself to a cup of coffee and sits down and gossips for a while. Harry's barge is a big one. It is a hundred and ten feet long and thirty-two feet wide. Except for narrow little decks at its bow and stern, it is covered with a superstructure made of heart-pine posts and white-pine clapboards. The superstructure is patched here and there with tar paper, and has a tar-paper roof. It is an old Delaware, Lackawanna & Western barge; on its sides are faded signs that say, "D L & W # 530." It is forty-two years old. When it was thirty years old, a fire that broke out in some cargo damaged parts of its interior; the Lackawanna repaired it and used it for two more years, and then sold it to Harry. Harry has partitioned off two rooms in the bow end of it—one for a galley and one for a bunkroom. In the middle of the bunkroom is a statuesque old claw-footed Sam Oak stove. Around the stove are seven rickety chairs, no two of which are mates. One is a swivel chair whose spring has collapsed. Built against one of the partitions, in three tiers, are twelve bunks. Harry usually makes a fire in the Sam Oak stove and works in the bunkroom; there is a stove in the galley that burns bottled gas and is much easier to manage, but he feels more at home with the Sam Oak, which burns coal or wood. He sometimes uses driftwood that he picks up on the riverbank. The galley and the bunkroom take up less than a third of the space in the barge. The rest of the space is used for storage, and scattered about in it are oars and sweeps and hawsers and kerosene lanterns and shad-bake planks and tin tubs and blocks and tackles and cans of boat paint and sets of scales and stacks of fish boxes. Hanging in festoons from the rafters are dozens of nets, some of which are far too old and ripped and rotten ever to be put in the water again.

ONE DAY IN LATE FEBRUARY, the weather was surprisingly sunny and warm. It was one of those balmy days that sometimes turn up in the winter, like a strange bird blown off its course. Walking back to my office after lunch, I began to dawdle. Suddenly the idea occurred to me, why not take the afternoon off and go over to Edgewater and go for a walk along the river and breathe a little clean air for a change. I fought a brief fight with my conscience, and then I entered the Independent subway at Forty-second Street and rode up to the 168th Street station and went upstairs to the Public Service bus terminal and got a No. 8 bus. This bus goes across the George Washington Bridge and heads south and runs through a succession of riverfront towns, the second of which is Edgewater. It is a pleasant trip in itself. At the town limits of Edgewater, there is a sign that says, "WELCOME TO EDGEWATER. WHERE HOMES AND INDUSTRY BLEND. EDGEWATER CHAMBER OF COM-MERCE." A couple of bus stops past this sign, I got out, as I usually do, and began to walk along River Road. I looked at my watch; I had made good connections, and the trip from Forty-second Street had taken only thirty-six minutes. The sunshine was so warm that my overcoat felt burdensome. All along the west side of River Road, women had come out into their front yards and were slowly walking around, looking at the dead stalks and vines in their flower beds. I saw a woman squat sideways beside what must have been a bulb border and rake away some leaves with her fingers. She peered at the ground for a few moments, and then swept the leaves back with one sweep of her hand. In the upper part of Edgewater, River Road is high above the river, and a steep, wooded slope lies between the east side of it and the riverbank. Just past the George Washington School, a public school on the site of the old schoolhouse, there is a bend in the road from which it is possible to look down almost on the tops of the shad barges drawn up close to the riverbank along there. I looked the barges over, and picked out Harry's. Smoke was coming from its stovepipe, and I decided to stop by and have a cup of coffee with Harry. Several paths descend from the road to the riverbank. Children like to slide on them and play on them, and they are deeply rutted. As I started down one of them, Harry came out on the bow deck of his barge and looked up and saw me and waved. A few minutes later, I crossed the riverbank and went out on the ramshackle footwalk that extends from the riverbank to his barge and climbed the ladder that is fixed to the bow and stepped on deck, and he and I shook hands. "Go inside and get yourself a cup of coffee and bring it out here, why don't you," he said, "and let's sit in the sun a little while."

When I returned to the deck, Harry motioned toward the riverbank with his head and said, "Look who's coming." Two men had just started up the footwalk. One was a stranger to me. The other was an old friend and contemporary of Harry's named Joe Hewitt. I have run into him a number of times, and have got to know him fairly well. Mr. Hewitt is six feet two and portly and red-faced. He lives in Fort Lee, but he is a native of Edgewater and belongs to one of the old Edgewater families. He went to school in the old schoolhouse at the same time as Harry, and fished and worked around the river for a few years, and then went to a business school on Park Row, in Manhattan, called the City Hall Academy. Through an uncle, who was in the trucking business and often trucked shad from Edgewater and other riverfront towns to Fulton Market during the shad season, he got a job as a clerk in the old Fulton Market firm of John Feeney, Inc. He became head bookkeeper in Feeney's, and subsequently worked for several other firms in the fish market. He retired over ten years ago. He spends a lot of time in Edgewater, and often hangs out in Ingold's garage. Years ago, Mr. Hewitt bought three tracts of cheap land along the Hackensack River, one in Hudson County and two in Bergen County; he speaks of them as "those mosquito bogs of mine." In recent years, two of these tracts have increased in value enormously, and he has sold sections of them for housing developments and shopping centers, and has become well-to-do. He is a generous man, and often goes out of his way to help people. Once in a while, a riverman gets in a bad jam of some kind and is broke to begin with and other rivermen take up a collection for him, and Mr. Hewitt almost always gives more than anyone else. However, despite his generosity and kindness, he has a bleak outlook on life, and doesn't try to hide it. "Things have worked out very well for you, Joe," I once heard another retired man remark to him one day in Ingold's garage, "and you ought to look at things a little more cheerful than you do." "I'm not so sure I have anything to be cheerful about," Mr. Hewitt replied. "I'm not so sure you have, either. I'm not so sure anybody has."

"Who is the man with Mr. Hewitt?" I asked Harry.

"I never saw him before," Harry said.

Mr. Hewitt came up the ladder first, and stepped on deck, puffing and blowing.

"The sun was so nice we decided to walk down from Fort Lee," he said, "and what a mistake that was! The traffic is getting worse and worse on River Road. Oh, it scares me! Those big heavy trucks flying past, it's worth your life to step off the curb. Slam on their brakes, they couldn't stop; you'd be in the hospital before they even slowed down. You'd be lying on the operating table with an arm off, an arm and a leg, an arm and a leg and one side of your head, and they'd still be rolling. And the noise they make! The shot and shell on the battlefield wouldn't be much worse. What was that old poem? How'd it go, how'd it go? I used to know it. 'In Flanders fields the poppies blow, between the crosses, row on row. . . ' And good God, gentlemen, the Cadillacs! While we were standing there, waiting and waiting for a chance to cross, six big black Cadillacs shot by, practically one right after the other, and it wasn't any funeral, either."

"Times are good, Joe," said Harry. "Times are good."

"Thieves," said Mr. Hewitt.

His companion reached the top of the ladder and awkwardly stepped on deck. "Gentlemen," said Mr. Hewitt, "this is my brother-in-law Frank Townsend." He turned to Harry. "Harry," he said, "you've heard me speak of Frank. He's Blanche's younger brother, the one who's in the sprinkler-system business. Or was. He's retired now." He turned to me. "Blanche is my wife," he said. Then he turned to Mr. Townsend. "Sit down, Frank," he said, "and get your breath." Mr. Townsend sat down on a capstan. "Frank lives in Syracuse," continued Mr. Hewitt. "He's been down in Florida, and he's driving back, and he's spending a few days with us. Since he retired, he's got interested in fishing. I told him the shadfishermen all along the Hudson are getting ready for shad season, and he's never seen a shad barge, and I thought I'd bring him down here and show him one, and explain shadfishing to him."

Harry's eyebrows rose. "Shadfishing hasn't changed much through the years, Joe," he said, "but it's been a long, long time since you lifted a net. Maybe you better let me do the explaining."

"I wish you would," said Mr. Hewitt. "I was hoping you would."

"I'll make it as brief as possible," said Harry, walking over to the edge of the deck. "Step over here, Mr. Townsend, and look over the side. Do you see those poles lying down there in the mud? They're shagbark-hickory poles, and they're fifty to seventy feet long, and they're the foundation of shadfishing; everything else depends on them. During shad season, we stick them up in the river in rows at right angles to the shore, and hitch our nets to them. When the season's finished, we pull them up and bring them in here in the flats and bed them in the mud on both sides of our barges until we're ready to use them again. They turn green down there, from the green slime, but that's all right—the slime preserves them. As long as we keep them damp, they stay strong and supple and sound. If we let them dry out, they lose their strength and their give and start to rot."

Mr. Townsend interrupted Harry. "How much do they cost you?" he asked.

"Shad is an expensive fish, Mr. Townsend, not to speak of shad roe," Harry said, "and one of the reasons is it's expensive to fish for. You can't just pick up the phone and order a shad pole from a lumberyard. You have to hunt all over everywhere and find a farmer who has some full-grown hickory trees in his woods and is willing to sell some, and even then he might not have any that are tall enough and straight enough and strong enough and limber enough. I get mine from a farmer who owns some deep woods in Pennsylvania. When I need some new ones, I go out there—in the dead of winter, usually, a couple of months before shad season starts—and spend the whole day tramping around in his woods looking at his hickories. And I don't just look at a tree—I study it from all sides and try to imagine how it would take the strain if it was one of a row of poles staked in the Hudson River holding up a shad net and the net was already heavy with fish and a full-moon tide was pushing against the net and bellying it out and adding more fish to it all the time. I study hundreds of them. Then I pick out the likeliest-looking ones and blaze them with an axe. The farmer cuts them down, and sends them up here on a trailer truck. Then I and a couple of men around the river go to work on them and peel their bark off and trim their knots off and smooth them down with adzes and drawknives and planes until there's no splinters or rough spots on them anywhere that the net could catch on. Then we sharpen their butt ends, to make it easier to drive them into the river bottom. I pay the farmer eighteen to twenty dollars apiece for them. After the trucking charges are added to that, and the wages of the men who help me trim them, I figure they cost me between thirty-five and forty dollars apiece. You need at least forty of them for every row you fish. Tugboats are always blundering into them at night and passing right over them and bending them down until they crack in two, so you also have to have a supply of spares set aside. In other words, the damned things run into money."

Some young girls—there were perhaps a dozen of them, and they were eight or nine or maybe ten years old—had come down one of the paths from River Road, and now they were chasing each other around on the riverbank. They were as overexcited as blue jays, and their fierce, jubilant, fresh young voices filled the air.

"School's out," said Harry.

Several of the girls took up a position near the shore end of the footwalk to Harry's barge. Two of them started turning a rope and singing a rope-jumping song, a third ran in and started jumping the rope, and the others got in line. The song began:

> *"Mama, Mama,*
> *I am ill.*
> *Send for the doctor*
> *To give me a pill.*
> *Doctor, Doctor,*
> *Will I die?*
> *Yes, my child,*
> *And so will I—"*

Mr. Hewitt looked at them gloomily. "They get louder every year," he said.

"I like to hear them," said Harry. "It's been sixty years since I was in school, but I know exactly how they feel. Now, Mr. Townsend, to get back to shadfishing," he continued, "the first thing a man starting out as a shadfisherman has to have is a supply of poles, and the next thing he has to have is a row—that is, a place in the river where he can stake his poles year after year. In the old days, a man could pretty much decide for himself where his row should be, just so he didn't get too close to another man's row or get out in a ship channel or interfere with access to a pier. However, the shipping interests and the tugboat interests were always complaining that the shadfishermen acted as if they owned the river, and vice versa, so the Army Engineers finally stepped in. The Engineers have jurisdiction over all the navigable rivers in the country, insofar as the protection of navigation is concerned. About twenty years ago, just before World War Two, they went out and made a study of the Hudson from the standpoint of shadfishing versus navigation, and the outcome was they abolished some of the rows and left some right where they were and moved some and laid out a few new ones. Every year, they re-survey the rows, and some years they move or abolish one or two more. The best rows are in what's called the lower river—the section from the mouth of the river, down at the Battery, to the east-and-west boundary line between New Jersey and New York, which is about twenty miles up. Now, all the way up to this point the north-and-south boundary line between the two states is the middle of the river, and it so happens that all this distance all the shad rows are in the half of the river that belongs to New Jersey—there can't be any over in the New York half, because the main ship channel is in it. At present, there are fifty-five of these rows. The first row is off the big New York Central grain elevator in the railroad yards in Weehawken, about on a level with Sixtieth Street in Manhattan. It's a short row, only five hundred feet across, and it's entirely too near the ocean-liner traffic to suit me. Now and then, a big Cunarder or a Furness Line boat or a Swedish American Line boat will back out of one of the piers in the Fifties, and when she gets out in the river she'll keep on backing to get in position to go down the channel, and her backwash will hit the first row and churn the net up and down and whip it against the poles and empty the fish out of it. Some days, the backwash of those boats can be felt practically all the way to Albany. The fifty-fifth row is off the village of Alpine, which is about on a level with Yonkers and just below the east-and-west boundary line. Up above this line, the whole river belongs to New York, and the New York shadfishermen take over. Some of them fish the same as we do, in rows, with nets hitched to poles, but most of them fish with nets that they drift from boats. Their rows aren't as good as ours. One reason is, you're bound to catch more fish if you have the first crack at them. And another reason is, the sooner shad are caught after they leave the sea—or, a plainer way of putting it, the less time they spend in the river water—the better they taste and the more they're worth. The Engineers have the say-so as to where a row can be placed, but the Conservation Department of the state in whose waters the row is located has the say-so as to who can fish it. The New Jersey rows don't change hands very often; once a man gets one, he can renew his rights to it every year, and he generally holds on to it until he dies, and then it goes to whoever's next on the waiting list. You don't rent a row—what you do is, every year you take out a license for each row you fish, and a license costs twenty-five dollars. Most of the rows off Edgewater and Weehawken are very old. One of the Edgewater rows has been fished for at least a hundred and fifty years, and maybe a good while longer. A man named Bill Ingold fishes it now, but it's still called the Truax row, after my grandfather, Isaac Truax, who fished it for many years. When my grandfather had it, it was called the Scott row, after the man who had it ahead of him. I've heard the name of the man who had it ahead of Scott and the name of the man who had it ahead of him, but they've faded out of my mind. I've got two rows in my name. They're the first two rows north of the George Washington Bridge. They're both twelve-hundred-foot rows, which is the length of most of the rows. The last few years, I've been fishing only one of them the whole season through. It's the lower one. If you ever drive over the bridge on the westbound roadway during shad season, look up the river a little ways and you'll see my poles."

Mr. Townsend had grown tired of standing, and he sat back down on the capstan.

"Sometime in the latter half of March," continued Harry, "I and three or four men that I swap labor with get together and move this barge up the river. They help me move mine, I help them move theirs; they help me stake my poles, I help them stake theirs. We tie the barge to a launch owned by one of the men and tow her up on the tide, and take her to a point beside the riverbank half a mile or so above the bridge, where she'll be convenient to both my rows. We run a hawser from that capstan you're sitting on to a tree on the bank and draw her up close to the bank, with the bow facing the bank, and then we anchor her with three anchors—port, starboard, and stern. She stays there for the duration of shad season. Then we get out on the bank and put up a rack to mend nets on and a gallows to hang a set of scales on. The land along there is owned by the Palisades Interstate Park, and a shadfisherman pays rent for the space he uses on the riverbank on the basis of how many rows he fishes—the rate is two hundred dollars a row for the season. Then we go back to the flats and start snaking my poles out of the mud and loading them on a peculiar-looking kind of craft called a double boat. A double boat consists of two forty-foot scows connected together side by side but with a narrow space left in between them. It resembles a raft, as much as it resembles anything. When we get it loaded, we tow it up the river on the tide, the same as we towed the barge, and then we start staking the poles. Until a few years ago, this was a job shadfishermen dreaded. We'd anchor the double boat over the place we wanted the pole to go, and we'd stand the pole up in the narrow in-between space I mentioned, to keep it steady. Then we'd lash a crosspiece on the pole, and two men, the heavier the better, would climb up and stand on the crosspiece and hold on to the pole and bend their knees and make a kind of jumping motion, keeping time with each other, until they drove the butt end of the pole into the river bottom. Sometimes they'd have to jump for hours to get a pole down far enough. Sometimes more weight would be needed and two more men would get up on the crosspiece. The two on the inside would hold on to the pole and the two on the outside would hold on to the two on the inside, and they'd jump and grunt and jump and grunt, and it was a strange sight to watch, particularly to people watching it from shore who didn't have the slightest idea what was going on out there. Shad poles are spaced from twenty-five to thirty feet apart, and you have to put down from forty-one to forty-nine poles on a twelve-hundred-foot row, counting the outside poles, so you can just imagine the jumping we used to have to do. Nowadays, it's much simpler. We have a winch sitting on a platform in the middle of the double boat, and we simply stand the pole in place and put a short length of chain around it up toward its upper end and hook a cable from the winch onto the chain, and the winch exerts a powerful downward pull on the chain and forces the butt end of the pole into the bottom.

"By the last week in March, the shad barges are in place all along the Hudson and the shad poles are up. There's a number of old retired or half-retired sea cooks and tugboat cooks in Edgewater and Weehawken, and they come out of retirement around this time and take jobs as cooks on shad barges. They work on the same barges year after year. As soon as the cooks get situated in the galleys, the shadfishermen start living aboard. Around the same time, men start showing up in Edgewater who haven't been seen in town since last shad season. You need highly skilled fishermen to handle shad nets, and for many years there hasn't been enough local help to go around, so every spring fishermen from other places come and take the jobs. A shadfisherman generally hires from two to five of them for each row he fishes, and pays them a hundred or so a week and bunk and board. Most of them are Norwegians or Swedes. Some come from little ports down in South Jersey, such as Atlantic Highlands, Port Monmouth, Keyport, Point Pleasant, and Wildwood. In other seasons, they do lobstering or pound-fishing, or go out on draggers or scallopers. Some come from a small dragger fleet that works out of Mill Basin, in Brooklyn. Some come from Fulton Market—old fishermen who work as fillet cutters and go back to fishing only during shad season. Some don't come from any particular place, but roam all over. One man didn't show up in Edgewater year before last, the best man with a shad net I ever saw, and last year he did show up, and I asked him where he'd been. 'I worked my way home on a tanker to see my sister,' he said, and by 'home' he meant some port in Norway, 'and then I worked on a Norwegian sealer that hunted harp seals along the coast of Labrador, and then I worked my way back here on a tanker, and then I worked awhile in the shrimp fleet in Galveston, Texas, and the last few months I worked on a bait-clam dredge in Sheepshead Bay.' They know how to do almost any kind of commercial fishing—and if they don't they can pick it up between breakfast and lunch and do it better by supper than the ones who taught them. When they come aboard a barge, all they ever have with them is an old suitcase in one hand and an old sea bag slung over one shoulder that they carry their boots and oilskins in, and they seldom say much about themselves. In times past, there were quite a few rummies among them, real old thirty-second-degree rummies, but the rummies seem to have dropped by the wayside. Oh, there's a few left.

"Every year, on one of the last days in March or one of the first days in April, the shad start coming in from the sea. They enter the mouth of the harbor, at Sandy Hook, and straggle around awhile in the Lower Bay, and then they go through the Narrows and cross the Upper Bay and enter the mouth of the Hudson and head for their spawning grounds. There are several of these grounds. The main one begins eighty miles up the river, up around Kingston, and extends to Coxsackie—a distance of twenty-five miles. This stretch of the river has a great many sandbars in it, and creek mouths and shallow coves and bays. As a rule, shad are four years old when they make their first trip in, and they keep on coming in once every year until their number is up. You can take a scale off a shad and look at the scars on it and tell how many times the shad has spawned, and every season we see quite a few who managed to escape our nets as many as five or six times and go up and spawn before they finally got caught, not to speak of the fact that they managed to keep from being eaten by some other fish all those years. Roe shad average around three and a half to four pounds, and bucks average around two and a half to three. The roes are always heavier. Once in a while, we see a seven-pound roe, or an eight-pounder, or a nine-pounder. I caught one once that weighted thirteen and a half pounds."

"Just think how many fish she must've spawned in her time," said Mr. Townsend. "If it had been me that caught her, I'd've patted her on the back and put her back in."

"A commercial fisherman is supposed to catch fish, Mr. Townsend, not put them back in," Harry said. "Anyway, as a matter of fact, I killed her getting her loose from the net. The shad won't come into the river until the temperature of the river water reaches forty degrees or thereabouts, and that's what we watch for. Day after day, when the water starts approaching this temperature, we go out just before every flood tide and hang a short net called a jitney in the spaces between several poles toward the far end of the row. This is a trial net. The shad may start trickling in, only three or four showing up on each tide, and continue that way for days, or avalanches of them may start coming in all at once, but as soon as we find the first ones in the trial net, however many there are, even if there's only one, we go to work in earnest. Just before the next flood tide begins, I and two or three of the hired fishermen take a regular-sized net out to the row in a shad boat. A shad boat is fifteen to twenty feet long and high and sharp in the bow and low and square and roomy in the stern. It has a well in its bottom, up forward, in which to sit an outboard motor—although you can row it if you want to—and it's unusually maneuverable. We have the net piled up in the stern, and we work our way across the downriver side of the row, and go from pole to pole, feeding the net out and letting the bottom of it sink and tying the top of it to the poles. It's like putting up a fence, only it's an underwater fence. Where my row is, the water ranges in depth from twenty to thirty feet, and I use a net that's twenty feet deep. The net has iron rings sewed every few feet along the bottom of it to weight it down and hold it down. In addition, on each end of it, to anchor it, we tie a stone called a dropstone. Several blocks north of here, there's a ravine running down from River Road to the riverbank. In the middle of the ravine is a brook, and beside the brook is an old abandoned wagon road all grown over with willow trees and sumac and sassafras and honeysuckle and poison ivy. Years ago, the main business of Edgewater was cutting paving blocks for New York City, and wagons carrying loads of these blocks to a dock on the riverbank used to come down this road. It was a rocky road, and you can still see ruts that the wheel rims wore in the rocks. Through the years, a good many paving blocks bounced off the wagons and fell in the brook, and the drivers were too lazy to pick them up, and that's where we get our dropstones. If we lose one in the river, we go up with a crowbar and root around in the mud and tree roots and rusty tin cans in the bed of the brook and dig out another one. Some of us have a notion the blocks are lucky. I wouldn't think of using any other kind of dropstone.

"By the time we have the net hung all the way across, the flood tide is in full flow, pushing and pressing against the net and bellying it out in the spaces between the poles. We go on back to the barge and leave the net to take care of itself for the duration of the tide. If enough shad to amount to anything come up the river in the tide, some of them are bound to hit it. They'll either hit it head on and stick their heads in the meshes and gill themselves or they'll hit it sideways and tangle themselves in it and the tide will hold them against it the way the wind holds a scrap of paper against a fence. In this part of the river, the tide runs from three and a half to six hours, according to the time of the month and the strength and direction of the wind, and it runs faster on the bottom than it does on the top, and it'll trick you. When we judge it's getting on toward the time it should start slowing down, we go back out to the row in the shad boat and get ready to lift the net. Quite often, we're way too early, and have to stop at the first pole and sit there in the boat with our hands in our laps and bide our time. We might sit there an hour. If it's during the day, we sit and look up at the face of the Palisades, or we look at the New York Central freight trains that seem to be fifteen miles long streaking by on the New York side, or we look downriver at the tops of the skyscrapers in the distance. I've never been able to make up my mind about the New York skyline. Sometimes I think it's beautiful, and sometimes I think it's a gaudy damned unnatural sight. If it's in the nighttime, we look at that queer glare over midtown Manhattan that comes from the lights in Times Square. On cold, clear nights in April, sitting out on the river in the dark, that glare in the sky looks like the Last Judgment is on the way, or the Second Coming, or the end of the world. Every little while, we stick an oar straight into the water and try to hold it there, to test the strength of the tide. We have to time things very carefully. We want the net to stay down and catch fish as long as possible, but if we wait too long to get started the tide will begin to ebb before we get across the row, and belly the net in the opposite direction, and dump the fish out. I sit beside the outboard motor and handle the boat, and I usually have three fishermen aboard. When I give the signal to let's get going, two of the fishermen stand up side by side in the stern, and one unties the net at the first pole. Then, while one holds on to the top of the net, the other pulls the bottom of it up to the top— that's called pursing it. Then they start drawing it into the boat, a little at a time. The third man stands a few feet farther back, and helps wherever he's needed most. We proceed from pole to pole, untying the net and drawing it in. As it comes aboard, the men shake it and jerk it and twitch it and seesaw it and yank it this way and that, and the fish spill out of it and fall to the bottom of the boat. The men tear a lot of holes in the net that way, but it can't be helped. As the net piles up in the stern, the fish pile up amidships. When we get to the end of the row, if we've had a good lift, we'll have over a thousand shad piled up amidships, bucks and roes all jumbled together, flipping and flopping and beating the air with their tails, each and every one of them fit to be cooked by some great chef at the Waldorf-Astoria and served on the finest china, and the boat'll almost be awash. I must've seen a million shad in my time, and I still think they're beautiful—their thick bodies, their green backs, their silver sides, their saw-edged bellies, the deep forks in their tails. The moment we draw in the end of the net, we turn about and head for the riverbank. We beach the boat, and all four of us grab hold of the net—it's dripping wet and heavy as lead— and heave it onto a kind of low-sided box with four handles on it called a net box. We carry this up on the bank, and spread the net on the net rack. Then, while one man starts picking river trash out of the net and mending it and getting it ready for the next flood tide, I and the two other men unload the fish and sort them and weigh them and pack them in wooden boxes, a hundred or so pounds to a box. The roes bring a much higher price than the bucks, and we pack them separately. I write my name on each box with a black crayon, and below it I write 'A. & S.' That stands for Ackerly & Sandiford, the wholesale firm in Fulton Market that I ship to. There's always some trucker over here who understands shadfishing and makes a business every spring of trucking shad to market. Joe's uncle, old Mr. John Hewitt, used to do it years ago, first with a dray, then with a truck. In recent years, a man named George Indahl has been doing it. Usually, about the time we get through boxing a lift, one of his trucks comes down the little one-lane dirt road that runs along the riverbank up where I anchor my barge, and the driver stops and picks up my boxes. Then he goes on down the line and stops at the next shadfisherman's place, and keeps on making stops until he has a load, and then he high-tails it for South Street."

"South Street is the main street in Fulton Market, Frank," Mr. Hewitt said to Mr. Townsend. "Most of the fishmongers have their stands on it. There's an old saying in the market, 'When the shad are running in the Hudson, South Street is bloody.'"

"My place on the riverbank is kind of hard to get to, although you can see it from the bridge," Harry continued, "but the first few days of shad season, every time we come in with a lift, we find a little crowd standing there. They're mostly old men. They stand around and watch us bring the fish ashore and sort them and box them, and the sight of the shad seems to do them good. Some are old men from Edgewater and Fort Lee. Others are old men I never see any other time. They show up year after year, and I say hello to them and shake hands, but I don't know their names, let alone where they come from. I don't even know if they come from New Jersey or New York. Several have been coming for so many years that I tell them to wait until the others have gone, and I give them a shad, a roe shad. They're well-to-do-looking men, some of them, and could probably buy me and sell me, but they bring a newspaper to wrap their fish in and a paper bag to carry it in, and the way they thank me, you'd think I was giving them something really valuable. One of them, who'd been showing up every spring for years and years with his paper bag all neatly folded in his overcoat pocket, didn't show up last spring. 'The poor old boy, whoever he was,' I said to myself, when I happened to think of him, 'he didn't last the winter.' Day by day, the little crowd gets smaller and smaller, and after the first week or so only an occasional person shows up, and things settle down to a routine. Not that they get dull. Lifting a shad net is like shooting dice—you never get tired of seeing what comes up. One lift, we may get only two or three fish all the way across; next lift, we may get a thousand. One lift, we may get mostly bucks; next lift, roes may outnumber bucks three to one. And shad aren't the only fish that turn up in a shad net. We may find a dozen big catfish lying in the belly of the net, or a couple of walleyed pike, or some other kind of fresh-water fish. A freshet brought them down, and they were making their way back up the river, and they hit the net. Or we may find some fish that strayed in from the

ocean on a strong tide—bluefish or blackfish or fluke or mossbunkers or goosefish, or a dozen other kinds. Or we may find some
ocean fish that run up the river to spawn the same as shad, such
as sea sturgeon or alewives or summer herring. Sea sturgeon are
the kind of sturgeon whose roe is made into caviar. Some of them
get to be very old and big. Going up the river, they keep leaping
out of the water, and suddenly, at least once every season, one of
them leaps out of the water right beside my boat, and it's so big
and long and ugly and covered all over with warts that it scares
me—it might be eight, nine, ten, or eleven feet long and weigh a
couple of hundred pounds. We get quite a few of the young ones
in our nets, and now and then, especially during the latter part of
the season, we lift the net and there's a gaping big hole in it, and
we know that a full-grown one came up the river sometime during
the tide, an old-timer, and hit the net and went right through it.
Several years ago, an eighty-one-pounder hit the net sideways while
we were lifting it, and began to plunge around in it, and it was as
strong as a young bull, but the men braced themselves and took a
firm grip on the net and held on until it wore itself out, and then
they pulled it aboard.

"The bulk of the shad go up the river between the middle of
April and the middle of May. Around the middle of May, we begin
to see large numbers of what we call back-runners coming down
the river—shad that've finished spawning and are on their way
back to sea. We don't bother them. They eat little or nothing while
they're on their spawning runs, and by this time they're so feeble
and emaciated they can just barely make it. If we find them in our
nets, we shake them back into the water. Shad keep right on coming
into the river until around the end of June, but during May the
price goes lower and lower, and finally they aren't worth fishing
for. In the last week in May or the first week in June, we pull up
our poles and move our barges back to the flats.

"The young shad stay up on the spawning grounds through the
summer. In October and the early part of November, when the
water starts getting cold, they come down the river in huge schools
and go out to sea. Way up in November, last year, they were still

coming down. One morning, a week or so before Thanksgiving, I was out in the flats, tied up to an old wreck, fishing for tomcod, and all of a sudden the water around my boat became alive with little shad—pretty little silver-sided things, three to five inches in length, flipping right along. I dropped a bucket over the side and brought up half a dozen of them, and they were so lively they made the water in the bucket bubble like seltzer water. I looked at them a few minutes, and then I poured them back in the river. 'Go on out to sea,' I said to them, 'and grow up and get some flesh on your bones, and watch yourselves and don't get eaten by other fish, and four years from now, a short distance above the George Washington Bridge,' I said, 'maybe our paths will cross again.'"

MR. TOWNSEND AND MR. HEWITT and I had been listening closely to Harry, and none of us had paid any further attention to the young girls jumping rope on the riverbank. Shortly after Harry stopped talking, all of us became aware at the same moment that the girls turning the rope were singing a new song. Just then, the girl jumping missed a jump, and another girl ran in to take her place, whereupon the girls turning the rope started the new song all over again. Their voices were rollicking, and they laughed as they sang. The song began:

> *"The worms crawl in,*
> *The worms crawl out.*
> *They eat your guts*
> *And spit them out.*
> *They bring their friends*
> *And their friends' friends, too,*
> *And there's nothing left*
> *When they get through. . . ."*

Harry laughed. "They've changed it a little," he said. "That line used to go, 'And you look like hell when they get through.'"

" 'The worms crawl in, the worms crawl out. They play pinochle on your snout,' " said Mr. Townsend. "That's the way I remember it. 'One little worm who's not so shy crawls up your nose and out your eye.' That's another line I remember."

"Let's go inside," said Mr. Hewitt. "It's getting cold out here. We'll all catch pneumonia."

"You know what they used to say about pneumonia, Joe," Harry said. " 'Pneumonia is the old man's friend.' "

"A lot of what they used to say," said Mr. Hewitt, "could just as well've been left unsaid."

Stooping, he stepped from the deck into the passageway of the barge and walked past the galley and into the bunkroom, and the rest of us followed. There is a bulletin board on the partition that separates the bunkroom from the storage quarters beyond. Tacked on it are mimeographed notices dating back ten years concerning new shadfishing regulations or changes in old ones—some from the Corps of Engineers, United States Army, and some from the Division of Fish and Game, Department of Conservation and Economic Development, State of New Jersey. Also tacked on the bulletin board is a flattened-out pasteboard box on which someone has lettered with boat paint: "OLD FISHERMEN NEVER DIE—THEY JUST SMELL THAT WAY." Tacked on the partition to the right of the bulletin board are several Coast and Geodetic charts of the river and the harbor. Tacked to the left of it are a number of group photographs taken at shad bakes run by Harry. One photograph shows a group of fishmongers from Fulton Market lined up in two rows at a shad bake on the riverbank, and Mr. Hewitt himself is in the second row. The fishmongers are looking straight at the camera. Several are holding up glasses of beer. All have big smiles on their faces. Mr. Hewitt went over to this photograph and began to study it. Mr. Townsend and I sat down in chairs beside the stove. Harry opened the stove door and punched up the fire with a crowbar. Then he sat down.

"Oh, God, Harry," said Mr. Hewitt after he had studied the photograph awhile, "it was only just a few short years ago this picture was made, and a shocking number of the fellows in it are dead already. Here's poor Jimmy McBarron. Jimmy was only forty-five when he died, and he was getting along so well. He was president of Wallace, Keeney, Lynch, one of the biggest firms in the market, and he had an interest in a shrimp company in Florida. And here's Mr. John Matthews, who was secretary-treasurer of Chesebro Brothers, Robbins & Graham. He was a nice man. A little stiff and formal for the fish market. 'How do you do, Mr. Hewitt?' he used to say to me, when everybody else in the market called me Joe, even the lumpers on the piers. And here's Matt Graham, who was one of the partners in the same firm. A nicer man never lived than Matt Graham. He went to work in the market when he was fifteen years of age, and all he ever knew was fish, and all he ever wanted to know was fish."

"I used to ship to him," said Harry. "I shipped to him when he was with Booth Fisheries, long before he went with Chesebro. I shipped him many a box of shad, and he always treated me fair and square."

Mr. Hewitt continued to stare at the photograph.

"This one's alive," he said. "This one's dead. This one's alive. At least, I haven't heard he's dead. Here's Drew Radel, who was president of the Andrew Radel Oyster Company, planters and distributors of Robbins Island oysters. He died only last year. Sixty-five, the paper said. I had no idea he was that far along. I ran into him the summer before he died, and he looked around fifty. He's one man I can honestly say I never heard a bad word spoken about him. Here's a man who kept books for companies all over the market, the same as I did. He worked for Frank Wilkisson and Eastern Commission and George M. Still and Middleton, Carman and Lockwood & Winant and Caleb Haley and Lester & Toner and Blue Ribbon, and I don't know how many others—a real old-fashioned floating bookkeeper. I ate lunch across from him at the front table in Sloppy Louie's two or three times a week year in and year out, and now I can't even think of his name. Eddie Something-or-Other. He's still alive, last I heard. Retired. Lives in Florida. His wife had money; he never saved a cent. Grows grapefruit, somebody said. If I felt I had to grow something, by God, it wouldn't be grapefruit. This man's alive. So's this man. Dead. Dead. Dead. Three in a row. Alive. Alive. Alive. Dead. Alive. And here's a man, I won't mention his name and I shouldn't tell about this, but a couple of years ago, when I saw in the *New York Times* that he was dead, the thought flashed into my mind, 'I do hope they bury him in Evergreen Cemetery.' "

He turned away from the photograph, and came over and sat down.

"And I'll tell you the reason that particular thought flashed into my mind," he said. "This fellow was the biggest woman chaser in the market, and one of the biggest talkers on the subject I ever heard. When he and I were young men in the market together, he used to tell me about certain of his experiences along that line out in Brooklyn, where he lived. Tell *me*—hell! he told everybody that would listen. At that time, Trommer's Brewery was the finest brewery in Brooklyn. It was at the corner of Bushwick Avenue and Conway Street, and out in front of it was a beer garden. The brewery maintained the beer garden, and it was a show place. They had tables in the open, and a large restaurant indoors with at least a dozen big potted palms stood up in it. During the summer, they had a German orchestra that played waltz music. And directly across the street from the beer garden was the main gate of Evergreen Cemetery. After a burial, it was customary for the mourners to stop in Trommer's beer garden and drown their sorrow in Trommer's White Label and rejoice in the fact that it was the man or the woman they'd left out in the cemetery's turn to go, and not theirs. On Sundays, people would take the streetcar out to the cemetery and visit the graves of relatives and friends, and then they'd go over to Trommer's beer garden for sandwiches and beer. Now this fellow I'm talking about, he used to dress up on Sundays and go out to the cemetery and walk up and down the cemetery paths until he found some young widow out there by herself visiting her husband's grave, and she didn't have to be too damned young, and he'd go over and get acquainted with her and sympathize with her, and she'd cry and he'd cry, and then he'd invite her over to Trommer's beer garden, and they'd sit there and have some beers and listen to the music and talk, and one thing would lead to another."

Mr. Hewitt leaned over and opened the stove door and spat on the red-hot coals. "To hear him tell it," he said, "he was hell on widows. He knew just what to say to them."

"Did this gentleman ever get married himself?" asked Mr. Townsend. He sounded indignant.

"He was married twice," said Mr. Hewitt. "A year or two before he died, he divorced his first wife and married a woman half his age."

"I hope some man came up to her in the cemetery when she was visiting his grave and got acquainted with her and sympathized with her," Mr. Townsend said, "and one thing led to another."

Mr. Hewitt had lost interest in this turn of the conversation. "It's highly unlikely she ever visited his grave," he said.

Mr. Townsend shrugged his shoulders. "Ah, well," he said. "In that case."

Mr. Hewitt got up and went over and scrutinized the photograph again. "I look a lot older now than I did when this picture was made," he said, "and there's no denying that." He continued to scrutinize the photograph for a few more minutes, and then returned to his chair.

"When I was young," he said, "I had the idea death was for other people. It would happen to other people but not to me. That is, I couldn't really visualize it happening to me. And if I did allow myself to think that it would happen to me, it was very easy to put the thought out of my mind—if it had to take place, it would take place so far in the distant future it wasn't worth thinking about, let alone worrying about, and then the years flew by, and now it's right on top of me. Any time now, as the fellow said, the train will pull into the station and the trip will be over."

"Ah, well," said Mr. Townsend.

"It seems to me it was only just a few short years ago I was a young man going back and forth to work," said Mr. Hewitt, "and the years flew by, they really flew by, and now I'm an old man, and what I want to know is, what was the purpose of it? I know what's going to take place one of these days, and I can visualize some of the details of it very clearly. There'll be one twenty-five-dollar wreath, or floral design, or whatever they call them now, and there'll be three or maybe four costing between twelve dollars and a half and fifteen dollars, and there'll be maybe a dozen running from five to ten dollars, and I know more or less what the preacher will say, and then they'll take me out to the Edgewater Cemetery and lay me beside my parents and my brothers and sisters and two of my grandparents and one of my great-grandparents, and I'll lie there through all eternity while the Aluminum Company factory goes put-put-put."

Harry laughed, "You make the Aluminum Company factory sound like a motorboat," he said.

"I don't go to funerals any more," said Mr. Townsend. "Funerals breed funerals."

"My grandfather used to like the word 'mitigate,' " Harry said. "He liked the sound of it, and he used it whenever he could. When he was a very old man, he often got on the subject of dying. 'You can't talk your way out,' he'd say, 'and you can't buy your way out, and you can't shoot your way out, and the only thing that mitigates the matter in the slightest is the fact that nobody else is going to escape. Nobody—no, not one.' "

"I know, I know," said Mr. Hewitt, "but what's the purpose of it?"

"You supported your wife, didn't you?" asked Harry. "You raised a family, didn't you? That's the purpose of it."

"That's no purpose," said Mr. Hewitt. "The same thing that's going to happen to me is going to happen to them."

"The generations have to keep coming along," said Harry. "That's all I know."

"You're put here," said Mr. Hewitt, "and you're allowed to eat and draw breath and go back and forth a few short years, and about the time you get things in shape where you can sit down and enjoy them you wind up in a box in a hole in the ground, and as far as I can see, there's no purpose to it whatsoever. I try to keep from thinking such thoughts, but the last few years almost everything I see reminds me of death and dying, and time passing, and how fast it passes. I drove through Shadyside the other day, and I noticed that some of those factories down there are getting real smoky-looking and patched up and dilapidated, and the thought immediately occured to me, 'I'm older than most of those factories. I remember most of them when they were brand-new, and, good God, look at them now.' And to tell the truth, I'm pretty well patched up myself. I've maybe not had as many operations as some people, but I've had my share. Tonsils, adenoids, appendix, gall bladder, prostate. I wear false teeth, and I've worn them for years— 'your dentures,' my dentist calls them; 'Oh, for God's sake,' I said to him, '*I* know what they are, and *you* know what they are.' And the last time I went to the eye doctor he prescribed two pairs of glasses, one for ordinary use and one for reading, and I can't really see worth a damn out of either one of them. I've got varicose veins from walking around on wet cement floors in Fulton Market all those years, and I have to wear elastic stockings that are hell to get on and hell to get off and don't do a damned bit of good, and I've got fallen arches and I have to wear some kind of patented arch supports that always make me feel as if I'm about to jump, and I've never known the time I didn't have corns—corns and bunions and calluses."

"Oh, come on, Joe," said Harry. "Don't you ever get tired talking about yourself?"

A shocked look appeared on Mr. Hewitt's face. "I wasn't talking about myself, Harry," he said, and his voice sounded surprised and hurt. "I was talking about the purpose of life."

Harry started to say something, and then got up and went out to the galley. It had become too warm, and I went over and opened the window. I put my head out of the window and listened for a few moments to the lapping of the water against the side of the barge. Two of Harry's shad boats moored to stakes in the flats were slowly shifting their positions, and I could see that the tide was beginning to change. I heard the click of the refrigerator door in the galley, and then Harry returned to the bunkroom, bringing four cans of beer. He paused for a moment in front of Mr. Hewitt. "I'm sorry I said that, Joe," he said. "I was just trying to get your mind on something else." Then he stood the cans on the bunkroom table and started opening them. "As far as I'm concerned," he said, "the purpose of life is to stay alive and to keep on staying alive as long as you possibly can."

(1959)

# Joe Gould's
# Secret

*J*OE GOULD WAS AN ODD and penniless and unemployable little man who came to the city in 1916 and ducked and dodged and held on as hard as he could for over thirty-five years. He was a member of one of the oldest families in New England ("The Goulds were the Goulds," he used to say, "when the Cabots and the Lowells were clamdiggers"), he was born and brought up in a town near Boston in which his father was a leading citizen, and he went to Harvard, as did his father and grandfather before him, but he claimed that until he arrived in New York City he had always felt out of place. "In my home town," he once wrote, "I never felt at home. I stuck out. Even in my own home, I never felt at home. In New York City, especially in Greenwich Village, down among the cranks and the misfits and the one-lungers and the has-beens and the might've-beens and the would-bes and the never-wills and the God-knows-whats, I have always felt at home."

Gould looked like a bum and lived like a bum. He wore castoff clothes, and he slept in flophouses or in the cheapest rooms in cheap hotels. Sometimes he slept in doorways. He spent most of his time hanging out in diners and cafeterias and barrooms in the Village or wandering around the streets or looking up friends and acquaintances all over town or sitting in public libraries scribbling in dime-store composition books. He was generally pretty dirty. He would often go for days without washing his face and hands, and he rarely had a shirt washed or a suit cleaned. As a rule, he wore a garment continuously until someone gave him a new one, whereupon he threw the old one away. He had his hair cut infrequently ("Every other Easter," he would say), and then in a barber college on the Bowery. He was a chronic sufferer from the highly contagious kind of conjunctivitis that is known as pinkeye. His voice was distractingly nasal. On occasion, he stole. He usually stole books from bookstores and sold them to second-hand bookstores, but if he was sufficiently hard pressed he stole from friends. (One terribly cold night, he knocked on the door of the studio of a sculptor who was almost as poor as he was, and the sculptor let him spend the night rolled up like a mummy in layers of newspapers and sculpture shrouds on the floor of the studio, and next morning he got up early and stole some of the sculptor's tools and pawned them.) In addition, he was nonsensical and bumptious and inquisitive and gossipy and mocking and sarcastic and scurrilous. All through the years, nevertheless, a long succession of men and women gave him old clothes and small sums of money and bought him meals and drinks and paid for his lodging and invited him to parties and to weekends in the country and helped him get such things as glasses and false teeth, or otherwise took an interest in him—some simply because they thought he was entertaining, some because they felt sorry for him, some because they regarded him sentimentally as a relic of the Village of their youth, some because they enjoyed looking down on him, some for reasons that they themselves probably weren't at all sure of, and some because they believed that a book he had been working on for many years might possibly turn out to be a good book, even a great one, and wanted to encourage him to continue working on it.

Gould called this book "An Oral History," sometimes adding "of Our Time." As he described it, the Oral History consisted of talk he had heard and had considered meaningful and had taken down, either verbatim or summarized—everything from a remark overheard in the street to the conversation of a roomful of people lasting for hours—and of essays commenting on this talk. Some talk has an obvious meaning and nothing more, he said, and some, often unbeknownst to the talker, has at least one other meaning and sometimes several other meanings lurking around inside its obvious meaning. The latter kind of talk, he said, was what he was collecting for the Oral History. He professed to believe that such talk might have great hidden historical significance. It might have portents in it, he said—portents of cataclysms, a kind of writing on the wall long before the kingdom falls—and he liked to quote a couplet from William Blake's "Auguries of Innocence":

*The harlot's cry from street to street*
*Shall weave Old England's winding-sheet.*

Everything depended, he said, on how talk was interpreted, and not everybody was able to interpret it. "Yes, you're right," he once said to a detractor of the Oral History. "It's only things I heard people say, but maybe I have a peculiar ability—maybe I can understand the significance of what people say, maybe I can read its inner meaning. *You* might listen to a conversation between two old men in a barroom or two old women on a park bench and think that it was the worst kind of bushwa, and *I* might listen to the same conversation and find deep historical meaning in it."

"In time to come," he said on another occasion, "people may read Gould's Oral History to see what went wrong with us, the way we read Gibbon's 'Decline and Fall' to see what went wrong with the Romans."

He told people he met in Village joints that the Oral History was already millions upon millions of words long and beyond any doubt the lengthiest unpublished literary work in existence but that it was nowhere near finished. He said that he didn't expect it to be published in his lifetime, publishers being what they were, as blind as bats, and he sometimes rummaged around in his pockets and brought out and read aloud a will he had made disposing of it. "As soon after my demise as is convenient for all concerned," he specified in the will, "my manuscript books shall be collected from the various and sundry places in which they are stored and put on the scales and weighed, and two-thirds of them by weight shall be given to the Harvard Library and the other third shall be given to the library of the Smithsonian Institution."

Gould almost always wrote in composition books—the kind that schoolchildren use, the kind that are ruled and spine-stitched and paper-bound and have the multiplication table printed on the back. Customarily, when he filled a book, he would leave it with the first person he met on his rounds whom he knew and trusted—the cashier of an eating place, the proprietor of a barroom, the clerk of a hotel or flophouse—and ask that it be put away and kept for him. Then, every few months, he would go from place to place and pick up all the books that had accumulated. He would say, if anyone became curious about this, that he was storing them in an old friend's house or in an old friend's apartment or in an old friend's studio. He hardly ever identified any of these old friends by name, although sometimes he would describe one briefly and vaguely— "a classmate of mine who lives in Connecticut and has a big attic in his house," he would say, or "a woman I know who lives alone in a duplex apartment," or "a sculptor I know who has a studio in a loft building." In talking about the Oral History, he always emphasized its length and its bulk. He kept people up to date on its length. One evening in June, 1942, for example, he told an acquaintance that at the moment the Oral History was "approximately nine million two hundred and fifty-five thousand words long, or," he added, throwing his head back proudly, "about a dozen times as long as the Bible."

In 1952, Gould collapsed on the street and was taken to Columbus Hospital. Columbus transferred him to Bellevue, and Bellevue transferred him to the Pilgrim State Hospital, in West Brentwood, Long Island. In 1957, he died there, aged sixty-eight, of arteriosclerosis and senility. Directly after the funeral, friends of his in the Village began trying to find the manuscript of the Oral History. After several days, they turned up three things he had written—a poem, a fragment of an essay, and a begging letter. In the next month or so, they found a few more begging letters. From then on, they were unable to find anything at all. They sought out and questioned scores of people in whose keeping Gould might conceivably have left some of the composition books, and they visited all the places he had lived in or hung out in that they could remember or learn about, but without success. Not a single one of the composition books was found, or has ever been found.

In 1942, for reasons that I will go into later, I became involved in Gould's life, and I kept in touch with him during his last ten years in the city. I spent a good many hours during those years listening to him. I listened to him when he was sober and I listened to him when he was drunk. I listened to him when he was cast down and meek—when, as he used to say, he felt so low he had to reach up to touch bottom—and I listened to him when he was in moods of incoherent exaltation. I got so I could put two and two together and make at least a little sense out of what he was saying even when he was very drunk or very exalted or in both states at once, and gradually, without intending to, I learned some things about him that he may not have wanted me to know, or, on the other hand, since his mind was circuitous and he loved wheels within wheels, that he may very well have wanted me to know— I'll never be sure. In any case, I am quite sure that I know why the manuscript of the Oral History has not been found.

When Gould died, I made a resolution to keep this as well as some of the other things I had inadvertently learned about him to myself—to do otherwise, it seemed to me at the time, would be disloyal; let the dead past bury its dead—but since then I have come to the conclusion that my resolution was pointless and that I should tell what I know, and I am going to do so.

Before I go any further, however, I feel compelled to explain how I came to this conclusion.

A few months ago, while trying to make some room in my office, I got out a collection of papers relating to Gould that filled half a drawer in a filing cabinet: notes I had made of conversations with him, letters from him and letters from others concerning him, copies of little magazines containing essays and poems by him, newspaper clippings about him, drawings and photographs of him, and so on. I had lost a good deal of my interest in Gould long before he reached Pilgrim State—as he grew older, his faults intensified, and even those who felt most kindly toward him and continued to see him got so they dreaded him—but as I went through the file folders, trying to decide what to save and what to throw out, my interest in him revived. I found twenty-nine letters, notes, and postal cards from him in the folders. I started out just glancing through them and ended up rereading them with care. One letter was of particular interest to me. It was dated February 12 or 17 or 19 (it was impossible to tell which), 1946; his handwriting had become trembly, and it always had been hard to read.

"I ran into a young painter I know and his wife in the Minetta Tavern last night," he wrote, "and they told me they had recently gone to a party in the studio of a woman painter named Alice Neel, who is an old friend of mine, and that during the evening Alice showed them a portrait of me she did some years ago. I asked them what they thought of it. The young painter's wife spoke first. 'It's one of the most shocking pictures I've ever seen,' she said. And he agreed with her. 'You can say that again,' he said. This pleased me very much, especially the young man's reaction, as he is a hot-shot abstractionist and way up front in the avant garde and isn't usually impressed by a painting unless it is totally meaningless and was completed about half an hour ago. I posed for this painting in 1933, and that was thirteen years ago, and the fact that people still find it shocking speaks well for it. Speaks well for the possibility that it may have some of the one quality that all great paintings have in common, the power to last. I may have written to you about this painting before, or talked about it, but I am not sure. If so, bear with me; my memory is going. There are quite a few paintings in studios around town that are well known to people in the art world but can't be exhibited in galleries or museums because they probably would be considered obscene and might get the gallery or museum in trouble, and this is one of them. Hundreds of people have seen it through the years, many of them painters who have expressed admiration for it, and I have a hunch that one of these days, the way people are growing accustomed to the so-called obscene, it will hang in the Whitney or the Metropolitan. Alice Neel comes from a small town near Philadelphia and went to the School of Design for Women in Philadelphia. She used to have a studio in the Village, but she moved uptown long ago. She is highly respected by many painters of her age and generation, although she is not too well known to the general public. She has work in important collections, but this may be her best work. Her best work, and it can't be shown in public. A kind of underground masterpiece. I wish sometime you'd go and see it. I'd be interested to know what you think. She doesn't show it to just anyone who asks, of course, but I will give you her telephone number and if you tell her I want you to see it I'm sure she will show it to you. . . ."

The day that I received this letter, I remembered, I had tried several times to call Miss Neel, but her telephone hadn't answered, and I had filed the letter away and Gould had never brought the matter up again and I had forgotten all about it. This day, on an impulse, I called Miss Neel and got her, and she said that of course I could see the Gould portrait, and gave me the address of her studio. The address turned out to be a tenement in a Negro and Puerto Rican neighborhood on the upper East Side, and Miss Neel turned out to be a stately, soft-spoken, good-looking blond woman in her middle fifties. Her studio was a floor-through flat on the third floor of the tenement. Against a wall in one room was a two-tiered rack filled with paintings resting on their sides. The Gould portrait, she said, was on the top tier. She had to stand on a chair and take out several other paintings in order to get at it. As she took them out, she held them up for me to see, and commented on them, and her comments were so offhand they sounded cryptic. One painting showed an elderly man lying in a coffin, "My father," she said. "Head clerk in the per-diem department." "Excuse me," I said, wondering what a per-diem department was but not really wanting to know, "the per-diem department of what?" "Excuse *me,*" she said. "Pennsylvania Railroad in Philadelphia." Another was a painting of a young Puerto Rican man sitting up in a hospital bed and staring wide-eyed into the distance. "T.b.," she said. "Dying, but he didn't. Recovered and became a codeine addict." Another was a painting of a woman in childbirth. Then came a painting of a small, bearded, bony, gawky, round-shouldered man who was strip stark naked except for his glasses, and this was the portrait of Gould. It was a fairly large painting, and Gould seemed almost life-size in it. The background was vague; he appeared to be sitting on a wooden bench in a steam bath, waiting for the steam to come on. His bony hands were resting on his bony knees, and his ribs showed plainly. He had one set of male sexual organs in the proper place, another set was growing from where his navel should have been, and still another set was growing from the wooden bench. Anatomically, the painting was fanciful and grotesque but not particularly shocking; except for the plethora of sexual organs, it was a strict and sober study of an undernourished middle-aged man. It was the expression on Gould's face that was shocking. Occasionally, in one of his Village hangouts or at a party, Gould would become so full of himself that he would abruptly get to his feet and rush about the room, bowing to women of all ages and sizes and degrees of approachability, and begging them to dance with him, and sometimes attempting to embrace and kiss them. After a while, rebuffed on all sides, he would get tired of this. Then he would imitate the flight of a sea gull. He would hop and skip and leap and lurch about, flapping his arms up and down and cawing like a sea gull as he did so. "Scree-eek!" he would cry out. "I'm a sea gull." He would keep on doing this until people stopped looking at him and resumed their conversations. Then, to regain their attention, he would take off his jacket and shirt and throw them aside and do a noisy, hand-clapping, breast-beating, foot-stamping dance. "Quiet!" he would cry out. "I'm doing a dance. It's a sacred dance. It's an Indian dance. It's the full-moon dance of the Chippewas." His eyes would glitter, his lower jaw would hang loose like a dog's in midsummer and he would pant like a dog, and on his face would come a leering, gleeful, mawkishly abandoned expression, half satanic and half silly. Miss Neel had caught this expression. "Joe Gould was very proud of this picture and used to come and sit and look at it," Miss Neel said. She studied Gould's face with affection and amusement and also with what seemed to me to be a certain uneasiness. "I call it 'Joe Gould,'" she continued, "but I probably should call it 'A Portrait of an Exhibitionist.'" A few moments later, she added, "I don't mean to say that Joe was an exhibitionist. I'm sure he wasn't—technically. Still, to be perfectly honest, years ago, watching him at parties, I used to have a feeling that there was an old exhibitionist shut up inside him and trying to get out, like a spider shut up in a bottle. Deep down inside him. A frightful old exhibitionist—the kind you see late at night in the subway. And he didn't necessarily know it. That's why I painted him this way." I suddenly realized that in my mind I had replaced the real Joe Gould—or at least the Joe Gould I had known—with a cleaned-up Joe Gould, an after-death Joe Gould. By forgetting the discreditable or by slowly transforming the discreditable into the creditable, as one tends to do in thinking about the dead, I had, so to speak, respectabilized him. Now, looking at the shameless face in the portrait, I got him back into proportion, and I concluded that if it was possible for the real Joe Gould to have any feeling about the matter one way or the other he wouldn't be in the least displeased if I told anything at all about him that I happened to know. Quite the contrary.

I FIRST SAW GOULD in the winter of 1932. At that time, I was a newspaper reporter, working mostly on crime news. Every now and then, I covered a story in Women's Court, which in those days was in Jefferson Market Courthouse, at Sixth Avenue and Tenth Street, in Greenwich Village. In the block below the courthouse there was a Greek restaurant, named the Athens, that was a hangout for people who worked in the court or often had business in it. They usually sat at a long table up front, across from the cashier's desk, and Harry Panagakos, the proprietor, sometimes came over and sat with them. One afternoon, during a court recess, I was sitting at this table drinking coffee with Panagakos and a probation officer and a bail bondsman and a couple of Vice Squad detectives when a curious little man came in. He was around five feet four or five, and quite thin; he could hardly have weighed more than ninety pounds. He was bareheaded, and he carried his head cocked on one side, like an English sparrow. His hair was long, and he had a bushy beard. There were streaks of dirt on his forehead, obviously from rubbing it with dirty fingers. He was wearing an overcoat that was several sizes too large for him; it reached almost to the floor. He held his hands clasped together for warmth—it was a bitter-cold day—and the sleeves of the overcoat came down over them, forming a sort of muff. Despite his beard, the man, in the oversized overcoat, bareheaded and dirty-faced, had something childlike and lost about him: a child who had been up in the attic with other children trying on grownups' clothes and had become tired of the game and wandered off. He stood still for a few moments, getting his bearings, and then he came over to Panagakos and said, "Can I have something to eat now, Harry? I can't wait until tonight." At first Panagakos seemed annoyed, but then he shrugged his shoulders and told the man to go on back and sit down and he would step into the kitchen in a few minutes and ask the chef to fix him something. Looking greatly relieved, the man walked hurriedly up the aisle between two rows of tables. To be precise, he scurried up the aisle. "Who in God's holy name is that?" asked one of the detectives. Panagakos said that the man was one of the Village bohemians. He said that the bohemians were starving to death—in New York City, the winter of 1932 was the worst winter of the depression—and that he had got in the habit of feeding some of them. He said that the waiters set aside steaks and chops that people hadn't finished eating, and other pieces of food left on plates, and wrapped them in wax paper and put them in paper bags and saved them for the bohemians. Panagakos said that all he asked was that they wait until just before closing time, at midnight, to come in and collect the food, so the sight of them trooping in and out wouldn't get on the nerves of the paying customers. He said that he was going to give this one some soup and a sandwich but that he'd have to warn him not to come in early again. The detective asked if the man was a poet or a painter. "I don't know what you'd call him," Panagakos said. "His name is Joe Gould, and he's supposed to be writing the longest book in the history of the world."

Toward the end of the thirties, I quit my newspaper job and went to work for *The New Yorker*. Around the same time, I moved to the Village, and I began to see Gould frequently. I would catch glimpses of him going into or coming out of one of the barrooms on lower Sixth Avenue—the Jericho Tavern or the Village Square Bar & Grill or the Belmar or Goody's or the Rochambeau. I would see him sitting scribbling at a table in the Jackson Square branch of the Public Library, or I would see him filling his fountain pen in the main Village post office—the one on Tenth Street—or I would see him sitting among the young mothers and the old alcoholics in the sooty, pigeony, crumb-besprinkled, newspaper-bestrewn, privet-choked, coffin-shaped little park at Sheridan Square. I worked a good deal at night at that time, and now and then, on my way home, around two or three in the morning, I would see him on Sixth Avenue or on a side street, hunched over and walking along slowly and appearing to be headed nowhere in particular, almost always alone, almost always carrying a bulging brown pasteboard portfolio, sometimes mumbling to himself. In my eyes, he was an ancient, enigmatic, spectral figure, a banished man. I never saw him without thinking of the Ancient Mariner or of the Wandering Jew or of the Flying Dutchman, or of a silent old man called Swamp Jackson who lived alone in a shack on the edge of a swamp near the small farming town in the South that I come from and wandered widely on foot on the back roads of the countryside at night, or of one of those men I used to puzzle over when I read the Bible as a child, who, for transgressions that seemed mysterious to me, had been "cast out."

One morning in the summer of 1942, sitting in my office at *The New Yorker,* I thought of Gould—I had seen him on the street the night before—and it occurred to me that he might be a good subject for a Profile. According to some notes I made at the time— I made notes on practically everything I had to do with Gould, and I found these in the file drawer with the rest of the Gould memorabilia—it was the morning of June 10, 1942, a Wednesday morning. I happened to be free to start on something new, so I went in and spoke to one of the editors about the idea. I remember telling the editor that I thought Gould was a perfect example of a type of eccentric widespread in New York City, the solitary nocturnal wanderer, and that that was the aspect of him that interested me most, that and his Oral History, and not his bohemianism; in my time, I had interviewed a number of Greenwich Village bohemians and they had seemed to me to be surprisingly tiresome. The editor said to go ahead and try it.

I was afraid that I might have trouble persuading Gould to talk about himself—I really knew next to nothing about him, and had got the impression that he was austere and aloof—and I decided that I had better talk with some people who knew him, or were acquainted with him, at least, and see if I could find out the best way to approach him. I left the office around eleven and went down to the Village and began going into places along Sixth Avenue and bringing up Gould's name and getting into conversations about him with bartenders and waiters and with old-time Villagers they pointed out for me among their customers. In the middle of the afternoon, I telephoned the switchboard operator at the office and asked if there were any messages for me, as I customarily did when I was out, and she immediately switched me to the receptionist, who said that a man had been sitting in the reception room for an hour or so waiting for me to return. "I'll put him on the phone," she said. "Hello, this is Joe Gould," the man said. "I heard that you wanted to talk to me, so I dropped in, but the thing is, I'm supposed to go to the clinic at the Eye and Ear Infirmary, at Second Avenue and Thirteenth Street, and pick up a prescription for some eye trouble I've been having, and if it's one kind of prescription it won't cost anything but if it's another kind it may cost around two dollars, and I've just discovered that I don't have any money with me, and it's getting late, and I wonder if you'd ask your receptionist to lend me two dollars and you can pay her back when you come in and we can meet any time you say and have a talk and I'll pay you back then." The receptionist broke in and said that she would lend him the money, and then Gould came back on the phone and we agreed to meet at nine-thirty the next morning in a diner on Sixth Avenue, in the Village, called the Jefferson. He suggested both the time and the place.

When I got back to the office, I gave the receptionist her two dollars. "He was a terribly dirty little man, and terribly nosy," she said, "and I was glad to get him out of here." "What was he nosy about?" I asked. "Well, for one thing," she said, "he wanted to know how much I make. Also," she continued, handing me a folded slip of paper, "he gave me this note as he was leaving, and told me not to read it until he got on the elevator." "You have beautiful shoulders, my dear," the note said, "and I should like to kiss them." "He also left a note for you," she said, handing me another folded slip of paper. "On second thought," this note said, "nine-thirty is a little early for me. Let us make it eleven."

The Jefferson—it is gone now—was one of those big, roomy, jukeboxy diners. It was on the west side of Sixth Avenue, at the conjunction of Sixth Avenue, Greenwich Avenue, Village Square, and Eighth Street, which is the heart and hub of the Village. It stayed open all day and all night, and it was a popular meeting place. It had a long counter with a row of wobbly-seated stools, and it had a row of booths. When I entered it, at eleven, Gould was sitting on the first counter stool, facing the door and holding his greasy old pasteboard portfolio on his lap, and he looked the worst I had ever seen him. He was wearing a limp, dirty seersucker suit, a dirty Brooks Brothers button-down shirt with a frayed collar, and dirty sneakers. His face was greenish gray, and the right side of his mouth twitched involuntarily. His eyes were bloodshot. He was bald on top, but he had hair sticking out in every possible direction from the back and sides of his head. His beard was un-kempt, and around his mouth cigarette smoke had stained it yellow. He had on a pair of glasses that were loose and lopsided, and they had slipped down near the end of his nose. As I came in, he lifted his head a little and looked at me, and his face was alert and on guard and yet so tired and so detached and so remotely reflective that it was almost impassive. Looking straight at me, he looked straight through me. I have seen the same deceptively blank expres-sion on the faces of old freaks sitting on platforms in freak shows and on the faces of old apes in zoos on Sunday afternoons.

I went over and introduced myself to Gould, and he instantly drew himself up. "I understand you want to write something about me," he said, in a chipper, nasal voice, "and I greet you at the beginning of a great endeavor." Then, having said this, he seemed to falter and to lose confidence in himself. "I didn't get much sleep last night," he said. "I didn't get home. That is, I didn't get to the flophouse I've been staying in lately. I slept on the porch at St. Joseph's R.C. until they opened the doors for the first Mass, and then I went in and sat in a pew until a few minutes ago." St. Joseph's, at Sixth Avenue and Washington Place, is the principal Roman Catholic church in the Village and one of the oldest churches in the city; it has two large, freestanding columns on its porch, behind which, shielded from the street, generations of unfortunates have slept. "I died and was buried and went to Hell two or three times this morning, sitting in that pew," Gould continued. "To be frank, I have a hangover and I'm broke and I'm terribly hungry, and I'd appreciate it very much if you'd buy me some breakfast."

"Of course," I said.

"Fried eggs on toast!" he called out commandingly to the counterman. "And let me have some coffee right away and some more with the eggs. Black coffee. And make sure it's hot." He slid off the stool. "If you're having something," he said to me, "call out your order, and let's sit in a booth. The waitress will bring it over."

WE TOOK A BOOTH, and the waitress brought Gould's coffee. It was in a thick white mug, diner style, and it was so hot it was steaming. Even so, tipping the mug slightly toward him without taking it off the table, he bent down and immediately began drinking it with little, cautious, quick, birdlike sips and gulps interspersed with little whimpering sounds indicating pleasure and relief, and almost at once color returned to his face and his eyes became brighter and his twitch disappeared. I had never before seen anyone react so quickly and so noticeably to coffee; brandy probably wouldn't have done any more for him, or cocaine, or an oxygen tent, or a blood transfusion. He drank the whole mug in this fashion, and then sat back and held his head on one side and looked me over.

"I suppose you're puzzled about me," he said. His tone of voice was condescending; he had got some of his confidence back. "If so," he continued, "the feeling is mutual, for I'm puzzled about myself, and have been since childhood. I seem to be a changeling or a throwback or a mutation of some sort in a highly respectable old New England family. Let me give you a few biographical facts. My full name is Joseph Ferdinand Gould, and I was named for my grandfather, who was a doctor. During the Civil War, he was surgeon of the Fourth Regiment, Massachusetts Volunteers, and later on he was a prominent obstetrician in Boston and taught in the Harvard Medical School. The Goulds, or my branch of them, have been in New England since the sixteen-thirties and have fought in every war in the history of the country, including King Philip's War and the Pequot War. We're related to many of the other early New England families, such as the Lawrences and the Clarkes and the Storers. My grandmother on my father's side was a direct descendant of John Lawrence, who arrived from England on the *Arbella* in 1630 and was the first Lawrence in this country, and she could trace her ancestry back to a knight named Robert Lawrence who lived in the twelfth century. She used to say that the Lawrence line, or this particular Lawrence line, was not only one of the oldest clearly traceable lines in New England but also one of the oldest clearly traceable lines in England itself, and that we should never forget it."

Gould abruptly began scratching himself. He went about it unselfconsciously. He scratched the back of his neck, and then he thrust his hand inside his shirt and scratched his chest and ribs.

"I should've been born in Boston," he continued, "but I wasn't. My father, whose name was Clarke Storer Gould, was also a doctor. He was a Bostonian, but he had been prevailed upon to move out and practice in Norwood, Massachusetts, and he and my mother had been living there only a few months when I was born. Norwood is a fairly good-sized old Yankee town about fifteen miles southwest of Boston. It's a residential suburb, and it also has some printing plants and some sheepskin tanneries and an ink factory and a glue works. I was born at high noon on September 12, 1889, in a flat over Jim Hartshorn's meat market. In Norwood, by the way, that's pronounced 'Jim Hatson.' A year or so later, my father built a big house on Washington Street, the main street of Norwood. Four-eighty-six Washington Street. It had three stories and twenty-one rooms, and it had gables and dormers and ornamental balconies and parquet floors, and it was one of the show places of Norwood. There was a mirror in our front hall that was eight feet high and decorated with gold cherubim. There were beautiful terra-cotta tiles around the fireplaces. There were diamond-shaped windows at the stair landings, and they had red, green, purple, and amber panes.

"As I said, my grandfather and my father were doctors, and when I was growing up I was well aware that my father hoped I would follow in his footsteps, just as he had followed in *his* father's footsteps. He never said so, but it was perfectly obvious to me and to everybody else that that was what he wanted. I loved my father, and I wanted him to think well of me, but I knew from the time I was a little boy and fainted at the sight of blood when I happened to see our cook wring the neck of a chicken that I was going to be a disappointment to him, because I really couldn't stand the idea of being a doctor; I kept it to myself, but that was the last thing in the world I wanted to be. Not that I had anything else in mind. The truth is, I wasn't much good at anything—at home or at school or at play. To begin with, I was undersized; I was a runt, a shrimp, a peanut, a half-pint, a tadpole. My nickname, when anybody thought to use it, was Pee Wee. Also, I was what my father called a catarrhal child—my nose ran constantly. Usually, when I was supposed to be paying attention to something, I was busy blowing my nose. Also, I was just generally inept. Not long ago, looking up something in the unabridged dictionary, I came across a word that sums up the way I was then, and, for that matter, the way I am now—'ambisinistrous,' or left-handed in both hands. My father didn't know what to make of me, and I sometimes caught him looking at me with a thoughtful expression on his face."

Gould stood up and took off his lopsided glasses and peered desperately at the counterman, who was evidently putting off starting on Gould's order until he had attended to everyone else in the diner, including some people who had come in after we had sat down, but the counterman deliberately ignored him and would not let him catch his eye.

"Anyhow," Gould went on, sitting back down resignedly, "when I was around thirteen, a couple of things happened that showed me pretty clearly where I stood in the world. At school, we used to do a lot of marching two by two. We'd march into assembly two by two, and we'd march out to recess two by two. I could never keep in step, so they used to put me on the end of the line and I'd bring up the rear, marching by myself. This particular day, I had been kept in after school, and the teacher had let me go to the library room to pick out a book to read, and I was alone in there and out of sight, squatting down at a bookcase in the back of the room trying to decide between two books, when the principal of the school, who was a man, came in with one of the men teachers, the math teacher. They each dumped some books down on the desk, and then they stood there for a few moments, talking about one thing and another, and all of a sudden I heard the principal say, 'Did you notice the Gould boy today?' The math teacher said something I didn't catch, and then the principal said, 'The disgusting little bastard can't even keep in step with himself.' The math teacher laughed and said something else I didn't catch, and then they went on out.

"Now, it so happened my father was on the school board and took a great interest in the school, and he and the principal saw quite a lot of each other. They were really very good friends; the principal and his wife used to come to our house for dinner, and my father and mother used to go to their house for dinner. Consequently, I was deeply shocked by the principal's remark. It hurt to overhear myself being called a disgusting little bastard, but it was the disrespect to my father that hurt the most. 'The Gould boy'! That brought my father into it. If he had just said 'Joseph Gould,' it wouldn't've been so bad. It would've confined it to me. I felt that the principal had insulted my father. I felt that he had betrayed him. At the very least, he had made fun of him behind his back. In some strange way, it made me feel closer to my father than I had ever felt before, and it made me feel sorry for him—it made me want to make it up to him. So that night, after supper, I went into the parlor, where he was sitting reading, and I said to him, 'Father, I've been doing some thinking lately about what I'd like to

be, and I've decided I'd like to study medicine and be a surgeon.'
I thought it would please him twice as much if I said I wanted to
be a surgeon. 'That'll be the day,' my father said. 'If you *did* become
a surgeon, and if you performed operations the way you do everything else, when you got through with a patient you'd have his
insides so balled up you'd have his heart hanging upside down and
his liver turned around backward and his intestines wound around
his lungs and his bladder joined on to his windpipe, and you'd have
him walking on his hands and breathing through his behind and
making water out of his left ear.' "

Gould sighed, and a look of intense sadness passed over his face.
"I held that remark against my father for a long time," he said.
"Every once in a while, through the years, I'd remember it, and it
would cut me to the quick. Then, years and years later, long after
I had left home and long after my father had died, I was walking
along the street one night here in New York and happened to think
of it, and it must've been the first time I had ever thought of it
objectively, for I suddenly burst out laughing."

At this moment, the waitress put a plate of fried eggs on toast
and another mug of coffee in front of Gould. As soon as she turned
her back, he took up a bottle of ketchup that was about half full,
and emptied it on the plate, encircling the eggs with ketchup. Then
he darted around to the next booth and brought back another bottle
of ketchup, which was perhaps a third full, and emptied this on
the plate also, completely covering eggs and toast. "I don't particularly like the confounded stuff," he said, "but I make it a practice
to eat all I can get. It's the only grub I know of that's free of
charge." He began eating, using a fork at first but quickly switching
to a spoon. "Sometimes I go in a place and order a cup of tea," he
said confidingly, "and I drink it and pay for it, and then I ask for
a cup of hot water. The counterman thinks I'm going to make a
second cup of tea with the same tea bag, which he doesn't mind:
that's all right. Instead of which, I pour some ketchup in, and I
have a very good cup of tomato bouillon free of charge. Try it
sometime." Gould finished his breakfast, and the waitress came to
take away his plate. Catching sight of the empty ketchup bottles,

she said, "You ought to have more self-respect than do a thing like that." "When I'm hungry, I don't have any self-respect," Gould said. "Anyhow, I didn't do it." He motioned with his head in my direction. "He did it," he said. "He turned both bottles up and drank them. You should've heard him. Glug, glug, glug! It was really quite embarrassing. Besides—and this is something you people can't seem to get through your heads—I'm not just an ordinary person. I'm Joe Gould—I'm Joe Gould, the poet; I'm Joe Gould, the historian; I'm Joe Gould, the wild Chippewa Indian dancer; and I'm Joe Gould, the greatest authority in the world on the language of the sea gull. I do you an honor by merely coming in here, and what do you do in return but bother me about such things as ketchup." This did not amuse the waitress. She was a portly, distracted, heavy-breathing woman, almost twice as big as Gould. "Who the hell do you think you are, you little rat?" she said. "One of these days, I'm going to pick you up by that Joe Gould beard of yours and throw you out of here." "Try it," said Gould, his voice becoming surprisingly intimidating, "and it'll be you and me all over the floor." He took a fistful of cigarette butts from a pocket of his seersucker jacket and put them on the table. As he did so, a shower of tobacco crumbs fell on his lap and on the floor and on the table, and I was afraid that he and the waitress would have some more words with each other. While she watched with disgust, Gould picked through the butts and chose one and fitted it in a long black cigarette holder. Paying no attention to the waitress, he lit it with an arch-elegant, Chaplinlike flourish, and she walked away.

"Now," he said, "to return to the story of my life for just a minute, I finished school in Norwood and then I went to Harvard. In 1911, I graduated from Harvard, and I spent the next few years debating in my mind what I should do next. By 1915, I had about given up hope of coming to any conclusion about this matter when I somehow became interested in the subject of eugenics. In fact, I became so interested that I borrowed some money from my mother and went to the Eugenics Record Office, at Cold Spring Harbor, Long Island, and took a summer course in eugenical field-work methods. After that, I decided I ought to put what I had learned to some use, and I borrowed a little more money from my mother and went out to North Dakota and began measuring the heads of Indians. In January and February, 1916, I measured the heads of five hundred Mandan Indians on the Fort Berthold Reservation, and in March and April I measured the heads of a thousand Chippewas on the Turtle Mountain Reservation, and then my money ran out. I wrote and asked my mother for more, and I received a telegram from her sending me my train fare and telling me to come home at once, which I did, whereupon she told me that she and my father were in financial difficulties to the point they had had to sell our house and were now renting it by the month from the new owner. It seems that some years previous to this my father had invested his own money as well as the money his family had left him in the stock of a company that had been formed to buy and develop a huge tract of land in Alaska. In other words, as smart as he was, my father had bought some gold-mine stock. And while I was out in North Dakota he and my mother had learned beyond all doubt that the stock was worthless.

"Well, I didn't see how I could be of any help to my parents, and I really had enjoyed measuring heads, so I went to Boston and called on various relatives and tried to raise money for another expedition to Indian reservations, but I was unsuccessful, to say the least. At this juncture in my life, my father took it upon himself to find a job for me. He had a friend in Boston, a Mr. Pickett, who was the lawyer for an estate that owned several rows of dwelling houses in Norwood. These houses were rented by the week to people who worked in the tanneries and the glue works, and Mr. Pickett offered me the job of collecting the rents. My father was tired of what he called my shilly-shallying, and I knew it was either take this job or leave Norwood. I was terribly mixed up in my feelings about Norwood. I really never had felt at home in it, but there were things about it that I liked very much, or had liked at one time. I used to like to walk beside a little river that winds along the eastern and southern edges of it, the Neponset. And I used to like to wander around in a weedy old tumbledown New England graveyard that was directly in back of our house on Washington

Street. The weeds were waist-high, and you could lie down and hide in them. You could hide in them and speculate on the rows upon rows of skeletons lying on their backs in the dirt down below. And I used to like some of the old buildings downtown, the old wooden stores. And I used to like the smell from the tanneries, particularly on damp mornings. It was a musky, vinegary, railroady smell. It was a mixture of the smells of raw sheepskins and oak-bark acid that they used in the tanning vats and coal smoke, and it was a characteristic of the town. And I used to like a good many of the people—they had some old-Yankee something about them that appealed to me—but as I grew up I gradually realized that I was a kind of fool to them. I found out that even some of the dignified old men that I admired and respected the most made little jokes about me and laughed at me. I somehow just never fitted in. So, little by little, through the years, I had come to hate Norwood. I had come to hate it with all my heart and soul. There were days, if wishes could kill, I would've killed every man, woman, and child in Norwood, including my mother and father. So I told my father that I couldn't accept Mr. Pickett's offer. 'I have decided,' I said, 'to go to New York and engage in literary work.' 'In that case, Son,' my father said, 'you've made your bed and you can lie in it.' I left Norwood a few days later. I left it with a light heart, even though I knew in my bones that I was leaving it for good, except I might possibly go back in the course of time for Christmas or summer vacations or such occasions as funerals—my father's funeral, my mother's funeral, my own funeral. I hadn't gone far, however, before I began having a reaction that took me by surprise. On the train, all the way to New York, I was so homesick for Norwood that I had to hold on to myself to keep from getting off and turning around and going back. Even today, I sometimes get really quite painfully homesick for Norwood. A sour smell that reminds me of the tanneries will bring it on, such as the smell from a basement down in the Italian part of the Village where some old Italian is making wine. That's one of the damnedest things I ever found out about human emotions and how treacherous they can be—the fact that you can hate a place with all your heart and soul and still be homesick for it. Not to speak of the fact that you can hate a person with all your heart and soul and still long for that person.

"I came to New York with the idea in mind of getting a job as a dramatic critic, for I thought that that would leave me time to write novels and plays and poems and songs and essays and an occasional scientific paper on some eugenical matter, and eventually I did succeed in getting a job as a sort of half messenger boy, half assistant Police Headquarters reporter for the *Evening Mail*. One morning in the summer of 1917, I was sitting in the sun on the back steps of Headquarters recovering from a hangover. In a second-hand bookstore, I had recently come across and looked through a little book of stories by William Carleton, the great Irish peasant writer, that was published in London in the eighties and had an introduction by William Butler Yeats, and a sentence in Yeats's introduction had stuck in my mind: 'The history of a nation is not in parliaments and battlefields, but in what the people say to each other on fair days and high days, and in how they farm, and quarrel, and go on pilgrimage.' All at once, the idea for the Oral History occurred to me: I would spend the rest of my life going about the city listening to people—eavesdropping, if necessary—and writing down whatever I heard them say that sounded revealing to me, no matter how boring or idiotic or vulgar or obscene it might sound to others. I could see the whole thing in my mind—long-winded conversations and short and snappy conversations, brilliant conversations and foolish conversations, curses, catch phrases, coarse remarks, snatches of quarrels, the mutterings of drunks and crazy people, the entreaties of beggars and bums, the propositions of prostitutes, the spiels of pitchmen and peddlers, the sermons of street preachers, shouts in the night, wild rumors, cries from the heart. I decided right then and there that I couldn't possibly continue to hold my job, because it would take up time that I should devote to the Oral History, and I resolved that I would never again accept regular employment unless I absolutely had to or starve but would cut my wants down to the bare bones and depend on friends and well-wishers to see me through. The idea for the Oral History occurred to me around half past ten. Around a quarter to eleven, I stood up and went to a telephone and quit my job."

A throbbing quality had come into Gould's voice.

"Since that fateful morning," he continued, squaring his shoulders and dilating his nostrils and lifting his chin, as if in heroic defiance, "the Oral History has been my rope and my scaffold, my bed and my board, my wife and my floozy, my wound and the salt on it, my whiskey and my aspirin, and my rock and my salvation. It is the only thing that matters a damn to me. All else is dross."

It was obvious that this was a set speech and that he had it down pat and that he had spoken it many times through the years and that he relished speaking it, and it made me obscurely uncomfortable.

"Just now, when you told the waitress that you were an authority on the language of the sea gull," I said, changing the subject, "did you mean it?"

Gould's face lit up. "When I was a child," he said, "my mother and I spent summers at a seaside town in Nova Scotia, a town called Clementsport, and every summer an old man would catch me a sea gull for a pet, and I sometimes used to have the impression that my sea gull was speaking to me, or trying to. Later on, when I was going to Harvard, I spent a great many Saturday afternoons sitting on T Wharf in Boston listening very carefully to sea gulls, and finally they got through to me, and little by little I learned the sea-gull language. I can understand it better than I can speak it, but I can speak it a lot better than you might think. In fact, I have translated a number of famous American poems into sea gull. Listen closely!"

He threw his head back and began to screech and chirp and croak and mew and squawk and gobble and cackle and caw, occasionally punctuating these noises with splutters. There was something singsong and sonorous in this racket that made it sound distantly familiar.

"Don't you recognize it?" cried Gould excitedly. "It's 'Hiawatha'! It's from the part called 'Hiawatha's Childhood.' Listen! I'll translate it back into English:

> *By the shores of Gitche Gumee,*
> *By the shining Big-Sea-Water,*
> *Stood the wigwam of Nokomis,*
> *Daughter of the moon, Nokomis.*

*Dark behind it rose the forest,*
*Rose the black and gloomy pine-trees,*
*Rose the firs with cones upon them . . . "*

Gould snickered; his spirits had risen the moment he had begun talking about sea gulls. "Henry Wadsworth Longfellow translates perfectly into sea gull," he said. "On the whole, to tell you the truth, I think he sounds better in sea gull than he does in English. And now, with your kind permission," he went on, standing up and starting to get out of the booth, a leering expression appearing on his face as he did so, "I'll step out in the aisle and give you my interpretation of a hungry sea gull circling above a fish pier where they're unloading fish." I had been aware, out of the corner of an eye, that the counterman had been watching us. Now this man spoke to Gould. "Sit down," he said. Gould whirled around and looked at the counterman, and I expected him to speak sharply to him, the way he had spoken to the waitress. He surprised me. He sat down meekly and obediently, without opening his mouth. Then, picking up his portfolio and putting it under his arm, as if preparing to go, he leaned across the table and began talking to me in a low voice. "You know the money I borrowed from you yesterday to get the eye prescription," he said. "Well, I started over to the Eye and Ear Infirmary, but on the way something came up, and when I got there the clinic was closed, and I'm in a worse fix today than yesterday as far as money is concerned, and the clinic closes earlier on Thursdays than on Wednesdays, and I wonder if you could lend me two or three or four or maybe five dollars, so I can go get the prescription and start using it. We can continue our talk some other time."

"Of course," I said.

"You won't mind?"

"Oh, no," I said. "Except I was hoping I could see some of the Oral History and maybe read some of it."

"I can easily arrange that," Gould said.

He sat his portfolio on his lap and untied it and opened it and dug around in it and brought out two composition books and put them on the table. "You'll find a chapter of the Oral History in each of these," he said. "I finished them only night before last. I've still got to polish them up a little, but you won't have any trouble reading them." He kept on digging around in the portfolio, using both hands. "In the twenties and thirties, a few bits and pieces and fragments of the Oral History were published in little magazines," he said, "and I have copies of them somewhere in here." He took a small, rolled-up paper bag with a rubber band around it from the deepest part of the portfolio and looked at it inquisitively. "What in hell is this?" he said, opening the bag and peering into it. "Oh, yes," he said. "Cigarette butts." He carefully put the bag back in the portfolio. "Sometimes, in wet weather or snow all over the streets," he said, "it's good to have some butts stuck away." Then he brought out four magazines one by one and stacked them on the table. They were dog-eared and grease-spotted and coffee-stained.

"Here's Ezra Pound's old magazine the *Exile,*" he said, riffling the pages of the one on top. "The *Exile* lasted exactly four issues, and this is the second issue—Autumn, 1927—and there's a chapter from the Oral History in it. I have E. E. Cummings to thank for that. Cummings is one of my oldest friends in New York. He and I come from pretty much the same kind of New England background, and our years at Harvard overlapped—my last year was his first year—but I got to know him in the Village. Sometime around 1923 or '24 or '25, Cummings spoke to Pound about me and the Oral History, and then Pound wrote to me, and we got into a correspondence that extended over several years. Pound became very enthusiastic about my plan for the History. He printed this little selection in the *Exile,* and later on, in his book 'Polite Essays,' after speaking of William Carlos Williams as a great, neglected American writer, he referred to me as 'that still more unreceived and uncomprehended native hickory, Mr. Joseph Gould.' And here's *Broom* for August–November 1923. It has a chapter from the History—Chapter C-C-C-L-X-V-I-I-I. At that time I was numbering the chapters with Roman numbers. And here's *Pagany* for April–June, 1931. It has some snippets from the History.

"And here's the greatest triumph of my life so far—the *Dial* for April, 1929. There are two essays from the Oral History in it. Marianne Moore, the poet, was editor of the *Dial,* and her office was right down here in the Village—on Thirteenth Street, just east of Seventh Avenue. It was one of those old houses—red brick, three stories high, a steep stoop leading up to the parlor floor, an ailanthus tree growing at a slant in front—that have always typified the Village to me. I used to drop in there about once a week and sit in her outer office all morning and sometimes all afternoon, too, reading back copies, and whenever I was able to wangle a little time with her I would try to get her to see the literary importance of the Oral History, and finally she printed these two little essays. Everything else I've ever done may disappear, but I'll still be immortal, just because of them. The *Dial* was the greatest literary magazine ever published in this country. It published a great many masterpieces and near-masterpieces as well as a great many curiosities and monstrosities, and there'll be bound volumes of it in active use in the principal libraries of the world as long as the English language is spoken and read. 'The Waste Land' came out in it. So did 'The Hollow Men.' Eliot reviewed 'Ulysses' for it. Two great stories by Thomas Mann came out in it—'Death in Venice' and 'Disorder and Early Sorrow.' Pound's 'Hugh Selwyn Mauberley' came out in it, and so did Hart Crane's 'To Brooklyn Bridge,' and so did Sherwood Anderson's 'I'm a Fool.' Joseph Conrad wrote for it, and so did Joyce and Yeats and Proust, and so did Cummings and Gertrude Stein and Virginia Woolf and Pirandello and George Moore and Spengler and Schnitzler and Santayana and Gorki and Hamsun and Stefan Zweig and Djuna Barnes and Ford Madox Ford and Miguel de Unamuno and H. D. and Katherine Mansfield, and a hundred others. For centuries to come, people will be going through the bound volumes looking up things by those writers, and now and then one of them will surely notice my two little essays and become curious about them and read them (God knows they aren't very long), and that's closer to immortality than a good many of my rooting and tooting contemporaries are likely to get—bestsellers, interviews on the radio, the dry little details of their dry little lives in *Who's Who,* photographs of their empty faces in the book-review sections, six or seven divorced wives, and all. Just look at some of the other things in this issue. A poem by Hart Crane. An essay by Logan Pearsall Smith. A couple of photographs of a sculpture of a nude by Maillol. A Paris Letter by Paul Morand. A piece about the theatre by Padraic Colum. A book review by Bertrand Russell."

Gould pushed the magazines and the composition books across the table to me. "Take them along and read them," he said.

Outside the diner, on the sidewalk, we agreed to meet again on Saturday night. "But not in the diner," Gould said. "I used to get along very well with the countermen and the waitresses in there. They used to kid around with me and I used to kid around with them. But they seem to have turned against me." A deeply troubled look appeared on his face, a haunted look, and he was silent for a few moments, reflecting. Then he shrugged his shoulders, as if dismissing the matter from his mind, but evidently the matter would not stay dismissed, for right away he started talking about it again. "In recent years," he said, "quite a few people have turned against me. Men and women all over the Village who once were good friends of mine now hate me and loathe me and despise me. You're bound to run into some of them, and they'll probably give you various reasons why they feel that way, and I guess I ought to get in ahead of them and give you the real reason. Would you like to hear it?"

I said that I would.

"The real reason," he said, "is a certain poem I wrote."

We walked slowly along Sixth Avenue.

"In the early thirties, because of the depression," he went on, "a good many people in the Village got interested in Marxism and became radicals. All of a sudden, most of the poets down here became proletarian poets and most of the novelists became proletarian novelists and most of the painters became proletarian painters. I know a woman who's married to a rich doctor and collects art and has a daughter who's a ballet dancer, and I ran into her one day and she informed me very proudly that her daughter was now a proletarian ballet dancer. The trouble is, the more radical these people became, the more know-it-all they became. And the more self-important. And the more self-satisfied. They sat around in the same old Village hangouts that they had sat around in when they were just ordinary bohemians and they talked as much as they ever had, only now it wasn't art or sex or booze that they talked about but the coming revolution and dialectical materialism and the dictatorship of the proletariat and what Lenin meant when he said this and what Trotsky meant when he said that, and they acted as if any conclusions they arrived at on these matters might have a far-reaching effect on the future of the whole world. In other words, they completely lost their sense of humor. The way they talked about the proletariat, you'd think they were all the sons and daughters of iron puddlers, but the truth was, a surprisingly large number of them came from families that were either middle-class or upper-class and either very well-to-do or really quite rich. As time went on, I began to feel like a stranger among them. It wasn't so much their politics that bothered me, beyond the fact that politics of any kind bores the living hell out of me; it was the self-important way they talked about politics. As much as anything else, it was the way they said 'we.' Instead of '*I* think this' or '*I* think that,' it was always '*We* think this' or '*We* think that.' I couldn't get used to the 'we.' I began to feel intimidated by it. Once, trying to make a joke and lighten the atmosphere, I blurted out to one of them that I belonged to a party that had only one member and the name of it was the Joe Gould Party. He said that every time I made such remarks and joked about serious matters I showed myself in my true colors. 'We're on to you and people like you,' he said. 'When you act the clown, all you're doing is trying to hide the fact that you're a reactionary. To be frank about it,' he said. 'we would classify you as a parasite, a reactionary parasite. As for the Oral History,' he said, 'all you're doing in that, as far as we're concerned, is collecting the verbal garbage of the bourgeoisie.'

"At that time, in the summer, one of the novelties of the Village was the sidewalk café in front of the Brevoort Hotel, at Fifth Avenue and Eighth Street. It was just a couple of rows of tables set back behind a hedge growing in a row of wooden boxes painted white, but people thought it was very European and very elegant. For some reason, this café was a great gathering place for the Village radicals. One afternoon in the summer of 1935, I was walking past it and I didn't have a penny in my pocket and I was hungry—not just a little hungry, the way I usually am, but so hungry I was dizzy and my eyes wouldn't focus right and my gums were sore and I had a sick headache and a dull, gnawing pain in the pit of my stomach—and a number of them were sitting there drinking the best Martinis money could buy and eating good French cooking and gravely discussing some matter no doubt having to do with the coming revolution, when a poem popped into my mind. I called it 'The Barricades.' That night, at a Village party, I stood up and said I had a proletarian poem I wanted to recite, and I recited this poem. It really wasn't much of a poem—in fact, it was just a piece of doggerel—but a surprising thing happened. Some of the people were mildly amused by it and laughed a little, which was all I had expected and all I had wanted, but there were several Village radicals and radical sympathizers present, including the man who had let me in on the fact that I was a reactionary parasite, and they were shocked. At first, I thought they were kidding me, pulling my leg, but they weren't, they were genuinely shocked—they looked at me the way deeply religious people might look at someone who had done something horribly sacrilegious—and when they got over their shock they became angry. They became so angry and hysterical that I left the party, which was away over on the east side of the Village, and started walking back to the west side. On Ninth Street, near University Place, I looked in the window of a restaurant called Aunt Clemmy's and saw a miscellaneous group of Villagers sitting around a table in there, some of whom I vaguely knew, and I decided to try 'The Barricades' out on them. I went in and recited it to them, and the same thing happened—some laughed politely and some got blazing mad. Then I went into a real old-time Village restaurant on Eighth Street, called Alice McCollister's—the kind of place that has red water glasses—and recited it to some people in there, and the same thing happened. Then I went over to Sheridan Square and went into a cafeteria that was the most popular late-at-night bo-hemian hangout in the Village at the time, a Stewart's cafeteria, and recited it in there, and the same thing happened. I was amazed at the fanatical reaction some people had to the poem. They practically foamed at the mouth. At the same time, I was delighted. I began to spend a good many evenings just going around the Village looking for opportunities to recite 'The Barricades.' Pretty soon, I found a way to make it even more inflammatory. Instead of reciting it, I would work myself into a state and chant it. I would chant it in a highly excited voice, the voice of a flaming revolutionary, and shake my fist at the end of each line. It got so, in some places in the Village, late at night, all I had to do was stand up and say that I had a proletarian poem I wanted to recite and half the people would leap to their feet and try to stop me and the other half would leap to their feet and egg me on.

"I go to as many Village parties as I can. I go for the free food and liquor and for material for the Oral History. I'm invited to some, and I hear about others on the Village grapevine and just go. One Saturday night a few months after I wrote 'The Barricades,' I showed up at a big party in a studio on Washington Square South. I hadn't been invited, but I knew the man and his wife who were giving it, and I had been going uninvited to their parties for years. When I rang the bell, the wife came to the door, and it didn't seem to me that she was as friendly as she had been in times gone by, but she asked me to come in. I went over and sat in a corner and had a number of drinks, after which it occurred to me that I should create a little diversion and repay my hosts by singing a song, so I stood up and announced that I had a proletarian poem I wanted to recite. Everybody suddenly became quiet, and I took a quick look around the room. It was a big room and there were a lot of people in it, and every face I looked at looked back at me with hatred. That didn't particularly disturb me. I'm used to that. Then I took a closer look around, and here and there, in among the faces of total strangers and the faces of people whom I knew but who meant nothing to me, I saw the faces of several men and women who had always been ready and willing to give me a little money or stake me to a meal or help me out in various other ways, and their faces were as cold and hostile as the others. And that did disturb me. That sobered me up immediately. I suddenly woke up to the fact that without quite realizing what I was doing I had made God only knows how many enemies. Since then, I've been trying to repair the damage, but it doesn't do any good. I never recite 'The Barricades' in public anymore—oh, I do if I'm sure of my audience— and quite a lot of time has gone by, but the Village radicals haven't forgiven me. They cut me dead on the street. If a group of them are sitting in a cafeteria and I sit down near them, they move away. If I stand near them at a bar, they move away. Some of them used to welcome me when I showed up at parties at their places, but now they shut the door in my face. And I've found out that every time my name comes up in conversation they revile me and disparage me and vilify me. And the worst thing is, they communicate the way they feel about me to others. Sooner or later, they'll turn everybody in the Village against me. The countermen and the waitresses in the diner, for example—I'm sure they've turned against me simply because they've heard some of the Village radicals making remarks about me and running me down. Oh, well, what's done's done. Here," he said, handing me his portfolio, "hold this, and I'll recite 'The Barricades' for you."

He straightened his tie and buttoned his dirty seersucker jacket. He drew himself excessively erect, like a schoolboy pledging allegiance to the flag. Then, raising his right fist in the air, he recited the following poem:

> "This prissy hedge in front of the Brevoort
> Is but a symbol of the coming revolution.
> These are the barricades,
>     The barricades,
>         The barricades.
> And behind these barricades,
>     Behind these barricades,
>         Behind these barricades,
> The Comrades die!

> *The Comrades die!*
> *The Comrades die!*
> *And behind these barricades,*
> *The Comrades die—*
> *Of overeating."*

Gould took back his portfolio. "On the other hand," he said, "as far as the people in the diner are concerned, it may not be that at all. I've been terribly run down and nervous this summer, and when I get that way, I scratch a lot. It's just a nervous habit—I've been doing it since childhood. The people in the diner have undoubtedly noticed me scratching, and they may have gotten it in their heads that I'm lousy, and *that* may very well be why they've turned against me." He had been speaking calmly, but now his manner changed. His face was abruptly contorted by an expression of pain and fury, and he spat on the street. "The absolutely hideous and disgusting and unspeakable God-damned truth of the matter is," he said, "I *am* lousy. I discovered it this morning while I was sitting through all those Masses in St. Joseph's. It's the second time in a month. I'll have to go to the Municipal Lodging House tonight and take a bath and let them put my clothes in the fumigator." He shook his head, vaguely. "This is no way to live," he said—and his voice sounded defeated—"but it's the only way I *can* live and work on the Oral History."

I started to try to say something optimistic but sensed that I ran the risk of being presumptuous; a man who has no lice on him is not in a very good position to minimize the disagreeableness of lice if he is talking to a man who is crawling with them, so I changed the subject to where we should meet on Saturday night. We decided that we would meet in Goody's, one of the saloons on Sixth Avenue in the Village. Then we said goodbye, and Gould started across the street. After he had gone a few steps, he suddenly did an about-face and hurried back to me.

"I just remembered something else I want to tell you," he said. "Something about the *Dial*. For a magazine of its kind, the *Dial* had a long life. It lasted nine and a half years. As I told you, the issue that has my contribution in it—the one I just gave you—was the issue for April, 1929. It lasted only three more issues. After the July issue, it discontinued publication, and that was a great shock to everyone who had any interest whatsoever in the cultural life of this country. In the Village, about the only thing people wanted to talk about for weeks was *who* killed the *Dial* or *what* killed the *Dial*. I wrote a poem about this."

Gould drew himself erect, as he had done before, and recited this poem:

> " 'Who killed the Dial?'
> 'Who killed the Dial?'
> 'I,' said Joe Gould,
> 'With my inimitable style,
> I killed the Dial.' "

As he recited it, he watched my face. When he finished it, I laughed more than he had expected me to, I think, and I was struck by how much pleasure this gave him. His bloodshot little eyes glowed with pleasure. Then, giggling, he hurried off.

IT WAS A CLOUDY DAY and looked as if it might pour down any minute, but I disregarded the weather and went over and sat on a bench under the big old elm in the northwest corner of Washington Square and opened one of Gould's composition books. On the first page was carefully lettered, "DEATH OF DR. CLARKE STORER GOULD. A CHAPTER OF JOE GOULD'S ORAL HISTORY." The chapter was divided into an introduction and four sections. The sections were headed: "FINAL ILLNESS," "DEATH," "FUNERAL," and "CREMATION." "The first thing I must deal with in this account of my father's death," Gould wrote in his introduction, "is that, for me, he died twice. In the summer of 1918, I left New York City, where I was getting down to work in earnest on the Oral History, and went up to Norwood to spend a month with my mother. The first World War was going on at that time, and my father was serving as a captain in the Medical Corps of the United States Army and was stationed at Camp Sherman, Chillicothe, Ohio. He was assistant adjutant of the base hospital. The second afternoon I was home, my mother went to the nearby town of Dedham to visit a friend, and I took a walk downtown, to the business district of Norwood. While we were both absent from the house, a doctor in Boston who was a friend of my father's telephoned my mother, and our cook, an old German woman who didn't understand English any too well and wasn't any too bright to begin with, took the call. The doctor in Boston said he was calling to ask my mother to inform my father the next time she wrote to him that another Boston doctor who was also a friend of my father's and had in fact been stationed with him for a while at Camp Sherman had died that day of blood poisoning in another camp out in the Middle West, but the old cook got it all balled up and understood him to say that my father had died that day of blood poisoning out at Camp Sherman. When I came home in the middle of the afternoon, she was sitting in the kitchen crying, and she told me that my father was dead. I went upstairs to my room and drew the shades and sat there mourning my father. I was overwhelmed with grief. Late in the afternoon my mother came home and immediately got on the telephone and called the doctor in Boston and ascertained what he had really told the cook. And then a curious thing happened to me— even though, intellectually, I knew that my father was not dead, I could not stop mourning him. For me, the blow had fallen. I sank into a mood of deep sorrow and could not rouse myself from it. I mourned my father all the rest of my visit to Norwood, and I continued to mourn him for several weeks after returning to New York City. My father was honorably discharged from the Army on December 28, 1918, and returned at once to Norwood and resumed his practice. After he had been back in Norwood for less than three months, he became seriously ill and was taken to the Peter Bent Brigham Hospital in Boston, where he died early in the A.M. of Friday, March 28, 1919, aged fifty-four. And now I must put down the fact that his illness was septicemia, or blood poisoning, which was and is to me an astonishing coincidence. When I received the news of his death, I did not mourn him at all. As far as I was concerned, he was already dead. When I write my autobiography, I am going to make the flat statement in it that my father died of blood poisoning in an Army camp in Ohio during the first World War, and I am going to insist that this be so stated in any biographical material that is written about me as long as I am alive and have any control over such things, for to me my father's untrue death was his true death. I have no misgivings about this. In autobiography and biography, as in history, I have discovered, there are occasions when the facts do not tell the truth. However, in this account, I am going to deal only with what was, I must admit, my father's actual and factual death."

Gould's writing was very much like his conversation; it was a little stiff and stilted and mostly rather dull, but enlivened now and then by a surprising observation or bit of information or by sarcasm or malice or nonsense. It was full of digressions; there were digressions that led to other digressions, and there were digressions within digressions. Gould's father had belonged to the Universalist Church and the Masons, and his funeral service had been conducted jointly by the pastor of the local Universalist church and the chaplain and the Worshipful Master of the local Masonic lodge. Gould described the Universalist part of the service, and went from that to a discussion of the subtle differences between the members of the Universalist, Unitarian, and Congregational churches in New England towns, and went from that to a discussion of the differences between an Easter service he had once attended in an Albanian Orthodox Catholic church in Boston with a friend of his, an Albanian student at Harvard, and Easter services he had attended in Roman Catholic churches, and went from that to a description of a strange but unusually good meat stew he had once eaten in a basement restaurant in Boston frequented by Albanian shoe-factory workers that the Albanian student had taken him to ("They said it was lamb and it may have been mutton," he wrote, "but it was probably goat, either that or horse meat, not that I have any objection to goat meat or horse meat, having had the experience of eating boiled dog with the Chippewa Indians, which incidentally tasted like mutton, only sweeter, although I should point out here that eating dog has a ceremonial significance to the Chippewas and might be compared to our communion services and consequently the taste per se is not of great importance"), and went from that to a description of a baked-bean pot he had once seen in the window of an antique store on Madison Avenue that was exactly like the baked-bean pot used in the kitchen of his home in Norwood when he was a child. "Gazing at that so-called ANTIQUE baked-bean pot," he wrote, "I felt for the first time that I understood something about Time." He then began a description of the Masonic part of his father's funeral service, but went astray almost immediately with a digression on the importance of the Masons and the Elks and the Woodmen of the World and similar fraternal orders in the night life of small towns, which he interrupted at one point for a subsidiary digression on the subject of life insurance. "I wonder what Lewis and Clark would have thought of life insurance," he wrote in the course of the latter digression, "never mind Daniel Boone." (He had run a line through "never mind" and had written "let alone" just above it; then he had run a line through "let alone" and had written "not to speak of" just above *it;* then he had run a line through "not to speak of"; and then, in the margin, beside "never mind," he had written "stet.") Scattered throughout the book were many sentences that were wholly irrelevant; they seemed to be thoughts that had popped into his mind as he wrote, and that he had put down at once, because he didn't want to forget them. In the description of the Easter service in the Albanian church, for example, apropos of nothing that went before or came after, was this sentence: "Mr. Osgood, the Indian teacher at Armstrong, N.D., said that whiskey made the Sioux murderous and the Chippewa good-natured."

On the cover of the other composition book was lettered, "THE DREAD TOMATO HABIT, A CHAPTER OF JOE GOULD'S ORAL HISTORY." I couldn't make much sense out of this chapter until I skipped around in it and found that it was mock-serious and that its purpose was to make fun of statistics. Gould maintained that a mysterious disease was sweeping the country. "It is so mysterious that doctors are unaware of its existence," he wrote. "Furthermore, they do not want to become aware of its existence because it is responsible for a high percentage of the human misfortunes ranging from acne to automobile accidents and from colds to crime waves that they blame directly or indirectly on microbes or viruses or allergies or neuroses or psychoses and get rich by doing so." Gould devoted several pages to a description of the nature of the disease, and then stated that he knew the cause of it and was the only one who did. "It is caused by the increased consumption of tomatoes both raw and cooked and in the form of soup, sauce, juice, and ketchup," he wrote, "and therefore I have named it solanacomania. I base this name on *Solanaceae*, the botanical name for the dreadful nightshade family, to which the tomato belongs." At this point, Gould began filling page after page with unrelated statistics that he had obviously copied out of the financial and business sections of newspapers. "If this be true," he wrote after each statistic, "this also must be true," and then he introduced another statistic. He filled twenty-eight pages with these statistics. "And now," he wrote, winding up the chapter, "I hope I have proven, and I have certainly done so to my own satisfaction, that the eating of tomatoes by railroad engineers was responsible for fifty-three per cent of the train wrecks in the United States during the last seven years."

I was puzzled. These chapters of the Oral History bore no relation at all that I could see to the Oral History as Gould had described it. There was no talk or conversation in them, and unless they were looked upon as monologues by Gould himself there was nothing oral about them. I turned to the little magazines Gould had given me, and found that his contributions to them were brief but rambling essays, each of which had a one- or two-word title and a subtitle stating that it was "a chapter of" or "a selection from" the Oral History. In the *Exile,* his subject was "Art." In *Broom,* his subject was "Social Position." He had two essays in the *Dial*—"Marriage" and "Civilization." And he had two in *Pagany*—"Insanity" and "Freedom." By this time, I had read enough of Gould's writing to know what these essays were. They were digressions cut out of chapters of the Oral History by the editors of the little magazines or by Gould himself and given titles of their own. In other words, they were more of the same. I read them without much interest until, in the "Insanity" essay, I came across three sentences that stood out sharply from the rest. These sentences were plainly meant by Gould to be a sort of poker-faced display of conceit, but it seemed to me that he told more in them than he had intended to. In the years to come, as I got to know him better, they would return to my mind a great many times. They appeared at the end of a paragraph in which he had made the point that he was dubious about the possibility of dividing people into sane and insane. "I would judge the sanest man to be him who most firmly realizes the tragic isolation of humanity and pursues his essential purposes calmly," he wrote. "I suppose I feel about it in this way because I have a delusion of grandeur. I believe myself to be Joe Gould."

ON SATURDAY NIGHT, June 13, 1942, I went into Goody's to keep the appointment I had made with Gould. Goody's (the proprietor's name was Goodman) was on Sixth Avenue, between Ninth and Tenth streets, directly across the avenue from Jefferson Market Courthouse. I had often noticed the place, but this was the first time I had ever been in it. Like most of the barrooms on Sixth Avenue in the Village, it was long and narrow and murky, a blind tunnel of a place, a burrow, a bat's cave, a bear's den. I learned later that many of the men and women who frequented it had been bohemians in the early days of the Village and had been renowned for their rollicking exploits and now were middle-aged or elderly and in advanced stages of alcoholism. I arrived at nine, which was when Gould and I had agreed to meet. He was nowhere in sight, and I went over and stood at the bar. "I'm just waiting for someone," I said to the bartender, who shrugged his shoulders. In a little while, I got tired of standing and sat on a bar stool. After I had been sitting there for half an hour or so, peering into the gloom, I recalled something that one of the first persons I had talked with about Gould had told me—a man who had been at Harvard with him. "If you're going to have any dealings with Joe Gould," he had said, "one thing you want to keep in mind is that he's about as undependable as it's possible to be. If he's supposed to be somewhere at a certain time, he's just as likely to arrive an hour or two early as an hour or two late, or he may arrive on the dot, or he may not show up at all, and in his mind Tuesday can very easily become Thursday." Around a quarter to ten, the telephone in a booth up near the front end of the bar began to ring. One of the customers stepped inside the booth and reappeared a few moments later and shouted out my name. When I stood up, startled, he said, "Joe Gould wants to speak to you."

"I'm sorry, but I won't be able to meet you tonight," Gould said, his voice sounding a little boozy. "I completely forgot that I had to go to a meeting of the Raven Poetry Circle. In fact, the meeting is going on right now, and I just slipped out and came down here to a phone booth in a drugstore to call you, and I have to go right back. I don't belong to the Ravens; they won't let me join—they blackball me every time my name comes up—but they let me attend their meetings, and now and then they give me a place on the program. The Ravens are the biggest poetry organization in the Village, and there isn't one real poet in the whole lot of them. The best parts of all of them put together wouldn't make one third-rate poet. They're all would-bes. Pseudos. Imitators of imitators. They're imitators of bad poets who themselves were imitators of bad poets. I can't stand them and they can't stand me, but the hell of it is, I enjoy them and I enjoy their meetings. They're so bad they're good. Also, after the program they serve wine. Also, there's a high percentage of unmarried lady poets among them, and sooner or later I'm going to bamboozle one of them into free love or matrimony, even if it has to be a certain tall, thin, knock-kneed drink of water I've had my eye on for some time now who's supposed to have a private income and writes poems about the eternal sea and has a Dutch bob and a long nose and an Adam's apple and always has cigarette ashes in her lap and cat hair all over her. 'Roll on, roll on,' she says, 'eternal sea,' and her big old Adam's apple bobs up and down. But the main reason I didn't want to miss tonight's meeting is I see a chance to poke some fun at the Ravens. Tonight is Religious Poetry Night, and I talked them into putting me on the program. I asked for a place right at the end. You can just imagine the kind of religious poetry they're capable of. Mystical! Soulful! Rapturous! 'Methinks' or 'albeit' in every other line, and deep—oh, my God, they're deeper than John Donne ever hoped to be. When they've all recited theirs, I'm going to stand up and recite mine. Listen, and I'll recite it for you. 'My Religion,' by Joe Gould:

> In winter I'm a Buddhist,
> And in summer I'm a nudist."

Gould giggled. He asked me if I had read the chapters of the Oral History he had given me. I said that I had, and that they had been a good deal different from what I had expected, and that I would like to read some more.

"The great bulk of the Oral History is stored away in a place that's quite inaccessible," he said, suddenly becoming serious, "but I have a few chapters stuck away here and there around town where they're easy to get at. I'll tell you what. I have an old friend named Aaron Siskind, who's a kind of avant-garde documentary photographer, and he has his darkroom and his living quarters in a flat up over a second-hand bookstore at 102 Fourth Avenue, and I must have six, seven, eight, nine, ten, or a dozen composition books stuck away up there. He'll be in now—he works in his darkroom at night—and it's only a short walk from Goody's over to his place. Why don't you take a walk over there and read those chapters? He won't mind getting them out for you. And let's meet in Goody's tomorrow night. I promise you I'll be there this time."

Siskind's flat was over the Corner Book Shop, at Fourth Avenue and Eleventh Street, right in the middle of the second-hand-bookstore district. He came to the door, a short, jovial man with skeptical eyes, and I told him what I was after, and he laughed. "Good God!" he said. "Haven't you got anything better to do with your time than that?" However, he went at once to a clothes closet in the hallway of the flat and squatted down and looked around among the shoes and the fallen coat hangers on the floor of it and picked up five composition books. "Joe's a little off in his calculations," he said. "He has only five up here at present." He slapped the dust off the books and handed them to me, and I sat down and opened one. On the first page of it was carefully lettered, "DEATH OF DR. CLARKE STORER GOULD. A CHAPTER OF JOE GOULD'S ORAL HISTORY." This turned out to be another version of Gould's account of his father's final illness, death, funeral, and cremation. The facts in it having to do with these matters were the same as those in the version I had already read, although they were differently arranged, but the digressions were completely different. I opened the second book, and the title was exactly the same: "DEATH OF DR. CLARKE STORER GOULD, A CHAPTER OF JOE GOULD'S ORAL HISTORY." This was still another version. The title in the third book was "DRUNK AS A SKUNK, OR HOW I MEASURED THE HEADS OF FIFTEEN HUNDRED INDIANS IN ZERO WEATHER. A CHAPTER OF JOE GOULD'S ORAL HISTORY." This appeared to be an account of the trip that Gould had made to the Indian reservations in North Dakota. The title in the fourth book was "THE DREAD TOMATO HABIT, OR WATCH OUT! WATCH OUT! DOWN WITH DR. GALLUP! A CHAPTER OF JOE GOULD'S ORAL HISTORY." This was another version of the statistical chapter. The title in the fifth book was "DEATH OF MY MOTHER. A CHAPTER OF JOE GOULD'S ORAL HISTORY." This was the shortest of the chapters. It took up only eleven and a half pages, and most of it was a digression on the subject of cancer.

"Joe comes up here every few days and hits me for a handout, or what he calls a contribution to the Joe Gould Fund, and if he happens to have a finished composition book with him he goes over and tosses it in the closet," Siskind told me as I looked through the books. "He's been doing that for quite a long time now. He leaves the books in the closet until anywhere from half a dozen to a dozen or so have accumulated, and then, one day, he gathers them up and puts them in his portfolio and takes them away. By and by, he starts a new accumulation. He used to ask me to read them, and I would, but I don't anymore. He writes on the same subjects over and over again, and I'm afraid I've lost interest in the death of his father and the death of his mother and the dread tomato habit and the Indians out in North Dakota and all that. He seems to be a perfectionist;

he seems to be determined to keep on writing new versions of each of his subjects until he gets one that is absolutely right. One cold day last winter, he came up here and sat by the radiator and started correcting and revising one of his books. He went through it once, changing a word here and a word there and scratching out sentences and writing new ones in. Then he went through it again and changed some more words and scratched out some more sentences. Then he went through it again. Then he tore the whole thing up and threw it in the wastebasket. 'Jesus, Joe!' I said. 'You certainly improved that one. You improved it right out of existence.' "

"When he gathers up his composition books and puts them in his portfolio, where does he take them?" I asked.

"He's always been kind of vague and remote about that." Siskind said. "As a matter of fact, I've never really understood why he takes them away in the first place. I've often told him that he can leave them here as long as he likes, and that he can have the whole closet to himself if he wants it. He's such a perfectionist I wouldn't be surprised if he tears them up and throws them in the first trash basket he comes to. Then he starts all over again. Starts fresh. Oh, I guess he has some secret place or other where he takes them and stores them away."

THE NEXT NIGHT, I went into Goody's again. Gould was sitting at a table across from the bar. There was an empty beer glass in front of him. He was wearing the same dirty seersucker suit that he had been wearing at our first meeting, only now it was much dirtier and had a bad rip at the shoulder. It looked as if somewhere along the line someone had given his left sleeve an angry jerk, ripping it half off at the shoulder. I went over and sat down and returned the composition books and the little magazines that I had got from him, and thanked him for letting me read them.

"You were disappointed," he said accusingly.

"Oh, no," I said.

"Yes you were," he said. "I can tell."

"To be honest," I said, "I was. I understood from what you told me that the Oral History was mostly talk, but there wasn't any talk in the chapters you lent me or in the ones I saw at Siskind's."

Gould threw up his hands. "Naturally there wasn't." he said. "There are two kinds of chapters in the Oral History—essay chapters and oral chapters. As it happens, all those you read were essay chapters."

This remark instantly cleared up my puzzlement about the Oral History; it seemed to explain everything. I took Gould's empty glass over to the bar and got him a beer. Then, sitting down, I told him I would like very much to read some of the oral chapters.

"Oh, Lord," Gould said. "Since we've gone this far, there's something about the Oral History I'll have to tell you—something about its present whereabouts. I was hoping I could keep it quiet, but I can see now I would've had to let people know about it sooner or later anyhow." He frowned and cocked his eyes at the ceiling and stroked his bearded chin and seemed to be casting around in his mind for the simplest way to tell about something that was extraordinarily involved. "Oh, well, to go back a little," he said, "a woman I know who used to work in the main branch of the Public Library retired several years ago and bought a duck-and-chicken farm on Long Island, and last Thanksgiving she invited me out there. I'm not going to tell you her name or the exact location of her farm, so don't ask me any questions. It's an isolated place, out on a dirt road. Huntington is the nearest railroad station, but it's a considerable distance from Huntington. There are two houses on the place. One is a frame house, and a Polish farmer and his wife live in it and look after the ducks and chickens. The other is an old stone house, and my friend and a niece of hers live in it. My friend showed me over the house, including the cellar. The cellar was snug and dry and whitewashed, and it was partitioned into one large room and three small rooms. The small rooms were built to be used for storage, and had good strong doors. And the doors had locks on them—set-in locks, not padlocks. Now, early in January of this year, a month and a half or so after I was out there, a painter friend of mine told me that an art dealer had told him that the Metropolitan Museum was moving a good many of its most precious paintings to a bombproof location outside the city for the duration of the war, and I decided I'd better get busy and do something about the Oral History. I immediately thought of those rooms in my friend's cellar, and it seemed to me that one of them would be an ideal place for the Oral History. So I wrote to my friend and inquired into the possibility. She didn't think much of the idea at first— didn't want the responsibility—but I wrote to her again and said that a good librarian such as herself ought to be able to understand the importance to posterity of what I was asking her to do, and I promised her that generations yet unborn would be grateful to her and rise up and call her blessed, and finally she wrote and said for me to get the Oral History together and wrap it in two layers of oilcloth and tie some ropes around it—in other words, bale it up. I did so, and the following Sunday she and her niece drove in and picked it up and took it out and deposited it in her cellar. And that's where it is. And if you'll pay my train fare out to Huntington and back and my taxicab fare from the station out to her place and back and give me money enough to buy her a box of candy for a present, I'll take a run out there early next week and open the bale and select a couple of dozen representative chapters—oral ones, that is—and bring them in."

We figured out how much money he would need for the trip, and I gave it to him.

He took his time about making the trip. I didn't see him again until the following Thursday, when he came to my office and said that he had gone out to his friend's farm the day before but hadn't been able to get at the Oral History. "My friend wasn't home," he said. "According to her niece, she's been away a couple of months. She's down in Florida. She has a brother who's a retired high-school English teacher, a bachelor, and he was spending the winter in St. Augustine, and sometime around the middle of April he had a stroke. She's very attached to him, and she went down there to look after him. And just before she left, the niece said, she locked up half the place, including the three rooms in the cellar, and took the keys with her. This upset me, and I begged the niece to write her at once and ask her to send back the key to the room the Oral History

is in. 'Write her yourself,' the niece said. 'It's none of my business.'
Then I decided it might be a lot wiser to telephone her, so the
niece gave me the number of the place where she's staying, and I'd
appreciate it very much if you'd let me have money enough to make
the call."

I said I could arrange for him to make the call right then, through
the office switchboard.

"That would be fine," he said, "except I'm not supposed to call
her during the day. The niece told me I should call her at night,
because she's at the hospital during the day. If you'll just let me
have the money, I'll call her tonight from the pay phone in Goody's."

Next morning, shortly after I got to the office, Gould telephoned
and said that after calling the woman person-to-person several times
he had reached her around midnight. "She must be all tired out
and nervous," he said, "because she scolded me severely. She reminded me that when she agreed to store the Oral History she had
made it clear that I couldn't be taking it out and putting it back in
but that I'd have to let it stay put for the duration of the war. 'You
wanted it in a safe place,' she said, 'and it's in a safe place, so just
relax.' I asked her when she expected to return, but I didn't get
much satisfaction out of her. 'It might be weeks,' she said, 'and it
might be months, and it might be years. And in the meantime,' she
said, 'quit bothering me.' I tried to reason with her, and she hung
up on me."

"Would it do any good if I called her?" I asked.

"As soon as she found out what you were calling about," Gould
said, "she'd hang up on you."

This put me in a predicament. Ever since my first interview with
Gould, I had been tracking down friends and enemies of his and
talking with them about him. Most of these people had known
Gould for a long time and either were regular contributors to the
Joe Gould Fund or had been in the past. In fact, several of them—
E. E. Cummings, the poet; Slater Brown, the novelist; M. R. Werner,
the biographer; Orrick Johns, the poet; Kenneth Fearing, the poet
and novelist; Malcolm Cowley, the critic; Barney Gallant, the proprietor of Barney Gallant's, a Village night club; and Max Gordon,

the proprietor of the Village Vanguard, another Village night club—had been giving him a dime or a quarter or a half dollar or a dollar or a couple of dollars once or twice a week for over twenty years. Each person I saw had suggested others to see, and I had looked up around fifteen people and spoken on the telephone with around fifteen others. All of them had been willing, or more than willing, to tell what they knew about Gould, and I had got a great many anecdotes and a great deal of biographical information about him from them. I had read the clippings concerning him in the morgues of three newspapers. (The oldest clipping I found was dated March 2, 1934, and was from the *Herald Tribune*. In it, Gould told the reporter that the Oral History was 7,300,000 words long. In another clipping from the *Herald Tribune*, dated April 10, 1937, he said that the Oral History was now 8,800,000 words long. In one from *PM*, dated August 24, 1941, Gould was called "an author who has written a book taller than himself." "The stack of manuscripts comprising the Oral History has passed 7 feet," *PM* said. "Gould is 5 feet 4.") At the suggestion of one of his classmates, I had gone to the library of the Harvard Club and hunted through the reports of his class—the class of 1911—for references to him. I had spent a day in the genealogy room in the Public Library looking through New England genealogies and town and county histories for information about his ancestors and family connections, and had been able to verify most of the statements he had made about them. Now all I needed was one more thing, a look at the oral part of the Oral History, but that seemed to me to be essential. As far as I was concerned, the Oral History was Gould's reason for being, and if I couldn't quote from it, or even describe it first hand, I didn't see how I could write a Profile of him. I could postpone further work on the Profile until the woman returned from Florida and let Gould into her cellar, but I knew from experience that postponing a project of this nature usually meant the end of it; I knew that my interest in it would fade as soon as I got involved in other matters, and that before long simply having it hanging over me would very likely cause me to turn against it. Furthermore, I was growing leery of Gould; I had begun to feel that, whatever the reason, he really didn't want me to see the oral part of the Oral History, and that when the woman returned, some brand-new difficulty might very well present itself. I decided on the spur of the moment that the best thing to do was to abandon the project right then and there and go on as quickly as possible to something else.

"I'm sorry, Mr. Gould," I said, "but I think we'd better just drop the whole thing."

"Oh, no!" Gould said. His voice sounded alarmed. "Look," he said. "I have an abnormal memory. In fact, people have often told me that I probably have what the psychologists call total recall. I've lost chapters of the Oral History several times and reconstructed them entirely from memory. Once, I lost one and reconstructed it and then found the one I had lost, and a good many pages in the two of them matched almost word for word. If you'll meet me in Goody's tonight, I'll recite some chapters for you. I'll recite dozens of chapters. If you've got the patience to listen, I'll recite hundreds. You'll get as good an idea of the oral part of the Oral History that way as you would by reading it. Considering my handwriting, you may even get a better idea."

That night, around eight, Gould and I sat down at a table in a quiet corner in the back of Goody's. First, he drank two double Martinis, doing so, he said, for a particular pupose. "I have found," he said, "that gin primes the pump of memory." Then he began telling the life story of a man he said he used to run into in flophouses who was a kind of religious fanatic and was called the Deacon, telling it in the first person, just as the Deacon had told it to him. The Deacon was a gloomy periodical drinker. He was a backslidden member of some schismatic Lutheran sect, he was under the impression that he had lost his soul, he believed that he had discovered hints in the Bible concerning the exact date—year, month, day, and time of day—of the end of the world, and he often saw things at night. One summer night, for example, while he was sitting in a doorway on Great Jones Street, near the Bowery, he smelled sulphur and looked up and saw the Devil walk past and felt the heat of Hell emanating from him. Later the same night, he saw two mermaids in the East River. They were off Pier 26, at the foot of

Catharine Street, frolicking in the moonlight. "They weren't exactly half women, half fishes," he told Gould. "They were more like half women, half snakes. When they saw me sitting on the pier looking at them, they held out their arms and wriggled and made certain other motions trying to tempt me to come in with them, and if I had done so they would've wrapped themselves around me and dragged me to the bottom."

Gould spent an hour or so on the Deacon's visions and torments. Then, after drinking another double Martini, he quoted some re- marks that he said had been made to him by a doleful old Hungarian woman, known as Old Budapest or Old Buda the Pest, who used to sit in bars on Third Avenue, around Cooper Square, and talk on and on to anyone who would listen. Gould said he had filled many composition books with her talk. Old Buda had been three times a wife and three times a widow; she had had some connection with the dope trade through one of her husbands; she had been a madam, or, as she defined it, "the operator of a furnished-room house for women over in the Navy Yard district in Brooklyn"; and she had wound up working in the kitchen of a city hospital. Her talk was made up for the most part of descriptions of and reflections on awful things that she had experienced or observed. Gould recited a few of her soliloquies verbatim and paraphrased others and sum- marized others. Finishing with Old Buda, he drank a fourth Mar- tini—a regular one this time. Then he ordered another, but decided not to drink all of it. Instead, he ordered a large beer, drank it, and then ordered a small beer and drank it. At this point, he described an eating place in which he said he had spent a lot of time during the early thirties. It was called Frenchy's Coffee Pot; it was on First Avenue, near Twenty-ninth Street, just across from the Pathological Building of Bellevue Hospital, a building that also housed the City Mortuary; it stayed open until two in the morning and opened again at six; and it was patronized by nurses, internes, orderlies, ambulance drivers, morgue attendants, embalming-school students, and other people who worked in the hospital and the mortuary. Whenever he could, Gould said, he would engage these people in conversation, and now he began to quote some of the things they had told him.

"This part of the Oral History is pretty gory," he said. "It is called 'Echoes from the Backstairs of Bellevue,' and it is divided into sections, under such headings as 'Spectacular Operations and Amputations,' 'Horrible Deaths,' 'Sadistic Doctors,' 'Alcoholic Doctors,' 'Drug-Addicted Doctors,' 'Women-Chasing Doctors,' 'Huge Tumors, Etc.,' and 'Strange Things Found During Autopsies.' "

Presently, after quoting at some length from each of his sections on Bellevue, Gould ordered another small beer and drank it, and then said that he would now quote for a little while from the longest and most important part of the Oral History. He said that he called this part "An Infinitude of Bushwa," and that it was about the Village, and that it ran through approximately seventy-five composition books. "It contains an enormous number of monologues, conversations, and disputes about a wide variety of art, literary, political, theological, and sexual matters that I overheard in the Village," he said, "and this will be very valuable to social historians in centuries to come, but the most valuable thing it contains is gossip—the things that people in the Village said about each other behind each other's backs during the twenties and thirties. As I say somewhere in my introduction to this part, which in itself takes up nine composition books, 'Malicious gossip, vicious and malicious. Spite and jealousy and middle-aged lust and middle-aged bile.' You can mention just about anybody who was around the Village during the last quarter of a century, and I've probably got something about him or her in this part of the History—something nasty. However and nevertheless and notwithstanding and be that as it may," he said, suddenly getting to his feet, "please excuse me a minute."

I had been so busy taking notes that I hadn't looked up for some time, and now I looked up and saw that Gould was drunk, or close to it. His eyes were blank and staring; he stared at me as if he had never seen me before. I was surprised, for his voice had been clear and his talk had been coherent. "I'll be right back," he said. Starting to step away from the table, he lurched into the aisle. Then, recovering himself, he made his way to the men's room, shuffling along cautiously and holding his arms out in front of him for balance, like a feeble old man.

When he returned, I said I was afraid that he was tired of talking, and suggested that we adjourn and meet again the following night. He shook his head vigorously. "I'm not in the least bit tired," he said. I closed my notebook and started to put it in my pocket. "You're the one who's tired," he said. He reached over and grabbed my sleeve. "Don't go yet," he said. "I want to say something about my mother. I didn't say much about her the other day in the diner, and I feel I should. Don't bother taking notes. Just listen."

His mother had been a good mother, he said, except for one thing: She had never treated him as a grownup. While he was at Harvard, he said, and even after he had been living in New York City for years and had become well known as a bohemian and had grown a beard, she had occasionally sent him packages of a kind of penny candy, called peach pits, that he had liked as a child. This was typical of her, he said. "My mother did one thing to me when I was a boy," he said, "that I've never been able to forgive or forget. It may seem like a trivial incident to you, not worth thinking about twice, but I must've thought about it a thousand times. We were sitting in the parlor of our house in Norwood one evening after supper. I was studying, and I happened to look up and I saw that she was looking at me and apparently had been for some time and that tears were running down her cheeks. 'My poor son,' she said." Gould's eyes blazed. He was silent for a few moments. Then he forgot all about his mother and began talking about his father. He got wound up talking about his father; he couldn't seem to stop. His father had been a railroad enthusiast, he said, and a collector of timetables and of pictures of locomotives. Norwood is on a branch line of what was then the New England Railroad and is now the New York, New Haven & Hartford, and his father had been local surgeon for the railroad and a member of the International Association of Railway Surgeons. "One evening," Gould said, "my father put down his newspaper, which was the Boston *Evening Transcript,* you may be sure, and announced that he was going in to Boston in the morning to see a new locomotive that the railroad was getting ready to put into service, and then he announced that he was taking me with him. This was when I was around nine or ten, back before he had given up on me, so to speak, and it was one of the happiest days of my life. We got up before day and had breakfast together, and then we went in on an early train and stopped in the station restaurant in Boston and had a second breakfast. He had coffee and a cinnamon bun, and I had hot chocolate and a cinnamon bun. Then we went out in the yards. There was a crowd of railroad men standing around the locomotive, looking it over, and my father knew one of them. 'How do you do, Mr. Delehanty,' my father said. 'This is my son Joseph.' "

Gould was so moved by this recollection that his voice broke and his eyes filled with tears and he was unable to continue talking. A few moments later, while he was dabbing at his eyes with a paper napkin and trying to regain his composure, one of the old bohemians at the bar came over to him and said, "I know how you feel, Joe. It was really quite a shock." Gould stared at the old bohemian. "What shock?" he asked. The old bohemian stared back at Gould. "Hearing about it," he said. "Hearing about what?" asked Gould. "Bob," said the old bohemian. Then, giving Gould a searching look and seeing that he was mystified, the old bohemian said that a man named Bob Something-or-Other (I didn't catch his last name), who was evidently another old bohemian and a friend of both of them, had keeled over in Goody's during the afternoon, while he was sitting at the bar, and had been taken to St. Vincent's Hospital, where, according to a telephone call the bartender had just received, he had died not long after he arrived. Gould was visibly delighted by this piece of news. "Well, I must say," he said, "I think that was very commendable of Bob. In fact," he went on, "it's probably the most commendable thing he ever did." The old bohemian was taken aback, but a moment later his face changed and he laughed heartily. "Poor old Bob," said Gould, in mitigation. Then he and the old bohemian became engrossed in an intensely serious discussion about Bob's age—whether he had hit seventy or was still in his sixties—and I took the opportunity to say good night and depart.

Next night, Gould and I met again in Goody's. We met at six, and I listened to him until around midnight. We skipped the following night, which was Sunday night. On Monday night, we met again at six, and once again I listened to him until around midnight. I thought that we had agreed to meet at eight on Tuesday night, but when I arrived at eight I found that I had not made this clear to him and he had been waiting for me since six and was so anxious to start talking that he was in a state of agitation. To square myself, I listened to him until Goody's closed, at four o'clock in the morning. I saw him again on Wednesday night, and again on Thursday night, and again on Friday night. These sessions followed a pattern. Gould would quote from the Oral History while the gin and beer were gradually taking hold, and then he would lose interest in the Oral History and talk more and more about himself, until presently he would give up and talk about nothing but himself. He seemed to think that no detail of his life was too trivial to tell about. He would tell about the first time he caught a fish or about the removal of his tonsils, he would tell fatuous family anecdotes, laughing all the while, and he would recall the ins and outs of conversations that he had had long ago with boyhood friends about the mysteries of the adult world. Once, he pointed out several scars on his cheeks and forehead and told how he got each one; I remember that he got a couple of those on his forehead when a Mason jar of stewed tomatoes that his mother had put up exploded. Late one evening, he paused for a moment and asked me if I was tired of listening to him, and I started to be polite and say "Oh, no!," but weariness made me frank and I said that I was, whereupon he snickered and said that he could sympathize with me but that he had been waiting for years to talk to someone about himself and really go into detail, and now that he had an opportunity to do so he was going to make the most of it. "And since you're going to write about me," he said, "you can't help yourself—it's your duty to listen to me, it's part of your job."

After the Friday-night session, which lasted ten hours—it started at 6 P.M. and ended at 4 A.M.—I decided that I had become sufficiently familiar with a representative group of chapters of the Oral History and that enough was enough and that I wouldn't listen to him any longer, although it was obvious that he had scarcely got started and could go on for weeks; I simply didn't have the endurance. I tried to tell him this but found myself hesitating and dissembling, and he interrupted me. "If you're trying to tell me that you don't want to hear any more," he said, a little angrily, "you don't have to apologize. I'm perfectly well aware that I talk too much."

On the following Monday, which was June 29th, I started writing the Profile of Gould. On Tuesday, around noon, Gould telephoned and said he was worried about the facts concerning his family background that he had given me, and wanted to come up and interpret them for me. There were subtleties involved that I might miss, he said, since he was a New Englander and I was not. He came and stayed until deep in the afternoon, but he didn't interpret any facts; he simply talked some more about himself. On Wednesday, bright and early, he telephoned and said he had spent most of the previous night going over our talks in his mind, and had been shocked to discover that he had forgotten to tell me a great many very important things. He said he wanted to come up and give me this additional information. I told him that I was sinking and suffocating and drowning in information, and begged him not to tell me anything else until I had finished writing the first draft of the Profile and he had read it. He could point out the gaps in it then, I said. On Thursday, in the middle of the morning, the receptionist came in and said that he was outside and wanted to see me. "He says it's very important," she said. I asked her to tell him that I had gone to a funeral. He sat in the reception room for an hour or so, and then left a note for me with the receptionist and went away. "It is my recollection that I told you the title of the Greenwich Village part of the Oral History was 'An Infinitude of Bushwa,' " he wrote in the note. "After much thought, I have decided to change this title, and I felt that I should inform you of this decision at once. The new title is 'The Bughouse Without Bars, or Descents by Day and Descents by Night Into the Intellectual Underworld of Our Time.' If you have occasion to refer to this part of the O.H., please keep this in mind." On Friday, he telephoned, and I lied to him. I told him that I was going on vacation and would be away for two weeks. During these two weeks, I came to my office early and left late, I had no interruptions, and I finished writing the Profile. Then I did go on vacation.

Soon after I returned, early in August, Gould telephoned. By that time, the Profile had been put in proof, and I asked him to come up and read it. He read it slowly and carefully, and said he was pleased with it. "Is there anything in it you want me to change?" I asked. "Not a word," he said. Next day, he came in and said he thought that a paragraph having to do with his knowledge of sea gulls should be made much longer. "People are going to want to know a lot more about that matter." he said. Two days later, he came in with a similar suggestion about another paragraph. Three days after that, he came in with a similar sugestion about still another paragraph. He got in the habit of coming in at least once a week and trying to talk me into adding a few sentences here or a paragraph there. He never tried to get me to change anything; he just wanted me to put more in. On the majority of the days that he didn't come in, he telephoned me. The sound of his voice began to make me wince.


THE PROFILE OF GOULD was printed in the issue of *The New Yorker* for December 12, 1942, under the title of "Professor Sea Gull." The day before this issue went on the newsstands, I had to go down South, because of the sickness of a relative. I ran into some bad luck down there—I was thrown from a horse jumping a ditch and dislocated a shoulder, and while I was laid up from that I had pneumonia—and it was over three weeks before I returned to New York City; it was after the first of the year, in fact. When I got back to my office, there was a pile of letters on my desk from readers of the Profile. There were forty-five addressed to me, and seventeen addressed to Gould in care of me. Among the letters addressed to me was one from Gould himself.

"I have always had a feeling of being way ahead of my time," Gould wrote. "Consequently, I have always taken it for granted that the importance of the Oral History would not be recognized until sometime in the distant future, long after I am dead and gone, but now, thanks to your little piece, I am beginning to see signs that it may happen in my own lifetime. Strangers passing me on the street used to look at me with reactions ranging from bafflement to outright hostility, but now a steadily increasing number of them seem to know who I am and look at me with respect, and every now and then one of them stops me and ask questions about the Oral History. Serious and sensible questions. And people who really know me and have known me from old are beginning to look at me in a different light. I'm not just that nut Joe Gould but that nut Joe Gould who may wind up being considered one of the great historians of all time. As great as Froissart. As great as John Aubrey. As great as Gibbon. I have even noticed a change in the Village radicals. One of them who has been cutting me dead for a long time spoke to me the other day. He was patronizing, but he spoke. 'I know that you don't intend any such thing,' he said, 'but the Oral History may very well turn out to be a sort of X-ray of the soul of the bourgeoisie.' 'What makes you think you know what I don't intend?' I asked him. It may also interest you to learn that the countermen and waitresses in the Jefferson Diner have begun to kid around with me again. When I go in there now, they call me the Professor or the Sea Gull or Professor Sea Gull or the Mongoose or Professor Mongoose or the Bellevue Boy, just as they used to, and I don't know why, but that pleases me. Sometimes, when they are kidding around, ignorant people like that have a kind of inspired audacity that is very cheerful and infectious. It lifts one's spirits. Book ignorant, that is. On some matters, I wish I knew one-tenth as much as they know. I still make the rounds of the places on Sixth Avenue, but I have a new hangout—the Minetta Tavern, at the corner of Macdougal Street and Minetta Lane, in the Italian part of the Village. The Minetta is an old-fashioned neighborhood bar-and-restaurant that attracts a few tourists now and then. The proprietor wants to encourage this, and he and I have reached what you might call an unspoken agreement. I sit at a table in there from late in the afternoon until around nine, ten, or eleven at night and work on the Oral History and give some Village atmosphere to the place. I am the resident bohemian, the house bohemian. In return, he sees to it that I get the table-d'hôte dinner free of charge so long as I order spaghetti and meat balls or something like that for the main course, and if I have to I can get by on one meal a day. Also, there are always people around who will buy me a beer or a glass of wine or if my need is great a Martini. Also, while talking to tourists and explaining the Oral History to them, I manage to pick up quite a few contributions to the Joe Gould Fund. . . ."

That night after work, I put the letters to Gould in my pocket and went down to the Minetta Tavern. Gould was sitting at the most conspicuous table in the place—it was up front and across from the bar and visible from the front window, on Minetta Lane—and he was busily writing in a composition book. I gave him the letters, and he looked at them with suspicion. Then, after reading a few, he got into a state of excitement and began ripping them open and glancing through them and murmuring appreciatively to himself. All the letters were complimentary in one way or another. One was from a woman in Norwood who had been in his class in high school. It was written in pencil on ruled paper, it was six or seven pages long, it contained news about a number of people Gould said he had not heard of since he'd left home, and it was very friendly. Gould's face shone as he read it. "Your old home is still one of the nicest-looking places in Norwood," the woman wrote. "People my age and older call it the old Dr. Gould house. It is now a rooming house for teachers and nurses and widows and women in general of the better class living alone. Do you recall Mrs. Annie Faulkner? She owns it and runs it. Her capacity is eighteen women. Inside it looks pretty much the same as when you lived there. Some of the furnishings are the same, such as that big tall mirror in the front hall with the gold cupids on it. If I remember right, you had some relatives living in Boston and other places in Massachusetts who were very well fixed, and sooner or later maybe one of them will leave you a little something and if this ever happens (and you know as well as I do such things do happen in widely related old families like yours full of old maiden aunts and cousins who might just as well leave it to you as to their dearly beloved old cats or dogs or the Christian Science Church the way they're always doing it) why don't you come on back up here and buy back the old house and live part of the year anyway in Norwood? I was very proud to read about the history book you are writing, and I heard others say the same, and someday I predict there will be a statue of you in Norwood. . . ." Several of the letter writers had enclosed dollar bills. "Buy yourself a drink on me," they wrote, or something to that effect. One, a Harvard classmate, had enclosed a five-dollar bill. Another, a retired Navy officer, had enclosed a check for twenty-five dollars. The retired Navy officer wrote that he spent a huge part of his time sitting on the pier of a crab-picking plant near his home, in Annapolis, Maryland, watching sea gulls and listening to them. "I love sea gulls very much the way you do," he wrote, "and I sometimes feel that I, too, can understand their language."

I told Gould that I hoped he would write these people and thank them.

"Write them!" he said. "I'm going to get busy tonight and try my best to start a correspondence with each and every one of them. Maybe I can persuade some of them to become regular contributors to the Joe Gould Fund."

Gould went over to the bar to show one of the letters to a man he knew who was standing there. The composition book in which he had been writing was lying open on the table, and I looked at it. On the first page, in big, careful capital letters, was "DEATH OF DR. CLARKE STORER GOULD. A CHAPTER OF JOE GOULD'S ORAL HISTORY." I reflected that this was the fourth version of this chapter I had seen. When he returned, I said, "I see you're still working on the chapter about your father's death." This made him irritable. "Is there anything wrong in that?" he asked. "The other night, I got into a discussion about this very thing with Maxwell Bodenheim and some other old bohemians in Goody's. Max knows from perpetually looking over my shoulder that I've been working on my father's death for years. He knows I keep putting it aside and returning to it. And he was making fun of me for spending so much time on it. 'Don't tell me you're still trying to bury your father,' he said to me. Max himself has written a whole shelf of books—a whole shelf of novels, that is; a whole shelf of no-good novels; a whole shelf of *long* no-good novels—and he thinks that gives him the right to tell everybody else how to do. I told him that all I'm trying to do is write an account of the matter that will be a little masterpiece and last forever. That's all. 'Quality,' I told him, 'not quantity.' I told him that that little five-line poem I once wrote on the death of the *Dial* was worth more than all his claptrap novels put together. 'One five-line poem that's perfect of its kind,' I said, 'is worth more than any number of huge, formless, shapeless books.' "

The thought crossed my mind that this was an odd way for the author of a book as huge and formless and shapeless as the Oral History to be talking.

I had taken the letters to Gould on a Monday night. On the following Wednesday morning, another letter arrived for him. I forwarded it to him at the Minetta Tavern. On Friday morning, four more letters arrived for him, and I decided to go by the Minetta that night on my way home and give them to him. Instead of which, shortly after lunch the receptionist stuck her head in my office and said that Gould was outside in the reception room and wanted to know if there was any mail for him. My heart sank. Oh, God, I remember thinking, I'm in for it now. He'll come in looking for letters practically every day from now on. And every time he comes in, he'll talk and talk and talk. And he'll keep on doing it, year in and year out, until I die or he dies. "Please send him in," I said. He came into my office, and I gave him the letters, and he looked each one over, front and back. "I wrote to all those people who wrote to me, just as I said I would," he said, "and these are the first replies."

"If you're going to keep on writing to them," I said, "wouldn't it be better to use the Minetta Tavern as your mail address?"

"If you don't mind," he said, his voice suddenly becoming indignant, "I'll continue to use *The New Yorker* as my address. The people at the Minetta are nice to me now, but they might get tired of me at any time and freeze me out, and if they did, I wouldn't like to have to go back there inquiring about my mail." Then he said something that brought me up short. "Look," he said. "You're

the one who started all this. I didn't seek you out. You sought me
out. You wanted to write a story about me, and you did, and you'll
have to take the consequences."

"Please forgive me," I said. "You're right."

The next moment, Gould became conciliatory. "In other words,"
he said, giggling, "if you lie down with dogs, you have to expect
to get up with fleas."

After that, just as I had feared, Gould started coming in frequently.
He would come in two or three times a week, usually in the
afternoon. When he was cold sober, Gould was shy—shy but desperate. He was a little like one of those men who are too shy to
talk to strangers but not too shy to hold up a bank. If he was in
this state when he came in, he would walk right past the receptionist
and burst into my office without knocking and pick up his mail, if
he had any, and collect a contribution to the Joe Gould Fund and
snatch that morning's *Herald Tribune* out of my wastebasket and be
out and gone in a matter of minutes. If he had been drinking when
he came in, he would sit down and talk, and I would have to drop
everything and listen to him. I didn't really mind this so much—
in this state, he was apt to be full of whatever gossip was floating
around at the moment in the barrooms and dumps of the Village,
and I had developed a morbid interest in such gossip. Also, I could
generally count on getting him out in half an hour or so. If he
happened to be suffering from a hangover when he came in, however,
my afternoon was shot. In this state, he was driven to talk, he was
determined to talk, he would not be denied, and I would be lucky
if I got him out in an hour and a half or two hours, or even three.
He would sit on the edge of an old swivel chair in a corner of my
office, his portfolio on his lap, his clothes smelling of the fumigants
and disinfectants used in flophouses, rheumy-eyed, twitching,
scratching, close to hysteria, and he would talk on and on and on.
His subject was always the same—himself. And I would sit and
listen to him and try my best to show some interest in what he
was saying, and gradually my eyes would glaze over and my blood
would turn to water and a kind of paralysis would set in. I was
young then, and much more courteous to older people—and to

everyone else, for that matter, as I look back on it—than I should have been. Also, I had not yet found out about time; I was still under the illusion that I had plenty of time—time for this, time for that, time for everything, time to waste.

I kept hoping that Gould would talk himself out, but the months went by and he showed no sign of doing so. He continued to come in as often as ever. One afternoon in August, during one of his visits, I suddenly realized, to my dismay, that as time passed, talking to me was becoming more and more important to him, instead of less and less. After a little reflection, I thought I saw why this was so. It didn't have much to do with me as a person. In fact, I don't think that Gould particularly liked me. He once said that he couldn't stand Southerners and that I was no exception, and although he was drunk when he said it, and apologized later, he probably meant it at least as much as he didn't mean it. It was simply that by listening to him for long sessions while I was working on the Profile and by continuing to listen to him whenever he came in and insisted on talking, I had probably come to know more about his past than anybody else in the city and perhaps than anybody else in the world, and had become a kind of stand-in relative of his, or fellow ex-Norwoodian. Despite the difference in our ages, when he talked to me he might have been talking to someone who had known him all his life. When he spoke of his Uncle Oscar, for example, he knew that I knew he was referring to his mother's brother, Oscar Vroom, whom his mother virtually worshipped, and he knew that I knew what his father thought of Oscar Vroom and what Oscar Vroom thought of his father. When he mentioned various people he had known while he was growing up in Norwood, such as Mrs. Betty Allsopp, he knew that I knew the parts they had played in his life. (He believed that Mrs. Allsopp was responsible for the fact that he had had a great deal of dental trouble and had had to start wearing false teeth before he was thirty. Mrs. Allsopp was a family friend and lived across the street. She was a widow, she was his mother's age, and she was small and delicate and pretty. One hot summer day when he was around fourteen, she invited him into her kitchen for a glass of lemonade and he tried to pull up her dress and she slapped him so hard, according to him, that she deadened the nerves of eight of his teeth—four upper and four lower—and ruined his bite.) When he mentioned the Bigelow Block and the Folan Block and the Sanborn Block, he knew that I knew he was referring to store-and-office buildings that were landmarks in Norwood, and he knew that I was aware of some of the emotional connotations that their names had for him. When he spoke of Ed Goodbird or of Water Chief or of Ash-kob-dip, he knew that I knew he was referring to old Indians he had known in North Dakota, and he knew that I knew how much he admired each of them, and why. In his years in the Village, he had pursued a succession of women bohemians, most of whom had been would-be poets or would-be painters, and many of whom had been alcoholics or extreme eccentrics, or both, and several of whom had wound up in state mental hospitals, and when their names came into his talk he knew that I knew which ones had been responsive to him and which ones had been unresponsive and which ones not only had been unresponsive but had complained about him to the police. He had given behind-their-back nicknames to many people in the Village, and when he referred to the Spitter or to the Nickel Snatcher or to Old Aunt Cousin Little Sister Susy Belle Susy Sue, he knew that I knew whom he meant. By knowing so much about his past, I had, in effect, I realized, become a part of his past. By talking to me, he could bring back his past, he could keep it alive. I realized also that there was no getting away from the fact that the more he talked to me the more I would know about his past, and the more I knew about his past the more important talking to me would become to him. This scared me, and I set out deliberately to get him off my back and, if necessary, onto somebody else's back as soon as possible.

The best way to do this, I decided, was to get an editor or a publisher interested in the Oral History. Gould had once told me that he had lugged armfuls of the Oral History into and out of fourteen publishing offices and had then given up trying to find a publisher for it. "Half of them said it was obscene and outrageous and to get it out of there as quick as I could," he said, "and the others said they couldn't read my handwriting." I had an idea that

Maxwell Perkins, the editor at Scribner's who had worked with
Thomas Wolfe, might possibly take an interest in Gould, and I called
him first. His secretary said he was out of town. I told her a little
about Gould and asked her if she thought Mr. Perkins would see
him and have a talk with him. "No," she said. "I don't." "Why?"
I asked. "Mr. Gould has already been here," she said. "He came in
out of the blue one day not long ago and insisted on seeing Mr.
Perkins. I saw him instead, and he gave me two perfectly filthy
copybooks to give to Mr. Perkins, each containing a manuscript
chapter of his history. He seemed to think he might be able to get
a large advance from Mr. Perkins on the strength of them. I spent
most of the next day deciphering his handwriting and making copies
of the chapters for Mr. Perkins to read. One chapter was about the
death of his father, although it wandered all over the Western
Hemisphere, and the other was something about Indians. Mr. Perkins
read them and was not impressed. Some days later, Mr. Gould
returned, and Mr. Perkins saw him and told him he was sorry but
he couldn't give him an advance, whereupon Mr. Gould became
quite difficult. I don't think Mr. Perkins would be at all eager to
see him again."

A friend of mine named John Woodburn was an editor at Harcourt, Brace, and I called him next. Woodburn said that it had
occurred to him several times that a representative selection of
chapters from the Oral History might make a book, and that he
would like very much to have a talk with Gould, but that he was
too busy. He was working day and night going over a manuscript
with a novelist who was leaving for Europe, he said, and he himself
was supposed to leave on a business trip in a few days. Then,
impulsively, he said that he would see Gould. "Ask him to come
in at noon tomorrow," he said. "I have a luncheon date that I've
been looking forward to, but I'll break it and have a sandwich sent
in, and we can talk for at least half an hour. I have a number of
questions I'd like to ask him about the Oral History, and you never
can tell—maybe something will come of it." I telephoned Gould
at the Minetta that night and told him about the appointment. He
wanted to know if I knew anything about Harcourt, Brace's policy

in regard to giving advances to authors against royalties and if so
how much of an advance should he ask for, and he also wanted to
know if I had ever seen a Harcourt, Brace contract and if so did it
stipulate that the total amount of the advance would be paid upon
the signing of the contract between author and publisher or did it
stipulate that a certain percentage would be paid upon the signing
of the contract and the rest upon the delivery of the manuscript.
I begged him not to talk to Woodburn about such things—it was
entirely too early for that—but to spend the time describing the
Oral History and answering Woodburn's questions. The next afternoon, Woodburn telephoned me. He was in a rage. Gould hadn't
shown up. That night, I went down to the Minetta and saw Gould
and asked him what had happened. He said he had gone into a
bookstore and picked out some Harcourt, Brace books and looked
them over and had come to the conclusion that Harcourt, Brace
would not be the appropriate publishers for the Oral History and
had decided not to keep the appointment. By the way he said
"appropriate," he strongly implied that he did not think Harcourt,
Brace was good enough to publish the Oral History. "Oh, for God's
sake, Mr. Gould," I said. "Harcourt, Brace is one of the best publishing houses in the country, and you know it is."

I had another friend in the publishing business—Charles A.
Pearce, of Duell, Sloan & Pearce—and a few days later I called him
and discussed the matter with him. It turned out that he, also, had
thought of the possibility of putting out a book of selections from
the Oral History. "I'd like to have a talk with Gould and explore
the idea," Pearce said, "but I don't want to make an appointment
with him. If he broke an appointment with Woodburn, he'd most
likely do the same with me. Also, I'd prefer to have a casual talk
with him, so he won't start right away thinking about advances and
royalty percentages and movie rights and North American serial
rights and world-wide translation rights, and all that. Who does he
think he is, anyway—Mary Roberts Rinehart? Suppose we do it
this way. My office is only a few minutes from yours. The next
time he comes in and sits down and it looks as if he's going to stay
a while, why don't you call me, and I'll take a cab right up. I'll

make it appear that I just happened to drop in." At that time, Pearce's firm was at 270 Madison Avenue, which is on the northwest corner of Madison Avenue and Thirty-ninth Street, and the distance from his office to mine was only four blocks up and one and a half over. On Friday afternoon, September 3, 1943, around three o'clock, Gould showed up in my office. He said that he had lost his fountain pen and that he wanted me to make a contribution to the Joe Gould Fund so he could buy a new one. He also needed some composition books, he said. Then he sat down in the swivel chair and began talking. He had a hangover, but it didn't seem to be a particularly bad one; that is, he was unduly talkative but he wasn't unduly incoherent. I excused myself and went into the next office and telephoned Pearce. Twenty minutes later, Pearce put his head in my door and said he had happened to be in the neighborhood and thought he'd drop in and say hello. "Please come in," I said, and I introduced him to Gould.

Pearce and Gould talked for a few minutes about a Village poet they both knew, and then Pearce said that he had been hearing about the Oral History for years and would like to read some of it.

" 'Some of it'!" said Gould. "Everybody wants to read 'some of it.' Nobody wants to just read it. From now on, I'm not going to let anybody read some of it. They'll read all of it or none of it."

"Well," Pearce said, "I'll do that. It may take me a long time, but if you'll bring it to my office or tell me where to go and get it, I'll make a start today or tomorrow."

"It's entirely too bulky," Gould said.

"Bring it in a little at a time," said Pearce. "When I finish reading one batch, I'll drop you a line and you can bring in another. I've often worked that way with authors of long books."

"It's stored in a place out on Long Island that's hard to get to," Gould said.

"We could hire a car over at Carey's limousine service, at Grand Central," Pearce said, "and drive out and get it. If you aren't too busy, we could drive out right now."

"I don't want to bring it back into New York City," Gould said. "I don't think it would be safe here. I don't think anything is safe here. I expect the whole place to go up in smoke any day now."

"We have some fireproof cabinets in the office that we keep manuscripts in," Pearce said, "and you could store it in one of them. We also have a big fireproof safe that we keep contracts in, and other important papers, and you could store it in there."

"What's the use?" said Gould. "After you got it, you probably couldn't read my handwriting."

"That's no problem," said Pearce. "We have a secretary in our office who's a wizard at reading hard-to-read handwriting. She prides herself on it. You could come in for a day or two and sit down beside her and help her until she got the hang of your handwriting, and then she could type up some chapters from various sections, and then, eventually, maybe we could publish a book of selections from the Oral History."

"No, indeed!" said Gould. "Absolutely not! It has to be published in its entirety. All or nothing."

"Well, now," said Pearce, "unless you let me read it—and you really don't seem to want me to—how can I tell if it's feasible to publish it in its entirety?"

Gould took a deep breath. "I've always been resolved in the back of my mind that the Oral History would be published posthumously," he said, "and I'm going to stick to that." He hesitated a moment. "There are revelations in it," he continued, "that I don't want the world to know until after I'm dead."

This stopped Pearce. He and Gould talked for a few minutes about things unrelated to the Oral History, and then he said he had to be running along.

"If you ever change your mind," he said to Gould, "please give me a ring."

Gould gazed at him morosely and said nothing.

I was exasperated. As soon as Pearce was out of the room, I turned on Gould. "You told me you lugged armfuls of the Oral History into and out of fourteen publishing offices," I said. "Why in hell did you do that and go to all that trouble if you've always been resolved in the back of your mind that it would be published posthumously? I'm beginning to believe," I went on, "that the Oral History doesn't exist." This remark came from my unconscious, and I was barely aware of the meaning of what I was saying—I was simply getting rid of my anger—but the next moment, glancing at Gould's face, I knew as well as I knew anything that I had blundered upon the truth about the Oral History.

"My God!" I said. "It doesn't exist." I was appalled. "There isn't any such thing as the Oral History," I said. "It doesn't exist."

I stared at Gould, and Gould stared at me. His face was expressionless.

"The woman who owns the duck-and-chicken farm doesn't exist," I said. "And her brother who had the stroke doesn't exist. And her niece doesn't exist. And the Polish farmer and his wife who look after the ducks and chickens don't exist. And the ducks and chickens don't exist. And the cellar that the Oral History is stored in doesn't exist. And the Oral History doesn't exist."

Gould got up and went over to the window and stood there looking out, with his back to me.

"It exists in your mind, I guess," I said, recovering a little from my surprise, "but you've always been too lazy to write it down. All that really exists is those so-called essay chapters. That's all you've been doing all through the years—writing new versions of those chapters about the death of your father and the death of your mother and the dread tomato habit and the Indians out in North Dakota and maybe a dozen others or a couple of dozen others, and correcting them and revising them and tearing them up and starting all over again."

Gould turned and faced me and said something, but his voice was low and indistinct. If I heard him right—and I have often wondered if I did hear him right—he said, "It's not a question of laziness." Then, evidently deciding not to say any more, he turned his back on me again.

At that moment, one of the editors knocked on the door and came in with proofs of a story of mine. He said that some last-minute changes were having to be made in a story that had been scheduled to run in the next issue, and that because there might not be time enough to complete them, my story had been tentatively scheduled to run in its place, and that he would like to go over the proofs with me.

"Does it have done to be done right now?" I asked.

"Well, as you might gather," he said, rather sharply, "we're kind of in a hurry."

I saw that I couldn't very well put this off, and I asked Gould if he would mind waiting in the reception room until I got through. He picked up his portfolio and went over and stood at the door. "No," he said, "I don't think I'll wait. I think I'll go on back downtown. The only reason I came up here today was to ask you for a contribution." I said that I would give him the contribution but that I wanted to ask him some questions about the Oral History first and that I hoped he would wait. He mumbled something and started down the hall toward the reception room.

The proofs took around half an hour. The second I got through with them, I went out to the reception room. Gould wasn't there. The receptionist said he had sat there for five minutes or so and had then left without saying a word. Well, anyway, I thought, I've got him off my back. God knows this wasn't the way I intended to do it, but I've probably got him off my back for good.

I returned to my office and sat down and propped my elbows on my desk and put my head in my hands. I have always deeply disliked seeing anyone shown up or found out or caught in a lie or caught red-handed doing anything, and now, with time to think things over, I began to feel ashamed of myself for the way I had lost my temper and pounced on Gould. My anger began to die down, and I began to feel depressed. I had been duped by Gould— I didn't think there was much doubt about that—and so had countless others through the years. He had led me up the garden path, just as he had led countless others up the garden path. However, I had thought about the matter only a short while before I came to the conclusion that he hadn't been talking about the Oral History all those years and making large statements about its length and its bulk and its importance to posterity and comparing it to such works as "The History of the Decline and Fall of the Roman Empire" only in order to dupe people like me but also in order to dupe himself. He must have found out long ago that he didn't have the genius or the talent, or maybe the self-confidence or the industry or the determination, to bring off a work as huge and grand as he had envisioned, and fallen back on writing those so-called essay chapters. Writing them and rewriting them. And, either because he was too lazy or because he was too much of a perfectionist, he hadn't been able to finish even them. Still, a large part of the time he very likely went around believing in some hazy, self-deceiving, self-protecting way that the Oral History did exist—oral chapters as well as essay chapters. The oral part of it might not exactly be down on paper, but he had it all in his head, and any day now he was going to start getting it down.

It was easy for me to see how this could be, for it reminded me of a novel that I had once intended to write. I was twenty-four years old at the time and had just come under the spell of Joyce's "Ulysses." My novel was to be "about" New York City. It was also to be about a day and a night in the life of a young reporter in New York City. He is a Southerner, and a good deal of the time he is homesick for the South. He thinks of himself as an exile from the South. He had once been a believer, a believing Baptist, and is now an unbeliever. Nevertheless, he is still inclined to see things in religious terms, and he often sees the city as a kind of Hell, a Gehenna. He is in love with a Scandinavian girl he has met in the city, and she is so different from the girls he had known in the South that she seems mysterious to him, just as the city seems mysterious; the girl and the city are all mixed up in his mind. It is his day off. He has breakfast in a restaurant in Fulton Fish Market, and then starts poking around the parts of the city that he knows best, gradually going uptown. As he wanders, he encounters and reencounters men and women who seem to him to represent various aspects of the city. He goes up Fulton Street and walks among the gravestones in St. Paul's churchyard, and then goes to certain streets on the lower East Side, and then to certain streets in the Village, and then to the theatrical district, and then to Harlem. Late at night, on Lenox Avenue, he joins a little group of men and women, some white and some Negro, who have just come out of a night club and are standing in a circle around an old Negro street preacher. He had seen the old man earlier, preaching at a street corner in the theatrical district, but had not listened to him. Now he listens. The old man is worldly wise and uses up-to-date New York City slang and catch phrases, but he also uses a good many old-fashioned Southern expressions, the kind that are mostly used by country people, and the young reporter realizes that the old man is also a Southerner, and, like himself, a country Southerner. His sermon is apocalyptic. There are fearful warnings and prophecies in it, and there are phrases snatched from bloody old Baptist hymns, and there are many references to Biblical beasts and fruits and flowers—to the wild goats of the rocks and to the pomegranates in the Song of Solomon and to the lilies of the field that toil not, neither do they spin. The old serpent is in it, and the Great Whore of Babylon, and the burning bush. Like the Baptist preachers the young reporter had listened to and struggled to understand in his childhood, the old man sees meanings behind meanings, or thinks he does, and tries his best to tell what things "stand for." "Pomegranates are about the size and shape of large oranges or small grapefruits, only their skins are red," he says, cupping his hands in the air and speaking with such exactitude that it is obvious he had had first-hand knowledge of pomegranates long ago in the South. "They're filled with fat little seeds, and those fat little seeds are filled with juice as red as blood. When they get ripe, they're so swollen with those juicy red seeds that they gap open and some of the seeds spill out. And now I'll tell you what pomegranates stand for. They stand for the resurrection. The resurrection of our Lord and Saviour Jesus Christ and your resurrection and my resurrection. Resurrection in particular and resurrection in general. All seeds stand for resurrection and all eggs stand for resurrection. The Easter egg stands for resurrection. So do the eggs in the English sparrow's nest up under the eaves in the 'L' station. So does the egg you have for breakfast. So does the caviar the rich people eat. So does shad roe." The young reporter intends to stay for only a few minutes, but he is held fast by the old man's rhetoric. Even though he feels that he has heard it all before a hundred times, he is enthralled by it. The old man reminds him of the Fundamentalist evangelists who were powerful in the South while he was growing up and who went from town to town holding revival meetings in big tents. He had hated and feared these evangelists—their reputations were based on the hideousness of their descriptions of Hell; the more hideous the description and the wilder the sermon, the better the evangelist was considered to be—but nevertheless they had left him with a lasting liking for the cryptic and the ambiguous and the incantatory and the disconnected and the extravagant and the oracular and the apocalyptic. He finds himself drawing oblique conclusions from the old man's statements in order to make them have some bearing on his own spiritual state. "All you have to do," the old man says, "is open your eyes and see the light, the blessed gospel light, and you can enter into a new time. You can enter into it and live in it and dwell in it and reside in it and have your being in it. You can live in the three times in one time. At one and the same time, believing in Him, you can live in the time gone by, you can live in the time to come, and you can live in the now, the here and now." As the young reporter listens, it dawns on him that it is not the South that he longs for but the past, the South's past and his own past, neither of which, in the way that he has been driven by homesickness to think of them, ever really existed, and that it is time for him to move out of the time gone by and into the here and now—it is time for him to grow up. When the sermon is over, he goes back downtown feeling that the old man has set him free, and that he is now a citizen of the city and a citizen of the world.

I had thought about this novel for over a year. Whenever I had nothing else to do, I would automatically start writing it in my mind. Sometimes, in the course of a subway ride, I would write three or four chapters. Almost every day, I would discard a few characters and invent a few new ones. But the truth is, I never actually wrote a word of it. Time passed, and I got caught up in other matters. Even so, for several years I frequently daydreamed about it, and in those daydreams I had finished writing it and it had been published and I could see it. I could see its title page. I could see its binding, which was green with gold lettering. Those recollections filled me with almost unbearable embarrassment, and I began to feel more and more sympathetic to Gould.

Suppose he *had* written the Oral History, I reflected; it probably wouldn't have been the great book he had gone up and down the highways and byways prophesying it would be at all—great books, even halfway great books, even good books, even halfway good books, being so exceedingly rare. It probably would have been, at best, only a curiosity. A few years after it came out, copies of it would have choked the "Curiosa" shelves in every second-hand bookstore in the country. Anyway, I decided, if there was anything the human race had a sufficiency of, a sufficiency and a surfeit, it was books. When I thought of the cataracts of books, the Niagaras of books, the rushing rivers of books, the oceans of books, the tons and truckloads and trainloads of books that were pouring off the presses of the world at that moment, only a very few of which would be worth picking up and looking at, let alone reading, I began to feel that it was admirable that he *hadn't* written it. One less book to clutter up the world, one less book to take up space and catch dust and go unread from bookstores to homes to second-hand bookstores and junk stores and thrift shops to still other homes to still other second-hand bookstores and junk stores and thrift shops to still other homes ad infinitum.

I suddenly felt a surge of genuine respect for Gould. He had declined to stay in Norwood and live out his life as Pee Wee Gould, the town fool. If he had to play the fool, he would do it on a larger stage, before a friendlier audience. He had come to Greenwich Village and had found a mask for himself, and he had put it on and kept it on. The Eccentric Author of a Great, Mysterious, Unpublished Book—that was his mask. And, hiding behind it, he had created a character a good deal more complicated, it seemed to me, than most of the characters created by the novelists and playwrights of his time. I thought of the variety of ways he had seen himself through the years and of the variety of ways others had seen him.

There was the way the principal of the school in Norwood had seen him—a disgusting little bastard. There was the way Ezra Pound had seen him—a native hickory. There was the way the know-it-all Village radical had seen him—a reactionary parasite. There were a great many of these aspects, and I began to go over them in my mind. He was the catarrhal child, he was the son who knows that he has disappointed his father, he was the runt, the shrimp, the peanut, the half-pint, the tadpole, he was Joe Gould the poet, he was Joe Gould the historian, he was Joe Gould the wild Chippewa Indian dancer, he was Joe Gould the greatest authority in the world on the language of the sea gull, he was the banished man, he was the perfect example of the solitary nocturnal wanderer, he was the little rat, he was the one and only member of the Joe Gould Party, he was the house bohemian of the Minetta Tavern, he was the Professor, he was the Sea Gull, he was Professor Sea Gull, he was the Mongoose, he was Professor Mongoose, he was the Bellevue Boy.

I was still adding to the list when the receptionist cracked my door open and put her head in. "Mr. Gould has just come back," she said. "He was down at the lunch counter in the lobby all this time, having coffee."

"Bring him right in," I said. Then, for some reason—perhaps because of my new-found respect for Gould—I changed my mind. "No, don't," I said. "I'll go out myself and bring him in."

I stood up, and as I did so, a thought entered my mind that caused me to sit back down. If I asked Gould the questions I had planned to ask him, I suddenly realized, and if he came right out and admitted that the Oral History did not exist—that it was indeed a mare's-nest—I might be put in the position of having to do something about it. I might very well be forced to unmask him. I found this thought painful. The Oral History was his life preserver, his only way of keeping afloat, and I didn't want to see him drown. I didn't want to blow the whistle on him. I didn't want to tear up his meal ticket, so to speak, or break his rice bowl. I didn't want to have to take any kind of stand on the matter at all. He wasn't harming anybody. He lived off his friends, it was true, but only off crumbs from their tables. Given a long life, he might yet write the Oral History. It would be better for me to leave things the way they were—up in the air. This was probably cowardly, but if it was, so it was. I was thankful now that when I pounced on him he hadn't admitted anything—he hadn't said yea, he hadn't said nay, he had said merely that it wasn't a question of laziness. And there was no law that said I had to ask him questions and try to trip him up and pin him down and worm the pure truth out of him. Suppose he chose to deny everything, and suppose he turned on me and denounced me, leaving it up to me to make the next move. I might be pretty close to certain of this, that, and the other, but I might have a hell of a time proving it. While I was trying to make up my mind what to do, Gould walked in, not bothering to knock.

"Are you going to give me the contribution?" he asked.

"Yes, I am," I said.

I gave him the money he wanted. He didn't thank me but said what he usually said when someone gave him a contribution to the Joe Gould Fund—"This will come in handy." Then he went over and sat in the swivel chair and put his portfolio on the floor at his feet. "You said you had some questions you wanted to ask me," he said.

"I did have," I said, "but I don't now. There were some things I thought I wanted to know, but I guess I really don't. Let's just forget it."

A look of relief appeared on Gould's face. Then, to my surprise, seeming to sense that I didn't intend to go one bit further into the matter, he looked disappointed. I could see from his expression that he wanted very much to confide in me—it was that half-noble, half-fatuous expression that people put on when they have decided to bare their souls—and once again my attitude toward him changed. I became disgusted with him. I was doing my best to keep from unmasking him, and here he was doing his best to unmask himself. "Oh, for God's sake," I felt like saying to him. "Don't lose your nerve now and start confessing and confiding. If you've pretended this long, the only decent thing you can do is to keep right on pretending as long as you live, no matter what happens." Instead, I said, "Please forgive me, but you really must excuse me now. It's getting late and I have some things I have to do."

This gave him the right to be huffy. "Oh," he said, "I'm ready to go. I've been ready to go for what seems like hours, but you held me up. After all, I've got things to do myself."

He picked up his portfolio and walked out without saying good-bye.

FOR QUITE A WHILE AFTER THAT, Gould distrusted me. He continued to come to see me, but nowhere near as often and never just to talk. He came only when he wanted a contribution to the Joe Gould Fund, and only, I suspect, when he was stony broke and couldn't run down any of his old reliables. He walked in and asked for what he wanted in as few words as possible and got it or some part of it and then stood around awkwardly for a few minutes and then hurried off. Although he continued to use *The New Yorker* as his mail address, he stopped asking for his letters the moment he came in, and, to preserve his dignity, waited for me to give them to him. Hoping to make things easier for him, I began forwarding letters to him at the Minetta. However, as an excuse to see how he was getting along, I would occasionally let a few accumulate and then go by the Minetta and give them to him. The first few times I did this, I behaved as if nothing had happened, and sat down at his table as I always had, no matter whether he was alone or others were there, but I soon found that if others were there my presence made him ill at ease. If someone asked him something about the Oral History, or even brought it into the conversation, he would glance at me uneasily and try to change the subject. I think he was afraid that at any moment I might stand up and announce that there was no such thing as the Oral History, that it was all imagination and lies. I made him self-conscious; I got in his way; I cramped his style. From then on, I never sat down with him unless he was alone. If others sat down, I would look at my watch, and pretend to be surprised at how late it was, and leave. Then, one evening, Gould suddenly became his old self again. I was sitting at his table when a couple of tourists, a man and his wife, came over from the bar and asked him a question about the Oral History. Without glancing at me and without any hesitation, he started describing the Oral History for them, and in no time at all was comparing himself to Gibbon—speaking of what he called "the fortunate immediacy" of his position in relation to New York City as contrasted with what he called "the unfortunate remoteness" of Gibbon's position in relation to the Roman Empire. I was greatly relieved to hear him talking like this, not only because I could see that he had got over his distrust of me but also because I could see that he had got his mask firmly back in place. Furthermore, I couldn't help admiring his spirit. He was like some down-on-his-luck but still buoyant old confidence man. He put his heart into his act. Right before my eyes, he changed from a bummy-looking little red-eyed wreck of a barfly into an illustrious historian. And the most he could hope to get out of the tourists was a few drinks and a dollar or two.

IN THE SPRING OF the next year—the spring of 1944—a chance encounter that Gould had with an old acquaintance set some things in motion that made life easier for him for a while. Around eight o'clock one morning early in May, he left the Hotel Defender, at 300 Bowery, where he had spent the night, and started out on his daily round of soliciting contributions to the Joe Gould Fund. He was hungry, and he was suffering from a hangover, a bad case of conjunctivitis, and a bad cold. He intended to go first to the subway station at Sheridan Square and stand for an hour or so near the uptown entrance and waylay friends and acquaintances hurrying to work. On the way over, trying to pull himself together, he sat down on the steps of a tenement in one of the pushcart blocks on Bleecker Street. He threw his head back and started squirting some eye drops in his eyes, and at that moment a woman named Mrs. Sarah Ostrowsky Berman, who had come down to the pushcarts from her apartment on Union Square to buy some of the small, sweet Italian onions called *cipollini,* caught sight of him and impulsively went over and sat down beside him. Mrs. Berman was the wife of Levi Berman, the Yiddish poet, and she was a painter. She had come here from Russia when she was a girl, and while making a living sewing in sweatshops she had taught herself to paint. Although her paintings were awkward, they were imaginative and they had a hallucinatory quality, and they had been admired and highly praised by a number of people in the art world. She was a gentle, self-effacing woman, and somewhat other-worldly, and she was maternal but childless. She had often run into Gould at parties in the Village in the late twenties and early thirties and had had several long talks with him, but she had not seen him for years, and she was shocked by the changes that had taken place in him. She asked him how he was getting along on the Oral History, and he groaned and shook his head and indicated that he didn't have the strength right then to talk about the Oral History. She asked him about his health, and he pulled up his pants legs and showed her some sores that had recently appeared on his legs. Mrs. Berman got a cab and took him to her apartment. She made some breakfast for him. She washed his feet and legs and put some medicine on his sores. She gave him some clean socks and a pair of her husband's old shoes. She gave him some money. Then, after he had gone, she sat down and made a list of all the people she knew who had known Gould in the period in which she had known him, including some who had moved to other parts of the country or to Europe, and she spent the rest of the day writing impassioned letters to them.

"Joe Gould is in bad shape," she wrote in one of these letters. "He is using up time and energy he should be devoting to the Oral History running around all over town getting together enough dimes and quarters for the bare necessities, and it is killing him. I have always felt that the city's unconscious may be trying to speak to us through Joe Gould. And that the people who have gone underground in the city may be trying to speak to us through him. And that the city's living dead may be trying to speak to us through him. People who never belonged anyplace from the beginning. People sitting in those terrible dark barrooms. Poor old men and women sitting on park benches, hurt and bitter and crazy—the ones who never got their share, the ones who were always left out, the ones who were never asked. Sitting there and dreaming of killing everybody that passes by, even the little children. But there is a great danger that Joe Gould may never finish the Oral History and that those anonymous voices may never speak to us. Something must be done about him at once. If it isn't, some morning soon he and a part of us will be found dead on the Bowery. . . ."

Among the people Mrs. Berman wrote to were two old friends of hers who had once been married to each other and had been divorced—Erika Feist and John Rothschild. Miss Feist was a German-born woman who had come here in the early twenties and had become a painter. Rothschild was a New Englander who had roomed with Malcolm Cowley for a while at Harvard and had got acquainted with Gould at a party in the Village soon after coming to New York City to make a living, and had been contributing to the Joe Gould Fund ever since. He was the director of a travel agency called The Open Road, Inc. One night a week or so later, Mrs. Berman received a long-distance call from Miss Feist, who, after her divorce, had moved from a studio in the Village to a farm in Bucks County, Pennsylvania. Miss Feist said that while she was married to Rothschild she had got to know and respect an old friend of his, a very reserved and very busy professional woman who was a member of a rich Middle Western family and had inherited a fortune and who sometimes anonymously helped needy artists and intellectuals, and that she had spoken to this woman about Gould. Independently of her, she said, Rothschild had also spoken to the woman about Gould. Miss Feist said that the woman had agreed to help Gould to the extent of sixty dollars a month. There were two conditions. First, Gould must never be told who the woman was or anything about her that might enable him to find out who she was. Second, some discreet and responsible person in New York City who knew Gould would have to receive the checks from the woman—they would come once a month—and disburse the money, passing it on to Gould in weekly installments and seeing to it that he spent it on room and board and not on liquor. It would have to be someone Gould respected and would heed. When Mrs. Berman heard this, she said, "Someone like Vivian Marquié," and Miss Feist said, "Yes, exactly." Mrs. Vivian Marquié was an old friend of Gould's and the proprietor of an art gallery on Fifty-seventh Street called the Marquié Gallery. As a young woman, she had been a social worker and had lived in the Village. She had met Gould at a party in 1925 or 1926 and had been helping him ever since. In recent years, she had been providing him with most of his clothes; she knew several men who were close to him in size, and she kept after them, and every now and then they gave her some of their old suits and shirts to give to him. He went to her gallery a couple of times a week for contributions to the Joe Gould Fund.

The following day, Miss Feist telephoned Mrs. Marquié at her gallery and explained the situation. Mrs. Marquié said that she herself had been worried about Gould and that she would be glad to handle the money and make it go as far as possible. Mrs. Marquié's maiden name was Ward, and she was a native of Lawrence, Long Island. Her husband, Elie-Paul Marquié, was a Frenchman. He was an engraver and etcher, and he was also a gourmet and an amateur chef. Through him she had become acquainted with a good many French people in the restaurant business. One of these was a man named Henri Gerard, who operated three rooming houses on West Thirty-third Street, between Eighth and Ninth avenues, just across the street from the General Post Office, that were known collectively as the Maison Gerard. They were old brownstones, and their numbers were 311, 313, and 317. In the basement of No. 311, he ran an unusually inexpensive restaurant that was also known as the Maison Gerard. Mrs. Marquié had a talk with Gerard about Gould. Gerard was used to the problems of people who had to get by on very little; most of his tenants were in that category. He said that for sixty dollars a month he could give Gould room and board and also see to it that he had a little left over for such things as cigarettes and carfare. His room would cost him three dollars a week, and he could get breakfasts for twenty-five cents, lunches for fifty cents, and dinners for fifty cents. Mrs. Marquié agreed to send Gerard a check at the end of each week covering Gould's approximate expenses, and Gerard agreed to deduct what Gould owed from the check, and give him whatever was left over in cash. If he skipped a meal, he wouldn't be charged for it. If he skipped what seemed to be an undue number of meals, Gerard would let Mrs. Marquié know, in case he might be going without them in order to have some money to spend on liquor. Before the week was out, Gould was installed in a room on the fifth floor, which was the attic floor, of No. 313. In the days when the brownstone houses of this kind were private houses, all the rooms on this floor had been maids' rooms, and Gould's room had obviously been the one that was customarily occupied by the newest, greenest maid. It was around behind the banisters at the top of the stairwell, it had a skylight instead of a window, and it was just big enough for a bed, a chair, a table, and a dresser.

At first, Gould wasn't able to get much pleasure out of living at the Maison Gerard or out of anything else connected with his new way of life, for the mystery of the identity of his patron tormented him. It was all he could think about. For a while, he turned up at Mrs. Marquié's gallery at least once a day, and sometimes as often as three or four times a day, and asked her seemingly innocent questions in an effort to trick her into giving him some clue. She begged him to stop it, but he couldn't. The speculation that seemed most likely to him was that it was someone who had been in his class at Harvard, and Mrs. Marquié encouraged him to believe this. Then, one day, instead of using the phrase "your patron," she forgot herself and used the word "she," and that inflamed Gould's imagination. He spent every afternoon for a couple of weeks going through newspaper files in the Public Library and searching for information about rich women in general and rich women who were patrons of the arts in particular, but he wasn't able to find any clues. His mind was dominated for several days by the idea that the woman might somehow be one or the other of two well-to-do old spinster sisters who were cousins of his and lived together in Boston. He had always been afraid of them, and he hadn't seen or heard of them since a few years after he got out of Harvard, when he had asked them to lend him some money with which to revisit the Indian reservations in North Dakota and they had refused. However, he finally got up his nerve and called them collect. One of them accepted the call and listened to him for about a minute while he tried in a roundabout way to find out what he wanted to know, and then interrupted him and said that she couldn't imagine what he was leading up to but that, whatever it was, she didn't want to hear it and that if he ever called her or her sister again she would put the police on him. Two or three nights later, lying in bed unable to sleep, he recalled an elderly woman, reputed to be very rich, whom he had once met at a party on Washington Square and with whom he had had a pleasant conversation about Edgar Allan Poe, and he decided that *she* might be the woman. In the morning, after a chain of telephone calls, he found out that she was dead. Next, he got it in his head that it might be some woman who had become interested in him through reading the Profile and that I knew who she was, and he came to me and asked me for her name. He demanded her name. Years later, quite by chance, I did find out who the woman was, and went to see her and had a talk with her, but at that time I didn't know who she was, and I told Gould so. He went away unconvinced and returned a few days later with a long letter that he had written to the woman. He wanted me to read it and send it on to her. The letter had a preamble, all in capitals, which read, "A RESPECTFUL COMMUNICATION FROM JOE GOULD TO HIS UNKNOWN PATRON (WHO WILL BE CHERISHED BY POS-TERITY FOR HER GENEROSITY TO THE AUTHOR OF THE ORAL HISTORY WHETHER SHE CHOOSES TO REMAIN ANONYMOUS OR NOT) PROPOSING THAT INSTEAD OF 60 DOLLARS MONTHLY SHE GIVE HIM A LUMP SUM OF 720 DOLLARS YEARLY THE PRINCIPAL ARGUMENT BEING THAT THIS WOULD PERMIT HIM TO GO ABROAD AND LIVE IN FRANCE OR ITALY WHERE BY EXERCISING A LITTLE PRUDENCE WHICH HE IS FULLY PRE-PARED TO DO THE MONEY WOULD GO TWICE AS FAR." It seemed to me that Gould's purpose in writing this letter was to provoke the woman into some kind of communication with him, no matter what, and this alarmed me. I urged him to tear the letter up and forget about lump sums and living abroad, and all the rest of it, or the woman might hear that he was already complaining and get annoyed and cut the money off. If he went ahead and finished the Oral History, or at least got some work done on it, I said, maybe she would come forth and make herself known to him. He told me to stop giving him advice; he could handle his own affairs. Then, a moment later, an agonized look appeared on his face and he exclaimed, "I'd almost rather know who she is than have the money!" He stopped talking until he had got control of himself. "How would you feel," he went on presently, "if you knew that somewhere out in the world there was a woman who cared enough about you not to want you to starve to death but at the same time for some reason of her own didn't want to have anything to do with you and didn't even want you to know who she was?" He watched me craftily. "A woman who had an illegitimate baby when she was young and hated the father of it and let it be adopted might behave that way," he said, "if she got to be old and rich and respectable and suddenly found out by reading a Profile in *The New Yorker* that the baby was now a middle-aged man living in poverty on the Bowery." He paused for a moment. "I know I sound crazy," he continued, "but when I was a boy I used to daydream that I had been adopted, and lately I've been having those daydreams all over again." He left the letter on my desk and went away, and a few days later he returned and retrieved it and took it up to Mrs. Marquié and asked her to read it and send it on to the woman. Mrs. Marquié had always been gentle with Gould, but at this point she spoke sharply to him, and something she said must have brought him to his senses, for from that time on he kept his curiosity about his patron to himself.

Not long after this, Gould stopped coming to my office (I had begun forwarding letters to him at the Maison Gerard), and I lost track of him for a while. I saw him around the middle of June. During the next six months, for one reason or another, I spent more time out of New York City than in it, and I didn't see him again until one afternoon in December. On that afternoon, I was walking past the Jefferson Diner when I heard the peremptory sound of metal rapping on glass, and looked up and saw Gould staring out at me from a booth in the diner and rapping on the window with a coin to get my attention. I went in and sat down with him. "Hold on to yourself and don't faint," he said, "and I'll buy you a cup of coffee."

It was the same booth we had sat in when I had my first talk with him. His face and hands were as dirty as ever, but his color was good and his eyes were clear and he had put on a little weight. As usual, he had on a suit that was a size or two too big for him. It was somebody's castoff—the ruins of a suit—but it was well cut and it was made of some kind of expensive, Scottish-looking material, and it had been a good suit in its time. He even had on the vest. He wore a hat whose sides were deeply dented and whose brim was turned up on one side and down on the other. It was an extraordinarily rakish hat, and almost any veteran Villager could have identified it at a glance; it was one of E. E. Cummings's old hats. I told Gould that he looked the best I had ever seen him, and I was surprised at the smugness of his response.

"Oh, I'm doing all right," he said, smiling complacently. "I'm doing fine. I didn't much care for the Maison Gerard at first, or the Maison G., as the inmates call it—it's too out-of-the-way, the food is too starchy, and the stairs are a damned nuisance—but I've gotten used to it. If fact, I'm quite happy there. I come down to the Village and make the rounds the same as ever and scratch around for contributions to the Joe Gould Fund, but it isn't a life-and-death matter any longer. I've even stopped bothering with some people—the dime ones and the maybe-tomorrow ones. I just hit the ones I'm sure of, and I don't hit them as often as I used to. A peculiar thing has happened. I thought I'd be ruined in the Village if the news got out that I had a patron who was paying for my room and board, and I tried to keep it under my hat, but I couldn't; I told a few of my friends and they told others, and one by one all of them found it out, and what do you know—instead of reducing the amount of their contributions or refusing to give me anything at all anymore, they've become far more generous than they used to be. People who used to give me a quarter and give it grudgingly now give me fifty cents, and sometimes even a dollar, and give it willingly. You know the old fundamental rule: 'Them as has gits.' Sometimes, these days, I have three, four, five, six, seven dollars in my pocket. I don't bum cigarettes any longer, let alone smoke picked-up butts; I buy my own. Sometimes I even drop in a place and order a drink and pay for it myself. And I'm taking better care of myself. Most mornings, if I don't have a hangover, I get up around eleven and have a big breakfast, and then I walk up to the main branch of the Public Library and read the papers or look up something, or I might go to a few exhibitions in the galleries on Fifty-seventh Street and see if there are any good nudes, or I might take a run up to the Metropolitan or the Frick or the Museum of Natural History or the Museum of the American Indian, or I might just walk around the streets. After a while, I go back to the Maison G. and lie down for an hour or so, and then I have an early dinner, and then I get on the subway and go down to the Village. I knock around the Village until the bars close at 4 A.M. and everybody goes home, and then I head on back to the Maison G. Compared to the way things used to be, I'm living the life of a millionaire." He hummed the tune of a bitter old Bessie Smith song and then sang a few words. " 'Once I lived the life of a millionaire,' " he sang in his squeaky, old-Yankee voice. " 'Spending my money, I didn't care. . . .'

"Of course," he went on, "there's one thing I *do* keep under my hat, and that's the fact that I don't know who my patron is. I don't give a damn anymore who she is, but I have my pride. People keep asking me, and I tell them I'm not allowed to say. It's a famous name, I tell them, and they'd recognize it if I mentioned it—one of the richest women in the world. I call her Madame X, and I hint that I have the inside track with her. You know how bohemians are. They profess to disdain money, but they lose all control of themselves and go absolutely berserk at the slightest indication of the remotest hint of the faintest trace of a smell of it. Ever since the word got out that I have a patron, and not only that, a *woman* patron, and not only that, a *rich* woman patron, the poets and the painters have been getting me aside and buying me drinks and asking me to tell Madame X about their work. I try to be as helpful as I can. 'Let me have a few of your best poems,' I say if it's a poet, or 'Let me have a few of your best sketches,' I say if it's a painter, 'and I'll take them up and show them to Madame X the next time I go up to see her in her huge town house just off Park Avenue.' I take the poems or the sketches up to my room at the Maison G.

and put them on the dresser and leave them there for a week or two, and then I take them back to the genius who produced them. 'Madame X looked at your work,' I tell him, 'and she asked me to thank you very much for letting her look at it.' 'But what did she say about it?' the genius asks. 'She strictly forbade me to tell you,' I say, 'but we've been friends for a long time, and I know you too well and respect you too much to lie to you, and I'm going to tell you exactly what she said. She said that she couldn't detect the slightest sign of any talent whatsoever in your work, and she said she feels it would be very wrong of her to encourage you in any way.' "

Gould's eyes flashed, and he giggled. "Oh," he said, "I've put quite a few people in their places that way. I've settled quite a few old scores that way."

I found myself getting annoyed with Gould, not because of his gloating over the settling of old scores—that was all right with me; I believe in revenge—but because of his general air of self-satisfaction, and I asked him a malicious question. "How are you getting along on the Oral History?" I asked.

"Fine!" he said, not batting an eye. "I'm making a lot of progress on it." His portfolio was beside him in the booth, and he patted it. "I've added an enormous number of words to it lately," he said. "It's growing by leaps and bounds."


AS TIME WENT ON, Gould grew accustomed to having his room and board paid for by his unknown patron. He came to take it for granted and to look upon it as a permanent arrangement. One morning in November, 1947, after he had been living at the Maison Gerard for almost three and a half years, I had a telephone call from him, and the moment I heard his voice I knew that something was wrong. "Mrs. Marquié called me yesterday afternoon and asked me to come up to her gallery at once," he said. "I went up there, and she broke the news to me that some weeks ago she had received word that Madame X was thinking of stopping her subsidy to me but that a man and a woman she knows who are old friends of

Madame X were trying to persuade her to keep it going. She hadn't wanted to tell me anything about it, she said, until she had found out for certain just what Madame X was going to do. Well, she found out for certain yesterday. Madame X sent word to her that she was putting a check for December in the mail but that that would be the last." Gould paused for a moment and I heard him take a deep breath. "I asked Mrs. Marquié to tell me why Madame X had turned against me," he said. "I begged her to tell me. She said she simply didn't know." He paused again. "Not knowing who she is was bad enough," he said, "but not knowing why she's turned against me is nerve-racking." He paused once again. "It's the worst news I've ever had in my life," he said. "I haven't been able to keep anything on my stomach since I heard it."

Gould sounded hurt and bewildered and terribly forsaken, and he also sounded humiliated. There was something in his voice, a hint of panic, that stayed in my mind and made me uneasy. In the middle of the afternoon, I left the office and took a taxicab to the Maison Gerard. A porter vacuum-cleaning the carpet in the vestibule said that Gould had gone out but that he might have come back in. "Go on up and see," he said. "His room'll be open. He never locks it." Gould wasn't in. Standing in the door and peering into his room, I saw some composition books on his dresser, and I went over and looked at them. There were five of them. I took the liberty of opening the one on top. On the first page was the old familiar title: "DEATH OF DR. CLARKE STORER GOULD. A CHAPTER OF JOE GOULD'S ORAL HISTORY." I went ahead and opened the second one. The title read, "THE DREAD TOMATO HABIT. A CHAPTER OF JOE GOULD'S ORAL HISTORY." I opened the third one. The title read, "DEATH OF DR. CLARKE STORER GOULD. A CHAPTER OF JOE GOULD'S ORAL HISTORY." I opened the fourth one. The title read, "DEATH OF DR. CLARKE STORER GOULD. A CHAPTER OF JOE GOULD'S ORAL HISTORY." I opened the fifth one. The title read, "DEATH OF DR. CLARKE STORER GOULD. A CHAPTER OF JOE GOULD'S ORAL HISTORY." I put the books back the way they were and left the room. "God pity him," I said, "and pity us all."

When Gould's subsidy ran out at the end of December, he told

Gerard that he wanted to keep on staying at the Maison Gerard. He would give up the board part of his room-and-board arrangement, at least for a while, he said, and concentrate on trying to hold on to his room. It was obvious that he hoped to do this by redoubling his efforts in soliciting contributions to the Joe Gould Fund. However, he forgot the old fundamental rule that he had once referred to—"Them as has gits"—and made the mistake of telling his friends that he had lost his patron. Consequently, a good many of them, fearing that he would now become too dependent on them, began cutting down on their contributions. Before long, it became hard for him to get together three dollars in a lump sum for his weekly rent, and Gerard refused to let him pay by the night. "You are penalizing me because I don't live the way most people do," Gould told him. "Most people live on a week-to-week basis or on a month-to-month basis. I live on a day-to-day basis, and some days I live on an hour-to-hour basis." "I know all that, and I would like to help you," Gerard replied, "but the Maison Gerard is not a flophouse." By the end of February, Gould was in debt to Gerard. He had set fire to his bed at the Maison Gerard several times by falling asleep while smoking. In March, he set fire to it again, and, using this an an excuse, Gerard asked him to leave. At that time, there was a cluster of cheap hotels around Tenth Avenue and Forty-second Street. In one of them, the Watson Hotel, at 583 Tenth Avenue, it was possible to get a room—that is, a narrow cubicle furnished with a metal cot—for thirty-five cents a night, and Gould began staying there. Late one night, leaving a barroom in the lower Village and feeling too tired to take the subway and go uptown to the Watson, he walked over to the Bowery and got a bed in a flophouse, and found himself right back where he had started from in May, 1944. Next day, he decided that he might as well keep on staying in Bowery flophouses, since the Bowery was so convenient to the Village, and from that time on almost every step he took was a step going down.

It soon became apparent to people who had known Gould through the years that a change had taken place in him. "What's the matter with you, Joe?" I heard one of the old bohemians in Goody's say to him one night. "You don't seem to be yourself." "I'm *not* myself," he answered. "I've never been myself." He made the rounds in the Village as he always had, turning up during the afternoon and night in at least a dozen barrooms, cafeterias, diners, and dumps, but he began to look as if he didn't belong in these places. More often than not, he was abstracted or gloomy or withdrawn or had a faraway look in his eyes. One night, I went into a place in the Village called Chumley's for dinner. As I sat down in the dining room, I glanced through an archway at the bar, which was in an adjoining room, and there was a crowd of loud, laughing, joking, overstimulated men and women sitting or standing two deep along it, and down at the end of it I saw Gould's somber, bearded face. He was standing by himself, holding a beer, observing the others, and he had on a ragged suit and an old dog's bed of an overcoat, and he was all hunched up, and he looked remarkably separate and set off from everybody else. He looked like the ghost of Joe Gould come back to haunt the bar in Chumley's. He looked like a zombie.

He continued to go to the Minetta every night and sit for a few hours at his customary table and scribble in a composition book in full view of any tourists who might happen to be around, but when tourists came over and asked him what he was working on he rarely made big, bragging speeches any longer. His replies were more likely to be sarcastic or scurrilous or wearily offhand. Not that the tourists minded; they seemed to think that that was exactly the way a bohemian should behave, and they showed just as much interest in the Oral History and contributed just as much to the Joe Gould Fund as the ones he used to knock himself out trying to impress.

It began to take him longer and longer to get over the effects of drinking, and his drinking habits changed. While he was living at the Maison Gerard, he had got used to holing up in his room all day if he had a hangover and sleeping it off, but he couldn't do that in flophouses, and he developed a dread of hangovers. Instead of drinking anything and everything every chance he got—the stronger the better, the hell with tomorrow—as he had been doing, he began sticking to beer. No matter how hard a party of tourists might try to persuade him to order something stronger, he would insist on beer. Even so, by spacing the beers out, he managed to stay in a fairly constant state of mild intoxication. In this state, he was easily irritated, and his speech became looser all the time. He began to make spiteful or uncomfortably frank remarks to old friends, and he began to tell people whom he had always pretended to like what he really thought of them. Once, staring across a cafeteria table at a man he had known ever since they were young men in the Village together, he said, "*You* certainly sold out." "You're slipping," he once told Maxwell Bodenheim. "You were a better poet twenty-five years ago than you are now, and you weren't any good then." On another occasion, he told Bodenheim that he wasn't a real poet anyhow. "You're only an artsy-craftsy poet," he said. "A niminy-piminy poet. An itsy-bitsy poet. And you're frightfully uneducated. You don't know how to punctuate a sentence, and all you've ever read is Floyd Dell and Ethel M. Dell and the Rubáiyát."

In those years, I used to go downtown at night on the Fifth Avenue bus. I usually got off at my stop, at Tenth Street, around seven-thirty. Gould knew this, and about once a week he would be waiting for me. When I stepped off the bus, he would appear out of the shadows in the doorway of the Church of the Ascension, on the corner, and hurry over to the bus stop and join me. He would walk a little way up the street with me and I would give him a contribution, and then he would dart off into the night. Sometimes we would stand on the street and talk for a few minutes. One night in the summer of 1952, as we were standing talking, he told me rather hesitantly that he was worried about his health. He had been having dizzy spells, he said. "The other day," he said, "I got on the subway at Fourteenth Street, intending to get off at the Twenty-third Street station, and a moment after I sat down, I had a kind of blackout, and when I came to, the train was pulling into the station at Seventy-second Street." I told him that a doctor I knew had read the Profile of him with great interest, and often asked me questions about him and about the progress he was making on the

Oral History. "He said one time that if you ever needed medical attention he'd be glad to see you and wouldn't charge you anything," I told Gould. I asked him to let me call the doctor and make an appointment for him. Gould shook his head. "Ah," he said, looking vaguely up the street, "what's the use?"

Around the middle of December of that year, I became conscious of the fact that I hadn't seen Gould at the bus stop for several weeks, but I didn't think much about it. It wasn't at all unusual for Gould to disappear from the Village for a few days or a few weeks, or even a few months, and then suddenly reappear and give an odd explanation for his absence. "I went on a bird walk along the waterfront with an old countess," he once said after such an absence. "The countess and I spent three weeks studying sea gulls." Another time, after he had been away unaccountably for most of a summer, he told people that he had been on a cruise on a yacht. "J. P. Morgan's yacht," he said.

In January, 1953, I went to a party at the house of a psychiatrist I had known ever since I was a young reporter and covered Bellevue Hospital and the Medical Examiner's office. Among the other guests was a woman psychiatrist who was on the staff of Pilgrim State Hospital, which is out in Suffolk County, Long Island, at a place called West Brentwood. I had seen her several times before at my friend's house and had always enjoyed talking with her, not about psychiatry—we never talked about that—but about things like the feeding habits of striped bass; she was an obsessed surf caster. This evening, when I spoke to her, she told me that she was taking a leave of absence from the hospital to have a baby. Then she said she had something she wanted to tell me, and we walked over and stood by a window. "We have an old friend of yours out at Pilgrim State," she said. "The man you wrote about who's the author of 'An Oral History of the World,' or whatever it is he calls it. Joe Gould." She said that Gould had collapsed on the Bowery one afternoon around the middle of November and that an ambulance from Columbus Hospital had picked him up. He was found to be suffering from "confusion and disorientation," and Columbus, which doesn't have a psychiatric service, had transferred him to the psychiatric division at Bellevue. Bellevue had kept him under observation until sometime around Thanksgiving, and had then transferred him to Pilgrim State.

"What's the matter with him?" I asked. "What do you call it?"

"It's nothing at all strange or unusual," she said. "Arteriosclerotic senility. The same thing a lot of us will have if we live long enough. Only, in his case it hit him rather early—he's only sixty-three. Also, he has something wrong with his kidneys. Also, since he's been out at Pilgrim State he's had a staggering number of minor ailments, one right after another. That often happens to men of his type, the Bowery type, once they finally get into a hospital. Among other things, he's had the worst case of conjuctivitis I've ever seen, an acute attack of bursitis, a terrible boil on the back of his neck, a series of chills, a series of earaches, and a persistent pain of some kind in his stomach. And I suspect he's just getting started."

I asked about visiting him

"I wouldn't, if I were you," she said. "Right now, he's so suspicious and confused it might do him more harm than good. He probably wouldn't know you. And if he did, trying to talk to you would just tire him out. As a matter of fact, if you want to do him a great favor, don't tell his friends in the Village where he is. At least, not now. Just keep it to yourself. Just forget I ever told you. We had another well-known bohemian in Pilgrim State a year or so ago, and people from the Village came out in droves to visit him, men bohemians and women bohemians, big bohemians and little bohemians, old bohemians and young bohemians, their tongues going a mile a minute, and they certainly didn't do him any good. Every time we got him to the point where he seemed to be almost reaching shore, so to speak, some of them would come out and push him back in. They'd push him back in and hold his head under. The main reason they came out wasn't to see him anyway but to try and get one of the psychiatrists aside and impress him or her with how much they knew about psychiatry—a subject, I might add, about which they were fantastically ill-informed."

I decided that for the time being I would do as she said and keep Gould's whereabouts to myself.

Pretty soon, a number of rumors about Gould sprang up in the Village. The most persistent rumor was that he had inherited a little money and had gone back to Massachusetts to live, and this gradually became the accepted explanation for his absence. A good many people did not believe this, I feel sure, or did not quite believe it, but they chose to appear to believe it, thereby washing their hands of Gould.

By and by, I told several people that Gould was in Pilgrim State. I told them in confidence. The first person I told was an old, old friend of Gould's named Edward Gottlieb, who was managing editor of the *Long Island Press,* a daily newspaper published out in Queens, at Jamaica. In his youth, Gottlieb had lived in the Village and had written poetry for little magazines and had hung out in bohemian joints, in one of which he had got acquainted with Gould. After deciding that he wasn't a poet and never would be, he had become a newspaperman. He had worked for the *Press* for twenty-five years, progressing from reporter to city editor to managing editor, and at least once a month, and sometimes several times a month, during all those years, Gould had taken the subway out to Jamaica and had gone to his office and had got a contribution from him. I told Gottlieb for two reasons. He had called me a couple of times about Gould and sounded worried about him, and I felt guilty about not telling him. The principal reason I told him, however, was that I happened to know he knew a great deal about state mental hospitals. In 1943, he and his newspaper had done an investigation of Creedmoor State Hospital, in Queens Village, that had led to an improvement of conditions not only in Creedmoor but also in other state hospitals, including Pilgrim State, and Governor Dewey had appointed him to the Board of Visitors at Creedmoor. I had once had a talk with him about this investigation, and I knew that he had a number of friends in medical and administrative capacities at Pilgrim State, and it seemed to me that he was in a position to be very helpful to Gould.

Gottlieb said he would talk with his friends at Pilgrim State and do everything for Gould that he possibly could do. "The way it sounds," he said, "I'm afraid there isn't a hell of a lot that can be done. I'm afraid poor Joe is getting on down toward the end of the line."

From time to time thereafter, Gottlieb telephoned me and gave me news about Gould. "Joe's worst symptom is apathy," he said during one of these calls. "He mostly just sits and stares into the distance. However, every once in a while, the doctors say, something seem to stir in his mind and a smile comes on his face and he rouses himself and gets up and scampers around the ward and waves his arms up and down and makes strange, unearthly screeches until he wears himself out. He seems to be trying to communicate something with these screeches. The doctors and the nurses and the other patients don't know what he's doing, of course—they're completely mystified—but I know what's he's doing, and I'm sure you do."

ON SUNDAY, AUGUST 18, 1957, around eleven o'clock at night, Gottlieb telephoned me and said he had just been notified that Gould had died. We spoke for a few minutes about how sad it was, and then I asked him if Gould had left any papers.

"No," he said. "None at all. As the man at the hospital said, 'Not a scratch.' I was hoping that he had. I was particularly hoping that he had left some instructions about what he wanted done with the Oral History. He used to say that he wanted two-thirds of it to go to the Harvard Library and the other third to the Smithsonian Institution, but it doesn't seem right to split it up that way. When scholars start using it as source material, it will be a nuisance if they have to go up to Cambridge to see one part of it and then down to Washington to see some other part. Maybe one institution could be prevailed upon to relinquish its share to the other, and then it could be kept intact. By the way, where is the Oral History?"

I said that I didn't know.

Gottlieb's voice instantly became concerned. "I took it for granted that you knew," he said. "I took it for granted that Joe had told you."

I said that I didn't know where the Oral History was, and that I didn't know anybody who did know where it was.

*"Well,"* said Gottlieb, "we'll just have to start hunting for it. We'll just have to start telephoning and get in touch with all the people who knew him best and call a meeting and form a committee and get busy and start hunting for it. It's probably scattered all over. Some of it may still be stored in the cellar of that farmhouse near Huntington where he put it during the war—that stone cellar he was always talking about, the cellar on the duck farm—and some of it may be stored in the studios of friends of his in the Village, and some of it may be stored in storerooms in some of those hotels and flophouses he lived in. Do flophouses have storerooms? They must. People must leave things with the clerks in them for safe-keeping during the night the same as they do in other hotels, and then go off and forget all about them the same as they do in other hotels, and the flophouses must have to make some kind of provision for this. I confess I have no idea where to start. The first thing we'll need is a list of addresses of places he lived in. Maybe you could start right now making such a list. You will help with this, won't you? You will be on the committee?"

I didn't know what to say. Gottlieb was an energetic man, the kind of man who gets things done, and I could tell by the way he talked that he was going to get to work the first thing in the morning and start forming a committee, and that very soon the members of the committee would be rummaging around in farmhouses all over Long Island and in studios all over the Village and in flophouses all over the Bowery. I could save him a lot of trouble if I spoke up right then and told him what I knew about the Oral History—I could save him and his committee quite a wild-goose chase—but one of the few things I have learned going through life is that there is a time and a place for everything, and I didn't think that this was the time or the place to be telling one of Joe Gould's oldest friends that I didn't believe the Oral History existed. Joe Gould wasn't even in his grave yet, he wasn't even cold yet, and this was no time to be telling his secret. It could keep. Let them go ahead and look for the Oral History, I thought. After all, I thought, I could be wrong. Hell, I thought—and the thought made me smile—maybe they'll find it.

Gottlieb repeated his question, this time a little impatiently. "You will be on the committee, won't you?" he asked.

"Yes," I said, continuing to play the role I had stepped into the afternoon I discovered that the Oral History did not exist—a role that I am only now stepping out of. "Of course I will."

(1964)

# About the Author

JOSEPH MITCHELL came to New York City from a small farming town named Fairmont in the swamp country of southeastern North Carolina in 1929, when he was twenty-one years old, looking for a job as a newspaper reporter. He arrived at Pennsylvania Station on Friday, October 25, the day after the stock-market crash that is generally considered to have been the beginning of the Great Depression. He eventually managed to find a job as a kind of bottom-depths apprentice crime reporter at Police Headquarters for *The World*. He worked as a reporter and feature writer—for *The World*, *The Herald Tribune*, and *The World-Telegram*—for eight years, and then went to *The New Yorker*, where he has been off and on ever since.

Aside from writing, Mr. Mitchell's particular interests are Gypsies, Southern agriculture, Irish literature, commercial fishing, and the architecture of New York City. He has served several terms on the board of directors of the Gypsy Lore Society, an international organization of students of Gypsy life and the Gypsy language, founded in England in 1888. *Bajour,* a musical comedy based on the stories about Gypsies in this book, ran for 232 performances on Broadway in 1964–65. He is an architecture buff and frequently spends a day wandering around the city with a pair of binoculars studying the facades of old buildings. He was one of the founders of the South Street Seaport Museum, he was one of the original friends of the Friends of Cast-Iron Architecture, and for five years he was one of the Commissioners of the New York City Landmarks Preservation Commission. His favorite institutions in the city are the Metropolitan

Museum, the Grand Central Oyster Bar, McSorley's alehouse, the Belmont racetrack, the Staten Island ferry, Fulton Fish Market, the Gotham Book Mart (he has been going to meetings of the James Joyce Society on the second floor of the Gotham for thirty years), and the William T. Davis Wildlife Refuge in the Staten Island marshes. For several years, he has been going back to North Carolina more and more often and spends months at a time down there helping reforest some cut-over timberland and worn-out farmland along the edge of Ashpole Swamp, going into the swamp now and then to look for wildflowers and for woodpeckers and hawks, which are his favorite birds. Once, deep in the swamp, looking through binoculars, he watched for an hour or so as a pileated woodpecker tore the bark off the upper trunk and limbs of a tall old dead black-gum tree, and he says he considers this the most spectacular event he has ever witnessed.

Mr. Mitchell's wife, Therese Mitchell, the photographer, died in 1980. He has two daughters, Nora Sanborn, of Eatontown, New Jersey, and Elizabeth Curtis, of Atlanta, Georgia, three granddaughters, two grandsons, and one great-granddaughter.

P. 316   fuss, fight & gumption

P. 664